CONTEMPORARY CURRICULUM

In Thought and Action

SIXTH EDITION

CONTEMPORARY CURRICULUM
In Thought and Action

JOHN D. MCNEIL
University of California, Los Angeles

JOHN WILEY & SONS, INC.

ACQUISITIONS EDITOR   *Brad Hanson*
EDITORIAL ASSISTANT   *Lindsay Lovier*
SENIOR PRODUCTION EDITOR   *Valerie A. Vargas*
MEDIA EDITOR   *Lisa Schnettler*
EXECUTIVE MARKETING MANAGER   *Jeffrey Rucker*
SENIOR DESIGNER   *Kevin Murphy*
PRODUCTION MANAGEMENT   *Ingrao Associates*
COVER ART   © Vera Siffner/Stock Illustration Source/Images.com

This book was set in 10/12 Times Roman by Indianapolis Division of John Wiley & Sons, Inc., and printed and bound by Hamilton Printing. The cover was printed by Phoenix Color Corp.

This book is printed on acid free paper.   ∞

Library* of *Congress Cataloging in Publication Data:
McNeil, John D.
  Contemporary curriculum in thought and action / John D. McNeil.--6th ed.
    p. cm.
  Rev. ed. of: Curriculum. 5th ed. c1996
  Includes bibliographical references and index
  ISBN 0-471-45975-5 (pbk.)
    1. Education--Curricula.   2. Curriculum planning.   I. McNeil, John D. Curriculum.   II. Title.

  LB1570.M3178 2005
  375'.001--dc22

                                                                                2004065919

ISBN-13 978-0-471-45975-0

Printed in the United States of America

10 9 8 7 6 5 4

CONTENTS

PREFACE   **xi**

PART I
CONCEPTIONS OF CURRICULUM   1

CHAPTER 1   *THE HUMANISTIC CURRICULUM*   **3**

Characteristics of the Humanistic Curriculum   **5**
    Purpose   **5**
    Role of the Teacher   **5**
Directions in Humanistic Curriculum   **5**
    A Confluent Curriculum   **6**
    Consciousness and Transcendency   **7**
    Responses to Depersonalization   **8**
Psychological Foundations of the Humanistic Curriculum   **13**
    Third Force Psychology   **13**
Historical Antecedents to the Humanistic Curriculum   **17**
    Ancient Greeks and Romans   **17**
    Traditional Humanities   **18**
    Progressive Education   **19**
    Spiritual Images   **19**
Criticisms of the Humanistic Curriculum   **19**
Concluding Comments   **21**

CHAPTER 2   *THE SOCIAL RECONSTRUCTIONIST CURRICULUM*   **24**

Characteristics of the Social Reconstructionist Curriculum   **24**
    Purpose   **24**
    Role of the Teacher   **25**
Social Reconstruction in Practice   **25**
    Changing the Community   **25**
    Freire's Social Reconstructionism   **27**
    Neo-Marxists   **29**
    Futurologists   **32**

Social Adaptation versus Social Reconstruction   **34**
Psychological Foundations of Social Reconstruction   **35**
    Cultural Psychology as a Source   **35**
Psychoanalytical Psychology and Social Reconstruction   **37**
    Historical Antecedents to Social Reconstruction   **37**
Criticisms of Social Reconstructionism   **40**
Concluding Comments   **41**

CHAPTER 3   *THE SYSTEMIC CURRICULUM*   **44**

Alignment   **45**
Accountability   **45**
Standards-Based Curriculum   **46**
    Policies for Standards-Based Curriculum   **46**
    Standards-Based Curriculum in the Classroom   **49**
Psychological Foundations of the Systemic Curriculum   **51**
Historical Antecedents to the Systemic Curriculum   **52**
Consequences of Systemic Curriculum   **54**
Concluding Comments   **57**

CHAPTER 4   *THE ACADEMIC CURRICULUM*   **60**

Approaches to the Academic Curriculum   **62**
    The Forms of Knowledge Approach   **63**
    Structure in the Disciplines Approach   **64**
    Reaction against a Structure of Knowledge   **66**
    Revival of the Disciplines Approach   **68**
    Liberal Arts and the Academic Core   **71**

Cultural Literacy   **73**
Making Subject Matter More
Appealing to Growing Minds   **75**
Psychological Foundations of the Academic
Curriculum   **77**
Historical Antecedents of the Academic
Curriculum   **79**
Concluding Comments   **83**

PART II

CURRICULUM DEVELOPMENT   87

CHAPTER 5   *DECIDING WHAT SHOULD BE*
TAUGHT   **89**

Arena for Deciding What to Teach   **89**
Levels of Decision Making   **89**
Curriculum at Different Levels   **91**
Contexts for Development of
Curriculum   **92**
Range of Activity   **92**
Development of Materials   **92**
State, Regional, and Local Curriculum
Planning   **93**
Institutional Curriculum Planning   **93**
Functions of the Curriculum   **94**
Determining What to Teach   **96**
Rational and Technical Models in
Curriculum Decision Making   **97**
Needs Assessment Model   **97**
The Futuristic Model   **100**
The Rational Model   **101**
The Vocational or Training
Model   **104**
Alternative Approaches to Determining
Curriculum Purposes   **107**
Disjointed Incrementalism   **107**
Emergent Approaches in Curriculum
Decision Making   **108**
A Comment on Models and Approaches for
Curriculum Building   **111**
Concluding Comments   **112**

CHAPTER 6   *DEVELOPING AND SELECTING*
LEARNING OPPORTUNITIES   **115**

Standards for Teaching Impact Classroom
Curriculum Development   **116**
Principles for Developing Learning
Opportunities   **118**

Learning Opportunities for Higher Order
Thinking   **120**
Transfer and Problem Solving   **121**
Creativity   **122**
Creating New Knowledge   **123**
Procedures for Developing Learning
Activities   **125**
Current Orientations in Developing
Learning Activities   **126**
Criteria for Selecting Learning
Activities   **130**
Philosophical Criteria   **130**
Psychological Criteria   **130**
Political Criteria   **133**
Practicality as a Criterion   **133**
Scientifically Based Research
Criteria   **134**
Criticisms of Textbooks and Learning
Opportunities   **135**
Criticisms of Criteria for Selecting Learning
Opportunities   **136**
Concluding Comments   **136**

APERTURE 6   *HOW TECHNOLOGY IS USED*
WITH CURRICULUM ORIENTATIONS   **139**

Technology in Humanistic Classrooms   **139**
Social Reconstruction and Technology   **140**
Technology in a Systemic Curriculum   **142**
Technology in the Academic
Curriculum   **144**
Building Web Sites   **145**

7 ORGANIZING LEARNING OPPORTUNITIES   **146**

Key Concepts in Curriculum
Organization   **146**
Organizing Centers   **146**
Organizing Elements   **147**
Principles for Sequencing Centers and
Activities Related to Elements   **150**
Organizing Structures   **150**
Structure at the Institutional
Level   **151**
Structure at the Classroom Level   **152**
Organizational Patterns and
Conceptions of the Curriculum   **156**
Unified Disciplines: The New
Academic Pattern   **158**
Empirical Studies of the Effects of
Patterns   **163**
Issues in Curriculum Organization   **165**
Concluding Comments   **168**

PART III

CURRICULUM MANAGEMENT **171**

CHAPTER 8 *MANAGING CURRICULUM* **173**

Schools and the Institutionalized Curriculum **173**
    Curriculum Change in the Context of Restructuring **175**
Roles in Restructuring Curriculum **179**
    The Principal as Director of Learning **179**
    The Principal in Shared Leadership **179**
    Department Heads in Curriculum Management **181**
Administrative Arrangements **181**
    Stratifying Students **183**
    Staffing Patterns and Scheduling **184**
    Supplementary Personnel **185**
    Nongrading **186**
    Facilities **186**
    The Middle School **186**
    Alternative, Magnet, Charter, and Specialist Schools **187**
Directions in the Reform of School Organizations **190**
    Options in the Schools **190**
Administration for Instructional Effectiveness **191**
    Coordinating the Curriculum **192**
    Effective Research and Curriculum Policy **194**
Concluding Comments **196**

CHAPTER 9 *EVALUATING THE CURRICULUM* **199**

Models for Evaluation **200**
    Consensus Models (Traditional and Technical Evaluation) **200**
    Pluralistic Models (Humanistic and Social Reconstructionist Evaluation) **204**
Controversial Technical Issues in Curriculum Evaluation **206**
    The Form of Objectives (Goals, Standards, Benchmarks, and Indicators) **206**
Measurement of Intended Outcomes versus Goal-Free Evaluation **208**
    Norm-Referenced Tests and Criterion-Referenced Tests **208**

Tests and Invasion of Privacy **209**
Authentic Assessment of Student Performance **210**
Assessment as Learning **211**
Techniques for Collecting Data **212**
    Measuring Affect **213**
    Sampling **214**
    Hazards in Conducting Traditional Evaluation **214**
    Value Added Assessment **216**
Concluding Comments **217**

CHAPTER 10 *THE POLITICS OF CURRICULUM MAKING* **220**

Curriculum Policy **223**
    The Politics Involved **223**
    Political Decisions about What Will Be Taught **223**
Concepts for Interpreting the Process of Political Decision Making **224**
    The Professionalization of Reform **224**
    Forces of Stability **225**
    Constraints on Policy **226**
Participants in Determining Curriculum Policy **227**
    School-Based Participants **227**
    Community Participants **230**
    State Agencies **232**
    Testing Agencies **233**
    Publishers **233**
    The Courts **234**
    The Federal Government **235**
    Foundations **236**
    Special Interests **237**
Conflicts in Curriculum Control **238**
Concluding Comments **239**

IV

ISSUES AND TRENDS **241**

CHAPTER 11 *CURRENT ISSUES DEMANDING RESPONSES* **243**

Curriculum for Thinking **243**
    The Focus of a Thinking Curriculum **245**
Curriculum Competition: An International Comparison **247**
    Invidious Comparisons **247**

Vocational Education **253**
   Contrasting Purposes for Vocational
   Education **254**
   Access to Vocational Education **255**
   Content of Vocational Education **257**
   Reorganizing Vocational
   Education **258**
   Trends in Vocational Education **259**
Moral Education **259**
   Phenix's Basic Questions in Moral
   Education **259**
   Kohlberg's Theory of Moral
   Development **261**
Character Education **262**
School Safety **263**
Concluding Comments **265**

CHAPTER 12 *DIRECTIONS IN THE SUBJECT
FIELDS* **268**

Mathematics **268**
   Mathematics in Our Schools **268**
   Trends in Mathematics **269**
   Science **272**
   Evolution of Science Teaching **272**
   New Approaches in Science
   Education **274**
   Recommendations for the Future
   Science Curriculum **275**
Physical and Health Education **276**
   Its Place in the Curriculum **276**
   Guidelines for Future Physical
   Education Programs **277**
   English **279**
   English as a Subject **279**
   Current Trends in the Teaching of
   English **281**
Reading **282**
   The Curriculum of Reading **282**
   Trends and Directions **283**
History and Social Studies **285**
   History as a Subject **285**
   An Evaluation of History
   Curriculum **285**
   History and Geography in the
   1990s **286**
   History and the Social Studies in the
   Standards Movement **287**
   Social Studies **288**
   The Future of Social Studies **289**

Foreign Language **291**
   The Rise and Fall of Foreign
   Language **291**
   Efforts to Revive Language
   Instruction **291**
The Arts **294**
Concluding Comments **295**

V

**CURRICULUM INQUIRY:
RETROSPECT AND PROSPECT** **299**

CHAPTER 13 *A HISTORICAL PERSPECTIVE OF
CURRICULUM MAKING* **301**

Curriculum Historians **302**
   Context for Formulation of the
   Curriculum Field **303**
Founders of the Field of Curriculum **304**
Herbartism and the McMurrys **305**
   Basic Tenets of Herbartism **305**
   The McMurrys' Thinking **305**
Dewey's Opposition to Herbartism **308**
   Dewey's School **308**
   Dewey's Curriculum **309**
Scientific Curriculum Making: Franklin
Bobbitt and Werrett W. Charters **310**
   Societal Influences on the Scientific
   Movement **310**
   Key Ideas of Scientific Curriculum
   Making **310**
   Bobbitt's Contribution to Curriculum
   Making **311**
   Charters's Contribution to the
   Curriculum Field **313**
Improvement of Instruction **314**
   Local Development of
   Curriculum **314**
   The Course of Study Movement **314**
   Caswell's Influence on the Curriculum
   Field **315**
Rational Curriculum Making **316**
   Tyler's Curriculum Inquiry **317**
Feminine Enactment of Curriculum **320**
   Hilda Taba **320**
   Mary Sheldon Barnes **321**
   Lucy Maynard Salmon **321**
   Lucy Sprague Mitchell **321**
   Concluding Comments **322**

CHAPTER 14 *THE PROMISE OF THEORY AND
INQUIRY IN CURRICULUM* **325**

State of the Field **326**
The Need for Curriculum Theory **326**
The Need for Curriculum
Conceptions **327**
The Need for Studies of Correlation
and Integration **329**
The Need for Studies of
Sequence **330**
The Need for Analyzing Education
Objectives (Standards) **331**
The Need for Process–Product
Research **332**
Directions in Curriculum Inquiry **334**
Forms of Inquiry **334**
Synoptic Activity as Curriculum
Inquiry **334**
Inquiry in the School and Classroom **336**
Narrative **336**
Qualitative Inquiry in School
Settings **336**
Action Research as Curriculum
Inquiry **337**
Concluding Comments **339**

NAME INDEX **342**

SUBJECT INDEX **346**

PREFACE

It is impossible to ignore the onslaught of criticism that today's schools have received from the media in recent years. In many of our nation's public schools, students are scoring poorly on standardized tests, being victimized by school violence, and failing to graduate. Unfortunately, these figures increase exponentially for public schools that reside in and serve under-resourced communities. So the question that is often posed and rarely answered is a difficult one: How do we improve the quality of education for our students?

Curriculum is one of the most potent and influential tools that we can use to effect serious change in schools today. Society, schools, classrooms, students, and parents look to the curriculum as a primary force in shaping a student's identity, expectations, and life-long trajectory. As a result, it should come as no surprise that there is interest in who should control the formal curriculum, since its emphasis on what should be learned strongly impacts not only the lives of students but, in addition, society as a whole.

Contemporary Curriculum In Thought and Action prepares readers to participate in the discussion of curriculum control and other matters important to K–12 and university educators. It also provides the intellectual and technical tools educators and administrators will need for constructing and implementing curriculum in the classroom.

This textbook is not a monograph dealing with a small corner of the curriculum field, nor does it narrow curriculum into a study of history, sociology, or any other specialization. In addition, it is not a text written to support a particular view of how the curriculum should respond to such issues as multiculturalism, globalization, or maintaining the best of civilization—though these issues and more are treated in depth.

Contemporary Curriculum In Thought and Action lays out practical tools for *doing* curriculum at all levels: policy, institutional, and classroom. In contrast to books that offer one procedural strategy for dealing with a particular curriculum problem, *Contemporary Curriculum In Thought and Action* offers multiple strategies, along with explanations as to when, why, and how each applies in given situation.

Though intended primarily for use in college and university courses in curriculum, the book does not require that readers have a prior knowledge of the technical skills of curriculum making. On the contrary, it is designed to serve those with a wide range of backgrounds and expectations, including administrators, teachers, parents, concerned citizens, and others who are serious about improving curriculum in local contexts.

TEXT ORGANIZATION

Contemporary Curriculum In Thought and Action is divided into five parts. Part 1, Concepts of Curriculum, provides a framework for presenting many subsequent topics. The curriculum conceptions reveal significant new developments, such as the movement within the academic curriculum from students reproducing knowledge to a focus on contributing knowledge through real-world inquiry.

Part 2, Curriculum Development, features the technical skills of curriculum: how to determine goals and purposes, how to provide optimum learning opportunities, and how to organize for effective and continuous learning. This part draws heavily from current research on how people learn.

Part 3, Curriculum Management, is timely for its descriptions and analysis of school reforms—the restructuring of schools and innovations. Evaluation is given extended treatment. Also, the politics of curriculum making is treated in detail, and new departures, such as the privatization of education, are examined for their consequences for schools and society.

Part 4, Current Issues and Subject Matter Trends, presents issues from a wide context. Taking a broader view, international curriculum comparisons, in Chapter 11, reveal how high-achieving European and Asian countries are moving to progressive schooling with an emphasis on flexibility, creativity, and lifelong learning, while the United States is focused on a measured curriculum and standardized expectations. Key views of other issues are also given, including responses to multiculturalism, character and moral education, and curriculum for safe schools. Chapter 12 on trends in school subjects examines changes in the teaching of science, math, history, social studies, English, and the arts, as well as curriculum development in programs for physical education, health, literacy, and foreign language.

Part 5, Curriculum Inquiry: Retrospect and Prospect, opens with accounts of the emergence of the field at the end of the nineteenth century, and shows that inherited ways of thinking may limit curriculum work or, conversely, resurrect good ideas for today's problems. Of special interest are the dominance of males in constructing the institutional curriculum and the contributions of women to the enacted curriculum. Also described are scholars on the growing edge of curriculum inquiry: their questions, approaches, and impact on curriculum theory and practice in schools and classrooms. This content balances the current press for scientifically based research as the determinant of curriculum and its values.

TEXT FEATURES

Contemporary Curriculum In Thought and Action fosters interactive learning and a lively classroom experience using several noteworthy features.

Part Opener Cases Each part opens with a case or problem that invites opinions and discussion. These openers start the curriculum conversation, activate awareness, and reveal the learner's background, general motivation, and purpose for studying the chapters. Openers may be revisited after reading the chapters.

Multiple Orientations Using an even-handed treatment, the text shows how humanistic, social reconstructionist, systemic, and academic orientations to curriculum can each be valuable in curriculum development. Having a breadth of curriculum perspectives is important for today's teachers, who want to think beyond the day-to-day demands of an increasingly mandated curriculum and understand how knowledge of the different orientations can contribute to their sense of empowerment.

Strategic Research Suggestions All chapters include suggested research strategies—over 70—and give guidance for a number of important curriculum questions that have *not* been answered. These strategies may be the basis for master's theses, doctoral dissertations, or activities that will enhance the long-term retention and transfer of chapter concepts and skills.

Linking Curriculum and Teaching Methods   Unlike texts that focus only on curriculum or pedagogy, *Contemporary Curriculum In Thought and Action* illustrates the connection between curriculum and instruction and examines the relationship between the institutional curriculum and the curriculum as enacted by teachers and students. The text also shows how to reconcile the press for content standards with the professional preparation of teaching standards promoted by professional educators.

Historical, Psychological, and Philosophical Foundations   To help the reader better understand current curriculum theory and practice and to make economical use of teaching and learning time, foundations are integrated throughout the text.

Flexibility   The topical divisions and their order are flexible and can be changed, since each topic can be a separate unit of study for one or more class sessions. For example, an instructor who wants to define the curriculum field before embarking on its study may start with Part 5. Similarly, an instructor may prefer to introduce particular chapters by beginning with the questions posed at the end of the chapter.

Helping our schools evolve into positive institutions of learning, where every student graduates and receives a quality education, is probably the world's biggest challenge for the twenty-first century. I believe that curriculum can be used as a powerful tool to change what and how students learn, and *Contemporary Curriculum In Thought and Action* provides future administrators, policy makers, and educators with the knowledge and resources to make informed decisions that will affect not only the lives of students, but society's direction as well.

ACKNOWLEDGMENTS

A major contribution to the prospectus and development of this new text came from Dr. Jaye Darby, especially in emphasizing the importance of multicultural and gender perspectives in curriculum and the desirability of bringing historical and psychological foundations to the study of curriculum. The writing and shortcomings of the text are my responsibility.

I also appreciate the reviewers who made helpful suggestions to ensure that the book is applicable in a range of contexts.

The assistance of Mary Ellen McNeil in preparing the manuscript and in clarifying content was indispensable.

The initiation of this text and guidance in all phases were made possible by the leadership of Mr. Brad Hanson. Lindsay Lovier kept the writing on schedule and fostered good author–publisher relations.

Special thanks are given to Valerie A. Vargas, Senior Production Editor, to Suzanne Ingrao for managing production, and to Connie Parks and Brian Rose for their considerate copyediting of *Contemporary Curriculum In Thought and Action*.

J. D. M.

CONTEMPORARY CURRICULUM

In Thought and Action

PART 1

CONCEPTIONS OF CURRICULUM

Like the schoolboy or girl who is surprised to find that they know more about prose than they realize, having spoken it all their lives, so readers of Part 1 of this text will find that by focusing on a curriculum dilemma, they will bring to light their taken-for-granted curriculum experiences and begin to question the different categories for interpreting these experiences.

As a vehicle for activating your and your peers' thinking about curriculum, consider the unresolved problem of equity and closing academic gaps. Although a litany of factors have been mentioned as important to closing the gaps—quality of teachers, remediation, desegregation, resilience of the at-risk, cooperation of parents, school finance—curriculum has a disproportionate positive effect on students from groups traditionally underachieving.

I suggest beginning Part 1 by your thinking about how curriculum will close the gaps. If possible, share your reflections with others. Then, after individuals or groups have read particular chapters in Part 1, revisit the dilemma and note if my treatment of curriculum conceptions has changed your thinking on the issues. You may wish to begin by considering how one or more of the following curriculum conceptions could contribute to improved learning of all.

Humanistic. A humanistic curriculum is seen by students as important in helping them be what they want to be; it is a curriculum where learning is high in personal relevance, feeling, and probable success.

Social Reconstruction. The social reconstruction curriculum is an instrument for effecting social reform, including exposing how institutions, such as schools, maintain existing hierarchies of privilege.

Systemic. A systemic curriculum aligns goals, standards, programs, and instructional materials with tests for assessing the outcomes. A measured curriculum reveals whether the school and its teachers are advancing the learning of all and whether diverse groups are acquiring prespecified knowledge and skills.

Academic. In an academic curriculum knowledge is organized in ways that are best for learning a particular subject matter and for introducing students to the big questions that drive inquiry in the academic disciplines. Familiarity with subject matter concepts and a matching pedagogy is a central focus.

CHAPTER 1

THE HUMANISTIC CURRICULUM

IN **VIEW** of the negative connotations and the imperatives for academic mastery, more rigorous standards, firm codes of discipline, and warnings against teaching anything but factual information, can we simply write off a humanistic orientation to curriculum? Such a dismissal would be unfortunate, as there are strong arguments in favor of the humanistic approach.

The American people have a commitment to self-actualization. Repeatedly, parents express interest in self-understanding, and in fostering the emotional and physical well-being of their children as well as the intellectual skills necessary for independent judgment. The humanistic curriculum supports the American ideal of individualism, helping students discover who they are, not just shaping them into a form that has been designated in advance.

Americans place a premium on innovation and creativity. Thus it is a mistake for educators in the United States to respond to competition from abroad by imitating curriculum which emphasizes shaping a whole population to a high level of rigorous discipline and the same basic academic subjects for all. Although the average amount of learning in some areas may be higher in Japan and Singapore, the range of knowledge is narrower, and educators in these countries are uneasy about emphasizing rote learning at the expense of thinking and creativity.

Instead of adapting curriculum so that students score higher on multiple choice examinations, Americans might be concerned with maintaining their advantage in creativity, problem-solving skills, and innovation. The humanistic curriculum features activities that are exploratory, puzzling, playful, and spontaneous—all of which are vital for innovation and self-renewal. The best interests of Americans lie in providing students with a curriculum that is fixed on an uncertain future—on what is possible and potential, not on what is merely utilitarian or what will make the learner a helpless captive to what is already known.

The humanistic curriculum also goes a long way toward solving a fundamental problem: that much of what is taught is not learned, and much of what is presented and tested is not assimilated. Critics who think that greater learning is achieved by pouring more facts into children's minds are mistaken. Earlier reformers who tried to raise standards in the curriculum with rigorous academic programs met with failure. What went wrong? The new programs were often too far removed from the background of both students and teachers and did not take into consideration how learners might construct meaning. This should not be interpreted that subject matter must be easy. Rather, it must be brought to life, taught in a way that demonstrates its relevance to the learner. The humanistic curriculum offers an alternative to dull courses and depersonalization.

Widespread dissatisfaction with much of the present curriculum is evidenced by high dropout rates, vandalism, and discipline problems among the bored, the unhappy, and the angry. The problem is not just one of motivating students to acquire academic content. A larger concern is determining the appropriate educational response to students who live desperate lives—students who lack a purpose for living, good personal relations, and self-regard. The humanistic curriculum addresses these concerns.

There are signs that the new century will see a revival of the humanistic curriculum. Current reforms in medical education, for example, have introduced a blend of humanism and science. Medical educators recognize that one-eighth to one-fourth of their students suffer from serious depression, and they see a need for doctors who are more skilled in human relations. Hence, many of the nation's 127 medical schools are designing humanistic curricula. Instead of using a lecture hall with the sole mission of transmitting anatomy, biochemistry, and physiology, there are human values courses, which focus on emotional skills and understanding.[1] Students at the Albert Einstein College of Medicine helped to design their human values curriculum so that they could learn how to respond to their psychological needs at various stages of life and to understand their own feelings. In this curriculum, students may face each other in a circle and talk about topics that were once almost taboo—their fears about talking with dying patients, their fears of dying themselves. In learning to face an inability to cure every problem, doctors are more likely to avoid overaggressive treatment and prolongation of a patient's pain.

In 1994 the C. Everett Koop Institute attempted to produce a new kind of medical student sensitive to the human side of the doctor–patient relationship. Accordingly, the curriculum allocates less time to lectures and labs and more time to working with needy families, learning to recognize emotions and telling students it is OK to feel weird and upset about what they are doing. Instead of being pressured to maintain stoic composure, students are encouraged not to suppress their emotions; rather, they are allowed to cry, laugh, or leave the room if they want when they walk into a place with 22 dead people, cadavers ready for dissection.

Similarly, postindustrial employers have adopted the learning-to-learn and problem-solving skills of the child-centered curriculum in their efforts to improve productivity. The value of cooperative learning and the importance of every worker learning to work with others is a common priority in industry. Industrial training includes how to resolve conflicts peacefully—for example, by acknowledging feelings before addressing surface concerns, by finding ways to increase respect for those of different backgrounds, and by making team decisions through democratic processes. Increasingly, employers are prizing the humanistic goal of self-awareness. They realize that workers who know something about themselves are more likely to persist, to be productive and responsible, and to defer gratification.

Executives, too, are participating in leadership programs for training emotions and building trust. Programs such as Outward Bound allow people to face physical and mental challenges (e.g., rappelling down sheer cliffs so they can learn their strengths and weaknesses

---

[1]*Clinical Education and the Doctor of Tomorrow* (New York: New York Academy of Medicine, 1994).

and how they confront fears). Intensive courses in team leadership use humanistic techniques: "ice breakers" to get people to feel at ease and to form close working relations, and problem-solving thought games that parallel the behavior of the workplace.

A further reason for not writing off the humanistic curriculum rests on the connections between motivation, emotion, belief about self, and the cognitive component of student learning. Without attending to motivations, teachers are unlikely to effect desired conceptual changes related to science, math, social studies, and other academic areas.

CHARACTERISTICS OF THE HUMANISTIC CURRICULUM

Purpose

Humanists believe that the function of the curriculum is to provide each learner with intrinsically rewarding experiences that contribute to personal liberation and development. To humanists, the goals of education are related to the ideals of personal growth, integrity, and autonomy. Healthier attitudes toward self, peers, and learning are among their expectations. The ideal of self-actualization is at the heart of the humanistic curriculum. A person who exhibits this quality is not only coolly cognitive but also developed in aesthetic and moral ways, that is, a person who does good works and has good character. The humanist views actualization growth as a basic need. Each learner has a self that must be uncovered, built up, taught.

Role of the Teacher

The teacher provides warmth and nurtures emotions while continuing to function as a resource and facilitator. He or she should present materials imaginatively and create challenging situations. Humanistic teachers motivate their students through mutual trust. They encourage a positive student–teacher relationship by teaching out of their own interests and commitments while holding to the belief that each child can learn. Those who assume a leadership role in affective approaches to learning get in touch with themselves and students. Albert Einstein's comment, "The supreme act of the teacher is to awaken joy in creative expression and knowledge," belies a humanistic orientation.

Three essentials for the humanistic teacher as seen by students are the following:

- Listens comprehensively to the student's view of reality. ("She cares about my feelings and understands what I wish to say when I have difficulty in expressing it.")
- Respects the student. ("He used my idea in studying the problem.")
- Is natural and authentic, not putting on appearances. ("She lets us know what she feels and thinks and is not afraid to reveal her own doubts and insecurities.")

DIRECTIONS IN HUMANISTIC CURRICULUM

There have been two prevalent forms of humanistic curriculum, *confluent* and *consciousness*. Although there are different definitions for confluent education, there is general agreement that it infuses affect with content.[2] Confluent education generally supports the

---

[2]Stewart B. Shapiro, *The Place of Confluent Education in the Human Potential Movement: A Historical Perspective.* (Lanham, MD: Lanham Press of America, 1998).

existing subject matter curriculum. Some applications, such as "a curriculum of concern," take learners to be the subject matter and their emotions, feelings, and thoughts are the basis for inquiry and learning. A consciousness curriculum is tied to spirituality and transcendence—what we experience privately in our subjective awareness, such as a sense of connectiveness and the world around us. It may entail intuition, the mysterious, and the mystical as students search for meaning and purpose in their work and life. It rests on the belief that there is a better way of being in the world, better expression of feelings, and more just relations with others.

Aspects of humanistic curriculum have been preempted by those working with other curricular orientations. Both academic and social reconstructionist orientations are introducing humanistic factors. Academicians are beginning to realize that the emotional qualities of the humanistic curricula, such as flow, are necessary for improving complex achievement. Social reconstructionists who want to take advantage of the humanists' success in increasing student personal power and sensitivity to feelings (consciousness of self) are building on self-awareness to develop *critical awareness* of patterns in the society.

A Confluent Curriculum

Rationale for Confluence   The essence of confluent education is the integration of an affective domain (emotions, attitudes, values) with the cognitive domain (intellectual knowledge and abilities). It is an *add-on curriculum*, whereby emotional dimensions are added to conventional subject matter so that there is personal meaning to what is learned. Confluentists do not downplay public knowledge, such as scientific information, in favor of subjective or intuitive (i.e., direct and immediate) knowledge. The confluent teacher of English, for example, links affective exercises to paragraphing, organization, and argumentative and other discursive forms of writing. By beginning with the student's personal, imaginative, and emotional responses and working out from these, the confluentist helps learners both to acquire language skills and to discover themselves.

Confluentists do not believe that the curriculum should teach students what to feel or what attitudes to have. Their goal is to provide students with more alternatives to choose from in terms of their own lives, to take responsibility for appreciating the choices available, and to realize that they, the learners, can indeed make choices.

Shapiro and others have analyzed examples and nonexamples of confluence, concluding that a confluent curriculum includes the following elements[3]:

1. *Participation.* There is consent, power sharing, negotiation, and joint responsibility by coparticipants. It is essentially nonauthoritarian and not unilateral.

2. *Integration.* There is interaction, interpenetration, and integration of thinking, feelings, and action.

3. *Relevance.* The subject matter is closely related to the basic needs and lives of the participants and is significant to them, both emotionally and intellectually.

4. *Self.* The self is a legitimate object of learning.

5. *Goal.* The social goal or purpose is to develop the whole person within a human society.

---

[3]Stewart B. Shapiro, "The Instructional Values of Humanistic Educators: An Expanded Empirical Analysis," *Journal of Humanistic Education and Development* 24, no. 3 (June 1987):155–170.

Consciousness and Transcendency

Mysticism   Although humanistic psychologists typically emphasize the affective and cognitive domains, some humanists are interested in treating higher domains of consciousness as well. Accordingly, the curriculum involves not only a cognitive mode of consciousness but an intuitive receptive mode—guided fantasy and various forms of meditation. For example, *transcendental meditation* (TM) is concerned with altering states of consciousness, voluntary control of inner states, and growth beyond the ego. It has been tried as an adjunct to the high school curriculum partly because it is seen as a way to diminish drug abuse among students. Essentially, TM is a simple technique for turning attention "inward toward the subtler levels of thought until mind transcends the experience of the subtlest state of thought and arrives at the source of thought. This expands the conscious mind and at the same time brings it in contact with the creative intelligence that gives rise to every thought."[4] TM has been used to reach some very commonplace curriculum goals, such as reduction of social tension, increased learning ability, and improved athletic performance. It has also inspired more novel goals, such as growth in consciousness and in other ways of knowing.

The Maharishi International University (MIU) at Fairfield, Iowa, offers degrees in a number of fields, such as physics, mathematics, biology, business, and education. However, as a university founded on a philosophy that uses transcendental meditation, it also offers opportunities for students to experience higher states of consciousness. Everyone at MIU—faculty, students, staff—practices a twice-daily hour-long routine of mediation. In addition, in all courses an effort is made to foster a principle of interdependence by which personal individuality is related to consciousness of whatever subject matter has been taught. As concepts are introduced in one course, students and teachers seek to recall corresponding concepts in other disciplines and how the concepts might be experienced in meditation. The probable consequence of this practice is a sense of personal relevance to knowledge and an integration of the different academic disciplines.[5]

One caution concerning transcendental mediation, practiced in such courses as the Science of Creative Intelligence, is that its inclusion in the curriculum may violate legal precedents opposed to sectarian indoctrination. The "science" of TM is held by some to be essentially a religious philosophy because its presuppositions about the source of life and energy reflect monistic Hinduism with pantheistic consciousness.

The religious concept of transcendence (i.e., the experience of going beyond any state or realization of being) has implications for curriculum. It suggests that students should learn how a particular mode of investigation in a subject field relates to other specializations. A transcending consciousness also helps us recognize the incompleteness of any subject. To learn that no discipline provides the full and final disclosure of the nature of things may help learners discern new possibilities, new directions, and new questions. A curriculum of transcendence should foster a spirit of criticism toward existing practices and encourage undeveloped potential and hope in improving one's existence.

In his essays *The Lure of the Transcendent*, Dwayne Huebner has illustrated how the arts can enhance awareness, meaning, and the beauty of life and how the humanistic teacher puts emotional and intellectual needs of students before institutional demands. Noteworthy is Huebner's illustration of how humanistic teachers risk themselves, accepting newness, surprise, pain, and happiness as they reshape their own values and listen to their students.

[4]Maharishi Mahesh Yogi, *Maharishi Mahesh Yogi on the Bhagavad-Gita: A New Translation and Commentary* (Baltimore: Penguin, 1969),470.
[5]Ira Shor, *Empowering Education: Critical Teaching for Social Change* (Chicago: University of Chicago Press, 1992).

Huebner views teacher insecurity as an indication of the doubt that allows them to "respond afresh to that which is given when afraid."[6]

Since 9/11, students are showing more interest in why they are here and who they are. A national survey is underway regarding spirituality among college students. Preliminary findings from entering freshmen indicate that during high school 40% of students rank spirituality as of great importance to them. Similar interest in spirituality has been found among college faculty.[7]

Transpersonal Techniques   Biofeedback for controlling brain waves, deep hypnosis, yoga, and the use of dreams are additional transpersonal techniques that have implications for curricula. In English, for example, dreams may be used as a basis for creative writing because they contain the emotional impact of messages from the unconscious. Physical education, too, may use aspects of the transpersonal in learning to control one's body for optimum health and physical fitness through biofeedback and yoga.

The use of such techniques as relaxation and imaginary journeys are sometimes used in academic courses. Teacher relaxed his class by having them imagine they were electrons being pulled and pushed by the fields around induction coils. When these students later read a chapter dealing with induction coils, they had no trouble visualizing the forces described, and the quality of their lab work seemed to bear this out.

A review of hundreds of studies regarding self-improvement techniques led the National Research Council (NRC) to conclude that many nonconventional techniques, such as sleep learning and mental imagery, can help people improve their abilities and that other techniques, such as extrasensory perception and psychokinesis (mind over matter), exist only in the minds of believers. Mental imagery and mental rehearsal help a person to perform better on skills that require a thoughtful, systematic approach. Some techniques like biofeedback and cohesion (the process by which members of a group become committed to each other and their common goals) have useful application but may not improve a person's abilities. Biofeedback can reduce muscle tensions, but the relaxed state it produces does not necessarily make for better performance. Although cohesive groups exhibit loyalty, altruism, and a willingness to take risks, no clear evidence exists that cohesion is linked to sharper skills.

Emotions can be changed to promote higher intellectual activity as well as mental and physical health. Exposing people to nature, in the form of gardens or other natural vistas, can reduce blood pressure, pulse rate, and increase the brain activity that controls mood and lifts feelings.[8] Positive emotions are associated with higher level processing such as reflection and problem solving than are negative emotions. Similarly, painful emotional states are transformed by using music and sound. Musical exercises that activate memories shared with loved ones and that reflect an aura of safety and trust in the world can evoke a mood of wonder, joy, celebration, and love.[9]

Responses to Depersonalization

Self-Directed Learning   Self-directed learning is one response to the threat of depersonalization brought about by a narrow focus on basic skills in reading, writing, and arithmetic. Humanists believe that the basics should include a sense of ability, clarity of

---

[6]Dwayne E. Huebner, *The Lure of the Transcendent: Collected Essays*, V. Hillis, ed., A. W. F. Pinar, coll. (Mahwah, NJ: Lawrence Erlbaum, 1999).

[7]A. W. Astin and H. S. Astin, *Meaning and Spiritualism in the Lives of College Faculty: A Study of Values and Stress* (Los Angeles: Higher Educational Research Institute, UCLA, Nov. 1998).

[8]Michael Waldholtz, "Flower Power: How Gardens Can Improve Your Mental Health," *Wall Street Journal*, no. 74 (Aug. 26, 2003): D3.

[9]Louise Montello, *Essential Musical Intelligence* (New York: Crest Books, 2003).

values, positive self-concept, capacity for innovation, and openness—characteristics of the self-directed learner.

The following are key ideas to consider in planning a curriculum for self-directed learning:

> *Achievement motivation.* Those persons who are motivated by hope of success have an incentive to learn when the task is not too easy and when there is an expectation of success. Persons motivated by fear of failure, on the other hand, tend to select tasks that are either so easy they cannot fail or so difficult that no embarrassment results when they do fail.

> *Attributive theory.* Achievement-oriented individuals are more likely to see themselves as a cause of their success.

> *Children's interests.* When children find schoolwork distasteful and yet are driven to engage in more of the distasteful work, they acquire learned helplessness, having no interests related to learning. Freedom to undertake a self-directed study of something that concerns the learner seems to be an important condition for developing channeled effort.

The late Evan Keislar developed a curriculum model for self-development.[10] The goal of this curriculum is to optimize future growth and development of the individual learner. Learners are helped to mediate key decisions by reflecting on their level of cognitive development and testing proposed courses of action. Resources are provided for helping learners deal with uncertainty, take risks, try out ideas, and profit from mistakes. The teacher's role is to make sure that the student faces situations that arouse questions and lead to exploration. Challenges are matched to the child's pattern of development. Although the teacher is available to help students find needed resources, the teacher does not do so when information is readily available. Because growth proceeds through encounters with conflict and tension, this curriculum promotes an optimum level of uncertainty.

As with other humanistic curricula, the self-directed curriculum aims at development in several areas:

> *Cognitive.* Children respond to the requirements of problematic situations, not simply to external directions. By anticipating consequences, they learn to make wise choices about goals. Allowances are made for those children whose thinking is tied to immediate perceptions and for those who are ready for inferential thought.

> *Affective.* Children learn to deal at an emotional level with such uncertainties as social conflicts, evaluation, and challenge. They learn to view failure as a learning experience.

> *Social.* Assertiveness training, role training, and experimenting with competitive and cooperative groups are among the activities provided.

> *Moral.* Moral development is fostered through consideration of moral conflicts that arise from the social activities of the class and the wider community.

> *Ego development.* The development of self-respect and self-confidence occurs through a social climate in which a person's world does not depend on ability or level of maturity. Each individual has an opportunity to attain success for there is no scarcity of rewards.

In many ways, self-directed curriculum is consistent with what John Dewey suggested more than 60 years ago: a curriculum that poses problems rooted within the present

---

[10]Evan R. Keislar, "A Developmental Model for a Curriculum in the Primary Grades" (unpublished paper, UCLA Graduate School of Education, Los Angeles, 1983).

experience and capacity of learners, problems that arouse an active quest for information and invite the production of new ideas.[11]

Finding the Personal in the Academic   In concentrating on academic knowledge, the learner may be depersonalized. To counteract this danger, there are two courses of action: (a) recognizing the limitations of academic knowledge while acknowledging other forms of knowledge and (b) finding personal meaning to subject matter.

The optimally developed person has not merely accumulated encyclopedic knowledge, but can live well, acting wisely in a wide range of circumstances and situations. The kind of knowledge that permits optimal development is not likely to be found only in academic knowledge but requires know-how achieved through active expression of one's existence and by interactive engagements with others and the natural environment. Walking and talking have led to great achievements through active expression. Good manners and the skills of actors, mechanics, artisans, physicians, and engineers are examples of knowledge acquired by emulating master practitioners. In short, there are many ways to gain knowledge other than through the academic fields.

Although academic knowledge is not sufficient for personal development, under some circumstances, it can enhance personal knowledge, and enable a person to live better. What are these circumstances?

Literature   Kenneth Resch believes that it is imperative for teachers to find their own personal connections in subject matter, to share these connections with students, and to hope that students will share their understanding. In reading a passage from Wordsworth's *The Prelude* (in which Wordsworth picks up a piece of stone rubble left from the destroyed Bastille and begins to muse of his youthful and lost past), Resch shares with his students some of his own seemingly trivial possessions and the memories they evoke. In turn, students share their memories sometimes by bringing things to class or by simply talking about possessions and the memories associated. In such an approach, poetry is related to personal experiences as students begin to sense their own relationships and the romantic notion of responding to the past.[12]

The Arts   The late Philip Phenix believed that there is personalization when the arts—music, art, dance—are taught with the idea of knowing how to produce patterns of the field and competencies in expressive movement or when they are taught so that the learner is at least able to emphatically participate in the activity.[13]

Margot Grallert has developed arts programs based on the belief that every person has an inner sense of self that must provide direction for learning and that the environment can stimulate individuals to find their personal directions, all with the conviction that there are no final answers.[14] Grallert's curriculum maintains a balance between expression and craftsmanship. Students are given help in learning to use the tools and skills they need to express themselves.

Mathematics   Unless the student is helped to become a participant in the process of mathematics, symbol making, and manipulation according to the accepted canons of the mathematics community, the study of math is likely to be depersonalized.

[11]John Dewey, *Experience and Education* (New York: Macmillan, 1939).
[12]Kenneth E. Resch, "Wordsworth, Whitman and Us: Finding Personal Relationships," *English Journal* (April 1988): 19–22.
[13]Philip H. Phenix, "Promoting Personal Development through Learning," *Teachers College Record* 84, no. 2 (winter 1982): 301–317.
[14]Margot Grallert, "Working from the Inside Out: A Practical Approach to Expression," *Harvard Educational Review* 61, no. 3 (Aug. 1991): 260–269.

Alvin White along with 30 other mathematicians promote humanistic mathematics through the *Humanistic Mathematics Network Journal,* now available online. This journal gives accounts of how teachers of math are promoting feelings as well as thinking in mathematics, transcending traditional goals of classroom learning and emphasizing questions over answers.

In Chapter 12, the newer trends in mathematics curriculum are shown to be consistent with personalization. However, Nel Noddings carries personalization in this field to a new level.[15] She argues that secondary school students should not have to take mathematics unless they want to study it, and, if they do, they will find it helpful to scatter their energies over a spectrum of studies. They will connect writing, history, philosophy, science, and the like to mathematics.

Science and Social Science   Personalization is enhanced through application and transcendency. Students see how knowledge of the material may be applied to the satisfaction of human need through technology and through the use of knowledge of science in understanding self or seeing how the natural world supports personal life. Personalization exists when students are helped to see mysteries yet unprobed by scientific undertakings as well as by shifting perspectives and alternatives.

In a curriculum that tries to reduce suicide among Native Americans, students draw on Zuni and Cherokee cultures and traditions in helping them cope with their personal difficulties. For example, they focus on the Indian way of dealing with anger, recognizing that there is much for Indians to be angry about. They also learn about Indian ways to cope with grief and loss, composing poems, singing, and meditating as well as addressing cultural factors that may contribute to self-destructive behavior.[16]

An illustration of a personalized science, aesthetics, and ethics curriculum is David Orr's "Earth centered" curriculum, where students transcend abstract knowledge by transforming the ecologically unstable culture of their campus. Students learn to critically study the ecological implications of their culture, including the hidden costs of the way we irresponsibly consume and create waste in our schools. Through this curriculum, students begin by learning to reflect on their reality and to live by the garden ethic. The school is transformed from a decorative, pretty, vacuous landscape to one that sustains the value of bioriginal self-sufficiency, caretaking, and community participation.[17]

History   Personal development occurs in the study of history when the past is dramatically recreated and made available for persons now living and when the students feel personally involved in the historical happening. History as only chronicle is depersonalizing. An outstanding example of teaching history as personal development is found in Arye Carmon's Teaching the Holocaust,[18] a curriculum that helps students formulate a set of moral rules for self through a confrontation with the Holocaust. The curriculum, which has been introduced in the United States, Germany, and Israel, places the adolescent at the focal point of the education process. The Holocaust serves as the subject matter used to respond to the needs of today's adolescents.

The theory of Erik Erikson underlies the construction of Carmon's curriculum.[19] Erikson felt that persons are confirmed by their identities and societies regenerated by their

[15]Nel Noddings, "Excellence as a Guide to Educational Development through Learning," *Teachers College Record* 94, no. 4 (summer 1993): 730–743.

[16]Jessica Porter, "Drawing on Indian Traditions and Culture, New Curriculum Seeks to Reduce Suicide Rate," *Education Week* (Feb. 24, 1993): 6–7.

[17]David W. Orr, *Ecological Literacy—Education and the Transition to a Post Modern World* (Albany: State University of New York Press, 1992).

[18]Arye Carmon, *Problems in Coping with the Holocaust: Experiences with Students in a Multinational Program,* American Academy of Political and Social Sciences, *Annals* 450 (July 1980).

[19]Erik Erikson, *Identity, Youth and Crisis* (New York: Norton, 1968).

lifestyle. To enter history, students must be able to relate their childhood to the childhood experiences of former generations. They must be able to identify with the ideals conveyed in the history of their culture. According to Erikson, in youth, childhood dependence gives way; no longer is it the old teaching the young the meaning of life. It is the young who by their actions tell the old whether life as represented to them has some vital promise.

The major objective of this Holocaust curriculum is to heighten each student's awareness of the critical function of adult responsibility. This objective is achieved by fostering awareness of the human tendency toward stereotyping, prejudice, ethnocentrism, obeying authority, and thus escaping responsibilities.

The subject matter is organized into units—the socialization of a German adolescent in Nazi Germany, the socialization of a secret service man, the moral dilemmas of individuals and groups during the Holocaust, and the meaning of life in the post-Holocaust era. In each unit, students are given documents from the historical period. These documents provide historical background and serve as stimuli for discussion of the moral dilemma. The method of instruction is a combination of individual inquiry and group integration. Each person deals with a specific document; students form small groups to exchange feelings and opinions regarding the topics and their individual studies; then the entire class completes the discussion of the topic at hand. The content is not alien to the students and they cannot remain apathetic to it. Students face questions that are relevant to their own lives: Why sanctification of life rather than martyrdom? What are the dilemmas that confronted the individual and which confronted Jews as members of a community? Which of these dilemmas touch you personally? Why? What is the common denominator of the dilemmas? Discussion manifests a dialogue between the student and his or her conscience, and between student and peers.

During the first phase of the curriculum, resistance toward the subject matter increases. Students tend to resist giving up their stereotypical attitudes and other protective mechanisms. Gradually this resistance fades, only to be replaced by a feeling of helplessness. At this point the study has opened students to the possibility of critical thinking and moral judgment. Students then begin to formulate the universal rule for confronting moral dilemmas: "How would I have behaved if I had been in this situation? How should I have behaved?"

Connecting Individual Learning and Social Learning Although the humanistic curriculum enables students to become knowledgeable about self and feelings, it has been faulted for not offering the societal perspectives necessary for social change. Hence, humanists are giving more of their attention to social, political, and historical connections to inequality and evil in the world rather than sole attention to the psychological factors that form people.

An example of how curriculum can be developed to synthesize personal and social change is found in the work of Lee Bell and Nancy Schniedewind.[20] In their curriculum, the teacher focuses on personal competition and uncritical acceptance of competition in the larger society. Questions as to why students need to feel superior to others and their uncritical belief in the superiority of American institutions and values are treated. The teacher begins by creating a trusting classroom and tries to develop the student's sense of personal power. Affirmation activities are implemented by which students validate their own and others' strengths. Students explore put-downs and how put-downs weaken personal power. Group support is developed through cooperative activities involving shared leadership and

[20]Lee Bell and Nancy Schniedewind, "Reflective Minds/Intentional Hearts: Joining Humanistic Education and Critical Theory for Liberating Education," *Journal of Education* 169, no. 2 (1987): 55–79.

conflict resolution. Students examine the costs of competition on self-esteem and inter-personal relationships as well as on political and economic relationships in society.

This curriculum is ordered so that the concepts of personal power, group support, critical consciousness, and action are applied first to the personal level and then to the community, nation, and world. At the personal level, students explore their feelings about ability grouping and standardized grading procedures. They consider alternative proce-dures that will validate everyone's strengths. At the community level, students explore the effects of cooperation and competition in the workplace. At the national level, they study examples of political cooperation, like the successful farmworkers' boycotts. At the global level, students engage in high-level activities, such as comparing personal egotism to social egotism in the context of nations.

PSYCHOLOGICAL FOUNDATIONS OF THE HUMANISTIC CURRICULUM

Donald Moss has written an historical view of humanistic psychology from the beginning in Ancient Greece to its flowering in the modern age.[21] Moss highlighted moments that influenced humanistic psychologists.

Kierkegaard in the nineteenth century posited higher individual consciousness. Subjective individuals make personal choices, avoid dependency on science and objectiv-ity, but take "leaps of faith" as they move from a sensuous state where emotions dominate to a state of understanding universal humanity and finally entering a religious state of unity with God. Nietzsche in the same century explored the ways an individual could transcend conventional values and constraints becoming a "superman."

Buber in the twentieth century was concerned with the absurdities that individuals face because of their inhumanity and their tendency to construct relationships characterized as "I–It" where "I–It" is used for selfish ends. Buber instead offered an "I–Thou" relationship—a mutual sensitivity of feeling or empathy where there is sharing of knowledge and feel-ing that makes life more spiritual.

Heidegger contributed to the notion that people can create better possibilities for liv-ing by his phenomenological idea that one's view of the world has been shaped by histor-ical events and that there is a need for reinterpreting this view based on revised views of the present and future. Sartre extended the idea of personal freedom with responsibility for our choices and actions, arguing that nothing restricts us from fashioning our own mean-ings and becoming what we desire.

Existential/phenomenological ideas are tied to both confluence and consciousness. Humanistic curriculum in its focus on conflict, war, hunger and the like, brings human conditions to student awareness and addresses their questions of whether these conditions are natural, thereby opening new possibilities for themselves and their world.

Third Force Psychology

Confluent curriculum has been influenced by a third force psychology, so called because it addressed inadequacies in both behaviorism and Freudian psychologies. The third force psychologist believes that behaviorism is mechanistic and that behaviorists view the learner as a detached intellect, ignoring affective responses and higher order aspects of

---

[21]Donald Moss, "The Roots and Genealogy of Humanistic Psychology," *Journal of Humanistic Education and Development* 7 (2002): 5.

the personality such as altruism. Likewise, to the third force psychologist, Freudian psychologies appear overly cynical about the motives of persons and emphasize humankind's pathological and unconscious emotional forces.

The late Abraham Maslow was a key figure in the development of third force psychology. Maslow viewed self-actualization as having several dimensions. He saw it as a life achievement, a momentary state, and the normal process of growth when a person's deficiency motives are satisfied and his or her defenses are not mobilized by threat. Maslow assumed that the human being has a biological essence. Hence the search for self means attending to impulses from within which indicate that a person is a part of nature as well as a unique being.[22]

If third force psychology is a foundation of the humanistic curriculum, it follows that this curriculum must encourage self-actualization, whereby learners are permitted to express, act out, experiment, make mistakes, be seen, get feedback, and discover who they are. Maslow thought that we learn more about ourselves by examining responses to peak experiences which give rise to love, hate, anxiety, depression, and joy. For Maslow, the peak experiences of awe, mystery, and wonder are both the end and the beginning of learning. Thus a humanistic curriculum should value and attempt to provide for such experiences as moments in which cognitive and personal growth take place simultaneously.

Consider this anecdote from a chemistry class:

The teacher was trying to teach us about sugars and we yawned as he added glucose to some Fehling's solution. But when he heated the mixture and the blue solution turned into a red solid, I sat up straight and recognized the moment as a turning point in my life. Within a day I had bought a Gilbert chemistry set and began threatening my attic and the peace of mind of my parents.[23]

Believing in the need to discover one's potentials and limitations through intense activity, Mihaly Csikszentmihalyi (pronounced Chick-sent-me-high) began his studies of optimal and enjoyable experiences in which there is a deep concentration on the activity at hand—the person forgetting his or her problems and temporarily losing the awareness of self.[24] Such experiences are termed "flow" and at their most challenging level allow the person to transcend self. "I am so involved in what I am doing I don't see myself as separate from what I am doing." Those who find their activities to be intrinsically enjoyable (in flow) develop their intellectual ability to the fullest. Flow experiences occur when environmental challenges match a person's competencies and skills. In contrast, negative experiential states occur in overchallenged situations (anxiety) or when one is overskilled for the task (boredom). As our capabilities grow, we must take in increasingly greater challenges to stay in flow.

Csikszentmihalyi exhorts us to develop complexity in our consciousness, to acquire multiple interests and abilities because our future depends on it. He holds that without resolving our personal conflicts, we will not be concerned for or do effective work for others. Complexity is made up of two closely linked processes: *differentiation* when individuals feel free to pursue individual goals and to become as different as they can be from each other and *integration* when individuals become aware of the goals of others and help them to realize their goals.

---

[22]Abraham H. Maslow, "Humanistic Education," *Journal of Humanistic Psychology* 19, no. 3 (summer 1979): 13–27.

[23]R. M. Ramette, "Exocharmic Reactions," *Journal of Chemical Education* 57, no. 1 (Jan. 1980): 68–69.

[24]Mihaly Csikszentmihalyi and Isabella Selega Csikszentmihalyi, *Optimal Experience: Psychological Studies of Flow in Consciousness* (London: Cambridge University Press, 1988).

How can the curriculum contribute to flow experiences and awareness of complexity? Although persons differ in their ability to experience flow—it is easier for some people to enjoy everyday life and to transform routine and threatening situations into opportunities for action—the ability to experience flow may be learned. Through meditation and spiritual discipline, a person can learn to control consciousness. Yoga can provide training in concentration memory control and the formulation of specific goals. Offering a range of learning opportunities increases the possibility of matching appropriate challenge and competency. A curriculum goal might be to educate students so that they will be able to experience flow and avoid boredom and anxiety, regardless of social conditions. To this end, students would learn how to recognize challenges, turn adversity into manageable tasks, and trust their skills. Awareness of complexity may occur through the arts—dance, music, painting—which are generally enjoyed by students and can be taught to advance both differentiation and integration. However, the funneling of knowledge into narrow channels of abstract material, such as chemistry, biology, mathematics, and geography, works against awareness of the complexity of society and the need for interdependence. Instead of each academic subject being taught as if it had a separate existence, Csikszentmihalyi advocates a curriculum that will help students put academics together, showing the interconnectedness of causes and effects—how physics is related to ethics, how molecular biology can enhance empathy, and how history can relate ecology, economics, sociology, and the like in understanding human action.[25] His curriculum would not enshrine the creative solutions of the past but make it possible for creativity to reassess itself. As students perceive the network of causes and effects in which actions are embedded and their emotions and imaginations are trained to respond to the consequences of these actions, students will grow in awareness of complexity and have a chance at surviving in the future.

Carl Rogers has provided a framework for a humanistic curriculum. He was a third force psychologist who identified conditions that enable humans to grow and seek fulfillment, showing the importance of emotional relationships where participants have positive regard and empathize understandings for each other. His writings offer practical illustrations of how teachers can change the way we think about students and learning.[26] Rogers believed that all individuals have a positive orientation and that they can become better to the degree that they are willing to be real, empathetic, trusting in their own experiences, and expressing what they truly feel. He thought everyone has a natural ability to learn and wants to continue learning as long as the experience is positive. His research studies confirmed that learning best takes place when:

- The self is not threatened (external threats are reduced to a minimum).
- Students choose and pursue their own projects, selecting resources and procedures but accepting responsibility for the consequences.
- If independence of mind, creativity, and self-confidence are the goals, self-evaluation and self-criticism precedes evaluation by others.
- Emphasis is placed on learning how to learn, which is usually more useful than learning a specific. Learning how to learn means being open to experience and to change.

Rogers saw teachers as facilitators of learning rather than directors of learning. Humanists are willing to trust and to take risks, not afraid to express their own thoughts and feeling: "You make me uncomfortable when you swear!"

---

[25]Mihaly Csikszentmihalyi, *The Evolving Self: A Psychology for the Third Millennium* (New York: HarperCollins,1993).
[26]Carl Rogers, "Researching Person-Centered Issues in Education," *Freedom for the '80s* (Columbus, OH: Merrill, 1983), 197–227.

Although the golden years of humanistic psychology and the human potential movement from the 1950s to 1980s are associated with the work of Maslow and Rogers, these leaders learned from many contemporaries. By way of example, Rollo May showed the importance of listening to the individual's perception rather than assuming the cause for another's behavior. Wilhelm Reich focused on how the body defends against unacceptable feelings and creates techniques for overcoming these defenses. Fritz Perls similarly developed therapeutic activities in which peers helped individuals reconcile their self-perceptions and their desired potentials. *The Handbook of Humanistic Psychology* features articles describing applications of humanistic psychology in a variety of contexts in which the emotions, intellect, and the body contribute to self-actualization and health. The articles also treat the history of the field and reveal the tension between those who want humanistic psychology to be more empirical or scientific and those who are seeking ways for individuals to reach higher levels of consciousness, including practices drawn from the sages and mystics of the world. Humanistic psychologists are challenged by the findings from genetic and neurological studies that give new answers to old questions: "What does it means to be human?" and "Is there a protean self or are our identities predetermined by genes or shaped by socially imposed categories and language?"

The following trends are noticeable in humanistic psychology. First, those with an empirical bent are responding to the call from the 1998–1999 president of the American Psychological Association, Martin E. F. Seligman, for a positive psychology that would focus on what makes people succeed, looking for how affect helps with existential questions together with the effects of hope and optimism.

Second, transcendentalists are using nontheistic spiritual traditions from Asia, such as Buddhism, aiming at high levels of consciousness and alternative ways to relate to the world. This direction is sometimes termed as *fourth force psychology*.

In contrast with typical efforts to develop skilled use of an analytic mind whereby students learn to use given categories and systems to evaluate something or someone and to analyze the present from past experiences, the transcendentalist encourages additional ways of learning and knowledge, such as being guided by intuition—an inner voice, feeling, thought, or image. The interplay between the rational and nonrational is necessary for creative imagination and a prerequisite to logical thought.

Awareness makes possible a higher level of thinking that is beyond that found in formal operations. As Albert Einstein said, "No problem can be solved with the same consciousness that created it. We must learn to see our world anew." Vision logic is an example of transcendency to a higher level. Accordingly highly actualized persons move from a single point in time and space to multiple positions with their different perspectives giving rise to insight and the possibility of transformation.[27]

Third, new findings from the fields of neurology and genetics challenge the humanists by suggesting that consciousness is a chemical and neural activity and that personality factors, like sense of humor, romantic love, cooperation, and aesthetics, are genetically predetermined.[28] On the other hand, brain scientists are reminded that brains do not work in isolation, that we are not fixed from birth and can change or be changed depending on the environment. Neural connections depend on experiences which are the basis for our identity. We do not know how brain structures activate their correlated functions when a phenomenon occurs.

---

[27]K.Wilbur, *The Eye of the Spirit: An Integral Vision for a World Gone Slightly Mad* (Boston: Shambhala, 1997).
[28]S. Quartz and T. Sejnowsici, T. *Liars, Lovers and Heroes: What the Brain Science Reveals about How We Become Who We Are* (New York: William Morrow, 2002).

Humanists continue to believe that each self is unique with a subjectivity that allows individual interpretations of events and a potential to exercise choice and responsibility.

Psychological and neurological studies indicate the importance of overcoming negative emotions by enhancing emotional competence and by cognitive control of the emotions. Accordingly, schools are developing programs to help students stop and inhibit impulsive tendencies, to identify feelings, and to think of alternative solutions to their problems. It is believed that as students understand and recognize their emotions, they improve in problem solving and facilitate their cognitive flexibilities.

Unlike school models for self-regulation that draw from a cognitive psychology with its strategies for comprehending text and lecture and metacognitive strategies for planning, monitoring and controlling cognition, humanistic models center on motivation and emotions, including strategies for boosting self-confidence or self-efficacy such as positive self talk ("I can do this") or increasing interest by making a game out of a required task, overcoming negative emotions such as anxiety in order to achieve their own goals.

HISTORICAL ANTECEDENTS TO THE HUMANISTIC CURRICULUM

In his description of the origin of confluent education, Shapiro likened it to the history of the humanities, involving different philosophies of the humanistic movement in psychology and the human potential movement including the countercultural programs of the 1960s and 1970s. Shapiro concluded that sporadically there is a humanistic impulse to express strivings and yearnings.

Ancient Greeks and Romans

The classical conception of the humanities originated in the Greek tradition of an education to develop a harmonious and balanced person. This education attempted to answer what it meant to be human: to actualize the meaning of life and death and to experience the greatest happiness while achieving excellence in performance. Both the Greeks and the Romans, who adopted the Greek civilization, thought it was not enough to add to a student's knowledge but to add to a student's happiness.

The Athenians emphasized freedom and development of physical, psychological, and artistic capabilities. Of course, the Greek ideal for education applied only to the few, and education varied with social conditions at given times. The late Athenian period, for example, a time of prosperity, brought a demand for fame and fortune rather than a demand for knowledge for its own sake.

Greek philosophers with contrasting beliefs founded their own schools. Stoicism, for example, is one of these philosophies and of current interest because of its relation to self-control and character. The Stoics followed the Socratic ideals of self-sufficiency, endurance, and virtues by teaching students to be indifferent to painful circumstances and to accept what life brings. Later the Emperor Marcus Aurelius and the early Christians promoted stoicism.

Today stoicism is hot with authors such as Peter Gibbon who advocate the reintroduction of heroes into the curriculum in an effort to renew America's greatness. As with Greek and Roman classics, the study of heroes is a search for better selves, to see how heroes can lift and improve our lives, and to realize that one's character is as important as one's intellectual ability. Clinton, while president, said he read Marcus Aurelius twice a year.

As seen in Table 1.1, humanistic metaphors and ideas for teaching have continually reappeared—"The original is not the original." Although these ideas for advancing the individual have been around for a long time, they have seldom been part of an institutionalized curriculum, which has a bias toward authority and control.

Traditional Humanities

The Greek and Latin cultures are periodically revived as repeating the best of civilization and humanity. They are justified on the basis of their aim at freedom of thought, creativity, and self-expression. However, this curriculum often becomes elitist, limited to selected classrooms and the imitating of Greek and Roman masters.

During the Renaissance in Italy, humanists stressed personal development, culture, and freedom, borrowing from the Greeks the idea of harmonious development of mind, body, morals, with the goals of individualization and self-realization. Their centering on the beautiful, including sensual beauty, is noteworthy.

The issue of how the traditional humanities relate to the present humanistic curriculum has been studied showing that both deal with values, deep subjectivity, students' feelings, and personal identity as well as inquiry. Continuity lies in the same goal, namely, enlargement of the human spirit.

As with science and other disciplines, the humanities can be taught for personal significance or for lifeless reproduction. The difference can be seen by asking whether the study contributes to one's self-understanding, inspiration, imagination or wonder. Examples of this is shown by teachers like Kingsley Amis who, when teaching the British novel, asked his students to rank works, not in order of their importance, but by their "sheer enjoyableness."

Table 1.1   Humanistic Ideas in Conflict with Institutionalized Curriculum

Humanistic Ideas	Distant Voices
"Know thyself—the unexamined life cannot succeed."	Socrates (469–399 B.C.)
"The learner is not an empty vessel to be filled, but a flame to be ignited."	Plato (427–347 B.C.)
"Education is an internal process assisted by external agencies in which the individuals actualize their potential."	Aristotle (384–322 B.C.)
"Education should aim for freedom, creativity, and self-expression."	Petrarch (1304–1374)
"Individuals have the responsibilities and ability to live their own lives.")	Erasmus (1469–1536)
"Character and the ability to evaluate one's own personality, to determine and fulfill one's own physical and spiritual needs, and to understand and cooperate with others are far more important than mastery of verbal or factual lessons."	Montaigne (1533–1592)
"Mind and body are closely interrelated and cannot be separated."	Locke (1632–1704)
"Children are born good with both an instinct for self-preservation and sympathy and good feelings for their companions."	Rousseau (1712–1778)
"No human being should control the will or decisions of another individual."	Kant (1724–1804)
"The relationship between student and teacher should be like that between mother and child—a shared process motivated by friendship, cooperation, mutual aid and love."	Pestalozzi (1746–1827)

Progressive Education

The ideas of Pestalozzi, Rousseau, and other humanists influenced Francis W. Parker (1831–1902) in his leadership as Superintendent of Schools in Quincy, Massachusetts, and at the University of Chicago where he advocated student choice and the student as the object of instruction not the content fields. John Dewey followed Parker at Chicago where his school curriculum added civic and social learning to the practical uses of content as well as a focus on individual development. Dewey's views on student responsibility and learning by experience are consistent with confluent curriculum. However, he departed from the transcendental approach to inquiry and the doctrinal answers to the moral question of right and wrong.

Spiritual Images

The Greek classics along with the Bible and formal religion were the sources for personal development and existential questions of most people until the twentieth century. Today there is a transcendental movement in curriculum that goes beyond formal religion and draws from the writings of Ralph Waldo Emerson (1803–1882) who proposed that education could awaken new possibilities by "bringing forth" the inner person rather than simply "putting in" information. Emerson advocated self reliance, attending to one's own intuition as to what is right or wrong, and being optimistic about one's capabilities to transform his or her self.

The humanistic legacies have given rise to issues that are central in curriculum today. How can the individual escape from social conventions and the constraints of economic and political pressure for conformity? Can the curriculum advance personal affiliations and relationships necessary for living in an uncertain world? Should the curriculum develop student capacity to make choices in accordance with their dreams or merely help them to respond to the perspectives of government and employers?

CRITICISMS OF THE HUMANISTIC CURRICULUM

Three charges are commonly made against the humanists. (1) Critics maintain that humanists prize their methods, techniques, and experiences instead of appraising them in terms of consequences for learners. The humanists, they say, have been lax in seeing the long-term effects of their programs. If they were to appraise their systems more thoroughly, the humanists might see that their uses of emotionally charged practices such as sensitivity training and encounter groups can be psychologically or emotionally harmful to some students. The self-awareness they encourage is not always a change for the better. The use of humanistic techniques such as deep-breathing exercises have been attacked by some parents as "new age" religious practices. There are anecdotes about an 8-year-old girl who supposedly was taken on an internal "minivacation" and "left there" and a kindergartener who used deep breathing to drown out the sound of her mother's voice when she was being disciplined. There have been suits alleging that the mental health component of the humanistic curriculum amounts to "unauthorized practice of psychology by teachers." There is fear among some parents of a curriculum that is effective in changing children's values, attitudes, and behavior through a process of open decision making. (2) Other critics maintain that the humanist is not concerned enough about the experience of the individual. Indeed some programs appear to demand uniformity of students and appear to regard open questioning as a dangerous deviance, getting in the way of development.[29] Although humanists say that their curriculum is individualistic, every student in a given classroom is actually exposed to the same stimuli. For example, everyone may be expected to take part in group fantasy, hostility games, and awareness exercises. (3) On the other hand, as we have shown, critics also charge that humanists give undue emphasis to the individual. These critics would like humanists to be more responsible to the needs of society as a whole.

Rebuttals to these attacks take varied forms. Humanists admit that their educational approach can be misused. However, teachers who would abuse their teaching role would do so whether or not they had affective techniques available. Furthermore, because humanism helps teachers learn more about themselves, those teachers are likely to demonstrate fewer instances of negative and destructive behavior. Not all students should have to participate in the humanistic curriculum because it may not be appropriate for everyone at the curriculum's present stage of development. This curriculum promises a fuller realization of the democratic potential of our society. The goals of the humanistic curriculum call for students who can perceive clearly, act rationally, make choices, and take responsibility both for their private lives and for their social milieu.

F. Hanoch McCarty believes it is necessary to combat the perceptions of humanistic education as chaotic, lacking in purpose, and bereft of a set of common goals. He would change the phrases of the 1970s—"If it feels good, do it" and "Do your own thing"—by adding "as long as it does not rob others of their dignity and potential."[30] In other words, McCarty believes that humanists must be involved with the welfare of others and that one should not seek personal pleasure while others slave.

Shortly before his death, Maslow addressed the question of whether we can teach for personal growth and at the same time educate for competence in academic and professional fields.[31] He thought it was possible, though difficult, to integrate the two goals. (The teacher's role of judge and evaluator in teaching to standards is often seen as incompatible with the humanistic role.) In his last article, Maslow expressed uneasiness over some practices in curricula of the ESALEN type. (ESALEN is a center in California that provides many approaches to consciousness and shows trends toward anti-intellectualism and opposition to science, discipline, and hard work.) He worried about those who considered competence and training irrelevant. For Maslow, the learning of content need not be the denial of growth. He thought subject matter could be taught humanistically with a view to enlightenment of the person. Study in a subject field could be a help toward seeing the world as it really is, a training in sensory awareness, and a defense against despair. To believe that real knowledge is possible and that weak, foolish human beings can band together and move verified knowledge forward toward some small measure of certainty encourages us to count on ourselves and on our own powers.

Many Americans view the humanistic approach negatively. Although most people would support increased human potential and self-worth as ends, they may be suspicious of what appear to be bizarre procedures, such as exploring the senses through touch and feel exercises and emphasizing the sensual, if not the sexual. If thought, feeling, and action cannot be separated, then neither should feelings be separated from injustices faced by one's fellows. Rather than feel the "joy" of a "blind walk," students might *feel* the "revulsion" and "outrage" of abused children.

---

[29]Richard Adams and Janice Haaken, "Anticultural Culture: Lifespring's Ideology and Its Roots in Humanistic Psychology," *Journal of Humanistic Psychology* 27, no. 4 (fall 1987): 501–517.

[30]F. Hanoch McCarty, "At the Edges of Perception: Humanistic Education in the '80s and Beyond" (paper delivered at annual meeting of the American Research Association, Montreal, April 1983).

[31]Abraham H. Maslow, "Humanistic Education," *Journal of Humanistic Psychology* 19, no. 3 (summer 1979): 13–27.

Social reconstructionists demand that the humanists do more than strengthen present courses. New teaching techniques that involve learners and their feelings in each lesson are not enough. They want to broaden the boundaries of the humanistic curriculum from self-study to political socialization; they would like humanistic curriculum to include such problem areas as medicine, parental care, sexism, and journalism. These critics want humanistic curriculum to deal with the exposure of injustice so that the learner's growth would be less restricted. The blending of humanism and social reconstructionism tries to answer this complaint.

CONCLUDING COMMENTS

Listening, self-evaluation, creativity, openness to new experiences, and goal setting are important curriculum goal areas. Learners have a real concern about the meaning of life, and curriculum developers should be responsive to that concern. Putting feelings and facts together makes good sense. It is alarming that studies of classroom interaction show that only 1% of instructional time assesses student feelings about what they are learning. We should also help learners acquire different ways of knowing. Still, few persons would want the humanistic curriculum to be the only one available or to be mandated for all. We have much to learn before we can develop curricula that will help students become self-directed.

Our best thinking today suggests that self-direction may follow from a climate of trust, student participation in decisions about what and how to learn (typically students report 95% of instruction on the *what* and only 5% on the *how* to learn), and efforts to foster confidence and self-esteem. The obstacles to be overcome are a desire by some institutions and persons to maintain power over others, a distrust of human nature, and a lack of student experience in taking responsibility for their own learning.

A fruitful approach to improving humanistic curriculum has begun. It includes focusing on the physical and emotional needs of learners and attempting to design learning experiences that will help fulfill these needs. The idea that curriculum standards and activities should match emotional issues that are salient at particular times is powerful. Curriculum developers might ask how a particular subject matter could be structured in order to help students with developmental crises. Adolescents, for example, who are experiencing an identity crisis and trying to reconcile conflicts with parents might study history to illuminate the origins of parental attitudes and beliefs, considering the present validity of these origins. Students might use the sciences in meeting their needs for coherence and understanding the world rather than studying isolated subjects. Or, they might use the arts to express their feelings and their natural desire to be themselves.

A related idea is for teachers to give more attention to the motivational and affective orientations that students bring with them. Inasmuch as the intentions, goals, and beliefs of students drive and sustain their thinking, then the enacted curriculum would encourage student expression and examination of their beliefs along with other perspectives. Through challenge, choice, novelty, fantasies, surprise, functionality, and other features of the humanistic curriculum, teachers cultivate students as whole persons who care about others and pursue their own dreams not just follow the trajectories set by government and employers.

Capitalism and scientism through mandated institutionalized curriculum aim at "filling empty vessels," while many teachers enact a humanistic curriculum that "ignites the fires in learners."

QUESTIONS

1. Consider a topic of interest to you. How could this topic be taught to avoid depersonalizing learners?

2. What is your response to those who believe that schools should not undertake the complicated responsibilities that an affective curriculum implies and that such programs may infringe on the civil liberties of children?

3. Discuss the expected outcomes from a primary classroom in which there are the following: (a) a "sad corner"; (b) an "I feel" wheel, with an arrow that points to "fine," "tired," "sick," "scared"; and (c) two plants, one that is ignored and another that is loved, to show children that "the plant we love more, will grow more, like people."

4. Designers of affective programs have been accused of equating good mental health with conformity. They are said to promote compliance with school routines and instruction and to discourage the kind of initiative, individuality, and creativity that demands change, "rocks the boat," and gives learners control over the institution in which they exist. To what extent are these accusations true?

5. Reflect on some of the ideas, concerns, and activities associated with the humanistic curriculum. Which of these are likely to prove fruitful and have a continuing effect on what is taught? You may wish to consider (a) psychological assumptions about the importance of freedom, learning by doing, and risk taking; (b) views of knowledge such as those stressing subjective or intuitive knowledge and the idea that the subject that matters is one in which the learner finds self-fulfillment; and (c) instructional techniques (values clarification, cooperative games, use of dreams, etc.).

6. What is your stance on human nature? Do you believe evil is inherent or are persons essentially constructive? What are the curriculum implications of your answer?

7. Why have great thinkers throughout history called for freedom in learning, yet schools as institutions have chosen mostly to control learning?

SUGGESTED STRATEGIC RESEARCH

READING EMOTIONS OF STUDENTS
Observe or video students in a learning situation and ask teachers if students are expressing positive emotions (hope, pride, empathy, joy, etc.) or negative emotions (fear, frustration, shame, anxiety). Compare teacher judgments with students' self-reports on recalling their feelings. How do students' emotions intersect with performance and desire to learn?

LEARNING WITHOUT OFFICIAL CATEGORIES
Ask students to use their intuition *before* introducing subject matter categories and procedures. For example, before teaching fractions or measurement, let students express their core intuitions and feelings about a beaker filled with water. Compare performance in learning the concepts with a group that did not preface their learning with an intuitive experience.

IDENTIFYING THE FACTORS IN A SCHOOL OR CLASSROOM THAT MAKE FOR ALIENATION AND THOSE THAT FACILITATE SELF-ACTUALIZATION
Ask students to describe the factors that make their school or classroom a good place to be and the factors that make it more like a prison. Students may document using digital videos.

IDENTIFYING A RESEARCH QUESTION
A profitable way to begin research is to regard a published source as the beginning of research, not the end product. Select a statement or reference in Chapter 1 and determine what is missing that you might address.

DIFFERENTIATING LEARNING ORIENTATION

We believe persistency in the face of difficulty depends on whether one is "performance oriented" (worries about making errors) or "learning oriented" (likes new challenges). Are these orientations stable traits of an individual, or do they vary with the subject matter or context?

DETERMINING THE POWER OF THOUGHT VERSUS THE POWER OF EMOTIONS

The emotional system tends to monopolize brain resources, making it easier for an emotion to control thought than for a thought to control an emotion. Create a "thought experiment" that would show the value of trying to activate the two systems.

SELECTED REFERENCES

CSIKSZENTMIHALYI, MIHALY, AND ISABELLA SELEGA CSIKSZENTMIHALYI. *Optimal Experience: Psychological Studies of Flow in Consciousness.* Cambridge, England: Cambridge University Press, 1988.

LEVINE, SARAH L. *Promoting Adult Growth in Schools.* Newton, MA: Allyn and Bacon, 1988.

NODDINGS, NEL. *The Challenge to Care in Schools.* New York: Teachers College Press, 1992.

PURKEY, WILLIAM W., AND P. H. STANLEY *Invitational Teaching, Learning and Living.* Washington, DC: NCA Professional Library, 1991.

SCHNEIDER, KIRK J., JAMES F. T. BUGENTAL, J. FRAZER PIERSON, EDS. *Handbook of Humanistic Psychology: Leading Edges in Theory, Research, and Practice.* Thousand Oaks, CA: Sage Publications, 2001.

SCHNEIDEWIND, N., AND E. DAVIDSON. *Cooperative Learning, Cooperative Lives: A Source Book of Learning Activities for Building a Peaceful World.* Dubuque, IA: William C. Brown, 1987.

CHAPTER 2

THE SOCIAL RECONSTRUCTIONIST CURRICULUM

SOCIAL RECONSTRUCTIONISTS are interested in the relationships between curriculum and the social, political, and economic development of society. Optimistic social reconstructionists are convinced that education can effect social change, citing, for example, literacy campaigns that have contributed to successful political revolutions. Pessimists, on the other hand, doubt the ability of the curriculum to change existing social structures but want the curriculum to be a vehicle for fostering social discontent. They think learners should understand how the curriculum is used to consolidate power and to define society.

This chapter presents the premises of social reconstruction and the directions taken by different social reconstructionists: revolution, critical inquiry, futurism. A distinction is also made between a curriculum of reconstruction, which attempts to change the social order, and a curriculum of social adaptation, which helps students fit into a world they never made.

CHARACTERISTICS OF THE SOCIAL RECONSTRUCTIONIST CURRICULUM

Purpose

The primary purpose of the social reconstructionist curriculum is to confront the learner with the many severe problems that humankind faces. Social reconstructionists believe that these problems are not the exclusive concern of "social studies" but of every discipline, including economics, aesthetics, chemistry, and mathematics. We are now in a critical period, they claim. The crisis is universal, and the widespread nature of the crisis must be emphasized in the curriculum.

The social reconstructionist curriculum, however, has no universal objectives and content. For example, the first year of such a curriculum might be devoted to formulating goals for political and economic reconstruction. Activities related to this objective might include the following: (1) a critical survey of the community (e.g., one might collect information on local patterns of savings and expenditures), (2) a study relating the local economy to national and worldwide situations, (3) a study treating the influence of historic causes and trends on the local economic situation, (4) an examination of political practices in relation to economic factors, (5) a consideration of proposals for change in political practices, and (6) a determination of which proposal satisfies the needs of the most people.

Objectives in later years of the curriculum might include the identification of problems, methods, needs, and goals in science and art; the evaluation of the relationship between education and human relations; and the identification of aggressive strategies for effecting change.

Role of the Teacher

Teachers relate national, world, and local purposes to the students' goals. Students can thus use their interests to help find solutions to the social problems emphasized in their classes. If a community wants to encourage participation of different ethnic groups in public meetings, for example, a foreign language class could help facilitate this participation by interpreting. Such a program provides an opportunity for students to use their special skills and interests to promote community goals in discussion groups, general assemblies, and other local organizations.

The teacher stresses cooperation with the community and its resources. Students may, for example, spend time away from the school participating in community health projects (for science classes) or in community acting, writing, or dance programs (for arts and literature classes). The arts might be integrated with other concerns in the program. The interconnections between art and science and art and economics, for instance, might be strengthened as the art student looks at art in home and city planning, contrasts unhealthy communities with "ideal garden cities," and attempts to see how the desire for business profits affects the quality of life.

In the primary school, the emphasis is on group experiences. Projects demand interdependence and social consensus. Children of different ages join in community surveys and other cooperative activities. The curriculum of an upper elementary school keeps the Utopian faith by providing generous exercises in social imagination. Children might create rough models of the future and more just institutions, such as imaginary hospitals, television, or schools, and thus stimulate the children's awareness of grave contemporary problems and how institutions might be modified to address these problems.

Also, as a resource person and catalyst, the teacher seeks opportunities for youth to work as equals with adults in social projects and political activities. The school and neighborhood project of Boston, for instance, channels funds to students who, with adults, make grants to deserving neighborhood undertakings, such as attempting to clean up Boston Harbor and serving meals to homeless women.[1] However, more than encouraging social service, the teacher should challenge the beliefs of students and develop their critical consciousness.

Social reconstructionists hold that all teachers are political persons who must choose either to serve whomever is in power (conservatives) or be opponents to those in power (social reconstructionists). This is not to say that the teacher neglects course content simply to politicize students but that students learn to recognize that content is never neutral and to continually ask, "For whom and for what do we use our knowledge?"[2]

SOCIAL RECONSTRUCTION IN PRACTICE

Changing the Community

Few schools have tried to develop a curriculum completely within the framework of social reconstructionism, although with the current explosion of schools of choice, there are occasionally schools that focus on social justice. The Los Angeles Leadership Academy is

[1]*The Forgotten Half: Pathways to Success for America's Youth and Young Families* (Washington, DC: William T. Grant Foundation on Work, Family and Citizenship, 1988).
[2]Paulo Freire, "Letter to North American Teachers," in *Freire for the Classroom,* Ira Shor, ed. (Portsmouth, NH: Boyston/Coor, 1987), 211–216.

one such school. This public middle school exposes students to social injustices in the world and reveals the roles capitalism and the U.S. government have played in these situations. Students hone their learning skills and academic knowledge by actively engaging in social protests aimed at securing better working conditions for marginalized peoples.[3]

Members of the Peace Corps and revolutionaries in Third World countries have attended to the concept of social betterment and have tried to apply it, primarily in rural areas.

Project Ixtliyollotl in the community of San Andres, Mexico, is an alternative to conventional schooling.[4] The project began with members of the community recognizing that their high loss of human resources, illiteracy, family disorganization, and poverty was not addressed by educational agencies. Shortly thereafter, more than 600 persons—children, youth, and adults—pooled their limited resources and formed their own school with related community activities. Subject matter is taught in the context of improving the social and economic conditions of San Andres. Science is taught in relation to local health improvement and history to understand the origins of their situation and to create a future. As an example of the close tie between school and daily life, one learning opportunity involves youth analyzing the political orientations of newspapers (social studies) and then issuing their own newspaper (writing) to serve the particular interests of San Andres. Under the leadership of the school, community members meet to acquire the mental outlooks, knowledge, and skills for establishing new industry central to the development and self-sufficiency of the community. Building on traditional understanding of cattle, textiles, and agriculture, adults find ways to adapt this knowledge to a changing world. The project focuses on strengthening the economic, political, and social capacities of women because they are seen as the key to the quality of life. Success has been hard won. The financial sacrifices of those on the brink of survival comprise one hurdle; another is harassment (vandalism, threats on life, legal challenges) instigated by political powers who fear an empowered community and educational bureaucrats who are made uneasy by Ixtliyollotl's achievement with tasks that they should address but do not.

In a similar fashion, Myles Horton founded Highlander Folk School in Tennessee, a leading educational center for activists in labor, civil rights, and other social struggles.[5] Horton's curriculum guidelines call for starting with the people's problems. (They may not be able to state what they want in educational terms, but they know what they want in practical terms.) The program must be based on the people's perception of the problem, not the educator's. The curriculum maker must induce people to use what they already know and to share it. The curriculum maker helps people diagnose their problem and helps learners supplement their knowledge. Limited use is made of the professional when the need for technical advice is obvious. At Highlander, participants are encouraged to take action, such as picketing the welfare office, and then to analyze their action in order to understand its importance and to internalize it.

Workshops are held each summer at Highlander and are characterized as argumentative places where students hash over their ideas on everything from how to gain control, to sex education, and to the public school curriculum. Students also get experience in trying to have an impact on problems that are devastating their communities. Typical projects are those planned by students from Lexington, Mississippi, who sought to expand a school curriculum devoid of their own culture. Students gathered oral histories from local residents and successfully lobbied for inclusion of the social history into local schools.

[3]Richard V. Colvin, "Reading, Writing and Revolution—Welcome to the LA Public Charter School Dedicated to Social Justice," *Los Angeles Times Magazine* (Oct. 5, 2003): 12–16.
[4]Ixtliyollotl Education Center, Cholula, Puebla, Mexico, 1994.
[5]John N. Glenn, *Highlander: No Ordinary School 1952–1962* (Lexington: University of Kentucky, 1988).

Other projects by students at the workshops include a public relations campaign to gain community approval of an unwanted recycling program and ways to service communities that are prime targets for landfills and undesirable development because they are open to the promises of jobs and economic benefits.

Student activities conducted according to reconstructionist principles are also found in volunteer programs in which students attempt to solve local poverty problems, to organize community resources in the interests of consumers, to help foreign-born nursing home residents, to correct discriminatory employment practices, to determine community needs, to establish facilities for mental patients, and to reform state utility laws.

Freire's Social Reconstructionism

Today, social reconstructionists draw from the theory and practice of the late Paulo Freire.[6] Although Freire concentrated on the challenges facing Latin America and one African country, he believed that other areas of the developing world differ only in small details and that they must follow his "cultural action for conscientization" if they are to be liberated from political and economic oppression.

Conscientization   Conscientization is the process by which individuals, not as recipients but as active learners, achieve a deep awareness both of the sociocultural reality that shapes their lives and of their ability to transform that reality.[7] It means enlightening people about the obstacles that prevent them from having a clear perception of reality. One of these obstacles is a standardized way of thinking—acting, for example, according to the perspectives received daily from the communications media rather than getting other views and attending to local realities. Other obstacles and dehumanizing structures that control learning are schools that are instruments for maintaining the status quo and political leaders who mediate between the masses and the elite while keeping the masses in a dependent state. Conscientization means helping persons apprehend the origins of facts and problems in their situations rather than attributing them to a superior power or to their own "natural" incapacity. Unless students see these facts objectively, they will accept the situation apathetically, believing themselves incapable of affecting their destiny.

Freire put his philosophy into action. For example, his plan and materials for teaching reading to adult illiterates aimed at transformation not reproduction. Table 2.1 shows the contrast between Freire's approach and the conventional approach in teaching reading in adult literacy campaigns.

Freire contended that oppression comes from within the person as well as from without. Hence, the felt needs and beliefs of individuals must be challenged if they are to be freed from blind adherence to their own world views as well as to the uncritically examined views of others. If farmers came to Freire demanding a course in the use of pesticides in order to increase yields of their crops, for example, Freire assisted them by examining the causes of why they wanted such instruction, thereby rediagnosing their perceived needs. Probing into causes that often led the participants to conclude that a course in the use of pesticides, as initially wanted, is less important than a course on marketing practice or a study of the long-term effects of agrobusiness practices versus farming for community needs. The aim of education in Freire's approach was not to accommodate or adjust learners to the social system but to free them from slavish adherence to it.[8]

[6]Paulo Freire, *Pedagogy of the Oppressed* (New York: Herder and Herder, 1970).
[7]Paulo Freire, *Education for Critical Consciousness* (New York: Continuum, 1989).
[8]Paulo Freire and Donaldo Macedo, *Literacy: Reading the Word and the World* (South Hadley, MA: Bergin and Garvey, 1987).

Table 2.1 **Contrasting Approaches to the Teaching of Reading**

Conventional Approach	Freire Approach
Teacher chooses words and selections to read and presents them to learner.	Poor people create texts that express their own thought-language and their perceptions of the world.
Literature selected has little to do with the students' sociocultural reality and does not reflect the lives and experiences of many of the children.	Words are chosen for their (1) pragmatic value in communication within learner's group. "Dangerous" words (i.e., love and lust, lease and license, prison and power), for example, the significant concepts that exist among the most broken of the poor; (2) connotations of indignation, (3) generative features, such as syllabic elements by which learners can compare and read new words of importance to themselves.
Teacher implies that there is a relationship between knowing how to read and getting a good job.	Teacher stresses that merely teaching students to read and write does not work miracles. If there are not enough jobs, teaching reading will not create them.
Learning to read is viewed as decoding words and sentences (phonics and structural) and reproducing generalizations (main ideas) in passages rather than constructing personally relevant meanings from text.	Learning to read is viewed as important in reflecting critically on the cultural milieu and in awakening students to the dehumanizing aspects of their lives.

Eradicating Illiteracy Despite attempts to cope with illiteracy, adult illiterates in the United States exceed 25 million. Typical reports on the efforts to eradicate illiteracy in the United States attest to the inadequacy of curricula that are not immediately relevant to people's lives and interests and failure to enlist illiterates in designing programs based on their own interests.[9] Creating a network of community-based literacy programs in poor neighborhoods could potentially win the confidence of those who would otherwise be suspicious of solutions that they perceive as imposed on them from the outside.

In Cuba, Nicaragua, and China national literacy campaigns using many of Freire's techniques, such as enlisting volunteer teachers and other students, resulted in great gains in literacy and laid the foundation for social development. Although the leaders of these campaigns were optimistic that curriculum would develop a critical consciousness in students and prepare people to reinvent society, it did not always happen.

Curriculum seldom alters the structural problems of inequality and poverty, or the domination of the many by the few. There is little evidence that educational reform has had a positive influence on economic development; most curriculum reforms support the status quo. Even leaders of revolutionary regimes use the curriculum to consolidate their power. In fact, the political revolutions in Cuba and Nicaragua preceded literacy; literacy did not lead the revolt. Curriculum can, however, contribute to the building of a social order by promoting political awareness and strengthening challenges to the existing society.

In the United States, Ira Shor has adapted Freire's critical process in teaching for social change, integrating (a) generative theories that come from student culture (problems in their daily life) and (b) social and academic themes that are raised by the teacher and go beyond the present thinking of students.[10] By way of example, in one of Shor's writing

---

[9]David Marman, *Illiteracy: A National Dilemma* (New York: Cambridge Book Company, 1987).
[10]Ira Shor, *Empowering Education: Critical Teaching for Social Change* (Chicago: University of Chicago Press, 1992).

classes, students chose "personal growth" as their generative theme. Students wrote on questions related to the self-selected theme: What does personal growth mean to me? What helps personal growth? What are the obstacles to personal growth? The resulting essays served as texts for discussion and revealed that students saw personal growth as an individual matter—personal strength, self-reliance, and the like. Students appeared to be unaware of how social factors—inequality, discrimination, corporate domination—affected their personal success.

When Shor introduced the topical theme "personal growth is affected by economic policy," students read about corporations fleeing the city for cheap labor areas and governments giving tax breaks to corporations as inducements to stay. The students discussed how these practices would affect their taxes, services, education, and personal growth. Other topical themes affecting personal growth were also introduced, and subsequent essays on the different themes were written and discussed.

Finally, the students' original essays on personal growth were revised to consolidate ideas from the critical dialogues and to integrate the topical issues. Importantly, students were not forced to discuss a given theme, which is consistent with Shor's belief that forced discussion is contradictory to critical-democratic education. A case in point: a number of students defended tax breaks for giant companies as the only way to keep jobs in the city. The issue became an open public debate instead of being hidden under the rug of self-reliant ideology.

Neo-Marxists

A new left evolved in the 1970s that sought social reforms using the schools to awaken allies in labor, civil rights, and other groups with the need for control and power. These revolutionaries accused older social reconstructionists of being naive in the belief that they could transform society by using a "new wave of students who have been nurtured (in the schools)." According to the neo-Marxist, the older reconstructionists failed to recognize that oppression and exploitation are a fundamental characteristic of class structure in the United States and cannot be altered by tinkering with the school. These neo-Marxists advocated that curriculum specialists recognize that the success of the schools is tied to conditions in the larger society. Just as conflicts over the curriculum arise outside the school, so the solutions to these problems require efforts by the larger society. Parents, concerned citizens, organized labor, students, and other groups must be involved in studying, for example, the prevailing patterns of financing, ways to create more jobs, and the possibility of redistributing income.

A Neo-Marxist Manifesto Indeed, in 1975 an Association for Supervision and Curriculum Development (ASCD) Yearbook committee presented a call to action, encouraging educators to protect their own living standards by uniting with other educators, students, workers, and minority organizations. The manifesto in the yearbook urged educators to demand democracy for students and a curriculum designed to serve the interests of the dominated: the broad working class. Public school educators were given guidelines for action:

1. Develop a core of progressive teachers in each school for the purpose of examining instances of class discrimination—materials, tests, methods, policies—that show differential bias.
2. Encourage students to study the presence or absence of democracy in the school and to report whose interests are being served by existing policies and procedures.

3. Present the findings of dominant class interests at meetings with progressive parents, members of other schools, the teachers' union, and other professional organizations.

4. Expose the class content of your school program publicly-for example, at PTA and union meetings.

5. Enlist the help of community and working-class organizations in developing a curriculum based on the interests of the working class. The curriculum at a minimum would include (a) the teaching of modern history focused on the struggles of Western-dominated Third World countries, the working classes, oppressed minorities, and women against exploitation; (b) full equality for the language and culture of oppressed national minorities; (c) instruction in fundamentals of socioeconomic analysis of social relations; and (d) development of cultural activities aimed at the acceptance of working-class culture.

6. Establish an area-wide committee for a curriculum based on the interests of the dominated groups, enlisting students in the struggle for liberation.

7. Introduce a plan for disseminating revolutionary demands and form a united front among all dominated groups against the increasingly centralized and rigid control by the power structure.[11]

Critical Theory against Reproductive Knowledge   Recently, Michael Apple and Henry Giroux have argued that the knowledge "reproduced" in schools creates a stratified social order and perpetuates the values of dominant social class interests. Only rarely has the curriculum reflected on what is happening outside of the school, and instead it embeds a restricted range of social and economic values.[12] Both authors believe that we should broaden the curriculum to include community action. Through this, they hold, students develop social and political responsibility and skills while learning to question the ethnic of their institutions and to criticize them when they fail to meet ideals. Giroux wants teachers to change the nature of schooling so that it is more emancipatory and less a feeble echo of the demand for social order.[13] He holds that teachers have the potential to overcome the social form that oppresses them. He also believes that schools as well as media are sites where personal identities are formed and re-formed. Conflict must be made part of the curriculum both because it is a legitimate means of getting recourse in unequal societies and because it is a positive source of vitality and renewal.[14] Teachers may oppose the official curriculum based on their own experiences, critical readings, and discussions with others. Although it is naïve to think that the school can create the conditions for changing the larger society, teachers and students can try to transform their own practices and consciousness as part of a larger strategy to change society.

By way of example, in Marilyn Frankenstein's statistics curriculum, students learn to understand the importance of quantitative reasoning in the development of critical consciousness and the ways in which math anxiety sustains hegemonic power and ideologies.[15] Students explore the fact that statistics are neutral but that official statistics are chosen to be more useful to conservative than to radical thinkers. Students analyze statistical knowledge

---

[11]James A. MacDonald and Esther Zaret, eds., *Schools in Search of Meaning,* ASCD Yearbook (Washington, DC: National Education Association, 1975), 158–161.

[12]Michael Apple, *Ideology and Curriculum,* 2nd edition (New York: Routledge and Kegan Paul, 1990).

[13]Henry Giroux, *Ideology and the Process of Schooling* (Philadelphia: Temple University Press, 1981).

[14]Henry Giroux, "Critical Pedagogy; Cultural Politics and the Discourse of Experience," *Journal of Education* 67, no. 2 (1987): 23–41.

[15]Marilyn Frankenstein, "Critical Mathematics Education," in *Freire for the Classroom,* Ira Shor, ed. (Portsmouth, NH: Heinemann, 1987), 180–204.

to reveal underlying interests and methods of collection as well as to consider what new knowledge might be produced that is consistent with humanization and with the improvement of their own lives. Students learn how the government makes the proportion of the federal budget for military spending appear smaller by such practices as including funds "in trust" as social services while assigning war-related expenditures, such as the production of nuclear warheads, the space program and veterans' programs, to various nonmilitary categories within the Department of Energy budget. Frankenstein's students address such myths as the belief that social welfare programs are responsible for a declining standard of living by asking students to research, using arithmetical operations, the amounts given to the poor versus the amounts given to the rich to uncover the fact that "welfare" to the rich dwarfs subsidies to the poor.

In seeking to understand the causes of math anxiety, students learn how structures in our society result in different groups being more affected than others by this anxiety, and how people participate in their own mathematical disempowerment. Students see how differentiated treatment based on race and class is related to math avoidance and question those whose research on math anxiety focuses only on the relationship between gender and mathematics learning.

Evidence in support of the "reproductive" theory of curriculum—namely, that the knowledge taught in school perpetuates existing political and economic structures—has been provided by Jean Anyon.[16] In her case study, Anyon collected data on school knowledge in elementary schools in contrasting social class settings. Her data suggest that while topics and materials are similar among working-class, middle-class, affluent, and elite schools, dramatic differences exist in students' experience of the curricula in these schools.

In the working-class schools, students never were taught their own history—the history of the working class—and the curriculum emphasized rote behaviors rather than creative thinking. The dominant theme was student resistance. The teacher had to discipline the class physically at times in order to impose the curriculum, which consisted only of the basics and worksheets. In contrast, the middle-class school students viewed knowledge as facts and generalizations which could be exchanged for college entrance or a better job. Possibility was the dominant theme.

In the affluent school, students perceived knowledge as a personal activity related to things or ideas. They were taught ways to use ideas for their own purposes. The dominant theme in the affluent school was individualization because these students thought for themselves and engaged in creative projects and personal discovery. Their schooling stressed individual values over collective ones.

In the executive elite school, excellence was the theme. Students viewed knowledge as the result of rational rules and consensus by experts, not personal discovery. Children were provided with socially prestigious subject matter and were given analytical insights about the social system. They were being prepared to govern, to exercise and exert power.

Though Anyon concluded that the curriculum reproduced the maintenance of social class, she felt it also offered possibilities for transformation. The resistance of working-class students might force a restructuring of capitalistic ideology. The middle-class students, on the other hand, might become disillusioned with false promises about big rewards for working hard and become critics of the system. Students in the affluent school might recognize irrationalities in society as they engage in their individual efforts at making sense of the world. Students in the elite school might discover the difference between using knowledge for pleasure and using it to maintain power in the face of competition from others. Furthermore, elitist learners might perceive a need for destroying the system because they see how under capitalism one must exploit others.

---

[16]Jean Anyon, "Social Class and School Knowledge," *Curriculum Inquiry* 11, no. 1 (1981): 3–41.

Anyon's optimistic view that transformation through resistance is possible in the face of reproduction signals a new direction in critical theory. Whereas previous critiques of curriculum have been too deterministic, offering weak roles to human actors; today some critical thinkers are recognizing that schools do more than reproduce dominant social relations or serve capitalistic demands. The language of critique is being modified to include the language of possibility.

Environmental Reconstruction The Neo-Marxist idea that the past represents domination and that the future offers an expanding range of possibilities is questioned by those who would restore the life-affirmative traditions of distant and Third World peoples and challenge the view that there can be progress by destroying nature. William Pinar and C. A. Bowers have faulted critical scholarship for its unresponsiveness to the environmental crisis (human population in excess of food distribution, loss of species, pollution, etc.).[17] They argue that the ecological crisis calls for a different way of thinking about human freedom and the forms of knowledge that will sustain this earth. They would include in their curriculum appropriate techniques—agricultural traditions from earlier periods, folk knowledge in arts, and narrations from other cultures that have maintained ecologically sustainable relationships.

Curricula that bring children and nature together are increasing.[18] Programs such as that found in the Gullett Elementary School in Austin, Texas, aim at developing empathetic environmental sensibility, moral views toward nature, knowledge about the environmental crises, and a personal investment in the world's well-being. At this school, children own, respect, and care for more than 100 animals of a wide variety, engage in extensive recycling, and maintain a large organic garden and greenhouse. Similarly, Project Wild (Workshop in Learning Design), a widely used environmental program features an interdisciplinary approach emphasizing awareness of wildlife, human values as they relate to nature, ecological systems, conservation, environmental issues, and responsible human action. It may be that environmental reconstruction will recast the Neo-Marxist curriculum debate from reproduction, resistance, and critical pedagogy to concern for the knowledge that primal peoples have regarding ecological relationships and technologies that are consistent with the view that we humans cannot survive independent of our habitat, that our freedom and progress is dependent on the larger biotic community of which we are a part.

Futurologists

Curriculum futurologists advocate making deliberate choices about the world of the future (Utopia). They study trends, estimate the social consequences foreshadowed by the trends, and then attempt to promote probable futures seen as "good" and prevent those seen as "bad."

There are many futurologists in society at large. The World Future Society alone, a nonprofit, nonpolitical organization, has 16,000 members from economists and philosophers to Venus watchers. Generally, futurologists do not attempt to predict what is going to happen in 10 to 15 years but rather attempt to decide on what they want to happen so that they can then make more intelligent choices.

---

[17]William F. Pinar and C. A. Bowers, "Politics of Curriculum: Origins, Controversies, and Significance of Critical Perspectives," *Review of Research in Education* (Washington: AERA, 1992): 163–191.
[18]Yvonne B. Estes, "Environmental Education," Kappan special report, *Phi Delta Kappan* 74, no. 9 (May 1993).

The Use of Future Planning   The late Harold G. Shane, a professor at Indiana University, was representative of those social reconstructionists who would use future planning as a basis for curriculum making.[19] Shane urged a program of planning the future, not planning for the future. As with other social reconstructionists, he stressed the power of persons to shape their own destiny and to believe that they are not bound to an inescapable future to which they must conform.

Shane would obligate curriculum developers to study trends first. Trends may be technological developments that have been identified with the help of specialists in academic disciplines. Such trends include reduction of hereditary defects, increase in life expectancy, chemical methods for improving memory, and home education via technology. Trends also may be inventoried problems such as those found in the literature of disaster (e.g., famine, dwindling resources, pollution). Shane would have educators who have studied trends engage with a wide number of participants in analyzing their consequences. Such consequences might be mandatory foster homes for children whose natural homes are harmful to their physical and mental health, psychological prerequisites for candidates seeking public office, use of biochemical therapy for improving mood, memory, and concentration, reversal of counter-ecological trends, and controlled growth. Professional specialists (those with expert knowledge) would decide whether the promised consequences would humanize or dehumanize. Final judgment about desirability, however, must rest with the people concerned. (Procedures used by futurists in setting purposes are described in Part 2.)

Most social reconstructionists are very clear about the role of the professional expert in the determination of social policy. Although they use experts in analyzing complicated social problems, they do not entirely relegate the solution of these problems to the experts. "In the realm of social policy, the decisions of the whole people, when they have full access to the facts, are in the long run typically wiser than those made by any single class or group. The cult of the expert is but the prelude to some form of authoritarian society."[20] Reconstructionists favor pressing society for decisions and for the development of a clear social consensus as to what is the "good life." In achieving this consensus, the ideas of children, parents, administrators, and teachers should be considered. Those ideas that the group sees as having merit must become the basis for "mutual coercion" control for a socially worthy purpose.

Typical Futurists' Recommendations   In their futuristic curriculum, reconstructionists focus on the exploitation of resources, pollution of the air and water, warfare, the effect of the population increase and the unequal use of natural resources, propaganda, especially in the media, and the need for self-control in the interests of one's fellow humans. For example, in his view of the future, the late Neil Postman saw television as a dangerous curriculum—an information system specially constructed to influence, teach, train, and cultivate the mind and character of the young—competing with the school's curriculum. It is a dangerous curriculum because it is (a) present-centered (does not encourage deferred gratification); (b) attention-centered (entertainment takes precedence over content); (c) image-centered (weakens ability to use abstract, propositional reasoning); (d) emotion-centered (nonintellectual); and (e) largely incoherent (it creates discontinuity). Postman would create a future in which the curriculum of the school would counter TV

[19]Harold G. Shane, *Educating for a New Millennium* (Bloomington, IN: Phi Delta Kappan, 1981).
[20]B. Othanel Smith et al., *Fundamentals of Curriculum Development* (Yonkers, NY: World Books, 1950): 638.

and offer a sense of purpose, meaning, and the interrelation of disciplines. The historical development of humanity, for instance, could be used to integrate the teaching of philosophy, science, language, religion, and cultural expressions.[21]

Social Adaptation versus Social Reconstruction

Both social adaptation and social reconstruction derive aims and content from an analysis of the society that the school is to serve. Curriculum development in response to social needs, such as AIDS and sex education, parenting programs, and antidrug campaigns, is often more adaptive than reconstructive. Such curriculum represents a mechanism for adjusting students to what some groups believe to be an appropriate response to critical needs within society. Social adaptation differs from social reconstruction in that usually no attempt is made to develop a critical consciousness of social problems and to do something about them. The approach of social adaptationists is to give students information and prescriptions for dealing with situations as defined rather than to seek a fundamental change in the basic structure of the society underlying the problems. Whereas social adaptationists look at society to find out what students need to achieve, to protect themselves in the real world, and to fit into society as it is; social reconstructionists look at society with the intent of building a curriculum by which students can improve the real world.

Learning through services—projects where students volunteer at nursing homes, tutor, take part in environmental cleanups and the like—support learning and reconnect students to the community. However, service projects are generally instances of social adaptations rather than social reconstruction. The difference between adaptation and reconstruction may be illustrated by the following account of a teacher and students who did not intend to enact a curriculum of reconstruction but did so because of unfolding events.

Students were involved in a biology project whereby water quality studies, including the monitoring of bacteria levels, were to be undertaken. The students' investigations showed that bacteria counts were high in nearby beaches. Before informing the public about the results of their findings, the students attempted to discuss the issue with the local water board whose sewage treatment plant voids effluents into the ocean via an outfall offshore from the popular beaches. However, the students were rebuffed and denied access to the board's own records of bacteria levels. Hence, the teacher and students lodged a freedom of information request so they could compare findings.

Subsequently, public disclosure triggered responses from the community. The media ran stories publicizing the school's activities, the issue, and the relationship to marine pollution elsewhere; the local health center began to keep records of complaints about infections associated with the bacteria in the seawater. Ultimately the water board was requested by the state's Ministry for Environment to undertake improvements to their sewage treatment facility. The project that unfolded can be characterized as social reconstruction because students played a role in changing community consciousness about the human impact on the environment. Changes in community consciousness brought a redistribution of resources aimed at environmental protection, and perhaps students gained both a sense of empowerment through their activities and the notion of subjecting to the dominant ideology of the state expressed in the role of the water board.[22]

---

[21]Neil Postman, "Engaging Students in the Great Conversation," *Phi Delta Kappan* 64, no. 5 (March 1983): 310–317.

[22]Annette G. Gough and Ian Robottom, "Towards a Socially Critical Environmental Education: Water Quality Studies in a Coastal School," *Journal of Curriculum Studies* 25, no. 4 (1993): 301–316.

PSYCHOLOGICAL FOUNDATIONS OF SOCIAL RECONSTRUCTION

In their efforts to challenge beliefs that take their toll in death, suffering, and displacement, social reconstructionists draw on sociocultural findings about dangerous individual and group world views. Roy and Judy Eidelson,[23] for example, marshaled findings on how five core beliefs lead to stereotyping, dehumanizing, and conflict:

Superiority—"We are special people."

Injustice—"My group has been treated unfairly."

Vulnerability—"Our position is precarious."

Distrust—"Others have acted against us."

Helplessness—"There is nothing we can do."

Yet there is wide variability within groups because of education, occupation, personal experience, and innate predispositions. Sociocultural interpretations underscore the idea that within societies and groups shared beliefs and assumptions about the world develop through common experiences. A key strategy among social reconstructionists is to bring shared frames of reference to full consciousness and to engage learners in evaluating their origins, the interests they serve and their consequences. For example, in her literary curriculum for participating democracy, Rebecca Powell[24] challenges students of varying ages and backgrounds to look beyond their limited cultural assumptions to see that they are part of a larger human dialogue and to find how their lives can make a difference. Her psychological approach to literacy assumes that people can move from (a) acquisition of the written language code to (b) comprehension of a range of texts and to (c) a higher level where they use literacy to transform cultural aspects of society.

Cultural Psychology as a Source

Cultural psychology explains how cultural forces control the thoughts, beliefs, and actions of individuals. Explanations include how taken-for-granted attitudes are formed, how cultural forces define what is real and what is to be valid. Social reconstructionists might act on these explanations as they try to help victims, protect against injustice, and reform or destroy an institution.

Michael Cole[25] is a cultural psychologist who attends to how thinking takes place in given contexts, particularly how distinctive groups organize the activities of their everyday lives. However, instead of regarding individuals as passive recipients of information from their environment, Cole holds that through social action people trigger both intellectual and cultural development. Key beliefs in Cole's psychology are as follows:

- People do not always act in settings of their own choice.
- The mind emerges through joint mediated activity of people. Therefore, the mind is coconstructed and distributed.

---

[23]Roy J. Eidelson and Judy I. Eidelson, "Dangerous Ideas: Five Beliefs that Project Groups Through Conflict," *American Psychology* 58, no. 3 (March 2003): 182–197.

[24]Rebecca Powell, "Literacy as a Moral Imperative" in *Handbook of Language and Social Psychology,* H. Giles and W. P. Robinson, eds. (New York: Wiley, 1990).

[25]Michael Cole, *Cultural Psychology: A Once and Future Discipline* (Cambridge, MA: Harvard University Press, 1996).

- The mind emerges through activity in local contexts and everyday life events.
- Changes in a culture or a community of practices that transmit meanings and form identities occur when the existing culture fails to meet community or society needs.

Richard Schweder[26] also has the basic idea that no cultural environment is independent of the meanings humans make from it and that individuals are altered by their participation in the sociocultural environment. Schweder writes of "intentional worlds" where things exist because of the meanings (representations) we give to them and our reactions to them. Intentional worlds influence our judgments, practices, intuition and the like, determining how individuals think and act. In addition, Schweder categorizes people as the "intentional persons"—the individuals whose own intentions and views of reality can perturb and disturb aspects of the intentional world. The interaction between a culture's contributed realities and the reality-constituted person may determine the stability or transformation of a society. Table 2.2 outlines five types of relationships identified by Schweder as found between culture and personal intentions.

Local guardians of the intentional world—parents, teachers, leaders, and researchers—present this world and decide how resources and opportunities, such as rituals and routines, are arranged and managed to strengthen student identification with it and how sanctions can be allocated to ensure conformity. In their critical pedagogy, social reconstructionists expose how the guardians are shaping student identity as well as creating student awareness of unofficial shapers—corporate society and its tools—media, technology, government institutions, and policies.

Social reconstructionists, along with curriculum specialists of different orientations, have resurrected the sociohistorical psychology of Lev Vygotsky (1896–1934). In "Mind and Society," Vygotsky introduced the concept of the zones of proximal development (ZPD) that differentiate the ability of the student to solve problems when helped by someone else. This idea includes the beliefs that (1) learning with the assistance of others can enhance growth (one does not have to wait until a certain developmental stage before engaging in higher intellectual activity) and (2) in interacting cooperatively with teachers, peers, parents, and others, one internalizes the culture's social relationships and learns to think in cultural rather than individual ways.

Like Dewey, Vygotsky envisioned the classroom as a social organization that is representative of the larger society, but instead of regarding the individual as an agent for social change, Vygotsky saw the curriculum and classroom organization as the agency for changing the individual. Students were to be melded into the norms and culture of the larger social structure and become productive members of that society.

Table 2.2 Cultural and Personal Intentions

Relationship	Culture	Person
Positive	Supports intention of the person	
Negative	Diminishes personal intention	
Active		Creates or selects own intentional world
Reactive	Others create or select an intentional world in light of that individual's intention.	
Passive	Person lives in a world created or selected by others	

[26]R. A. Schweder, "Cultural Psychology—What Is It?" in *Cultural Psychology: Essays on Comparative Human Development,* J. W. Stigler, R. A. Schweder, and J. Herdt, eds. (New York: Cambridge University Press, 1990).

How then can Vygotsky be a contributor to social reconstruction? For one thing, he identified the prestigious and dominant representations of knowledge that should be the ends in view for all learners—the symbolic or abstract knowledge found in academic language, math, science, history and aesthetic subject matters—identifying powerful concepts and the tools for their expression. Second, he presented classroom activities that engaged small groups of learners and their mediators in tasks that, although they came from the everyday world of the student, were building blocks to the ends in view. These activities featured ZPD experiences for all learners regardless of age, gender, and background. Indeed differences in students were regarded as a social advantage that can lead to differences in development and employment of one's subcultural background in learning and shared construction of knowledge. Hence inequalities in opportunities to learn were minimized. Third, Vygotsky's curriculum offered open spaces for spontaneous learning and encouragement for students to use their newly acquired tools for their own purposes, thereby contributing to relevance and generalization.

PSYCHOANALYTICAL PSYCHOLOGY AND SOCIAL RECONSTRUCTION

Psychoanalysts believe that children are assimilated into the social traditions of their particular culture by the process of identifying first with parents and then with representatives of the wider culture.

Freud theorized that children are originally coerced through rewards and punishment to accept cultural rules and customs but that later the superego assumes the role of an external authority exacting social conformity as one becomes socialized. Rebellion is attributed to weaknesses in identifying with authorities and failure to find satisfaction with social traditions.

Freud regarded culture as civilization whereby necessity imposes prohibitions on one's freedom of action. For him, the ideal of society is not liberty by equality of treatment for all members. In a culture, individuals give up much of their pursuit of pleasure in the interest of security.[27]

An unjust society is one where the privileged few are accorded special favors, while the many are held to a different standard of conduct. Discontent is when society imposes excessive severity of hardship and prohibitions exceed rewards. Freud thought such a society was unstable and that the masses would rise up against such injustice.

Historical Antecedents to Social Reconstruction

Social reconstructionists' ideas have existed for centuries. Plato in his *Republic* saw education as building a better society. Augustine in his *City of God* raised the reconstructionist question as to whether ideal goals can be reached. Although Marx believed that education has been used to support the ruling class through both the formal and the hidden curriculums, he believed that education could alone overthrow the moneyed interests and serve the people. Early educational figures in the United States, such as Horace Mann, Francis Parker, and John Dewey, looked to education as a way to change both individuals and society although they were more reformists than revolutionaries.

In his analysis of Dewey's laboratory school curriculum, writings, and political activism, Aaron Schultz has found that Dewey lost faith that the school can be the main

[27]S. Freud, *Civilization and the Discontents* (London: Hegarts Press, 1930).

agency in changing society but that individuals could make improvements in their local situations and that schools could ally with social currents that are moving against the economic, media, and political forces that are obstacles to a more just society.[28]

Aspects of reconstructionism appeared in American curriculum thought in the 1920s and 1930s. Harold Rugg was concerned about the values for which the school should work. He tried to awaken his peers to the "lag" between the curriculum, a "lazy giant," and the culture, with its fast-paced change and its resultant staggering social dislocations. Rugg's textbooks, teaching, and professional leadership had one overriding quality—the spirit of social criticism. He wanted learners to use newly emerging concepts from the social sciences and aesthetics to identify and solve current social problems. Rugg and his colleague, George Counts, author of *Dare the School Build a New Social Order?*, were among the pioneer thinkers who called on the school to begin creating a "new" and "more equitable society."[29]

In the early 1950s, Theodore Brameld outlined the distinctive features of social reconstructionism.[30] First, he believed in a commitment to building a new culture. Brameld was infused with the conviction that we are in the midst of a revolutionary period from which the common people should control all principal institutions and resources if the world is to become genuinely democratic. Teachers should ally themselves with the organized working people. A way should be found to enlist the majority of people of all races and religions into a great democratic body with power to enforce its policies. The structure, goals, and policies of the new order must be approved at the bar of public opinion and enacted with popular support.

Second, Brameld believed that the school should help the individual, not only to develop socially, but to learn how to participate in social planning as well. The social reconstructionist wants no overstating of the case for individual freedom. Instead, the learners must see how society makes a people what they are and must find ways to satisfy personal needs through social consensus. Third, said Brameld, learners must be convinced of the validity and urgency of change. But they must also have a regard for democratic procedures. Ideally, reconstructionists are opposed to the use of intimidation, fear, and distortion to force compromise in the attempt to achieve a "community of persuasion." However, the reconstructionists take sides and encourage all to acquire a common viewpoint about crucial problems, to make up their minds about the most promising solutions, and then to act in concert to achieve those solutions. The social reconstructionists believe they are representing values that the majority—consciously or not—already cherish. Most people are not now able to act responsibly, they say, because they have been persuaded and stunted by a dominating minority—those who largely control the instruments of power. Hence most persons do not exercise their citizenship on behalf of their own interest—their cherished values—but on behalf of scarcity, frustration, and war.

Although today's reconstructionists are less likely to present detailed visions of what society might be, preferring to center on giving learners hope in the future and a sense of possibilities, Utopian thinking has always been a part of social reconstruction. Robert Owen (1771–1850) was one of many Utopians that influenced education. In his textile mill in Scotland, he established shorter working hours, better housing and health conditions for all employees, schools for child laborers, and the first infant school for toddlers of working mothers. In 1825 he started a cooperative community on the American frontier at New Harmony in Indiana dedicated to improving human progress through fundamental changes

---

[28]Aaron Schutz, "John Dewey's Conundrum: Can Democratic Schools Empower?," *Teachers College Record* 13, no. 2 (April 2001): 267–302.

[29]George Counts, *Dare the School Build a New Social Order?* (Yonkers, NY: World Book, 1932).

[30]Theodore Brameld, *Toward a Reconstructed Philosophy of Education* (New York: Dryden, 1956).

in social and environmental conditions. In the mid-nineteenth century there were nearly 100 such community settlements (many organized by religious sects) founded on the principles of a cooperative social system.

Social adaptation was also common in rural areas in the 1930s and 1940s when schools applied academic learning to improving the quality of life in their local communities. Some features of social adaptation can be found in the school program in 1940 in Holtsville, Alabama, a consolidated rural high school located in a poor area, which had as its ideal better living conditions in the community.[31] In Holtsville, the students were challenged to study their local economy. They found many problems: heavy meat spoilage in the stores, purchase of canned fruits and vegetables from outside the community as opposed to purchase of the same fruits and vegetables grown in the community, and an overemphasis on the production of a single crop.

With the cooperation of local farmers, the students secured a loan from a governmental agency to construct a slaughterhouse and refrigeration plant. Guided by a teacher, the students began processing meat and renting lockers to the farmers. Soon, they had paid off the loan. Then they did more. The started a hatchery and arranged to sell chicks to the farmers and buy back eggs below the market price, making money on the enterprise. Subsequently, they undertook to manage a cannery at the school; installed a water supply; helped install modern facilities in homes and restored homes; purchased modern machinery, which they rented or used in working for the farmers; planted more than 65,000 trees to prevent erosion; planted, sprayed, and pruned 50,000 peach trees for farmers; and set up woodwork and machine shops, a beauty shop, a local newspaper, a movie theater, a game library, a bowling alley, and a cooperative store in which many of their own products were sold, including toothpaste made in their chemistry department.

Equalitarian programs flourished in the 1960s and 1970s with the creation of Project Head Start, magnet schools, Upward Bound, racial desegregation and storefront schools that promoted cultural awareness and celebrated cultural roots. Teachers initiated curriculum activities against the Vietnam War, environmental degradation, and gender discrimination—all of which led to the 1980s reaction and a tightened curriculum aimed at transmitting a basic core of knowledge and minimal skills of literacy and numeracy to everyone and more academic programs in high schools.

Deschooling was a controversial theory of the 1970s. This theory holds that the school as an institution is so vicious it should be disestablished as soon as practicable. In his book *Deschooling Society*,[32] Ivan Illich presented a vision of education as the pursuit of learning through nonformal means from peers, elders, models, and things, whereby information, knowledge, and skills would be accessible through technology and real-life activities. Teachers would assume the role of facilitators to assist learners in satisfying what they wanted to learn—putting learning ahead of schooling.

Illich was opposed to the school's monopoly in certifying people for different vocations and establishing the curriculum required for gaining certification. He protested the commodification of knowledge divorced from real situations, inert, packaged and sold. Illich argued that people should have access to richer situations than schools for learning—situations that would be open to every person throughout his or her life.

According to deschooling, the content to be learned would be a matter of personal need and drawn from both sources of information and critical responses to it. Illustrations of such resources include: (a) cultural references—libraries, laboratories, theaters, and museums already available; (b) factories, airports, and parks that could be available to students; (c) skill exchanges whereby persons offer skills and the conditions for their mastery;

---

[31]*The Story of Holtsville: A Southern Association Study School* (Nashville: Cullum and Ghertner, 1944).

[32]Ivan Illich, *Deschooling Society: Social Questions* (New York: Marion Bayers Publisher, 1999).

(d) peer matching through networks where students partner in inquiry; and (e) reference services where professionals and experts list opportunities for learning.

Today's technology makes deschooling possible. Also, today's atmosphere of choice connects with deschooling. However, the privatizing of schooling and the establishing of class structures and distributions of jobs or income on the basis of preacquired privileged knowledge and attendance at given schools maintains the hidden curriculum of schooling.

CRITICISMS OF SOCIAL RECONSTRUCTIONISM

Reconstruction is appealing because it is based on faith in the ability of humankind to form a more perfect world. Furthermore, it claims to use the best of science in determining consequences and suggesting possibilities. Among the difficulties of reconstruction, however, is the fact that scientific findings permit varied interpretations and do not prescribe how everyone should respond to the findings. Established empirical and general conclusions are scant. Even the futurologists have been divided into the "bleak sheiks" (pessimists) and the "think-tank Utopians" (optimists). Also, there are no direct implications for curriculum. What one sociologist or economist considers true may be refuted by another. Few agree about the special conduct that is best for a planned society.

Reconstructionists with a Marxist orientation fault older reconstructionsts for failing to recognize that oppression and exploitation are fundamental characteristics of class structure in the United States and cannot be altered by teachers within the schools. Although older reconstructionists did not speak of the school as remaking the society in any total sense, they did believe that the school might influence behavior in regard to social problems. They realized that attitudes and beliefs would not be sustained unless supported by changes in the structure of society. However, older reconstructionists thought that the primary task of the school was a moral and intellectual reconstruction. Unlike the neo-Marxists, they did not believe that the school should be an instrument for subversion and political revolution. Instead, they wanted to use the school to extend the ideals to which the people were already committed.

Neo-Marxists also have been faulted. Peter McLaren[33] is a leading proponent of critical pedagogy. His interpretation of the relationship between power and culture and the school's role in issues of class, race, and gender has been a target for criticism. J. Martin Rochester acknowledges McLaren's wide influence in criticizing capitalism and how it is transforming the global world through exploitation and oppression, but faults him for putting ideology above inquiry.[34] Rochester believes McLaren fosters cynicism and that McLaren's account of the struggle for the suffering fails to fulfill the school's traditional purpose of generating foundational knowledge, love of learning, and the intellectual tools for pursuing that learning. Noteworthy, however, is Rochester's omitting of any discussion of the validity of McLaren's ideology and the knowledge that it contributes. Rochester fails to acknowledge McLaren's scholarship in showing how corporations and government are affecting lives throughout the world.

The theory of cultural reproduction, namely, that the school reproduces the social inequalities of the society, has been challenged because few have tried to collect evidence to show that schools have been deliberately oppressive in the interests of the larger society.

---

[33]Peter McLaren and F. Jarmillo, "Critical Pedagogy as Organization Practices: Challenging the Demise of Civil Society in a Time of War," *Educational Foundations* (Fall 2002): 1–20.

[34]J. Martin Rochester, "Critical Demagogues," in *The Writings of Henry Giroux and Peter McLaren* (Palo Alto: Hoover Institute, Stanford University, 2003).

Daniel Liston has faulted Marxists for not providing sufficient evidence in support of their claims and for associating a particular consequence without showing that it is the practice itself which produces the result.[35] With respect to tracking, for example, little evidence exists that this grouping arrangement was selected for capitalistic purposes or that it persists because it serves capitalistic interests.

Although the work of Freire in developing curriculum through dialogue with learners is generally highly regarded, he, too, has his critics. Jim Walker, for instance, doubts that Freire's educational ideas and methods are truly liberating because they do not give enough attention to effecting a revolution. Freire had little to say, Walker charges, about the nature of political leadership and how to achieve unity among a divided people.[36]

C. A. Bowers, on the other hand, believes that Freire's approach reflects Western culture and therefore might undermine the traditional worldviews of people in non-Western cultures. Bowers questions whether Western assumptions such as knowledge is power, change is progressive, and people are the masters of their own fates are appropriate in non-Western traditional societies.[37]

CONCLUDING COMMENTS

Social reconstructionists are concerned with the relation of the curriculum to society as it *should* be as opposed to society as it *is*. Many tenets of this group are consistent with our highest ideals, such as the right of those with a minority viewpoint to persuade those of a majority viewpoint, and with faith in the intelligence of the common people and in their ability to shape their own destiny in desired directions. Neo-Marxists within the social reconstructionist ranks would pit class against class, disregarding the differences within classes, groups, and genders. The futurists in the movement are far less ideologically oriented and would be happy if the curriculum would help learners "want well"—that is, conceive of a desirable future after taking into account crucial social trends.

The reconstructionist commitment to particular social ideas determined by "social consensus" may not be readily accepted in an individualistic United States. Americans have so many competing interests and different views regarding moral, religious, aesthetic, and social issues that it is difficult for them to agree on an ideal. Some also voice concern about the reconstructionists' efforts to create a collective society in which solutions are reached through social consensus.

We can expect accelerated curriculum development along reconstructionist lines whenever a resolution of conflict in values is needed. Such a need often exists in multicultural neighborhoods. Cultural groups frequently have different interpretations of history, different conceptions of nature, different levels of aspiration, and different views of social conduct. The prediction also applies whenever there is a breakdown in the barriers that isolate the school from the community. Accelerated curriculum development should thus occur when parents and community members become involved in teaching and social service roles, when students and adults participate in effecting changes outside the school building, and when community members assess local social and economic needs or deficiencies

---

[35]Daniel Liston, "Faith and Evidence: Examining Marxists' Explanations of Schools," *American Journal of Education* 96, no. 3 (May 1988): 323–351.

[36]Jim Walker, "The End of Dialogue," in *Literacy and Revolution,* Robert Mackie, ed. (New York: Continuum, 1981), 120–151.

[37]C. A. Bowers, "Cultural Invasion in Paulo Freire's Pedagogy," *Teachers College Press* 81, no. 4 (summer 1983): 935–955.

and decide how the institutions in the community can contribute to the improvement of the selected priority needs.

Today's social reconstructionists are wrestling with world conditions as well as the impact of these conditions locally. Globalization, multiculturalism, health, and environmental problems favor a world curriculum that must deal with uncertainty.

It is difficult to implement social reconstruction in state schools in which conservation of the political status quo is the rule. Furthermore, social reconstruction is not viable as long as teachers view teaching as subject matter transmission rather than personal and social transformation. Also, professional teacher organizations tend to clash with reconstructionists favoring local community groups and parents. Rivalry between professional teacher and parent power movements regarding *what* should be taught and *how* it should be taught has already surfaced. The challenge, therefore, is to apply the principle that calls for a "community of persuasion," probably by including teachers in the decision-making process but also by giving the community—parents, students, and others—more of a controlling voice.

QUESTIONS

1. What circumstances would be most likely to give rise to a curriculum along social reconstructionist lines?

2. Paulo Freire spoke of the curriculum obstacles preventing a clear perception of reality (e.g., control of learning from mandates from government and educational agencies, content and methods that foster learner dependency, and standardized ways of thinking). Can you provide specific examples of these obstacles to reconstructionists in schools which you have known?

3. Consider computer literacy, drug education, and dropout prevention programs known to you. Was their approach social adaptation or social reconstruction? Why?

4. Are you optimistic or pessimistic about the ability of curriculum to change existing social structures or institutions? Why?

5. What predictions about the world future appear "good" to you? Which predictions appear "bad"? How should a curriculum be designed in order to prevent the bad future?

6. Whose interests are served by the curriculum with which you are familiar?

SUGGESTED STRATEGIC RESEARCH

DISPROVING A THEORY ABOUT SOCIAL INJUSTICE
There is danger in finding an event that supports a theory in that it may be only a coincidence. State one of your theories regarding the cause for the widening gap between rich and poor. Collect (if possible) evidence that might *refute* this theory.

IDENTIFYING HOW SCHOOL PURPOSES ALTER THE CURRICULUM
Describe how curriculum differs in schools that put one of these purposes first: (1) ladders of mobility; (2) source of potentially qualified employees; (3) inducement to buy consumer goods and services; (4) indoctrination in civic responsibility and social order.

FINDING WINDOWS OF OPPORTUNITY FOR SOCIAL CHANGE
Social change is thought to occur when there is an open period or space where "taken for granted" beliefs or practices are beginning to be questioned. Some refer to this condition, which applies to both individuals and societies, as liminality—"twilights", tipping points or moments of cultural tran-

sition when we are "betwixt and between," ready to challenge established thought and behavior. Identify liminality in a situation known to you. How would you take advantage of it to shape the curriculum?

DISCOVERING THE SOURCES OF BETTER LEARNING

It is important to know the educational background of those who are best informed about phenomena related to world, national, or local conditions. Did they gain their knowledge and wisdom through the media, the school curriculum, or personal experiences in social reconstruction? Your findings may point to recommendations for changing how people can best be educated.

EVALUATING A KNOWN CULTURE

Select a culture either large (nation, state) or small (school or classroom). What evidence can you provide that this culture is meeting the following universal criteria for a good society?

- One does not have to conform.
- There is no role conflict such as "follow the golden rule" one moment and "business is business" the next.
- It allows for meeting biological needs.
- Subgroups share ideals, goals, and frames of reference.
- The transition from childhood to adulthood is smooth.
- Use of force is effectively controlled.
- There is no discrepancy between what the culture promises and what it delivers.

SELECTED REFERENCES

FREIRE, PAULO. *The Politics of Education.* Amherst, MA: Bergin and Garvey, 1985.

GIROUX, HENRY. *Schooling for Democracy: Critical Pedagogy in the Modern Age.* London: Routledge, 1987.

JOSEPH, P., ET AL., EDS. *Cultures of Curriculum.* Mahwah, NJ: Lawrence Erlbaum, 2000.

SHOR, IRA, ED. *Freire for the Classroom: A Sourcebook for Liberating Teaching.* Portsmouth, NH: Heinemann, 1987.

STANLEY, WILLIAM B. *Curriculum for Utopia: Social Reconstruction and Critical Pedagogy in the Post-Modern Era.* Albany: State University of New York Press, 1994).

CHAPTER *3*

THE SYSTEMIC CURRICULUM

THE **SYSTEMIC** curriculum is easily camouflaged. Sometimes it is presented, as in the No Child Left Behind Act of 2001 (NCLB) and standards-based exit examination requirements, as serving egalitarian interests, proclaiming that all students should have access to basic and prestigious subject matters that will prepare for life and college. Other times the systemic curriculum is promoted as the chief tool for preparing the nation's future workforce, enabling the United States to meet the twenty-first century's demand for those with high-level thinking and extensive knowledge in science, mathematics, and technology.

Some groups see the systemic curriculum as the vehicle for efficiency and effectiveness in delivery of content. It makes possible employment of a differentiated staff whereby coaches and mentors ensure reliability of teacher performance or even circumvent dependence on the classroom teacher by putting students in touch with a range of educational providers.

The systemic curriculum can be found in many contexts. Training programs for the military, industry, and religious orders rely on a systemic curriculum to ensure uniformity in what is to be learned. The current standards-based curriculum attests to the dominance of this curriculum orientation.

The overarching theme of the systemic curriculum is control. Prescribed goals are given along with standards to be attained. Instructional objectives, benchmarks, test results, and other indicators are used to evaluate progress toward the goals and standards and to signal the need for modifications.

As seen in Table 3.1, content standards are tied to the goals and give expectations for what students are to learn. Although teachers and students may sometimes initiate projects, start inquiries, and engage in matters of local and personal relevance, such activities are to be connected and reconciled to the content standards. Performance standards and benchmarks are intended to lay out for the teacher the sequencing of lessons and to support the content standards by focusing on specific skills and facts that contribute to the more encompassing scope of the content standards.

Performance standards are used by both students and teachers to clarify expectations and to make explicit criteria that will be used in judging performance. These standards enable the teacher and students to recognize their strengths and to identify areas that need improving.

Table 3.1 Anatomy of a Standards-Based Curriculum

Unified Goals

Standards sequenced by age, grade, school subjects

Content standards (what students must know)

Performance standards (what students must be able to do)

Alignment	Classroom Subsystems
State, district, school instructional program materials, teacher preparation and monitoring	Instructional objectives and benchmarks
Achievement measures results—feedback, modifications, rewards, punishment	Assessment measures
	Elements—grouping of students, time or space allocations
	Functions—assessing and motivating students, academic diagnosis
	Process—gaining students' attention, presenting, guiding, giving feedback, and demanding applications

ALIGNMENT

Parts should relate to the whole. It is not rational to set goals if there are no means for attaining them, nor to prescribe unproven methods that might be incompatible with the goals. Policies, curricular frameworks that describe what should take place in the classroom, particular instructional programs, staff development, tests, and other measures of student achievement should be consistent or coherent.

The success of a standards-based system depends on having both strong standards and measures for assessing what the standards call for. The Center for the Study of Evaluation at UCLA has found that although in general current tests may be matching the standards developed by state agencies, only a few test items measure the full range of objectives and standards.[1] The most challenging standards and objectives are the ones that are undersampled or omitted entirely. Standards and objectives that call for high-level reasoning are often left out in favor of simpler cognitive processes for recalling information and procedures. Also, tests do not measure attitude and metacognition.

There is ongoing improvement in the tools for determining the alignment between content standards, textbooks, and measures of achievement.[2] One can use these tools to determine how well instructional materials and the elements of classroom teaching are aligned with the standards in terms of topics introduced and their cognitive demands.

ACCOUNTABILITY

Accountability aims at assisting educators and policy makers to meet educational expectations and to identify deficiencies, such as the lack of resources and inability to apply

---

[1] Richard Rothman, Jean B. Slattery, and Jennifer L. Vranek, *Benchmarking and Alignment of Standards and Testing* (Los Angeles: Center for the Study of Evaluation, GSOE, University of California Los Angeles, May 2002).

[2] Andrew C. Porter, "Measuring the Content of Instruction: Uses in Research and Practice," *Educational Researcher* 30, no. 7 (2002): 3–14.

practices known to increase student achievement. Accountability is also a way (a) to exercise political power and the promotion of a particular view of knowledge or teaching methodology and (b) to shift responsibility to others. Linn characterizes educational accountability systems as having the following features[3]:

a. Developing challenging content and performance standards that focus on student learning.

b. Emphasizing the measurement of student achievement as a basis for school accountability.

c. Developing a measure for evaluating schools.

d. Introducing rewards, penalties, and interventions for improving achievement.

Katherine Ryan sees accountability systems as structured by a hierarchical approach to improving educational achievement. Policy makers are committed to an efficiency model that uses test scores as indicators of productivity whereby gains in standardized achievement scores represent the productivity of schools and districts. These scores are monitored closely by federal and state policy makers. School administrators and teachers are under pressure to be accountable, particularly to the state and federal agencies.[4]

Although systemic curriculum is most often associated with curriculum centralization and uniformity, a system may have windows for experimentation. Accountability may be a safety valve in the interests of curriculum innovations and choices when accountability is exchanged for flexibility. In return for being accountable for boosting achievement, districts and schools may be free to introduce alternative ways of teaching and learning. Policy makers who support decentralization of school programs, materials, and qualifications of teachers may give waivers to districts and schools in exchange for evidence of student achievement.

STANDARDS-BASED CURRICULUM

The United States is embracing centralization and standardization of the curriculum at federal, state, and local levels.

Policies for Standards-Based Curriculum

National subject matter associations that represent numerous areas such as mathematics, science, social studies, and English have developed curriculum standards for their fields as they vie to infuse their content into the schools. Typically, these standards indicate the scope of topics and skills along with the sequence for presenting them by grade level. States use these national standards as guides and models as they formulate their own standards and frameworks.

The NCLB requires that states develop content standards in reading and mathematics and administer tests that are linked to these standards in grades 3 through 8. Science content standards and assessment will follow.

The NCLB requires that states measure yearly progress toward objectives for improved achievement by all students and that at least 95% of students reach the goal of performance at the "proficient level" or above by the end of the 2013–2014 school year. Students representing diverse groups—ethnic, racial, languages, and disabilities—must participate in the assessment. Schools that fail to progress toward these objectives for two

---

[3]R. Linn, "Assessment and Accountability," *Educational Research* 29, no. 2 (2003): 4–16.
[4]Katherine Ryan, "Shaping Educational Accountability Style," *American Journal of Evaluation* 23, no. 4 (2002): 453–468.

consecutive years will be marked as needing improvement or closure. In addition to holding students and districts accountable for student progress in the rudiments of literacy and numeracy, the federal government requires states and districts to focus their secondary school programs on academic preparation, encouraging more students to make the transition from K–12 to college.

All but one state has adopted some form of statewide standards, and most have state tests that are more or less aligned with the standards. Many states have high school graduation standards keyed to scores derived from new statewide tests. States and organizations are developing comprehensive curriculum aligned with the standards and assessments, usually laying out a grade-by-grade continuum of content so that teachers will be aware of what students should already know and would need to know to succeed in subsequent grades.

California, by way of example, began its systemic curriculum by emphasizing elementary school reading and math, adopting a limited number of textbook series in reading and mathematics that appeared to offer a desired methodology. These systemic commercial programs, which allocated content by grade level, featured (a) scripted lessons for direct instruction, (b) classroom activities, and (c) procedures for continuous assessment of the learning progress. The state also mandated the use of an academic progress index whereby individual schools were evaluated on the basis of student yearly gain (allowing for differences in expectations on the bases of socioeconomic background, race or ethnic group, and English-language proficiency). Until the collapse of the state's economy, bonuses were given to schools for teachers associated with the best results.

At the local level, the Los Angeles Unified School District mandated particular reading and math programs as the curriculum content for all students in 400 low-achieving elementary schools that were lagging on their standardized test scores. In addition, hundreds of teachers were selected as literacy and mathematics coaches and trained to support the implementation of these programs by preparing and monitoring the teachers. Coaches modeled classroom lessons, observed and guided their colleagues in organizing the assessment of student learning, and sometimes supplemented classroom materials with materials aligned with the state standards. In this way, the coaches assured that instruction was consistent in all low-performance schools.

Other states differed in their approach. In New York, the United Federation of Teachers took on the task of the writing a K–12 curriculum, including sample lessons, lists of resources, and guides on how to teach the material. Their first K–12 curriculum was for English language and math with other curriculum to follow.[5]

Colleges and universities have influenced K–12 content standards by issuing subject matter requirements for admission. Generally, higher educational institutions specify math, literacy skills, history, and the like as requirements before high school graduates can be considered as applicants. A general systemic curriculum for high schools has been developed at the Center for Educational Policy and Research at the University of Oregon. This curriculum and an accompanying CD-ROM, "Understanding University Success," outlines the knowledge and skills students need to progress during the first year on a higher education campus and is available to all high schools in the country. In addition to the standards, the document provides work samples, assignments, syllabi, and information about standards, exams, and assessments in all 50 states.

Early in the 1990s many states participated in a systemic approach known as "competency-based and outcome-based education" (OBE) aimed at defining and evaluating student deficiencies. Proponents shared the idea that curriculum should center on essential far-reaching outcomes that all students would master, not merely putting in "seat work."

---

[5]Randi Weingarten, "Writing a Curriculum—It's Union Work," *Education Week* 22, no. 18 (Jan. 15, 2003): 28–33.

At least 30 states described outcomes although their scopes differed. Much controversy followed about whether the outcomes should be in terms of achievement in traditional subject matters or in having students demonstrate their ability to use knowledge in everyday life as complex thinkers, responsible citizens, ethical and high quality workers, and the like. Most promoters of outcome-based curriculum opposed deriving objectives from the existing traditional curriculum. Instead, they preferred general outcomes likely to be needed in future life experiences considering trends and conditions that students might meet as adults. The OBE curriculum lost force because there was considerable controversy and concern that outcome-based education was usurping local curriculum decision making, infringing on the privacy rights of parents, and replacing the church by taking responsibility for moral development of learners.

Subsequently, a diverse group promoted the idea of a standards-based system. Represented players included: a preselected advisory panel, a labor and political committee on the needed skills for the American workforce, the National Educational Goals Panel, the National Council on Education Standards, and the National Center on Education and the Economy to name a few. (The political nature of the standards movement is described in Part 3.)

One influential corporation active in promoting standards-based curriculum "driven by results" is the New American Schools (NAS).[6] NAS aims at a coherent system that encourages innovations and parental choice. NAS calls for national education goals, uniform standards, better assessment, and improved teacher training. Their approach has been to form whole school reform at the elementary school level and to encourage secondary schools to contract with other agencies. NAS has launched alternative designs for schools in keeping with the promise to exchange the permission to innovate in return for accountability for results. A current study indicates that their projects have had mixed results. Without strong school district support and continued assistance from the curriculum reformers, many projects are unsustainable. NAS has subsequently joined a contractor from the U.S. Office of Education in reform efforts.

The similar organization ACHIEVE was created by the nation's governors and business leaders to advance standards and to assess programs.[7] ACHIEVE helps states to develop high, internationally benchmarked standards. This organization has posted state standards by grade level for major curriculum areas and linked lesson plans to these "national standards." ACHIEVE has a long-range vision where citizens question the adequacy of local standards against the "national" standards, and work for enactment of legislation to authorize local education agencies to contract out instruction and the management of schools to qualified groups, granting local autonomy in return for accountability for results.[8]

The National Center on Education and the Economy through its "New Standards" program has influenced curriculum by providing tools, resources and training to implement standards-based education.[9] The philosophy of those at the Center is to offer standards that include key concepts from the disciplines as well as ability to apply the concepts to real-world problems. New Standards specifies what the standards look like, how to assess student progress, what the curriculum looks like, materials to be used, the pedagogy, and how the classroom should be organized.

---

[6]New American Schools (merged with American Institute for Research), *New American Schools: A Decade of Experience 1991–1995* (Arlington, VA: The American School Development Corporation, 2002).

[7]ACHIEVE—an organization founded in 1996 by state governors and heads of large corporations. Achieve, 1775 Eye Street N.W., Washington, DC.

[8]David T. Kearns and James Harvey, *A Legacy of Learning: Your Stake in Standards and New Kinds of Public Schools* (Washington, DC: Brookings Institute, 2000).

[9]Mark S. Tucker and Judy B. Codding, *Standards for Our Schools: How to Set Them, Measure Them, and Reach Them* (San Francisco: Jossey Bass, 2001).

In the process of developing their curriculum, New Standards found little agreement on which topics in each core subject should be taught at given grade levels, resulting in publishers cramming many topics in their textbooks at the expense of the conceptual base of the subject. Further there were inadequate provisions for students at different levels of understanding and experience. New Standards derived their performance standards from the National Content Standards developed by four national professional organizations. Each standard has a performance description, samples of student work, and commentaries that reflect on the work samples.

In their recommendations for setting high standards for everyone, the National Center on Education and the Economy argue for standards that are (a) competitive with standards in other countries and (b) realistic with what can be taught and learned in a given period of time. Parenthetically, Robert Marzano[10] cited a study where 350 teachers who, when asked how long it would take them to adequately address each benchmark for a variety of standards in different subject matters, reported that the elementary school years would have to be extended by nine years.

Perhaps less is more. A focus on key core concepts and real-world applications might allow many parts and procedures to be learned incidentally and much knowledge to be combined and better learned as the same concepts are used and represented in different content fields.

Standards-Based Curriculum in the Classroom

Local schools and teachers typically develop their standard-based curriculum planning backwards from the standards and benchmarks deciding what will be addressed at each grade level. Starting with these standards, teachers prioritize the standards and try to find a way to measure progress toward as many standards as possible as they examine state content standards and state performance standards. Teachers decide what key topics must be addressed and what student work might show that the standards are met. The focus on key topics means deciding on what is most important and how much time can be devoted to the topic. Determining which students are ahead or behind with respect to particular benchmarks and standards helps determine allocation of effort. Teachers also consider safety nets in the form of instruction by tutors and peers.

In one school, teachers focused on research-based language standards for speaking and listening and coupled them to standards for reading and writing. They created an instrument for tracking the language, literacy skills, and interests of children. The use of this instrument was an impetus to planning systemic instruction for a grade level resulting in greater efforts to engage children in conversation and more opportunities for children to write and use books.[11]

Instructional Alignment   Instructional alignment is another example of the measured curriculum and involves "teaching to the test." In his review of instructional alignment, S. Alan Cohen presents evidence that when instructional stimuli match assessment, effects occur that are about four times what is ordinarily seen in typical classrooms.[12]

---

[10]Robert Marzano, *What Works in Schools* (Alexandria, VA: Association for Supervision and Curriculum Development, 2003).

[11]David K. Dickinson, Allyssa McCabe, and Kim Sprague, "Teacher Rating of Oral Language and Literacy (TROLL): Individualizing Early Instruction with a Standards-based Rating Tool," *The Reading Teacher* 56, no. 6 (March 2003): 540–570.

[12]Alan Cohen, "Instructional Alignment: Searching for a Magic Bullet," *Educational Researcher* 16, no. 8 (Nov. 1987): 16–20.

Alignment proceeds by matching the stimulus conditions of criterion performance and the instructional sequence. Tests are generally created *before* designing the curriculum. Mastery learning and personalized systematic instruction are older models to enhance alignment.

Mastery Learning Mastery learning is a systemic curriculum. Instructional objectives, arranged in an assumed hierarchy of tasks, are the keystone of the system, and lesson materials are built around that arrangement. The objectives are the intended outcomes of instruction. Each student must master them before going on to the next step in the learning hierarchy. Mastery is indicated by successful responses to criterion-referenced tests matched to the content and behavior specified in the objective. Objectives in the teaching of mathematics, for example, are grouped by topics such as numeration, place value, and subtraction.

Lesson materials are matched with the objectives and allow the pupil to proceed independently with a minimum of teacher direction. The pattern for involving the student with the system has three parts:

1. *Finding out what the student already knows about the subject.* Usually a general placement test is administered to reveal the student's general level of achievement. The student is also given a pretest to reveal specific deficiencies.

2. *Giving the student self-instructional materials or other carefully designed learning activities.* Such activities focus on one of the student's specific deficiencies previously identified.

3. *Giving the student evaluative measurements to determine his or her progress.* Such measurements help the teacher decide whether to move the student ahead to a new task or to provide additional materials or tutoring. Materials usually include placement tests, pretests and posttests (criterion-referenced), skills booklets, a record system, games and manipulatives, and cassettes and filmstrips. Paid aides and volunteers (such as parents) assist students, check response sheets, and help to keep the materials organized.

Mastery learning is sometimes employed by teachers implementing outcome-based programs in that it allows individuals more time and additional clarification for mastering units of curriculum related to the desired outcomes before proceeding.

Personalized Systematic Instruction More schools are using technology to transmit some portion of their curriculum to students. Media, for example, is an ancillary means to extend conventional pedagogy. Lectures are videotaped and CDs are made available for viewing at the convenience of the student. The teacher tends to change from the role of imparter of knowledge to that of facilitator. The content of instruction and its applications are set in advance. In contrast to traditional education, the boundaries of knowledge are not fluid, and the results obtained are more important than the process. When course content is viewed as finite, it can be packaged in advance, duplicated and transmitted. Although the view may narrowly define content, it also allows students to work at their own pace.

A personalized system of instruction (PSI) is a soft technology involving persons, content, and materials as opposed to a hard technology, which involves only devices such as television, video, and other programmed sequences. PSI uses the principles of behavioral science that call for frequent active responses from students, immediate knowledge of results, and a clear statement of objectives. It also allows for individualization; different students may use different amounts of time and different approaches for attaining mastery of the instructional tasks.

With PSI, a course or subject is broken into small units of learning, and at the end of each unit learners take tests to determine whether they are ready to proceed. They go to a "proctoring room" staffed by advanced students who administer the test, score it, and give feedback to the students. If less than "unit perfection" performance is shown, the proctor becomes a tutor, explaining the missing points and guiding the student in restudy. There is no penalty for failing a unit, but one must study further and try again. Frequent interaction with proctors often develops affect and contributes to understanding.

PSI permits one teacher to serve many students. Instructors are responsible for conducting one- or two-hour weekly large group sessions for motivating students and clarifying content. They also have overall responsibility for planning the course, including the procedures and procurement or development of materials and examinations.

Although many teachers of the systemic curriculum directly focus on the content they are expected "to cover" so that students will have the skills needed for the next course or for standardized exit tests; others try to elicit initiating questions that students might have before engaging in the "laid out" curriculum. In these classrooms, student-generated questions are chosen if they appeal to the interests of the students and can serve as a link to the concepts that are to be introduced. For example, a math class might ask, "How do numbers create order?" before the teacher introduces the prescribed treatment of nonrational numbers.[13]

PSYCHOLOGICAL FOUNDATIONS OF THE SYSTEMIC CURRICULUM

Behavioral psychology is one foundation for the traditional transmission of teaching and learning where students acquire prespecified skills and content related to specific outcomes or objectives and assessments determine if desired changes in behavior (learning) have occurred. A prime precept of behaviorism is that the association of stimuli, responses, and reinforcement result in a changed behavior.[14]

The policy of states and districts to reward or punish schools and teachers based on the results of their efforts is an example of reinforcement. Recitation lessons in classrooms by teachers and media illustrate the behavioral model of (a) instructional presentation, (b) eliciting a student response, and (c) correcting or affirming feedback. Other features of curriculum based on principles from behaviorism include the following:

- Differentiating the types of learning outcomes sought (simple, complex, low or high order thinking).
- Task analysis—breaking complex tasks into more manageable units.
- Parts to whole instructional sequences.
- Direct instruction—clear directions, examples, opportunities to practice and apply what has been taught.

Cognitive psychology and information processing theories have also influenced the systemic curriculum by drawing attention to how students' beliefs influence their learning and how conceptual thought can best take place. It was cognitive psychology that redirected

---

[13] Alison Zonuda and Mary Tomaiho, *Competent Classroom: Aligning High School Curriculum—A Creative Teaching Guide* (Washington, DC: National Education Association, 2001).

[14] B. F. Skinner, *Verbal Behavior* (Englewood Cliffs, NJ: Prentice-Hall, 1957). Reprinted by B. F. Skinner Foundation, 2002.

concerns to the learner's state of mind and away from the behavioral emphasis on external performance alone.[15]

Cognitivists have the idea that by studying the structures of experts (their ways of thinking about problems) they can identify thought processes that can be mapped into the heads of learners. This idea has led to the study of how experts in different subject areas approach their work—the specific information and procedures and their ways of thinking.

The systemic curriculum has drawn from cognitive psychology the importance of:

- Accommodating new information into existing schemes or beliefs.
- Knowing where and when to apply knowledge and strategies.
- Chunking information into meaningful units.
- Modeling through flowcharts, simulations, and other representations to pinpoint errors and to target a need.

In contrast with psychologies for shaping behavior or programming minds, alternative psychologies such as social constructionism act on the participation metaphor for learning that is responsive to (a) the tentativeness of knowledge, (b) conflicts in beliefs and understandings that students bring to schools, and (c) recognition that young children have capabilities to engage in sophisticated levels of thinking.

Systemic-based curriculum is weakened when psychological assumptions and learning theories are not in alignment. While most state standards rely on behaviorism and cognitivism, constructivist psychology fits the national standards for science and mathematics that focus on key ideas and the relations among them rather than on a mélange of isolated facts and skills unlikely to be taught as tools for dealing with real-world situations.[16] A serious issue is the press by professional teacher educators for social constructivist pedagogies whereby students and teachers construct meanings from classroom activity. Such teaching methods conflict with scripted lessons that put acquisition of official knowledge in place of student views.

State and district policies have failed to implement the fundamental changes in content and pedagogy advocated by national standards.[17] Instead accountability and an emphasis on students' test scores has precluded many teachers from particular practices, such as sharing different interpretations and engaging in multiple solutions derived from constructivist theory. In the systemic curriculum teachers are expected to use methods that are strategically aligned with cognitive and behavioral principles.

HISTORICAL ANTECEDENTS TO THE SYSTEMIC CURRICULUM

The Jesuit schools in the sixteenth century were an early example of a systemic curriculum for teaching the classical liberal arts, philosophy, and theology—all aimed at the ideals of a Christian gentleman fit for leadership in citizenship, commerce, and the affairs of court.[18] The Jesuits systemized school-keeping by specifying the development of instructional materials, methods for teaching, scripted lessons, and frequent testing so that the curriculum was effective over broad regions of space and time.

[15]E. Major, "Learners as Information Processors: Legacies and Limitations of Education's Second Metaphor," *Educational Psychologist* 3, no. 3/4 (1996): 151–161.

[16]National Research Council, *National Science Educational Standards* (Washington, DC: National Academy Press, 1996).

[17]James P. Spillane and Karen P. Callahan, "Implementing 'State Standards for Science Education,'" *Journal of Research on Science Teaching* 37 (2000): 401–425.

[18]E. A. Fitzpatrick, *St. Ignatius and the Studiorum* (New York: McGraw-Hill, 1933).

Other elements in today's systemic curriculum have also been tried and abandoned. Until 1890, the English and Irish used payment by results whereby there was an annual oral exam where inspectors assessed the knowledge of reading, writing, arithmetic, grammar, and geography of every student. Funds to schools and payments to teachers from public sources depended on percentages of individual success in the approved subjects.[19] This practice led to such consequences as

- Prescribed syllabi and teaching to the examination.
- Employment of underprepared and unsupervised teachers inasmuch as results would monitor their effectiveness.
- Teachers investing their instruction efforts toward middle achievers where positive gains were more likely than among the top and bottom students where instruction was either not needed or unlikely to make a difference.

In the late 1800s, written tests began to replace the oral examination in determining the degree to which students had mastered the material in their textbooks, and, in the early 1900's, testing took new prominence in the context of a drive to manage schools in the interest of efficiency and modeled after practices in business and industry.[20]

The "cult of efficiency" gave rise to most of today's educational tools (e.g., norm-referenced achievement tests, portfolios, and rubrics for assessing student work). This early period saw the introduction of statistical concepts and language for interpreting the measures—standard deviation, means, correlations. Authorities began to collect statistical data about schools and to replace ineffective methods with practices that would produce better performance in less time.

The use of achievement tests changed curriculum, goals, and content. These tests put emphasis on the acquisition of information and the learning of basic algorithms instead of on the older goals and content which aimed at the development of mind and character. The twentieth century also saw changes in the concept of schooling from an informal local institution where a community introduced children to the rudiments of literacy and moral beliefs to a formal institution that was responsive to the needs for graduates who were prepared differently—some for work in new vocations and industry and others educated for professional opportunities—in keeping with their likely future role in society.

Although testing in the early 1900s was used to assess the efficiency of teachers and schools, by the 1930s the purpose and nature of tests had changed from assessing schools and teachers to making judgments about students. Tests no longer held teachers and schools accountable but were developed for the purposes of (a) diagnosing student strengths and weaknesses, (b) placing students in classrooms and groups (tracking), and (c) for giving grades. As schools began to undertake more goals in order to serve more purposes and to prepare students for a greater range of life occupations, curriculum standardization disappeared and curriculum differentiation was the norm within each school and classroom.[21]

Regions and states differed in the degree to which they centralized control of the curriculum. Southern states and California, for example, practiced statewide adoption of textbooks in contrast with states and districts that allowed local choice. Nationwide, however, even with different instructional materials, the curriculum of elementary schools was common, at least on its focus on the basic skills of literacy and numeracy.

[19]J. Doven Wilson, ed., *The Schools of England* (Chapel Hill: The University of North Carolina Press, 1929).
[20]Raymond Callahan, *Education and the Cult of Efficiency* (Chicago: University of Chicago Press, 1962).
[21]Reba Page and Linda Valli, eds., *1990 Curriculum Differentiation Interpretive Studies in U.S. Secondary Schools* (Albany: State University of New York Press, 1990).

External influences on the secondary school curriculum were directed at the academic program for those preparing for college, ignoring the general vocational and elective programs. The New York Regents Examinations, for instance, brought curriculum uniformity to the academic track. The measurement-driven curriculum with its commercially developed standardized tests declined throughout the mid-twentieth century although elementary schools continued to give the tests in order to compare their standings with other normed populations but seldom to use the results for school improvement or accountability.

Curriculum coherence by states or districts in the 1930s and 1940s was chiefly through the development of courses of study, curriculum guides, and frameworks. Boards of education would authorize the development of detailed courses of study for all schools to match the board's stated philosophy for the curriculum and general curriculum objectives. Committees of teachers and others would plan the scope (topics) and sequence of curriculum topics and other elements (skills, appreciations, and concepts) that were to be expanded throughout the course or program and used to guide plans for attaining the objectives, including suggested methods, activities, and materials. The courses of study and the curriculum guides were written for different subject areas and grade levels.

In the 1960s, there were incremental changes in the systemic curriculum. There were national efforts to strengthen curriculum through disciplinary programs that engaged students in activities that mirrored the practices of scientists and scholars in different academic disciplines. This academic aim was to have students learn some of the ideas and ways that scholars were describing and exploring the world. Elaborate materials were centrally produced (texts, films, laboratory manuals, teachers' guides) but insufficient attention was given to developing the background and confidence of teachers for teaching the curriculum. Also there was a public backlash against what was seen as a federal intrusion on state and local control. At the same time, there were curriculum efforts by behavioral psychologists to develop programmed instruction with questions, prompting, and reinforcement leading to achievement of specific instructional objectives. These efforts took the form of modules, scripted lessons, and computer-assisted instruction minimizing the role of the teacher. One explanation for the failure of such programmed instruction to dominate the curriculum in the 1970s was that there was an excessive number of minuscule objectives: "Too many targets turned out to be no targets at all."[22]

CONSEQUENCES OF SYSTEMIC CURRICULUM

Twenty years after the National Commission for Excellence in Education issued the *Nation at Risk* report, which gave impetus to the current movement for systemic reform, advocates for curriculum reform continue to fault secondary schools for lack of a central purpose and too often offering a diverse curriculum. An updated 2003 report calls for more rigorous standards and higher requirements for high school graduation with all students evidencing a solid base in English, math, science, social studies, and computer sciences. In contrast to the first national risk report, children in preschool through the eighth grade are targeted for achieving the skills and knowledge presumed to be necessary for continued academic learning.

The systemic "reformers" also want each school or provider of educational services in all states to adhere to common academic standards, make public their records, and give

---

[22]W. James Popham, "Measurement as an Instructional Catalyst," *New Directions for Testing and Measurement* 17 (1983): 17–30.

parents the right to select the provider that will best serve their child.[23] The systemic approach has narrowed the breadth of subject matter and learning experiences in K–12 schools. The National Center for Educational Statistics show that students are taking more academic courses than before. The percentage taking the "new basics" quadrupled from fewer than 14% of graduates in 1982 to 56% in 1998. However, fewer than one-fourth of high school students describe the classes as challenging.[24] In contrast, colleges and universities are increasing their own curriculum options with interdisciplinary studies, innovative courses, and individually pursued off-campus learning experiences.

The Council of Great City Schools evaluated the nation's 59 largest urban districts, tracking math and reading scores by grades over five years, and found that under accountability programs those that focused on improvement made significant student achievement gains on statewide assessment exams. In math, 87% of the pupils in the Great City Schools posted gains by 2002 and fewer than 12% lost ground. In reading, the results were similar with 47% doing better that the state's average. However, students in these urban schools still trailed students in wealthier suburban schools.

Controversy surrounds the impact and direction of systemic curriculum. Although 49 states now have content standards for most subjects as well as assessments to measure student achievement, the quality of these standards and assessments varies. Some state standards are either hopelessly vague or encyclopedic. There has been widespread reliance on off-the-shelf tests and teaching to these tests instead of what might have been taught, narrowing instruction instead of deepening and broadening knowledge as envisioned by the professional associations that issued the National Standards for Math and Science, the members of the National Research Council, and general educational groups, such as the Coalition of Essential Schools and the High Success Network. These groups and organizations promote systemic curriculum that focuses on major concepts and themes rather than discrete items of isolated information and the accumulation of facts. The national standards also connect major concepts across disciplines as opposed to isolated ideas within separate disciplines or subject areas.

A major concern is that state standards and tests have failed to give importance to the teaching of high order thinking and problem-solving skills. Results of the 2002 International Mathematics Study show that although American students rank near the top in the fourth grade they fall into lower rank among developed nations by the twelfth grade. Lower achievement and grade inflation is also a concern of members of the National Research Council who recommended that credit no longer be given for advanced placement scores below the highest level of 5 because students taught largely through recitation are unable to reason mathematically and scientifically when they get to college.

The high-stakes testing associated with systemic reform curriculum is very controversial. Audrey Amsein and David Berliner challenged the benefits of high-stakes testing after examining what happened to both students' motivation to learn and academic achievement when states used exams to grant or withhold diplomas.[25] They found that tests decreased student motivation and increased the proportion of students who dropped out. Also, student achievement did not improve on a range of measures, such as assessments by the National Assessment of Education Progress (NAEP), the Stanford Achievement Test or Scholastic Assessment Test (SAT), AET, or Advanced Placement (AP), although

---

[23]Paul E. Peterson, ed., *Our Schools and Our Future: Are We Still At Risk?* (Koret Task Force on K–12 Education, 2003)

[24]Michael Casserly, *Breaking the Odds* (Washington, DC: Council of Great City Schools, 2004).

[25]Audrey L. Amsein and David C. Berliner, "The Effects of High Stakes Testing on Student Motivation and Learning: A Research Report," *Educational Leadership* 60, no. 5 (Feb. 2003): 32–39.

scores on state assessment often improved, perhaps owing to narrowing of the curriculum and to teachers teaching to what would likely be on the test.

On the other hand, Edwin A. Lock found setting specific, challenging goals leads to higher performance than setting easy goals or no goals. Martin Carnoy and Suzanna Loeb found that NAEP score gains, particularly among African-American and Hispanic students, were higher in those states with stronger accountability systems—extensive testing, exit examinations, and consequences for principals and teachers. An evaluation of the National Science Foundation's Systemic Initiative Program, aimed at changing classroom practice, found small but consistent positive relationship between teachers' reported use of standards-based instruction and student achievement.[26]

The public, too, is supportive of the measured curriculum and sees standardized test scores as important indicators of school effectiveness and a basis for determining what needs improving. Much of the opposition to both mandated tests of basic skills and to high-stakes testing so far has come from parents and students who question the validity of the tests and the arbitrary setting of passing scores. Also, many parents of high achieving students resent the time required for taking tests that are inappropriate for their children. In response some districts have excluded high performing schools from required tests of rudimentary skills and instead assess students' progress only in those schools in need of improvement.

State tests have influenced instruction. Teachers attend to what is tested.[27] The influences of testing have been greatest in the elementary schools and in states with high-stakes testing. For example, 40% of teachers in high-stakes schools report that their testing results influenced their teaching daily, compared with 10% of teachers in nonstake schools.

Testing also influenced teachers to use a variety of specific methods—whole group instruction, individual seat work, cooperative learning, and tasks similar to those expected on the tests. Exit tests have become the medium through which curriculum standards are interpreted. The teachers see the benefits of removing unneeded content, giving emphasis to important topics, and more teaching of such skills as writing and critical thinking. They also see the negatives of minimizing creativity, giving increased time for test preparation, and addressing concern for breadth rather than depth.

Systemic demands on the school, for example, the mandating of a common textbook series or the implementation of district schoolwide programs, have the virtue of engendering teacher solidarity. Sometimes collegiality comes as teachers redirect their stress brought about by the pressure for results, but more often it comes from confronting common problems as teachers implement a coordinated system—a departure from the old isolated classroom where each teacher put his or her own values and knowledge into play.

Teachers' views of standards-based curriculum may differ because of their time in the profession and their sense of efficacy. Great teachers thrive under autonomy. Good teachers want structure but seek windows for responding to student-generated concerns and interests. Many beginning teachers welcome scripted lessons, guiding questions, suggestions and activities for students, and easy to use materials along with tools for assessing student progress. Different opinions are seen in these statements:

"What I see as important is not on the test."

"One of my groups is struggling. If I were in control of my classroom, I could redirect and reteach."

[26]Laura S. Hamilton et al., "Studying Large Scale Returns of Instructional Practice: An Example from Mathematics and Science," *Educational Evaluation and Policy Analysis* 25 (Spring 2003): 1–29.

[27]Boston College, National Board on Educational Testing and Public Policy, "Perceived Effects of State-Mandated Testing Programs on Teaching and Learning," 2003, www.bc.edu/nbetpp.

"Now all the kids leave the school with the same experience."

"I wouldn't have a clue about what to teach without the standards."[28]

CONCLUDING COMMENTS

The systemic curriculum is viable because it matches so many conventional beliefs. There is general acceptance in American life of the importance of having a goal and then planning backwards to determine what would it take to reach the goal together with continually assessing to ensure that the parts are contributing to the desired outcome or to make modifications if necessary.

The acquisition metaphor dominates whereby the school, its curriculum, and teaching should present prespecified knowledge and skills and see that learners acquire them. There is a notion that the curriculum should order content and activities so there is a cumulative effect on learning and development. As indicated in other chapters, this belief is in contrast to the belief that instead of effort to predict and control, it is better for students and teachers to be free to adapt and have diverse experiences provided there is opportunity to collaborate and reflect with others on the meaning of these experiences.

The systemic curriculum confronts several challenges. One centers on the problem of measuring achievement of standards and progress toward goals. Misalignment and invalid measures are part of the problem. Albert Einstein's quote is appropriate: "Not everything that can be counted counts, and not everything that counts, can be counted." Similarly, the current systemic curriculum centers on measuring basic skills at the elementary school level and foundation knowledge in selected school subjects at the secondary level. There is little measurement of critical and higher order thinking or testing to see what students have learned about confronting situations of uncertainty for which there are no established "right answers." The uncertainty of knowledge is both a measurement and an instructional problem for the systemic curriculum. The drive to ensure that all students complete college preparatory courses or programs that lead to specific careers assumes an unwarranted certainty about educational trajectories and future employment. Some "break the mold schools" are moving away from the acquisition metaphor with its emphasis on individual attainment, abstract knowledge and information that can be exchanged as a commodity, that is, good grades lead to admission to a good school, a good school leads to a good social network, which leads to a high paying job.

There are evidence-based programs that follow the participation metaphor by encouraging student collaboration and promoting the concrete nature of learning that extends beyond the school. The Coalition of Essential Schools Programs and the Accelerated School Programs are examples of innovative approaches that are part of the reform movement that give local participants responsibility for developing curriculum plans in accordance with general principles rather than expecting implementation of a one size fits all curriculum.

A serious problem is the proliferation in curriculum standards by the states. The practice of laying out taxonomies of what should be taught at different levels of schooling is questionable. Lists of content and skills are contributing to fragmentation, leading to little coordination among the subjects and distraction from key concepts. Also unresolved is the matter of student variability and the goal of giving all students access to challenging

---

[28]Amber Winkler, "Division in the Ranks: Standardized Testing Draws Lines between New and Veteran Teachers," *Phi Delta Kappan* 84, no. 3 (Nov. 2002): 219–225.

opportunities to learn, avoiding tracking but not expecting all to learn the same way and at the same time.

Finally, systemic reform is undertaken in response to a perceived threat to an institution. For the last two decades, the public has been told that the public schools are failing. Public opinion now supports a systemic curriculum reform to meet this threat and gives wide approval for measuring curriculum results and holding schools and teachers accountable. Accountability is seen as necessary for determining how to improve a curriculum as well as to ensure the public of its quality.

A demand is growing for research-based evidence that particular curriculum programs are effective and sustainable in a range of contexts.

QUESTIONS

1. List the probable consequences from the systemic approach to curriculum whereby state and local governments (a) specify the competencies or outcomes to be acquired by all students and (b) maintain tight control by testing students and monitoring implementation of approved programs while helping teachers develop effective teaching practices.

2. Should technology be "domesticated" by the systemic curriculum in the interest of students acquiring officially prescribed content and objectives? (No free access to the Internet.)

3. The measured curriculum tends to use test scores in making critical decisions about students, teachers, programs, and schools. What other information is important?

4. In order to sense the difficulty of making a task analysis, compare your list of basic elements for achieving a given task or understanding with the prerequisites identified by your peers.

5. Should the systemic curriculum deal with the question of values, ethics, and morality, going beyond basic skills and less contested aspects of subject matter?

SUGGESTED STRATEGIC RESEARCH

DETERMINING CURRICULUM ALIGNMENT

Consider using Andrew Porter's instrument for alignment of standards, teaching practices, materials, and assessment measures. You can adapt this instrument for your purpose to find out how well two or more curriculum components are aligned in a situation of interest to you.

VALIDATING TEST RESULTS

Take a representative sample of students and compare their scores on a standardized test with your own assessment of their abilities and knowledge when they are given opportunity to draw on their own language and culture, to know what you are asking them to do, and to show in their own way what they know. Compare the external assessment results with your internal assessment. Where does validity lie?

ANALYZING CURRICULUM STANDARDS

Select a school subject or area of interest to you and the curriculum standards for this subject. Analyze how the standards might be applied in daily living outside the school. Examine the standards through one or more grade levels. Organize a panel to use your analysis eliminating items that can best be acquired incidentally or disregarded because of their limited transfer value.

IDENTIFYING CORE CONCEPTS THAT TRANSFER

Help a faculty group which represents different program areas identify the core concepts in their fields that can be presented and applied in all of their areas. Subsequently, decide on the value for deepening understanding and transfer by systematically embedding these concepts in a range of contexts.

DETERMINING TEACHER EFFICACY

There are teachers who value their autonomy, preferring to develop their own courses and programs; others prefer to have guidelines such as standards and suggested allocation of content before responding to students' interests and taking advantage of external opportunities for extending student learning; and some teachers welcome scripted lessons, units of instruction, matched materials, activities, and assessment devices as a ready-to-teach program. Identify the curriculum preferences of a few teachers and the degrees of freedom they have in their teaching situations. What is the match between their preferences and their teaching situations? Does the match or mismatch bear on their satisfaction and likely retention in teaching?

SELECTED REFERENCES

DUFFY, THOMAS M., AND DAVID H. JOHASSEN. *Constructivism and the Technology of Instruction.* Hillsdale, NJ: Lawrence Erlbaum, 1992.

FLODEN, ROBERT. "Policy Tools for Improving Education," *Review of Research on Education* (theme issue), Robert Floden, ed. Washington, DC: American Educational Research, 2003.

HESS, FREDERICK, ANDREW J. ROTHERMAN, AND KATE WALSH, EDS. *A Qualified Teacher in Every Classroom? Appraising Old Answers to New Ideas.* Cambridge, MA: Harvard Education Press, 2004.

KAUFMAN, ROGER. *Planning Educational Systems: A Result-Based Approach.* Lancaster, PA: Technonic Publishing, 1988.

TUCKER, MARK S., AND JODY B. Codding. *Standards for Our Schools: How to Set Them, Measure Them, and Reach Them.* San Francisco: Jossey Bass, 2001.

CHAPTER 4

THE ACADEMIC CURRICULUM

THE ACADEMIC curriculum is a mirror of broader cultural trends. One overarching trend is the commodification of education which puts economic gains at the fore with knowledge as a commodity to be exchanged by (a) individuals that seek chances at high paying jobs, (b) schools as institutions that offer the kind of knowledge that will bring enrollments (tuitions), institutional rankings, grants, inventions, and mergers with for-profit corporations; and (c) government that will pay for research that produces results for money expended on behalf of security, health, and economic competitiveness. This trend plays out in the academic curriculum as *instrumentalism*—knowledge for use.

The test-driven accountability curriculum described in Chapter 3 with its emphasis on skills, competencies, and performance standards is a manifestation of an instrumental view of knowledge although it is only quasi-academic because it aims at transmitting facts and skills rather than providing intellectually challenging opportunities for learners to either acquire the powerful conceptual maps of the academic disciplines or engage in inquiries where they can go deeply into a study to create and validate their own ideas.

Instrumentalism in academic learning is occurring in universities and some secondary and elementary schools. There is a major reorganization in universities in order to address real-world problems that require collaboration across disciplines. More funding agencies now require students to have mentors from two or more fields. Faculty are asked to improve their data collecting and create new research strategies for the real-world problems. Increasingly, problems are seen as not answerable by a single discipline. National priorities require new knowledge that comes from connecting the disciplines and harnessing their potential. Departments of engineering are combining with biology. Chemistry and anatomy are taught concurrently and "just in time," as medical students confront particular cases.

Academicians are developing more encompassing "interdisciplines" as they select a research theme. The theme conceptualizes the problem in new ways and generates novel research strategies, fusing the disciplines. Preliminary to their undertakings, team members may engage in short intensive programs where they learn to understand the fundamental aspects of their partners' disciplines.

Just as interdisciplinary studies, such as systems biology that combines physics, computer science, biology, and physiology using a quantitative approach, are racing through universities, many secondary and elementary schools are introducing a new academic curriculum that revitalizes the "structures of the disciplines" approach of an earlier decade that promoted student inquiry. Like the older approach, the revitalized curriculum calls for students either to think about unanswered questions in a discipline or to address problems in their local community. There is a difference, however, in that the new academic structuring of the disciplines takes advantage of technology by putting learners in touch with resources that make their investigations more fruitful. Access to both archives of data and collaboration with scientists in data collection is introducing students at earlier ages to what science is really like, starting their trajectories as experts. In the new academic curriculum, students learn to present their findings and recommendations together with this evidence and convincing arguments.

The Knowledge Integration Environment (KIE), for example, uses Web technology to support learner-constructed evidence purporting to answer scientific phenomena, for example, "How far does light travel?" Learners make observations from their experiences to use in interpreting and explaining, browse data bases for evidence that may support or reject their positions, and deliberate their divergent views. Varied methods and perspectives are seen as critical to the thinking process.

An exemplar of the new academic curriculum with young children is found in Fostering Communities of Learning, a mid-city schools program for grades K–8. This program draws from the discipline of biology and prepares children to want and to be ready to contemplate disciplinary research.

Although guidelines are given in Part 2 for the development of such curriculum, it is important to recognize that the new academic curriculum offers students opportunities to experience what research is like and to learn what counts as knowledge. Students undertake investigations that foster particular ways of thinking as modeled by the experts with whom they work.

Obstacles in implementing the academic curriculum include the difficulty of getting students to ask appropriate questions, hypothesize, synthesize information, master scientific procedures, design investigations and draw valid conclusions. However, the spirit of this curriculum is found in Nobel prize winner Barbara McClintock's recall of her high school science class: "I would solve some of the problems in ways that weren't the answer the instructor expected. It was a tremendous joy—the whole process of finding that answer."

Postmodern thought and multiculturalism are associated with a second major trend that has fragmentalized the academic curriculum. Postmodern thinking distrusts single explanations and generalizations, thereby stimulating broad ranges of new studies and methods of inquiry that give better explanations for local situations. Postmodernists have a critical view of experts and authorities. Conflicts abound about the knowledge base for decisions affecting society and the natural environment. Science itself has historically regarded knowledge as tentative and subject to revision. There is more questioning of the objectivity of specialists with rising public awareness of the connections between science and economic interests.

Multiculturalism has revealed the intellectual strengths of diverse people and created cultural forms of knowledge beyond the traditional liberal arts derived from Ancient Greece and Rome and the modern Western world. This broadened knowledge has enriched the curriculum, and its economic counterpart of globalization has enlarged its academic curriculum. Multiculturalism has influenced academicians in history and social sciences to reach beyond traditional parochialism and to become more interested in understanding the behavior of people in other countries.

The cultural wars of the last decade opened curriculum content to alternative literary canons and to multiple interpretations of the classics and the social sciences. "Teaching the conflicts" made the curriculum more challenging than a "set out to be learned" approach.

Because the structure of a discipline is more stable than particular facts and topics, the academic curriculum is able to accommodate to cultural change. For example, many musicology departments are offering popular courses, such as "History of Rock 'n' Roll," which can transition to traditional studies of classical music.

The liberal arts curriculum still holds a firm place in academic institutions as indicated by a recent poll among university presidents that asked: "Which five books should every undergraduate read and study if they are to engage in the intellectual discourse and public duties of the twenty-first century?" Their answer: the Bible, the *Odyssey*, the *Republic*, *Democracy in America*, and the *Iliad*.[1]

Nonetheless, traditionalists are under siege, and fewer students pursue the liberal arts. Defenders use different arguments. Some point to the economic value of education and justify liberal education as valuable in the job market because it teaches people how to write and how to think, embodying students with a flexibility of mind.[2] Others are opposed to economic instrumentalism that "sells" liberal education on the basis of salaries and sophistication. Instead they believe that the value of liberal education lies in its potential to develop moral agents by causing students to reflect on how the choices they are making will turn them into the persons they become.[3]

APPROACHES TO THE ACADEMIC CURRICULUM

The various academic subjects represent a range of approaches to truth and knowledge. Some academicians define knowledge as *justified belief*, as opposed to ignorance, mere opinions, or guesses. Others appeal to traditional sources.

The academic curriculum is incoherent. Although those holding an academic conception believe that the development of a rational mind is the primary goal, they do not agree on how best to achieve this goal. Some look at the radically plural world of knowledge and believe that if students are to find their way about this world and learn how to acquire meaning in human experience, they should participate in the different forms of knowledge and acquire a unique mode of thought associated with each.

Those who value inquiry or habit of mind recommend teaching the concepts, attitudes, and processes of inquiry used in particular selected disciplines as the way to develop

---

[1] International Association of University Presidents, Oct. 2003 FDU press release. inside.fdu.edu/prpt/iaupsurvey .html-7R.
[2] John Feedman, *Liberal Education and the Public Interest* (Iowa City: University Iowa Press, 2003).
[3] Marshall Gregory, "A Liberal Education Is Not a Luxury," *The Chronicle of Higher Education* (Sept. 12, 2003): B16.

thinking persons. They put students in touch with the controversial issues in a given field and let them participate in its discourse.

Although it may be unrealistic to expect students to emerge from the secondary schools as experts in any academic domain, it is not unusual for students to make significant progress beginning in the early years and increase their competence in the use of tools for analyzing and responding to unsolved problems.

Classicists look to the ancient teachers as the source of judgment and argue for teaching the great books of the modern world, using the Socratic method to eliminate inconsistencies in thinking. Other conservatives believe that the transmission of cultural literature associated with affluent America is a necessary basis for intelligent participation in the national culture. In contrast to the traditionalists, multiculturalists want an academic curriculum that opens choice in liberal studies, drawing from abundant transcultural literacies ranging from elite populations to popular culture; from didactic to revolutionary; from traditional to experiential; and from the local to the global.

The Forms of Knowledge Approach

The forms of knowledge approach addresses the problem of selecting from among the more than 1,000 academic disciplines that could be part of the school curriculum. The problem is not new:

> Good Lord! how long is Art,
> And life, how it goes flying!
> It is so hard to gain the means whereby
> Up to the source one may ascend.
> And ere a man gets half-way to the end,
> Poor devil! He's almost sure to die![4]

It is impossible for a person to delve deeply into many disciplines. How shall those administering the curriculum decide which disciplines to offer? A number of measuring rods are proposed: (1) comprehensiveness with respect to ways at arriving at or justifying truth or knowledge, (2) social utility—the usefulness of the discipline for all citizens, (3) prerequisite knowledge—the importance of certain disciplines as a basis for others or for subsequent education.

In the interest of comprehensiveness, it would be well to sample disciplines that emphasize different avenues for justifying knowledge. The late Philip Phenix, for example, illustrated how to achieve comprehensiveness in the fundamental disciples. In *Realms of Meaning,* he described and analyzed six basic types of meaning, each of which has a distinctive logical structure.[5] Art, with its concern for subjective validation, can balance a discipline like science, which uses objective observations to confirm an expected occurrence. History can be used to illustrate the criteria of coherence and verifiability to show that ideas have to fit together and that new conclusions can be weighed against past events. Mathematics can prepare learners to gain knowledge through reason and logic. It may be possible to find a form that will help students recognize that some forms of knowledge can be validated by intuition and divine revelation. Such a curriculum would preclude the exclusivity of contemporary schools, which tend to emphasize the scientific mode of learning.

Similarly, Paul Hirst believes that the curriculum must develop the mind and that this is best done by mastering the fundamental rational structure of knowledge, meaning, logical

---

[4]Johann Goethe, *Faust*, trans. and ed. J. F. L. Raschen (Ithaca: Thrift Press, 1803), 29–31.
[5]Philip H. Phenix, *Realms of Meaning* (New York: McGraw-Hill, 1964).

relations, and criteria for judging claims to truth. Hirst offers an answer to the classical curriculum question "What knowledge is of most worth?" He proposes a number of forms of cognitive knowledge for understanding the world. Each of these forms is said to meet four criteria: (1) certain concepts are peculiar to the form (e.g., gravity, acceleration, and hydrogen are concepts unique to the physical form); (2) each form has a distinct logical structure by which the concepts are related; (3) the form, by virtue of its terms and logic, has statements or conclusions that are testable; and (4) the form has methods for exploring experience and testing its statements (e.g., in mathematics the "truth" of any proposition is established by its logical consistency with other propositions within a given system, while in physical science, knowledge is validated by data from observation). Hirst's forms include mathematics, physical sciences, knowledge of persons, literature and the fine arts, morals, religion, and philosophy. This range in forms allows for many different kinds of meaning.

Hirst's belief that all meaning, all understanding, and the whole of intelligible experience are subsumed within the forms of knowledge is not too different from Howard Gardner's belief that there are multiple forms of knowing or intelligences. Gardner thinks that curriculum should change students' intuitive understanding of the world by leading them to the theoretical objective knowledge of the scholars about the world as found in the forms of knowledge.[6]

In proposing forms of knowledge rather than stipulating a particular fixed substance of subject matter (particular facts and operations), such as in basic skills programs, Hirst argues for a dynamic curriculum. His forms do not, however, encourage a subjective or relative view of knowledge. To him, knowledge consists of ways to structure experience so that it can be public, shared, and instrumental or useful in daily living.[7]

Criticisms of Hirst's views of knowledge and the curriculum center on whether he has indeed discovered distinct forms and whether he has slighted the idea of subject matter as substance. Some concepts in one form have more in common with some concepts in another form. A focus on the forms of knowledge might result in an absence of attention to specific knowledge or what has been learned about the world. Learning a form should include learning the substance within it, not just acquiring knowledge of concepts, rules, and criteria for claims to truth. Hirst admits that there is no complete agreement on the descriptions of the forms of knowledge and that mastery of the formal features of a discipline should not be mistaken for mastery of a particular area of knowledge itself. Therefore he wants students to acquire both substantive knowledge that has significance for them and knowledge of the general principles and ways of thinking that are the inherent features of the forms by which knowledge is gained.

A recent reassessment of Hirst and his critics acknowledges the importance of a broad range of theoretical knowledge and the skills of higher thinking. But the central question of whether such education is attainable by all people or is appropriate only for abstract thinkers who look at the world in fresh ways and use theory only after relevant practice in real situations, particularly in the early stages of intellectual growth,[8] remains unanswered.

Structure in the Disciplines Approach

In his celebrated book, *The Process of Education*, Jerome Bruner proposed that curriculum design be based on the structure of the academic disciplines. He proposed that the curriculum of a subject should be determined by the most fundamental understanding that can

[6]Howard Gardner, *The Unschooled Mind: How Children Think and How Schools Should Teach* (New York: Basic Books, 1993).

[7]Paul H. Hirst, *Knowledge and the Curriculum* (London: Routledge and Kegan Paul, 1974).

[8]D. C. Mulcahy, "Jane Roland Martin and Paul Hirst on Liberal Education," *Journal of Thought* (spring 2003): 19–30.

be achieved of the underlying principles that give structure to a discipline. The basis for his argument was economy. Such learning permits generalizations, makes knowledge usable in contexts other than that in which it is learned, and facilitates memory by allowing the learner to relate what would otherwise be easily forgotten, unconnected facts. "The school boy learning physics is a physicist, and it is easier for him to learn physics behaving like a physicist than doing something else."[9] Years later Bruner, caught up in the social movements of the day, urged a deemphasis on the structure of history, physics, mathematics, and the like and called for an emphasis on subject matter as it related to the social needs and problems of the American people.[10]

Recently, he has shown more concern with how one can control and select knowledge as needed rather than letting knowledge control and guide the person.[11] The concept of structure in the disciplines was widely heralded as a basis for curriculum content. The concept refers to rules for pursuing inquiry and for establishing truth in particular disciplines. These kinds of structure are posited:

1. *Organizational structure:* definitions of how one discipline differs in a fundamental way from another. The organizational structure of a discipline also indicates the borders of inquiry for that discipline.

2. *Substantive structure:* the kinds of questions to ask in inquiry, the data needed, and ideas (concepts, principles, theories) to use in interpreting data.

3. *Syntactical structure:* the manner in which those in the respective disciplines gather data, test assertions, and generalize findings.

The particular method used in performing such tasks makes up the syntax of a discipline. Sociologists, for example, generally observe in naturalistic settings, identify indicators believed to correspond to the theoretical framework guiding the inquiry, and often rely on correlational data to show relationships among factors observed. Experimental psychologists, on the other hand, manipulate their treatment variables in an effort to produce desired consequences. Experimentalists believe they have found knowledge when they are able to produce a predicted result.

A useful view of the structure of knowledge has been given by D. Bob Gowin. Gowin offers five questions that can be asked in any order to establish the structure of knowledge in a curriculum or other text:

1. What is the telling question (the generative question or discourse)? The telling question directs our thinking, our inquiry, our sense of what is going on. It also organizes our actions. For example, the question "Is the human mind just an extension of the animal mind?" could be a telling question.

2. What are the key concepts? What concepts are used to ask the question? In the example above, the concepts *mind, animal, extension* would be crucial.

3. What method(s) is to be used to answer the question. In our example, both philosophical and scientific methods are appropriate.

4. What are the major claims of the work? The claim may be factual, depending on the method and its relation to the question. Logic and evidence support the claim.

5. What value claims are made? What are the consequences of the findings? Utility, aesthetic, and moral justifications may be used in judging the worth of the findings.

---

[9]Jerome S. Bruner, *The Process of Education* (Cambridge: Harvard University Press, 1960), 31.

[10]Jerome S. Bruner, "The Process of Education Revisited," *Phi Delta Kappan* 53, no. 1 (Sept. 1971): 18–22.

[11]Jerome S. Bruner, *Actual Minds: Possible Worlds* (Cambridge: Harvard University Press, 1986).

The relation of knowledge claims to moral and social matters is shown in Figure 4.1.[12] The context of inquiry is expanded in moving up the left and right side of the V. The V can be used to establish consistency among the components of the curriculum—methods, for instance, are unlikely to be implemented or accepted unless these changes agree with the practitioners' world view or unless the world view is also changed.

The structure of the disciplines concept was widely used in designing curriculum whereby students were to learn how specialists in a number of disciplines discover knowledge. An intellectual emphasis was the basis for most nationwide curriculum development projects of the 1960s. Curriculum builders of this period were primarily subject matter specialists who organized their materials around the primary structural elements of their respective disciplines: problems or concerns, key concepts, principles, and mode of inquiry.

Scholars in colleges and universities prepared materials focused on single subjects. These programs began as early as kindergarten and were designed on the assumption that all pupils should understand the methods of science and the basic properties of mathematics. This was in contrast to the prevailing practice of teaching scientific facts and a style of treatment in mathematics best characterized as rote and applied. Algebra, in the "reform" course, was treated as a branch of mathematics dealing with the properties of various number systems rather than as a collection of manipulative tricks.

What little debate there was regarding the "new programs" centered on the argument that what was being taught would be needed only by students who were to become professional scientists and mathematicians. The rebuttal offered these arguments:

1. There is need for appreciation from the general culture that we need well-trained scientists and their fields.

2. It is better to develop a deeper comprehension of the fundamentals than to touch on many facts that are often outdated conclusions of science. A discipline approach, for example, can help the learner deal with the "knowledge explosion."

3. True understanding of the facts in more fields of learning comes only from an appreciation of various interpretations, and a continuing investigation is far more interesting to the student than a set piece. There is a growing realization that the process of inquiry itself is a form of knowledge to be acquired.

4. A discipline is an internal organization, a subject matter suitable for efficient learning.

In almost every field—from English and social studies to art, and health education—there was an updating of content, a reorganization of subject matter, and fresh approaches to method. Typically, the stress was on a separate entity—not science, but biology, chemistry, or physics; not social studies, but history, geography, or economics; not English, but literature, grammar, or composition.

Reaction against a Structure of Knowledge

Not all went as well as hoped through the structure of knowledge approach. Teachers who themselves had never produced knowledge, who had not made an original scientific finding or historical interpretation, had difficulty leading students in the ways of discovery. The validity of the concept of structure as a basis for curriculum development was questioned, with opponents claiming that the concept was only an after-the-fact description of the way knowledge can be organized by mature scholars and not the way it was really won and that such structure is not necessarily the best way to organize knowledge for instructional purposes or to start and direct significant inquiry and reflection. Enrollments in

[12]D. Bob Gowin, *Educating* (Ithaca, NY: Cornell University Press, 1981), 107.

CURRICULUM

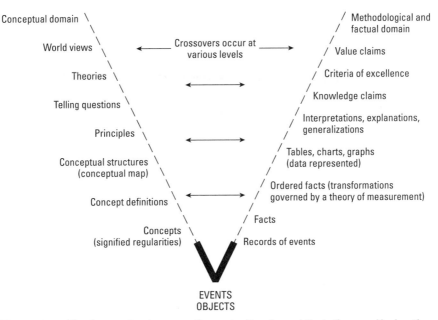

Figure 4.1   The Connection between Concepts, Events, and Facts Seen as Having the Shape of a V.

advanced physics courses declined. Many students, in both high and low ability groups, did not achieve as well as intended.

We now know that most of today's leading scientists are products from structure of the disciplines approach. Other factors, such as students' changing social attitudes in an era of social discontent, might have been more influential. The availability of numerous programs created problems of maintaining balance and organization. Many subjects had to be omitted from a school's offerings. Furthermore, the subject specializations were so narrowly focused that it was difficult to combine their concepts into broader fields.

The 1970s saw a decline in the academic approach to curriculum making. The popularity of a disciplined approach to the science curriculum waned with a growing distrust of science. It was argued that scientists should be doing more to solve humanity's problems. Also, those with nonacademic curriculum bents attacked the structure of knowledge approach to curriculum development through opposition to a well-publicized exemplar of this approach: MACOS. MACOS, the acronym for *Man: A Course of Study*, was to have been the primer for curriculum in the 1970s.[13] Bruner himself established the initial guide for this curriculum and directed much of its development, which was supported by the National Science Foundation (NSF) and the U.S. Office of Education in order to reform the teaching of social sciences and humanities. MACOS is a curriculum designed for students in the elementary school and consists of books, films, posters, records, games, and other classroom materials. More important, it sets forth assumptions about humans. Three central questions define the intellectual concerns and reveal the assumptions of MACOS: What is human about human beings? How did they get that way? How can they be made more human? The developers of the course wanted children to explore the major forces

---

[13]*Man: A Course of Study* (Washington, DC: Curriculum Development Associates, 1970).

that have shaped and continue to shape humanity: language, tool use, social organization, mythology, and prolonged immaturity. Through contrast with other animals, including the baboons, children examine the biological nature of humans. By comparing American society with that of a traditional Eskimo group, they explore the universal aspects of human culture.

The intellectual models used to get ideas across to children are disciplinary. Children are given examples of field notes and encouraged to construct their ideas about animals and humans in the ways ethnologists and anthropologists do. The principal aims of MACOS are intellectual: to give children respect for and confidence in the powers of their own minds and to provide them with a set of workable models that make it simpler to analyze the nature of the social world. Its values include the scientific mode of observation, speculation, hypothesis making and testing; understanding of particular social science disciplines; and the joy of discovery.

Attacks on MACOS came from those with different curricular concerns. Humanists criticized Bruner for failing to recognize the potential of MACOS for fostering emotional growth. Social reconstructionists opposed MACOS on the ground that it was created by a scholarly elite. A ruling class should not foster ideas in teachers and students, they said. The topics that children are asked to study are not related to improving the social life of the community in which they live. Congressman John B. Conlan criticized the course on the House floor as depicting "abhorrent and revolting behavior by a nearly extinct Eskimo tribe." Conlan said the material was full of references to adultery, cannibalism, killing of female babies and old people, trial marriage, wife-swapping, and violent murders. Many congressmen and others began to view the National Science Foundation as indoctrinating children and showing preference for certain scientists and curriculum makers. The controversies surrounding MACOS led to restricted NSF funding for educational research and greater surveillance of NSF by Congress. A suit in federal court asked that the state be enjoined from compelling children to participate in MACOS. The plaintiffs charged that this curriculum espoused secular humanism and that the United States Supreme Court had defined this as a religion. They argued that this course violated the First Amendment.

Revival of the Disciplines Approach

A revival of the structure in the disciplines approach is underway. Nearly every national report on education calls for curriculum concentrating on "higher-order" skills in reading, writing, mathematics, problem solving, and abstract reasoning. Accordingly, curriculum is supposed to engage students in emergent learning rather than merely reciting known conclusions. The new mathematics curriculum in algebra and geometry, for instance, insists on developing analytic reasoning and the student applying concepts in the solution of unfamiliar problems. Students are expected to formulate hypotheses about problems at hand and then test them against available data.

A study of policy for science education recommended that the NSF take the lead again in developing a high-quality K–12 science curriculum.[14] Among the arguments for having NSF generate alternative curricula as it did in the 1960s and early 1970s is that new evidence shows that the structure in the disciplines curriculum of those times was much more effective than critics thought. For example, a majority of those holding a bachelor's degree in physics had received high school instruction using the NSF-sponsored Physical Science Study Committee (PSSC) materials.[15]

[14]James H. Scheur, *The Education Deficit* (Washington, DC: Subcommittee on Education and Health for the Joint Economic Committee, 1989).
[15]George Pallrand and Peter Linderfeld, "The Physics Classroom Revisited—Have We Learned Our Lessons?" *Physics Today* 38 (1985): 39–44.

The National Research Council is promoting an academic curriculum based on the structure of the disciplines and giving students the intellectual tools and strategies for understanding different subject matters.[16] In this curriculum students learn to frame questions from the perspective of experts and how to transfer what is learned to new settings. The Council recognizes that there is no way a curriculum can cover the information and knowledge in any discipline but that students can acquire and apply key ideas or concepts from a discipline in real-world problem-solving situations.

This academic reform curriculum rests on the evidence that lectures, laboratory and recitation courses are ineffective at helping students master and retain important concepts over the long term. Moreover, traditional curriculum does not develop the creative thinking, investigative, and co-problem-solving skills that employers seek. The new curriculum has an absence of sets of facts to be learned, and instead addresses the difficulty in conceptualizing and analyzing information related to unsolved problems. By way of example, Edward Ayres, a history teacher, involves his students in compiling a vast archive of Civil War documents, telling them to handle the evidence of the past for themselves and struggle with its loose ends, silences, and surprises. Similarly, Thomas Goodman in his chemistry course engaged his students in a previously unanswered problem of identifying the chemical components that may reveal how elephants communicate.

Although the immediate aim is to lay the foundation for students to be successful thinkers, learners, and decision makers throughout their lives, the new structure of the disciplines rests on the assumption that means approximate ends—what students do in the present represents future expectations. Hence, as described in Part 2, students in the new academic curriculum "do" science, math, history, and the like, learning from their peers and from thoughts and actions of experts.

Technology has given students opportunities to bring their ideas to bear and to test their feasibility. Today there are more virtual classrooms that connect learners with like-minded peers and worldwide experts in real world investigations.

Conflicting Views of Knowledge Proponents of the forms of knowledge and structure of disciplines reject the fixed view of knowledge and instead hold that knowledge is tentative. The creation of knowledge—valid statements, conclusions, and truth—occurs by following the inquiry systems of the specific discipline or cognitive form. Proponents of these approaches reject the practice of students reciting conclusions apart from the methods and theories by which they are established.

Current reform in the academic curriculum reflects the disciplines approach and its view of knowledge as social construction. Students give more attention to the evidence for knowledge claims than to the recall of so-called knowledge facts. Classrooms are regarded as centers of inquiry where the different subject matters are seen as different cultures. Each culture has its own values, language, and ways of constructing meaning. More recognition is given to the social nature of learning and to the importance of dialogue through which practitioners maintain, modify, and develop the theories and interpretations that constitute the different disciplines or cultures.

Although Chapter 12 reports trends in the subject matters, the current disciplines approach can be introduced by references to changes in mathematics, science, and history. Table 4.1 contrasts the traditional mathematics and recommended practices that reflect new views about the structure of mathematics.[17]

---

[16]National Research Council, *How People Learn: Brain, Mind, Experience and School* (Washington, DC: National Academy Press, 2002).

[17]Robert B. Davis and Carolyn A. Mayer, eds., *Schools, Mathematics, and the World of Reality* (Boston: Allyn and Bacon, 1993).

Table 4.1   Traditional Mathematics Curriculum versus Structure of the Discipline Approach

Traditional	Structure of Knowledge
Lessons One- or two-day lessons.	Students work with an important mathematical idea over an extended period—sometimes as long as 6 weeks.
Instruction, examples, and practice narrow contexts.	A variety of contexts and real investigations.
Assignments Daily assignments from a textbook or worksheets.	A broad and complex problem or investigation that requires mathematical power.
Authority Teacher and textbook determine right answers.	Students explain their findings and engage in dialogues about what is acceptable.
Computation Students learn the steps to perform an algorithm.	Emphasizes "number sense"; students invent and use different procedures.
View of mathematics A collection of concepts and skills.	A cultural product; something people do—solve, communicate, reason.
A body of knowledge. Fixed "truths."	Context changes the kinds of math needed.

An example of a science curriculum in which students learn how theories are made can be found in *Properties of Matter*.[18] In this curriculum, students discuss and compare their views of phenomena and use their differences as the basis for constructing meaning. Situations are provided for students to test their ideas and to compare their efficacy. The program leads to the idea that piles of apparently unconnected data can be related by a theory and that the generation of a theory often involves searching for a pattern as well as "imaginative leaps."

The history curriculum as an academic study expects students to "do" history through inquiries by which they learn to judge conflicting evidence and draw their own conclusions. Each student's position is valid if researched, reasoned, and well articulated. Students are not expected to reach absolute conclusions but to learn how to judge evidence, to see the other side, and to recognize the biases of interpreters. Secondary school students might question the traditional views of Jefferson, Jackson, and Lincoln. They might examine the treatment of native peoples in the United States and the historical records of the Spanish–American War as well as Vietnam and other recent events. The approach is not without criticism. Some scholars fret about the loss of chronology and the absence of traditional content. Others believe the approach develops cynics who do not have the belief in heroism and virtues necessary for clear ideals and confidence.

Many oppose the forms and disciplines approaches. Humanists claim that all knowledge is personal and subjective. For them, knowledge is the result of a person's unique perceptions of the world. Social reconstructionists, on the other hand, see knowledge not only as a human product but as a product of specific social groups whose knowledge reflects their ideologies. Reconstructionists regard attempts at imposing a discipline in the same way they regard imposing an ideology—as a form of social control.

---

[18]*CLIS Approaches to Teaching the Particular Theory of Matter* (Leeds, England: University of Leeds, Center for Studies in Science and Mathematics Education, 1987).

Other opponents are academicians who work in the tradition of the liberal arts and those who believe in the transmission of "essential" information derived from the dominant cultural experience. The latter opponents fault the disciplines and forms approaches for (1) failing to inculcate traditional values and (2) fostering vocationalism, relativism, and pluralism at the expense of a coherent curriculum and common learning.

Liberal Arts and the Academic Core

From its early association with the study of Latin and Greek, the liberal arts have been expanded to the study of language, creative arts, expressive arts, and other subjects believed to have the power to stir the imagination, develop appreciation for beauty, and disclose the nature of humankind. The push for excellence fixes on wisdom of the past and cultural heritage.

Liberal Arts in Higher Education Higher education is under attack for failing to disseminate the great traditions of philosophy, literature, and the arts. Allan Bloom's popular *The Closing of the American Mind* attributes major moral and social changes to the failure of colleges and universities to teach the traditions from Plato through Rousseau. According to Bloom, students lack a sense of intellectual adventure and, because of their pursuit of careers, believe they have no time or need for the classics of Western culture. To solve the problem, Bloom suggests something similar to the old Great Books approach to learning, whereby students study classical Western thoughts. Another critic, Lynne Cheney, former chairman of the National Endowment for the Humanities, indicts colleges for failing to teach the best that has been thought and said. Cheney alleges that colleges have pandered to new interest groups and mixed the universal ideals of art and morality with politics, gender, and race.[19] Cheney might have been thinking of the instance of the Stanford University faculty voting to replace the university's Western cultural requirement with a new year-long program called "Culture, Ideals, and Values," which gives substantial attention to the issues of race, gender, and class and includes the study of works by women and minority-group members.

Since the 1980s, conflict has existed between those who want coherence (a unifying purpose and structure for the undergraduate college curriculum) and those who want to offer students more opportunities to engage in specialized studies of their own choice. In 1982, Harvard University implemented a new undergraduate core curriculum designed to bring a common purpose and coherence to courses of study. This curriculum replaced 80 to 100 highly specific courses, ranging from the historical origins of inequality to lectures on law and social order, with academic requirements in five areas: literature and the arts, history, social analysis and moral reasoning, science, and foreign culture. Harvard's students were also required to show proficiency in writing, mathematics, and the use of computers. Knowledge was not to be conveyed by rattling off facts but by helping students understand the modes of thought employed by a range of disciplines in a spectrum of fields.

In 2004, the Harvard College Curriculum Review recommended major changes in the curriculum in the interest of helping students develop multiple perceptions of themselves and the world and a foundation for their lives. The new curriculum calls for:

1. An international experience—study research or work abroad as well as study in a foreign language.

2. Every student broadly educated in the sciences.

---

[19]Lynne V. Cheney, *Humanities in America: A Report to the President, the Congress and the American People* (Washington, DC: National Endowment for the Humanities, 1988).

3. Fewer requirements in a major field with more exploration before in-depth work.

4. Encountering the major intellectual controversies of the day through work on topics that cross disciplinary boundaries.

It is not clear if other institutions will follow Harvard's recommendations as they did 10 years ago when nearly 95% of all institutions of higher education followed Harvard in completing curriculum reviews, with a host of these colleges instituting core requirements.[20] The teaching of Western culture was emphasized as colleges reshaped core courses to reflect the theme of "cultural legacies."

Traditionalists wanted core courses to feature classical texts of enduring value although many scholars believed that a national core curriculum or list of books would be both a recipe for unimaginative teaching and a restriction on intellectual liberties.[21]

Underlying the problem of what content should be taught in the core curriculum are these two questions: What is to be the relationship between works traditionally taught as great and writing reflecting the experiences of other people, either within Western society or from other societies? Should "great books" be used to blaze a trail back to shared values and traditional content, or can contemporary research and contexts be reinvestigated in new ways to think about the classics?

At the start of the twenty-first century, the liberal arts curriculum is fragmented. Major academic disciplinary associations, such as the Modern Language Association and the more recently established Association of Literary Scholars and Critics, have taken opposite stands on the liberal arts curriculum. The former is responding to new areas of scholarship—feminism, multiculturalism, gender—by encouraging literary studies of themes, such as homosexuality, that accompany new scholarship. The canon has been broadened to include works by females, minority, and non-Western authors. The latter organization continues the traditional study of the Great Books of Western civilization. However, the trend is toward greater choice, interdisciplinary studies, and communities of learners. The curriculum in liberal studies is more likely today to be jointly planned by students and faculty teams of four to five faculty and 60 to 100 students who invent their curriculum each year as they dig deeply into a big idea. The rise in feminist teaching practices also is influencing not only the content of the liberal arts but the way it is taught. If feminists are less hierarchial, the distance between the instructor and students is lessened and there is greater coconstructing of knowledge among peers and instructor. The goal of the emerging collaborative curriculum in the liberal arts is to emancipate students from oppressive structures, beliefs, and values.

Few schools offer a curriculum based on the proposition that there is a body of eternal and absolute truth, valid under all conditions, or that reason can be enhanced by familiarity with the most profound and grandest of humankind's intellectual works. St. John's College in Maryland is an exception. When students take biology at St. John's, they are handed a stiff frog and an Aristotelian treatise. In this school an older view of academic education, including science, mathematics, Greek, French, music, and the Great Books seminars, is maintained. In preceptorals, similar to electives, seven or eight students and a tutor work intensively on one of the Great Books or on a limited subject like Freud. In the all-required curriculum, third- and fourth-year students study physics, measurement theory, and chemistry in their science course. Sophomore biology emphasizes anatomy, embryology, and genetics in the framework of evolution. When they dissect their frogs, students read Aristotle's book *On the Parts of Animals* and ponder his notion of aliveness. They also

---

[20]Elaine El Kwawes, *Campus Trends* (Washington, DC: American Council on Education, Report 75, Aug. 1987).
[21]George Levine et al., *Speaking for the Humanities* (New York: American Council of Learned Societies, 1989).

read Galen, the second-century physician whose works were definitive for more than 1000 years, while they dissect rabbits. When they progress to the rabbit's circulatory system, they discuss William Harvey's treatise, "On the Motion of the Heart and Blood in Animals," published in 1628.

Rather than presenting only the most current research to students to memorize and repeat in exams, tutors encourage students to practice scientific inquiry. To do that, they believe, students must confront the great minds. Almost half of the biology sessions are spent in laboratory dissections and experiments that demonstrate genetics and embryological theory. Although students read from a half-dozen contemporary books, they also read and discuss the works of such trailblazers as Claude Bernard, Gregor Johann Mendel, and Karl Ernst Von Baer. In the language tutorial students study ancient Greek, in part because they read many Greek works, and one modern language, French. Students are not taught that all Western ideas are right and good. The materials inspire discussion and raise fundamental questions provoking much disagreement. Many students come out of St. John's as skeptics of any Western scholarly tradition.[22]

Liberal Arts in the Elementary and Secondary Curriculum In 1982, Mortimer Adler proposed a common liberal education for all students from ages 6 through 18. His Paideia Proposal has been the basis for many of the school reform movement's curriculum changes. According to this proposal, there should be a single program and common academic core in which students learn their own language, literature, fine arts, mathematics, natural science, history, geography, and social studies. This required curriculum allows only one elective—a second, foreign language. Students also take industrial arts, physical education, and hygiene. They are involved in drama, music, and the visual arts, and they learn how to exercise critical and moral judgment. The Paideia Proposal jettisons many conventional offerings: vocational education, electives, specialized courses, and tracking. This mandatory curriculum emphasizes three modes of teaching (learning at successive gradations of complexity): didactic instruction for acquiring organized knowledge; coaching, exercises, and supervised practice for developing intellectual skills; and Socratic dialogue for understanding ideas and values.

Noteworthy among the central claims of the Paideia Proposal are the following: (1) universal education and universal suffrage are inseparable and (2) education for all (grades 1 through 12) must be liberal, not specialized or occupational.[23]

Although states differ in their policies toward curriculum reform, a surprising number of state curriculum changes are consistent with the Paideia Proposal. More students are taking courses in the academic subject areas and enrollments are up in advanced placement courses that value analytical thinking and cultural literacy.

Cultural Literacy

For nearly 40 years, the Council for Basic Education, a conservative political group, lobbied consistently for the teaching of fundamental intellectual subjects, including history and geography with an emphasis on facts rather than process. The Council closed its doors in 2004, unable to compete for funding. New proponents, Diane Ravitch and Charles Finn, Jr., launched a campaign for the national revival of the teaching of history and literature by presenting data that reveal that 17-year-olds exhibit "a distressing lack of knowledge about

[22]Ruth Bond, "St. John's Clings to the Classics," Education Life, *New York Times* (Jan. 10, 1993): Education 18–19.
[23]Edwin H. Delattye, "The Paideia Proposal and American Education," *The Humanities in Precollegiate Education*, 1983 Yearbook of National Society for the Study of Education (1984), 143–154.

major historical and literary events."[24] Finn's work through the Heritage Foundation is anti-multiculturalism. The new revivalists want the curriculum to present more than "just the facts." They want factual knowledge to be linked to the world of culture and to make sense to students. They emphasize knowledge of important literary works and historical events related to nationalism.

California was one of the first states to respond to the cultural literacy revival by including a new history curriculum stressing content and historical chronology. In the early grades, students were exposed to fairy tales, myths, legends, and biographies of dramatic historical figures. In every grade, history was tied to literature—both literature of given historical periods and literature about the period under study. Acknowledging the importance of religion in history, the curriculum introduced the basic ideas of major religions and the ethical traditions of each time and place. The curriculum plan called for study of the fundamental principles of the U.S. Constitution and the Bill of Rights by examining how these principles were formed. Three goals directed the plan: (1) knowledge from other cultural understandings, incorporating learnings from history and the other humanities, geography, and the social sciences; (2) democratic and civic values of understanding our national identity and constitutional heritage; and (3) participation skills for citizenship.[25]

Among the essential learnings of this curriculum are a sense of time and chronology, understanding history as society's "common memory" and understanding the importance of religion and other belief systems. Learnings in ethical literacy indicate respect for life and the dignity of the individual. An interesting feature is that study of the modern world and controversial issues of the twentieth century are reserved for grades 10 and 11 when it is assumed that students are intellectually able to understand the issues.

Criticism of this new history centers on the particular vision of democratic institutions and culture; that is, it leans in the elitist direction and ignores the social reconstructionist's views about root causes of today's problems, including an economic system that demands consumption. The curriculum is faulted for not going far enough in its treatment of racism and other issues.

In contrast to those who would tie concepts to a depth of experience and reflective thinking and do not settle for decontextualized learning and cursory examination, E. D. Hirsch, Jr., has recommended a curriculum comprising background information that relates to competent literacy.[26] Hirsch argues that an American who lacks certain basic information cannot effectively participate in the national culture. For example, a person cannot grasp the meaning in newspapers and magazines without knowing to what particular terms allude. To be culturally literate, a person must have appropriate associations for Peter Pan, NATO, 1776, *The Grapes of Wrath*, Greeks bearing gifts, "win one for the Gipper," and more pages of such items. Although Hirsch concedes that the information represented by his list is elementary and superficial, he says that possession of this information is necessary for students to acquire more detailed information and that the list is descriptive rather than prescriptive. The content is seen as especially important for the student from nonaffluent families who are likely to be more unfamiliar with the items than privileged groups. Hirsch subsequently established the Cultural Literacy Foundation, now called the Core Knowledge Foundation, which produces tests and booklets to further the goal of providing Americans with common knowledge to draw on.

---

[25]*History–Social Science Framework for California Public Schools—Kindergarten through Grade Twelve* (Sacramento: California State Board of Education, 1988).

[26]E. D. Hirsch Jr., *Cultural Literacy: What Every American Needs to Know* (Boston: Houghton Mifflin, 1987).

[24]Diane Ravitch and Charles E. Finn, Jr., *What Do Our 17-Year-Olds Know: A Report on the First National Assessment of History and Literature* (New York: Harper and Row, 1987).

The chief argument for a common lexicon is that a body of shared background knowledge is necessary for conversation and debate within the nation. Criticisms of Hirsch focus on his choice of terms and his failure to recognize that inert knowledge (ability to define items as in a game of Trivial Pursuit) does not equip students to transfer the knowledge to problem-solving contexts in which they have to think about new situations. Hirsch recognizes the importance of parents and others to offer rich experiences in daily life in order to enhance the curriculum.

Hirsch has been charged with being disturbingly ignorant of some very common aspects of culture—for example, women, the Civil War, and the New Deal.[27] World culture is absent from Hirsch's dictionary.

Making Subject Matter More Appealing to Growing Minds

The academic curriculum has been indicted for putting the logic and orderliness that appeals to the academic mind over the psychological logic of the learner. The failure of the subject organization to inspire learners is a common challenge. The fact that teachers often are not willing or able to carry out the curriculum plans of the academic scholars with the intended enthusiasm and insight is related to this criticism. Academicians are also said to be guilty of two curriculum fallacies: the fallacy of content and the fallacy of universalism.

Those who commit the *fallacy of content* are preoccupied with the importance of *what* students study rather than *how* they study. They emphasize content that they believe is intellectually rigorous and difficult and that they presume will make the necessary demands on students. As indicated in Chapters 1 and 12, the goal of teaching science as inquiry is rarely observed. Instead, textbook information is emphasized—terminology and definitions. Laboratories tend to be used for demonstrations of information already presented rather than for discovery.

There is concern about the lack of emphasis on application. Academic studies are treated as if they are important chiefly for future studies, a means of advancing up the academic ladder. Certainly students should have access to the very best concepts, principles, and generalizations which civilization has created, but they should seldom be instructed before they are prepared to engage in examining and testing what they are being taught. The process of learning is more important than the content. It is not *declarative* knowledge (knowledge of facts) that students lack. The deficiency is in *operative* knowledge (understanding of how the facts are known and the capacity to apply this knowledge in new situations).

The *fallacy of universalism* rests on the belief that some content areas have universal value regardless of the characteristics of specific learners. One extreme of this view is found in the Paideia Proposal and in the statements by one of America's best known educators, the late Robert Maynard Hutchins, who said that "Education implies teaching. Teaching implies knowledge as truth. The truth is everywhere the same. Hence, education should be everywhere the same."[28] Another instance of universalism is the presumption that academicians can adapt the disciplinary mode of university scholarship for wide use in elementary and secondary schools by pupils who are anything but budding knowledge specialists.

Partly in response to these criticisms, efforts are being undertaken to improve the academic subject matter curriculum. Newer academic subject matter encourages intuition (clever guessing) as a handmaiden of the recognized analytical thinking of the disciplines.

---

[27]Richard Simonson and Scott Walker, eds., *The Graywolf Annual Five: Multicultural Literacy* (Saint Paul, MN: Graywolf Press, 1989).

[28]Robert Maynard Hutchins, *Higher Learning in America* (New Haven: Yale University Press, 1936), 66.

School people are supplementing, adapting, and developing the scholars' curriculum materials, not regarding them as panaceas for given local educational needs. For example, teachers are preparing extra resources for less able pupils, as well as additional ways to stimulate the gifted child. Local facilities are being organized for introducing more creative elements into programs, illustrating the techniques of disciplines in a different environment than that intended by the original planners. Instead of studying biology solely from a textbook, students learn the nature of biology from studies of tidepools and animal husbandry. Homegrown academic programs are flourishing. Indeed, they may survive better than the national transplants.

The curriculum designed by the Biological Science Curriculum Study for kindergarten through high school is a good example of how subject matter, such as genetics, can be made valuable in the personal public lives of students.[29] In this curriculum, kindergarten and first-grade children are provided opportunities that introduce basic scientific concepts and modes of investigation. For example, as the basis for the concept of continuity, children observe the growth and development of seeds, sort organisms of various species into family groups and identify physical resemblances between parents and their offspring in human and nonhuman families.

In grades 2 through 4, pupils have experiences with the idea of variety by comparing body measurements and individual preferences for foods, color, and hobbies. They are helped to be made aware of the concept of change by studying their own patterns of daily living, making predictions about certain days and times of day in their routines. The principle of continuity is reinforced for students in the middle grades by their study of families and other organizations and their constructing of family trees.

Fifth and sixth graders begin population studies considering their own class and other classes as prototypes. They conduct scientific experiments with preschoolers to see how little ones think about problems. The principle of continuity is extended as the children examine the transmission of specific traits and genes from generation to generation.

The curriculum for the junior high or middle school learners, "Genes and Surroundings," stresses individuality, continuity, variability (both in time and in relation to others), and adaptation. Variability is featured because it is an important developmental concept for the adolescent. The activities in this curriculum require students to apply knowledge about human genetics to their personal growth and to the local physical and social environment.

Basic genetics for the high school and adult learner emphasizes the physical, psychological, and social delineation of health created by new knowledge in genetics. Although students learn as a traditional class would about gene segregation, blood types, pedigrees, and genetic disorders, they also learn the content from a human point of view. In the study of inheritance, for example, human beings are featured in preference to animals. Most important, students learn the principles of genetics, not as ends in themselves, but in connection with personal and familial concerns such as genetic counseling, prenatal diagnoses, and prenatal care and in connection with social concerns—the ethical issues of such matters as prenatal screening and abortion.

Improvement in the quality of the academic curriculum requires attending to several interdependent aspects. Although learning, especially what student should learn, receives much attention, more effort should be given to helping students criticize academic assertions. The idea of teaching the conflicts, putting students in touch with conflicting studies about science issues such as whether electromagnetic fields cause cancer or about literacy issues such as the place of popular culture in literature is a promising direction. More attention is needed in helping students learn strategies for applying knowledge and predicting consequences: "What must I do with what I know?" "How do I take action?" "How do

[29]"You, Me, and Others," "Genes and Surroundings," "Basic Genetics: A Human Approach," and "Living with Cystic Fibrosis" (Boulder, CO: Biological Sciences Curriculum Study, 1982).

I make desirable outcomes more likely?" "Do I know what would happen?" Lastly, teachers should develop an academic curriculum that students will value. Currently, few academic programs exploit the need for students to answer questions which they themselves regard as important: "Where do I fit in?" "Do I care?" "Do I value the outcome?"

In short, some curriculum makers are attempting to provide learning opportunities that are appealing and well within the learners' capacities to serve as the starting point for organizing subject matter intellectually as the specialist does. They are able to differentiate between those activities that lead to growth and those that do not. These developers have taken a long look ahead. They know the academic forms (facts, principles, and laws) in which the children's present activities relate and are giving children opportunities for intelligent activity, for seeing how things interact with one another to produce definite effects, not aimless activity.

PSYCHOLOGICAL FOUNDATIONS OF THE ACADEMIC CURRICULUM

Although there are differences among approaches to the academic curriculum, their proponents confront the challenges of enculturing learners into a discourse community—science, the humanities, mathematics. Inculcation means learning the language of the academic discipline—particular ways of saying, writing, doing, and believing—new ways of making sense of one's experiences. The disciplines, as secondary discourses, are frequently at odds with the students' primary discourse from home and street. Not only will much of the new discourse be foreign to the student, but abstract concepts and explanations probably are counterintuitive to the students' ways of making sense. "The sun does not rise in the east."

Psychologists sometimes speak of "spontaneous concepts" that are naturally developed and "nonspontaneous concepts" that are academically invented and used in interpretations and explanations and which are subject to change in light of new knowledge claims—the universe is expanding at increasing speeds.

In contrast with quasi-academic programs that transmit canned conclusions, isolated facts, and information that can be acquired by using behavioral psychology with its emphasis on reward and memorization, a rigorous academic curriculum aims at higher thinking whereby students engage in the discipline's ways of knowing and using academic concepts as frameworks in thinking and organizing their experiential world. This more challenging curriculum draws from cognitive, developmental, and sociocultural psychologies. The difficulty of getting students to change their spontaneous beliefs and to accept academic perspectives has long been recognized.

Jean Piaget differentiated between "assimilation" whereby one merely adds features and properties to an already-held belief or schema for an object—a three-wheel vehicle may be a car—and "accommodation" where one needs to modify a fundamental belief, schema or mental frame in order to fit changed circumstances.[30] Leon Festinger termed the conflict "cognitive dissonance" and showed its importance in learning and exploring new ideas.

Dissonance occurs when one loses faith in the capacity of a current concept to solve a problem.[31] Strategies for changing beliefs rest on studies showing that after creating initial dissatisfaction with one's existing concepts, the new alternative should be intelligible, plausible, and fruitful.[32]

[30]*Piaget's Theory in Carmichaels's Manual of Child Psychology* (New York: Wiley, 1970).
[31]Elliot Aronsu, "The Theory of Cognitive Dissonance," in *The Message of Socio Psychology*, Craig McGarty and S. Alexander Haslow, eds. (Cambridge, MA: Blackwell, 1997).
[32]George Posner, "A Cognitive Science Conception of Curriculum and Instruction," *Journal of Curriculum Studies* 14, no. 4 (1982): 342–343.

The student's background knowledge and beliefs are both a predictor of academic success and a basis for initial instruction. David Ausebel, a psychologist famous for his concepts of "advanced organizers, outlines, or cognitive maps," believes that "the most important single factor in improving learning is attending to what the learner already knows."[33]

Nevertheless, the laying out of a conceptual map is often helpful. Teachers may present a map of topics showing their relationships to orient students to a study and to build on the ideas that students bring. Students may enlarge on their maps after their study.

As described in Part 2, "cognitive mapping" is helping students see the organizational and structural patterns in particular disciplines—cause–effect, problem–solution, part–whole—thereby contributing to higher levels of abstract thinking.

Newer psychological ideas about academic learning reflect a blend of cognitive, cultural, and social psychology. The social construction of knowledge has gained influence whereby peers, teachers, and others interact to reconcile individual meanings and public concerns while learning the norms, conventions, and ways of representing knowledge and other practices of a discipline.[34]

Cultural psychology emphasizes the use of abstract concepts as tools, believing that knowledge is only acquired when it is used in concrete situations. Accordingly, students are placed in real-world situations with scholars to learn how knowledge originates and how it is used.

Problem-solving learning is consistent with the view that it is more important for students to learn how to retrieve information and when, where, and why to use knowledge than to acquire a breadth of facts and formulas. Students learn the strategies of experts—what they notice, how they represent and interpret information. In addition, students represent their experiences as abstract principles and concepts so they can go beyond or transfer their learning to other situations and events.[35] Core concepts or "big ideas" in the discipline tend to guide the thinking of the inquiries—knowing more means connecting facts and information, posing alternative explanations, and offering collaborative evidence.

However, social learning requires changes in classroom norms, roles, and interactions. Research studies that have tested social interdependent theory have shown the relative merits of cooperative, competitive, and individualistic efforts and describe the conditions where each is appropriate. This theory predicts that cooperation induces mutual assistance, trust, and exchange of needed resources. Competition obstructs the other's success through coercion, threat, deceptive commercials, and "win" conflicts.

Individualistic efforts induce avoidance of others.[36] More than 700 resource studies over 12 decades show that cooperative experiences promote the use of higher level cognitive and moral reasoning strategies than do competing and individualistic experiences. This is true when the cooperation includes shared common goals and acceptance as responsible members who help each other.

Competition is constructive when winning is relatively unimportant, and all have a reasonable chance to win. Individual efforts are appropriate when cooperation has high costs, the goal is important, one is expected to succeed, and that which is individually accomplished will be used subsequently in a cooperative effort.

In his view of knowledge-centered curriculum, John Bradford recommended looking at a world in which people will eventually operate and then design learning experiences,

[33]David P. Ausebel, *Educational Psychology: A Cognitive View* (New York: Holt, Reinhart & Winston 1968).
[34]*Constructivism in Education,* Ninety-ninth Yearbook of National Society for the Study of Education, D. C. Phillips, ed. (Chicago: University of Chicago Press, 2000).
[35]"Situated Learning and Education," *Educational Researcher* 25, no. 4 (May 5, 1996).
[36]David W. Johnson, "Social Interdependence: Interrelationships among Theory, Research and Practice," *American Psychologist* 58, no. 11 (Nov. 2003).

working backward from that perspective.[37] His psychological theory supports students engaging in inquiry with experts and with "what we don't know." as the foundations for the inquiry.

Other psychologists provide metacognitve strategies to teach what it means to be a good thinker in different disciplines, fostering both cognitive and social development. Metacognitionists attempt to help students know themselves as learners and their roles in learning a discipline. Metacognition means reflecting on what one knows and how that knowledge can be useful. Usually it involves learning how to monitor one's own learning by identifying goals, generating ideas, trying the ideas out, and improving on them. Often metacognition strategies are applied to learning a general strategy for unlocking meaning, such as reciprocal teaching where students learn to summarize, clarify, infer, and self-test for understanding as a key procedure for understanding text.[38]

HISTORICAL ANTECEDENTS OF THE ACADEMIC CURRICULUM

The academic ideal of developing minds capable of improving both how students think and the quality of their ideas is old. Plato (427–347 B.C.) believed that the lowest kind of thinking was mere opinion; the higher forms that captured generalizable concepts and enlarged on their meaning in real-world contexts were more powerful and enduring. Theoretical concepts and their approximations as understood by others in dialogue and as used in everyday life continue in today's academic curriculum.

Plato's Academy offered the first academic curriculum aimed at turning persons and government in the direction of temperance and justice. Students in the Academy advanced the world's knowledge of mathematics and astronomy as they made the unseen visible and awakened students to new dimensions. Plato himself contributed to advancements in geography and mathematical subjects. In his *Republic*, Plato outlined education for young learners, advocating musical and gymnastic training beginning in the early years and continuing through life. Music included responding to the great poets and their literature, presumed to be stimulated by the Muses—spirits thought to preside over different arts and sciences. Students set their works to musical harmonies and rhythms. Music without gymnastics was thought to be insufficient.

In the Academy, knowledge was regarded as something that could enable people to live better together, not as an end in itself. Social negotiation of meaning was prized. It is clear also that Plato's Academy was not for those who could not deal with abstractions, and in his ideal Republic all were not equal. Elitism sticks today to the academic curriculum.

Academicians have always followed Plato in seeing experience as a force coming and inevitably passing away. Without extracting lessons or generalizations from experiences there is no knowledge. Hence like Plato, academicians seek generalizations, principles or laws, and, like him, recognize that generalizations have instrumental and predictive value but that they are forever subject to correction by further experiences.

In his dialogues, Plato illustrated the social discovery of knowledge through questioning and discussing human concerns. Aristotle (384–322 B.C.), a former student at the Academy, subsequently divided knowledge into separate subjects and greatly influenced

---

[37]John Bradford, *How People Learn: Brain, Mind, Experience in School* (Washington, DC: National Academy Press, 2001).
[38]*Metacognition in Learning and Instruction: Theory, Research and Practice,* H. Hartman, ed. (Norwell, MA: Kluwer, 2003).

the academic curriculum. In contrast to Plato, Aristotle regarded the pursuit of generalizations (knowledge) as an end, not as a means.

Aristotle founded a lyceum for instruction, research, and investigation. Although biology was his leading interest, his works in a variety of subjects, such as logic, rhetoric, politics, ethics, and history of science, were colossal, more than 140 separate books. These books became fundamental textbooks for the academic curriculum. Aristotle also introduced two methods for deriving knowledge that are common in today's schools: (1) *deductive*, deriving conclusions logically from stated assumptions, and (2) *inductive*, describing and classifying objects of study and then generalizing from the observations.

Aristotle's classifying and compartmentalizing of human knowledge has encapsulated curriculum organization to this day. His biological interest in the divisions of the human body probably led him to skeletonize knowledge by subjects and their parts setting a pattern that is found in today's scope and sequence charts and lists of content standards by separate disciplines.

Aristotle also differentiated knowledge as (a) *theoretical* or intellectual (physics, mathematics) and *contemplative* (cosmology of the universe and the mysteries of life) and (b) *practical* studies concerned with things humans can modify—the arts, medicine, economics, and agriculture—giving rise to the hierarchical status among different studies common among academicians.

Alexander of Macedon (356–323 B.C.), who had been tutored by Aristotle, carried Greek literature with him on his conquest of the world. He especially held the *Iliad* and the Greek tragedies in high esteem.

Acting on a suggestion from Aristotle, the kings of Egypt in 331 B.C. established a museum and laboratory at Alexandria that became a center of learning. Scholars there gave priority to literature, mathematics, geography, and natural history. Euclid's *Elements of Geometry* was written at Alexandria about the year 300 B.C. and became the curriculum for instruction in that subject for more than 2000 years. Archimedes (287–212 B.C.) was another great scholar at Alexandria who wrote among other works a mathematics text that anticipated integral calculus.

Greek epic poetry, such as the *Odyssey*, became an intellectual source for the Romans who copied and adapted Greek culture. Early Romans, such as Cicero (106–43 B.C.), Virgil (70–19 B.C.), and Horace (65–8 B.C.) added much to literature as a subject. The Romans expanded rhetoric to include powerful speech by identifying the elements of persuasion (in fact, great speeches by modern leaders, such as President John Kennedy's inaugural speech with the lines, "Ask not what your country can do for you—ask what you can do for your country." are drafted from Roman models).

Rhetoric was the core of academic learning throughout the Roman Empire for more than 800 years. Virgil's epic poem *Aeneid* and Horace's lyrical poems became classical studies for generations. Rhetoric with its stress on moral education, writing, and discussion has been a foundation for university study and is currently being revised. The Association of Rhetorical Societies has redefined rhetoric as the study of the effect of text on audience. "Although rhetoric is the oldest branch of higher education, its subject matter is as new as the morning's headlines."[39] Roman rhetoric, civil law, and the liberal arts were considered studies that liberated students from everyday crafts and the customary activities of ordinary workers. These Greek and Roman texts continue to be models and are used by conservative essentialists who want to transmit a common core of ideals and ideas and who want to promote a cultural heritage that stimulates higher level thinking through exact and exacting subjects, freeing minds from conventional opinion.[40]

---

[39]*Association of Rhetorical Societies* (Palo Alto: Stanford University, 2003).
[40]J. Barzun, *From Dawn to Decadence—500 Years of Cultural Life: 1500 to Present* (New York: HarperCollins, 2000).

On the fall of the Roman Empire, the monastic schools incorporated in their religious studies and teaching the seven liberal arts from the Greeks and Romans, offering all instruction in Latin.

Scholastics is the term for academic learning in the cathedral schools and universities of the Middle Ages. Beginning the twelfth century, church doctrine was presented as orthodoxy with religious premises used as the basis for deductive reasoning. Along with the Bible, authoritative Latin and Greek works comprised much of early Christian literature supplemented with lectures and manuscripts by Christian scholars.

Although scholastics is usually associated with dogma and opposition to inquiry, Rodney Stark asserts that because early Christian scholars saw God as a rational being, they thought the natural world must be a "rational, lawful, stable structure, awaiting (indeed inviting) human comprehension."[41] Certainly Thomas Aquinas used this argument in reconciling Aristolean philosophy with Roman Catholic theology in saying that knowledge comes through the senses and reasoning but the new knowledge is in harmony with religious faiths. This argument is useful today in the tensions between science and religion.

Other events moved the academic curriculum in the direction of inquiry. The Crusaders' contacts with Greeks and Arabs led to their discovery of the former glories of the Roman Empire, the Byzantine culture and the intellectual and artistic achievements of Moorish Spain.

In the fifteenth century and periodically thereafter, Greek and Roman cultures have been reinvented. In the Italian Renaissance, the children of aristocrats attended classical schools that borrowed Greek ideas for harmonizing mind and body, while learning to read, write, and speak Latin. Italian rulers and aristocrats supported artists who created masterpieces of painting, sculpture, architecture, and music, inventing new techniques that resulted in works of splendor and inspiration.

Nevertheless acceptance of the arts as academic disciplines has been controversial. In part, this is because, unlike scientists, artists do not start with an abstraction but with their own perception of the world and they express themselves by uniquely organizing their materials.

It has been difficult to overcome the notion that an academic discipline for teaching purposes should be for intellectual development rather than for personal enjoyment and expression. Throughout the centuries the valued academic subjects were expected to have substance, rules, and organized knowledge and to demand rigorous mental effort if they were to be mastered. Art as a discipline versus art as creative expression has always been an issue—should the arts curriculum be (a) disciplined centered and taught by giving the meaning of artworks, familiarity with materials and processes, and knowledge of forms and standards for judgment or (b) a curriculum best delivered through authentic apprenticeships with recognized artists.

In the enlightenment period, some individuals responded to Locke's call, "Dare to Know," and entertained the possibility that both nature and institutions can be controlled. Newton (1642–1727) with his theories of gravity and mechanics and his invention of differential calculus and Boyle (1627–1691) whose law regarding how pressure of a confined gas varies with volume are but two whose findings triggered a science of mechanics and applications that transformed agriculture, transportation, industry, economics and other ways of life. Knowledge of astronomy, biology, chemistry and physics increased as new disciplines—history, psychology, sociology, and anthropology—were created. It is debatable if these new social disciplines promoted or merely responded to the conditions of the French Revolution. Most of this intellectual upheaval took place outside of schools. Experiments and technological inventions were conducted by many innovators, such as

---

[41]Rodney Stark, *Christianity and the Creation of Science* (Washington, DC: American Enterprise Institute, 2003).

Michael Faraday (1791–1867) who pioneered chemistry and physics, had very little formal education but associated themselves informally in newly formed academic societies.[42]

In contrast with the old academic practice of separating one's self from the everyday world contemplating and searching for wisdom in authoritative texts, those of the enlightenment period participated intellectually in a deschooled curriculum as they pursued new knowledge and practice. These investigators formed networks among those with common interests and shared their findings and ideas openly in journals and handbooks, giving public lectures, experiments and demonstrations. Amateurs—lovers of learning—became informed investigators. The availability of new forms of literacy—novels and newspapers—along with discussions at reading clubs allowed ordinary people to develop their curiosity and excitement for the future. This period offered opportunities to criticize, contest, and exchange ideas, such as whether the new search for knowledge was mere idolatry that would undermine standards of right and wrong.[43]

The belief in research to uncover facts, in theories that explain the facts, and in the benefits that will follow from applying newly found knowledge in both natural and social worlds became known as *positivism*, and those who enjoyed secular and scientific studies became "explorers of the future" and challengers in contrast to "guardians of the past" who saw the classics' relevance for training the mind and developing ethical, moral, and transcendental character.

Formal schooling, particularly the Latin Grammar School and Harvard University in colonial and the early American Republic, opted for morality and classicism. The study of Latin and Greek along with Hebrew was undertaken to gain better understanding of Christian scripture. New forms of knowledge were slow in entering the curriculum. It was not until the nineteenth century that some university students were allowed to do their own experiments, and those were more for confirmation than for discovery. Social sciences were viewed as not having sufficient breadth and depth of knowledge. In order to gain acceptance as an academic study, English and French languages and literatures had to be reconstructed to be as rigorous a study as that of the classical languages. Latin grammar was borrowed and applied to English syntax and usage. Grammatical categories, rules, and principles for English and French were derived from Greek and Roman poetry and rhetoric. Only after English was transformed into something difficult to learn and to analyze, were the works of Shakespeare, Pope, and Milton considered sources suitable for study.[44] Although *belles lettres* was in the culture of the wealthy and suitable for aesthetic and status reasons, they were not acceptable for didactic and informative academic purposes.

In the Victorian age, educational leaders such as Mathew Arnold tried to strengthen English poetry by imitating poems that were faithful to Archetonics of the ancient classical poets. Some of his poems were studied well into the twentieth century in secondary schools.

The inability of the Latin Grammar School and the universities to adjust to changed conditions during colonialization and the beginning of the New Republic led to competing private schools that offered professional courses in natural sciences, commercial subjects, navigation, and modern languages for communication purposes. Interestingly, these schools were called *academies* or *adventure schools*. The academies became the precursors of the public high school which initially was a preparatory school for college.

---

[42] David Layton, *Science for the People* (London: Allen and Unwin, 1973).

[43] John C. Thackray, *To See the Fellows Fight: Eyewitness Accounts of the Meetings of the Geological Society of London and its Club* (Faringdon, UK: British Society, 2003).

[44] Edward Finegan, *Attitudes toward English Usage: The History of the War of Words* (New York: Teachers College Press, 1980).

At the beginning of the twentieth century a small number of high school students had a laboratory experience in a science and even this experience was for acquiring techniques, appreciation of method, and confirmation of an existing knowledge, not discovery. Mathematics was taught as a closed unified system, not as a way to analyze and understand the world. College domination of the curriculum assured that the high school curriculum would remain classical until, at the end of the nineteenth century, the president of Harvard University, Charles W. Elliot, headed a Committee of Ten[45] and advocated an academic curriculum consisting either of (a) a scientific program, (b) a classical program, or (c) a modern language and English program. A subsequent committee (1899) signaled diminution of Latin and Greek. Whereas in 1900, nearly half of the students in grades 9–12 studied Latin, 5 years later only 8% were enrolled.

The academic curriculum in the secondary schools—whether in the liberal arts or scientific tradition—lost ground to programs adapted for an influx of students with widely varied backgrounds to new purposes for schools in light of pressing social conditions. It was not until the mid-twentieth century, when the U.S. government supported the development and implementation of academic programs to engage students in learning how to participate in inquiry, that the academic curriculum was vitalized.

CONCLUDING COMMENTS

Academic specialists have at different times attempted to develop a curriculum that would equip learners to enter the world of knowledge with the basic concepts and methods for observing, noting relationships, analyzing data, and drawing conclusions. They wanted learners to act like physicists, biologists, or historians so that as citizens they would follow developments in disciplines with understanding and support and, if they continued their studies, become specialists themselves. One weakness in the approach was the failure to give sufficient attention to integrative goals. Learners were unable to relate one discipline to another and to see how the content of a discipline could be brought to bear on the complex problems of modern life not answerable by a single discipline. Two current movements to overcome this weakness are (1) "integrated" studies, in which content from several fields is applied to important social problems and historical topics, and (2) the teaching of the forms of knowledge so that learners acquire a range of perspectives for understanding experience.

A second weakness in the academic conception of curriculum is a tendency to impose adult views of the subject matter on students. Academic specialists and cultural literacy advocates have given insufficient attention to the present interests and backgrounds of individual learners. They might use those interests as sources for problems and activities by which learners might acquire the intellectual organization and powerful ideas that constitute academic subject matter.

If the academician's goal is to teach people to think better, there must be more consciousness of the kind of thinking that needs to be done and more engagement of students in genuine problem solving, inventing, and critical appraisals. For example, to encourage science programs that involve scientific ideas and allow students to use these ideas in their daily life, the National Science Foundation has funded projects for elementary and secondary students that promote questions and problems of local interest. In these projects, students acquire the knowledge they need as they consider and try solutions. Projects at the

[45]National Education Association, *Report of the Committee on Secondary School Studies* (Washington, DC: U.S. Government Printing Office, 1893).

University of Iowa involve more than 300 teachers who have reorganized their school program to solve local problems with applications of science.[46] Subject matter reform through standards described in Chapter 3 are inadequate in not going beyond each subject's boundaries and engaging learners in seeking solutions to their problems in a range of fields. In contrast, planners of the mathematics and science curricula have already taken a giant step by adopting newer views of learning from psychology. The increased use in these subjects of activities by which students construct and negotiate meanings is a case in point. Whether teachers can accept the philosophical change required for the new curriculum, which entails world views emphasizing uncertainty, conflict, and the inevitability of contradiction remains to be seen.[47]

QUESTIONS

1. Science and English successfully challenged the classics, Greek, and Latin as useful academic subjects in teaching students to think. What are the possibilities that technology with ability to use it in problem solving may become a leading contender for a basic academic competency?

2. The capacity to discriminate and judge is a central goal of all education. For centuries, languages, literature, history, philosophy, and the arts have been viewed as the sources of knowledge for best attaining this goal. Is this true today? Why? Why not?

3. The issue of "elitism" versus "populism" shows clearly in curriculum changes from personal and social relevance to academic excellence. Are the goals of relevance and excellence mutually exclusive? Is it possible for the curriculum to reflect the different directions simultaneously? If so, how?

4. The daily lives of most people are going to be complicated and constantly changing. They will be assailed by new laws, new traffic schemes, and new sex roles; these will loom larger in their lives than the works of Shakespeare or the Third Law of Thermodynamics. They will not be able to find textbook answers to their daily problems. Neither will they be able to categorize the problems into subjects like history or physics. And so, more value should be placed on education for ordinary life than on academic education. How would you respond to both the premises of this argument and the conclusion which shows a belief in educating students for life rather than for academic achievement?

5. Judge each of the following definitions of the academic curriculum in terms of feasibility (ease of learning and teaching), utility (extent to which it contributes to learners' basic needs for survival, independence, and respect), and idealism (degree to which it is consistent with the highest ideas about human nature):

   a. Academic subject matter as the intellectual tools (questions, methods, concepts, processes, and attitudes) by which knowledge is currently acquired

   b. Academic subject matter as conclusions (facts, principles, and laws) carefully chosen from those derived by specialists on the basis of their relevancy to the conduct of daily living

   c. Academic subject matter as the finest achievements of our cultural heritage, the works of those great minds that have had an effect on civilization

SUGGESTED STRATEGIC RESEARCH

SELECTING MULTIPLE REPRESENTATIONS OF A SUBJECT

What are the effects that follow from introducing a subject—math, biology, art—as it might be used in music and film, science and engineering, or economics and business? How does representation of the discipline impact motivation, retention, and understanding?

---

[46]"What is S/T/S?" Science 1986 (Iowa City: University of Iowa Science Education Center, 1986).

[47]Jean Schnittac, "Mathematics Education in the 1990s: Can It Afford to Ignore Its Historical and Philosophical Foundations?" *Educational Theory* 41, no. 2 (1993): 121–133.

LINKING UNIVERSALS TO THE EXEMPLARS

In an interview, Howard Gardner illustrated how an academic curriculum could connect great ideals and memorable experiences. He would show *truth* through Darwin's evolutionary theory with its focus on the variations of species, and survival; *beauty* through Mozart's "Marriage of Figaro" that brings forth previously unrealized emotions and inspiring new creation; *goodness* through a study of the Holocaust to show that humans are capable of doing good and bad things and a way for students to learn how others deal with extreme pressure and moral dilemmas. What links are best in given local contexts? Are the "universals" universal and, if so, can their variations be reconciled?

ASSESSING STUDENT KNOWLEDGE OF "BIG" IDEAS

In light of greater access to knowledge through the Internet, students may be more advanced in their conceptual understanding than assumed by writers of their formal curriculum and text material. Compare student knowledge of a selected big idea for a discipline and compare this knowledge with what current standards say students should know about the idea. Which sources give students the richer and deeper levels of understanding? What are the curriculum implications from your findings?

PREPARING SYMBOLIC ANALYSTS

Increasingly, societies are depending on people who can analyze, manipulate, and communicate things and ideas through numbers, shapes, and words and who seek new problems and solutions in meeting human needs. Identify some leading academics who are breaking the mold and describe the critical features of the curriculum that prepared them to make these contributions.

OVERCOMING OBSTACLES TO INQUIRY IN CLASSROOM LEARNING

Consider beliefs that mitigate against student-initiated inquiry—beliefs in fixed capacities on the basis of age, gender, or social class; beliefs that facts and information are prerequisite to inquiry; and beliefs that it is more important to deliver *what should be taught* than to teach *how to learn*. Relate the extent of classroom inquiry to the teachers' beliefs. What strategies might be most useful in changing beliefs that limit student inquiry?

DETERMINING POTENTIAL CUMULATIVE EFFECTS IN TEXT MATERIALS

Deep understanding of a discipline and the ability to transfer what is learned depends on knowing the key principles and representative ideas in a discipline. Select a subject—history, math, a social science. Review a sample of the units of instruction or text material for teaching the discipline and determine if key concepts underlie the content and activities in the materials.

SELECTED REFERENCES

BRADFORD, JOHN D., ET AL., EDS. *How People Learn: Brains, Experience, and School.* Washington, DC: National Resource Council, National Academy Press, 2001.

CHEEK, DENNIS. *Thinking Constructively about Science, Technology, and Society Education.* Albany, NY: State University of New York Press, 1992.

Mathematical Science Education Board Curriculum Framework for K–12 Mathematics. Washington, DC: Mathematical Science Board, 1994.

SISKIN, LESLIE. *Realms of Knowledge: Academic Departments in Secondary Schools.* Bristol, PA: London, Palmer Press, 1994.

WESTBURY, IAN, AND ALLAN C. PURVIS, EDS. *Cultural Literacy and the Ideas of General Education.* Eighty-seventh Yearbook of the National Society for the Study of Education, Part 2. Chicago: University of Chicago Press, 1988.

PART II

CURRICULUM DEVELOPMENT

What do you expect to do with curriculum? Are you thinking of starting a school and know you will need one? Might you build a curriculum in order to change an existing school? Or are you interested in developing a curriculum that will be more responsive to the needs of your own students? Perhaps you want to know how to tell a great curriculum from a weak one. Can you see yourself as a curriculum consultant to a developing nation, a business, or a governmental agency? Would you consider preparing an educational after-school program for children, a training program for a new industry, or a distance Online program to make knowledge in your field more accessible to underserved populations? Perhaps your goal is to create materials for teachers and students—texts, instructional games and activity booklets. The chapters in Part 2 contain core knowledge as "tools" for use in such curriculum undertakings.

If you are in a class or faculty situation, you might preface your reading of these chapters by finding out what your peers or colleagues expect to do with curriculum. Then after reading the chapters, you can see which of the tools are most appropriate and why for given purposes.

CHAPTER 5

DECIDING WHAT SHOULD BE TAUGHT

THE DECISION about what should be taught in an institution, corporate training program, academic department, classroom, or other instructional situation is a decision about curriculum purposes. Persons differ in their desire to determine what should be taught. On the one hand, there are those who want to be free from curriculum responsibility. They acquiesce to the decisions of others. For example, teachers sometimes accept without question and justification the goals of boards, administrators, or textbook writers and do not respond to needs of individuals beyond the offered curriculum. Trustees and administrators sometimes avoid making decisions about curriculum and what should transpire in classrooms, excusing themselves on the grounds of academic freedom. Responsibility is sometimes avoided by denying the need for the decision, claiming that the present curriculum is good enough. A more subtle way to avoid responsibility is to apply a systemic approach, in which determination of curriculum ends is treated as nonproblematic.

On the other hand, many individuals and groups want to propose what should be taught. They may have special concerns and interests, such as AIDS, drug abuse, ethnic studies, suicide prevention. Similarly, prospective employers and those at the next rung in the academic ladder often are eager to say what should be taught in preparation for future jobs and study.

Rather than avoiding responsibility and mandating curriculum purposes without justification, those at all levels of schooling should constantly question the purpose of curriculum. Changing circumstances make even the most enduring of subject matter questionable. Of course, some situations offer instructors little freedom to determine ends, for instance, the military instructor ordered to train recruits in a certain task. However, having curriculum goals chosen by the largest number of people involved in an educational enterprise is still the best general principle. Thus, in this chapter basic approaches to setting curriculum purposes are stressed. Although not all the approaches give equal opportunity to discover new directions, the reasons why one of the approaches is more appropriate than another in a particular situation is recognized.

ARENAS FOR DECIDING WHAT TO TEACH

Levels of Decision Making

Curriculum planning, including decisions about what to teach and for what purpose, occurs at different levels of remoteness from intended learners. These levels are *societal, institutional, instructional,* and *personal.* Participants at the societal level include boards of education (national, local, or state), federal agencies, publishers, and national curriculum reform committees. At the institutional level, administrators and faculty groups are prominent actors. Parents as well as students may play a role in institutional decision making about curriculum. The instructional level refers to teachers deciding on purposes that are appropriate for the learners at hand, and cautionary teachers link student personal purposes to the official curriculum, if possible. However, the student or personal determination of goals is at a fourth decision level in curriculum making. This level is consistent with the view that learners generate their own purposes and meanings from their classroom experiences and are not merely passive recipients of curriculum ends and means.

The scope and basis for curriculum decisions vary according to the level. At levels remote from the learner there are policy decisions, which either prescribe procedures to be followed by others in formulating the curriculum or establish the character of curriculum by specifying what must be taught or what will be tested. Societal level decisions are based ideally on theoretical data and are influenced by the norms and pressure groups in the society. Intermediate between policy and the learner are curriculum decisions which translate policy into specific terms.

Different techniques and personnel are involved in curriculum making at the different levels. Curriculum making at the national societal level includes development of standards, goals, and objectives as well as textbooks and other instructional materials for wide use. Increasingly, national educational goals and standards are set by politicians and corporate leaders although professional organizations are also influential. Curriculum designers at this level often do not focus on a wide range of educational goals such as critical thinking, self-expression, manual dexterity, or general social attributes. Instead, they center on domains that are specific to a single subject, grade level, or course. In this arena, specialized personnel—subject specialists, curriculum experts, and editors—make most of the decisions about *what* should be taught and *how.* These specialists do, however, attend to professional and public opinion as reflected in the yearbooks published by national subject matter organizations such as the National Council for Social Studies (NCSS), professional journals, and popular media. Publishers also seek the advice of representative teachers, textbook salespersons, and other consultants. Results from marketing efforts and trials of preliminary versions also bring about changes in both the ends and the means of their curricula.

Curriculum development at the state level involves the production of curriculum standards, guides, and frameworks. These materials are prepared by professional staffs in state departments of education assisted by representative teachers, college and university personnel, and curriculum specialists. The purposes and goals set forth in these materials are usually formulated by advisory committees composed of professional educators, representatives from educational agencies, and selected nonprofessionals. Since the 1990s, the influence of economic and business interests has increasingly dominated the development of curriculum purposes at societal levels. State departments of education personnel also engage in curriculum making in response to state laws pertaining to the teaching of such topics as narcotics, health, and English-language learners.

As indicated in Chapter 3, policy makers are attempting to control by having a direct pipeline from the Capitol to students' minds. In contrast with the early 1990s when policies and standards were promulgated as guidance for local implementation and teachers were expected to find their own ways to help students achieve in the mandated directions, the policy makers now are prescribing methods and materials as well as outcomes they want.

The most common arena for curriculum planning now is the state, although districts continue to offer local programs and the rise of charter schools encourages curriculum decisions at individual school sites. Districts usually involve specialized personnel in curriculum as well as curriculum generalists, subject matter specialists, consultants, representative teachers, and some nonprofessionals. Ideally, all these persons are concerned with adapting and designing curriculum to local situations and problems. They should consider the implications of the regional economy, history, and resources for learning in altering curriculum for local schools. Curriculum making at the individual school level involves all classroom teachers and administrators, and representative parents and students. Their activities may focus on goals, materials, organization, and instructional strategies. Teams of teachers often derive curriculum they believe to be appropriate for students keeping in mind the overall goal of the school as well as official standards.

The relative importance of the levels of decision making varies from country to country, state to state, and school to school. Centralized educational systems such as those in Japan and France give the Ministry of Education more authority over curriculum ends. In the United States, local authority for curriculum decisions was greatest in New England and among the states of the Midwest. State control has always been more evident in such states as Texas, Florida, New York, and California. Now, however, the state role is more apparent in all states although it is recognized that no curriculum derived from outside agencies is successful without teacher commitment.

Curriculum at Different Levels

Persons reading casually about curriculum get inconsistent messages. On the one hand, they read that the curriculum is rapidly changing—a new program in mathematics, health education, more challenging content for the gifted, and mastery learning for the slow. On the other hand, reports indicate that schools are teaching the same thing in the same way as always—reading, writing, arithmetic in the elementary school and vocational and college preparatory programs in the secondary school.

One explanation for the conflicting reports is that there is a curriculum of rhetoric, official proclamations, and a curriculum of practice behind the classroom door. A curriculum formulated at one level is not necessarily adopted and implemented at another. John Goodlad and his associates, for example, have proposed five different curricula, each operating at a different level.[1]

1. *Ideal curriculum.* From time to time foundations, governments, and special interest groups set up committees to look into aspects of the curriculum and to advise on changes that should be made. Curriculum recommendations proposed by these committees might treat mathematics, science, multicultural curriculum, a curriculum for the talented, early childhood curriculum, computer literacy, or something else. These proposals might represent ideals or describe desired directions in curriculum as seen by those with a particular value system or special interest. The proponents of such ideal curricula are competing for power within the society. It should be clear, however, that the impact of an ideal curriculum depends on whether the recommendations are adopted and implemented.

2. *Formal curriculum.* Formal curriculum includes those proposals that are approved by state and local boards. Such a curriculum may be a collection of ideal curricula, a modification of the ideal, or other curriculum policies, guides, syllabi, or texts sanctioned by the board as the legal authority for deciding what shall be taught and to what ends.

3. *Perceived curriculum.* The perceived curriculum is what the teachers perceive the curriculum to be. Teachers interpret the formal curriculum in many ways. Often there is little relationship between the formally adopted curriculum and the teachers' perceptions of what the curriculum means or should mean in practice.

[1] John I. Goodlad et al., eds., *Curriculum Inquiry* (New York: McGraw-Hill, 1984), 344–350.

4. *Operational curriculum.* Operational curriculum is what actually goes on in the classroom. Observations by researchers and others who make records of classroom interaction often reveal discrepancies between what teachers say the curriculum is and what teachers actually do.

5. *Experienced curriculum.* The experienced curriculum consists of what students derive from and think about the operational curriculum. Each student's background interacts with classroom activities contributing to unique meanings from common instruction. This curriculum is identified through student questionnaires, interviews, and inferences from observations of students.

CONTEXTS FOR DEVELOPMENT OF CURRICULUM

Range of Activity

Major categories of plans derived from curriculum efforts are curriculum policy, programs of study, courses, instructional units, and lesson plans. *Curriculum policy* is usually a written statement of what should be taught and is a guide to curriculum development. Graduation requirements, curriculum mandates, and frameworks outlining the content for a field of knowledge are examples. Curriculum policy making is the authoritative allocation of competing values. Elaboration of the political nature of curriculum decisions is given in Chapter 10.

Programs of study are designed for particular disciplines and broad fields: mathematics, science, language arts, vocational education. Each program allocates content activities and resources to different grade levels or courses, providing curricular linkage by specifying the common abstractions (skills, concepts, attitudes) to be extended in each course of the program. A *course* is a set of learning opportunities within a field of study for a year, semester, or quarter. Within courses, there are *instructional units*, plans aimed at one or more topics, problems, themes, or activities (foci). The particular focus of a unit is not only an important study in itself, but allows for the integration of learning experiences and gives purpose to the classroom activities. *Lesson plans* indicate teaching strategies and procedures for student engagement.

Development of Materials

There are curriculum developers who produce detailed instructional materials: textbooks, videos, activity kits. These materials often require the developer to detail suggestions for the teacher or child and to prepare tests and record-keeping systems, as well as procedures for training the teacher on how to use the materials.

Before undertaking the production of any materials, the curriculum developer will consider time and the intended learners. Will the material serve an hour's lesson, a year's work, a 6-year program? What are the ages, mental and physical characteristics, and experiential backgrounds of the future users of the materials?

In determining what the individual or target population should learn, curriculum developers take either a restricted or an unrestricted approach. In the restricted approach, the developer looks for possible standards and objectives from within a domain of knowledge and practice. Mathematics, health, and vocational education are typical domains. Usually the systemic and academic curriculum developers use the restricted approach. Developers with other curriculum conceptions use the unrestricted approach, willing to regard any problem, idea, or situation as appropriate for what should be taught. Of course, the curriculum maker's task of conceiving possible outcomes does not mean that all proposed ends will be accepted and acted on. Boards of education, principals, teachers, and students all have ways of rejecting the best-conceived purposes. However, persons who propose outcomes should be able to justify them. Later in this chapter, we describe the ways in which developers formulate their purposes and justify them.

In addition to the development of goals and materials as a curriculum activity, there is the enacted curriculum where teacher and students create their own meanings in teaching and learning.

State, Regional, and Local Curriculum Planning

According to Seaton, those planning curriculum for state, regional, or local communities are drawn by two functions: (1) *the attraction function*—the need for curriculum to produce the human capital that will attract investment, business, and jobs as well as the attendant infrastructure and (2) *the amelioration function*—curriculum policies that can close disparities in such areas as unemployment, displacement, population movement and problems related to health, environment, and safety.[2]

Institutional Curriculum Planning

Those who plan to develop curriculum within a given institution attend to the nature of that school, especially to the school's manifest purposes. Why? One reason is that the selection of an appropriate model or set of procedures for the formulation of standards and objectives depends on the central purpose of that school. Often vocational and other training schools, for example, are expected to prepare students for specific jobs. Hence, the use of *job analysis*, a technique for deriving objectives that directly contribute to helping students find jobs and keep them, is warranted. This technique seeks to ensure a match between what the student learns and what he or she will do on the job. The method can be modified, of course, with procedures for collecting data that will help anticipate likely future job requirements. Job analysis would be a less appropriate tool to use in the formulation of objectives within an institution whose mission is to further humanistic goals. Such an institution would use a different technical tool to formulate objectives, that is, a tool more consistent with actualizing learners as individuals, such as a personal "concerns" survey.

Illustrations of how institutional purposes match procedures for curriculum development can be seen in the familiar practices of the community college. There is more freedom in the formulation of curriculum goals in community colleges than in traditional schools devoted to the liberal arts because they frequently have a very broad goal, that of community service, an invitation to meet the educational needs of the community. Because of such goals and the state legislature's practice of funding community colleges on the basis of student enrollment, the curriculum problem becomes a search for courses that will attract students. Anything that appeals to aged persons, young mothers, veterans, and immigrants must be considered. The appropriate technical tool for the formulation of objectives in this case is needs assessment, a procedure for uncovering local deficiencies and trends to decide what might be taught, and a way to sample and stimulate interests in various kinds of learning.

In higher education, departmental chairs often face faculty conflict in introducing new programs, courses, or modifications in course goals and content. Proposed programs usually require approval from a college or university committee or from state regulatory

---

[2]Andrew Seaton, "Reforming a Hidden Curriculum," *Curriculum Perspectives* 22 (April 23, 2003): 9–15.

bodies, and later they must confront accreditation standards and externally mandated student examinations.[3]

Social reconstructionists and transformists do not want curriculum standards and objectives to be shackled to institutional purposes. Indeed, they believe that curriculum developers have been shaped by the bureaucratic nature of the schools, and thus have mistakenly formulated purposes that serve an industrial model of education with an emphasis on efficiency. They would prefer curriculum workers to advance futuristic, transformative, and humanistic ends, helping institutions to focus on getting people to define problems that they did not perceive before and to make contact with one another in stronger ways.[4]

Martha Nussbaum is an example of one who believes that the best preparation for an uncertain future world is to show students what they are able to do and be informed about life worthy of a human being. She puts curriculum emphasis on the development of such capabilities as *practical reason*—whereby students form concepts of their goals and critically reflect about planning their life; and *affiliation*—the ability to live with and toward others, to recognize and show concern for others, to engage in various forms of social interactions, to have empathy for others (imagining oneself in the values of others) and to develop the capacity for both guidance and friendship.[5]

Hence, the role of the curriculum worker is not determined by the constraints of educational institutions; instead, curriculum workers create new institutional forms and environments. The introduction of forms such as nondirective teaching roles, student goal setting, women's studies, service learning, cooperative learning, and therapeutic modes of working broaden the function of a traditional school to include newer ends.

Functions of the Curriculum

Before preparing any curriculum plan—whether for a textbook, lesson, course of study, document, product, or program—one should be clear about the functions the proposed curriculum will serve. We have already alluded to the use of attractive and ameliorative functions in state and regional planning. Those responsible for total curriculum offerings of a school can also find a functional concept useful in bringing balance to their program of study. Four such foundational functions are as follows:

1. *Common or general education.* The function of common education is met through a curriculum that addresses the learner as a responsible human being and citizen, not as a specialist or one with unique gifts or interests. It means, for instance, including as content the ground rules (the Bill of Rights) for participating in the civic affairs of the community and developing those minimal competencies essential for the health, welfare, and protection of all. Successful general education enables everyone to support and share in the culture; hence, a curriculum worker decides what the individual needs in order to communicate with others. The planner considers what outcomes and experiences all should have in common.

2. *Supplementation.* Individuality is the key to understanding supplementation. Objectives consistent with it deal with both personal deficits and unique potentials. To serve this function, a curriculum might be designed for those whose talents and interests enable them to go much farther than the majority or those whose defects

[3]Dennis Baron, "New Programs; New Programs," *The Chronicle of Higher Education,* Section B (Feb. 27, 2004): 1–4.

[4]Jerry L. Patterson et al., *Productive School Systems for a Non-Rational World* (Alexandria, VA: Association for Supervision and Curriculum Development, 1986).

[5]Martha Nussbaum, *Women and Human Development: The Capabilities Approach* (Cambridge, MA: Cambridge University Press, 2000).

and deficiencies are severe enough to require special attention. Such a curriculum is personal and individual, not common or general.

3. *Exploration.* Opportunities for learners to discover and to develop personal interests capture the meaning of exploration. When well executed, exploration enables learners to find out that they do or do not have either the talent or the zeal for certain kinds of activities. Exploring experiences should *not* be organized and taught as if their purposes were to train specialists. Nor should they be conceived as shoddy. Exploration demands a wider range of contacts within a field, realization of the possibilities for further pursuit, and revelation of one's own aptitudes and interests.

4. *Specialization.* A specializing function is rendered by a curriculum in which the current standards of a trade, profession, or academic discipline prevail. Students are expected to emulate those who are successfully performing as skilled workers or scholars. Entry into such a curriculum requires that students already have considerable expertise and drive.

Each curriculum orientation serves a function: humanistic, development of the person; social reconstruction, social change; systemic, social control and stability; academic, knowledge production.

The balance among the different functions and the curriculum conceptions associated with them varies every few years. With secondary schools, for example, academic specialization was in the ascendancy in the 1960s. In the early 1970s, general education was weakened in favor of exploration, minicourses, optional modules, alternative curriculum, and other electives. In the early 1980s, the demand for basic skills by parents and some educators pushed the curriculum back in the direction of general education. Although vocational specialization, too, received attention, particularly training on the job site itself, the 1990s saw the core of common learning and academic specialization driving the curriculum. As indicated in Chapter 3, the new century began with a quasi-academic and basic skills emphasis through systemic delivery.

In higher education, general education is today fragmented. Conservatives favor the liberal arts as a common core, while the humanists and academic specialists believe it best for teachers and students to select their own area of interest for study. In their defense of specialization, a scholar's gavel holds that research must be specialized in order to focus effort and delve deeply. To be specialized is not to be trivial, because the best specialized research has broad implications. As a countercharge to the charge of narrowness, the academic specialist says that by understanding one's field in depth, the student will learn to appreciate a wider array of intellectual tools and artistic achievement. This notion has not gone unchallenged. Elliot Eisner, for instance, views teaching a specialized curriculum with skepticism.

> *I'm not convinced by the thesis that specialization breeds general understanding, or that it cultivates an appreciation of the variety of ways in which meaning can be secured.... If attention to a wide range of problems and fields of study is necessary for the type of personal and intellectual range one wished to develop in students, how then can one cultivate, in depth, those idiosyncratic interests and attitudes which almost all students have.*[6]

Latent or hidden functions abound in schools. For example, there are the *consummation functions* (whetting student demand for material things such as a car or the latest

---

[6]Elliot W. Eisner, "Persistent Dilemmas in Curriculum Decision Making," *Confronting Curriculum Reform* (Boston: Little Brown, 1971), 168–169.

computer), the *custodial function* (warehousing students from job markets and entertaining them), and the *socializing function* [encouraging students to meet members of the opposite sex and gain access to powerful social networks (social capital)].

DETERMINING WHAT TO TEACH

The power to frame educational purposes is central in the curriculum field. Those who are not sensitive to the need for this power, who merely accept what others have proposed, are, in one sense, instruments. The following paragraphs describe the ways in which individuals and groups generate and select curriculum ends, content, and experiences. Usually the stated ends or aims indicate the purposes for which programs and lessons are undertaken. They give direction to what otherwise would be blind activities and enable practitioners to prepare plans of action. Note, however, that unplanned activities and experiences may imply the need for new goals and influence their attainment. A curriculum goal is more than a whim or desire. Its formulation is a complex intellectual operation involving observation, study of conditions, collection of relevant information, and, most of all, judgment. Curriculum planning demands an intellectual anticipation and evaluation of consequences.

It is important to note the difference in curriculum work by (1) conservative curricularists who seek to justify existing goals, content, and experiences by showing how these answers are relevant to cultural realities and (2) curriculum inquirers who use cultural analyses as a basis for generating alternative goals, contents, and experiences.

In order to plan curriculum based on a justifiable selection from the culture, it is necessary to have a process. Denis Lawton recommends analyzing the kind of society that exists and then mapping out the knowledge and kinds of experiences that are most appropriate for this culture.[7] According to Lawton, it is necessary to identify both cultural invariants and cultural variables. Cultural developers should have access to many dimensions in the dominant cultures and subcultures: social and economic level, communication, nationality, technology, morality, belief, and aesthetics. Alternative and existing curriculum can be compared for their fit to the realities described. Although social reconstructionists and transformists draw from culture, they are not narrow but international, transcending national boundaries and cultural differences.

It is true that many curriculum plans are drawn in response to perceived inadequacies or single issues without comprehensive cultural analysis. Current curriculum reform policies, for example, are responses to business and industrial concerns about American economic growth, and they are based upon limited data regarding present and future work.[8] Furthermore, these policies neglect consideration of the educational functions. To the extent that these policies operate at a high level of abstraction and aim at uniformity in curriculum they will fail. Reform policy succeeds when it accommodates to cultural regional and individual variability. Policy is best when it initiates local curriculum development in which people in schools fashion solutions to their real problems.[9]

In addition to familiarity with policy and the analyses underlying it, those developing curriculum at the school and classroom levels require data from cultural analyses of their particular community. Consideration of the implications of local data for what to teach is the essential task of their undertaking.

[7]Denis Lawton, *Curriculum Studies and Education Planning* (London: Hodder and Stoughton, 1993).
[8]*Global Competition: The New Reality* (Washington, DC: Report of the President's Commission on Industrial Competition, 1988).
[9]Richard Elmore and Milbray W. McLaughlin, *Steady Work: Policy, Practice, and the Reform of American Education* (Santa Monica, CA: Rand Corporation, 1988).

RATIONAL AND TECHNICAL MODELS IN CURRICULUM DECISION MAKING

In most rational models, the decision-making process follows an orderly pattern. The determination of goals is the first priority. Other decisions about structure, content, activities, materials, and accountability are tied to the goals. Goals themselves are determined by means of a logical problem-solving approach. The following paragraphs feature the most widely known rational models for formulating goals; these models are adaptable for use at societal, institutional, and instructional levels.

Needs Assessment Model

Needs assessment is the process by which educational needs are defined and priorities set. In the context of curriculum, a need is defined as a condition in which a discrepancy exists between *an acceptable* state of learner achievement or attitude and an *observed* learner state.

Needs assessment is one of the most frequently used ways for justifying curriculum goals and objectives. Several reasons underlie the popularity of needs assessment as a tool for formulating desired outcomes. Some people are motivated by efficiency. They want to identify and resolve the most critical needs so that resources can be employed in the most efficient manner. They want to avoid the practice of trying to do a little bit in many problem areas and solving none of them. Other people are concerned about social disorganization, the lack of consensus among the school community. They see needs assessment as a way to effect shared values and mutual support. The discussion of alternative ends by parents, students, teachers, and other citizens is an educational activity in itself. Other people want new value orientations to be reflected in the curriculum and see needs assessment as a vehicle for influence. Cultural pluralists, for example, use needs assessment to ascertain the values of subcultures such as those of Hispanics, African-Americans, and Asians. They also try to persuade the dominant society to accept these values as worthy goals to be advanced through the curriculum.

Steps in Needs Assessment A needs assessment requires four steps: formulating a set of tentative goals statements, assigning priority to goal areas, determining the acceptability of learner performance in each of the preferred goal areas, and translating high-priority goals into plans.

Formulating a Set of Tentative Goals Statements Comprehensive sets of goals that reflect the dominant culture are readily available. Such goals statements are collected from curriculum guides, textbooks, evaluation studies, and basic research studies by psychologists and educators. These goals refer to the conventionally sought outcomes in most schools; fundamental competencies for reading, writing, mathematics, health, citizenship, and aesthetics or in four areas: academic, social and civic, vocational, and personal. Goals statements may also include attributes of character such as friendliness, respect, and independence.

In order to apply needs assessment in multicultural contexts, additional goals statements that reflect multicultural values are necessary. Cross-cultural investigations reveal fundamental differences among the values of different cultural groups. Although stereotypical generalizations are inadequate, some Hispanic parents, for example, believe that learners should make their choices in terms of family interests rather than acting only from personal desires. The goals of those from a particular culture may contrast sharply with those of the dominant culture and with goals of other subcultures. Goals statements from a diverse group may reflect a desire to gain better treatment for their children in the school. Such a goal might be that "learners will see school as a friendly and helpful place."

Goals statements about community values are also obtained. Those conducting needs assessments consider more than the conventional goals available from state and federal publications. Participants focus on their own perception of what they want their learners to think, feel, or be able to do as a result of school instruction.

Typical techniques for eliciting data for needs assessment are *concerns conferences* and *sponsor speakups*. Concerns conferences, organized by school administrators and curriculum specialists, are attempts to identify local problems, and later, in small discussion groups, problems are articulated and suggestions made for their solution. Frequently, new educational goals are proposed in order to attempt a solution to the identified problem. In sponsor speakups, students are organized into groups so that they work cooperatively to identify the most pressing needs of their school situation. Efforts are made to encourage uninhibited student expression. Although many of these needs may be met by actions that are not curricular in nature, it is important to consider the curriculum goals that might contribute to resolving the perceived difficulties. A perceived problem in health, for example, may involve a different goal for medical health agencies than for a school. The school's curriculum goal might be limited to helping students understand the reason for the health problem and explaining some ways the learner can cope with it. A medical agency might take more direct action-that is, inoculate students to prevent disease. Of course, the trend to integrate the activities of different agencies within the context of the school makes needs assessment a procedure for planning a coordinated answer to priority problems.

Assigning Priority to Goal Areas   The second phase consists of gathering preference data, typically from parents, staff, students, and community members. Members of these groups are given goals statements and asked to rank them in terms of importance. Opportunities are provided for the respondents to add to the set of goals presented. Usually they rate the goals on a five-point scale (a rating rather than a ranking allows more goals to be considered). Samples of goals *can* be given to different persons to effect average group estimates. Later, the combined ratings of all the people sampled will reveal those goals considered very important, important, average, unimportant, and very unimportant.

Determining the Acceptability of Learner Performance in Each of the Preferred Goals Areas   In the third phase either a subjective or an objective approach can be taken. A subjective approach calls for a group of judges to rate the acceptability of present learner status on each goal. No direct measure of the learners with respect to the goals is undertaken; judges estimate the present status of learners with respect to each goal. Their impression might be gained by whatever they have observed or been led to believe by the media and reports from the children and other neighbors. Judges' ratings become indices of need. The objective approach requires actually measuring the status of students relative to each goal. Measures must be congruent with the goals, of course. To this end, instructional objectives within each goal area are selected. Matching assessment devices are chosen and administered to representative samples of pupils. If the students' level of performance on a measurement is less than the acceptable level, a need is indicated. Levels obtained on each measurement are compared. Those showing the widest gap indicate a greater priority. However, one must also consider the relative importance of the goal as indicated by preference data.

Translating High-Priority Goals into Plans   In the fourth phase, goals that are preferred and for which a need has been identified become the bases for new curriculum instructional plans. The selection of new target outcomes, goals, and objectives has implications for course offerings and for instructional materials and arrangements because the realization of new goals requires new facilitating means. Learning activities, teaching strategies, and evaluating techniques must be changed. For example, having once identified a need for students to learn to read and write in Spanish and acquire minority cultural values as well as positive attitudes toward school, the school may need to develop a two-way immersion or bilingual program. Consequently, the staff will acquire new materials in the Spanish language and offer activities consistent with particular values—group cooperation and family involvement. Furthermore, teachers can be helped to use teaching strategies that are effective with the culture, such as learning how to indicate nonverbal acceptance.

Problems in the Needs Assessment Technique   Technical and philosophical problems are resolved before needs assessment can fulfill its promise. One technical problem involves making the meaning of the goals clear so that respondents are choosing the same goals. A vague goal, such as citizenship, creative fluency, or application of scientific methods, indicates only a general direction. On the other hand, making a vague goal specific often results in numerous objectives, so many in fact that no single person could rank them according to their value. More than 50 years ago, Boyd H. Bode commented on Franklin Bobbitt's claim that 1200 high school teachers in Los Angeles had given an almost unanimous judgment on a long list of objectives. Bode said, "If the list really represents common judgment, we are bound to conclude that men and women are more amenable to reason in Los Angeles than anywhere else on the globe.... One almost wonders whether the teachers of Los Angeles did not mistake Bobbitt's list of abilities for a petition to be signed."[10] One answer to the problem of how to discriminate among objectives is to rely on broad-scope but measurable objectives and benchmarks that represent significant competencies rather than to stipulate the many objectives that contribute to the general competency. Another answer is to have different persons rate different goals and objectives, with no single person having to evaluate carefully more than seven (a digestible number). It is helpful to ask all who are to rate goals to engage first in common discussion and to ascertain that particular goals or standards satisfy these three criteria: (1) the goal is needed for future learning and contributes to fundamental needs, such as making a living and gaining the respect of others, (2) the goal is teachable, and (3) is not likely to be acquired outside the school.

Needs assessment is frequently used by social adapters as a way to ensure that the curriculum is responsive to changing social conditions. It can also be used by social reconstructionists who want not so much to prepare students to adapt to changing conditions but to alter the social institutions that are creating undesirable social conditions. Group deliberation and judgment thus become factors in needs assessment. There must be opportunity for sharing facts and logical persuasion, that is, facts and ideas brought by the participants themselves, not by outsiders, and deliberation involving normative philosophical considerations. The fact that something exists does not mean it is desirable. The reflective curriculum worker inquires about both what is desired and whether it is worthwhile, right, and good.

Systemic planners who favor "data driven" decisions regard needs assessment as nothing more than a scientific information-gathering procedure and see it as a way to avoid ethical issues by justifying the curriculum merely on the basis of the popularity of certain goals and the magnitude of the discrepancy between where learners *are* and where learners *should be* with respect to these popular goals. Needs assessment has been opposed when it is regarded solely as an information gathering procedure on the grounds that "No

---

[10]Boyd H. Bode, "On Curriculum Construction," *Curriculum Theory* 5, no. 1 (1975): 39–59; reprinted from *Modern Educational Theories* (New York: Macmillan, 1927), 17.

scientifically derived information can yield a judgment about 'what should be' because science deals not with normative considerations but with facts."[11]

It remains to be seen whether the dominant groups in schools will attend to the goal priorities of other groups. Can the curriculum reflect the priorities of all groups within the community or must a consensus be reached? If there is group conflict, how will the conflict be resolved?

The Futuristic Model

There is a growing realization that the world of the future is going to be different from the present, that it will demand new kinds of people, and that the time is short to prepare the citizens of the future. Hence, efforts have been made to develop educational objectives consistent with this realization and specific enough to imply action.

Common Ingredients   Although there are slight differences among authors' conceptions of the model, the following techniques and phases are regarded as important:

1. *The multidisciplinary seminar.* Professional educators and specialists from outside education (political scientists, economists, medical psychologists) meet for several days to discuss possible future developments that would affect curriculum planning. Members of this seminar prepare papers examining the research frontiers in their field. The results of literature searches on educational innovations and goals are also presented.

2. *Judgment of projected trends.* Major anticipated changes are ordered according to their importance to society and probability of occurrence. The difficulty of bringing about these changes in terms of time, money, and energy is considered. A period of occurrence is estimated. The potential social effects of these changes are classified as good or bad on the basis of carefully examined opinions on which there is a consensus. Participants rate each change from "very desirable" to "very undesirable."

3. *Educational acceptance for creating the future.* After the social consequences of trends have been established and rated, school persons and others suggest how they think the schools should respond. In deciding the educational responsibility to be taken, consideration is given to the certainty of a future occurrence, the social consequences of that occurrence, and the possibility that educators can effect it or can prepare students for it. Educational objectives, thus formed, should support "good" futures and resist "bad" ones. The educators also decide what items in the present curriculum are unlikely to prepare students for the future world and suggest that these items no longer be supported.

4. *Scenario writing.* A group of writers prepares at least two descriptions. One is a description of what learners will be like if action is taken on the decision in phase 3 and implemented by the school. The second is a description of the necessary related changes in subject matter, learning activities, curriculum organization, and methods. Attention is also paid to institutional arrangements that will bear on the new curriculum.

The Strategy Planning Network, consisting of 23 schools and sponsored by the Association for Supervision and Curriculum Development attempts to analyze changes for which the schools should be planning if they are to have a program suitable for all students

[11]Maurice L. Monett, "Needs Assessment: A Critique of Philosophical Assumptions," *Adult Education* 29, no. 2 (1979): 83–95.

in the twenty-first century. An example of strategy planning within the network is "Project 2001" undertaken by Lake Washington School District in Washington state. In this project futurists were commissioned to write reports on the skills schools should teach in 2001, so they asked other members of the community for their views on what schools should be doing.

The Delphi method is used by curriculum workers to obtain a consensus on goals and objectives for the future. By this method one tries to obtain the intuitive insights of experts and then uses these judgments systematically. In vocational education, content is often selected through Delphi as a way to find what is likely to be useful to future graduates of the school. Members of an employers' advisory council to the school are sent a series of questionnaires. The first questionnaire indicates present content offerings and asks participants to indicate their recommended changes in course subject areas in light of anticipated futures and to state the amount of time to be spent on each. In an attempt to gain consensus, questionnaires are sent again to collect information about the participants' responses to the previous ones. Participants are asked to reconsider their first recommendations and to give their reasons. Usually survey participants begin to form a consensus.

Problems with a Futuristic Model The difficulty that any group faces in trying to predict or invent the future is a problem. However, difficulties are also associated with getting a broad enough base of participation within and outside the school systems and with understanding the complex factors that affect school curriculum. Different community contexts and different views of the school's role delay consensus. There is no consensus about the goals different educational institutions should be trying to achieve. A related aspect of the problem is that many people do not like to make choices and find it difficult even to make hypothetical choices. Even when groups arrive at a consensus on some preferred alternatives, many dissentions remain unresolved. Educational standards and objectives frequently are not consistent with one another or have more than one meaning even for one person. One objective may call for the learner to show initiative; a second objective may call for the learner to follow directions. Respondents experience a tension in deciding between creativity on the one hand and order and tradition on the other.

The Rational Model

The late Ralph Tyler's *Rationale* is the best-known rational model for answering questions about formulating educational purposes, selecting and organizing education experiences, and determining the extent to which purposes are being attained.[12] It is called an ends–means approach because the setting of purposes, standards, or objectives as ends influences the kinds of activity and organization (the means) most likely to assist in reaching the goal. Evaluation, too, according to this model is undertaken to see how well the learning experiences as developed and organized are producing the desired results.

Deriving Standards and Objectives Tyler's assumption is that standards and objectives will be more defensible—will have greater significance and greater validity—if certain kinds of facts are taken into account. One source of facts consists of studies of the intended learners. A second source is found in studies of contemporary life outside the school, and a third source is made up of suggestions from subject matter specialists regarding what knowledge is of most worth in their disciplines for citizens. The following elaborates how standards and objectives are derived from data provided by the different sources.

---

[12]Ralph W. Tyler, *Basic Principles of Curriculum and Instruction* (Chicago: University of Chicago Press, 1950).

Learners   In order to derive standards and objectives from this source, learners should be studied to find their deficiencies in knowledge and behavior as well as their psychological needs for affection, belonging, recognition, and a sense of purpose and their interests.

Essentially, the process of deriving an objective from studies of the learner demands that an inference be drawn about what to teach after looking at the data. Making inferences also involves value judgments. If the data show that learners are chiefly interested in video games, it must be decided whether this is a desirable interest to be extended or a deficiency to be overcome.

Let us assume that the curriculum worker had discovered this fact: "During adolescence, learners are likely to have the cognitive skills of intuition, generalization, and insight; and their sensibilities toward justice are awakened." The curriculum planner can use this information to infer what to teach, perhaps deciding that learners should acquire knowledge of Utopian thought and the methods for effecting a more perfect social order. The curriculum planner might also infer that students should suppress the tendency to believe that wars, tyrannies, and the like are caused by human nature and believe instead that changes in social structure may preclude injustices.

Social Conditions   Facts about the community—local, national, or world—can be taken into account if what is to be taught is to be made relevant to contemporary life. Again, a value judgment is made in deciding what kind of facts to collect. Comprehensiveness is sometimes sought: one might collect data on health, economics, politics, religion, family, and conservation. The educational responses to these facts often provoke controversy. After discovering from health data that venereal disease is at an epidemic level, the curriculum worker might make inferences that range from (a) learners should be taught the causes and means for preventing communicable diseases to (b) learners should be taught those moral principles governing conduct which uphold the sanctity of marriage. It is obvious that a curriculum worker's responses in such a case could be controversial.

Subject Matter Specialists   In rational curriculum making, scientists and scholars, the discoverers of disciplined knowledge, are consulted in order to find out what the specialist's subject can contribute to the education of the intended learners. Suppose that a curriculum planner asked this question: "What in your field might best contribute to the aim that learners generate fruitful new questions and that they conceptualize alternatives and their consequences?" The planner would receive different answers from specialists in different fields. A historian might reply, "You should teach the principles for interpreting historical events and help students to comprehend such schemes as the great-man theory, cultural movements, and economic determinism as explaining factors." A linguist's response might be, "You should teach concepts that show the unitary and meaning-bearing sequences of language structures, such as intonation patterns." An anthropologist might want to stress the processes of inquiry that illuminate culture or might say, "Be sure learners understand the difference between nature and the symbolic devices, institutions, and things constructed by people."

Selecting among Education Goals, Standards, and Objectives   After formulating tentative purposes, the rationalist applies the following criteria before accepting them as suitable for the selection of learning activities:

Congruency with Values and Functions   Standards and objectives should relate to the values and functions adopted by the controlling agency. If authorities for the institution value general education, objectives must further common understanding; if authorities value specialization, then standards must be related to the development of specialists in a field.

Comprehensiveness   Standards that are more encompassing, that do not deal with a minuscule sort of learner behavior, are more highly valued. Often many such standards can be coalesced into a single powerful standard.

Consistency   Standards should be consistent with one another. One should not have standards stressing both openness or inquiry and dogmatism or unconditional acceptance.

Attainability   Standards should be capable of being reached without great strain. The curriculum maker considers teacher and community concurrence, costs, and availability of materials.

As guides to instructional planning, educational standards and objectives are then stated in a form that makes clear the content that the learner must use, the *domain* or situation in which the knowledge is to apply, and the kind of thought and *behavior* to be exhibited by the learner. The following objective is an illustration: "In different writing samples (domain), the learner will be able to recognize (thought and behavior) unstated assumptions (content)."

The learning activities that follow allow the learner to work with the defined substantive element at a level consistent with that called for in the standard of objective and benchmark. Activities designed to teach prerequisites to that terminal task can also be provided, of course.

Problems with the Tyler Model

The Tyler model represents conciliatory eclecticism. In recommending the three sources to use in formulating objectives, Tyler confronts the decision maker with three warring conceptions of the curriculum. The learner as a source is consistent with the humanistic conception, especially when data regarding the learner's own psyche needs and interests are considered. Society as a source is in keeping with social adaptive and some reconstruction orientations; while the subject matter specialist as a source tends to recognize the academic conception of curriculum.

Little help is given in the way of assigning weight to each source when one must take precedence over another. On the other hand, the model offers the possibility of treating learners, society, and subject matter as part of a comprehensive process rather than as isolated entities.

Not all criteria by which some standards and objectives are excluded are stipulated by the model. Users of the model must identify their own set of philosophical axioms for screening their purposes. The fact that standards and objectives are consistent with one another does not in itself indicate the value of the objectives formulated.

The role of values and bias is not highlighted in the model. Values and bias operate at all points in the *Rationale*—in the selection of specific data within the sources, in drawing inferences from the data, in formulating the objectives, and in selecting from among the standards and objectives.

Three other criticisms remain. The model has been criticized for locking curriculum making into the "top-down" tradition, with those at the top setting the purposes and functions that narrow the school's goals, standards, and objectives, which in turn control classroom instruction. The predetermined purposes that guide all other aspects, such as learning experiences, have been likened to a production model with its input (students), processes (learning experiences), and output (prespecified objective or product). The criticism of those who would shackle the *Tyler Rationale* to a management function has been repudiated.[13] The *Rationale* is the way most curriculum specialists refer to key ideas in Tyler's

---

[13]Peter S. Hlebowitsch, "Amid Behavioral and Behavioral Objectives: Reappraising Appraisals of the Tyler Rationale," *Journal of Curriculum Studies* 24, no. 6 (1992): 533–547.

Basic Principles of Curriculum and Instruction. The *Rationale* was not based on the pre-supposition that administrative authority is the exclusive ground for curriculum decision making. Rather, it was intended to be used by committees of teachers in given schools for their planning and developing of curriculum.

The second criticism that the model takes time to implement is related to the third: the resolving of disagreement over values. The practical difficulties of getting the right data sources and being able to infer appropriate implications for schools require imaginative thinkers. The model does not resolve the political conflict in curriculum policy making even if common values are accepted. Even those characterized as devout members of the same value persuasion may have their disagreement over methods:

> *Those who agree that the truths honored in our tradition should be the primary curriculum elements may still disagree over whether certain classics should be taught in English translation, Latin translation, or the original Greek. They may argue whether to include Virgil together with Tacitus and Julius Caesar in a fixed time of study. They may differ over the amounts of time to be allotted to the Bible and other more strictly oriented texts. The resolution of such problems requires a decision procedure in addition to a value base.[14]*

Curriculum specialists have tried to improve on the Tyler model. Usually the improvement consists of reversing the order of procedures by placing the statements of educational values or aims as the first step and then refining these aims in light of information about learners, social conditions, and new knowledge in the subject fields. In working with students of curriculum, I often randomly divide the students into two groups: (1) those who follow the procedures outlined by Tyler, beginning with sources and ending with the application of philosophical and psychological screens and (2) those who follow the revised procedures, making value orientations explicit before looking at data from the sources. I give both groups the same facts or generalizations from each of the three sources and then observe how variations in ordering of the procedures influence the number and kinds of objectives generated. Table 5.1 illustrates the contrast in procedure.

The difference in number and kind of objectives generated by the two procedures is considerable. The Tyler model results in many more standards and objectives about learners and the community. The difficulty experienced by the revisionist group in getting agreement on educational aims is much greater than the difficulty of establishing a philosophical framework after forming tentative objectives.

The Vocational or Training Model

Training usually implies narrower purposes than educating. Educating allows for objectives that include the wholeness of a student's life as a responsible human being and a citizen. Training tends to look at the student's competence in some occupation. Although these two sides of life are not altogether separable, different procedures are used in deriving training objectives than in formulating educational objectives. The training model for formulating proposed outcomes has essentially two functions: one is to reveal particular manpower needs or occupations that the institutions or programs should serve. A second purpose is to determine the specific competencies that must be taught in order for learners (trainees) to take their place within the target occupations.

---

[14]Michael W. Kirst and Decker F. Walker, "An Analysis of Curriculum Policy Making," *Review of Educational Research* 41, no. 4 (Dec. 1971): 485.

Table 5.1   Comparison of Tyler and Revisionist Procedures for Generating Objectives

Tyler	Revisionist
1. *Data* Facts about learners indicating that they do not feel responsible for their successes or failures in school. Facts about the community indicating perhaps ideological confusion about traditional ways of doing things and newer technology. 2. *Tentative objectives* Suggested objectives in response to the facts and generalizations. 3. *Philosophy* State what you think the goals of the schools should be (cognitive development, development of respect for others, desire for continued learning, ability to enter the world of work) or the aims and functions most important for the school and programs you have in mind (general, remedial, or vocational). 4. *Final objectives* Accept or reject the tentative objectives on the basis of your educational values, educational aims, and functions of schooling.	1. *Philosophy* State what you think the goals of the schools should be (cognitive development, development of respect for the rights of others, desire for continuing education, ability to enter the world of work). 2. *Data* Facts about learners indicating that and generalizations. 3. *Objectives* Objectives are derived by keeping in mind detailed educational aims and functions and responding to facts and generalizations.

Determining Occupational Targets   Procedures for determining needed occupations rely initially on existing studies and plans. Most states release detailed area manpower requirements for more than 400 key occupational categories, reflecting for each category current employment, anticipated industry growth, and personnel replacement. The annual *Manpower Report of the President* issued by the U.S. Department of Labor gives an overall picture of the employment problems facing the nation.

Specific organizations such as the military, large industries, and businesses have projected their own manpower needs, which indicate the types of training that will be necessary. State and regional planners attempt to estimate future employment opportunities and to foresee fluctuations in mobility within the area and in mobility likely to result as firms enter or leave an area. These planners try to coordinate the programs that determine vocational services with those aimed at developing jobs. They take into account job market analysis, program reviews, curriculum resources, and state, local, and national priorities.

It is customary to use advisory councils in connection with planning vocational programs. Usually these councils are made up from employers in a given occupational field, but sometimes they are composed of parents, students, representatives from labor, and potential trainees. Members help supply more information both on what will happen in a community and on what kind of employee employers are seeking. Furthermore, they help inform the community of the forces affecting the job market.

Determining the Objectives for Training Programs or Courses   Job descriptions and task analysis procedures are used to enhance the relevancy of the training program to the job to be performed. A job description is a paragraph or two listing the tasks involved and any unusual conditions under which those tasks are carried out. All classes of tasks are listed. The task analysis begins with a study of the particular job or jobs. The curriculum developer tries to answer these questions: What tasks are required on this job? How frequently are they required? What skills and information are the graduate of the training program expected to bring to each task?

A task is a logically related set of actions required by a job objective. The first step in the task analysis is listing all tasks that might be included in the job. Second, for each of these tasks an estimate is made of the frequency of performance, relative importance, and relative ease of learning. Third, the task is detailed by listing what the person does when performing each task. Note that what is done is not necessarily the same as what is known.

Task identification occurs through interviews, questionnaires, reports of critical incidents, and hardware analysis. Observation shows what the employees *do* while being observed; questionnaires and interviews reveal what they *say* they do. Critical incident techniques also indicate what people say they do. A critical incident report may describe a specific work assignment which an employee carried out very effectively or very ineffectively. Such reports are especially valuable in identifying unforeseen contingencies, difficult tasks, and interpersonal aspects of a job. Reports are sorted into topics such as equipment, problems, or groups of incidents that go together. The features common to these incidents are categorized. Each incident is judged effective or ineffective and characterized by the presence or absence of some skill or knowledge. The records may be further classified by such dimensions as work habit, management effectiveness or ineffectiveness, and method problem. From these data new training objectives are derived for courses. Critical incident reports are completed by representative samples of job holders and supervisory persons who interact with job holders.

The job analysis and a knowledge of the characteristics of the intended learners are all that is necessary for the blueprint of expected student performance. The course objectives can be obtained by subtracting what the student is already able to do from what he or she must be able to do. Course objectives are not the same as task analyses. Objectives specify the abilities that a beginning learner must have after training; task analyses describe the job as performed by a highly skilled person. Subtracting what students are already able to do from what they must be able to do helps one to decide the course objectives. One cannot go directly from a task analysis to the formulation of objectives for a course. It is necessary to decide which skills demanded by the occupation may be better taught on the job and which skills are best taught in the course.

Problems with the Vocational Model   There are several criticisms of the training model. First, the objectives derived from it usually prepare a learner for work as it is rather than as it should be. Related to this criticism is the charge that the model is associated with presentism, a focus on the current situation rather than on a likely future condition. Most critics admit, however, that the model is ahead of the practice of deriving objectives only from tradition, convention, and the curriculum maker's personal experiences.

A second criticism is that the task analysis procedure is valid only for aspects of jobs that are certain. If we know what an employee must do in a situation, the training model is effective. However, many aspects of jobs are uncertain—what to do in light of unanticipated circumstances, what to do when the situation is altered. Furthermore, not many developers know how to make task analyses for situations demanding political, economic, or moral judgments. Preparing students for instances in which the grounds for decision are not clear or unique requires a different model for curriculum development, a model that is unrealized but probably will take the form of critical inquiry as suggested by Habermas.[15]

---

[15]Thomas McCarthy, ed., *The Critical Theory of Jurgen Habermas* (Cambridge: MIT Press, 1981).

Briefly, a critical inquiry model would call for participants to (1) relate proposed decisions to common norms of the institution, (2) question the validity of the common norm in light of how well they serve human needs, and (3) use the weight of evidence and reason (not political inference) in arriving at the best solution.

ALTERNATIVE APPROACHS TO DETERMINING CURRICULUM PURPOSES

Disjointed Incrementalism

Disjointed incrementalism is not really a model; it is a nonmodel. It occurs when curriculum decisions are made without following a systematic procedure. In the nonmodel, decisions about what will be taught occur through a political process. Advocates of a particular curriculum try to justify the ends they already have in mind. Advocates of the liberal arts and fundamental skills appeal to tradition; advocates of cognitive skills appeal to psychological and educational research; advocates of relevant vocational skills appeal to the workplace; and advocates of self-improvement appeal to personal judgment. Those who must resolve the conflicting pressures—politicians, school boards, advisory councils, textbook publishers, professional educators—tend to use informal methods of decision making. Disjointed incrementalism is a strategy and it has these rules:

1. Contemplate making only marginal changes in the existing situation.
2. Avoid making radical changes and consider only a few policy alternatives.
3. Consider only a few of the possible consequences for any proposed change.
4. Feel free to introduce objectives consistent with policy as well as to change policy in accord with objectives.
5. Be willing to look for problems after data are available from implementation.
6. Work with piecemeal changes rather than making a single comprehensive attack.

Decisions made under disjointed incrementation are based on unchallenged assumptions and rhetoric and the interests of special groups, not on educational considerations. Hence, political processes are used to resolve conflicts.[16] In Chapter 10 we describe this process in detail.

Goals 2000 is an example of unrealistic goal setting. This political document stated eight national goals, such as American students will be first in the world in math and science achievement and every adult will be literate and possess the knowledge necessary to compete in a global economy and experience the rights and responsibilities of citizenship. Set by state governors on the basis of political grounds and passed into law by Congress in 1994, the program gave no attention to the attainability of the goals in view of learner characteristics, constraints of time, and resource limitations. Neither was the criticism of American education leveled in setting these goals validated. Indeed governmental industrial policies and defective management decisions have had more to do with the failure of industries to compete than have shortcomings in schools. Further, in viewing curriculum as a collection of things to be learned rather than a process for equipping students to tackle unpredictable problems, the governors can be faulted for not preparing students for the twenty-first century.

---

[16]Evans Clinchy, "Sustaining and Expanding the Educational Conversation," *Phi Delta Kappan* 76, no. 5 (Jan. 1995), 352–355.

Problems with Disjointed Incrementalism in Curriculum Making

Disjointed incrementalism in making curriculum decisions about what to teach is not very different from what occurs in other areas of government and industry. It tends to result in an unbalanced and fragmented curriculum. The main defect in the procedure is associated with gaps in the democratic process: the lack of well-informed citizens who exercise wide participation, assume responsibility for starting social improvements, and have competency in the skills of political action.

At local and institutional levels, disjointed incrementalism is used frequently in times of affluence; programs and courses are added rather than hard choices being made about their elimination. It represents a realization that conflict over what to teach is not merely a conflict of ideas but a conflict of persons, groups, and factions. Accordingly, conflicts over goals and objectives are not resolved on the basis of principles, logic, and evidence but by political power.

Emergent Approaches in Curriculum Decision Making

Emergent approaches differ from rational models in that they are guided by principles rather than by specified procedures. Furthermore, the process of determining desired outcomes is seen as the goals themselves. Ends and means are not separated. Hence, participants in the curriculum-making process are the prime benefactors; this makes wide empowerment of persons—teachers, parents, students—important in curriculum development. In addition to an emphasis on deliberation, these approaches aim at curriculum consciousness. Three such approaches, namely, deliberation, inquiry, and student generation of experience, can be identified.

Reflective Deliberation

Guiding principles for reflective deliberation are (1) policy and action should be determined locally rather than at a centralized level; (2) policy is not developed prior to action but through it; (3) understanding of participants is as important as the outcomes or list of action priorities; (4) both oral or conventional modes of expression (the mode in which participants operate most easily) and written codification of what is decided (authentic account of the particular ideas) are important.

Steward Bonser and Shirley Grundy have illustrated the principles in their description of a faculty facing the need to develop a school curriculum policy regarding use of technology in the schools.[17] In this case, teachers and an outside consultant go through four phases. In each phase, planning, data production, and reflective deliberation are present. In phase 1, planning consists of focusing on the approach to be taken for data generation and teachers sharing their understanding about computer education. Data production is in the form of audiorecorded accounts from individual interviews. Reflective deliberation occurs when the transcribed statement is returned to the individual participant for personal reflections and the preparation of a jointly authored statement.

In phase 2, the planning centers on how to code the information contained in each of the jointly authored statements. Data production occurs as participants meet in small groups and identify each member's issues and concerns. In reflective deliberation in this phase, the "owner" of each statement elaborates on points. The consultant summarizes the concerns of the group as a whole for subsequent documentation.

---

[17]Steward A. Bonser and Shirley A. Grundy, "Reflective Deliberation in the Formulation of a School Curriculum Policy," *Journal of Curriculum Studies* 20, no. 1 (Jan./Feb. 1988): 35–45.

In phase 3, whole group planning takes place with the purpose of classifying concerns from all groups according to those implicated (teachers, pupils, community), teaching and learning tasks and strategies for teaching, managing, and staff development. Data production in phase 3 occurs as members from opposite groups focus on classifying the intergroup data and attempting to get a consensus through group discussion.

The plan for phase 4 calls for the outside consultant to take information from the previous phase and to develop from it a school statement about technological education. Data collection consists of teachers' knowledge, viewpoints, concerns, and issues relevant to the subject. A statement prepared from the data collected is returned to the participants for affirmation. This statement provides the basis for curriculum documents delineating the school's policy for computer education.

Joint Fact Finding   Joint fact finding is the latest in a multistep participatory process for making decisions at institutional and governmental levels. This approach calls for a neutral facilitator to ensure that participants have an opportunity to advise on all value decisions involved in the analyzing and assessing impacts of decisions. The local knowledge of stakeholders is given equal weight to that of experts, thus avoiding the delay and extra costs that develop over policy decisions.[18]

Critical Inquiry in Curriculum Renewal   The heuristics of critical inquiry can be applied at any level of curriculum-making policy, institutional or classroom. An aspect of curriculum—a particular policy, course of study, textbook, or school practice—is identified and then participants attempt to answer a series of questions: What problem or central question does this curriculum purport to address? What are the historical antecedents to this curriculum? What are the assumptions about schooling, learning, or knowledge that underlie this curriculum? What are the consequences that follow from this curriculum? What information do we need? What is missing in this curriculum?

Critical inquiry in the classroom is consistent with active learning. By way of example, John Willinsky's language arts curriculum involves elementary school children in answering the question "Why do people write?" In so doing, students relate historical antecedents and popular culture to their own need for expression. In addition to development of the cognitive processes of reading and writing, these students become conscious of the political and social implications of literacy.[19]

In the setting of controversial curriculum policy and the planning of courses in areas where conflict is high, the critical framework is useful. Consider, for example, sexual education. Participants can look at critical reviews of health programs that show variations among them and their effectiveness, potential, and limitations.[20] Critical discourse on the issue can then occur by sharing the traditional, progressive, libertarian, and radical perspectives. Participants consider the power relations involved. The curriculum planners are able to make educational contributions rather than address all aspects of the social problem or limit the curriculum to a form of indoctrination.

---

[18]C. J. Andrews, *Humble Analysis—The Practice of Joint Fact-Finding* (Westport, CT: Praeger, 2002).
[19]John Willinsky, *The New Literacy: Redefining Reading and Writing in the Schools* (New York: Routledge, 1990).
[20]Luciana Laguna and David M. Hayes, "Contraceptive Health Programs for Adolescents: a Critical Review," *Adolescence* 28, no. 10 (summer 1993): 347–361.

Student-Generated Curriculum   Student-generated curriculum is consistent with principles of humanistic and social reconstructionist conceptions. The curriculum is situated in the students' culture: their literacy, their affective levels, their aspirations, and their daily lives. The derived goals will reflect personal background and experience as much as the academic subjects. This approach is not always easy for teachers to use. It will be rejected by those who see their role as transmitting "right" answers to predetermined problems. Unless mediated by teachers and peers, the measured curricula are counterproductive to student creation of knowledge and curriculum.

The teacher's role in these student-generated approaches require studying the life and language of the students, generalizing themes that can be used in linking student and teacher realities to learning. The themes vary with the context, the students, and the era. When students engage in critical dialogue about their generative themes, they connect their concrete ideas to more abstract ones. Words like *drugs* and *gang* may mean money, security, escape. With understanding teachers, dialogue may extend these themes to their implications for becoming more human and to ways of negating and overcoming, rather than passively accepting the given. Students learn to identify persons who are served by situations involving drugs and gangs and those who are negated and crushed by them. Tomas Graman has shared his experiences with student-generated curriculum in teaching English as a second language to farm workers.[21] Graman fosters active dialogue about reality so that the immediate need to confront real problems and resolve them can be met. Instead of emphasizing practical language for tourists or the empty artificial words in language textbooks, his students analyze their own experiences and build their own words to describe and understand their experiences.

After discussing their generative words, such as *bonus* (growers' deduction of money from paychecks until all crops are picked) and *short hoe* (a tool that is painful to use), the students began thinking about the practices and conditions of their work. Their analyses, construction of meanings, and choice of words became acts for overcoming what many had considered to be their unfortunate lot in life. Graman generates themes for discussion and writing by having students examine pictures, photographs, and newspaper articles (unedited for second language students) that contain such themes at early linguistic levels. Students read and discuss articles on familiar topics. Students do not merely practice language by answering questions to which students and teacher already know the answers. The goal is to become more critically conscious, not only to acquire language as a tool.

The student-generated curriculum requires examining beliefs and the basis for them, aiming at supporting arguments that reflect intelligent ways to resolve problems. The point is not to learn *what* to think and say, but *how* to think for oneself and express these thoughts in a new language.

Curriculum planning is an opportunity for teaching and learning. Joan Scott, for example uses the French word *partage*, signifying dividing and sharing, to characterize the approach.[22] Individuals and groups contribute to the setting of purpose without losing their different identities and viewpoints. *Partage* is open to the diversity of people and views found in contemporary society and operates on these assumptions:

- Knowledge and meaning are contributed by examining, discussing, and rediscovery.

- Engaging with differences is indispensable for constructing new knowledge.

- Difference is essential for curriculum change.

- Although teachers introduce extant knowledge, students share their knowledge to create new meanings and purposes.

---

[21]Tomas Graman, "Education for Humanization: Applying Paul Freire's Pedagogy to Learning a Second Language," *Harvard Educational Review* 58, no. 4 (Nov. 1988): 433–449.
[22]Joan Scott, *The Campaign Against Political Correctness* (Bloomington, IN: UP, 1986).

A COMMENT ON MODELS AND APPROACHES FOR CURRICULUM BUILDING

Thus far, we have focused on models and approaches for determining the purposes that curriculum should fulfill. Other decisions must be made about how to achieve stated purposes and how best to evaluate progress toward intended goals. The choice of emphasizing purpose and content as a first step in curriculum development is arbitrary. Alan Purves has been building curriculum for many years. When asked to think about the processes by which he developed and arranged materials to effect learning, he realized that existing models are a fine way to look at curriculum but that they do not tell a person how to proceed any more than a blueprint tells where to begin building a house. Purves knows that curriculum reflects the maker's view of the society, the people who are to be affected, and the nature of what is to be learned. However, he thinks the metaphor of a game is the best way to describe the process by which curriculum is built.

Rules for playing the curriculum game center on these pieces: legal constraints and administrative structure. Who is the decision maker in the school—the principal, the teacher, or some more remote body? How does the proposed curriculum fit with other curricula? Other pieces include teacher attitude and capacity, student interests, principles for sequencing activities, activities themselves, and the constraints of time and resources. Obviously, formulating purposes and anticipating possible outcomes are important pieces. Purves believes that the formulating of purposes might take place at the same time as the selection and arrangement of materials, just as evaluation can take place during the course of devising the curriculum or as the starting point.

Curriculum is like a board game. Just having the pieces does not mean that a person knows how to play the game. Some start with a sense of the overall look of the classroom either structured or open. Others begin with a view of how society should be. Purves says, "A number have started with evaluation and built a dog to fit the tail."[23] Some begin with standards and objectives and others with a set of materials or activities. Others start with a theory about subject matter.

Purves' rules indicate that a player may start with any piece, as long as all the pieces are picked up. His next rule is that all pieces must be perceived in some relationship to one another. Activities should relate to purposes and theories of learning. A final rule is that there are several ways to win the game. One way is to have all the pieces placed in some relationship to one another. Another way to win is to have the finished board approximate a model of rationality with standards and objectives determining learning activities, organization, and evaluation. A person can also win by showing that the intended outcomes were achieved by the learner; that is, if the learner achieves the stated purposes, no matter what else is learned, it is a winning curriculum. It is even possible to have a winning curriculum by virtue of the attractiveness of the materials or their modernity. Conflicting views of winning make curriculum one of the most controversial games in town.

There is some evidence that the curriculum development model influences what is taught. The effects of three models have been shown in creating a curriculum in mathematics: (1) a naturalistic model with an emphasis on subject matter as the principal source for deciding on purposes; (2) a deliberative model that stresses student concern and participation in planning as the basis for determining content; and (3) a situational approach that proceeds from needs in a real-life context and determines purposes and content from analysis of the qualifications required. The subject-centered approach results in a traditional subject matter structure; the student-centered approach results in a variety of activities and

---

[23] Alan C. Purves, "The Thought Fox and Curriculum Building," in *Strategies for Curriculum Development*, Jon Schaffarzick and David Hampson, eds. (Berkeley: McCutchan, 1975), 120.

in-depth development of content; and the situational approach favors prescriptive type applications.[24]

CONCLUDING COMMENTS

The needs assessment model for determining curriculum has been a popular means of curriculum making. It is seen as a way of restoring community confidence in the school and of advancing the interests of previously ignored groups when it allows clients to determine what they want to learn and not merely to select from a list of meaningless choices. It is closely associated with the adaptive and social reconstructionists' conception of curriculum but may also be used by those with other philosophical orientations.

As the name implies, the futuristic model emphasizes future conditions more than present status. It is a form of needs assessment in that future needs are anticipated. For this model, the curriculum maker decides what students should be like in light of some desirable future.

The vocational training model is most appropriate in institutions claiming to prepare students for jobs. Those using the model must be aware, however, that its use may tend to perpetuate the status quo.

Few models are as idealistic and comprehensive as the rational model. It is appealing because it gives attention to the interests of learner, society, and the fields of knowledge. In practice, however, curriculum makers often fail to respond equally to these interests. If specialization is accepted as the overriding function of a school program or course, the outlooks of subject matter specialists carry the most weight. Similarly, when those in an institution prize the general education function—that is, wanting to develop shared values and to make schooling relevant to social needs—they tend to respond to generalizations about society to the exclusion of other considerations.

Emergent approaches aim at raising consciousness. However, these approaches differ in what consciousness is to be raised. Social critics attack the technical efficiency model and the systemic curriculum produced by it and aim at arousing curriculum consciousness by revealing reductionism, simplistic solutions, hidden values, and ideologies of the technical model and its curriculum. Social reconstructionists focus on developing student consciousness of the deficiencies in the local community and the larger society with the aim of promoting political action. In their emergent approach, humanists regard curriculum as the process of bringing the students' private meanings and concerns into consciousness and using the social interactions and resources of the classroom to extend and share these meanings in a public way, and perhaps to transform persons in the process.

Curriculum purposes should not be narrowly conceived. A curriculum that is relevant to present and likely future conditions, to the concerns of the learners, and to a wide span of cultural resources is better than a curriculum that relies solely on tradition. The final acceptance of what is to be taught or learned is a value judgment. The decision to accept, however, should be influenced by evidence that shows that the purposes will be of value to the learner, that they are attainable, and that they probably will not be achieved without instruction.

To keep curriculum workers in touch with reality, it is important to admit that there will be disagreements on the proper base for assessing the worth of the curriculum and that political processes will be used for dealing with the value conflicts.

---

[24]Carl Frey, Alfons Frey, and Rolf Langeheime, "Do Curriculum Development Models Really Influence Curriculum?" *Journal of Curriculum Studies* 21, no. 6 (1989): 553–559.

QUESTIONS

1. Consider one of the following curriculum tasks, and indicate the model or approach you would take to determine purposes for the following endeavors:

   a. To generate a curricular vision for a school.

   b. To determine curriculum goals for a program in science, the arts, or health.

   c. To select purposes and content for a new course of instruction.

   Give reasons for your answer.

2. In using the needs assessment model, would you want the preferences of special groups—parents, teachers, students—to be given equal or weighted importance? Why or why not?

3. State an aim of importance to you, such as health, ecology, self-worth, or vocational skill. How would you refine this aim into an educational goal? What might be taught in order to help learners make progress toward this aim?

4. Read the following generalizations and then infer what should be taught in light of one or more of the generalizations.

   a. Students construe moral issues in terms of power relationships and physical consequences. They see morality as something outside their control.

   b. Adults are strangers who grant neither substance nor interest in one another and do not see a society larger than their private world.

   c. The cry for law and order is a fundamental demand for cognitive order, for normative clarity, and for predictability in human affairs.

   d. The average person will change jobs seven times and find work less a source of satisfaction than in previous years.

5. What do you believe is the function of the school? Is there something the school can do better than any other agency? Indicate how your answer might be used in deciding what and what not to teach.

6. How do you think the use of emergent models will impact our lives?

SUGGESTED STRATEGIC RESEARCH

EVALUATING GOALS IN DIVERGENT SCHOOLS

State action in setting curriculum goals may be crumbling in light of growing numbers of charter schools, homeschools, preschools, and sectarian schools. Are the local goals of these new forms of schooling more fulfilling than those mandated by the state?

DETERMINING VIABILITY OF PERFORMANCE STANDARDS AND BENCHMARKS

Curriculum objectives are not viable if teachers do not have sufficient time to teach for them. Replicate Kendall and Marzano's study[25] to determine if there is adequate time to address the prescribed standards and benchmarks for a classroom of interest to you.

JUDGING BALANCE IN CURRICULUM DECISIONS

Are school curriculum decisions more tied to economic development than to sensitive issues such as wealth distributions and the role of the United States in the world? Examine samples of frameworks, standards, textbooks, tests, or other artifacts associated with a program or course. Whose interests are best served?

---

[25]J. S. Kendall and R. J. Marzano, *Content Knowledge: A Compendium of Standards and Benchmarks for K–12 Education*, 3rd ed. (Alexandria, VA: Association for Supervision and Curriculum Development, 2000).

DETERMINING VALIDITY OF TEACHER ASSESSMENT OF ACHIEVEMENT

Ask teachers to select the girl and boy who are the best "readers" in the class, Compare the performance of the teacher-selected students with the performance of two randomly selected students.

COMPARING SCHOOL GOALS WITH WHAT STUDENTS DESIRE TO LEARN

Consider a familiar school or classroom. Examine the stated curriculum goals or content standards. Ask a sample of students for whom these goals are intended, "What would you like to know?" "Why?" How do the official goals compare with student-initiated goals in terms of their likely contribution to lifelong learning and ability to relate to others?

ASSESSING PROPOSED INTERNATIONAL CURRICULUM GOALS

The Consortium of Institutions for Development and Research in Education (cidree@s/o.nl) has proposed new outlooks for schools in European countries. The outlooks move away from reproducing knowledge and test scores and instead place learners and development in the central position. Communicate with CIDREE and find implications for curriculum development in the United States.

COMPARING CURRICULUM ORIENTATIONS AT STATE, DISTRICT, AND CLASSROOM LEVELS

Compare state frameworks and their standards in a subject area with samples of a teacher's lessons or instructional units. To what extent are the teacher's plans consistent with the standards given by policy makers?

SELECTED REFERENCES

DOYLE, WALTER. "Curriculum and Pedagogy," in *Handbook of Research on Curriculum*, Philip Tacker, ed. New York: Macmillan, 1992, 486–516.

McNEIL, JOHN D. *Curriculum: The Teacher's Initiative*. Englewood Cliffs, NJ: Prentice-Hall, 2002.

SEEL, NORBET, M., AND SANNE DIJKSTRA, EDS. *Curricula, Plans, and Processes in an Industrial Design: International Perspectives*. Mahwah, NJ: Lawrence Erlbaum, 2004.

CHAPTER 6

DEVELOPING AND SELECTING LEARNING OPPORTUNITIES

ONE OF the three purposes of this chapter is to critique the principles that guide development of classroom learning opportunities—that is, activities, experiences, lessons, and interactions between learners and conditions arranged by teachers. A second purpose is to describe how different conceptions of curriculum are enacted. An aperture to this chapter offers ways to use technology in the different curriculum orientations. The third purpose is to examine criteria used in selecting instructional materials such as textbooks, films, and software.

In contrast to the 1990s when teachers were expected to create rich and varied experiences tailored to students' strengths and interests, today's teachers are more often disenfranchised from curriculum development and required to use prespecified activities found in adopted textbooks and to follow officially approved standards for teaching. Although teachers draw on aspects of students' backgrounds, interests, and prior learning by teachers, these designs are valued by their contributions to official curriculum goals. Nonetheless, teacher creativity is required to make lessons effective and in many ways teachers and students enact their own curriculum.

Adaptation of instruction is best undertaken by teachers who are sensitive to learner responses and are able to learn from students and to vary instruction according to hypotheses about how learning takes place. In hundreds of ways, teachers modify curriculum for the needs of their classes—by preparing handouts, making arrangements for visiting speakers, creating learning games, designing learning packets, planning field trips, arranging original displays, suggesting individual studies, and posing novel questions. Teachers recognize the inadequacies of available instructional materials in matching the requirements for each child. It is as if textbooks, curriculum guides, and other instructional material developed by those outside the classroom are highways, which are satisfactory for general planning but from which the teacher must at times turn off and take a different route to provide something more appropriate for a learner or a group of learners. Usually the development and modification of curriculum by teachers are undertaken for the following reasons:

1. The individual learners require learning opportunities that are closer to their present background and level of attainment. Students may need explanations drawn from familiar instances or more simple or more advanced tasks than have been provided.

The development of a lesson in the language of a non-English-speaking child is one example.

2. The individual learners or their community have pressing questions or problems that lead to new activities and materials.

3. Teachers desire to provide opportunities that are motivating. Hence, they create learning opportunities in accordance with motivational principles such as the following:

   a. *Choice.* Learners choose from among activities. A range of opportunities is offered to accommodate the learner's purpose and mode of learning.

   b. *Utility.* Opportunities encourage learners to use what is learned in satisfying unmet physical and psychological needs and to satisfy motives such as curiosity, exploration, and manipulation.

   c. *Link to other values.* Opportunities place learners in contact with highly valued persons or activities.

   d. *Interests.* Opportunities are related to special interests of learners at hand.

   e. *Models.* Older peers, parents, and other significant persons are selected as exemplary models.

   f. *Success.* Adaptations in conventional materials are made in order to ensure success, including prompting, flexible standards, and provision for learners to recognize their own success.

4. Teachers' interests, capabilities, and style make departures from standard materials desirable or necessary.

STANDARDS FOR TEACHING IMPACT CLASSROOM CURRICULUM DEVELOPMENT

In addition to national, state, and district content standards, teachers are influenced in their planning by standards for the teaching profession. There are national standards for teachers promulgated by such organizations as the National Board for Professional Standards (NBPT), which certify experienced teachers as accomplished, and the National Council for the Accreditation of Teacher Education (NCATE), which affect practice by their evaluation formats. Also there is the Interstate New Teaching Assessment and Support Consortium (INTASC) which has moved states to develop tests of teacher proficiency. These new performance tests assess the ability of the novice to apply principles of cognitive constructivism. That is, does the teacher use *ideas* that students bring and strategies that challenge? Does the teacher give opportunities for learners to put forth and discuss diverse ideas and apply them in a range of contexts.[1]

Standards for teaching are aligned with new academic goals aimed at student understanding of concepts, higher order thinking, and transfer of knowledge. Table 6.1 illustrates how a state's standards for teaching affects the learning opportunities as perceived by students.

[1]Mark Windschitl, "Framing Constructivism in Practice as the Negotiation of Dilemmas: An Analysis of the Conceptual, Pedagogical, Cultural, and Political Challenge Facing Teachers," *Review of Educational Research* 72, no. 2 (2002): 133–175.

Table 6.1   Teaching Standards and Student Perceptions of Learning Opportunities

Standards	Perceptions
1. Making subjects comprehensible	"We start with a big and messy problem and everyone tries to solve it." "We look for different ways to solve a problem." "We explain our solutions." "We look for patterns and relationships."
2. Engaging students in learning	"Most problems are solved by us." "We know how to give and receive help." "Other students and the teacher really listen to me." "My classes make me question my own beliefs." "First, we work alone to have something to share and then we discuss and argue in small groups or with the whole class."
3. Designing learning experiences	"We choose, design, revise, carry out, and evaluate our projects." "We do projects that help our school and neighborhood." "We collect information and resources from the community." "Our projects connect math, science, language, and the arts."
4. Creating and maintaining effective learning environments	"We apply what we are learning to situations outside of school." "We seek new information to settle arguments." "Everyone expresses opinions and gives reasons." "I know when to give help and when I shouldn't."
5. Assessing learning	"I test myself to see if I really understand."

In evaluating the curriculum plans of teachers, standards-based assessors use the following criteria to identify those at accomplished levels:

- *Access to curriculum.* The plan gives opportunities for active involvement of all students and student processing what they have learned by summarizing, analyzing, and reflecting.

- *Instructional design.* Learning is scaffolded and extended in response to student needs, including new challenges. There is a balance between (a) a focus on the big ideas associated with the meaning and higher order thinking; and (b) anchoring activities that will put students in touch with substantive facts, procedures, and conventions. The design takes into account the diversity (cultural and psychological) represented in the class.

- *Engagement.* Proposed interactions deepen student thinking in contrast to carrying out formalistic recitations of questions and answers.

- *Assessment.* The plan shows how students will analyze their own work and the work of others. It indicates different ways students can show what they know and the depth of their understanding.

Teaching standards based on constructivist views of learning are controversial. Social reconstructionists fault the absence of critical discourse and actions in behalf of social justice. Humanists fear the standards are weakening the moral responsibilities of teachers and standardizing expectations for both teachers and students. Pseudoacademic and curriculum essentialists believe the new standards for teaching with their emphasis on projects and interdisciplinary inquiry fail to provide the breadth of information and skills necessary for understanding separate subjects. Those with a deregulatory or privatizing agenda oppose the professional standards for teachers because the standards are tied to educational programs and courses that are biased in favor of pedagogy and multiculturalism instead of viewing quality teaching as a product of subject matter knowledge and good verbal ability.

PRINCIPLES FOR DEVELOPING LEARNING OPPORTUNITIES

John Amos Comenius (1592–1670) was a prophet of modern curriculum principles who looked at nature for his guide to pedagogy. Among his principles were the following:

- Prepare the mind to receive new knowledge.
- Go from the general to the specific.
- Go from what is easy to the more difficult.
- Follow the natural development of the learner.
- Consider how the content will be used.[2]

In modern history of curriculum thought, Ralph Tyler proposed five general principles for developing learning experiences: (1) appropriate practice, (2) satisfaction, (3) success, (4) multiple approaches, and (5) multiple outcomes.[3]

Appropriate Practice Tyler viewed the principle of appropriate practice as a means–ends context in which objectives (ends) determine learning opportunities (means). Accordingly, this principle is commonly used by those with a systemic orientation. Learning opportunities give the student practice in what is called for by the objective. If the objective is to develop the skill of problem solving, students have opportunities to solve problems and not merely to watch how others solve problems.

The match between practice and the desired learning outcome varies. For an objective such as swimming, students should have practice in the water. Hands-on opportunities are important in the learning of procedural tasks; however, conceptual knowledge can be acquired without having the practice identical with the situation called for by the objective. In conceptual learning it is important that the practice situations (simulations, partials, imaginary and symbolic rehearsals) induce the mental representation of the desired concepts and relationships. It is effective to give students practice with artificial tasks that have no surface resemblance to real-world tasks but direct students' attention to difficult and crucial aspects of the real-world task.[4] With the use of computers, more learning opportunities free mental resources (memory) that would otherwise be involved in noncrucial tasks.

The means–ends view of planning dominates the systemic curriculum and is a common fixture in teachers' lesson plans. However, among many humanistic and new academic teachers, there are those who put means ahead of ends by not specifying their objectives or goals in advance but providing exploratory activities from which students find the content and tools that will be useful as they take on tasks and questions of their own choosing.

[2]John Amos Comenius, *The Great Didactic*, trans. M. W. Keatinge (London: Adam and Charles Black, 1896), 279.
[3]Ralph W. Tyler, *Basic Principles of Curriculum and Instruction* (Chicago: University of Chicago Press, 1949).
[4]Henry Halff et al., "Cognitive Science and Military Training," *American Psychologist* 41, no. 10 (October 1986): 1131–1139.

Satisfaction According to the principle of satisfaction, the learning opportunity should be satisfying to learners. As indicated in Chapter 1, cognitive abilities do not guarantee success. A person must like what he or she is good at. Unless students enjoy the process, they will not cross unexplored frontiers. Satisfactions are derived from several sources. The research on flow experience suggests the importance of activities that offer continuous challenge, social approval, and the meeting of physical needs; and success itself contributes to satisfaction. For younger and many older *persons, physical manipulation*—that is, activities that allow for making things go, pushing buttons, constructing something, or handling objects—is satisfying. Also satisfying is *incongruity*—that is, the exposure to novel and puzzling situations, to events that are inconsistent and incompatible. An illustration comes to mind: that of Robert Prigo, an expert physics teacher, lowering his body onto a bed of nails, with an assistant placing a second board spiked with nails on Prigo's chest, putting a cinder block on top of that, and, to the crescendo of death scene music, bringing down a sledge hammer that shatters the block, after which Prigo gets up smiling. Prigo first captures student interest before embarking them on pursuit of the theories behind the demonstrations.

Interacting with *significant others* such as parents and friends is often satisfying. *Confluence*—that is, activities that combine thinking, feeling, and physical movement—are generally well received.

Not everyone is satisfied by the same activity. Hence, there are attempts to adapt learning activities to learning styles. Learning styles may have different dimensions. The cognitive dimension refers to different ways in which students mentally perceive and order information; the affective dimension is the effect that students' social and emotional responses have on their learning; the physiological dimension indicates such elements as auditory, visual, or tactile preference for learning, and how the learner is affected by light, temperature, and room design; and the psychological dimension involves inner strengths such as self-esteem of the student.

A current concern of teachers is that some students are oriented more toward performance—wanting to finish quickly and accurately for a good grade rather than oriented toward learning and gaining understanding of a task domain. We are not sure that these orientations are stable by personality or modifiable by changing classroom conditions.

Teachers also are aware of the cognitive development of their learners believing that those with low development do better with close guidance, such as direct teaching lessons; while students of high cognitive ability learn more effectively when free to explore and receive abstract hints from the teacher or others.[5]

Success The principle of success requires deciding whether the learning activity is within the range of possibility for the student. The student's background experience is the best predictor of success: what the student already knows determines what will be learned from the activity. Hence, teachers design activities that link new content to the student's prior experiences and teach prerequisites to critical tasks.

The theory of Vygotsky—what students can do today with parent or teacher, they can do alone tomorrow—is also applied.[6] First the teacher or peer models or guides the student's activity; later, the responsibility is shared by teacher and students, and finally the student has full responsibility. A successful experience may not be easy. Indeed, difficult and confusing tasks are best for successful understanding.

Sheila Tobias, an expert in mathematics anxiety, has devised a method of analyzing the teaching of mathematics and science for the purpose of identifying what makes these

[5] Vincent Aleven et al., "Help Seeking and Help Design in Interactive Learning Environments," *Review of Educational Research* 73, no. 3 (fall 2003): 277–320.
[6] L. S. Vygotsky, *The Development of Higher Psychological Processes* (Cambridge: Harvard University Press, 1979).

subjects hard. Her findings were the following: (1) The students lacked a framework and prior knowledge. As one student said, "I had no way of telling what was important and what was not." (2) Demonstrations often led to confusion instead of clarification. "I could follow what was described but I could not grasp what was actually happening in what was described." (3) Lectures moved along preordained tracks, making it difficult for students to slow down the train. (4) Students needed more time to think about ideas. (5) Words that were used caused confusion. To the teacher, zero is in the middle of plus and minus; to the student it meant absence or void. (6) Students were interested in *why* questions; the teacher in *how* questions.[7]

In addition to learning style, status variables, including sex, race, and socioeconomic factors, are sometimes considered in planning for success. However, Thomas Good and Deborah Stipek's review of the literature on individual differences in the classroom concludes that status variables do not provide a systematic basis for planning instruction.[8] The idea that all girls and boys need a particular level of learning opportunity is likely to be incorrect at least 60% of the time. Similarly, the problem of matching activities to high and low ability students is considerable. In classes of students of unequal ability, the outcomes are determined only in part by ability; the teacher and student expectations for success, effort, and other factors are as important in the selection of content and its organization.

Multiple Approaches   Many different activities can be used to attain the same purpose. I have found that when teachers are given the same objective, each teacher develops a unique approach for achieving the objective. One of the most rewarding aspects of teaching is the creativity that is possible. Nevertheless, studies indicate that teachers tend to rely on textbooks and paper and pencil activities, rather than activity centers, projects, simulations, debates, dramas, investigations, media, and meditation. One reason for teachers failing to adopt social construction of knowledge is that they are wedded to traditional activities and materials based on behavioral psychology. Also, teachers stress linguistic and logical mathematical activities rather than musical, spatial kinesthetic, interpersonal, and intrapersonal activities. Although several reasons for the lack of rich and engaging activities are possible, McNeil attributes minimal effort to the organizational context of the school in which school administrators emphasize order and student discipline (conduct) rather than valuing student creation of knowledge or supporting teaching and learning.[9]

Multiple Outcomes   In one sense there will always be multiple outcomes from a learning activity because each student interprets and applies ideas from the classroom in his or her own way, depending on prior experience. In another sense, it is economical to arrange learning activities that are likely to contribute to multiple desirable outcomes. A curriculum that provides a study of a historical event in the context of geography, writing, critical thinking, literature, and the like offers an increased possibility of maximizing outcomes.

LEARNING OPPORTUNITIES FOR HIGHER ORDER THINKING

In view of the current clamor for teaching higher order thinking to all students, a review of conditions appropriate to these ends is appropriate. John Goodlad has suggested that a significant change in instructional time allotted to various learning activities must take

---

[7]Sheila Tobias, "Insiders and Outsiders," *Academic Connection* (winter 1978): 1–4.

[8]Thomas L. Good and Deborah J. Stipek, "Individual Differences in the Classroom: A Psychological Perspective," in *Individual Differences and the Common Curriculum*, Gary D. Fenstermacher and John I. Goodlad, eds., NSSE Yearbook (Chicago: University of Chicago Press, 1983), 9–37.

[9]Linda McNeil, *Contradictions of Control: School Structure and School Knowledge* (London: Routledge and Kegan Paul, 1987).

place if improvements in problem solving and creativity are to occur. He recommends that instead of the current norm of 70% of instruction being aimed at declarative and procedural levels of learning, 70% should be given to learning opportunities that involve higher order thinking processes.[10]

Walter Doyle defines higher level academic tasks as tasks that require understanding rather than memory, routine, or opinion tasks.[11] Understanding tasks are often not reduced to a predictable algorithm. For example, writing a descriptive paragraph is not simply following steps but using complex procedures and a high-level executive process to generate a product. The student must understand not only the procedures but why they work and where they apply.

In Chapter 11, we ask questions about the best ways to teach thinking, such as "Is it better to develop within or without a domain of conventional subject matter?" At present, we will consider general guidelines for developing learning activities for problem solving and creative thinking, emphasizing processes for generating meaning rather than routine skills. We also attend to the conditions of learning that are necessary if student beliefs are to change in more fruitful directions.

Transfer and Problem Solving

Transfer occurs whenever a previous learning influences what is learned in a different situation. In order to promote wide transfer, teachers focus on abstract general principles and consider when the principles do or do not apply. Also students see how a principle or concept is represented in many contexts and how it is illustrated in varied formats, such as tables, stories, and pictures. An appropriate activity involves students looking for analogies that may or may not be useful.

It is important to emphasize that transfer and long-term retention are enhanced by learning conditions that introduce difficulties in learning initially and even impair performance during training. This finding runs counter to the commonplace belief that successful performance during training is a reliable index of learning. In fact, errors and mistakes during instruction are essential in promoting transfer.[12] Meaning (the formation of schemata) is the key to problem solving, including the ability to learn a new task. In addressing problems for which a solution is not readily available, students relate various facts and ideas. Without the conceptual structure (schemata) with which to analyze the problem and to deal with its various elements, students will not have success. Hence, the teaching of problem solving centers not only on practice in using basic concepts and schemata for viewing specific phenomena so that students acquire the mechanisms for analyzing the facts and conditions that must be considered but also on ways to activate relevant analogies. Persons who fail at a problem often say they could have been more successful if they had taken more time to sort out its crucial elements before adopting a strategy.

Problem solving also depends on combining knowledge with metacognitive strategies such as having a plan, identifying subproblems, and examining alternative solutions (brainstorming). Students should have learning opportunities that feature generalized procedures for problem solving in situations in which the problems are not clearly stated, all the needed information is not available, and no algorithm or simple correct answer exists. Nevertheless, the acquisition of problem-solving procedures for a specific domain may be more useful than generalized procedures.

---

[10]John I. Goodlad, *A Place Called the Classroom* (San Francisco: Freeman, 1984).
[11]Walter Doyle, "Academic Work," *Review of Educational Research* 53, no. 2 (summer 1983): 159–201.
[12]Robert J. Bjork, "On the Challenge of Becoming Metacognitively Sophisticated as a Learner and Teacher," address, UCLA Department of Psychology, winter 2004.

Joseph Agassi's approach to teaching problem solving aims at guiding the natural activity of students seeking knowledge for themselves.[13] Hence, the problem is always based on a student's interest and desire for knowledge. In order to articulate the problem, the activity begins with the expression of discomfort or interest of the student. Analysis of the initial statement of interest helps make explicit the knowledge from the student's perspective. The awareness of a limitation may form the starting point for the development of a problem.

Agassi's approach to problem solving has two great strengths: (1) it is unlikely that a problem will be formulated that is beyond the range of the student's abilities or stage of development and (2) the problem will not be trivial because the student explains its importance so that an answer can be pursued. The student adopts prima facie explanations of how the solution may be pursued and may change the plan as the project goes along. If the plan breaks down, the student should be able to reformulate a clear and specific problem and a plan for solving it.

Similar approaches are found in *strategic teaching,* which aims at student construction of meaning by learning activities that take into account background knowledge, organizing patterns, and metacognitive strategies.[14] Strategic teaching begins with something that activates students' prior knowledge, so that students articulate how they think about a problem. Later, they are helped to confront inconsistencies or contradictions between their assumptions and the phenomena. After students perceive gaps, there are opportunities to reconstruct new meanings and to acquire alternative conceptions. By way of illustration, students count the number of grid sequences touched by the diagonal of each of several rectangles they have drawn on squared paper, attempting to see how that number relates to the dimensions of the rectangle. Students then debate what is to count as "touching" a grid square. Discussions of students' findings are followed by writing an account of the investigation, indicating whether they have reached a firm "result."

Some clue to the development of problem solving comes from studies of experts who (1) describe a problem in detail before attempting a solution, (2) determine what relevant information should go with the analysis of the problem, and (3) decide which procedures can be used to generate a problem description and analysis.[15] Experts tend to look for patterns or principles that are applicable while novices attend to surface features.

Creativity

As with problem solving, creativity can be enhanced not only by knowing much about the area in which a person is creative but by encouraging the transfer of training from one subject to another, the search for common principles, the stressing of analogies, similes, and metaphors, and the seeing of symbolic equivalents in the highest possible number of sensory images and modalities such as imaginative play. Obviously, creativity can be nurtured in other ways: by granting student autonomy, by avoiding criticism and rejection, and by encouraging students to solve problems for themselves.

Some view creativity as innate ability, although not all creative people are alike. Dean Keith Simanton differentiates between (a) functional creativity where a person engages in everyday problem solving and has the ability to adapt to change and (b) original creativity

[13]John Wellersten, "On the Unification of Psychology, Methodology and Pedagogy," *Interchange* 18, no. 4 (1987):1–14.

[14]Beau Fly Jones et al., *Strategic Teaching and Learning: Cognitive Instruction in the Content Areas* (Alexandria, VA: Association for Supervision and Curriculum Development, 1987).

[15]*How People Learn: Brain, Mind, Experience, and School,* John D. Bransford et al., eds. (Washington, DC: National Research Council, National Academy Press, 2000).

or coming up with something that hasn't been done before and that has an impact on how other people think, feel, and live their lives.[16]

Richard Sternberg regards creativity as a decision that people can make if they have the courage to go their own way—defining problems in unique ways, analyzing their own education so as to discard what does not work, persuading others to accept initially rejected ideas, overcoming difficult obstacles placed in their path, and recognizing that better ideas will eventually replace theirs.[17]

Can you teach children to be creative? The late E. Paul Torrance analyzed the results of 142 studies in the literature of the effects of attempts to teach creative thinking skills. The overall percentage of successes was 72%.[18] Some teachers believe that creative skills should be taught directly in courses that are separate from the rest of the curriculum. Edward de Bono, for example, has developed a set of independent materials aimed at helping students deal with novelty.[19] De Bono poses incomplete problems and encourages students to list the positive, negative, and interesting features of each alternative solution, getting them to see both familiar and unfamiliar problems in novel ways. On the other hand, Vera John-Steiner has uncovered clues to the nurturing of creative minds that can be an integral part of any curriculum.[20] She interviewed more than 100 creative men and women and sifted through the personal papers of distinguished artists and scientists, showing that these persons drew heavily from childhood play—the delight in nature, devices, and books.

Children everywhere have a drive to know, to wonder, and to invent. However, as they grow older, they lose their skill to dip into their own stores of pleasure and fantasy. The sense of wonder in early experience is kept alive only with the help of a caring and knowledgeable adult. Most great contributors single out a parent, teacher, or mentor (living or distant) who helped them have a dialogue across generations as they absorbed the values of their society and made their own fresh discourse, going from the known to the new, from immersion to exploration. A key to their creativity was a sustained concern about something. They recalled their engagement with play, ideas, and the world while they were young. Their childhood preoccupation with ideas, images, and questions gave intensity to their mental life. In Einstein's case, the questions he asked about space and time reached back to his early years and were childlike in their simplicity, but the answers were wrought through his concentration.

Suggestions for learning opportunities aimed at creativity focus on creating a climate for incubation and the freeing of that mind of influence that inhibits discovery. Teachers should treat students' imaginative ideas with respect and show the students that these ideas have value. An attitude of playfulness rather than evaluation is helpful as is a class in which there is freedom from time pressure.

Creating New Knowledge

Although knowledge has traditionally been regarded as beliefs publicly justified by authorities, it may also include the beliefs held by an individual who can convince others of their validity. In a general sense, all learning opportunities are intended to change or extend the beliefs held by the student. However, instead of telling students that their beliefs are

---

[16]Karen Kersting, "What Exactly Is Creativity?" *Monitor on Psychology* (Nov. 2003): 40–41.

[17]R. J. Sternberg, "Creativity Is a Decision," in A. L. Costa, ed., *Teaching for Intelligence II* (Arlington Heights, IL: Skylight Training and Publishing, 2000): 85–106.

[18]E. Paul Torrance, "Can We Teach Children to Think Creatively?" *Journal of Creative Behavior* 6 (1972): 114–143.

[19]Edward de Bono, "The Direct Teaching of Thinking as a Skill," *Phi Delta Kappan* 64 (1973): 703–708.

[20]Vera John-Steiner, *Notebooks of the Mind* (Albuquerque: University of New Mexico Press, 1985).

wrong and presenting them with what authorities know to be true, more teachers now arrange situations where students reveal what is in their heads and weigh new information against their present views, working through discrepancies with others and coming to a new understanding.

Increasingly, students are afforded opportunities to explore phenomena and ideas, make conjectures, share hypotheses with others, and revise their original thinking. The assumption underlying this trend to constructivism is that you can tell students all sorts of things, but you cannot make them believe it unless they construct it for themselves. Of course, students can parrot a correct response to an exam question or show that they understand new ideas very well, but they are unlikely to act on the information or belief if it conflicts with their current beliefs.

Psychologists have questions about how belief is related to knowledge and change.[21] Among these questions are those whose answers hold implications for learning opportunities.

- If one teacher believes that knowledge is certain as given by authorities and another teacher assumes knowledge to be temporarily uncertain and to be challenged by convincing evidence, how will learning opportunities in their classrooms differ?

- If a student who believes that knowledge must be handed down from authorities is a member of a class where peers argue and quiz each other, will the student change the beliefs of the peers or abandon the peers or will the peers change the student's beliefs?

- If students are predisposed to demand evidence and apply logic in familiar situations but not so in school contexts, how can teachers get students to transfer their out-of-school critical predisposition to the classroom learning of subject matter?

One of the most comprehensive reviews of how individuals respond to conflicting ideas and the factors that impel them to change to a new belief is that of Clark Chinn and William Brewer.[22] These authors describe what students do when they confront data that contradict their beliefs and change their thinking. When presented with information or data that differs from their own beliefs, students must answer three questions: (1) Is the information believable? (2) How can this information be explained? (3) How will my present views have to change in order to agree with the information? Table 6.2 shows seven ways in which learners respond to ideas that conflict with those they hold.

Table 6.2 Accounting for Responses to Contradictory Ideas

Factors Influencing the Responses	Responses to Contradictory Ideas
Do I believe the information?	
No	Ignore, reject, exclude
Yes	Hold in abeyance, reinterpret, make slight change, change belief
Can I explain the information?	
No	Ignore, exclude, hold in abeyance
Yes	Reject, reinterpret, make slight change, change belief
Should I change my belief?	
No	Ignore, reject, exclude, hold in abeyance, reinterpret
Yes	Make slight change, change belief

[21]Barbara Hofer, ed., "Personal Approaches to Understanding Students' Beliefs About Knowledge and Knowing," *Educational Psychologist,* special edition 39, no. 1 (winter 2000).

[22]Clark A. Chinn and William F. Brewer, "The Role of Anomalous Data in Knowledge Acquisition: A Theoretical Framework and Implications for Science Instruction," Review of Educational Research 63, no. 1 (Spring 1993): 1–49.

A number of conditions influence how individuals respond to conflicting ideas: prior knowledge, having an alternative explanation, the quality of the new information, and how carefully they attend to the contradictory information.

If a learner's prior knowledge includes an entrenched belief that satisfies personal or social goals, the belief will be difficult to change. Instead the person will reject, exclude, or reinterpret the idea, or hold the new idea in abeyance. Without a good explanation for the new finding, learners probably will not accept it. Accuracy, consistency, wide application, and simplicity (ability to understand the idea) are among the qualities of good explanation. Nevertheless, learners sometimes adopt a new idea without fully comprehending it. Information that is credible will not be rejected, but it may be excluded, reinterpreted, or effect a minor change in the learner's views. Credibility can be enhanced by using an expert's opinion, making an unbiased presentation, appealing to accepted ways of collecting and analyzing the data, replication, and allowing students to directly observe experiments. Of course, if the information agrees with what a person already believes, it will be regarded as credible. Reinterpretation is more likely when the information is ambiguous. Ambiguous information allows learners to reinterpret it so that it is consistent with the currently held framework. A key factor affecting responses to new information is involvement in the issues, including thorough examination of the contradictory arguments and attempts at justifying their opinions and reasoning to other people.

Teachers can help students create new knowledge by (1) arranging opportunities that will reveal why the beliefs of students are entrenched; (2) promoting enculturation whereby students regularly debate alternative views, discuss responses, and evaluate evidence; and (3) helping students see that knowledge is not a static condition but a process of change. Examples are teachers who introduce unresolved issues and problems and let students develop their explanations without telling them what experts believe or they might engage students in considering which competing idea is better supported. Of course, teachers must not overlook the importance of helping students construct needed background knowledge regarding an issue or problem and illustrating some of the techniques for studying it.

Students are more likely to change their beliefs if alternative beliefs and ideas are available. When unguided discovery is unfruitful, an alternative idea can be presented to those who do not discover it on their own.

The use of analogies, models, examples, and the examination of real data may help students understand the alternative view. Discussion of what should count as credible information is highly recommended. So, too, is the appeal to real-world data that students already know about but might not realize are relevant.

Similarly, issue involvement is promoted by having students explain their everyday experiences and attempt to justify their thinking. The typical model for activities that effect conceptual change begins with a problem or situation where the outcome is not yet known. Students next predict the outcome or propose solutions. In small groups, they advance different explanations and later evaluate their competing ideas, considering conflicting views in light of personal experiences. At the same time, students refine their understanding and indicate how they have changed their beliefs to fit new ideas.

PROCEDURES FOR DEVELOPING LEARNING ACTIVITIES

Selecting learning opportunities is not the same as developing them. Some persons can apply criteria in deciding among various textbooks and other materials but are not able or willing to produce them. The ability to carry out opportunities in the interactive phase with learners calls for additional skills. Development is a creative art and allows for personal expression of the developer's values and style. As indicated in Part 1 of this book, techniques of development can be categorized by the major categories of curriculum.

Current Orientations in Developing Learning Activities

Humanistic Guidelines   The humanistic curriculum had its roots in both the individual humanism of the Renaissance with its stress on personal culture, individual freedom, and development as the best way toward a full and rich life, and the naturalism of the eighteenth century which was a revolt against the cold aristocracy of intellect. The naturalists worshiped feelings and regarded education not as a preparation for life but as life itself. They believed that the activities which spring naturally from the interests of the pupils, from the needs of life, should make up the curriculum.

In contrast to other curriculum orientations, learning opportunities in the humanistic curriculum are not planned in the framework of a means–ends continuum. Indeed, many humanistic educators believe that *after* an opportunity has been experienced, purposes may be generated. Students may themselves establish plans for reaching a distant goal and have wide freedom in following their own routing. How then does one create a more humanistic experience? The answers from the neohumanists fall into three categories:

1. *Emphasize teaching as transformation of the student, not teaching as transmitting subject matter*. Instructional plans, textbooks, courses of study, and other artifacts designed to shape learners in specified ways all are seen as less important than interaction with the student. Interpersonal associations experienced with a teacher influence the student's growth. Humanists give more attention to method and the interactive phases of instruction than on advanced planning. Indeed, the planning of opportunities, activities, and experiences should be a cooperative process by students and teacher in which the student's own purposes are respected.

   This emphasis takes many directions. It may mean that the teacher prepares by developing procedures of reflective teaching, group dynamics, and sensitivity-training methods that may be of value in releasing the creative capacity of learners. It may mean that teachers anticipate what they will bring to students by "knowing" themselves. They try to recognize their prejudices, biases, fears, loves, strengths, and other attributes that bear on the ability to care, feel, and relate to students. As indicated in Chapter 1, the use of theater, autobiography, and reader response activities as a way for students to understand themselves is promoted.

2. *Create an environment that does not impede natural growth*. The most general guide to developing learning opportunities is focused on the conditions of learning. On the positive side, creating good conditions for learning includes attending to conditions such as the characteristics, interests, and growth patterns of each student; the richness of the environment; opportunities that stress wholeness and putting all senses to work; opportunities to wonder and be puzzled; and opportunities for the learner to feel independent by facing problems alone.

   On the negative side, some warn that such an environment implies that learners do not have to meet standards beyond their abilities, endure great tension, face destructive criticism, think in terms of previous solutions to problems, conform to tradition, regard achievement as the production of a similar rather than a unique product, and be denied choices.

3. *Arrange situations in which learners determine what they will learn*. The teacher as arranger considers physical conditions, including safe facilities as well as natural objects of beauty, and uses those from which the learner can benefit. The cultural environment, too, is a responsibility of the humanistic teacher. Cultural excellence in music, painting, and literature, and scientific equipment, musical instruments, and art supplies may constitute an invitation to learning. Arrangement of the social environment also may be planned. Association with others in a variety of shared

enterprises may permit self-activated students to respond and, through their own urge toward self-realization, bring the learning process to fulfillment.

Social Reconstructionist Guidelines The social reconstructionist wants learners to use knowledge and intelligence to help improve the quality of public decision that determines the conditions under which they live. Hence, student learning activities combine knowledge and action in effecting change in the community. The following are 10 key steps in the processes of developing a learning opportunity:

1. *Select an idea for a learning opportunity.* The developer might reflect on a topic or problem such as public opinion, elections, media, or conservation, which makes sense to the students and is related to school and course goals. Issues and problems in the community are among the best sources of ideas for learning opportunities. Persistent struggles and value premises also suggest areas for learning. A topic to consider may be apathy toward general welfare or the importance of keeping informed on public issues and informing others.

2. *Explore the idea.* The question to ask here is "What can students do about the issue or problem besides studying about it?" A learning opportunity for the reconstructionist requires that students take responsible action, whether working with community groups, providing information, or taking a stand on issues. Students may provide information to persons about a public issue, try to influence them to a point of view, serve the community, or work with and as adult citizens.

3. *Plan for action.* Surveys, field trips, and interviews are not what the reconstructionist means by action. Although these activities may contribute to the action phase, they do not constitute *taking action* in a political sense. Because the essence of the civic act is carrying knowledge into action, a student activity that omits persuasion, decision making, and so forth, is not viewed as satisfactory. Planning means thinking of the action or project desired—for example, organizing a public forum and indicating how students will carry it out.

4. *Test the idea or project for realness.* Students can perform real work in the community—for example, helping persons to get out to vote, campaigning for a candidate, talking on issues. Mock trials, mayor for a day, reading, and taking straw votes are not real to the reconstructionist; they are role playing. To the reconstructionist, action must promise to contribute to the solution of the situation and be seen by students as important.

5. *Specify the educational purposes that will also be served by the project.* The purposes might stress competencies such as persuasion, obtaining information, arriving at valid conclusions, predispositions toward recognition of others, acceptance of responsibility, and critical awareness of how institutions serve particular interests and disadvantage others.

6. *Limit the scope of the learning opportunity.* The project must be subject to reasonable limits of time and effort. Enough time must be allowed for students to complete the action phase. For most effective results, the project should be focused. One idea is to plan the project around the action of the city council on a particular issue rather than around a broad interest such as government. Include only those activities necessary to achieve the goals of the plan. Decide on the termination date at the outset and keep it in mind daily. The sixth consideration is met when teaching has limited student actions to a specific job, enumerated the students' tasks, and justified the time needed for completing the project.

7. *Involve others in the project.* Involve the school administrator and other persons in the community whose help is desirable.

8. *List the sources of first-hand information needed.* Consider interviews, polls, the Internet, surveys, films, and visits.

9. *Select study materials.* Collect textbooks, pamphlets, films, and other materials on the subject matter of the project that are pertinent to the educational purposes.

10. *Plan for evaluation.* Design an evaluation plan to determine what gains and losses accrue as a result of the project.

Systemic Guidelines The systemic product development procedures were delineated in Chapter 3. Although some in the systemic camp are adapting conceptual approaches to instruction, particularly in efforts to connect ideas within a subject matter and incorporate them into the learner's existing knowledge structure, the prevailing guidelines used by planners of the accountability movement, the military, and other institutions that want to impose uniformity into the curriculum continue to employ the following procedures.[23]

1. *Specify what is to be learned.* Content, standards, and performance guide development. The standards must be specific enough to remove ambiguity about what the learner is expected to know and do in particular situations or classes of situations. A posttest or other procedure for indicating achievement of the desired terminal behavior is often created in order to further designate all dimensions of the learning task.

2. *Make a task analysis.* An effort is made to list all prerequisite skills and knowledge believed necessary before learners can perform in accordance with the standards. After this list is prepared, the developer must indicate which of these prerequisites will be taught in the learning opportunity and which will be considered "entry behaviors" (requirements that the learner is expected to demonstrate on entrance to the learning opportunity).

3. *Specify the intended population.* At this point, an idea of the anticipated learner can be gained. In addition to entry skills, characteristics such as cultural differences, learning styles, personality, and interests are used to guide the developers.

4. *Formulate rules for development of the materials, activity, or product.* The following questions give direction to the developer and determine the characteristics of the learning program or activity:
   a. Concept presentation. Will the concept be taught by means of examples leading to a generalization (inductive), or will a generalization be given followed by examples (deductive)?
   b. Response mode. Will the learner be actively involved in speaking, writing, and touching? In addition to overt responding, are there anticipated covert responses? How often will learners be expected to respond overtly?
   c. Elicitation of correct responses. How can learners be helped to make a correct response and learn? Can all answers be confirmed as right or wrong? Can they be confirmed with reiteration of the reasons for correctness? How? Can the learner be prompted to make the right answer by hints, as through visual cues, questions, metaphors, and other verbal means?
   d. Learning sequences. How will en route objectives be ordered and reviewed? Will all learners be required to follow the same order? Will there be provision for "branching" (a point of choice at which students are sent to alternative material depending on their prior responses)?

---

[23]William E. Monague and John A. Ellis, "U.S. Military Developments in Instructional Technology," *Instructional Science* 21, no. 4 (1993): 223–240.

Early use of the computer featured computer-assisted instruction (CAI), a technological approach to curriculum in which the designer focused on specific objectives, made a task analysis of en route objectives, and then decided on a presentation strategy.

Academicians' Guidelines for Instructional Materials   To the academician, learning opportunities are chiefly inquiries, problems, and investigations demanding the collecting and analyzing of data. The Internet, textbooks, videos, teachers' guides, and laboratory apparatus are resources. These resources include tools for conveying the authenticity of content and method of given subject fields. Organizing centers for the courses are the questions or problems that will guide the class in its activities over an extended period.

The following criteria are used in the selecting of centers:

1. Do the centers stress major achievements, that is, powerful ideas? Do they show ways in which the ideas were conceived and sometimes improved on? Do they show how the ideas are interrelated?

2. Is the center appropriately ordered? Usually this answer rests on an assumed principle of dependency in which the basic concepts are given so that the student can have the understanding necessary for further study. The presentation is through general concepts rather than specific definitions so that the students make some contact with the subject matter they will deal with later in greater depth.

3. Consider specific instructional content and ideas. The content often includes methods that help students interpret data, examples that lead to important generalizations, background information that encourages generalizations, opportunities that lead students to apply generalizations, demonstrations that show the limits of the generalizations, and lists of useful materials such as maps, apparatus, and collections that might be used.

4. Choose teaching strategies. Unlike the system designers, academicians do not specify in detail the methods teachers are to follow; each teacher adapts the material to his or her methods. Academicians, however, prize one method of choice, learning how to inquire by doing it. Hence, they not only suggest different ways for students to discover important principles, they also model thinking and behavior. Furthermore, they preface the experimental and theoretical problems presented to students with a variety of possible solutions. However, the communication of method has turned out to be one of the weakest aspects of the academic curriculum. Teachers who have never themselves developed skill in scientific reasoning and problem solving have difficulty teaching methods of inquiry to others. Also, each teacher may have a favorite method and is likely to stress ideas and concepts different from those of other teachers, filtering the materials through their own perceptions.

Increasingly, constructivist views of learning have influenced the academic approach to learning opportunities. Accordingly, teachers aim to foster students' construction of powerful ideas in an academic field which took the community of scholars many years to develop. Constructivists believe that they can provide a structure and a set of plans that will support the development of informed exploration and reflective inquiry without taking control away from the student. The learning opportunity (project or task) must stimulate students to ask questions, pose problems, and set goals.

One of the best examples of a learning opportunity from the constructivist viewpoint is Marilyn Burns's *Math by All Means,* a multiplication unit for grade 3.[24] This unit offers a model for math instruction, allowing students to recognize the variety of situations that call for multiplication, to identify appropriate procedures for carrying out needed calculations,

[24]Marilyn Burns, *Math by All Means* (New Rochelle, NY: Cuisenaire Company, 1992).

to evaluate the reasonableness and accuracy of solutions, and to apply results in real-life situations. The unit integrates ideas from geometry, statistics, probability, and patterns and functions. Lessons in the unit engage the children in thinking, creating their own theories, investigating patterns, inventing and justifying solutions, and listening to the perspectives of others.

CRITERIA FOR SELECTING LEARNING ACTIVITIES

Different criteria are used for guiding and justifying the selection of learning activities: philosophical, psychological, political, and practical. The latest is the scientific or evidence-based criterion. Each curriculum orientation tends to place priority on different criteria. Humanists, for example, are more interested in the inherent qualities of a learning activity than in data indicating that the activity has had an effect in some specific but limited way. Learning activities are judged as good or bad when they meet our value expectations or philosophical assumptions. If a person holds human variability to be of great worth, then he or she will favor activities that advance learner variability rather than activities that stress common outlooks and capacities. Learning activities are also judged in accordance with psychological criteria. Those who have different viewpoints on whether learning should be painful or pleasant have different viewpoints on their assessments of learning opportunities. Those with a systemic orientation put foremost scientifically based evidence that the opportunity "works," that is, it causes achievement as measured by test scores.

Philosophical Criteria

Values are the chief basis for judging proposed learning activities and materials. Typically, these value positions parallel curriculum conceptions as illustrated in Table 6.3.

Psychological Criteria

Psychological beliefs about how learning best takes place often determine the acceptability of a learning activity. However, not all people agree on the specific learning principles to use. Some examples of conflicts are shown in Table 6.4.

Table 6.3   Curriculum Maker's Dilemma

Learning Activities Should...	But They Also Should...
Be immediately enjoyable.	Lead to desirable future experiences.
Show the ideal: the just, beautiful, and honorable.	Show life as it is, including corruption, violence, and profanity.
Treat the thought and behavior of the group to which the learner belongs.	Treat the thought and behavior of the groups other than those to which the learner belongs.
Increase variability by stressing individuality.	Minimize human variability by stressing common outlooks and capacities.
Stress cooperation so that individuals share in achieving a common goal.	Stress competition so that the able person excels as an individual.
Allow students to clarify their own positions on moral and controversial issues.	Instruct students in the values of moral and intellectual integrity rather than allowing students to engage in sophistry and personal indulgence.

Table 6.4   Conflicting Views of How to Enhance Learning

Closed View: Learning Activities Should...	Open View: Learning Activities Should...
Be under the direct influence of the teacher who demonstrates what is to be perceived so that the learner imitates and acquires.	Be removed from direct teacher influence, allowing self-actualization by finding meaning in a situation where the teacher is a resource person.
Be pleasant and comfortable for the student.	Allow for hardship and perplexity so that significant growth can take place.
Teach one thing at a time but teach it to mastery, simplifying the environment and giving enough instances to help the learner abstract desired generalizations.	Bring about several outcomes at once, helping students develop interests and attitudes as well as cognitive growth.
Allow the learner to acquire simple basic patterns before being exposed to higher orders of learning.	Allow the learner to grasp the meaning and organization of the whole before proceeding to study the parts.
Allow the learner to see and emulate the best models of talking, feeling, and acting.	Allow the learner to create and practice new and different ways of talking, feeling, and acting.
Feature repetitive practice on a skill not mastered. Do not let the learner practice error.	Feature novel and varied approaches to an unlearned skill. Recognize that learners can learn from error.

Behaviorists judge learning activities on the basis of whether they minimize errors by prompting and reinforcing correct responses. Cognitivists value activities that activate students' backgrounds, prod the students to hypothesize, predict, seek patterns, plan to confirm their predictions, and monitor and revise their plans, if necessary. Developmentalists emphasize opportunities that match the maturation of the student as a biological organism; believing that learning activities should be student-initiated and match student ability and interest.

Systemic designers follow different psychological principles both in the judging and developing of learning opportunities.[25] Until the early 1990s, some like Benjamin Bloom adapted behavioral and contiguity psychology to instructional development.[26] They accepted the revolutionary idea that all students can master a learning task if the right means for helping the student are found. Chief among the means was careful analysis and sequencing of tasks so that prerequisites were provided. They made sure that learners understood the task and the procedures to be followed. Systemic designers also adapted instruction to the characteristics of individual learners by giving some students more examples, frequent testing with immediate knowledge of results, reteaching if necessary, alternative procedures, and variation in time allowed for learning.

Systemic designers use the following criteria in assessing instructional materials:

1. The materials are aligned with content and performance standards.

2. The objectives for the activity or material are stated in performance or measurable terms, including the level of expected performance.

3. A task analysis (identification of components of a complex behavior) has been made, and a relationship between the tasks and the final objectives has been specified.

[25]Geneva D. Haertel et al., "Psychological Models of Educational Performance: A Theoretical Synthesis of Constructs," *Review of Educational Research* 53, no. 1 (spring 1983): 75–91.

[26]Benjamin S. Bloom, *All Our Children Learning* (New York: McGraw-Hill, 1982).

4. Learning activities are directly related to the benchmarks and specified content standards.

5. There is immediate feedback regarding the adequacy of the learner's responses.

6. There are criterion-referenced tests or benchmarks that measure progress toward stated objectives and standards as well as norm-referenced tests to differentiate levels of achievement of a common standard.

7. Attention is given to evaluating both process, by which the learner learns, and the product, or what the learner learns.

8. The product or activity has been carefully field-tested. A technical manual might cite sources of available evidence to document claims about effectiveness and efficiency, including reports of unintended outcomes.

In the 1980s, cognitive and constructivist learning theories began to replace behavioristic theories and the psychologically based criteria changed accordingly. These changes can be summarized as a movement to (1) higher levels of thinking as opposed to the mastery of discrete tasks or skills; (2) a concern for coherence and relationship among ideas, (3) student-initiated activities and solutions instead of recitation and prespecified correct responses; and (4) students, as opposed to the teacher or the text, as an authority for knowing. Students began constructing their own understanding by working through problems and synthesizing their ideas. The following are examples of the new criteria:

Goals. Do goals include conceptual understanding and higher order applications of content? Do the goals imply a network of key ideas? Do the goals integrate knowledge, procedures, attitudes, and dispositions? Are there cooperative learning goals?

Content. How does content put students in touch with the problematic nature of subject matter and with ways to serve their local community? Does the content help students learn how the world works and how it got this way? Does the content deal with the students' naïveté or perceptions?

Activity. Does the activity encourage a range of representations by students—from the visual to the oral symbolic? Are concepts represented in multiple ways? To what extent do students get the chance to explore and explain new concepts and defend their views as they interact with peers and teacher?[27]

Student-centered learning opportunities are taking many forms. *Learning by Design* (LBD) is a project where students design artifacts such as making parachutes from coffee filters to learning the relation between gravity and air restraint. *Apprenticeship-based* projects give opportunities for students to mix play and education as they engage in computer games with added related educational obligations and participate with older students. In *issue-based spaces* projects, students resolve controversial questions, concurrently learning domain knowledge that is appropriate, conducting experiments, and promulgating their findings. Student-centered learning rests on the theory that learning:

- is a process of making meaning by interacting with others and with artifacts in the environment.

- relies on dialogue to determine the truth of personal beliefs.

- is guided by our intentions and reflections to resolve dissonance between what we know and what we want to know.[28]

---

[27]Jere Brophy, "The De Facto National Curriculum in U.S. Elementary Social Studies: Critique of a Representative Sample," *Journal of Curriculum Studies* 24, no. 5 (1992): 401–447.
[28]David H. Jonassen and Susan M. Land, eds. *Theoretical Foundations of Learning Environments* (Mahwah, NJ: Lawrence Erlbaum, 2000).

Political Criteria

Some pressure groups have been successful in promoting new criteria for guiding the adoption of instructional materials. Although many of these new criteria reflect the philosophical belief that every human being is important, legal and political actions were necessary before the portrayal of racial, ethnic, and cultural groups, the handicapped, and the sexes began to change nationally. Typical of criteria that reflect political efforts on behalf of social justice are the following legal requirements:

1. Teaching materials must portray both men and women in their full range of leadership, occupation, and domestic roles, without demeaning, stereotyping, or patronizing references to either sex.

2. Material must portray, without significant omissions, the historical role of member of racial, ethnic, and cultural groups, including their contributions and achievements in all areas of life.

3. Materials must portray members of cultural groups without demeaning, stereotyping, or patronizing references concerning their heritage, characteristics, or lifestyle.

As a consequence of these standards, publishers and teachers count the pictures of boys and girls to be sure that both sexes are depicted in a range of roles, rather than traditional masculine and feminine ones. In addition, they are careful not to attach a color to an animal serving as the antagonist in a tale. They also modify the language by making changes in affixes and other structures. The singular *he* is replaced with *they* and *person* substituted for *man*.

At policy levels, curriculum planners attempt to meet the political criteria by designating curriculum domains or areas such as women's studies, Native American studies, and Hispanic studies. Curriculum planners at a policy level also confront the special interests of conservationists, religious and veterans' organizations, automobile-related industries, and other groups. Numerous admonitions to curriculum developers are the direct result of such pressures. They are told to teach the responsibilities of individuals and groups in preserving or creating a healthful environment, including appropriate and scientifically valid solutions to environmental problems, to present the hazards of tobacco, alcohol, and drugs without glamorizing or encouraging their use, and to be sure that the curriculum reflects and respects the religious diversity of people. Schools are adamant about the teaching of evolution. As indicated in Chapter 11, conservative Christian activists are questioning all materials which they say undermine their children's religious beliefs, particularly in such social areas as health and sex education, lifestyle, self-esteem, and values education. There is extensive documentation regarding the censorship of materials by both the Left and the Right. There is need for studying the consequences from the absence of honesty and accuracy in deference to sensitive issues and thought controls.[29]

Publishers are faulted for promoting materials that feature attractive colors, animations, and the like without evidence that these variables are directly related to attainment of specific standards. The systemic use of evidence-based data and its relation to achievement promises to change that.

Practicality as a Criterion

At the policy level, practicality generally takes the form of economy. Planners weigh the cost of providing a certain learning opportunity. In times of a financial pinch, for instance, curriculum planners may consider the cost of initiating an expensive laboratory course to

---

[29]Diane Ravitch, *The Language Policies: How Pressure Groups Restrict What Students Learn* (New York: Alfred Knopf, 2003).

be prohibitive. Instead, they may suggest a science course that features a less expensive instructional process such as a lecture and video demonstration format. Curriculum programs can be expensive in many ways, such as in the outright costs of purchase of materials, the costs of maintaining the materials, the costs of purchasing necessary supplementary materials, and the additional costs of acquiring or training personnel for these programs.

Costs of purchase and installation should be weighed against the expected level of goals or objectives to be achieved. If powerful forces outside the school are working against the attainment of a goal, the purchase of new means for attaining that goal is impractical. In times of economic austerity, curriculum planners consider diminishing returns in learning opportunities. There is a level of educational attainment beneath which dollars invested show a return in student progress. Beyond that level, however, gain occurs only at rapidly increasing cost.

At both policy and classroom levels, there are other practical concerns. Safety, durability, and adaptability of the activity must be considered. There also is the factor of *conditions of use:* Does it demand that a teacher interact with students or does it free the teacher from direct instruction? Is it appropriate for learners with given abilities and motivational levels?

With respect to the latter, Connie Muller and Melissa Conrad recommend "kid rating" as a method for textbook evaluation. The practice is a learning opportunity for critical thinking as well. A topic, concept, or skill is selected and alternative textbooks are examined by students to determine which book best addresses the learning task. Using criteria for considering texts, students seek consensus.[30]

Scientifically Based Research Criteria

In selecting instructional materials, teachers want to know now "what works." Just as in medicine, the physician or pharmacist wants to know that a medicine has been tested and how the drug will work for given patients and particular health needs. For years, a nonprofit corporation, Educational Products Information Exchange Institute (EPIE), has made impartial studies of the availability, use, and effectiveness of teacher time, costs, and staffing and stated the underlying assumptions or philosophy of the material, revealing the extent to which there has been verification. Surprisingly, although more than 90% of students' time is spent with some form of instructional text, fewer than 2% of all instructional materials rely on learner response as a source of revision. Readers want validated products.

Early in the twenty-first century national legislation and policy demanded that only instructional programs and materials deemed "scientifically based" were to be eligible for purchase with federal funds. In Part 3, I analyze the political nature of this federal policy and the interests it serves. Briefly, however, the concept "scientifically based" is ambiguous and contested.

The No Child Left Behind (NCLB) Act of 2001 and the Educational Science Reform (ESRA) Act of 2002 in describing the evidence to be used in assessing education tended to narrow the concept to data collected through empirical and experimental designs. Many educational researchers became concerned about the omission of other forms of inquiry— case studies, surveys, comparisons, participatory observations, and classroom narratives— as ways to provide evidence of effectiveness.[31]

---

[30]Connie Muller and Melissa Conrad, "Kid Rating: An In-Depth Textbook Evaluation Technique," *Educational Leadership* 46 no. 2 (Oct. 1988): 79–80.

[31]M. Eisenhart and L. Towne, "Contestation and Change in National Policy on 'Scientifically-Based' Educational Research," *Educational Researcher* 32, no. 7 (Oct. 2003): 31–38.

The National Research Council (NRC) then published a report which argued for the use of mixed methods depending on the questions under investigation.[32] Subsequently, legislation by ESRA gave space to the possibility of exploratory, descriptive, and naturalistic studies being scientific, and the newly organized Institute of Educational Science (IES) established a "What Works Clearinghouse" to assess and report on the strength and nature of scientific evidence on the effectiveness of different education programs, products, and practices which claim to enhance important student outcomes. Also, the IES hired the Coalition for Evidence-Based Policy, a Washington group that advocates randomized field trials in evaluating government programs to produce a guide to what constitutes evidence of effectiveness of educational programs and practices.[33] The guide is heavy on randomized controlled studies but acknowledged that other kinds of studies, such as comparison studies, can provide "possible" evidence.

There are many concerns about scientifically evidence-based selection of materials and practices. Such studies:

- Fail to explain *why* a product or a practice works or does not work.
- Are too narrowly focused on test results as the measure of effectiveness.
- Rely on standards that will be less defensive in light of world uncertainty.
- Place too much emphasis on basic skills and the sciences and too little on the arts, humanities, and civic actions.
- Curtail choice of newer innovations that may be better but not selected for testing.
- Ignore materials more appropriate for local context.

Some fear that use of the scientific-based criterion is a move to social engineering on behalf of a nationalized curriculum.[33]

CRITICISMS OF TEXTBOOKS AND LEARNING OPPORTUNITIES

Numerous problems have been identified with textbooks. Texts attempt to cover more topics than can be treated in depth, explanations are unclear, and readers are not provided with a context to make facts meaningful. Texts often do not assist students in understanding why certain ideas are superior to others for given aims but instead present the ideas as prescriptions. Neither do most texts give opportunity to use concepts from many fields of study in examining the same problem. However, under the guidance of a good teacher, textbooks become resources for developing critical studies rather than recipes for instruction.

In their conceptual analysis of learning activities that teachers expect students to do, Jere Brophy and Janet Alleman included instances of both faulty and good activities.[34] The faulty activities lacked purpose and were mostly busywork: word searches, cutting and pasting, connecting dots, memorizing. The faulty activities were peripheral to powerful ideas and had minimal application potential—for example, "Find a picture of products made but not used by people." Some faulty activities were unnecessary because students already knew what they were intended to learn; others called for students to use knowledge

[32]National Research Council, *Scientific Research in Education,* L. Towne and R. Shavelson, eds. (Washington, DC: Committee on Scientific Principles for Educational Research, 2002).

[33]Institute of Educational Science (Washington, DC: Coalition for Evidence-Based Policy, 2004).

[34]Jere Brophy and Janet Alleman, "Activities as Instructional Tools: A Framework for Analysis and Evaluation," *Educational Researcher* 20, no. 4 (1991): 9–23.

that had not been taught or likely to have been acquired elsewhere. Activities were faulty when they were not feasible within the constraints of time, space, or student characteristics.

The good activities had the potential to get students thinking about important ideas and applying the ideas in accomplishing some purposes. They were also likely to advance the student's basic understanding about how and why the world functions as it does and where and how they can best relate to it. These activities were at the appropriate level of difficulty—challenging but not so difficult as to leave students frustrated.

CRITICISMS OF CRITERIA FOR SELECTING LEARNING OPPORTUNITIES

Criticisms may be directed both at the criteria themselves and at their use. Simply having criteria does not take care of the problem of who will use them in making decisions; it may make a difference whether they are used by state curriculum committees, individual teachers, or boards of education. Furthermore, little thought has been given to decision rules. Answers are seldom given to these questions: How many criteria must be satisfied before adoption? What should the planners do if two alternative opportunities meet the same number of criteria? Will the decision require agreement among evaluators?

It is often difficult to obtain agreement on the evidence that a particular criterion has been met. Criteria demanding few inferences, such as the specification that standards be stated in measurement terms, present little difficulty. Criteria requiring high levels of inference, such as the requirement that materials be appropriate for the learners' motivation levels, allow for more subjective and varied judgments.

Disagreement on the worth of learning opportunities occurs because the value of activities and content depends on the time and place, and the persons involved. What was deemed worthwhile in the past is not necessarily worthwhile today. For example, the supremacy of calculus in the mathematics curriculum is being challenged by those who would substitute discrete mathematics on the ground that calculus deals with continuous problems whereas discrete mathematics allow for individual values to be treated—something more appropriate for use with computers that manipulate individual symbols and quantities. However, trying to justify an activity or content on the ground that it is instrumental to the pursuit of other ends leaves much to be desired. The instrumental argument is of little consequence if the ultimate justification cannot be sustained. Generally, an activity is justified if it satisfies a range of impulses, rises above mere partisan considerations, meets a social norm, and is highly prized by those who have reflected on the activity and its value.

CONCLUDING COMMENTS

The previous discussion of learning principles and ways to develop learning activities and to select programs and materials should have illuminated the kinds of choices that can be made. What has not been made clear is that some consistency should exist between these different guides to instructional planning and the curriculum domains and teaching modes to be used. Just as failure to match a domain with the right learning opportunities makes an ineffective curriculum, so, too, does a mismatch between goals and teaching modes. A teaching mode appropriate for achieving performance with isolated basic skills, for example, may be inappropriate for use when critical theory is the goal.

A serious deficiency in curriculum planning is the gap between concepts for designing learning activities and concepts guiding teacher preparation. Paradigms for teaching are not often related to specific kinds of learning opportunities or to the curriculum design teachers may want to use in their particular school settings.

There is tension between those who want to give greater autonomy to teachers in creating learning opportunities and those who want to restrict teachers' initiative to what school authorities have prescribed. Fenwick English, for instance, would align the curriculum by *mapping,* a technique for recording instructional and learning time given to classroom tasks and then by analyzing the data determine its suitability for the officially adopted curriculum and the tests that will be given for accountability.[35] Similarly, some teachers of the same grade or subject create "pacing guides", using a format by which they align short-term lessons, activity materials with specific objectives and the objectives in turn are aligned with key questions drawn from the mandated content standards.[36] In reality, learning opportunities will be developed at both policy and classroom levels. We need more information on how standards are set by those distant from the classroom, and the politics of selecting mandated instructional materials. We are beginning to learn how these materials are modified and used by teachers and students in meeting their own purposes in reconciling their own capabilities and circumstances. Students and teachers are creating their own learning opportunities and their own meanings from classroom events. Indeed, a promising direction in the curriculum field is the concept of curriculum as enactment, which assumes the active nature of learning whereby students set their own goals and their own plans and activities for achieving them, evaluating consequences and sharing their findings with an interested audience.

QUESTIONS

1. Think of an experience in school when your perception of your own abilities changed positively or when you found that a certain subject "made sense." What was different about the activity where this memorable experience occurred? Why was the activity so powerful? What does your recollection imply about criteria for effective experiences?

2. How do humanists, social reconstructionists, systematizers, and academicians differ in their models for developing learning opportunities?

3. Consider a learning opportunity that you might like to introduce as an innovation within a school system. What factors would you use in defending the proposed innovation? How would you justify the proposal? Would you use costs as a criterion?

4. What might you like to teach a given learner or learners? Describe a learning opportunity for this learner(s) consistent with the purpose, illustrating the following principles: (a) appropriate practice (opportunity to practice what you want the student to learn), (b) learning satisfaction (provision for the learners to find the opportunity rewarding), and (c) success (assurance that the learner has the background for participating in the opportunity).

5. Select a belief about the natural or social world that you think conflicts sharply with students' beliefs. Describe the procedures you would use in promoting change in the beliefs of students.

---

[35]Fenwick English, "Contemporary Curriculum Circumstances," in *Fundamental Curriculum Decisions* (Alexandria, VA: Association for Supervision and Curriculum Development, 1983).

[36]M. D. Rettig et al., *From Rigorous Standards to Student Achievement: A Practical Process* (Larchmont, NY: Eye on Education, 2003).

SUGGESTED STRATEGIC RESEARCH

IDENTIFYING CRITICAL LEARNING OPPORTUNITIES AS RECALLED BY PROMINENT STUDENTS

We continually read of students who make important contributions. Herbert M. Hedberg, 17, a high school student, for example, experimented with an enzyme in cancer cells and found a way to screen for its inhibitors and to possibly suppress local tumors. Locate entries in the Intel Science Search and other sources to identify students who have made outstanding contributions. Draw a sample from this population and through interview or other means determine what they recall as the defining situation and assistance that motivated and prepared them for their work. Extrapolate the common principles among the recalled events with implications for developing learning opportunities.

DETERMINING EFFECTS OF PERFORMANCE VERSUS LEARNING GOALS

Obtain and collate a puzzling activity. Form two groups and tell those in one group, "I want to see how smart you are, how you compete with each other, and how you talk to those in the other group." Tell the other group, "This activity will help you improve your abilities in math (or other subject)." Analyze your results, considering such factors as help-giving, solutions obtained, and student satisfaction for those under the separate conditions.

DETERMINING THE VALUE OF CHOICE IN LEARNING OPPORTUNITIES

If 3-year-olds are free to exercise their choices of color or other attributes in an activity, they are said to develop more positive attitudes toward the activity, showing more initiative and follow-through than children confined to directions without choice in how to proceed. Does this finding hold for older students and for those of different cultural backgrounds?

ENHANCING CREATIVITY

Does inducing a positive mood enhance creativity? Give half of the members of a class a pleasant offering—a gift such as a bag of candy or showing a 5-minute clip from a nonaggressive comedy video. Compare the performance of this group with a matched control group on a range of creative tasks.

RECONCILING CONFLICTING BELIEFS

We know little of how students reconcile the conflicting beliefs gained from parents, teachers, peers, and their own experience. Do young children and adolescents deal with these conflicts differently? Select an issue on which peers, parents, and scholars differ. Determine how particular students treat this issue in their presentations to peers or others or how they resolve the issue. Whose reasoning do they use? Or present a moral or scientific dilemma and determine through observations, analyzing student dialogues and self-reports, how they resolved the conflict.

SELECTED REFERENCES

Brown, Ann L. "The Advancement of Learning," *Educational Research* 23, no. 8 (Nov. 1994): 4–30.
Duckworth, Eleanor. *The Having of Wonderful Ideas.* New York: Teachers College Press, 1987.
Hennessey, Beth A., and Teresa M. Amable. *What Research Says to Teachers: Creativity and Learning.* West Haven, CT: National Association of Professional Librarians, 1992.
Jonassen, David H., and Susan M. Land, eds. *Theoretical Foundations of Learning Environments.* Mahwah, NJ: Lawrence Erlbaum, 2000.

HOW TECHNOLOGY IS USED WITH CURRICULUM ORIENTATIONS

TECHNOLOGY OPENS an array of possibilities for learning opportunities along with other changes in the conduct of schooling. Most people see both benefits and dangers from educational technology. There is danger in fragmenting members of society who have access to technology and those who do not. There are concerns about technology separating persons from each other as more people study and work at home instead of interacting at school and the workplace. Time spent on the computer may mean less time with friends and family. There are studies showing that the increasing use of computers is associated with more loneliness and depression. Conversely, the Internet promotes "cyber hegemony"—more collegial friendships and empathy.

TECHNOLOGY IN HUMANISTIC CLASSROOMS

Chatrooms, electronic portfolios, and teleconferences can build self-respect if participants are encouraged to know why they think what they think, to justify their beliefs, and to take responsibility. Students may not be immediately popular in expressing doubt about an idea, but they will not be seen as ridiculous as they might seem if they profess its certainty.

In the humanistic classroom, students tend more to use technology for personal expression than for getting information disconnected from personal concerns. In real-time electronic conferences, students dialogue back and forth among themselves or focus on a particular message on the computer screen, writing a collaborative essay or reinventing a work, such as making a collage from their e-mail.

The teacher can initiate discussion about where students send their e-mail responses and negotiate meaning. The teacher need not be the sole arbitrator, possessor, and communicator of knowledge.

Other techniques are put to humanistic purposes. One humanistic teacher challenged each of his students to make a video for presentation at a public gathering. Each video was to deal with a personal concern. One young student had a burning desire to come to terms with a father he had never known. His mother and stepfather had been silent on the matter. The student on finding a picture of this unknown father created a video which brought mother and son together, reconciling emotional needs.

Actualization trumps conformity. The development of an e-portfolio, for example, lends itself to collecting evidence of growth through self-reflection, peer collaboration, and teachers' comments, and often students learn to trust themselves, peers, and teachers as they evaluate themselves and others.

E-mail is helpful in learning how to write and to gain competency in multiple forms of discourse. In a networking computer class using e-mail, students may share their work with another or with a group, or put it on a document accessible to all. Distance makes it easier for students to be more honest. "We've found that students tend to disclose themselves more through interacting with others with e-mail than they do in the traditional classroom."

The humanistic interest in awakening the imagination—the inner force of an individual—can be met through technology. Electronic readers use their imagination in rerouting their own story line in books, flipping from Chapter 4 to Chapter 19, for example, in the quest for meaning or making sense as well as deliberately choosing other ways of thinking about the text. The nonlinear and multilinear interactions along with the multimedia features of e-literacy let authors convey aspects of their works and elicit reader interaction while they are performing with digital videos of the text being read.

James Gee uses video games to get people to use their imagination.[1] Instead of regarding video games as "dumbing down classrooms with sexism and violence," Gee sees games as stimulating students to think about values and ideologies. By way of illustration, Will Wright produces games that put students on the existential edge where they must grapple with real questions, such as "What makes a person happy?" In "Sim Ant," Wright engages players in a virtual version of ordinary life involving moral choices and imaginations. This game is based on Maslow's theory of needs, a fundamental building block of human behavior. It may be that programs for video games that put students in morally charged situations are better at teaching ethics than traditional instruction because games appeal to both emotions and cognition. Ian Boyost at the Georgia Institute of Technology also aims at preparing game developers who are inspired and capable of inspiring others with new visions, such as transforming poetry into video games that convey metaphors and imagery.

The great collections of historical and aesthetic artifacts available through the Internet is bringing humanism to the classroom. On the other hand, technology facilitates awareness of the negative in the world. On the issue of "protecting" students from a dangerous and overstimulating cyberworld, humanists come down on the side of helping students learn to discern and make choices rather than censorship. Tobin Hart, for example, asks students to project their own inner wisdom, to be aware of their own sense of what is right. Students can imagine what their key moral models would do in given situations and do likewise. The humanist assumes that students are able to cope if they use their intelligence, wisdom, freedom, and responsibility.

SOCIAL RECONSTRUCTION AND TECHNOLOGY

E-mail played a part in a student-led protest against the Massachusetts mandated exit test. A student coalition for alternative assessment against standardized tests led to students boycotting of a state exam. Worldwide electronic communication by students taking stances on social issues and attacking institutions is increasing. Technology is seen by reconstructionists as a tool for global and multicultural social activism in the interest of human betterment. High-speed technologies have been used effectively by activist groups, such as People's Global Action, an international network founded by the Zapatistas, and

---

[1] J. P. Gee, *What Video Games Teach Us about Learning and Literacy* (New York: Palgrave Macmillan, 2003).

Direct Action Network (DAN) which helped organize activists in the antiglobalization movement. Within schools teachers have also used technology to connect the official curriculum with social activism. The Internet makes universities and other data bases available to school children, revealing knowledge and statistics concerning worldwide problems— environmental degradation, health, unemployment—and other indicators of the diminishing quality of life. Students can then collect information on the severity of these problems in their own communities, and then form and carry out action plans in the local context.

It is becoming more common for students interested in water shortages, AIDS, and other issues to use Google or other search engines to access extensive information on the topics and then process the data for reliability and significance. Subsequently, the students use other techniques—digital cameras, tape recorders—to document local conditions followed by graphic spreadsheets for data analysis. Videos, radio, fax, and PowerPoint presentations are used to inform selected audiences. There is an increase in student Web sites for given causes. School projects by reconstructionists are opportunities for applying and improving performance in all subject areas, for example, numeracy and literacy.

Technology is also used in a very different way of raising social consciousness. Technology itself may be the focus of study making the familiar unfamiliar. Students may examine the technology in their own school to see if it is serving educational or economic interests. Stephen Kerr has written on technology for educators and human values as opposed to economic utility.[2] Students can see if technology in their school is preparing them for jobs characterized by routine or for employment as managers, creative artists, and analytic thinkers.

Other reconstructionist teachers will follow Henry Giroux's practice of involving students in finding out how films, TV shows, and other popular media are created to promote certain views of reality. The issue of how media is shaping student identity, such as that of consumer, is an example. Students learn to differentiate technologies as toys, entertainment with a view of the world as beautiful, safe, controllable, and unconnected to life itself versus students creating their own software and critically analyzing media presentations controlled by corporations.

In contrast, the Utopians within social reconstruction are likely to use simulations by having students work cooperatively on projects that feature solution strategies to selected problems along with likely consequences. Responses to global warming involving harnessing a variety of energy options including nuclear power form a prime candidate for such a simulation. Although social reconstructionists may envision Utopias, they are skeptical about the possible effects of dreams as played out through simulators. The variables selected for the simulation are unlikely to match the unexpected events of real life.

Outside of schools, those with a revolutionary bent are using music and visuals through radio, TV, CDs, and public spaces as ways to express criticism, rage, and scorn. Newer forms of talk (slang), singing (rap), dancing (break dancing), and writing (graffiti) are forms of political discourse. G. Butler calls these forms "reverse citations" in which hate speech is the appropriation of negative terms of identity and their reassessment as positive by marginal groups with the potential to destabilize the forces of order.[3] Albums that feature the exotic beats and rhythms of those like the King of Grime, Dizzee Rascal, illustrate how hip-hop artists use media in getting out the message from the urban disaffected.

Digital technology with software makes it possible for the consumer to control the means of film production—the visual equivalent of a rap CD.

[2]Stephen T. Kerr, "Visions of Curriculum: The Future of Technology, Education and the Schools," *Issues in Curriculum*, 98th Yearbook of the National Society for the Study of Education, Part II, Margaret Early and Kenneth J. Rehage, eds. (Chicago: University of Chicago Press, 1999), 169–199.
[3]G. Butler, *Excitable Speech: A Politics of the Performative* (New York: Routledge, 1997).

TECHNOLOGY IN A SYSTEMIC CURRICULUM

Technology has long been viewed as important for both its efficiency and its effectiveness. Indeed it was the development of an early educational technology—the textbook for different grade levels in the nineteenth century—that contributed to the laying out of content and skills (scope) for reading, arithmetic, history, and geography and the order in which the content and skills were to be acquired (sequence). Following World War I, there were several series of textbooks in reading, math, social studies, and science for the eight grades of the elementary schools. High school textbooks were introduced with the expansion of the high school in the twentieth century but unlike the textbooks for the elementary schools, textbooks were authored by individual college professors who selected and ordered content according to their beliefs of what the high school course should be. Today, of course, publishers of K–12 textbooks are challenged to produce texts that are aligned with the content standards of the states.[4]

The textbook with its supplementary features—media, activities, plans, and assessments—is a viable curriculum. Its coverage of specific topics and its explanations constitute a manifest curriculum. Its particular selections of content and manner of presentation make the textbook a hidden curriculum conveying inferential messages and values; and its suggestions and activities form a powerful pedagogical apparatus.[5]

More than other curriculum orientations, the systemic curriculum regards technology as instructional interventions chosen for their match to specific standards and objectives or as procedures for designing supplementary products that will clarify concepts and operations, enhancing the instructional process.

Technology is seen as an efficient way to achieve both the goal of knowledge acquisition and the proof of conceptual understanding. Knowledge acquisition refers to adding to one's store of facts, skills, and procedures, making links with units of knowledge. Conceptual understanding requires the ability to explain in one's own words the theories of how things work and to apply concepts in the real world. Table 6A.1 outlines the contributions and limitations of technology to these goals.

In the past decade, the systemic classroom used computers chiefly for word processing of stories and reports or drill and practice of the basic skills. Such practices are effective in producing achievement on tests and improving self concepts. In the twenty-first century, the teacher in the systemic classroom is expected to use technology more dynamically, choosing extra resources (CD-ROMs, encyclopedias, Web), presenting materials (multimedia software, PowerPoint), and clarifying concepts (simulation modules).

Individualized assistance might be given through Intelligent Tutoring Systems (ITS) that follow learners as they undertake specific problems, giving hints and feedback as students work through the program. Also, hypermedia that is Web-based makes it possible for learners to get information about a topic and can be adapted to present information according to the characteristics of the learner by filtering and ordering links displayed on the page or by tailoring the content in the information space.

Cognitive tutors, such as the Algebra Cognitive Tutor, turn problems for which the student has knowledge into an example from which the student can learn both the solution and why it is correct by constructing an explanation with guidance through help messages that are under the learner's control. Evaluation studies show that the curriculum in which the Algebra Cognitive Tutor is a part lead to better learning than typical classroom instruction.[6]

[4]Allison Zmuda and Mary Tomaino, *The Competent Classroom—Aligning High School Curriculum, Standards, and Assessment: A Creative Teaching Guide* (New York: Teachers College Press, 2001).

[5]Richard L. Venezky, "Textbooks in School and Society," *Handbook of Research in Curriculum*, Philip W. Jackson, ed. (New York: Macmillan, 1922), 436–463.

[6]K. R. Koedinger, J. R. Anderson, W. H. Hadley, and M. A. Mark, "Intelligent Tutoring Goes to School in the Big City," *International Journal of Artificial Intelligence in Education* 8 (1997): 30–43.

Table 6A.1   Contributions and Limitations of Technology to Knowledge Acquisition and Conceptual Understanding

Knowledge Acquisition	Conceptual Understanding
Contributions	
Facilitates access to accurate and updated information. Transcontinental electronic field trips are possible.	Use of real-life images, simulations, graphics, and voice-over exercises link content to real life, making transfer more likely.
Relationships among subunits in control of a system can be demonstrated graphically.	Simulations where the users' use of key variables may force them to form better mental models to account for results.
Students' errors can be tracked and remedied.	Learners learn to interpret a situation from multiple perspectives when responding to characters in filmed scenarios and seeing the consequences of human decisions.
Limitations	
Students cannot use natural language in questioning materials.	There is an element of artificial neatness in the selection of materials by the designers; situations are contrived.
Given so much information and so many tasks, students do not have time to think and to understand and generate new ideas.	Users cannot opt for solutions that have not been programmed. Courseware is an authoritative given, getting results that cannot be challenged. There are few opportunities for students to improve their interpersonal skills in development of the situations. Overuse of models might lead students to believe they can control and manipulate people in the real world.

Although the systemic curriculum is unlikely to use technology to serve a community larger than the classroom and to introduce concepts apart from the official curriculum, systemic teachers may turn to technology as a means to introduce authentic problems designed to stimulate learners to seek official knowledge that could help in finding a solution to the problem. Video-based macro contexts are used to overcome the charge that the school content is just so much inert knowledge. The Cognition and Technology Group at Vanderbilt has made available authentic problems in rich real-world environments.[7]

In their *Jasper Woodbury Series* of video disks, for example, learners engage in a fictitious problem with information relevant to solving it embedded in the program's story. In "Escape from Boone's Meadow," students must think they are saving an eagle. In another video, they want to know if there is sufficient time to bring a boat home before sunset and must consider fuel readings, time of day, distance, speed and other factors. In solving such specific problems, students are expected to develop the most efficient strategy, gaining experience in solving ill-structured problems, as well as acquiring mathematical and other subject matter skills and concepts of the systemic curriculum.

Surveys of video usage in schools show that teachers use the programs that are provided by their district although local Public Broadcasting System (PBS) programs are introduced as extension of instruction, not as replacements.

Simulation modules are helpful in clarifying concepts. Visualization tools such as "Sketch Pad" and "Model It" allow learners to construct models and then test their parameters. Although simulations and graphic depictions of the world may lead students

[7]Cognition and Technology Group at Vanderbilt, *The Jasper Project: Lessons in Curriculum, Instruction, Assessment, and Professional Development* (Mahwah, NJ: Lawrence Erlbaum, 1997).

to think as if they are present in viewing a real-world historical event, a chemical process, or a mathematical evaluation, they carry the danger that the representations are not the "true" view of reality.

TECHNOLOGY IN THE ACADEMIC CURRICULUM

The Massachusetts Institute of Technology's (MIT's) Open Courseware is a superb example of a rich knowledge source available on the World Wide Web. This courseware, which includes lectures, videos, handouts, notes, syllabi, problem-sets, and software from more than 2000 courses and interdisciplinary projects, is freely available to nearly anyone in the world. Although MIT does not itself conduct the courses as an open university, the archives are expected to speed up the preparation of students for advanced work, influence the ways courses are taught, and alter the way students learn.[8]

Inquiry drives the new academic curriculum with students (a) addressing domain-related dilemmas (such as what are the best prospects for extending the periodic table) or (b) tackling real-world problems that require interdisciplinary efforts.

Technology has made it easier for students and experts in distant academic communities to share the goals, discourses, and practices of particular disciplines. Also, opportunities for like-minded students and scholars to tackle real-world problems have increased because of technology. The site www.thinkcycle.org, for example, links students, researchers, and organizations in tackling obstacles hampering underserved communities, listing more than 100 health, environmental, and other challenges awaiting solutions. Student design teams submit their own ideas and proposals to academic and individual experts who help them refine their solutions.

The "Kids Network Curriculum" was an early academic program that linked school children in different classrooms and countries for research on acid rain. Students studied and discussed the issue as it related to their locality. Ten classes worked as a team to describe their local situation and to contribute to global comparisons.

Students familiarized themselves with data-collecting tools and gathered samples. Experts from Kids Network were available to discuss problems and offer guidance. Network staff integrated the data across sites. Summaries were prepared along with interpretations by a scientist who also models the way scientists think. The students, also, made their own interpretations and drew conclusions regarding their local community before presenting their findings to the local public audiences. Kids Network (with other areas of research) has been adopted by more than 250,000 children from 49 different countries.[9]

Similarly, the "Global School Bus" has served as a clearinghouse for over 900 science programs helping students find partners or join projects around the globe. Academic learners do not lack sites that offer data packed with current and past findings, methods, publications, and information about on-going studies that need students, teachers, and volunteers. Conversely, there are networks, like Computer-Supported Intentions Learning Environment (CSILE), where learners enter information into a common data base that can be borrowed, linked, and commented on by others.[10] CSILE helps learners identify their goals and makes their thinking overt so others can provide feedback or model their own thinking.

---

[8]"Why MIT Decided to Give Away All Its Course Material via the Internet," *Chronicle of Higher Education* (Jan. 30, 2004): B20–21.

[9]F. Tinker, *Teleco as a Progressive Force in Education*, unpublished manuscript (Concord, MA: The Concord Consortium, 1991).

[10]M. Scardamalia and C. Bereiter, "Text-Based and Knowledge-Based Questioning by Children," *Cognition and Instruction* 9 (1992): 177–199.

Currently, the "Neptune Project" proposes that students participate in exploring the last frontier on the earth—the deep sea. This project connects hundreds of instruments to the seafloor and in the ocean. Data and images will be transmitted to classrooms via the Internet.

The desirability of students working with experts is not new. The biochemist Peter Csermely has given more than 2000 high school students a chance to do exactly that by arranging for them to experience what research is really like. He has connected motivated students with working scientists who arrange laboratory stays and experiences for the students. "I was bored to death in high school" admits Csermely reference. With the help of a mentor, students make breakthroughs in knowledge, such as finding how the human brain functions or how the West Nile virus is transmitted. Web sites in science and other disciplines that offer telecommunications projects are growing. ILEARN telecommunication is a global network that involves K–12 students in working joint social and environmental projects of international importance.[11]

There are Web sites that offer teaching tools for the academic curriculum, such as animation that brings abstract subjects to life. Animation showing the role of calcium in muscle contractions or the mechanics of hearing are examples. Graphic simulations can provide models of cognitive processes and make visible events that are too small, dangerous, fast, or slow for ordinary viewing.

The Writing Partner is an illustration of a tool that helps one check about the writing process.[12] *Sense Maker* helps students construct arguments categorically and spatially with different claims about a topic.[13]

Less used but potentially important are technologies that enable students without strong backgrounds in the mathematics to use the tools they need for designing and analyzing experiments.[14] In addition to tools that develop cognitive skills important to an investigation, there are calculators, spreadsheets, charts, and other artifacts that free students to direct their cognitive efforts to other activities. The virtual world may also relate to the tradition of the liberal arts. Students who program robots to interact with each other must study community and other complex situations.

When considering the behavior of robots, students examine their own knowledge, like how to describe a political party or how to define something as good or evil. As described in the humanistic curriculum, technology can put students in morally charged situations that are opportunities for reflecting on ethical matters.

Building Web Sites

The Internet also offers learners possibilities to create and share web pages throughout the world. With streaming video capabilities and PowerPoint, students can build Web sites that address current and historical issues, introduce their community, or showcase a class's research. SchoolWorld's National (International) Math Trail invites students to provide "community-based math problems, along with photographs, illustrations, audio or video content, or web pages," which are posted on the Math Trail site.[15]

The Oracle Education Foundation sponsors ThinkQuest, an international competition for student Web sites. Over 5000 Web sites in a range of disciplines are available online.

---

[11]P. Cooper, "Connecting Classrooms through Telecommunications," *Educational Leadership* 53, no. 2 (1992): 4.

[12]P. Bell, "Designing for Students Science Learning Using Argumentation and Classroom Debate" (unpublished doctoral dissertation, University of California, Berkeley, 1998).

[13]M. Zellermayer et al., "Enhancing Writing—Related Metacognition through a Computerized Writing Partner," *American Educational Research Journal* 28 (1991): 373–391.

[14]W. Blake and D. Bosteir, "Science and Mathematics in Education," *Science* 303 (Feb. 2004): 788–798.

[15]SchoolWorld Internet Education Internet Projects, URL: http://www.schoolworld.asn.au/projects.html.

CHAPTER 7

ORGANIZING LEARNING OPPORTUNITIES

CHAPTER **6** focused on learning opportunities that are satisfying and that encourage students to pursue goals, along the way questioning their present beliefs and constructing more powerful understandings and ways of knowing the world. The present chapter considers how these opportunities might be organized to best help students (1) relate ideas so they are mutually reinforcing (the problem of integrating knowledge) and (2) deepen understanding of a concept or skill so that each successive encounter builds on the preceding ones (the problem of sequencing the development of knowledge).

Curriculum organization is an attempt to overcome the disarray and fragmentation found in many instructional programs. Too often, curriculum takes on the kaleidoscopic quality of television in presenting isolated pieces of information and sensations without showing their connections or cultivating their underlying meanings. There is a danger, however, in placing knowledge in too neat an integrative framework and in sequencing objects of thought that others have trimmed to fit their patterns. The curriculum plan becomes an instrument for control, an obstacle to the learners making connections to new unprogrammed ideas and dealing with the unexpected.

In this chapter, curriculum organization is treated as a pedagogical activity rather than a study of managerial arrangements. The managerial organization of the school is the subject of Chapter 8. However, management decisions related to scheduling courses and classes, allocating instructional time, tracking students, setting examination policies, and the like influence both what is learned and how.

KEY CONCEPTS IN CURRICULUM ORGANIZATION

Learning opportunities can be joined by two kinds of devices: *organizing centers and organizing elements.* The centers are foci by which learning activities are integrated and the elements are what the curriculum maker or teacher has in mind as the central knowledge or unifying ideas to be developed throughout the weeks, months, or years of instruction and the basis for selecting the next task or unit of work: a theme, a concept such as energy, a skill such as reading, or a value such as "plain speech," careful listening, or searching for the truth.

Organizing Centers

Organizing centers may consist of themes, topics, problems, questions, and projects that are significant in their own right but also important because they are likely to motivate students and give them opportunities to acquire and integrate the particular concepts and values specified by the curriculum elements as they pursue a selected focus of study or inquiry.

One fourth-grade class had as a learning center "cats." In their focus on this topic, students studied the history of cats from deification in ancient Egypt to persecution in the Middle Ages. Science and mathematics were introduced through cat anatomy and measurements. Language arts entered through the reading of works such as T. S. Eliot's "Old Possum's Organizing" in *Book of Practical Cats*. The students were also treated to a performance of the musical *Cats* and later performed a few of the numbers themselves.

A faculty science team restructured their smorgasbord of courses to an intellectually resourced multidisciplinary cluster centered on "Origin and Evolution of the Universe, the Earth, and Life."

In making a choice for a center, one might consider its appeal to students and its possibility for addressing widespread differences in student ability and interests, its social relevance, the availability of resources and time (manageability) of the undertaking, and, as mentioned before, whether it will put students in contact with the educational content related to the organizing elements.

Organizing Elements

In order for centers to be related, some common element must exist among them. Elements are the threads—the woof of the fabric of curriculum organization. Until recently curriculum specialists believed that activities and their implied learning experiences should be woven together to have a cumulative effect and to maximize understanding of powerful ideas and values. If they are not, they believe we will have a situation as described by Edna St. Vincent Millay:

> *Upon this gifted age, in its dark hour,*
> *Rains from the sky a meteoric shower*
> *Of facts... they lie unquestioned, uncombined.*
> *Wisdom enough to leech us of our ill*
> *Is daily spun; but there exists no loom*
> *To weave it into fabric....*[1]

Common Organizing Elements   The following are some of the more common elements used as the basis for organization:

1. *Themes and concepts.* Many academic sequential plans are built around such concepts as culture, growth, number, space, entropy, and metaphor—the ruling ideas in respective fields.

2. *Generalizations.* Generalizations are conclusions drawn from careful observations. Two examples are "In stable societies all educative influences operate consistently on the individual; in heterogeneous societies, there are inconsistencies and contradictions." "A person is both participant (subjective) and observer (objective) in all human behavior."

3. *Skills.* Skills are generally regarded as proficiency plans for curriculum organization. They are commonly used as the basis for building continuity in programs. Elementary schools sometimes organize learning experiences around reading comprehension,

---

[1]Excerpt from "Upon this age, that never speaks its mind" by Edna St. Vincent Millay. From *Collected Sonnets*, rev. and exp. (New York: Harper and Row, 1988). Copyright 1939, 1967 by Edna St. Vincent Millay and Norma Millay Ellis. Reprinted by permission.

fundamental operations in mathematics, and the skills for interpreting data. Metacognitive strategies in problem solving are the latest organizing elements in skill programs. These strategies include sifting out relevant information from irrelevant information, looking for patterns in the information to make it meaningful, and perceiving the relationship of old information to the newly acquired information.

4. *Values.* Philosophical values are cherished beliefs that are not questioned but taken as absolutes for governing behavior. Two examples are "respect for the dignity and worth of every human being regardless of race, nationality, occupation, income, or class" and "respect for self." When organizing a curriculum plan around values, most of the activities are designed so that they reinforce the particular value selected.

Understanding organizing elements is a distinguishing attribute of the curriculum expert. A child may be immediately aware of learning activities or centers only in their concrete form, but the insightful teacher or curriculum writer is always conscious of their deeper significance. When one asks children what they are learning, they are likely to respond, "We're learning about Indians" or "We're learning to speak a foreign language." The curriculum person, however, sees, in addition to such direct study, the powerful abstractions to which the activity points. The activity dealing with Indians may be pointing toward a generalization about basic needs that all people have always had. Learning to speak a foreign language may be most important for what it illuminates about the student's own language, language in general, language acquisition, and even some more fundamental elements such as communication among people.

Organizing elements are selected in light of the purposes of the curriculum. When the curriculum goals are technical and vocational, skills are an appropriate element to use. When the curriculum goals emphasize moral and ethical domains with an integrative function, values are the preferred element for organization. Table 7.1 outlines the use of organizing elements in connecting centers and contributing to the attainment of a long-range goal or purpose.

Elaborating on the outline, consider the following purpose and activities.

Purpose   Given new situations from life, the learner can predict the likely effect of technology on these situations. Characteristics, limitations, and capabilities of modern technology are used by the learner for determining the effect.

Within the first center or unit of instruction (defining technology), students are introduced to a systems approach for reducing complex problems. Students acquire one definition of technology and in the next unit they glimpse the ways in which technology helps

Table 7.1   Relating Organizing Elements to Organizing Centers

Organizing Elements	Organizing Centers					
	Defining Technology	People	Jobs	Society	Environment	Quality of Life
Technology (concept)	x	x	x	x	x	x
Value of persons (value)		x	x	x	x	x
Relationship of natural resources to quality of life (generalization)			x	x	x	x

people, the limits to its use, and its side effects. The concept of technology is further extended, and the student begins to judge the way in which technology decreases or enhances the value of people. Subsequent units involve students in problems about the application of technology to human uses, to societal needs, and to natural and artificial environments. Prior elements are extended and a new element—the relationship of resources to the quality of life—is introduced. Opportunity for students to assess the future effect on and value to persons is given in all subsequent units. The quality of life unit allows for an unusually large number of activities related both to individual and to societal values. As indicated in the matrix, no provision is made for treating values in the first unit; and the relationship of natural resources to quality of life is not dealt with until the third unit.

To illustrate how the element is used in connecting different fields, consider how learners taking a course in technology might be helped if teachers in other courses exchanged elements with the teacher of the course in technology. In their mathematics course, they could acquire other basic concepts for understanding technology and systems such as algorithms, probability, and binary systems. In their English course, they might be able to examine the interaction between technology and society in the mass media. They could appraise American societal values as reflected in newspapers, advertisements, and modern fiction. They could be helped to see how language is related to thought in both persons and machines.

Usually, the meaning of an organizing element through learning opportunities is extended in two ways. The designer can provide for more complex situations to which the element applies, or the complexity of the situation can remain constant but the level of competency expected from the learner becomes more demanding. For example, in early learning opportunities, the learners might be asked only to define and give examples of a concept; in later centers the learners are given the opportunity to apply the concept; and in a final unit they might be asked to evaluate the concept or show its limitations.

However, theory from cognitive psychology stresses that learning is the making of connections between information and the learners' existing network of knowledge. Hence, the idea of teaching lower level concepts before higher order learning seldom makes sense. For example, computational skills do not exist as lower order mathematical problem solving but are learned in relation to and as part of problem solving.[2]

If one wants long-term retention and transfer, the initial experiences should be complex and allow for the student to struggle with the task or questions. This approach is opposed to teaching an isolated skill where direct instruction and the minimizing of errors during the training or introductory period is more effective. Impaired performance during training enhances long-term retention and transfer.

The older view of ordering on the basis of logical dependency is also deficient because it does not take into account the unique ways in which children look at a task. Children differ from adults not only in the amount of previously learned subskills but in the number of subskills they are capable of coordinating at one time and in their ability to avoid applying incorrect subskills or concepts. In making a task analysis or hierarchy, the structure of the task from the *learner's point of view* is important. When such an analysis shows a mismatch between the capacities of the learners and the demands of the task, the sequence should be redesigned either to reduce the hierarchy or to differentiate concepts that are confusing to children.

---

[2]Penelope Peterson et al., "Using Knowledge of How Students Think About Mathematics," *Educational Leadership* 46, no. 4 (Dec. 1980–Jan. 1981): 42–46.

PRINCIPLES FOR SEQUENCING CENTERS AND ACTIVITIES RELATED TO ELEMENTS

Principles for sequencing learning opportunities go back hundreds of years. Most of these principles are being questioned in light of newer beliefs about how learning takes place. In 1636, Comenius admonished teachers to order activities from the simple to the complex. The principle *simple to complex* means introducing learning activities involving a few factors before activities involving many factors. It also means going from parts to the whole. However, this principle is challenged by the belief that it is better to start with the whole before attending to the parts—"A mirror constructed from broken parts doesn't give a true reflection." Other traditional principles of sequence—for example, going from *familiar to unfamiliar*—lead to activities where what learners know precedes completely novel activities. Children study their neighborhood before learning about their state and nation, and about foreign lands. This principle is challenged by those who point to children's interest in the exotic and the unfamiliar. Another principle of sequence is to progress from *concrete to abstract* by presenting opportunities for children to see, touch, taste, hear, or smell a phenomenon before asking them to verbalize and categorize. A common principle is to teach *dependent factors* first. Addition and subtraction, for example, precede multiplication. Authors of a new proposal for teaching physics, chemistry, and biology in that order use the argument of dependency. However, authors of another proposal advocate teaching biology, chemistry, and physics together for three years with the first year offering descriptive hands-on activities related to these subjects; the second year involving experimental and empirical investigation; and the third year introducing theories of what has been learned.

There are also several ways of sequencing a series of facts or subjects. Ordering by *chronology* means presenting events as they occurred in time. Ordering by *usefulness* means teaching particular school subjects at the time they are needed in everyday life.

In Chapter 13, there is a discussion of the *theory of cultural epochs,* which was used as the basis for sequencing studies at the turn of the twentieth century. This theory states that the learning processes of children follow the same pattern as the learning process of the human race. The notion is still very much alive. Some modern curriculum writers in the field of music are interested in the ideas of Carl Orff, a German composer who developed new plans and materials for teaching music to children based on the cultural epoch hypothesis. Orff reasoned that primitive peoples used free bodily movement in dance and also simple rhythmic drum patterns; therefore, children should begin with drums suited to their size and skill. Bodily movements should be combined with the beat of the drum, and rhythmic chants should synchronize the spoken rhythm with other movements.

Because primitive peoples first use only one or two pitches before finally progressing to the use of the five-tone scale, the musical experiences planned for children by cultural epochists to include songs with only two or three notes, and, at most, five notes from the pentatonic scale. Melodic vocabulary offers other steps only after many opportunities with the simple melodies.[3]

ORGANIZING STRUCTURES

An organizing structure divides time spent in the school into a series of periods for activities. The kind of structure used depends on (1) the level (institutional or classroom) at which curriculum decisions occur; (2) the conception of curriculum; and (3) the chosen

---

[3]Carl Orff and Gunhill Keetman, *Orff-Schulwek: Musik fur Kinder*, 5 vols. (New York: Associated Music, 1950–1953).

domain, function, or purpose of the curriculum (exploration, general education, specialization). Structure influences but does not determine social interaction. Indeed it is better to change the curriculum before altering the structure than to introduce new structures in expectation of changing the curriculum.

Structure at the Institutional Level

Institutions make use of a number of options in structuring curriculum. A *broad fields structure* focuses on fields of study—social studies, language arts, and vocational education—whereas *specific subjects structure* concentrates on individual subjects—science, mathematics, and English. A *core curriculum structure* draws content from a range of subjects or fields by addressing general problems or unifying themes. Amherst College, for example, once organized a program around "Problems in American Democracy," involving the entire faculty and student body. The arts, humanities, and sciences all were related in addressing the problems selected. Finally, a *free-form or open structure,* common in affluent times and when individuality and choice are priorities, offers a potpourri of courses and independent study to reflect different students' needs.

At intermediary levels, within departments, structures feature discrete courses such as health care and the law, women's movements, modern dance, or courses that make up a unified program such as first-year science, second-year science, and third-year science.

Whatever structure is chosen, it should be part of an overall design relating purposes (functions, domains, goals, standards, objectives) to organizing elements (concepts, values, skills) and to specific learning opportunities or activities. Such a design is shown in Figure 7.1 in which the designers in the school show that they have a wide range of purposes, domains, standards and objectives. They provide several organizing structures: broad fields for general education, undifferentiated or open structure for self-realization, and subjects or disciplines for specialization. The organizing elements derived from purposes indicate the kinds of learning opportunities that will be created within the structures.

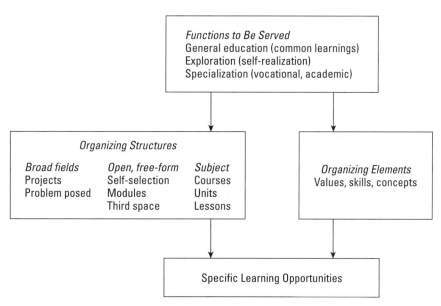

Figure 7.1 Outline of a Curriculum Design

Structure at the Classroom Level

Open Structure A popular structure in humanistic classrooms within the elementary school is an *open structure*. Time, space, materials, and human resources are arranged to integrate skills learned in isolation and to develop social skills. In one early childhood program, the curriculum is divided into three major areas: language, numbers, and drama. The thrust of most activities is to involve children in their own learning. Observers of the program sense a tremendous enthusiasm on the part of both teacher and children as they work together in small groups or as a whole class. The following account records observations of such a class during a typical school day:

Open Structure for the Teaching of Numbers In the number class three children were measuring flour, water, and orange juice in order to make cookies. After measuring the ingredients, they became involved with additional number activities by cutting out squares for each member of the class. After these children finished their project, other children became involved with the same procedure.

At the same time, another child was coloring numbers, another was counting, two other children were painting and finishing their projects, four children were individually taking a number count regarding an upcoming sports event, and four others were working with the teacher with counters. There was an abundance of activity, interest, and sustained effort on the part of each of the 31 children in the classroom. Those children who were not involved were questioned by the teacher as to their activity or lack of it. The room was alive with number concepts and activities, but also ample evidence of language and creative activities was present, such as science interest centers, art projects, writing, and verbalization. Other activities included:

Measuring each other to find the tallest, and the shortest boy or girl.

Measuring hand spans—number of hand spans needed to fill the inside of a truck.

Motor skill development.

Art.

Drawing pictures of their concept of football players on the field.

The flower shop—using tissue to make flowers, and selling them, which entails using money.

Using the water table to measure water—how many cups in a gallon jug, etc.

Figure 7.2 shows a typical day in a number class.

The Key School, an inner city elementary school in Indianapolis has an open structure aimed at stimulating multiple intelligence.[4] The school has a theme-centered curriculum that calls for introducing standard literacies and subject matter around themes such as "people and their environment." Themes change nearly every 10 weeks, and students are asked to carry out and present a project related to each theme. In addition, however, teachers have arranged "pods," activity centers where students work with peers of different ages using materials related to cognitive areas of intelligence—bodily kinesthetic, language, spatial, musicality, logical–mathematical, intra- and interpersonal, and nature study. These pods include centers such as architecture, gardening, cooking, "making money," "math pentalons," and "actors unlimited," with each pod emphasizing a particular intelligence.

---

[4]Howard Gardner, *The Unschooled Mind: How Children Think and How Schools Should Teach* (New York: Basic Books, 1991).

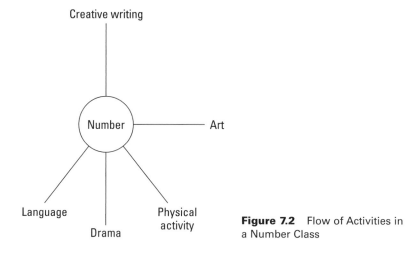

Figure 7.2 Flow of Activities in a Number Class

Third Space The third space is an organizational arrangement that capitalizes on disruption and conflict as opportunity for potential learning. Third space is an expanded zone or hybrid social space where conflicts between school and everyday life become the basis for new activities and outcomes. For example, in one second and third grade classroom conflict arose when a student called another a "homo," violating the school's expected mutual respect. A brief classroom conversation with the children about why people use insults revealed deep misunderstanding about sexuality and sexual reproduction. The teacher explained that the topic was something with which society and parents were not comfortable and before continuing, permission from parents and administrators would be needed to include the topic in the "third space." With parental approval and participation, the class decided to learn about the human reproductive system and to design a 6-week curriculum in the third space, bridging the official and unofficial space of home and school.[5]

The Lesson Plan The lesson plan is a major organizational structure. Currently, the systemic lesson plan prevails over alternative plans although teachers depart from it in actual practice.

The Systemic Lesson Plan Although structured lesson plans can reflect principles drawn from different curriculum orientations, it is the systemic view that features a prescriptive model for planning. Typically the plan includes the following:

1. *Diagnosis.* A major performance objective associated with a content standard is identified and there is some provision—a quick quiz or question perhaps—for determining the status of the learners in relation to the objective.

2. *Specific objectives or benchmarks.* On the basis of the diagnosis, a specific objective for a day's lesson is selected.

3. *Anticipatory set.* There is a plan for focusing the learner's attention, giving brief practice or relating learning previously achieved, and developing readiness for the instruction to follow.

---

[5]K. D. Gutierrez et al., "Rethinking Diversity, Hybridity and Hybrid Language Practices in the Third Space," in *Language Literacy and Education: A Reader,* Sharon Goodman et al., eds. (Sterling, VA: Trentham Books, 2003).

4. *Perceived purpose.* Learners are informed of the objective and told why it is important and relevant to their present and future situations.

5. *Learning opportunities.* Activities are selected that promise to help achieve the desired performance.

6. *Modeling.* Modeling is a demonstration or visual example of what is to be attained—product or process—and a verbal description of the critical features involved.

7. *Check for understanding.* This provision ensures that learners have acquired the essential information or skill.

8. *Guided practice.* Activities to test whether students can perform the task successfully are given so that the teacher can decide if students are ready to study on their own.

9. *Independent practice.* After learners can perform the task without major errors, they are given an opportunity to practice the new concept, skill, or process with little or no teacher direction either at school or outside of school.

Alternatives in Lesson Plans According to Shavelson and Stern, the prescriptive lesson structure is consistently *not* in teachers' planning.[6] A mismatch exists between the demands of classroom instruction and the prescriptive planning model. Teachers want to maintain the flow of activity during a lesson so that classes do not become unruly. Teachers, therefore, give first priority to planning activities that capture the attention of students during the lesson. The focus of teacher planning is on the learners' interests while at the same time attending to the content.

Perhaps preservice teachers differ in their approach to planning depending on the nature of their preparation for teaching. Those indoctrinated by experts into a traditional subject matter major introduce the principles of the subject matter first as prerequisite to student application—a "top-down" approach. Other preservice teachers from university programs that emphasize general education and pedagogy begin their planning with sensitivity to students' prior knowledge, interests and developmental needs—"bottom-up." *Progressive formulation* is a bottom-up approach that begins by having students describe their own solutions to problems. Later, they acquire the formal solutions.[7]

Alternative-style lesson plans call for the teacher first to engage in self-questioning: What idea am I to teach? What does this idea mean? How does it relate to other ideas within the subject, to ideas in other subjects? How is this idea related to my course goals and standards? Next, the teacher plans ways for relating the idea to the minds and motivations of the students. This may include preparing students for the activity, linking the new idea to something familiar, and the selection of teaching method (inquiry, project, didactic). The generating of guiding questions is important.

When appropriate, let students connect their own backgrounds and communities through collaborative social interactions, hands-on activities, arts integration, and student-generated questions. With partners and using contrasting materials, students engage in multiperspective inquiry. Note that these are guidelines, so the key words are "when appropriate." Therefore, sequence and range of activities overlap.

- *Connecting to learners and locating the context.* Teachers access students' prior knowledge and previous experiences through open-ended questions. They generate interest, encourage questions, and personalize through a variety of ways appropriate

---

[6]Richard J. Shavelson and Paula Stern, "Research on Teachers' Pedagogical Thoughts," *Review of Educational Research* 51, no. 1 (1981): 455–498.

[7]Mitchell J. Nathan and Anthony Petrosmo, "Expect Blind Spots among Preservice Teachers," *American Educational Research Journal* 40, no. 4 (winter 2003): 929–961.

to the learners and the goals. They provide multidisciplinary opportunities for learners to acquire necessary background knowledge, perspectives, and multidimensional contexts for understanding historical, sociocultural, aesthetic, political, and/or economic dynamics.

- *Engaging learners in interactions with the content, encouraging conversations, inquiry, and critical analysis.* Teachers involve students in exploring, examining, and interpreting, especially the students' own backgrounds, revising prior knowledge. Students look for different perspectives and bias.

- *Extending and deepening learners' experiences and knowledge.* Encourage further elaboration through more in-depth study, research, comparisons and contrasts to other content, and/or through culminating projects and actions.

- *Engaging learners in metalevel questions throughout each stage.* How have I come to know this? Where do I stand in relationship to this knowledge? What do I choose to do?

The Unit   The unit structure is cited by teachers as the most important teaching tool, followed by weekly and daily planning. There are two kinds of units: the resource unit and the teaching unit. The difference between the two lies in how closely the recommended practices are tailored for particular learners. The *resource unit* is a guide for teaching a potential and general population of learners. The teaching unit is developed for known persons. Both units have the same components: rationale (justification for the unit presented as an overview), standards, topics, activities, and materials.

The unit's length is usually from 2 to 6 weeks, and the body of the document includes activities to introduce the major topics and to prepare for the activities that follow. Problems, demonstrations, and guest speakers are common initiating activities. Development activities comprise the major portion of the unit. In these activities, students interact with the content by raising and formulating questions, collecting data, and trying to resolve the initially proposed problem.

In preparing such activities, the designer considers what resources (field site, materials, resource persons) will be necessary as students carry out their investigations and what skills they need to gather information and complete their projects. Culminating activities in the unit offer opportunities for students to evaluate and synthesize what has been learned, to present their findings with recommendations before specific audiences, and to summarize and formulate new questions for further study.

Topics for units reflect the curriculum orientation—subject matter, personal concerns, social problems, and basic skills. These topics are cast as organizing centers and arranged in a sequential order, thereby constituting a course of study.

The following example illustrates the different components in a resource unit for the middle grades entitled "Providing Education":

Organizing elements: relation of physical environment to quality of life (generalizations)—reading, writing, and thinking (literacy skills)

Organizing centers: the focus of the problem. "What is the function of education?" "How do the differences in living conditions between modern and earlier cultures account for differences in the educational system?" "What makes a good school?"

Activities: Compare a contemporary school with early schools, showing the contrast in enrollment, lessons, discipline, and materials. Read and write stories about the school days of pioneer children. Exhibit old textbooks and show how these books differ from current books. Dramatize a day in a colonial or frontier school.

Teacher's materials:

Cubberly, E. P. *History of Education.* Boston: Houghton Mifflin, 1920.

Mayhew, K., and A. Edwards. *The Dewey School.* New York: D. Appleton-Century, 1936.

Children's materials:

Dunton, Lucy. *School Children the World Over.* New York: Stokes, 1909.

Gordy, W. P. *Colonial Days.* New York: Scribner, 1908.

Wilson, Howard. *Where Our Way of Living Comes From.* New York: American Book, 1937.

Community resources: Schools (public and private), libraries, museums, and interviews with persons from other generations.

The Module   A module is a short course of between 20 and 60 hours, designed in terms of objectives, content, skills required on entry and anticipated at the end of the course, assessment techniques, and suggestions for methodology and resources. Modules are not mere chunks of content; they develop knowledge and skills in a balanced way. The key quality of the module is its relative brevity. This brevity allows students more choices about the composition of their whole course of studies than would be possible if they were committed from the start to a 1-year or 2-year block of work. Often students can negotiate the specific curriculum they need and want.

Organizational Patterns and Conceptions of the Curriculum

Most patterns of curriculum organization fall within particular curriculum orientations. Each of these orientations has its own view regarding the nature of knowledge, the purpose of education, and how learning is best acquired. Parenthetically, this section is written for the reader who has a special need for in-depth treatment of curriculum organization. We suggest that those with a general interest in the topic skip this section and go directly to the section "Issues in Curriculum Organization."

Academic Patterns   Five patterns have prevailed in the academic curriculum: (1) discipline, (2) broad fields, (3) concentration, (4) cross-discipline, and (5) unified disciplines.

   Discipline   The discipline, or single subject, approach is the oldest and most widely accepted form of curriculum organization. Accordingly, knowledge is classified as different forms: mathematics, science, arts, social sciences, and the like. Each form and the different subjects within the form presumably have a basic structure, a set of organizing principles, fundamental ideas, and relationships; pages 66 and 67 illustrate this form of organization. Typically, the academic discipline curriculum divides knowledge into separate subjects, each with its characteristic ideas, meanings, and methods. Ideally, students learn how to evaluate knowledge claims in subject matter and acquire ways to test what they know or what others think they know.

   This curriculum is designed to prepare students to enter the discipline as scholars and perhaps to contribute to the development of knowledge in the field. The goal is to help students think like subject matter specialists. The argument is that in studying several subjects, such as math, history, and science, students acquire the ideas, facts, and skills with which to understand the world.

   The discipline curriculum emphasizes exposition and explanation. Ideas are stated and elaborated on so that they may be understood. Main ideas are ordered by one of the following principles:

1. *Simple to complex.* Topics that contain few elements or subordinate parts are taught before complex topics are taught, as in chemistry where hydrogen and oxygen are taught before chemical compounds.

2. *Logical dependency.* Certain learnings are prerequisite to others, as in geometry when theorems are ordered by their logical relations.

3. *Whole to part.* In contrast to breaking a task down and teaching its elements, attention is given to the whole task to be learned, so that the learner has a frame of reference, a blueprint to help relate the parts as they are subsequently encountered. An instance is the whole language method of teaching reading that begins with a meaningful complex text rather than with letters and phonic elements.

4. *Chronological.* Facts and ideas are arranged in the order of their development over time. History courses present events in this manner.

The discipline pattern emphasizes building connections within a subject more than making connections with developmental concerns of students, with social problems, and to other disciplines. A study of course-planning activities in higher education reveals that faculties have been so strongly socialized in their disciplines that they do not have a systematic view of problems outside their fields.[8] Arrangement of content in courses varies by discipline. History professors structure according to chronology, mathematics and science faculty often hold dependency views, and those in literature and composition are more likely to order content according to the perceived needs of students and literary genres.

Broad Fields   The broad-field pattern is common in elementary and secondary schools and marks an effort to strengthen the interrelationship of ideas and interests in the direction of synthesis or integration. This modification in the academic program juxtaposes subject matter that is assumed to have more or less related ideas. Language arts is composed of what was previously taught separately: grammar, spelling, penmanship, literature, reading, and composition. Mathematics includes arithmetic, geometry, algebra, trigonometry, and topology. Social studies encompasses history, sociology, psychology, anthropology, economics, and geography. Generally, the content of each broad field is linked by generalizations, themes, or principles. For example, the thread of history may be the clarifying idea (organizational element) whereby the study of particular topics or problems (organizing centers or foci), such as those related to environment, education, democracy, and family, are viewed at different historical periods, showing how the concepts of the element are adapted to varying needs.

Concentration   All aspects of a particular object, event, location, or person are studied. An excellent example of concentration is a college course on fowl, which is dedicated to the idea that what is divided may once more be made whole. Described in the *Chicken Book,* this course illustrates how an organizing center—the chicken—can be used to bring together a wonderful compendium of history, science, medicine, religion, technology, economics, facts, and lore.[9]

Similarly, *Galileo,* a team-taught interdisciplinary course in the junior high school, included Galileo's writings, biographical and historical studies, and Bertolt Brecht's play *The Life of Galileo.*[10] This course involved students in making connections, judgments, and

[8]J. Stark and M. Lowther, *Disciplinary Influences in Faculty Planning of Courses* (Ann Arbor, MI: National Center for Research to Improve Post-Secondary Teaching and Learning, 1989).
[9]P. Smith and C. Daniel, *The Chicken Book* (Boston: Little, Brown, 1975).
[10]A. Kaplan, "Galileo: An Experiment in Interdisciplinary Education," *Curriculum Inquiry* 18, no. 3 (1988): 255–287.

understanding themselves in the recovery of one man's life, works, and character. The organizing theme of the course was the relationship between observations and inferences. During activities such as observing the night sky with the naked eye and the moon with a telescope, students attended to details and distinguished what Galileo observed from what he inferred about those details. Also, the course was a canvas for the study of authority between scientist and state, delineating the political problems of authority.

Cross-Discipline   One discipline is viewed from the perspective of another—for example, the history of psychology and the psychology of history. Teachers of mathematics sometimes create cross-disciplinary units such as "the mathematics of music."

Applications   Academic connections are made by using a skill or knowledge from one discipline in another (e.g., using writing skills to develop a science report or using math to interpret social science findings). Teachers resist using their subject as a tool in another subject. In her study of teachers planning integrative curriculum, Gehrke[11] shows the importance of teachers exchanging their explicit view of integration and their individual and common interests, goals, themes, and academic expertise. Others have found that science teachers rarely or never go beyond the boundaries of science content by trying to relate content to other domains of scientific literacy or provide a larger context for understanding facts or concepts.[12]

Unified Disciplines: The New Academic Pattern

The emergence of new frontiers of research and the need to solve real-world problems that cannot be resolved by a single discipline is creating new and dramatic curriculum landscapes that cross traditional disciplinary boundaries.[13] Faculty from different disciplines, such as math and science, are focusing less on textbook knowledge within the separate disciplines, and instead the teachers are learning to communicate with each other, using each other's academic or disciplinary language—such as the language of biology and the language of mathematics or physics—as they collaboratively design a curriculum focused on a problem that is likely to draw on the individual intellectual concepts, methods, and facts of each discipline, capitalizing on the synthesis from unifying seemingly disparate subjects.

Social Reconstruction Patterns   Basic categories of societal problems—leisure, protecting life and health, conserving natural resources, and making a living—have been the foci ordering social reconstruction learning. Courses treating women at work, technology and society, and issues in foreign policy are instances. When these problem areas are developed so that students (1) consider the value conflicts underlying the issues, (2) determine the social goals that should be pursued, and (3) take action in support of the goals, there is a curriculum of reconstruction. To reiterate, the emphasis is on social problem solving, the development of community norms, and participation in political action, not on acquiring subject matter as an end in itself. However, a variety of descriptions and theory often are useful in analyzing and addressing the problems.

[11]N. Gehrke, "Developing Integrative Curriculum. Some Discoveries in Process" (paper presented at the annual meeting of the American Educational Research Association, New Orleans, April 1988).
[12]A. C. Mitman, J. R. Mergenddler, V. A. Marchmen, and M. J. Packer, "Instruction Addressing the Components of Scientific Literacy and Its Relation to Student Outcomes," *American Educational Research Journal* 24, no. 4 (1987): 611–635.
[13]William Bialer and David Botstein, "Introductory Science and Mathematics Education for 21st Century Biologists," *Science* 303 (6 Feb. 2004): 788–793.

Although most social reconstruction activity occurs in nonformal settings, a social reconstructionist curriculum can be organized in formal education. In formal settings, sequencing occurs at two points: (1) in the ordering of social problems (foci) and (2) in the extending of the capacities and outlooks sought through the curriculum (organizing elements). The problems selected fall within the learners' range of experience or students work closely with others (older peers and adults) on aspects of the problem when the problems are advanced and complex.

Typically, only those problems that meet the following criteria are selected: (1) crucial; (2) connection to the local community and the real world; (3) potential for illuminating the power structure and developing values and critical thinking; and (4) opportunity for taking effective action.

Two principles for sequencing problems are common. First, psychological principles involve conception of what learners can do (independently and with assistance). Second, sociological principles concern attending first to problems of greatest importance.

An example of curriculum organization within the social reconstruction perspective is Ira Shor's account of how he uses critical-democratic pedagogy centered on issues from everyday life.[14] Shor often begins his writing course by encouraging students to generate a theme from their own lives. In one instance, the students chose personal growth as their primary theme—a theme that expressed their aspirations. Shor then asked students to indicate in writing what personal growth has meant to them, what helps personal growth, and what are the obstacles. The essays students wrote were used as anonymous discussion texts. In addition to talking about skills like paragraphing and sentence boundaries, Shor noticed that most students saw personal growth as an individual matter—that success or failure depends solely on your individual qualities and your personal strengths. Shor was concerned that this self-reliant ideology hides the influence of such social factors as inequality and discrimination. Hence, he intervened with a topical theme that was related to the theme they had chosen, "Personal growth is affected by economic policy." Shor introduced readings about corporations fleeing the city for cheap labor areas, and government decisions to give various companies huge tax breaks to keep them in the city. Students were asked how these economic policies would affect their taxes, city services, and the education available to them. "Would it impact their personal growth?"

The topical theme was expanded to other conditions influencing personal growth. After Shor presented racism as a theme, a Hispanic student claimed in his essay that racism had been an obstacle but student resistance crippled it. He thus decided to switch to sexism as an obstacle and theme. Shor read a news article about young women in Ireland doing cheap labor under male supervision for a runaway U.S. firm whose relocation was facilitated by the latest technology in satellite and cable contacts. Questions followed, such as "Were computers a good thing for working people or for management?" "Is high tech a neutral force in society?" Students also opened up the theme of sexual inequality, with many sharing their personal experiences.

Finally, students reworked their original essay in a new format with the paragraphing focused on separate issues, such as examining individual qualities that help or hinder growth as well as social factors that serve as remedies or obstacles.

It should be noted that Shor introduced the topical theme as a participation problem, not as a lecture. Students were free to reflect and disagree. Indeed, in the case of the corporate policy and personal power, some students defended tax breaks for giant companies as the only way to keep jobs in the city. What is important from the social reconstructionist

---

[14]Ira Shor, *Empowering Education: Critical Teaching for Social Change* (Chicago: University of Chicago Press, 1992).

view is that this curriculum brought the issue to open public debate instead of it being swept under the rug of self-reliance ideology.

In brief, the instructional sequences of reconstructionists typically follow these steps: (1) identifying the issue that is most problematic; (2) examining the realities of the participants" lives, including the constraints and root causes of their problems; (3) linking issues to institutions and structures in the larger society; (4) relating social analyses to the norms and ideals they have for their world and community and for themselves; and (5) taking some responsibility (action) for making reality agree more with ideals.

Humanistic Patterns   The image of the learner as a developing person guides the organization of the humanistic curriculum. It is a curriculum that considers the *whole person*: an individual who is not only intellectual but also developed in aesthetic and moral ways. It aims at helping the person integrate emotions, thought, and action. Subject matter is valued only as it matches the learner's psychological organization.

Developmental Stages   Theories of developmental stages have been used to interpret the conceptions of learners and to help them reconstruct their realities at a higher level. A teacher using a stage theory of mental growth, for example, is interested in whether a learner has attained the mental abilities that Piaget called *concrete operations* before introducing tasks requiring application of abstract principles.[15] The curriculum of the High/Scope Educational Research Foundation in Ypsilanti, Michigan, is based on Piaget's developmental theory. In this program, children are grouped by developmental stages (preoperational or concrete), not by age. Other examples of curriculum centered on the individual and ordered by the developmental perspective that knowledge is constructed by learners, reflecting the joint contribution of the subject and the object, are available.[16]

Kohlberg's theory that a person develops a moral sense through universal stages also has been used to sequence instruction. In this curriculum, the learner is encouraged to generate moral principles at the next higher level than present attainment. The procedure is to present moral dilemmas posing a cognitive conflict and to engage in cross-stages discussions in which students are guided to the next level.[17]

Humanistic curricula have been developed in accordance with Erik Erikson's theory of eight stages of growth in which there is a continuous progression throughout life in struggles between positive and negative outcomes. The curriculum becomes ordered as teachers attempt to help individual learners succeed in confronting the particular crises with which they are struggling.

There are criticisms of stage theories, such as the belief that students must reach a certain developmental level or age before engaging in abstract reasoning as moral thinking. Instead the critics believe that students can control their development if placed in environments where parents, peers, teachers, and others scaffold activities that exceed the students' current performance levels.[18]

Age appropriateness is an issue as seen in the question of when to begin formal instruction in reading. Bruce Joyce and others are introducing a formal reading program for kindergarten students in order to increase their achievement in the primary grades.[19]

---

[15]D. Elkind, "Developmentally Appropriate Practice: Philosophical and Practical Implications," *Phi Delta Kappan* 71, no. 2 (1987): 113–118.

[16]E. Duckworth, *The Having of Wonderful Ideas and Other Essays on Teaching and Learning* (New York: Teachers College Press, 1987).

[17]L. Kohlberg, "Education for a Just Society," *Moral Development, Moral Education, and Kohlberg,* B. Mussey, ed. (Birmingham, AL: Religious Education Press, 1980).

[18]K. Metz, "On the Complex Relation Between Cognitive Development Research and Children's Science Curriculum," *Review of Educational Research* 67, no.1 (1997): 151–163.

[19]Bruce Joyce et al., "Learning to Read in Kindergarten: Has Curriculum Development Bypassed the Controversies?" *Phi Delta Kappan* 85, no. 2 (Oct. 2003): 126.

Yet children in Finland do not start school until they are 7 years old and Finland's students are at the top of international comparisons in math, science, and reading achievement. The Finns believe preschoolers will love learning through play, not formal lessons.[20]

Confluence, the integrating of thought, feeling, and movement, has been presented in Chapter 1. A current example of research on integration experiences aimed at helping learners discover their potentials and limitations through intense activities is found in studies of flow in consciousness.[21] A *flow* experience is one in which people temporarily lose awareness of themselves, becoming so involved in a process that they do not see themselves as separate from what they are doing. When a person is in flow, intellectual ability is developed to the fullest. Such experiences occur when environmental challenges match competencies and skills.

The importance of individuals maintaining their own continuity and integration of experience by pursuing problems and interest of personal concern has been shown.[22] Those who make unusual creative contributions have such concerns and show an intense awareness of their active inner life as well as a sensitivity to the external world.

Open Classroom   In the 1960s, open curricula gave learners a voice in determining what and how to learn. Learners were encouraged to create their own knowledge and to pursue their own questions through a combination of spontaneous activity and a stimulating environment. The instructional sequence of problem solving—puzzlement, problem identification analysis, alternative solutions, and their consequences—was common. Recent research has revealed that an influential study that trumpeted the failure of open education but never gained public recognition was retracted because of statistical flaws. Moreover, extended studies of open education led to the conclusion that open classrooms effectively enhance attitude, creativity, and self-concept without detracting from academic achievement, unless classes are radically extreme.[23]

In brief, sequence and integration in humanistic curriculum tend to be structured by the learners. The task of the teacher is to find out what structure of knowledge and perspectives the learners already have and to help them reconstruct their knowledge so that it makes increasing sense to them. Newer instructional sequences based on theories of cognitive learning are consistent with learner-centered organization and do the following:

1. Activate the learner's prior knowledge with respect to the new situation and sensitize the teacher to what learners already know and the preconceptions that might be modified or evaluated against other conceptions.

2. Engage the learner in making predictions and clarifying through visual imagery, questioning, and assessing and applying new learning.

3. Allow the learner to integrate new knowledge with the old, elaborating and using knowledge in new ways.

Systemic Patterns   The systemic curriculum emphasizes the specification of curricula standards and performance indicators (goals), precisely controlled instructional sequences to achieve the objectives, and criteria for performance and evaluation. An underlying assumption of systemic organization is that without a conscious effort to organize the

[20]Lizette Alvarez, "Education Flocking to Finland, Land of Literate Children," *New York Times International* (April 9, 2004).

[21]Mihaly Csikszentmihalyi and Isabella Salega Csikszentmihalyi, *Optimal Experience: Psychological Studies of Flow in Consciousness* (Cambridge, England: Cambridge University Press, 1988).

[22]V. John-Steiner, *Notebooks of the Mind: Explorations of Thinking* (Albuquerque: University of New Mexico Press, 1985).

[23]B. J. Fraser, H. J. Walberg, W. W. Welch, and J. A. Hattie, "A Synthesis of Educational Productivity Research," *International Journal of Educational Research* 11 (1987): 145–252.

curriculum, learning experiences are isolated, chaotic, haphazard, and unlikely to produce significant change.

As described in Chapter 3, systemic curriculum is organized in a hierarchical goal-structured manner with both performance and learning mechanisms operating under the control of some standard, goal or subgoal. Mastery Learning,[24] Curriculum Alignment,[25] and Instructional Systems Design[26] are examples.

In these programs, a learning task (academic or job-related) is broken into parts, ordered, and taught one at a time, and then pulled together based on the resulting relationships. Gagné's system, for example, uses a hierarchical analysis with sequencing of intellectual skills whereby simple component skills are taught before more complex combinations of the parts: multiple discrimination to stimuli, concept learning, principle learning, and problem solving. The system has been used in developing courses for the military. However, its impact in practice is limited by several problems, and its use is being reconsidered by the services.[27] Among the problems are high developmental costs and lack of a strong cognitive theory. Analysis of cognition, as opposed to overt behavioral skills, is difficult or impossible within the system. Newer trends in systemic approaches to military training center on simulations that follow conceptual components useful for reasoning and problem solving.

Graphic depictions of the components are acted on by the learners who can see the effects of their manipulations. The displays suggest what people need to *understand* about a complex system in order to operate it. Hierarchical views of the system and subsystems mirror the understanding of competent experts. Physical principles underlying a system's functions are taught in the context of operation and maintenance.

Cognitive psychology also influences technological curriculum by suggesting that content should be progressively organized from more general ideas to more detailed ones. For example, the elaboration theory of Reigeluth and Stern proposes beginning a sequence with the most general ideas that epitomize (not summarize) the entire subject.[28] The first lesson in a sequence is the epitome lesson that presents a few of the most crucial ideas at a concrete, application-based level. Learners acquire ideas at the *use* level rather than at the remember level. Also, the theory varies sequencing procedures according to the types of content: procedural, theoretical, and expository.

Synthesis or integration of components in systemic organization in the past was thought to occur as the components were incorporated in the prespecified *terminal* objectives or domain specifications consistent with evaluation criteria. Newer strategies address problems of integration, retention, transfer, and motivation by focusing on strategies for integrating cognitive skills. These organizational strategies include *mapping,* a two-dimensional diagram representing the conceptual structure of subject matter in which content elements are organized in a hierarchical order,[29] and *synthesizers.*[30] The latter strategy

[24]B. S. Bloom, "The Search for Methods of Group Instruction as Effective as One-to-One Tutoring," *Educational Leadership* 41, no. 8 (1984): 4–17.

[25]S. A. Cohen, "Instructional Alignment: Searching for a Magic Bullet," *Educational Researcher* 16, no. 6 (1987): 16–20.

[26]R. M. Gagné, *The Conditions of Learning and Theory of Instruction*, 4th ed. (New York: Holt, Rinehart and Winston, 1985).

[27]H. M. Halff, J. D. Hollen, and E. L. Hutchens, "Cognitive Science and Military Training," *American Psychologist* 41 (1986): 1131–1139.

[28]M. Reigeluth and S. S. Stern, "The Elaboration Theory of Instruction," in *Instructional Design Theories and Models: An Overview of their Current Status*, C. M. Reigeluth, ed. (Hillsdale, NJ: Lawrence Erlbaum, 1983), 355–379.

[29]J. D. Novak and D. B. Gowin, *Concept Mapping and Other Innovative Educational Strategies* (Ithaca, NY: Cornell University, 1982).

[30]Reigeluth and Stern, 312–322.

involves a diagram depicting a particular type of relationship (conceptual, procedural, theoretical). A lesson synthesizer shows the relationships among ideas in a single lesson, and a set synthesizer shows relationships among ideas across lessons.

Systemic curriculum organization has been outcome driven; that is, clear statements of the outcomes are sought from instructional sequences. Indeed a critical feature of mastery learning is the creation of unit tests before design of the instructional program. Available evidence supports the idea that the closer the objectives, test, and instruction align, the higher posttest achievement will be.

Heidi Hayes Jacobs extends the systemic procedure of curriculum mapping by having teachers in a school collect data about what they are actually teaching and when it is taught.[31] Each teacher enters the data electronically, and colleagues instantly find out what is being taught. The teachers can also see what was taught the previous year and learn why each teacher modified the official curriculum. They also make planned revisions on their map, renegotiating content standards in the light of student needs, performance data, and changes in the world. Jacobs's e-mapping allows teachers to form a community of judgment that becomes a force in curriculum improvement and gives power to the teachers instead of making them blind acceptors of imposed standards.

EMPIRICAL STUDIES OF THE EFFECTS OF PATTERNS

Over 60 years ago in a classic study, Aiken evaluated different patterns of curriculum organization.[32] This study threw light on the question of how graduates of secondary schools unhampered by college entrance requirements and encouraged to break down barriers between subjects would perform in college. A problem-centered pattern predominated in the 30 experimental schools whereby subject matter from various fields was brought together as needed for understanding and solving a social problem. The findings supported the conclusion that students from the experimental program were more successful than their matches in the traditional programs.

A recent study in 14 Australian schools, contrasting the effects of traditional (externally set syllabi and examinations) and alternative courses (student participation in course direction, nongraded assessment, and content adapted to individual goals), found that alternative courses were more effective in developing positive feelings in students about themselves, the courses, their teachers, and the school.[33] Further, students in the experimental courses showed greater fulfillment in terms of academic, personal, social, and career development. An evaluation of the Sudbury learner controlled curriculum as described in Chapter 8 reported similar results.[34]

There have been studies that cast doubt on prescribed sequences for high-ability secondary school students who *have not* studied high school chemistry or physics. These students can succeed in college chemistry and physics as well as similar students who have completed high school courses in these subjects[35,36] However, in a study of the effects of

---

[31]Heidi Hayes Jacobs, "Creating a Timely Curriculum," *Educational Leadership* 6, no. 4 (Jan. 2004): 12–18.

[32]W. M. Aiken, *The Story of the Eight-Year Study* (New York: Harper and Row, 1942).

[33]M. Batten, "Effects of Traditional and Alternative Courses on Students in Post-compulsory Education," *British Educational Research Journal* 15, no. 3 (1989): 259–271.

[34]P. Gray and D. Charnoff, "Democratic Schooling: What Happens to Young People Who Have Charge of Their Own Education?" *American Journal of Education* 5, no. 2 (1986): 182–214.

[35]D. D. Hendel, "Effects of Individualized and Structured College Curriculum on Students' Performance and Satisfaction," *American Educational Research Journal* 22, no. 1 (1985): 117–122.

[36]R. E. Yaker and S. Kraskik, "Success of Students in a College Physics Course with and without Experiencing a High School Course," *Journal of Research in Science Teaching* 26, no. 7 (1989): 369–389.

curriculum continuity in physical science, Arzi, Ben-Zui, and Ganiel drew a different con-clusion.[37] They found that prior knowledge acquired in grade 7 facilitated learning in grade 8, and retention of the grade 7 subject matter was higher in the group that had studied physical science continuously during grades 7 and 8.

Results of studies treating outcome-based organizational plans, such as mastery learn-ing and hierarchical sequences, are mixed. A synthesis of research using mastery learning showed an average effect of 0.8.[38] Separating the organizational aspects of mastery learn-ing from other features—reinforcement, corrective feedback, and teaching to the test—is difficult. Indeed, the late John Carroll said that his model, which is the theoretical basis for mastery learning, does not require that the tasks be broken into small steps for drill and practice, although it does require clear specification of tasks to be learned.[39]

A synthesis of findings from 46 studies on group-based applications of mastery learn-ing showed great variation in the size of effects.[40] This variation is attributed to subject area, grade level, and duration of the study.

Descriptive studies of curriculum organization show little adherence to organizing principles. A study of elementary school programs in Michigan revealed that a large num-ber of mathematical topics are taught for exposure with no expectation of student mastery-that much of what is taught in one grade is taught again in the next.[41] Porter lamented that knowing a little about a lot of different things is valued more than deep understanding of a few key concepts. Teachers taught in light of what they thought best for their students and within the limits of their own knowledge, time, and energy. Frameworks, standards, sets of objectives, textbooks, and tests were inadequate for deciding what would be taught.

A similar study of curriculum continuity in geography in a British secondary school and its eight feeder primary schools revealed that geography in the primary grades did not fit with the work in secondary schools.[42] Projects were executed in a curriculum vacuum, not in an overall school plan.

An extensive review of instructional research on sequence and synthesis is available.[43] This review includes studies at macro levels (programs and courses) and at micro levels (single lessons). Its authors conclude that micro sequences (generality, example, and prac-tice) have more impact on learning than macro sequences. No consistent instructional ben-efits have been attributed to macro sequencing strategies. Sequences aimed at mastery together with overlearning have been found to improve academic achievement and long-range retention.[44] However, the previously cited research by Robert Bjork found the coun-terintuitive practice of accepting forgetting and impaired performance during training is a better way to enhance long-term retention and transfer. Initiating strategies, such as advanced organizers, contribute little to the learners' knowledge of subject matter structure and

[37]H. J. Arzi, R. Ben-Zui, and V. Ganiel, "Practice and Retroactive Facilitation of Long-term Retention by Curriculum Continuity," *American Educational Research Journal* 22, no. 3 (1985): 369–389.

[38]B. Fraser, H. J. Walberg, W. W. Welch, and J. A. Hattie, "Synthesis of Educational Productivity Research," *International Journal of Educational Research* 11 (1987): 145–252.

[39]J. Carroll, "The Carroll Model: A 25-Year Retrospective and Prospective View," *Educational Researcher* 18, no. 1 (1989): 26–32.

[40]T. D. Pigott, "Research on Group-based Mastery Learning Program: A Meta-Analysis," *Journal of Educational Research* 81, no. 4 (1988): 199.

[41]A. Porter, "Curriculum Out of Balance: The Case of Elementary School Mathematics," *Educational Researcher* 18, no. 5 (1989): 9–16.

[42]M. Williams and R. Howley, "Curriculum Discountability: A Study of a Secondary School and Its Feeder Primary Schools," *British Educational Research Journal* 15, no. 1 (1988): 61–75.

[43]J. Van Patten, C. I. Chao, and C. M. Reigeluth, "A Review of Strategies for Sequencing and Synthesizing Information," *Review of Educational Research* 56, no. 4 (1986): 437–473.

[44]Normand Peladeau et al., "Effect of Paced and Unpaced Practice on Skill Application and Retention: How Much Is Enough?" *American Educational Research Journal* 40, no. 3 (fall 2003): 769–780.

interactive strategies, such as mapping, networking, and elaborating on a generality, lack empirical support.

Although empirical studies of curriculum organization suffer from a lack of consistent terminology and adequate theory, it is doubtful that any organization pattern would explain more than 5% of the variance of what is learned. There is little likelihood that researchers will be able to control outcomes through organization, considering how the effects of any pattern changes in light of more important variables: subject matter, learner backgrounds, time, and cultural factors.

Research on curriculum organization is shifting from prediction and control to efforts that describe, appreciate, interpret, and explain, giving rise to new possibilities. There are signs that curriculum organization is departing from the Cartesian school of thought, which solves problems by separating them into sections and arranging them in logical order, and is becoming more consistent with views of an unpredictable and indeterministic world and a cross-disciplinary approach that will address real-world problems.

Recognition that individuals construct their own meanings from learning opportunities and that, without a lifelong direction, the individual is unlikely to fulfill potential, suggests that curriculum organization be judged both for its promise to raise learner awareness of possibilities and to sustain them so they keep their excitement in working and reworking their own generative ideas.

W. Ullrich and J. Beane[45,46] have categorized attempts at organizing middle school curriculum in the interest of connecting knowledge, casting curriculum on a continuum from (a) *multidisciplinary*—where individual teachers teach their separate subject matters but all relate their subjects to an agreed-on theme, such as "the environment," (b) *interdisciplinary*—two or more teachers involve their students in a problem-based unit whereby selected content and skills from each of the disciplines are repositioned and taught as tools and habits of mind as needed for addressing the problem; and (c) *integration*—students generate questions related to their own concerns about themselves and their world. These concerns are then clustered into projects and inquiries aimed at answering the questions and that require students to draw widely from disciplinary and multicultural resources, integrating their new experiences and findings with their original beliefs and capacities.

Table 7.2 illustrates some of the features that follow from choosing a particular organizational pattern.

ISSUES IN CURRICULUM ORGANIZATION

Curriculum organization is difficult because the fields of knowledge have not been organized in a way that makes them useful in daily life. Also, those in different disciplines express their findings in different terms with the result that the consumer does not know how to relate the findings. Curriculum efforts to integrate concepts from various disciplines have not been successful.

For example, designers at the Education Development Center in Newton, Massachusetts, tried to organize learning opportunities around interests that appear to be important to the prospective students, such as child-rearing practices, love and affection, expressions of fear and anger, and parent–offspring conflict. Using these interests, the staff

[45]W. Ullrich, "Connecting the Curriculum" (paper presented at Joint Doctoral Program in Leadership, CSU Fresno, Sept. 2003).

[46]J. Beane, *Curriculum Integration: Designing the Core of Democratic Education* (New York: Teachers College Press, 1997).

Table 7.2 Connecting Knowledge

Multidisciplinary	Interdisciplinary	Integrated
Focus or center		
Thematic	Problem-based	Student concerns
Purpose		
Show relevance of subject matter School unity	Cross subject boundaries Knowledge for use	Social construction of knowledge from various sources
Subject matter		
Separate subjects and possible contributions to a theme	Selected concepts and procedures necessary for solving real-world problems	Students investigate using both multiple disciplinary and multicultural resources
Role of teacher		
Traditional teacher plans	Work with colleagues in selecting problems and intellectual tools needed from separate disciplines	Facilitator—challenge students' levels of thinking Promote democratic processes
Role of student		
Traditional recitation	Collaborate with others Engage in guided inquiry	Collaboration in peer assisted learning and students plan with teacher
Structure		
Little change	Block schedule or laboratories Site visits	Data collection extended beyond school. Outside resource persons enter classroom and share alternative perceptions
Authority		
Text Teacher Content standards	Experts' reasoning Independent conclusions based on data and evidence	Negotiated meanings Restructured personal knowledge

sought content from different disciplines (biology, anthropology, psychology, sociology, linguistics) which would help students to meet these interests and at the same time to gain an understanding of their own uniqueness, of their kinship with others of the culture, and of the characteristics that unite the human race. The curriculum developers found that no academic discipline was adequate to cope with the questions they wanted to raise. They also found that academicians from different fields use different words to discuss similar phenomena and that these words are invested with different meanings. A biologist speaks of "bonding" when examining relationships between male and female or between parent and offspring; a psychologist may use the word "bonding" as well as words like "love" and "attachment" to describe the same relationships. A third problem was that the disciplines not only represented separate languages and analytical tools, but also drew from bodies of data that did not overlap. A final and deeper problem was the difficulty of trying to combine different points of view regarding human nature. There is, for example, much conflict over whether cultural evolution proceeds independently of biological factors or whether biological forces determine the direction of evolution.

Several solutions have been offered as broader approaches to the problem. Philosophers of science have argued that integration can be achieved by using concepts of knowledge about knowledge. One can draw from disciplines the content that represents the field as a whole. The curriculum person can select ideas and instances that exemplify the method of inquiry in these disciplines and offer instruction in *synoptics*—the integrative fields, like history, religion, and philosophy. These disciplines have as their function the making of coherent wholes.

A second proposal is that we live with the fact that scholars in any one discipline are incapable of resolving any complex human problem. In other words, students should try to examine personal and social problems from multiple perspectives, realizing that one of these views alone is entirely unsatisfactory. Perhaps the conclusion that students reach after attending to the different perspectives will be more valuable than any one discipline's answer to the problems.

The sequencing opportunities are equally problematic. In their attempt to sequence content that will reveal its logical relations and lay down a particular path to important knowledge, curriculum designers may deny learners participation in the intellectual conflicts among experts—opportunities to engage in the dialogues about incongruities in a discipline or fail to capitalize on the unexpected concerns and ideas of learners.

Curriculum integration is an overriding concern. The curriculum reform movement of the 1960s extended the scope of content to include new areas of knowledge but neglected to evolve a unifying purpose. Pluralistic and humanistic interests as well as governmental programs aimed at social and political causes of the 1970s extended even further the range of electives and the scope of content. Curriculum fragmentation resulted. The current efforts to set national curriculum standards in separate subjects are likely to impede efforts at interdisciplinary integration.

Also, there are practical problems that center, for example, on (1) the teachers' loss of identity and security by being isolated as teachers of English, science, history, or other subject fields; (2) the need for flexible scheduling during the school day, along with freedom for student choice of work and movement within the school building and community; (3) the need for material resources that go beyond the normal stock of books and equipment found in separate departments; (4) the difficulty of learning the teaching roles, skills, and attitudes required by the new curriculum; and (5) the need to answer the objection that an integrated curriculum does not prepare students for external examinations based on separate subject matter.

Perhaps we should forget about curriculum organization as a way to effect meaning for students. Even when there is a careful attempt to simplify and relate content so that students can follow it, the organization will fit any one student imperfectly. Students individualize their experiences anyway. Why not put the burden on the learners to make sense out of learning opportunities in any order? More positively stated, why not challenge students to pose their own questions, seek their own answers, make their own synthesis, and find satisfaction in so doing?

Peter Freyberg and the late Roger Osborne think that curriculum developers have erred in structuring curriculum from the perspective of the teacher.[47] They propose that no matter what curriculum framework is employed, learners are going to structure the subject matter in their own way. What is learned can be very different from what is taught. Progress in curriculum development rests on finding out the concepts and cognitive structures that learners bring with them to the learning opportunities. Usually, there are only three or four distinctly different viewpoints regarding a matter. Ascertaining the learners' conceptions and the procedures for dealing with conflicting preconceptions so that students can be helped to accommodate more adequate conceptions is now central. Learning is being viewed less as a process of knowledge accretion than as a process of conceptual change.

---

[47]Roger Osborne and Peter Freyberg, *Learning in Science* (Portsmouth, NH: Heinemann, 1985).

Curriculum design has been suspected of preventing learners from comprehending content in any other order and from learning content that is incompatible with adaptive teaching. Underlying most organizational issues, however, are disputes about purpose. Curriculum workers who favor academic specializations value organization as it relates to sequencing for depth, but they are not impressed by integrative arrangements. Those who seek integrated approaches, usually humanists and social reconstructionists, distrust pre-arranged sequences within a single field.

CONCLUDING COMMENTS

In this chapter emphasis was placed on two ways to organize learning opportunities: by means of organizing centers and organizing elements. Curriculum design was viewed as a plan showing the relationships among purpose, organizing structures, organizing elements, and specific learning opportunities. Illustrations of curriculum design were presented with special attention to the designing of classroom curriculum structures. Principles for sequencing and integrating content were critiqued, and the organizational patterns used by those with particular curriculum orientations evaluated. Issues in curriculum organization—particularly concern about the integration of subject matter and the dangers of tight sequencing—were discussed. The problem of linking curriculum planning undertaken at two levels of decision making (institutional and classroom) was also introduced.

Because the planning of a curriculum is a management and political matter as much as a technical one, the connection between the curriculum and these matters is treated more fully in Part 3.

QUESTIONS

1. Think of a familiar learning task such as tying shoes, operating an automobile, playing a game, or composing a musical or literary piece. Into what units would you divide the task you have in mind? In what order would you teach these steps? What principle of sequence determines your ordering?

2. State an organizing element—a concept, value, or skill—that you would like to build on throughout a number of activities in a course or program of interest to you.

3. Curriculum constructed in accordance with hierarchical theories (i.e., curriculum in which there is an attempt to specify prerequisites and to order them from simple to complex) is sometimes criticized for being boring, ineffective, and controlling. Critics charge that there are too many unnecessary steps for some learners and that many learners who successfully complete the en route steps fail at transfer tasks at the end of the programs. What is your response to this criticism?

4. Arno Bellack once suggested a program that would include the powerful ideas found in the humanities, natural sciences, and social sciences together with a coordinating seminar in which students dealt with problems "in the round" and in which a special effort is made to show the relationships between the ideas of the systematized fields of study as materials from these fields are brought to bear on a chosen topic or problem. What are the advantages and disadvantages of Bellack's suggestion? What conditions would have to exist in order for the proposed plan to work?

5. Assume that you are a member of a planning committee charged with recommending a curriculum organization for a school. You have been asked whether the new plan should attempt to provide for integration of subject matter and, if so, how it can best be achieved. What is your reply?

SUGGESTED STRATEGIC RESEARCH

EXPERIMENTING WITH TOP-DOWN AND BOTTOM-UP APPROACHES IN CURRICULUM PLANNING

Nathan and others ("Expect Blind Spots Among Preservice Teachers," *American Educational Research Journal*, winter 2003) suggest that in planning instructional units it is better to start with representations, applications, stories, and real-world situations that students bring than to begin with the symbolic principles and organizational patterns of the discipline. Order an instructional unit in two ways—begin one version following bottom-up rule with student-centered activities (use student informal ideas and help them see how they can be formalized) and the other version beginning with the top-down approach, that is, subject matter as ordered by principles and operations of the discipline. Both versions may treat the same concept. Note the effects (achievement and motivational) from each version.

UNCOVERING GAPS IN CURRICULUM ALIGNMENT OF STANDARDS AND CLASSROOM ENACTMENT

How does what gets taught in the classroom differ from what state and district content standards say should be taught? What are the reasons for teachers departing from official coverage of the subject matter? Engage teachers from two or more grade levels in the same school in reviewing the content standards for these grades and then elicit from them how much time, if any, they gave to teaching each standard. If possible, determine the activities and materials they used and their reasons for substituting or eliminating content.

DETERMINING REASONS FOR PLACING CONTENT AT GIVEN GRADE LEVELS

Little attention has been given why particular content is placed and its attainment assessed at specific grade levels. Is it because of the logic of the subject matter? Or a belief about what learners can do at a certain age? Is it only because of tradition? Are there survival needs to be met at given times? Weldon and Sharon Zenger are researching these questions and would welcome your findings collected in a local school or district (e-mail cofz@ksu.edu).

COMPARING KNOWLEDGE ACQUISITION AND COMPETENCY ACQUIRED UNDER (A) SINGLE-SUBJECT ORGANIZATION AND (B) INTERDISCIPLINARY ORGANIZATION

There is concern that interdisciplinary programs might not prepare students with the fundamentals of any discipline in as much depth as does a single subject approach. Select a population of students who have participated in a interdisciplinary program and a population who complete their work in one of the subjects as a single subject. Compare what is learned under each condition by student interviews, analyses of relevant achievement test data, teacher self-reports, and other indicators of understandings and competencies.

IDENTIFYING EXEMPLARY TEACHERS BY WHETHER THEY HELP STUDENTS LINK CONCEPTS TO OTHER SUBJECTS AND/OR THE EVERYDAY WORLD AS OPPOSED TO ONLY TEACHING KEY CONCEPTS IN A SINGLE DISCIPLINE

Select teachers recognized as accomplished—board certified, collegial reputations, teaching performance assessment, or other indicator—and then assess their work by interviewing them and collecting samples of students' work under their direction and accounts of their curriculum planning. Do outstanding teachers excel in helping students link key concepts?

SELECTED REFERENCES

BUCHMANN, M., AND ROBERT FLODEN. "Coherence: The Rebel Angel," *Educational Researcher* 21, no. 9 (Dec. 1992): 4–10.

DUFFY, THOMAS M. AND DAVID JONASSEN, EDS. *Construction and the Technology of Instruction: A Conversation.* Hillside, NJ: Lawrence Erlbaum, 1992.

GRANT, CARL A., AND CHRISTINE E. SLEETER. *Turning on Learning: Five Approaches for Multicultural Teaching Plans for Race, Class, Gender, and Disability*, 3rd ed. Hoboken, NJ: John Wiley & Sons, 2003.

JENKINS, J. M., AND J. TANNER. *Restructuring for an Interdisciplinary Curriculum.* Reston, VA: National Association of Secondary School Principals, 1992.

SHARP, VICKI F. *Computer Education for Teachers: Integrating Technology into the Classroom*, 5th ed. Boston: McGraw Hill, 2005.

PART III

CURRICULUM
MANAGEMENT

The chapters in Part 3 have much to do with a revolutionary change in schools and in their governance. Never have we seen so many alternative schools with such variety in curriculum enactments. Yet never has there been so much standardizing of curriculum by the federal and state governments.

Perhaps, before reading these chapters, you will discuss with others their views regarding schools of choice, privatizing schooling, and the kind of schooling they want for their own children. You and others may want to give your opinions regarding the political forces that are changing schools and making curriculum policies in the United States. What are the roles for parents, teachers, and students in the making of a curriculum? Is there a place for local developers at a time when national and state authorities are holding schools and teachers accountable for achieving predetermined curriculum outcomes?

CHAPTER 8

MANAGING CURRICULUM

CURRICULUM PRACTITIONERS at district and school levels are confronted with two dueling movements in curriculum management: (1) official curriculum as presented by professional bodies and government and legal agencies and (2) local and teacher empowerment in enacting curriculum to enhance learning and the personal growth of students.

The first movement is characterized by the setting of national and state academic standards and relying on test results as evidence of success or failure. The local empowerment movement advocates that issues about what to teach should be resolved as close to the school or classroom level as possible, dictated by the needs of students, rather than by bureaucratic mandates. The empowerment movement has been supported by the work of (1) John Goodlad, who has long argued for curriculum development at the individual school where the principal and the teachers take responsibility for curriculum dialogue and plans of action along with parents and students, and (2) Ted Sizer, who, as chairperson of the Coalition of Essential Schools, believes that every community and every school is necessarily different from any other. Hence, the Coalition Project encourages each school to shape ideas about intellectual development, personalization, and the like in a way that is respectful of the local situation. Coalitions begin with a group of people, including the principal, who are interested in what their school might do to better the intellectual development of all students.

Although federal and state control of the institutionalized curriculum has intensified with the enforcing of curriculum content standards and testing in publicly funded schools, there has been a dramatic increase in the number and kind of alternative schools—private, non- and for-profit, home, charter, democratic, open, religious, therapeutic, military, special need, college preparatory, international, and many more.

SCHOOLS AND THE INSTITUTIONALIZED CURRICULUM

The 500-year history of schooling has maintained the concept of "school" as a different kind of place from other situations in which teaching and learning occur. A school differs in having a curriculum that lays out a purpose, goal, mission, or vision of the kind of learner to be formed, and content is predetermined rather than introduced by chance, sporadically, or spontaneously. In school the curriculum has an appearance of sequence whereby some content is regarded as more advanced than other content; programs and courses have a beginning, middle, and completion; and there are provisions for monitoring student progress.

As institutions, schools have been given particular responsibilities and entitlements. They are obligated to teach the knowledge and skills thought to be of significance to society or their authorizing agency. Schools are supposed to have clear goals and criteria for judging that students have attained the goals. Individual schools differ in whether they are preparing students as experts, workers, consumers, or likely players in the dominant institutions of society—church, military, corporate, government, and civic life. Milton Schwebel puts schools into three categories: elite private and public schools that provide leaders for all fields; schools that prepare the vast array of middle level workers; and schools for marginal populations where they are to learn how to act in public situations, to comply with regulations and with work tasks.[1]

As an institution, the school has been given authority over its students, and, although particular schools are autonomous, they have to meet the obligations set by their authorizing and funding agency if they are to continue receiving resources and entitlements. As seen in Table 8.1, schools have options as to how they manage their institutionalized curriculum. A school with a particular curriculum conception may exercise the options that best reflect that conception.

When asked how college differed from elementary school, a freshman answered: "When I have to go to the bathroom, I don't have to raise my hand." David Olsen says that the failure to recognize the institutionalized responsibility of the school to shape students for prespecified social roles keeps one from understanding why it is so difficult for schools to change their controlling, bookish, ritualistic, and miseducative bureaucratic practices.[2]

In contrast to the institutionalized curriculum, there is the enacted curriculum whereby principals and teachers are committed to the local community and their students with a determination to help them gain understanding of the world, that is, to a curriculum meaningful and related to their lives and to broader contexts.

Table 8.1 Varied Responses (Options) to Key Organizational Decisions

Decisions to Make	Optional Bases for Decisions
Admissions	Ability, age, trait, intelligence, motivation
Graduation requirements	Grade points, number of credits, required courses taken, years of study, promotionpolicies, attendance records, intellectualproducts
Completion	Certificate, diploma, license, degree
Assessment	Diagnostic tests, embedded assessment, teacher-made tests, external tests and examinations (normative and criterion-referenced), portfolios, intellectualproducts, college admission, placementtests
Grouping	Ability, age, interest, gender, grade level, multi- and ungraded
Schedule	Length of school day, year-round, semester, quarter, 45-minute periods, block, flexible
Individualization	Individual pathway, tutoring, pullout, gifted programs and honors courses, early college program, independent study, online courses, internships
Levels of schooling	Primary (alphabetization and socialization) Elementary ("elements" of subject matter—basic skills and national political andcultural identity) Middle (respond to developmental needs or teach subject matter) Secondary (disciplined knowledge or preparation for careers) Higher (general, liberal, or specialized)

[1]Milton Schwebel, *Remaking America's Three School Systems* (Lanham, MD: Scarecrow, 2003).
[2]David R. Olson, *Psychological Theory and Educational Reform: How Schools Remake Mind and Society* (New York: Cambridge Press, 2003).

The enacted curriculum entails pedagogical practices based on what is known about how people learn and is dedicated to developing minds and personal growth for lifelong learning. The challenge is for school and classroom managers to reconcile the two curriculums. Can a principal or teacher, for example, attend to the intentions and concerns of learners, giving them responsibility and encouraging their autonomy, while satisfying the expectations set forth in the official institutionalized curriculum? Are the metaphors of the "filling of empty vessels" and "lighting the flame of the learner" mutually exclusive?

Olson places the teacher as a mediator between beliefs and intentions of students and the norms and standards represented by the official curriculum. Similarly, William Reid has shown how curriculum historically has been institutionalized learning. He cautions teachers who would depart from it in the interest of student learning and motivation to show how their innovative learning opportunities will support the school's official curriculum.[3] Both Olson and Reid see problems with official offerings because of their nationalistic focus, ties to the special interests of other institutions, and the doubtful centrality of their content in light of changing world conditions and emergent mechanisms such as E-learning that are more effective for teaching and learning than conventional methods.

There are those who think it is time to think seriously about bidding farewell to the school's conservative programs that prepare students for the past, not the present, and certainly not the future. These critics see new technology as opportunities to redesign the way we learn and transmit culture.[4]

For decades, school administrators such as superintendents, principals, and curriculum directors have been asked to act in accordance with models of curriculum that assume a close tie between decisions and their implementation. School leaders are expected to bind their district or school to common purposes and to embrace new models of operation in an environment characterized both by change and by a lack of consensus about policies and procedures.

Many administrators respond to curriculum reform and conflicting views regarding the importance of bureaucratic curriculum alignment and local emancipation by *strategic interaction*, seizing and adopting those policies that meet their needs and adapting policies to reflect their local priorities.

Curriculum Change in the Context of Restructuring

An agenda for restructuring schools is moving ahead throughout the nation influencing the management of curriculum. Several states are returning to school-based curriculum decision making along with accountability. In California, Governor Schwarzenegger's Secretary of Education is locking horns with the Superintendent of the Los Angeles City School District over the issue of central office management of schools versus giving budget and curriculum responsibility to individual schools. The secretary, Richard Riordan, favors the idea of having public schools compete for students and giving the principal authority but also accountability for results. William Ouhi has elaborated on this decentralized approach.[5]

Foundations and special interests are behind much of the restructuring effort. Carnegie schools, for example, receive state grants to restructure school organization and governance. The Association for Supervision and Curriculum Development has initiated a consortium of schools involved in changing school governance, roles, curriculum, and instruction, and the Rockefeller Foundation has recommended (1) that school administrators

[3]William A. Reid, "Curriculum as Institutionalized Learning: Implications for Theory and Practice," *Journal of Curriculum Studies* 31 (May 2004): 29–44.
[4]Jon Wiles and John Lundt, *Leaving School: Finding Education* (St. Augustine, FL: Matazanzar Press, 2004).
[5]William G. Ouhi, *Making Schools Work: A Revolutionary Plan to Get Your Children the Education They Need* (New York: Simon and Schuster, 2003).

make it possible for teachers to be active participants in curriculum development by giving them released time for joint planning, (2) that there be team instruction whereby teachers share their experiences with colleagues, and (3) that teachers be encouraged to develop their own curriculum programs.[6]

The Coalition of Essential Schools founded by Theodore R. Sizer and its associated program with the Education Commission of the States is a reform group of more than 300 secondary and elementary schools committed to restructuring around the following principles:

- The focus is on helping students learn to use their minds well.
- Students master a limited number of essential skills and areas of knowledge; "less is more."
- School goals apply to all students.
- Teaching and learning are personalized.
- The practical metaphor of the school is students as workers and teachers as coaches.
- The diploma is awarded on successful final demonstration of mastery, such as an exhibition.
- Student load does not exceed 80 per teacher (secondary school) and costs do not exceed 19% more than traditional schools.
- Students have the opportunity to discover and construct meaning from their own experience.
- The elementary school does not have age grouping, and families are vital members of the school community.[7]

Other prominent reform movements at the elementary school level are the School Development Program (Robert Comer), which tries to bring together adults to support the total development of children; the Accelerated School Project (Henry Levin), which hopes to speed up instruction so at-risk children can match advantaged peers; and the Success for All Program (Robert Slavin), which aims at helping low-achieving students.[8] The Foxfire Network and local school projects funded by such foundations as the Nabisco Foundation (active in support of bottom-up curriculum development), and the PEW Charitable Trust (active in promoting charter schools) are increasing.

Indications of what panels from education, business, and community organizations see as desirable reform is found in the story of the New American Schools Development Corporation.[9] This corporation, which was created by business executives in 1991, invited nationwide teams to foster a new generation of "break the mold" schools. Teams included school districts, business associates, colleges, and think tanks. The corporation offered one-year contracts of up to $3 million for refinement of plans, after which half of the teams would win two-year grants to test their ideas, with a smaller number to be chosen to put their plans into action.

Nearly 700 designs were received, from which 11 were selected. Researchers considered the winning designs as laudable but viewed them largely devoid of new ideas. Most

[6]*Helping Schools Work* (New York: Rockefeller Foundation Communications Office, 1989).

[7]Theodore R. Sizer, *Horace's School: Redesigning the American High School* (Boston: Houghton Mifflin, 1992).

[8]*School Development Program* (Washington: Widemeyer Group, 1994); *Accelerated Schools Project* (Stanford: Stanford University, 1994); *Success for All Project* (Baltimore: Center for Research on Effective Schooling for Disadvantaged Students, Johns Hopkins University, 1994).

[9]*New American Schools: Driven by Results and a Decade of Experience* (Arlington, VA: New American Schools, 2002).

of the designs carried out ideas already in place by celebrated innovators—Howard Gardner, James Comer, Robert Slavin, and Ted Sizer—or ideas that have a long tradition in curriculum—the project method, interdisciplinary studies, learning centers, and experiential learning, such as Outward Bound. The introduction of computer-based community networks is an exception. A project entitled the Modern Red Schoolhouse, associated with the politician and conservative William J. Bennett, returns to character education as its unique contribution to help schools meet world-class standards.

In general, the major themes of the winning proposals were multiage classrooms, individual learning, "personalization" of education through advisors, smaller grouping, and teachers who stay with students over several years (looping) of cooperative learning and project-oriented activities. Community service, character education, and a blurring of in- and out-of-school learning were also highlighted.

By 2004, it was clear that the New American Schools' strategy of establishing individual "Lighthouse Schools" was ineffective in expanding to entire districts and regions as well as being unsustainable when extra funding was not available. Consequently, the New American Schools Organization merged with a Washington think tank (American Institute for Research), a nongovernment contractor, to promote their reform agenda through regional and district contacts.

From 1995 until 2004, Congress approved funding for a Comprehensive School Reform Program (CSRP) to foster research-based models of school reform where the Department of Education gave grants to schools that would adopt proven models. These models featured adoption by a whole school rather than adoption by a state or district. The federal government detailed required components, such as benchmarks of student progress, evidence of replication, and parent and community participation in the school government. Through a competitive process, CSRP awarded a minimum of $50,000 per year for 3 years to qualifying schools.

Several CSRP school models that have been implemented for 5 years or more have shown strong effects, and the benefits are consistent across schools of varying poverty levels.[10] Table 8.2 illustrates CSRP models that have evidenced effectiveness. Some of the salient features of each are shown.

By 2004, in spite of Congress's hefty typical yearly $1.3 million for CSRP's program, the use of the national school improvement models declined. Homegrown and commercial programs were more likely to be adopted by schools and districts.[11] Explanation for the decline includes the following: what "works" with English speakers may not work in schools with concentration of English-language learners; high costs for training and materials; and there is a trend to districtwide strategies rather than schoolwide reform models. Instead of CSRP, the U.S. Department of Education is awarding contracts to private firms to collect scientific evidence through randomly controlled experiments with selected models to determine the programs that will be eligible for federal funding.

Definitions of curriculum restructuring vary. Federal political leaders have the following marked for reconstruction: greater choice in schools, creation of magnet schools, rewarding of merit schools, availability of child care, improved achievement in mathematics and science, and alternative certification of teachers. The National Government Association advocates (1) a greater variety of ways for students to learn, such as varied class sizes, cooperative teaching, peer teaching, and better use of instructional technologies; (2) teaching methods that deemphasize lectures and memorization, and include more

---

[10]Geoffrey D. Burmer et al., "Comprehensive School Reform and Achievement," *Review of Educational Research* 73, no. 2 (summer 2003): 125–130.

[11]"Reform Program Backed by Research Finds Fewer Takers," *Education Week* 23, no. 32 (April 21, 2004): 16.

Table 8.2 Highly Rated Comprehensive School Reform Models

Model	Primary Goal	Key Features
Accelerated school (K–12), Henry Levin	Achievement of students in at-risk situations	Opportunities are those given to gifted and talented students, whole school participation building on strength and powerful learning
Coalition of essential schools (K–12), Ted Sizer	Students learn to use their minds well	Personalized learning, mastery of basic skills, sense of community, local application of principles, student exhibits
Knowledge core (K–8), E. D. Hirsch, Jr.	Provide background knowledge for articipation in U.S. school and society	Grade by grade topics, published instructional materials for half of program, and parents and schools develop the remainder of the program including learningopportunities and methods
School development program (K–12), James Comer	Enlisting entire community in meeting students' needs	Planning and management teams, school support teams, parent teams, staff development, monitoring, community collaboration
Success for all (K–8), Robert Slavin	Every child learns to read	Reading, writing, and language arts, curriculum materials and staff development, one-to-one tutoring, family support, cooperative learning, on-site advisory team, materials adopted only with faculty approval

teaching of critical thinking and higher order skills; (3) school-based decisions with accountability for results; (4) students have more choice in selecting alternative school programs; and (5) experiments with the length of the school day and year.

The 1990s saw an increase in state and district deregulation of class schedules as well as an increase in open enrollment, theme schools, and innovative private schools. There were questions regarding the political aspects of these changes. Did they represent a ploy by federal and state authorities to reduce their financial obligations to public education without giving up their power to shape education in favored directions? What is the connection between deregulation and the countervailing centralizing of authority through national and state curriculum standards and testing? Site-based management reformers in the past failed to affect outcomes positively in large part because schools did not develop coherent models for guiding their work and decision making and failed to take into account the rigidity of the institutionalized concept of "school."[12]

Many of the celebrated changes in the Rochester City School District, for example, aimed at restructuring schools as centers of inquiry and of reflection, not of unexamined tradition. The Rochester contract provided for school-based planning, empowering all major stakeholders (parents, teachers, administration, and in high schools, students) to decide on such matters as budget, curriculum goals, school dynamics, and selection of new

[12]J. Murphy and L. Beck, *School-Based Management as School Reform* (Newbury Park, CA: Corwin, 1995).

teachers on the basis of the school's needs and ethos. Among their considerations were how to allocate time, use space, classify students, divide subject matter, and adapt to different types (not level) of intelligence and learning styles. They questioned the assumptions that one building means one school, that children learn best in 47-minute segments, that multiple-choice tests are the best indices of student learning, and that teaching is telling.

A special problem exists among well-off schools. Nothing is so likely to bring institutional failure as 40 years of success. Leaders in some of America's top high schools are concerned that parents do not want changes in their schools. Schools in central cities rather than affluent suburban counterparts have been the driving forces behind reform. The concern is that the affluent schools are unlikely to prepare students for changes in the economy and in society. Instead affluent students continue to focus on admission to competitive colleges, cramming honors courses into their schedules without any sense of purpose, seldom rewriting, rethinking, wrestling with ideas, or staying with a problem until they have solved it and made it theirs.

ROLES IN RESTRUCTURING CURRICULUM

The Principal as Director of Learning

System technologists put the principal in the forefront of designing curriculum plans consistent with state and district intents. For example, in California, administrators attend curriculum training centers where they are briefed on state and district curriculum goals and learn how to match classroom activities with the predetermined goals. As they create curriculum plans at the center, the principals are encouraged to look for ways to expand on what teachers are already doing in the classroom with the idea of seeing how teachers can organize and manage the classrooms envisioned by state and district curriculum makers. The principals shape a mental image of what is to be accomplished with students and how they might look in the various disciplines, including the setting of specific student performance measures consistent with the reformers' intents. District personnel review the performance expectations and make suggestions for modification until they are satisfied that each principal is clear on the operational meaning of state and district goals.

Later, in districtwide training sessions, teachers and administration have their performance expectations for specific grade levels approved, and they develop hypothetical yearlong plans in the various subject areas. The plans are critiqued and individual teachers create their classroom plans. The principal and teachers from the same school decide on the steps they will take to translate their curriculum plans into practice. As the plans are implemented, the principal provides support as the teachers experiment with new ways to modify classroom practice and arranges for groups of teachers to meet regularly for comparing notes and devising new strategies.

"Focused leadership" is where principals meet with teachers to analyze student progress as measured by required testing and benchmarks and then determine the implications for instruction. This leadership strategy highlights the school's responsibility for the transmission of knowledge.

The Principal in Shared Leadership

Under emancipation, the principal and teachers have the freedom to generate their own curriculum visions rather than merely create ways to achieve the purposes set by others. Instead of addressing the problems that state and district think the school has, the staff focuses on their own views of school problems. One approach is to focus on the school's culture, including beliefs, shared values, traditions, practices, expectations, and assumptions. The development of a mission statement and critical analysis of the existing curriculum practice, noting where there are consistencies, is a good way to begin curriculum revision. The idea of a school having an ethos, being distinct from other schools, and subjecting all aspects of school life to furthering this ideal quality is powerful. Quaker schools, for instance, have been singled out as unique in encouraging students to "go beyond their private interests and put their lives in historical, social, and ethical perspective." Among the principles in the Quaker essence is to get students to strive for excellence rather than to be concerned whether they reach it, and to stress the careful use of language, including "plain speech" and listening.

"Learner centered leadership" is influenced by contemporary social constructivists' views of how people learn whereby the principal and teacher focus on the meaning and understanding, (intellectually and emotionally) of school experiences.

Schools may choose to begin with principles as in the Essential Schools Projects where teachers create curriculum to match principles. Teachers and principal explore school regularities (grading policy, scheduling, textbooks, field trips, assemblies, and the like) for their consistency with the ideal professed by the school. In such an approach, the faculty meets to describe the practice or policy, interpret it, and give accounts of likely consequences. Usually, alternatives are introduced that are in keeping with the ideal. Under shared leadership, the principal's role is to release the creative capacity of the faculty, not control it. One aim of the planning sessions is that all should share their knowledge, observations, and interpretations and that there should be evidence and agreement about the validity of conflicting views. Decisions are based on a rational consensus, not on the principal's position or the popularity of certain teachers. Throughout the discussion, participants keep in mind the school's norms and values. However, sometimes the existing norms and values are subjected to more encompassing ideals; the possibility of creating new norms is important for the transformation of the school. The deliberation model of curriculum making as given in Chapter 5 is appropriate in this context.

A role for teachers in curriculum decision making is not new. Gary Peltier wrote of a program of curriculum construction in 1922 using teacher participation.[13] The account brings forth most of the arguments for the practice. As a result of participation, teachers became better informed about the aims of education, better able to interpret programs to others, and more accepting of new methods. Teachers changed to reflect newer views of subject matter, and to be more responsive to social needs, and learners.

History repeats itself. Recently, Israel wanted a new English curriculum and involved teachers in making the change. The old way of teaching English to foreigners was to directly teach the four language skills (speaking, listening, reading, and writing) as well as grammatical structures and patterns. The curriculum was a hierarchical program with a targeted vocabulary. In the new curriculum, language is learned when students have an authentic need for using the language. Skills are taught when needed to perform communicative tasks. There are no grammar and vocabulary lists but there is access to information and literature together with social interactions. Evaluation centers on "what kids can *do* in the language." The teachers were asked to stop thinking what they want their students to know and begin to think of what they want students to *do* and then think of the skills and knowledge needed. It is a bottom-up approach whereby teams of teachers accept the challenge to be "curriculum developers" and to collaborate in constructing materials, syllabi, lesson

---

[13]Gary Peltier, "Teacher Preparation in Curriculum Revision: A Historical Case Study," *History of Education Quarterly* 7, no. 2 (summer 1967): 1209–1217.

plans, and giving their own interpretations of the new curriculum and its use in their particular contexts. The teachers are free to choose their own methods and to bring their teaching alive.[14]

Department Heads in Curriculum Management

In secondary schools, principals have looked to department heads for curriculum leadership. Indeed, one survey reports that 73% of principals perceived department heads as functioning successfully in curriculum development.[15] Heads of departments often provide the structure and sense of purpose for inquiry, discussion, and decision making while enabling genuine participation by colleagues. Departmental curriculum decisions treat such issues as intentions or expected outcomes, content selection and sequencing, criteria for new materials and activities, teaching approaches, monitoring of implementation, and evaluation. A recommended technique by which a department ensures that overall themes permeate planning is "the network of ideas." Figure 8.1 is an adaptation of a network developed by a group of math teachers in response to the goal for students knowing something about the historical development of mathematical concepts.

ADMINISTRATIVE ARRANGEMENTS

In organizing the curriculum, administrators and staff decide how students are grouped, how much time is devoted to each subject, and how it will be taught. Since the functions of schooling change, each of these factors requires frequent alteration. In the decade of the 1980s, state-mandated reforms had a chilling effect on a wide range of school arrangements. Mandatory academic requirements resulted in reduced vocational offerings, fewer options for students, and reduced flexibility in scheduling.[16] The reform requirement substantially reduced the number of courses that students took in home economics, industrial arts, physical education, business, psychology, and the performing arts. Most reform reports recommended increasing instructional time, adding days to the school year, and lengthening the school day. Achievement replaced effort as the basis for promotion. Students spent more time retaking courses they failed. Most schools continued offering low and middle achieving students "dull" factual repetitive material through tracking. Although more math and science courses were required for low and middle achievers, these courses were focused on a low level of skills at the basic levels. In some cases, low quality courses replaced higher quality vocational ones.

A second reform wave of the 1990s promised to encourage greater freedom in school curriculum arrangements. The National Association of State Boards of Education recommended the abolition of the Carnegie unit.[17] The Carnegie unit is a measure used for accrediting high school work in which 120 hours of classroom work equals one unit of credit, based on the assumption that the school year would be from 36 to 40 weeks and the class period from 40 to 60 minutes in length. Since its adoption in 1909 by the College

---

[14]Lily Orland-Barac et al., "Seeing the 'New' in Light of the 'Old'—Evolving Interpretation of a New National English Curriculum," *Journal of Curriculum Studies* 31, no. 3 (May 2004): 321–331.

[15]Janice Adkisson, *High School Trends Study* (Alexandria, VA: Association for Supervision and Curriculum Development, 1986).

[16]William H. Clune et al., *School Responses to Curriculum Mandates* (New Brunswick, NJ: Center for Policy Research in Education, Eagleton Institute of Politics, Rutgers University, 1989).

[17]Rethinking Curriculum: A Call for Fundamental Reform (Alexandria, VA: National Association of State Boards of Education, 1989).

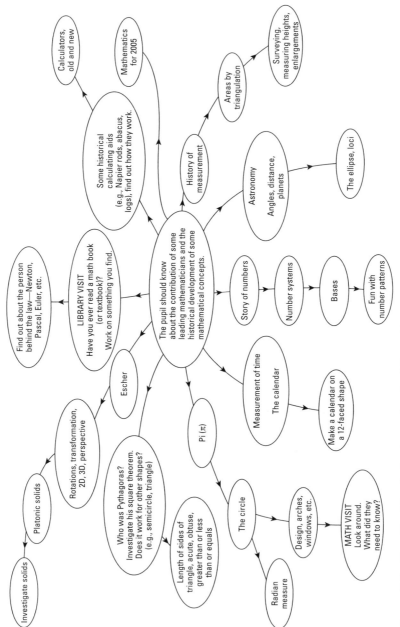

Figure 8.1 Cognitive Map for Implementing Goal (from *Managing Mathematics*, The Mathematical Association and Stanley Thornas Publishers, 1988)

Entrance Examination Board, it has become a fixed part of almost every secondary school program. The Carnegie unit has resulted in uniforming standards, crystallizing the curriculum, limiting freedom for experimentation, and defining education as an accumulation of units.

The National Association of State Boards of Education worked to replace the Carnegie unit with student achievement in the core areas of language arts, mathematics and science, citizenship, fine arts, health, and foreign languages and would give emphasis to the acquisition of central concepts rather than superficial knowledge.

Similarly, the National Education Association's Learning Laboratory's initiative was a project for freeing local communities "to turn their school systems upside down or inside out," to open school doors to 4-year-olds and end the arbitrary division of class periods into 50-minute chunks. Increasingly, states began to "trade off" greater flexibility in return for greater accountability.

Chief among the forces confronting the Carnegie unit is the trend to national standards; outcome-based education that establishes what students should be able to *do,* not how much time has been spent on a subject, and the coalition for Essential Schools' espousing of "less is more," which allows for in-depth learning rather than mere coverage.[18]

Stratifying Students

The practice of grouping students by apparent ability both along curriculum paths and within classes is under attack. Some schools are charged with perpetuating discrimination against minority students and poverty families by directing them toward lower educational tracks. Most educators reject the notion that curriculum inequality is intentional and regard tracking as a way to meet the special needs of a diverse student body. However, as a result of her study of tracking, Jeannie Oakes recommends "what we now provide for the most advantaged children, we need to provide for all children."[19]

Among recent efforts to organize curriculum to accommodate individual differences and ensure the same quality of instruction are the following:

1. Creating a core curriculum to which all students will be exposed even if different students take different approaches to the same material. The San Diego Unified School District, for example, introduced a common core curriculum to replace all remedial and lower level science and math courses. The aim of this program is to qualify all graduating high school students for four-year college entrance requirements. Also, accelerated school projects in inner city schools are offering the active, exciting, and fast-paced curriculum associated with gifted children to "kids who don't have anything going for them."

2. Eliminating the general track that is faulted for its lack of challenge and replacing it with a rigorous core curriculum that will prepare students for either college or technical training. In Tennessee, for example, all students complete core courses and then those electing the university preparation pathway complete a fine arts course and two courses of the same foreign language; those taking the technical pathway complete four courses related to a chosen occupational field.[20]

3. Encouraging within-classroom instruction to feature cooperative learning in small groups with students at different levels studying together and helping one another in place of permanent groups based on assumed ability and achievement.

[18]Gene I. Maeroff, "The Assault on the Carnegie Unit," *Education Week* (Oct. 13, 1993): 26–27.
[19]Jeannie Oakes, *Keeping Track: How Schools Structure Inequality* (New Haven: Yale University Press, 1985).
[20]Lynn Olson, "Tennessee Is Latest State to Eliminate the General Track," *Education Week* (Sept. 29, 1993): 18–20.

Empirical findings about the effects of stratification are numerous.[21] Adam Gamoran and Mark Berends's review of studies of stratification reveals patterns of instructional differences favoring high track classes and suggests that tracking polarizes students into pro- and antischool factions.[22] Grouping does affect achievement. Teachers reputed to be more skilled and successful are more often located in high track classes, which may produce cycles of low expectations, poor morale, and failure for both teachers and students in low track. Similarly, Robert Slavin's analysis of ability groupings in elementary schools has led him to conclude that ability grouping does not enhance student achievement in the elementary school.[23]

Attempts to reform tracking and ability grouping may be met with opposition from parents of gifted children concerned that their children will be held back by slower learners and lose advantages such as enriched rooms, better teachers, and more attention. However, recent findings show that when high achievers are placed in heterogeneous groups they gain more than when in a group comprised of high achieving peers, provided individuals in groups operate collaboratively rather than competitively.[24]

Staffing Patterns and Scheduling

A team of teachers can accept responsibility for 100 students for a two-hour block of time each day. This allows the staff to assume different roles such as planning, lecturing, leading discussions, and counseling. A teacher in a team may be involved with a large class for a lecture, with a seminar-sized group of 15, or with students engaged in individual study. Teaching teams determine in advance the specific students they need to teach, the size of the groups, the length of teaching time, and the materials to use. Team leaders provide information for preparation of a master schedule for student guidance. Often, in a daily 20-minute period, students determine their day's program from the choices available on the master schedule.

One brand of interdisciplinary teaming by teachers is found in some middle schools in which four-person teams are composed of one specialist from among the areas of language arts, mathematics, social science, art, and science. Each specialist serves as the resource person for a subject area, doing much of the planning and teaching of that subject. Each teacher on the team, however, teaches all four of the academic subjects. The advantage of this arrangement is that correlation of subject matter areas is easier and teachers are better able to attend to individual students.

Team teaching is not supposed to be a laborsaving device, like cooperative or rotating turn teaching. It is intended to bring about clear joint acceptance of objectives and better conditions for achieving them. Teams of teachers and groups of students can be together, for example, for about three hours each day in what is called a *fluid block*. Two hours are devoted to interdisciplinary activities, and the additional hour is given to one or more open labs in a variety of subcourse content. With 12 teachers operating across three teams for at least two of the three different hours, as many as 24 different minicourses can be offered during a nine-week period. Students from each of the three fluid blocks are able to schedule the minicourse of their choice. The fluid block team also schedules large-group, small-group,

---

[21]Laura Mansherus, "Should Tracking Be Derailed?" *New York Times* Section 4A (Nov. 1, 1992): 14–16.

[22]Adam Gamoran and Mark Berends, "The Effects of Stratification in Secondary Schools: Synthesis of Survey and Ethnographic Research," *Review of Educational Research* 57, no. 4 (winter 1987): 415–435.

[23]Robert E. Slavin, "Ability Grouping and Student Achievement in Elementary Schools: A Best Evidence Synthesis," *Review of Educational Research* 57, no. 3 (1987): 293–336.

[24]N. M. Webb, K. M. Nemer, and S. Zuniga, "Short Circuits or Superconductors? Effects of Group Composition on High-Achieving Students' Science Assessment Performance," *American Educational Research Journal* 39, no. 4 (winter 2002): 943.

and individual student activities, always with an option for student placement in the open labs, which operate concurrently on an individual basis. The balance of the school day is given to elective courses such as physics or to a vocational block in any of a number of different areas (Table 8.3).

Each student is assigned to a specific team or faculty member for the entire day, thus meeting accountability concerns. The organization of the team, advisement, and individualized labs offer several ways to meet student needs.

Modification in the standard schedule through double periods is not dependent on team teaching. Arranging for Tuesday–Thursday and Wednesday–Friday classes, which meet for 1 hour and 45 minutes, for example, has the advantage of giving a teacher more time to spend with each student and giving the students opportunity to reflect on their laboratory observations and experiments, not merely to carry them out.

There may be difficulties in changing schedules. The Masconomet Massachusetts Regional School District introduced 100-minute "macroclasses" whereby students took six courses, two each trimester, each for 100 minutes daily. With classes of 12 students instead of 25, teachers had more time to know their students and give more individual help. Students found it possible to delve more deeply into subjects and make connections in a way that never happened in a 45-minute class. Many formerly low achievers began to exceed students in the traditional program.

In spite of favorable evaluations from researchers from Harvard University, praise from students, teachers and parents, there was controversy. Some parents of honor students not in the program opposed giving honors credit for participation in the innovation. This opposition plus budget cuts that required teachers to teach both the new and traditional classes resulted in discontinuance of the plan.

Supplementary Personnel

Student tutors, adult volunteers, and inexpensive paraprofessionals allow teachers to serve more pupils effectively and efficiently. Cross-age tutoring, whereby older students tutor younger ones, is beneficial to both and has become very popular across the country. No other innovation has been so consistently perceived as successful. Ideally, tutoring is a regular class assignment and not a voluntary activity. Instructional modules are selected that will induce academic growth of the tutor as well as the tutees. Sixth graders, for example, may teach fractions to fourth graders if the sixth-grade teacher believes the tutors need to learn and practice fractions and the fourth-grade teacher would like his or her students to learn fractions.

Table 8.3   A Team-Teaching Outline

Hour	Types of Course	Individualized Labs
1	Fluid blocks: 100–120 Students in course (Minicourses or planning)	Music
2		Science
3		Art
		Drama
		Other
4	Elective	or 3-hour vocational block
5	Elective	
6	Elective	

Scheduling of one-to-one tutoring can occur when two classes get together regularly on two or three occasions per week. A room set up with pairs of enclosed desks (carrels) is most desirable, but regular classrooms, cafeterias, or libraries will suffice. The sending teacher prepares the tutors in special training sessions. In these sessions, tutors learn exactly what they are to teach. They may also practice their methods and prepare materials such as flash cards and tests for their tutees.

The tutoring sessions themselves should be supervised by the teachers concerned. Tutors should be free to ask for assistance, and the teacher can check whether the work is being taught correctly.

Nongrading

Nongrading occurs when content and experience are offered on the basis of learner interest and ability and are not restricted to a given grade level. The lack of grade levels permits students to progress at different rates and lets them take advanced or additional courses. A student may wish to take online courses, for example, or participate in advanced placement programs, taking college level courses for credit while in the secondary school. Also, instead of offering world history, U.S. history, and problems of democracy to tenth, eleventh, and twelfth graders, respectively, schools may offer one of these courses each year to all students. We will see more emphasis on proficiency than on age or grade level as a basis for school progress.

Facilities

Ideally, buildings, grounds, supplies, and equipment correspond to both the educational purposes and the means by which teachers and students achieve these purposes. Facilities for independent study means students have a place to work and a place to use the special materials of the subject matter they are learning. There may be a need for space in which to view films, read, practice music, and work with metals and clay.

Current changes in space allocation reflects changes in pedagogy and learning, such as collaborative work by teachers and greater use of technology and off-campus components—internships, community service, and community institutions like museums and libraries.

Classroom walls need not define the limits of the learning environment. Facilities can encourage communication and variations in lighting—less in small group discussion space than in independent study rooms. The budget for supplies and equipment does not always increase as the cost of school buildings increases. Unlike industry, which wisely puts only 25% of total capital outlay into structure, schools have put 75% of capital outlay into the building shell and only 25% into instructional tools. Although modernization procedures are less costly than building new structures, the politics of education usually means that school persons are vulnerable to the pressures of real estate and building contractors for expensive sites and buildings that are not necessary. Dade County schools have an interesting innovation in that some of their elementary schools are in quarters provided by businesses. Schools get their classrooms without capital outlay and businesses get a perk for their employees.

The Middle School

A major institutional change with implications for curriculum organization is found in the rise of the American middle school. This type of school has grown from a smattering of schools in the 1950s to, more than 10,000 in the new century and now is the predominant form of organization. This school is characterized by service to the 11- to 14-year-old age group. Typically, middle schools are centered on the child rather than on the subject matter. The schools usually offer the design components of a subschool within a larger middle school and an interdisciplinary teaching team. The team operates as a small four- or five-teacher school. The same group of students in the subschool may stay together for a period of three or four years. Another team of teachers offers a related unified arts program to students from all subschools. The unified arts program gives all students experiences in such subjects as art, shop, homemaking, music, and physical education, as well as focusing on career opportunities. Exploratory experiences on a nongraded basis are also provided to enrich the students and supplement their needs.

Middle schools are more likely to provide program characteristics needed by early adolescents.[25] However, simply placing grades 6 through 8 or 5 through 8 in a single building does not ensure that students will receive help with problems common to the age group: (1) emotional, social, and academic concerns; (2) making a smooth transition from the child-centered elementary school to more academically oriented institutions; (3) discovering interests and career options; and (4) integrating subject matter. Organizational responses to these problems include teacher adviser programs, transition and articulation activities, interdisciplinary teaching and block schedules, and a wide range of teaching strategies. Most middle schools have exploratory programs, but only 36% have adopted interdisciplinary, team teaching and intramural sports.[26]

Recently Rand conducted an international comparison study examining student achievement, learning conditions, leadership, and reform in middle schools. The findings are negative:[27]

- U.S. students are less enthusiastic about learning conditions and report more physical and emotional problems than their peers in other countries.
- Students experience more social isolation.
- The transition in U.S. middle schools compromises both developmental and academic progress.
- Team teaching is seldom implemented.
- Without preparation in collaborative methods or time to plan together, teachers do not teach and integrate content across disciplines.
- Many teachers do not have knowledge of adolescent development.
- Little is done to engage parents.
- Principals spend so much time on discipline, their academic leadership is limited

Alternative, Magnet, Charter, and Specialist Schools

Module scheduling, team teaching, flexible group instruction, and similar plans did not prove to be ideal solutions in the past, nor did they lead to more effective curriculum. Some call these innovations superficial tinkering and are demanding a much more basic reform. Alternative, magnet, charter, and specialized schools are seen as more enduring paths to reform.

---

[25]Gordon Cawelt, "Middle Schools: A Better Match with Early Adolescent Needs," in *Curriculum Update* (Alexandria, VA: Association for Supervision and Curriculum Development, November 1988).

[26]*National Study of Leadership on Middle School Education* (Reston, VA: National Association Secondary School Principals, 1993)._

[27]Jaana Juvonen et al., *Focus on the Wonder Years: Challenge Facing American Middle Schools* (Santa Monica, CA: Rand Corporation, 2004).

Alternative Schools   Active groups began to take daring steps toward the reorganization of schooling in the 1970s. Convinced that public schools were instruments of a racist and oppressive society, some community activists opened storefront schools that emphasized both basic skills and black culture. They also tried to enroll school dropouts from the street and prepare them for college. These "freedom schools" were financially supported by foundations and dedicated persons. Such schools encouraged a close, nonauthoritarian teacher–pupil relationship and an open concept of learning. Not surprisingly, content focused on the ills of the capitalistic society.

Today a new type of freedom school puts student choice first. These freedom schools are growing in popularity in reaction to the standards-based momentum. Many parents are frustrated with traditional public schools cutting out recess, music, art, and physical education. Free schoolers believe that children are natural learners and are unlike those who believe that knowledge must be forced into children "whether they like it or not." Not all free schools are alike—some lead students through lessons, but others let students decide for themselves what they want to learn.[28]

It is impossible to generalize accurately about alternative schools. By definition, each one is different. Much of the movement is directed toward making schools effective for students who have been school dropouts. Some alternative programs are organized to allow students to work in a congenial atmosphere consistent with their work style. Most people in alternative schools today are not working as social revolutionaries but either as humanists, who want pupils to have a choice in subject matter to be studied and in styles of learning, or as academic strivers, who want early development of talent in prestigious subject matter and careers.

Alternative schools have made us conscious of whether we should allow students to select freely a formal or an informal school, a structured or an individualized curriculum. An alternative school—either a separate institution or a unit within a comprehensive school—is an organizational answer to the old problem of fitting the curriculum to the enormous range of talents and traits that students bring to school and to the diverse expectations that they and their parents have for schooling.

Today's alternative school movement has broadened the definition of an elective from a choice of subject to a choice in ways of working. Generally, people in the movement recognize the need for structure, sequence, and discipline but assert that, for many students, a choice about the degree of structure in a learner's school life is as crucial as a choice of studying either Spanish or statistics.

In some alternative schools, students seldom enter a classroom. They pursue their individual interests outside the school. They may study the stars at an observatory, work with computers at a local firm, learn to make bread at the corner bakery, and discuss medicine with a physician—all for academic credit. Sometimes students travel from place to place in the city, learning from a variety of paid and unpaid teachers. A student may study physics at a university, elementary functions and world cultures from the school staff, contemporary American literature and French II from students at another university, museum methods from the museum staff, and understanding the stock market from a stock broker.

Magnet Schools   An *options* system has been introduced in which the choice of school curriculum (methods, activities, and environment) is offered to individual students and their families. Instead of a single alternative to an existing program, there are many options. In Minneapolis, for instance, students may attend the school selected by themselves and their parents. In most large cities, there are "magnet" schools which are consistent with the concept of options. These schools offer an especially strong curriculum in some areas, such as

---

[28]Michelle Galley, "Free Rein," *Education Week* 23, no. 36 (May 12, 2004): 27–32.

science, business, education, or health and medicine, as a way to further court-ordered integration by attracting students from different ethnic and socioeconomic populations.

An early purpose of magnet schools was to draw children from beyond the immediate neighborhood to foster integration. Now, however, magnet schools are sprouting because they bring together spirited students who want to link education to their visions of careers. Criticism of magnet schools comes from administrators of neighborhood schools who do not like the siphoning off of the brightest children and from those who believe that such schools isolate children, promoting elitism rather than a democratic society. A federal study casts doubt on the efficacy of magnet schools for desegregating school districts.[29] As a way of bringing options in the curriculum, however, the more than 2000 magnet schools, funded by the federal government's magnet school assistance program, have been a success.[30]

Chicago's college prep magnets have accepted only 5% or less of students who apply. Most schools bypass desegregation goals and enroll disproportionately more white and high-income students.[31]

Charter Schools   Charter schools are schools that are not required to follow many of the state and district curriculum mandates. Often they are small units within large comprehensive high schools (schools within schools) or separate elementary schools that request waivers from state and district rule in order to explore changes in curriculum. Usually, the charter schools comprise high performing schools and students who are eager to trade regulation for results. Typically, each charter has a distinctive theme or focus, such as multicultural studies or the humanities.

Charter schools are expanding as the state or local school agencies give a charter to a school along with public funding for a specific time period. Charters are opportunities for schools to be created. The charter school is responsible for its budget, assembling teachers, and the learning programs. Innovations have been wide ranging. In Minnesota, a group of teachers formed a partnership to run a learning program that features student Internet projects, rather than formal classes. Students with their teacher advisors and parents follow personal interests but see that they connect with the areas of knowledge the state requires for graduation.[32]

Specialist Schools   Other changes are occurring in response to the international competition in mathematics and science. There are "exemplary" schools specializing in mathematics and science at both elementary and secondary levels. State networkings for the talented are becoming more common. For example, the Louisiana School for Math, Science, and the Arts at Natchitoches is where the most talented juniors from the state's 66 school districts are brought together for an elite education.

Public schools currently available to students, parents, and teachers offer incredible variety. Some schools emphasize different instructional approaches (open schools, Montessori schools, continuous progress schools, behavioral modification schools); some feature distinctive curriculum (law and government, centers for world studies, environmental study centers, vocational centers); others focus on special students (maternity schools, bilingual schools, schools for the gifted and for dropouts). Yet throughout the country, schools are putting much emphasis on the content for college preparation.

[29]David Armor and Christine H. Rossell, *National Survey of Magnet Schools* (Palo Alto, CA: American Institute for Research, 1994).
[30]Evans Clinchy, "Magnet Schools Matter," *Education Week* (Dec. 8, 1993): 28–31.
[31]Pauline Lipman, *High Stakes Education: Inequality, Globalization, and Urban School Reform* (New York: Routledge Falmer, 2004).
[32]Edward J. Dirkswager, *Teachers as Owners* (Lanham, MD: Scarecrow Press, 2002).

Private schools also offer options. In 1993, for the first time in 30 years Catholic schools recorded significant gains in enrollment. The finding that Catholic schools may consider effort more important than ability and promote achievement among all students rather than perpetual academic stereotyping may be a factor.[33]

In 2004, the U.S. Supreme Court removed an obstacle to voucher plans by saying that a voucher plan that involved participation in private religious schools did not violate the establishment clause. Parents could obtain tuition grants to use in religious or nonreligious schools within the school district.

Private schools challenge our thinking of what is possible. The Sudbury Valley School where there are no grades, no required homework assignments, and no compulsory courses is a case in point. The school's classes only exist if there is student demand, and the classes disband if interest fades. That the Sudbury Valley students do so well in their subsequent lives as citizens and scholars is noteworthy.[34] Fairhaven and other schools are following the Sudbury model.[28]

Also, the growing popularity of Waldorf schools may indicate areas for consideration by leaders in public schools. Among the features of Waldorf schools are (1) placing as much emphasis on art, music, and crafts as academic subjects; (2) keeping a teacher with one group of children from grades 1 through 8 (looping); (3) encouraging students to write their own texts rather than rely on textbooks and worksheets; and (4) helping young people find the strength to change what is harmful and unhealthy in our civilization.[35]

It should be clear, however, that horror stories about public schools have been exaggerated and tainted by racial stereotypes. Also, many private schools present their own set of perils by creating a sheltered homogeneous world that may not prepare students for a diverse society. For this reason, because of many positive changes in public schooling plus the high tuition of private academies, more middle-class parents are organizing in defense of public schools.

DIRECTIONS IN THE REFORM OF SCHOOL ORGANIZATIONS

Options in the Schools

Two directions of organizational reform have emerged out of the ferment over social policy dilemmas and the innovations both from those who would make the school more humane and from those who would make it more productive. Various commissions and study groups bent on studying secondary schools in order to restore them to full strength and vitality agree on two directions.

First, reduce barriers between adolescents and opportunities in the community. Work or volunteer experience outside the school building is seen as desirable in increasing students' independence and helping them to encounter a broader range of people and experiences. Students' time is well planned, and off-campus programs are organized to allow for reflection. The study groups also realize that tracking can occur outside as well as inside the school. A combination of action and reflection is believed necessary for adolescents to mature in an integrative manner.

Second, create smaller schools or subschools with more specialized courses of study. Students who are unlikely to get training beyond high school can leave school with enough

---

[33]Reba Page and Linda Valli, eds., *Curriculum Differentiation* (Albany: State University of New York Press, 1992).
[34]David Ruenzel, "Classless Society," *Teacher* 5, no. 4 (Jan. 1994): 20–26.
[35]The Association of Waldorf Schools of North America, 3911 Bannister Road, Fair Oaks, CA 95628.

skill to procure a job. Rather than each school offering training in 15 or 20 skills, different schools each might offer three or five trades in depth. To facilitate such specialization, the school, satellite, or cluster within schools is smaller, with each unit focusing on fewer but more specific areas and skills. Basic academic subjects are still offered in all schools, but students may select a magnet school on the basis of the training it offers.

The reorganization of middle schools and senior high schools into houses is one possibility. Each house has its own curriculum. The students in each house are at all grade levels; that is, each student spends his or her entire middle school and senior high school career affiliated with one house. Teachers have the opportunity to adjust to the student's present attainment, and all students have the opportunity to reach mastery in the general curriculum; slower students are not tracked into different courses. Furthermore, the longer association of the students and their teachers is likely to reduce both student alienation and teacher frustration.

Teachers within smaller schools, with some of their students on alternating work and study programs outside the school, have more time to spend with fewer students. Teachers also perform more varied roles like that of advisor, work supervisor, and role model. The reports from the various commissions and panels trying to reform secondary education emphasize options in high school organization and the need for instruction in informal settings. These reports are not truly plans for curriculum development because they fail to attend to the questions of what should be taught and how. If we return to our metaphor of curriculum as a game, as found in Chapter 5 we might say that the authors of these reports fail to pick up all the curriculum pieces. Like so many administrators and policy makers, they assume that if the structure and organization are changed or if the setting and scene of schooling are moved, then appropriate and effective education will result. This is not so. The learning in the various settings often is not coordinated with that of the school, and not all work settings are appropriate for learning. The task of improving the learning of students in specific tasks has yet to be done. Unfinished, too, is the development of a conceptual framework for the creation of learning activities and the training and deployment of personnel.

ADMINISTRATION FOR INSTRUCTIONAL EFFECTIVENESS

The last decade has seen substantial growth in our understanding of the various conditions that account for achievement in individual schools. Unfortunately, achievement has too often been defined as performance on standardized tests of reading and mathematical skills, not creativity or concerns about social conditions that could be addressed by the institutions called "schools."

Over-reliance on test scores as indicators of quality education has diverted needed discussion of what should count as education. Richard Ingersoll, for example, sees test scores as serving two conflicting interests. There are (a) centralists who want top-down control of teaching so all students achieve and teachers become more competent in transmitting academic knowledge and (b) anticentralist teachers who believe that their denial of autonomy prevents them from arranging the conditions of learning by which their students would have greater success in gaining academic knowledge. Both sides depend on scores to operate their dependent variables rather than attending to a wider range of educational expectations than test performance.[36]

---

[36]Richard M. Ingersoll, *Who Controls Teachers? Power Accountability in America's Schools* (Cambridge, MA: Harvard University Press, 2003).

Coordinating the Curriculum

As with other administrative issues, the administrator can take either a systems approach or a school cultural approach to curriculum coordination.

Systems Approach to Curriculum Coordination The different aspects of the curriculum in effective schools (effective as defined by achievement tests) are carefully coordinated or "tightly coupled." School goals, classroom objectives and activities, and measures of student performance are all aligned. Curriculum alignment has become the most popular way to improve test scores. Alignment consists of three steps:

1. The essential outcomes to be achieved are defined and the lists of outcomes, standards, and performance benchmarks are distributed to teachers.

2. Test items for the essential outcomes are developed. A system for scoring the tests is in place and presented to teachers, principal, and district administrators. The teachers and the principal receive reports on student achievement for each grade level in the school. Teachers also receive a separate report for individual students.

3. Teachers focus their teaching on the desired outcomes. To this end, teachers work in grade-level groups, discussing each outcome and making sure they agree on its meaning in terms of classroom instruction. After priorities are set, groups of teachers plan instruction for the year, ensuring that adequate time and appropriate materials and methods are available. During the year, teachers monitor the program and meet to discuss how well plans are being carried out. Near the end of the year, teachers assess their accomplishments, discuss problems, and develop plans for improvement.

Tight coupling requires instructional standards and outcomes that are clear, public, and acceptable. Such a program must minimize differences in the treatment of students' allocated time to certain content, and expose all students to the same curriculum. It also means that the work of outside specialists (resource teachers, reading teachers, counselors) must support the efforts of the classroom teacher.

School Cultural Approach to Curriculum Coordination Administrators in schools with strong culture have a vision of quality schooling that does not equate high test scores with a good school. Their definition of a good school includes ethnic and racial pluralism, parent participation, shared governance, rich programs, personal attention to students, and supportive environments. One of the significant functions of culture is that it governs how members think, feel, and behave.[37] In schools with strong culture, the staff is cohesive in their beliefs and integrated in their efforts to achieve common goals.

Principals of secondary schools require more time to get a consensus on goal setting and problem solving than those in elementary schools. Secondary school teachers often view themselves as working, independently functioning departments and have little to do with overall curriculum goals. An answer to the problem is found in previously described empowerment and emancipation approaches to curriculum development, including matching practices to a predominant moral ideal (ethos). The development and promulgation of a school's "mission" statement of what it is about may help.

Shared Values Effective schools have a strong sense of community with shared goals and high expectations for student and staff performance.[38] In a successful school more members of the teaching staff discuss their teaching. The teachers are organized as a team,

[37]Terrance E. Deal, "The Culture of Schools," in *Leadership: Examining the Elusive*, L. T. Shelve and M. B. Schoenhelt, eds. (Alexandria, VA: Association for Supervision and Curriculum Development, 1987).
[38]Patricia Ashton et al., "A Study of Teachers' Sense of Efficacy," *NIE Report* 400-79-0075 (Gainesville, FL: University of Florida, 1982).

making collective decisions about instructional matters for a common population of students. Shared values also follow from the teachers' acceptance of the need for continuous improvement through analysis, evaluation, and experimentation. A school with shared values is often characterized by (1) talk among teachers about *manipulative variables*—methods of teaching, materials—and *external variables*—pupil background, community attitudes; (2) frequent observations by teachers of each other's teaching; and (3) co-teaching, teachers working together planning, designing, and preparing teaching materials.

The Hidden Curriculum   The hidden curriculum is part of the school's curriculum ethos. This curriculum sometimes refers to the hidden interests served by the institutionalized curriculum as it influences the identities of teachers and students. It also refers to the informal system of the school and classroom that affects what is learned—a hidden system of cliques that control much of the behavior of youth in school achievement and social conduct, such as dating—a network of personal and social relations. C. Wayne Gordon was one of the first to reveal this hidden curriculum and to show a student hierarchy from "big wheel" at the top to "isolates" at the bottom, presenting a source of conflict to the teachers.[39]

Ruth Hubbard found unofficial literacy prevalent in the sixth grade.[40] Her analysis of student self-initiated writing of signs and notices taped to their desks, and notes passed to each other, "the really important stuff," revealed that students were writing to present themselves, to share, and to order. In their notes from the underground, students make announcements about themselves and how they want to be perceived—for example, "A message from the Commander." They also wrote for social purposes—"Do you like me?"—and to escape—"Let's get out of here"—and to organize and find patterns in their environment—a list of popular phrases in *Star Trek*.

In order to deal with the hidden curriculum, teachers identify roles in the informal group —boss, brain, clown—and their motivations. Armed with this knowledge, teachers may decide to (a) advance individual goals that are not part of the institutionalized curriculum, (b) maintain fair relations with all students and run the risk of having conflicts, or (c) bestow affective and other rewards selectively.

Students deal differently with the school's regime, and the atmosphere may produce cheats, conformists, rebels, and recluses. Principals and teachers might ask, "What kind of character is being built by our practices of grading, grouping, eligibility, promotions, and detentions?"

Effective Principals   Principals can contribute to the development of collegiality and continuous improvement. They can express clearly the expectation that all staff members are to be knowledgeable about teaching and are to participate in activities for instructional improvement. Principals should themselves participate in instructional improvement activities and support such efforts by providing encouragement, time, and materials. For example, effective principals protect teachers who are trying curriculum innovations from competing demands and possible criticism.

Principals in successful schools are optimistic about the ability of students to meet goals. They are able to work well with others, manage conflict, and cope with ambiguity. Compared with less effective principals, they take more responsibility for instruction, discussing teaching problems, and protecting teachers from distractions.[41] As indicated in the research by Linda McNeil, good principals put more emphasis on learning than on order.[42]

[39]C. Wayne Gordon, *The Social System in the High School* (Glencoe, IL: Free Press, 1957).

[40]Ruth Hubbard, "Notes from the Underground: Unofficial Literacy in the Sixth Grade," *Anthropology and Education Quarterly* 28, no. 4 (1989): 291–307.

[41]Arthur W. Steller, *Effective Schools Research: Practice and Promise* (Bloomington, IN: Phi Delta Kappa Educational Foundation, 1988).

[42]Linda McNeil, *The Contradictions of Control* (New York: Routledge, 1986).

Effective Classroom Practices   As curriculum goals shift to the teaching of higher order thinking, the definition of effective teaching has changed. Instead of the effective teacher universally moving through materials at a good pace and engaging mostly in direct instruction such as structuring lessons, giving detailed explanations, providing examples, and demanding practice, professionalization of teaching is in the wind.[43] Under professionalism, teachers are free from the demands to teach a prescribed curriculum using stylized methods to prepare students for standardized tests. Instead teachers are compelled to teach students (1) to read for knowledge and enjoyment not simply for acquiring testable reading skills, (2) to think mathematically rather than simply to work problems, (3) to question and analyze, not merely to give right answers, and (4) to think and write creatively.

Effective Research and Curriculum Policy

Caution must be exercised before translating research on effectiveness to curriculum policy. In the first place, most of the findings are correlational, not causal. The fact that principals who concern themselves with instruction and students who try to accomplish clear learning goals are associated with high test scores may mask the underlying reasons for success. What is it in the school environment or training of a principal that makes it likely that the same principal will be effective with instruction in one school and not in a different school? How can teachers engage uninterested students in learning? The answers to such questions are more important than the mere association of an instructional variable with learning.

Furthermore, many of the associations are misleading. The use of time in school, for example, often has been discussed in connection with teaching. However, there is evidence that the amount of time spent on a task by itself is meaningless.[44] We need to know how much time is needed and to consider time spent in relation to decisions on content, mode of instruction, and students' willingness and ability to pay attention. In a well-organized school, trying to improve a time-on-task rate of 65% is probably constructive. However, in a school where the average attendance is less than 70% and the school day is characterized by disorder, more pressing issues than time on task should receive attention.

A serious limitation to the effectiveness studies is that they have ignored achievement in important areas—creativity, desire for further learning, ability to deal with uncertainty. Standardized achievement tests (most of which are skills for reading and math) focus on known tasks for which there are known procedures for teaching. Those interested in good education also attend to the problem of teaching complex concepts and a range of subject matters for which the teaching strategies are not known. Indeed, there are indicators that the focus on mastery of isolated skills such as decoding in reading is detrimental to the attainment of higher level cognitive processes—comprehension and critical reading.[45] The heavy emphasis on answering correctly may reduce curiosity and critical thinking in students. Investigators have found strong resistance from students as teachers make an effort to shift from routine or procedural tasks (teacher directed) to understanding tasks (student directed).[46]

Several implications follow from the findings of the effectiveness studies. The use of achievement test scores, profiles of school practices, needs assessment, and other tight-coupling mechanisms may help the staff to identify a curriculum problem. Sources for

---

[43]Arthur E. Wise, "Professional Teaching: A New Paradigm for the Management of Education," in *Schooling for Tomorrow*, Thomas J. Sergiovanni and John H. Moore, eds. (Boston: Allyn and Bacon, 1989).

[44]Time on Task: A Research Review (Baltimore: Center for the Social Organization of Schools, 1983).

[45]W. C. Becker and R. A. Gersten, "A Follow-up of Follow-Through: The Later Effects of the Direct Instruction Model on Children in Fifth and Sixth Grades," *American Educational Research Journal* 19 (spring 1982): 75–92.

[46]R. S. Brause and J. S. Mayher, "Teachers, Students, and Classroom Organizations," *Research in the Teaching of English* 16, no. 2 (1982): 131–148.

proposed solutions should include the effectiveness literature and the best thinking of the staff itself. If a school is not successful in a certain area, the first place to look for reasons might be the amount of time each teacher is allocating to that content area. After a solution is proposed, a plan outlining staff responsibilities and procedures for evaluating progress may be developed and put into effect.

Central administrators have several mechanisms for coordinating the curriculum. Districtwide testing programs can focus the curriculum on important goals. The practice of focusing on a limited set of goals and aligning these goals with outcomes, content, materials, and tests is a powerful tool. However, efforts to coordinate the system from above are insufficient. Enlistment of the faculty in each school will be necessary because different circumstances exist at each site and because staffs need to develop shared values within each school. Principal and teachers work together to plan, design, and prepare curriculum materials in order for a school to be effective. Rather than imposing school improvement plans from above. Administrators allow effective individual school faculties sufficient latitude to adapt new policies and practices to their situations, and their unique problems. Along with autonomy, the development of group norms requires time for the staff to talk with each other, observe each other, and engage in planning and preparation.

Student Use of New Material   The decisions students make about their involvement with a new curriculum are the most crucial in the process of curriculum change. Such decisions are determined by *internal_supports*. If students perceive the learning opportunity as relevant to their values, interests, and curiosities and if they receive feedback from their responses, they are more likely to learn from the material and experience the excitement of active search and discovery. Other determinants of student involvement are *external supports*. The innovator takes into account peer norms about student participation and cooperation in working with the teacher. Teachers also need to be aware of student norms and to be willing to share leadership with student leaders if students are to become involved. In like manner, the extent of collaboration of parents and other adults in the community influences student involvement with the changed curriculum.

As school superintendent, Larry Cuban successfully coordinated the curriculum at school level. However, he also recognized that the concentration on academic achievement and the coordination of the organization with this goal had undesirable consequences.[47] There was a press toward standardization, a uniform curriculum, and adoption of the same materials for each class in a grade level. (Fewer materials were appropriate for the range of individual differences in each of these grade levels.) Teachers tended to assume that there was a single best way of teaching (usually involving lecturing, recitation, and whole-group instruction). Teaching seemed to be focused on tests rather than on teaching students to think. Teachers were forgetting about responsibility for dealing with such serious matters as being sensitive to the welfare of others.

Tightly coupled procedures narrowly focused on standardized tests are a limited answer to the achievement of the broader and more complex goals of education. Major improvement in academic work depends on learning (1) to teach higher order tasks that may not lend themselves to direct instruction, (2) to present difficult material so that slower students can learn it, and (3) to ensure that subject matter is meaningful to teachers and students, not just material to be memorized for tests.

A recent extensive review of effective schools leads to the conclusion that efforts to reform schools—whether community control, school choice, school site autonomy, or any other proposal—will fail unless there is individual commitment. An ethic of caring conveyed

[47]Larry Cuban, "Effective Schools: A Friendly but Cautionary Note," *Phi Delta Kappan* 64, no. 10 (June 1983): 695–697.

through informal, face-to-face interactions among adults and students provides the bonding and animating force for the enterprise.[48]

CONCLUDING COMMENTS

More coherent school programs are needed. Reform by addition—costly innovations and courses for special interest groups—is not as effective as improving the curriculum by setting priorities, focusing on certain subject matter, and abolishing the tracking system in favor of a common core of knowledge. Guidelines have been presented in this chapter for establishing purposes as well as increasing options and making hard choices about what *not* to teach yet encouraging learner choices.

As the purposes of schooling change, so do organizational arrangements. When personal interests and social concerns are foremost, the curriculum features flexible scheduling, electives, minicourses, and a greater variety of theme schools. As the mode turns to challenging students in basic subjects, fewer electives are offered and the requirements for mathematics, science, and English are strengthened. Remedialism and pluralism, however, do not disappear. Administrators arrange through networks, magnet schools, and schools within schools ways to help students with special needs even in the midst of widespread standardization.

Finally, effective schools are characterized by shared values among staff and students. As found after a decade of work in 40 schools, Anthony Bryk and Barbara Schneider concluded that trust is imperative in improving schools and that trust requires the following from students: *respect*—listening to others and noting their subsequent actions; *personal regard*—willing to go beyond formal role requirements or contracts; *competence*—ethics, skills, and ability; and *integrity*—commitment to education and student welfare.[49] Curriculum development activities within successful local schools are undertaken and supported in the interest of developing a common vision of what the school is attempting to do for students.

QUESTIONS

1. There is much interest in ensuring that all students have equal access to powerful subject matter. Consider a school known to you. What are the criteria for student access to courses? What do students see as barriers to taking particular courses? On what basis are they assigned to courses? How do they select courses? Is there tracking and, if so, what effect does it have on instruction, content, self-image, aspiration, and preparation for advanced course work?

2. Which of the following are most important in developing a coherent curriculum for a school?

   a. Periodic analysis of course content, difficulty, and achievement.

   b. Students and teachers seeing connections and continuity in their work.

   c. Consistency in course content across teachers in terms of texts, topics, assignments, and entrance and exit criteria.

---

[48]Valerie E. Lee, Anthony S. Bryk, and Julia B. Smith, "The Organization of Effective Secondary Schools," *Review of Research in Education*, vol. 19 (Washington, DC: American Educational Research Association, 1993), 171–269.

[49]Anthony S. Bryk and Barbara Schneider, *Trust in Schools: A Core Resource for Improvement* (New York: Russell Sage Foundation, 2002).

3. Consider an educational situation familiar to you and describe the mechanisms that are used in order to focus the curriculum, such as a schoolwide, jointly developed mission statement by which curriculum goals, materials, and methods as well as policies of student promotion and review of student achievement are implemented.

4. Shared educational values among administrators, parents, teachers, and students are important to the success of a school. Describe some ways to foster shared values in a local school.

5. How will tests, textbooks, and school and classroom organization have to change if understanding, innovation, and creativity rather than rote tasks are to become the educational target?

6. Why has the move to site-based management been supported by conservative interests—business, school administrators, teachers, and nonpoor parents?

SUGGESTED STRATEGIC RESEARCH

DETERMINING WHY SIZE MAY MAKE A DIFFERENCE

The size of enrollments in schools and classrooms is often said to affect learning. Little research on how classroom conditions such as safety, light and air quality, and number of interruptions are related to class size and classroom organization. Compare classroom conditions with enrollment and academic and social effects.

RECONCILING THE INSTITUTIONAL (THE FILLING OF EMPTY VESSELS) AND THE PERSONALLY RELATED (LIGHTING THE LEARNER'S FIRE) CURRICULUMS

Identify schools or teachers where there is both high student engagement in learning and successful academic achievement. How do these successful schools and teachers connect their institutional curriculum with their students' own quests for meaning?

VALIDATING PEER HELP-GIVING AS A RESPONSE TO MIDDLE SCHOOL ALIENATION

Attention may be given to the finding that, in contrast with peers in 11 other nations, U.S. middle schoolers have more developmental problems such as feeling low, being nervous, and having dislike of each other. Richard Newman has found that relatedness, autonomy, and competence may be enhanced when students learn how to give and receive help [Richard Newman, "Social Influence on the Development of Children's Adaptive Help Seeking," *Developmental Review* 20 (2003): 350–404]. See if teaching students ways to both give and receive help can bridge both social and academic goals. Students learn to minimize competition and social comparison and instead learn to collaborate when they develop the questioning skills needed for help seeking. What happens when students strive for conditions that foster self-disclosure, intimacy, and mutual support?

CHALLENGING IDEOLOGY OF THE "ONE BEST SYSTEM"

The idea of a public school open to all, financed by taxpayers, and offering a standardized curriculum is challenged by magnet, charter, and other alternative schools. Study one or more alternative schools and determine which of the positive and the negative predictions (add your own) for these new schools are fulfilled.

Positive Predictions	Negative Predictions
Higher student attendance, aspirations, and achievement	Students with special needs lose out
	Social, racial, and economic
Money for schools is more effectively spent	The public school is weakened by flight of better students
More instructional innovations	
Faculty satisfaction is greater	

SELECTED REFERENCES

BOYD, WILLIAM L., AND DEBRA MIRETZEY, EDS. *American Educational Governance on Trial? Change and Challenges.* National Society for the Study of Education Yearbook. Chicago, IL: University of Chicago Press, 2003.

LIPMAN, P. *High Stakes Education.* New York: Routledge, 2004.

McNEIL, LINDA. *The Contradictions of School Reform.* New York: Routledge, 2000.

OLSON, D. R. *Psychological Theory and Educational Reform: How School Remakes Mind and Society.* Cambridge University Press, 2003.

REID, W. A. *Curriculum as Institution and Practice: Essays in The Deliberative Tradition.* Mahwah, NJ: Lawrence Erlbaum, 1999.

CHAPTER 9

EVALUATING THE CURRICULUM

CURRICULUM EVALUATION generates a host of responses. Some fear the power and control it gives central authorities. Local communities have been dismayed by those in government who seem to offer autonomy yet still demand that the school system be evaluated by standardized tests. Teachers interested in evaluation as a way to understand their students fault imposed tests as inadequate for diagnosing and motivating individuals.

Others are reassured by the evaluations. People often expect that evaluation will solve many pressing problems—the public who demands accountability, the decision maker who must choose among curriculum alternatives, the developer who needs to know where and how to improve curriculum materials, and the teacher who is concerned about the effect of learning opportunities on individual students all look to evaluation in their search for solutions.

The field of evaluation is full of different views about its purposes and how it is to be carried out. Humanists argue that measurable outcomes form an insufficient basis for determining the quality of learning opportunities. They believe it is simplistic to measure higher mental functioning, knowledge of self, and other lifelong pursuits at the end of the school year. Curiously, they have no difficulty in evaluating the classroom environment. For them, the learning experience is important in itself, not just a rehearsal whose value will be known only on future performance. On the other hand, systematists with faith in scientific-based evidence perceive evaluation as a set of verified guidelines for practice. They believe that if curriculum workers use these procedures, essential decisions regarding what and how to teach will be warranted.

David Hamilton has summarized the ideas and events in curriculum evaluation during the past 150 years, illuminating its relatively unchanging features.[1] According to him, curriculum evaluation falls within the sphere of practical morality. As such, it responds to both the ethical question "What should we do?" and the empirical question "What can we do?" He recognizes, too, that the importance of evaluation is heightened by social change and politics. Governments make evaluation compulsory, and curriculum evaluation can be seen as part of the struggle by different interest groups—educationalists, teachers, administrators, industrialists—to gain control over the forces that shape the practice of schooling. When more than one person is involved in the selection of criteria for use in an evaluation, agreement cannot be assumed.

---

[1]David Hamilton, "Making Sense of Curriculum Evaluation: Continuities and Discontinuities in an Education Idea," in *Review of Research in Education,* Lee S. Schulman, ed. (Itasca, IL: F. E. Peacock Publishers, 1979), 318–349.

Recently, debate has begun over the conduct of curriculum evaluation and over the particular evaluation model to be used. Systematists use *consensus models* and regard evaluation as a technical accomplishment—the demonstration of a connection between what is and what all agree ought to be. They require a consensus on educational goals and on the rules of evidence. If all agree on the ends, the selection and evaluation of appropriate means are only technical problems for them. In reality, systematists have been most active in determining achievement in rule-governed order such as the basic skills, academic knowledge, and the acquisition of information prized by the dominant culture. A central issue is whether systematists can legitimize emergent goals and assess self-constructed order in innovations and alternative logics.

Social reconstructionists and humanists have a *pluralistic* view of evaluation. This view holds that evaluators should be sensitive to the different values of program participants and should shift the judgment away from the evaluator to the participants. As evaluators, pluralists tend to base their evaluations more on program activity than on program intent and to accept anecdotal accounts and other naturalistic data rather than numerical data and experimental designs. For them, evaluation is an unfinished blueprint that can point out problems, not solutions. They are more concerned with the fairness of the evaluation than with its effectiveness as measured by changes in test scores, for example. Hence, those with a pluralistic bent advocate handing over control of an evaluation to those who have to live with the consequences and having it conducted by the participants rather than *for* the participants.

This chapter shows how to match specific evaluation procedures with specific curriculum decisions, for example, how to improve a course, how to decide which program should continue, and how to assess the long-term effects of the curriculum. A major issue is whether curriculum evaluation is best served by classic research models and experts in measurement or by adaptable procedures in which students and teachers judge their own curriculum. The emergence of *assessment* as the focus on the individual student as opposed to *evaluation*—the appraisal of a program, materials, or course of study—is an instance of adaptation in testing.

In addition to offering information about a number of evaluation techniques, this chapter covers common errors that prejudice evaluative studies and make it difficult to judge the relative effects of different programs. After studying this chapter, one should be able to take a personal stand regarding controversial technical issues—the value of criterion-referenced and norm-referenced tests, the worth of "authentic" assessments, and how best to use assessments as in the interests of learning instead of evidence of achievement.

MODELS FOR EVALUATION

Consensus Models (Traditional and Technical Evaluation)

In a general sense, curriculum evaluation to a systematist is an attempt to throw light on two questions:

1. Do planned learning opportunities, programs, courses, and activities as developed and organized actually produce desired results?

2. How can the curriculum offerings best be improved?

These general questions and the procedures for answering them translate a little differently at macro levels (e.g., evaluating the citywide results from several alternative reading programs) than at micro levels (evaluating the effect of a teacher's instructional plans for achieving course objectives). Classroom teachers often have an additional set of evaluation questions to guide them in making decisions about individuals:

1. *Placement:* At which level of learning should the learner be placed in order to challenge but not frustrate?

2. *Mastery:* Has the learner acquired enough competency to succeed in the next level?

3. *Diagnosis:* What particular difficulty is this learner experiencing?

Decisions and Evaluative Techniques If evaluation is to provide information useful to decision makers, evaluative models should be chosen in light of the kind of decisions to be made. In this connection, a useful distinction can be made between formative and summative evaluation. Formative evaluation is undertaken to improve an existing program. Hence the evaluation provides frequent detailed and specific information to guide the program developers. Summative evaluation is done to assess the effect of a completed program. It provides information to use in deciding whether to continue, discontinue, or disseminate the program. Summative evaluation is frequently undertaken in order to decide which one of several competing programs or materials is best.

Guidelines for conducting formative evaluation have been given by Lee J. Cronbach in a classic article treating *course improvement* through evaluation.[2] The following prescriptions are among the most important:

1. Seek data regarding changes in students as a result of the course.

2. Look for multidimensional outcomes and map out the effects of the course along these dimensions separately.

3. Identify aspects of the course in which revisions are desirable.

4. Collect evidence midway in curriculum development, while the course is still fluid.

5. Try to find out how the course produces its effect and what factors influence its effectiveness. You may find that the teacher's attitude toward the learning opportunity is more important than the opportunity itself.

6. During trial stages, use the teacher's informal reports of observed student behavior and thinking in aspects of the course.

7. Make more systematic observations, but only after the more obvious flaws in the early stages have been dealt with.

8. Make a study of events taking place in the classroom, and use proficiency and attitude measures to reveal changes in students.

9. Observe several results of the new program ranging far beyond the content of the curriculum itself—attitudes, general understanding, aptitude for further learning, and so forth.

[2]Lee J. Cronbach, "Course Improvement Through Evaluation," *Teachers College Record* 64, no. 3 (May 1963): 672–683.

Formative evaluation does not require all students to answer the same questions. Rather, as many questions as possible should be given, each to a different sample of students. Follow-up studies to elicit opinions regarding the ultimate educational contributions of the course are of minor value in improving the course because they are too far removed in time.

Summative evaluation has several purposes. One purpose is to select from several competing curriculum programs or projects those that should continue and those that are ineffective. To this end, an experimental design is highly desirable. W. James Popham has illustrated such designs.[3] There is the *pretest/posttest control group design.* As the design's name suggests, students are pretested on whatever dimensions are sought from the program. Then, after receiving instruction, students in each of the competing programs are tested for their status on a common set of objectives for which each program claims superiority. The posttest must not be biased in favor of one program's objectives. Objectives important to others, but not those of the designers of a particular program, can also be assessed.

The students are assigned to the programs randomly so that each student has an equal chance to be assigned to any one of them and differences in the performance of students may be attributed to differences in the programs. However, evaluators may not always know whether the respective programs were carried out as planned. It is desirable to try each of the programs in many settings, because the experimental unit for analysis is likely to be schools or classrooms, not students. Only in experiments in which the students in the same classrooms receive different programs can the student be the unit of analysis.

Evaluators need not allow ideas about what must happen in an ideal evaluation to discourage them; they should remember that no evaluation has been perfect. When faced with frustrations such as student absenteeism or the failure to give tests, they can remember that the curriculum evaluator is only responsible for providing the best information possible under existing circumstances.

Purposes of Traditional Evaluation   One purpose of evaluation is to decide on the value of a curricular intervention within a course. An *interrupted time series design* is useful for this purpose. In this design, a series of measurements is taken both before and after the introduction of the intervention. Unobtrusive records—absences, disciplinary referrals, requests for transfer—are frequently used with this design, although test scores and other data can also serve. A significant difference in student performance during and after the intervention may be taken as evidence that the intervention had a positive effect.

Another important purpose of evaluation is to decide on the long-term value of curriculum offerings. Longitudinal or follow-up studies are undertaken to indicate whether desired objectives are being realized and to reveal shortcomings. One of the better known longitudinal studies was conducted on a national level in Project Talent. This study was initiated in 1960 with the testing of 400,000 secondary school students. Miscellaneous data such as student interests, ability scores, and characteristics of a student's school, including courses offered, were collected. Fifteen years later, a representative sample of these persons was interviewed, and they reported on their satisfaction with their current status on different life activities. One overall generalization from the findings was that educational programs should be improved and modified to enable persons to achieve greater satisfaction in intellectual development and personal understanding.[4] Another example of the findings from Project Talent studies is that in 1960 47% of the graduating boys and 38% of the girls said their courses were not helpful in preparing them for occupations, whereas 11 years later 46% of the men and 40% of the women felt that high school had been adequate at best.

[3]W. James Popham, *Educational Evaluation*, 3rd ed. (Englewood Cliffs, NJ: Prentice-Hall, 1992).
[4]John C. Flanagan, *Perspectives on Improving Education* (Los Alamitos, CA: Southwest Regional Laboratory for Educational Research and Development, 1979).

National Assessment of Educational Progress (NAEP) is an information system designed to furnish information regarding the educational achievements of children and young adults and to indicate both the progress we are making and the problems we face. Unlike Project Talent, NAEP does not follow individual progress but samples different age groups. The project assesses a variety of curriculum areas. Information on factors that affect student performance is also provided. Test results are reported by age and grade level. Parents, school board members, legislators, and school officials all find the information useful.

An illustration of how the NAEP illuminates problems is the finding that students have improved their verbal and mathematical skills in the past 20 years, but most cannot apply them to complex intellectual tasks. In reading, 61% of 17-year-olds cannot find, understand, summarize, or explain complicated information. In math, 49% of 17-year-olds cannot compute with decimals, fractions, and percentages, recognize geometric figures, or solve simple equations, whereas 94% cannot solve multistep problems or use basic algebra. In science, 93% cannot infer relationships and draw conclusions using detailed scientific knowledge. The report calls for less emphasis on memorization and more on the promotion of thinking. "Teachers should act more as guides, and students more as doers and thinkers."[5]

Evaluating a Curriculum Project Systematists evaluate a curriculum project by assessing (1) the merits of its goals, (2) the quality of its plans, (3) the extent to which the plans can be carried out, and (4) the value of the outcomes. Illustrative of such models is the CIPP (Context, Input, Process, Product) model developed by Dan Stufflebeam and others. In the *context* phase of evaluation, the evaluator focuses on defining the environment, describing the desired and actual conditions, and identifying the problems (needs assessment). *Input* refers to the selection of strategies to achieve the educational objectives. Once a strategy has been selected, a *process* evaluation provides feedback to the implementer about faults in the design and the implementation. Finally, a *product* evaluation is undertaken to reveal the effects of the selected strategy on the curriculum.

In his analytical review of evaluation, David Nevo summarized in question and answer form the nature of consensual models and approaches:

1. What is evaluation? Educational evaluation is a systematic description of educational objects (projects, programs, materials, curriculum, and institutions) and an assessment of their worth.

2. What is the function of evaluation? Evaluation can serve four different functions: (a) formative (for improvement), (b) summative (for selecting and accountability), (c) sociopolitical (to motivate and gain public support), and (d) administrative (to exercise authority).

3. What kinds of information should be collected? Evaluators should collect information about the goals of the object, its strategies and plans, the process of implementation, and the outcome and impacts.

4. What criteria should be used to judge the merits of an object? In judging the worth of an educational object, consider whether or not the object (a) responds to identified needs of clients; (b) achieves national goals, ideals, or social values; (c) meets agreed-on standards; (d) does better than alternative objects; and (e) achieves important stated goals.

5. What is the *process* of doing an evaluation? The process should include three activities: (a) focusing on the problems, (b) collecting and analyzing empirical data, and (c) communicating findings to clients.

---

[5]*Crossroads in American Education* (Princeton, NJ: National Assessment of Educational Progress, 1989).

6. Who should do evaluations? Individuals or teams who have (a) competency in research methods and other data analysis techniques, (b) an understanding of the social context and the unique substance of the evaluation object, (c) an ability to maintain correct human relations and rapport with those involved, and (d) a conceptual framework to integrate the above-mentioned capabilities.

7. By what standards should an evaluation be judged? Evaluation should strike for a balance in meeting standards of (a) utility (useful and practical), (b) accuracy (technically adequate), (c) possibility (realistic and prudent), and (d) propriety (conducted legally and ethically).[6]

Pluralistic Models (Humanistic and Social Reconstructionist Evaluation)

Evaluation models with the pluralistic concern of humanists and social reconstructionists have had as yet a relatively limited impact. Pluralistic procedures are less frequently used than the research and technological procedures applied by teachers in course improvement, by school managers in rational decision making, by government evaluators in auditing new social programs in the schools, and by statewide evaluators in monitoring the curriculum for accountability purposes.

Pluralistic evaluation models tend to be used only when research is less attractive for reasons of politics, cost, or practicality. These newer models are chiefly used with curriculum that is out of the mainstream and is associated with aesthetic education, multicultural projects, and alternative schools. Pluralistic models are also increasing in supplementary experimental designs.

Responsive Evaluation Robert E. Stake[7] was one of the first evaluators to propose the pluralist argument that the evaluator should make known the criteria or standards that are being employed and who holds them. As a pluralist, Stake believes that sensitivity to the perceived needs of those concerned with the evaluation is essential. Accordingly, he urges initial evaluations to discover what clients and participants actually want from the program evaluation. These concerns should be discovered prior to designing the evaluation project. Stake places less emphasis on precisely specified objectives than do systematists, because he wishes to describe all intentions, even those not expressed in terms of student learning. The key emphasis in his model is on description and judgment. For him, an evaluator should report the ways different people see the curriculum. Hence, the evaluator's principal activities include discovering what those concerned want to know, making observations, and gathering multiple judgments about the observed antecedents, transactions, and outcomes. A variety of persons—outside experts, journalists, psychologists—as well as teachers and students may participate in the conduct of the evaluation.

The Connoisseurship Model Elliot W. Eisner has argued for an evaluation process that will capture a richer slice of educational life than test scores do.[8] One of his procedures is educational criticism in which an evaluator asks certain key questions: What has happened during the school year in a given school? What were the key events? How did they come into being? How did students and teachers participate? What were the consequences? How could the events be strengthened? What do such events enable children to learn?

[6]David Nevo, "The Conceptualization of Educational Evaluation," *Review of Educational Research* 53, no. 11 (Spring 1983):117–128.

[7]Robert E. Stake, "The Countenance of Educational Evaluation," *Teachers College Record* 68 (1967): 523–540.

[8]Elliot W. Eisner, The Educational Imagination: On the Design and Evaluation of School Programs (New York: Macmillan, 1985).

Other vehicles for disclosing the richness of programs, according to Eisner, are films, videotapes, photography, and taped student and teacher interviews. These tools, useful in portraying aspects of school life, are valuable channels for communication when supplemented by critical narrative.

Connoisseurship is involved in noting what is and is not said, how it is said, its tone, and other factors that indicate meaning. Another procedure recommended by Eisner is the analysis of work produced by children, including a critique to help evaluators understand what has been accomplished and to reveal some of the realities of classroom performance. As we shall see, this procedure is gaining popularity in the newer approaches that fall under the rubric of authentic assessment.

The fundamental thesis of the connoisseur approach is that the problem of communicating to some publics, such as parent, board, and state agencies, about what has happened in school (the good and the bad) can be usefully conceived as an artistic problem. In such an approach an evaluator fashions an expressive picture of educational practice and its consequences.

Connoisseurship and criticism are ways of seeing rather than ways of measuring and have been criticized as abstruse technology that requires special training in acquiring "interpretive maps" and ways to understand the meaning of what has been said. Judgments are established externally by the nature of artistic virtues and tradition. This approach, though informative and highly adaptive to unique local conditions, is subjective and thus potentially controversial. However, social interaction among participants in creating meaning from what is collected contributes to the validity of interpretations.

Evaluation as Critical Inquiry   Kenneth Sirotnik is a pluralist who believes that evaluation requires multiple perspectives on what constitutes knowledge by people in the school. For him, evaluation is rigorous *self-examination,* a process of critical inquiry. Critical inquiry is a dialectic using such questions as

What goes on in the name of X (any curriculum practice)?

How did it come to be that way?

Whose interests are and are not served by the way things are?

What information and knowledge do we have or need to get?

After getting the required information, is this the way we want it?

What are we going to do about all this? (What action is required?)[9]

The conduct of critical inquiry in schools is advanced by district encouragement and the support of collaborative networks where districts and schools address problems of mutual concern, and accept responsibility for carrying out the necessary research, development, and evaluations.

Critical inquiry allows for the collection of varied but pertinent information including the meanings generated by those in the school. Data are not limited to quality indicators and test scores that lend scientific credibility to superficial accountability systems. In evaluation through critical inquiry, moral questions are raised about the goals given by state and district and the human cost of achieving them, throwing light on why these goals are being achieved at a high or low level. For Sirotnik and others, evaluation is a valuing activity in which evaluators (members of the school community) make explicit their operant values, beliefs, interests, and ideologies as they critically examine school practices enlightened by experimental data.[9]

[9]Kenneth Sirotnik, "Evaluation in the Ecology of Schooling," *The Ecology of School Renewal* National Society for the Study of Education Yearbook (Chicago: University of Chicago Press, 1987), 41–63.

CONTROVERSIAL TECHNICAL ISSUES IN CURRICULUM EVALUATION

Curriculum specialists, teachers, and administrators often disagree on which techniques to use in evaluation. Many disputes about procedures occur because each party has different purposes and needs in mind. They argue over the merits of procedures and instruments such as formats for stating objectives or specifying goals, norm- and criterion-referenced tests, privacy, and the merits of authentic assessment. Their controversies will not be resolved by taking an uncompromising attitude but by showing the circumstances in which one approach is better than another.

The Form of Objectives (Goals, Standards, Benchmarks, and Indicators)

The value of and proper manner for stating objectives is uncertain. Part of the problem is philosophical. An extreme position is that an objective must specify the exact overt behavior that a learner is to display at the end of an instructional sequence. This overt response is seen as important in itself. A more moderate position is that the objective must specify performance or a product that indicates whether the objective has been attained. This position allows for covert responses on the part of the learner, but demands that some evidence be specified to indicate whether the desired change in the learner has occurred. Whether only a few high status objectives should be stated for a program is an issue. Another position is that there should be no stated objectives at all, that objectives represent external goals and manipulation, and they insignificantly indicate a learner's actual experiences from a situation.

Part of the problem is that these groups try to judge the form and value of objectives without understanding the reason for the evaluation. There are many uses for objectives: They can communicate general direction at a policy level, provide a concrete guide for selecting and planning learning opportunities, and set the criteria for evaluation of the learners' performance. To illustrate, there are at least four degrees of specificity for an objective. Very general statements are useful when trying to get a consensus on direction at a policy level. For this purpose, it is often sufficient to use *general goal statements:* to learn to respect and get along with people by developing appreciation and respect for the worth of individuals, to respect and understand minority opinions, and to accept majority decisions.

More specific objectives are useful when planning the learning opportunities for courses or when analyzing instructional materials. These objectives are called standard performance indicators or *educational objectives* and are illustrated in several taxonomies.[10-12] These taxonomies treat affective, cognitive, and psychomotor domains. The *Taxonomy of Educational Objectives: Handbook I*, for example, treats cognitive objectives and classifies them using six major categories and several subcategories. Categories range from simple recall of information to critical evaluative behaviors. One such category is application. *Application* is defined as using abstractions in particular and concrete situations. The abstractions may be general ideas, rules of procedures, or generalized methods. They may also be technical principles, ideas, and theories that must be remembered and applied. The taxonomy also gives sample objectives. The level of specificity of an educational objective

---

[10]Benjamin S. Bloom, ed., *Taxonomy of Educational Objectives: Handbook I—Cognitive Domain* (New York: David McKay Company, 1956).

[11]David R. Krathwohl et al., *Taxonomy of Educational Objectives: Handbook II—Affective Domain* (New York: David McKay, 1956).

[12]Anita Harrow, *A Taxonomy of the Psychomotor Domain: A Guide for Developing Behavioral Objectives* (New York: David McKay, 1972).

can be seen in this example: "The ability to predict the probable effect of a change in a factor on a biological situation previously at equilibrium." The objective can be further amplified by an illustration of the kind of test or test item that would be appropriate.

The taxonomies have influenced curriculum making by drawing attention to affective, cognitive, and psychomotor domains. Also, curriculum workers are now more sensitive to the level of performance expected from instruction. They are, for instance, more concerned that objectives and test items treat higher cognitive processes like comprehension, application, and analysis rather than dealing only with recall of information. Nevertheless, many scholars believe it does not make sense to assess separately cognitive, affective, and conative (concerned with persistence and will) components. Affective and conative components are integral to the ability to think. According to John Raven, for example, the classification of cognitive and affective objectives distorts and obstructs efforts to assess significant educational achievements.[13]

Recently, the most prominent of the taxonomies, Bloom's Taxonomy, has been revised, and the new framework allows one to classify standards, goals, objectives, and activities on the basis of the cognitive processes involved.[14,15] The processes range from simple remembering of relevant knowledge to creating from elements an original product. Like the original taxonomy, the revision cuts across subject matters. However, the new framework differentiates knowledge as factual, conceptual, and procedural and includes metacognitive (self) knowledge about one's own cognition and ways of learning. When the revised taxonomy is used to illuminate the cognitive demand and the language dimensions of standards, objectives, and activities, their relative emphasis, alignment, and missing educational opportunities are revealed.

Some persons still employ *instructional objectives*—a specific form for an objective—although they are losing popularity. This form is useful when teaching a specific concept. It is often called a Mager-like instructional objective after the person who advocated its use.[16] These objectives specify the behavior to be exhibited by the student, a standard or criterion of acceptable performance, and the kind of situation in which the behavior is to be elicited. An instructional objective might be, "Given a linear algebraic equation with one unknown (the situation or condition), the learner must be able to solve the equation (behavior and criterion) without the aid of references, tables, or calculating devices (additional conditions)."

Objectives seem valuable in providing guidance for the evaluation of instructional materials and student performance. Other functions of objectives, such as giving direction in teaching and aiding learning, arouse much difference of opinion. It is charged that a teacher who uses specific objectives may not give enough attention to the immediate concerns of learners. The research on this issue, however, is inconclusive. Some studies on the effect of objectives on learning, for example, have shown positive effects, but an equal number have not shown any significant differences. Objectives sometimes help and are almost never harmful. They seem to assist students in determining what is expected of them and in discriminating between relevant and irrelevant content. Charles Clark thinks objectives are all right, provided that students themselves generate or choose the objective(s).[17] A question remains about the number of objectives that should be provided to the

---

[13]John *Raven*, "The Barriers to Achieving the Wider Goals of General Education," *The British Educational Research Journal* 16, no. 2 (1990): 273–296.

[14]L. Anderson and D. Krathwohl, eds., Special Edition, "Revising Bloom's Taxonomy," *Theory Into Practice* 41, no. 4 (200x): 210–267.

[15]L. Anderson, D. Krathwohl, et al., *A Taxonomy for Learning, Teaching, and Assessing: A Revision of Bloom's Taxonomy of Educational Objectives* (New York: Longmans, 2001).

[16]Robert F Mager, *Preparing Instructional Objectives* (Palo Alto, CA: Fearon Publishers, 1961).

[17]Charles Clark, "The Necessity of Curriculum Objective," *Journal of Curriculum Studies* 20, no. 4 (Aug. 1988): 339–349.

student. If the list of objectives is extensive and detailed, both student and teacher are overwhelmed. On the importance of stating objectives, a reviewer cites the philosopher George Santayana, "The fanatic is one who redoubles his efforts when he has forgotten his aim."

Measurement of Intended Outcomes versus Goal-Free Evaluation

In the past Ralph Tyler told evaluators that it was impossible to decide whether a particular test would be appropriate for appraising a certain program until the objectives of the program had been defined and until the kinds of situations that would give an opportunity for this behavior to be expressed were identified. Tyler recommended checking each proposed evaluation device against the objectives and constructing or devising methods for collecting evidence about the student's attainment of these objectives.

More recently, Michael Scriven moved beyond Tyler's concern for data about intended outcomes to a concern for all relevant effects. His approach is called *goal-free evaluation.* This evaluation does not assess a situation merely in terms of goal preferences. It is evaluation of *actual* effects against a profile of demonstrated needs. It is offered as a protection against the narrow vision of those close to the program, against harmful side effects, missed new priorities, and overlooked achievement. To the extent that Scriven's approach is used, more evaluative measures will have to be used. Selection of these measures will be difficult, for there are thousands of such devices. Practicality will probably dictate the use of measures that assess most intended outcomes and a limited number of possible effects.

David Fetterman is also opposed to use of evaluations of programs based on their goals.[18] He believes that such evaluations are misleading. Goals are often part of the political rhetoric. They are often vague and therefore misrepresent the program. Focus on procedures, formulative evaluation, and ethnographic techniques may contribute to more accurate understanding of a program, revealing both the manifest and latent purposes of the program.

Among the anthropological tools that evaluators use are *phenomology*—attending to viewpoints of their students; *holism*—considering the larger picture rather than details and looking for patterns; *nonjudgmentalism*—making biases explicit; and *contexturalization*—placing acquired information in its own environment so that it is represented accurately.

Norm-Referenced Tests and Criterion-Referenced Tests

Standardized achievement tests are norm-referenced and designed to compare the performances of individuals with the performance of a normative group. The purposes of these tests initially were to find the most able persons and to sort out those who were most likely to succeed or to fail in some future learning situation. Only those test items that discriminate between the best and the worst are kept. The assumption that everyone can learn equally well is rejected in norm-referenced testing. These tests tend to correlate very highly with intelligence tests. In order to obtain items with high response variance, writers of norm-referenced tests are likely to exclude the items that measure widely known concepts and skills that have been most effectively taught.

Although norm-referenced tests identify persons of different ability, they are of questionable value in curriculum evaluation. They may not accurately measure what educational programs are designed to teach nor reveal particular problems that are keeping

---

[18]David M. Fetterman, "Qualitative Approaches to Evaluating Education," *Educational Researcher* 17, no. 8 (Nov. 1988): 17–24.

pupils from achieving. Teachers can sometimes improve scores on such tests, but usually such improvement results from tricks such as (1) telling children to respond to all items so that the possibility of getting more right answers is increased,* (2) testing at a time of the year different from that of the previous testing to show apparent but not real gains, (3) capitalizing on regression effects that make the poorest scores look better on the second testing, and (4) teaching students how to respond to the test items themselves and to the test format.

Congress has continued to require students in Chapter 1 (a federal program for the disadvantaged) to be tested on standardized norm-referenced tests although these tests do not reflect the curriculum and lead to rote learning. Efforts to introduce alternate tests, such as criterion-referenced and performance-based tests, have been resisted by some educational officials and by the publishers of the standardized tests.[19]

Criterion-referenced tests are meant to ascertain a learner's status with respect to a learning task, rather than to a norm. These tests indicate what learners can and cannot do in specified situations. The tasks selected can be those emphasized by the curriculum. The items used in the test match what is called for in the objective and should not be eliminated, as in the norm-referenced tests, merely because most students answer them correctly. Hence, these tests can be sensitive measures of what has been taught.

Criterion-referenced tests are also useful in showing whether a student has mastered specific material. Consequently, they are popular in instructional settings using continuous progress plans or other individualized teaching approaches. The tests indicate which instructional treatments are needed by individual learners and also indicate when learners are ready to proceed to other tasks.

Criterion-referenced tests are sometimes faulted because they have been based on objectives that are too narrow. The multiplicity of tests necessary to accompany many objectives has been a management problem for teachers. Trends indicate that particular courses in the future will use perhaps eight to ten very important final tests based on objectives that are applicable to many situations, rather than the large numbers of objectives. Tests that have items dependent on particular materials or programs will also diminish. Other ways of improving these tests are to include a complete description of the set of learner expectations that the test is to assess and to increase the number of items for each competency measured in order to have an acceptable standard of reliability.

Tests and Invasion of Privacy

The American Civil Liberties Union has taken up the cause of students who charge that tests are an invasion of privacy. Students have complained about the use of instruments, usually self-report devices, that probe their attitudes in such areas as self-esteem, interest in school, and human relations. Evaluators want such data in order to assess the effects of schooling. Protests against the use of tests to guide the learning process in academic areas are less frequent. ACLU lawyers argue that authorities have not made it clear that pupils may refuse to take tests that they believe to be invading their privacy. Students should also be told that the questions asked in a test might require self-incriminating responses that could later be used against them.

This issue is related to a larger problem, that of the effect of tests on students. Do they affect motivation and self-esteem by producing anxiety and encouraging cheating? Do they create labels and determine adult social status? How persons think of themselves

---

*A child needs to get only three to seven more items right to show one-year improvement on typical achievement tests.

[19]Mark Pitsch, "Test Changes for Chapter 1 Are Predicted," *Education Weekly* 13, no. 13 (Dec. 1, 1993): 11–14.

and what they believe about a test influence their test behavior. Students' attitudes about tests in general are negative. The more interested persons are in their test results, the more they perceive positive consequences of tests. Systematic reporting of test results helps students to understand their interests, aptitudes, and achievements. Tests are powerful, and their consequences are far-reaching.

Peter Airasian found that testing eroded local school control and shaped curricular goals in response to varied social groups; quality replaced equality.[20] He evaluates tests in light of the likely social and legal implications of their use. For example, instead of following the old maxim "don't teach to the test," Airasian believes that not to teach to a test may be a disservice to students in light of the consequences of failing a test.

Tests have often been criticized as inaccurate and biased against women and minority groups. Indeed, courts have in fact ruled that the awarding of scholarships based on scholastic aptitude test scores may discriminate against female students. Also, students who cannot afford to pay for coaching may be disadvantaged.

Authentic Assessment of Student Performance

Authenticity refers to *real,* nonroutine problems or tasks that represent the kinds of situations faced by citizens or professionals in a given field, and which require students to use knowledge efficiently and creatively in fashioning solutions. Students are given access to information and encouraged to contribute with others in their problem solving. Further, they are not required to work within arbitrary deadlines.

Ideally, students perceive the context of the task as realistic, such as publishing a school newspaper or, as in the case of an introductory physical science course, a multiday test where students chemically analyzed a sludgelike mixture of unknown solids and liquids, simulating real-world tests of chemical analysis.

Although authentic tasks are clear about both what the student is to do and the criterion for judging performance, the tasks do not call for pat routines, procedures, or recipes. On the contrary, the tasks permit alternative ways of responding and allow for different ways (representations) for making public their interpretations and solutions.

Roles and activities common to professional life serve as possible "templates" for test design. Grant Wiggins, for instance, suggests giving students a task related to the role of museum curator by asking them to design an exhibit on a given topic or to compete with one another in designing grant proposals.[21] For sample problems faced by engineers, Wiggins would give tasks that require students to bid and meet specifications or to design and build a working catapult or herbarium. Other illustrations of authentic tasks might include advertising campaigns for a product; designing a book jacket; or developing a travel brochure, including research on the costs and logistical information from a computer reservation system.

Reasons for the movement to authentic assessment are of interest to curriculum workers. In part, authentic assessment, which couples evaluation to the context of instruction, is a reaction to the excesses of the reform movement of the 1980s. As indicated in Chapter 8, the demand for higher standards set by policy makers could not be met by mandating formal testing and tougher tests. Improved learning and teaching were needed. Authentic assessment gives teachers the opportunity to introduce new instructional methods that favor investigation, exploration, and the students' creation of knowledge.

---

[20]Peter W. Airasian, "State-Mandated Testing and Educational Reform: Context and Consequences," *American Journal of Education* 95, no. 3 (May 1987): 393–420.

[21]Grant Wiggins, "Assessment, Authenticity, Context, and Validation," *Phi Delta Kappan* 75, no. 3 (Nov. 1993): 200–215.

Other reasons are the influence of findings from research: (1) studies of metacognition for authentic assessment point to the importance of learners controlling their own thinking; (2) studies of understanding show that the manipulation of formulas and shadow learning of information does not result in understanding and applying fundamental principles; (3) studies of situational knowledge reveal that tests that have little resemblance to life yield scores that have poor predictive value for daily living; and (4) studies of cognition support the value of holistic activities whereby students constructed personal and shared meanings in complex situations rather than activities that followed a narrow sequence of facts to concepts, and concepts to problem solving. In brief, the mapping of valued educational outcomes, such as the ability to communicate, cooperate, create, and solve complex problems, cannot be translated into objective pencil-and-paper test items.

There are, however, controversies regarding authentic assessment. There is concern that evidence of a student's ability to perform on a task may not adequately represent abilities needed for performing other tasks of a broadly defined domain (lack of generalizability). Also, the challenge of developing criteria for judging performance is an issue. The problem of setting an acceptable performance involves determining what is developmentally appropriate and what will be useful in profiling strengths and weaknesses.

Costs and practicality are additional concerns. Although there is interest in teachers sharing tasks across school districts, collaborating cohorts of teachers through the Internet are slow in coming. Generally, tasks are prepared by teams made up of teachers who identify the major ideas of a domain, create the tasks that will be motivating for students, and the scoring criteria. Students may be involved in clarifying the task.

Perhaps the most controversial aspect of authentic testing is political. Traditional tests are instruments for control by governmental and educational agencies who seek to define what will count as knowledge. Usually, these authorities promote inert and reproductive knowledge—*knowing that*. In contrast, authentic testing considers local norms and emphasizes knowledge in use—*knowing how*—which encourages learners to create new solutions and interpretations. How far will official groups go in permitting teachers and students to substitute performance assessment for traditional standardized tests in making high-stakes decisions involving sanctions and rewards on the basis of test results? Which evaluative currency will be acceptable within the political realm?

Assessment as Learning

Paul Black and Dylan Wiliam have shown how to improve classroom assessment so that it is not a test of what the student has learned (summative evaluation) but instead an integral part of learning (formative evaluation).[22] These experienced evaluators claim that traditional classroom assessment practices, such as marking, grading and fostering competition, and ranking have negative impacts. The mislabeling of students as lacking in ability, which minimizes the value of effort, is but one example.

In contrast, assessment as learning consists of practices that improve learning and performance. These practices include encouraging students to reflect on their work and allowing more time for students to work in small groups with their peers where they assist each other by clarifying tasks, sharing knowledge and points of view, and helping each other improve performance. Students may work individually first and then share their work and thoughts with peers. Important problems, dialogue, and the willingness to explore "wrong" and "dumb" questions are features of assessment in learning.

---

[22]Paul Black and Dylan Wiliam, "The Formative Purpose: Assessment Must First Promote Learning" in *Toward Coherence between Classroom Assessment and Accountability*, Mark Wilson, ed. (Chicago, IL: National Society for the Study of Education, 2004), 20–51.

The feedback that students receive from the teacher and peers is not a "grade" or a score, but a comment—a way to communicate what has been achieved and what the student needs to do next; An action plan with appropriate support follows.

The focus of assessment as learning does not compare one student with another. The criteria for evaluating achievement is known to all, and it is helpful to highlight the criteria through examples and modeling. Tools by which students develop the microcognitive knowledge for reflecting on their inquiries are now being developed. These tools show positive effects, particularly for lower achieving students.[23] Table 9.1 illustrates the difference between assessment of achievement by those outside the classroom and ways that teachers and students determine progress in student learning.

TECHNIQUES FOR COLLECTING DATA

Newton S. Metfessel's and William B. Michael's list of multiple criterion measures for evaluating school programs is an old but useful survey of ways to collect data.[24] One class of indicators of change in learners includes informal devices, short answer techniques, interviews, peer nominations, sociograms, questionnaires, self-evaluation measures, projective

Table 9.1 Testing for Outsiders versus Testing for Learning in the Classroom

External Summative Assessment	Internal Formative Assessment
Purpose	*Purpose*
Accountability	Student learning
Ranking	Knowledge of how to improve
Acquisition of prescribed content	
Measures	*Measures*
Standardized tests	Student work
Textbook tests	Observations or interviews,
Benchmarks	projects
External criteria	*Internal criteria*
Levels of proficiency, passing scores	Criteria generated with students and used
Grades	in judging work
Norm referenced:	*Criterion referenced*
Independent effort	Group participation
Feedback	*Feedback*
Delayed	Immediate
Score	What has been accomplished
Rank	Reflection
	How to improve
Audience and use of data	*Audience and use of data*
Teacher and authorities external to	Student, teacher, parents
the classroom	Used in diagnoses and in forming action
Decision makers in placement of students	plans
selecting areas for school improvement	Progress map for school and for individual

[23]J. R. Frederksen and B. Y. White, "Designing Assessment for Instruction and Accountability," in *Toward Coherence between Classroom Assessment and Accountability*, Mark Wilson, ed. (Chicago, IL: National Society for the Study of Education, 2004), 74–102.

[24]Newton S. Metfessel and William B. Michael, "A Paradigm Involving Multiple Criterion Measures for the Evaluation of the Effectiveness of School Programs," *Educational and Psychological Measurement* 27, no. 4 (1967): 931–934.

devices, and semantic differential scales. The authors also describe the many ways of assessing the effect of programs without influencing the outcomes. These methods are called *unobtrusive measures*; they include attending to absences, anecdotal records, appointments, assignments, stories written, awards, use of books, case histories, disciplinary actions, dropout, and voluntary activities.

As indicated in the previous discussion regarding authentic testing, creative indicators can be devised if persons think beyond the use of formal tests. Other useful indicators are (1) the learners' products, such as compositions, paintings, and constructions; (2) the learners' self-reports on preferences and interests; and (3) the learners' solutions to problems, their conduct in discussions, and their participation in physical games and dances. The use of student portfolios where student and teacher maintain a record of work and reflections that will tell a story of the student's learning is a case in point. With these methods, the teacher or evaluator should use an accompanying checklist stipulating what is to be exhibited by the student and the qualities to be found in the student's product.

Michael Patton has written on ways the evaluator can get closer to students and situations being evaluated in order to understand the curriculum as the students experiencing it do.[25] His suggestions for observation and interviewing are extensive and consistent with pluralistic notions. Patton stresses the importance of understanding the point of view and experiences of others. For example, he believes that evaluators, with their own personalities and interests, are naturally attuned to some people more than others. Favoritism may hinder the observer from acting naturally and being integrated into the program. The evaluator as observer must decide about personal relationships and group interest, without losing perspective or the experience of students with whom the evaluator is less directly involved. Similarly, in interviewing, Patton is opposed to having participants fit their knowledge, experiences, and feelings into the evaluator's categories. Instead, the evaluator should provide a framework for the respondents' understanding of the program, not asking "How satisfied are you with this program?" but asking "What do you think of this program?"

Measuring Affect

Although it is a controversial activity, the assessment of affect is gaining interest. Special techniques are used for this task, because it is believed that persons are more likely to "fake" their attitudinal responses. Hence, mild deception is often used so that learners will not know the purpose of the inquiry or that they are being observed. A student may be asked, for example, to respond to several hypothetical situations, only one of which is of interest to the examiner. The examiner may ask, "Where would you take a visitor friend from out of town—to the market, the movie, the school, the library, or the bank?" If "school" is the answer, it is presumed that the respondent tends to value that institution. Another, less direct approach, is to use high inference and theoretical instruments. The examiner might ask, "Would you play the part of a degenerate in a play?" or "Which of the following names (one of which is the respondent's own) do you like?" (The inference is that students with high self-concepts will play any role and will like their names.) Situations are sometimes contrived, and students' reactions are interpreted to indicate particular attitudes. Student observers may collect unobtrusive data and report their observations later, for example. Audio recordings are sometimes made of student small group discussions and analyzed later.

Sometimes, too, students are offered ways to respond anonymously. In evaluating the affective consequences of a curriculum, students need not be identified. One only has to know what effect the curriculum is having on students as a group. Furthermore, the

[25]Michael Q. Patton, *Creative Evaluation* (Beverly Hills, CA: Sage Publications, 1987).

measures or scores obtained with most high inference instruments are not reliable enough for making predictions about individual students.

In an effort to improve the credibility of their findings, evaluators may use *triangulation* (the use of three different measures in concert). If a similar attitude is found by all three measures, they have more confidence in the findings. Locally developed instruments also are thought to be more valid when two or more persons score students' responses the same and when several samples of student behavior are consistent.

Sampling

Sampling is the practice of inferring an educational status on the basis of responses from representative persons or representative tasks. W. James Popham has said, "Sampling should make a Scotsman's values vibrate. It is *so* terribly thrifty."[26] Sampling is controversial mainly because it is sometimes imposed in inappropriate situations. When students are to be graded on their relative attainment of common objectives, it is not proper to assess only certain students nor is it valid to test some students on one set of objectives and others on another set.

Administrators rightfully use sampling when they estimate the typical reactions of students from a few instances of their behavior. It is not necessary to collect all the compositions that students have written in order to judge their writing ability. Samples will suffice—perhaps one at the beginning of the year and one at the end—to show change, if any, as a result of instruction. Similarly, to determine a student's knowledge in one subject, it is not necessary to ask the student to respond to all the items that are involved in this knowledge. A sample of what is involved is enough to draw an inference about the student's status. To find out whether the student can name all the letters of the alphabet, one can present only five letters at random from the alphabet and ask the student to name them. The responses indicate ability to respond to the total population of letters. If all five are named correctly, there is a high probability that the child could name all of the letters. If the child cannot name one or more of the letters, obviously the objective has not been reached. Controversy arises over sampling because teachers have concerns that do not lend themselves to sampling. If sampling indicates that a child cannot name all of the letters of the alphabet, then the teacher wants to know specifically which ones must be taught. Sampling is unlikely to reveal this information.

Controversy may also arise between legislators and others who want achievement records of individual students and evaluators who prefer to use a technique like *matrix sampling* to determine the effects of a program. In this sampling technique randomly selected students respond to randomly selected test items measuring different objectives. Thus, different students take different tests. The advantages of the technique are many: reduced testing time required of the student, attainment of information concerning learners' knowledge with respect to many objectives, and reduced apprehension on the student's part because examinees are not compared. The disadvantage is that sampling does not tell us the status of an individual on all the objectives. But again, this is not necessary to get an indication of abilities within groups of students.

Hazards in Conducting Traditional Evaluation

Donald Horst and colleagues at the RMC Research Corporation have identified 12 hazards in conducting evaluations. Each hazard makes it difficult to know whether students do better in a particular program than they would have done without it.

---

[26]W. James Popham, *Educational Evaluation*, 3rd ed. (Englewood Cliffs, NJ: Prentice Hall, 1993).

1. *The use of grade-equivalent scores.* One should not use grade-equivalent scores in evaluating programs. The concept is misleading; a grade-equivalent score of 7 by fifth graders on a math test does not mean that they know sixth- and seventh-grade math. Such scores do not comprise an equal interval scale and, therefore, it is difficult to obtain an average score. The procedures for obtaining these scores make them too low in the fall and too high in the spring.

2. *The use of gain scores.* Gain scores have been used to adjust for differences found in the pretest scores of treatment and comparison groups. Using them in this way is a mistake, because raw gain scores (posttest scores minus pretest scores) excessively inflate the posttest performance measure of an initially inferior group. Students who initially have the lowest scores have the greatest opportunity to show gain.

3. *The use of norm-group comparisons with inappropriate test dates.* A distorted picture of a program's effect occurs when pupils in the new program are not tested within a few weeks of the norm group's tests. Standardized test developers might collect performance scores in May in order to obtain a norm for the test. If the school's staff, however, administers the test during a different month, the discrepancy might be due to the date of testing rather than to the program.

4. *The use of inappropriate test levels.* Standardized norm-referenced tests are divided into levels that cover different grades. The test level may be too easy or too difficult, and thereby fail to provide a valid measurement of achievement. The test might differentiate sufficiently among groups at either end of the scale. Such effects may also occur with the use of criterion-referenced tests. Hence, tests should be chosen on the basis of the students' achievement level, not their grade level in school.

5. *The lack of pre- and posttest scores for each treatment participant.* The group of students ultimately posttested is not usually composed of exactly the same students as the pretest group. Eliminating the scores of dropouts from the posttest may raise the posttest scores considerably. Conclusion of a program's report should be based on the performance of students who have both pre- and posttest scores. The reason for dropping out also should be reported.

6. *The use of noncomparable treatment and comparison groups.* Students should be randomly assigned to groups. If they are not, students in a special program may do better or worse than those in other programs, because they were different to start with.

7. *The use of pretest scores to select program participants.* Groups with low pretest scores appear to learn more from a special program than they actually do because of a phenomenon called *regression toward the mean.* Gains of high-scoring students may be obscured.

8. *The use of mismatched comparison groups.* The correct procedure for matching groups is to match pairs of pupils and then randomly assign one member of each pair to a treatment or comparison group. If, for example, you want to control for age, you should choose pairs of pupils of the same age. Each member of the pair must have an equal opportunity to be assigned to a given treatment. Do not consciously try to place one member in a certain group.

9. *Careless administration of tests.* Students from both treatment and comparison groups should complete pre- and posttests together. Problems arise when there is inconsistent administration of tests to the two groups. If, for example, there is a disorderly situation in one setting and a different teacher present, the results may differ.

10. *The assumption that an achievement gain is due to the treatment alone.* The Hawthorne effects—unrecognized "treatments," such as novelty—may be responsible for the gain. Plausible rival hypotheses should be examined as a likely explanation.

11. *The use of noncomparable pretests and posttests.* Although conversion tables allow one to correct scores on one test to their equivalent on other tests, it is best if the same level of the same test is used for both pre- and posttesting. Often it is possible to use the identical test as both pre- and posttest. Obviously, this does not suffice if teachers teach to the test and if there are practice effects from taking the test.

12. *The use of inappropriate formulas to estimate posttest scores.* Formulas that calculate expected posttest scores from IQ or an average of grade-equivalent scores are inaccurate. The actual posttest scores of treatment and comparison groups provide a better basis for evaluating treatment effects.[27]

Value Added Assessment

The No Child Left Behind Act of 2001 requires that schools, districts, and states report the percentages students score on the "Proficiency Level" or higher on standardized tests. This requirement makes value added assessment a likely tool. Value added assessment is an attempt to find out how much value school adds to the academic progress of students over time. The results are used in judging the school, the teacher, and the individual student. It is an effort to use test scores as the basis for determining the present level of a student in a given academic area and from this score set an expected rate of growth during a future given period of time. Measurement of performance through elementary and secondary school levels are recorded as well as accumulated scores for particular teachers, subject areas, and schools. Reviews of the test scores (data) reveal where schools and teachers need improvement. Action plans are devised to address "trouble spots."

There is some variation in value added methodology: (1) a simple regression model that predicts each student's expected performance based on prior attainment and not taking into account other factors and (2) multilevel models that attempt to control for individual and school characteristics: limited English speakers, absenteeism, mobility of students, gender, economic status, and subgroup membership.

Most districts use the simple model and compare schools in terms of the percentage of students in top, middle, or bottom quartiles. Feedback of results to a school comprises a "snapshot" of performance and the school's relative standing. The snapshot or profile can be the basis for analyzing where changes are needed and developing the action plan for improvement.

Although the value added method is better than using raw test results, there are concerns about it and its consequences:

- The academic targets (percentage desired at proficiency level) set by officials are unrealistic.
- The curriculum narrows as school and teacher center on those subject areas that are to be tested.
- Teachers spend time on practicing for the test rather than enrichment of learning; they also give major attention to the middle range of students where changes in scores are more manageable.
- Schools with many high-ability students excel initially but have difficulty showing growth over time.
- Scores tend to plateau.

[27]Donald P. Horst et al., *A Practical Guide to Measuring Project Impact on Student Achievement*, Monograph Series on Education, no. 1 (Washington, DC: Office of Education, 1975).

- Many important outcomes from schooling are not measured.
- Factors other than prior attainment as the basis for prediction are often ignored.
- The variability in performance across subjects is not always recognized.
- The assessment and the subsequent planning add to the teacher's workload.
- Small numbers of students in subgroups or small schools create a sampling problem affecting reliability and making it difficult to be confident that one year's class is from the same population as members in a subsequent class.

England, which has had a longer history with value added assessment, is trying to overcome some of these concerns by proposing that schools (a) set their own academic targets on the basis of student performance and taking into account school variances and (b) give more emphasis to the teacher's classroom assessment of student progress; In brief, to use formative evaluation for both learning and accountability.[28]

CONCLUDING COMMENTS

Evaluation does not fulfill its promise if conclusions are not drawn from the data and acted on in modifying the curriculum. Looking at test scores and filing them away mock the evaluative process, although admittedly evaluation serves purposes other than those that are curricular. Consensus evaluation may be undertaken because it is a necessary basis for requesting monies or reassuring a public that the school is doing its job. A clear purpose for using the data, however, is improvement of the curriculum. Hence, some schools now have curriculum groups that study the findings and then make plans both for the whole school and for individual teachers.

Scores or descriptive terms summarize learner performance and give study groups the opportunity to see the strengths and weaknesses of their programs. Analyses of different populations of students reveal how well the curriculum is serving major cultural subgroups, such as the physically handicapped, or how different groups compare with each other. Teachers attempt to ascertain from the data what individual students need. Diagnosing needs becomes a basis for giving personal help. Study groups also discuss the reasons for a curriculum's strengths and weaknesses. Members try to explain the results of particular learning opportunities, the time spent on an objective, the arrangement of activities and topics, the kinds and frequency of responses from learners, the grouping patterns, the use of space, and interactions with adults. Explanations are verified by determining whether all the data lead to the same conclusion. Plans are made to modify the curriculum in light of deficiencies noted and the cause of the deficiencies.

The results from consensus evaluation can be used in at least two ways. First, they can be used to strengthen ends—to select more defensible standards. Results can be the basis for deciding on new instructional objectives aimed at meeting revealed needs. If evaluation of a program or particular learning opportunity results in the selection of more important objectives than were originally held, the evaluation is valuable. Dewey said it well: "There is no such thing as a final set of objectives, even for the time being or temporarily. Each day of teaching ought to enable a teacher to revise and better in some respect the objectives arrived at in a previous work."[29]

[28]Lynn Olson, "English Refines Accountability Reform," *Education Week* 23, no. 34 (May 5, 2004): 20.
[29]John Dewey, *The Sources of a Science of Education* (New York: Horace Liveright, 1929).

Results can also be used to revise means. They can serve as a guide to the need for new learning opportunities and arrangements that might remedy deficiencies in the curriculum. That is, evaluation pinpoints needs and guides a person in the selection of new material, procedures, and organizational patterns. These innovations in turn must be tried out and their results appraised. In short, evaluation is only one part of a continuing cycle.

Pluralistic evaluation, especially critical inquiry and authentic assessment, is consistent with the rise of professionalism and the school as the center for evaluative focus. Accordingly, responsibility, learning, and change become more important than scoreboard accountability. Such evaluation includes teachers, students, administrators, parents, community members, and possibly a researcher from the university. As they focus on curriculum matters like content, goals, learning opportunities, and grouping, participants create a new awareness, knowledge, and values, at least if they engage in inquiry for action and try to answer Sirotnik's generic questions. Conditions for critical inquiry include trust among participants, understanding (comprehension) of one another, and sharing of feelings, observations, and interpretations. In the evaluative process, any statement can be challenged. Evaluation of the statement rests solely on the strength of the evidence and supporting arguments. All curriculum practices are subject to question and to examination of their consequences. "Deep" critical evaluation even allows for evaluation of the school's normative structure in which local values are assessed in light of larger values for human life. The relevancy of deep critical evaluation to the issue of authentic performance assessment should not be overlooked.

QUESTIONS

1. How would you respond if faced with the choice of obtaining important data about the learner through deception or obtaining less important data in a straightforward manner?

2. What kind of student progress is best revealed by (a) products of learners, (b) self-reports, and (c) observation of students?

3. Compare the purpose and construction of norm-referenced and criterion-referenced tests.

4. Think of a learning opportunity that you might select for learners (a particular educational game, lesson, field trip, experiment, textbook article, or story). Then indicate what you would do in order to find out whether this opportunity produced both intended outcomes and unanticipated consequences.

5. Whose criteria should be used in an evaluation situation known to you: experts, participants, or those affected by its consequences? Explain your answer.

6. Discuss the strengths and weaknesses of each of the following evaluative purposes and accompanying approaches:

Purpose	*Approach*
To measure student progress	Determine gain by standardized testing
	See how students perform on real-world tasks that invite alternative responses
To resolve curriculum crises and increase perception of school as legitimate	Blue ribbon committee
	Analyze portfolios of student work over time
To make rational curriculum decisions	Critical inquiry
To help students learn	Small groups' criteria help each other meet criteria at stages of their work

SUGGESTED STRATEGIC RESEARCH

USING CLASSROOM FORMATIVE ASSESSMENT FOR ACCOUNTABILITY PURPOSES

We are accustomed to seeing how external evaluations, such as high-stakes testing, might be a wake-up call for improvement of teaching, but how might internal assessments in the interests of student learning provide data to the schools and others that real progress is taking place? Collect evidence from teachers that show how their students are progressing as measured by *both* external testing and indicators of student growth while learning.

EVALUATING THE POWER OF ASSESSMENT ON LEARNING

Pose an important problem as a step in students doing something about it:

- Small groups of students brainstorm ideas and contribute "dumb questions."
- Plan with students how they might find answers to some of their questions.
- As students complete their tasks and assignments, ask them to review each others' work and suggest how it can be improved (no grade).

What were the results? What difficulties had to be overcome?

COMPARING EXTERNAL ASSESSMENT IN THE TEST WITH CLASSROOM OPPORTUNITY TO LEARN

Select a high-stakes test (graduation exit test, college placement, or admissions test) and determine the topics (content) and the cognitive level of the items. Compare this analysis with the content and cognitive level of the textbook or learning activities found in a course designed for preparing student for the high-stakes exam.

EXPLAINING THE RESULTS OF A PROGRAM THAT "WORKS"

Select a curriculum program or instructional material recommended by the "What Works Clearing House"[30] or other consumer report. What is the "mechanism" that makes this material more likely to be associated with academic achievement than other programs? Is this mechanism generalizable? Can it be used with other programs or materials to get similar results?

SELECTED REFERENCES

ALKIN, MARVIN L. *Evaluation Roots Tracing Theorist's Views and Influence*. Thousand Oaks, CA: Sage, 2004.

BERLAK, HAROLD, ET AL., *Toward a New Science of Educational Testing and Assessment*. Albany: State University of New York Press, 1992.

EISNER, ELLIOT W. *The Educational Imagination: On the Design and Evaluation of School Programs*, 2nd ed. New York: Macmillan, 1985.

ROMBERG, THOMAS A. *Reform in School Mathematics and Authentic Assessment*. Albany: State University of New York Press, 1994.

WILSON, MARK, ED. *Toward Coherence between Classroom Assessment and Accountability*. Chicago, IL: National Society for the Study of Education, 2004.

---

[30]*What Works Clearing House* (Washington, DC: U.S. Department of Education, Institute of Education Science, 2004).

CHAPTER 10

THE POLITICS OF CURRICULUM MAKING

POLITICAL DEBATES and conspiracy theories abound about curriculum and schooling, pressing the need to reexamine the concept of the public school. In the nineteenth century, a common public school meant a school publicly open to all (with exceptions), paid for by public funds, and serving the public interest by making the community a better place in which to live (civic order and preparation for a new economy).

Today there is less social consensus, and the myth of the unitary community has collapsed. The politics of the curriculum are intensifying in the light of multiculturalism and other changing aspects of society.

The early decades of the twentieth century saw the collapse of small schools and districts into large bureaucracies where professional administrators, teachers, and other experts constructed the curriculum within general regulations from the state and local school boards. Student attendance was compulsory, and parental and community participation in curriculum-making decisions was minimal in these bureaucratic schools.

The widespread popular uprisings in the 1960s and 1970s against war, traditions, institutions, and authority impacted schools and curriculum. Political activities on behalf of civil rights involving race, ethnicity, gender, disabilities, and the like brought more equitable court decisions and federal and state educational policies that weakened the power of local school boards and other factors that isolated schools from community activists.

In the last decades of the twentieth century, political power shifted even more to state and federal levels. The Excellence Movement of the 1980s reflected economic interests and concerns for social order. States mandated policies that narrowed the curriculum in the direction of basic skills and academic subjects.

Next the Accountability Movement, based on business models for efficiency through result-driven decision making, intensified the emphasis on basic literacy and academic preparation which were seen by government and corporate leaders as key to regional and national economic competition. These movements also were responses to a perception that the public schools were becoming less efficient and the curriculum more fragmented because of the growing influence of new special interest groups—teachers unions, bilingual and special education advocates, and others.

The concept of *public schooling* altered to *public funding* for diverse forms of schooling—both for-profit and nonprofit and a range of instructional delivery systems. Alternatives to bureaucratic schooling were given freedom to innovate in exchange for results.

A combination of business leaders and state governors was instrumental in getting educational standards for all in place. Initially they aimed at a national curriculum, but in order to win state and local support, they relegated standards setting to the states. Federal enactment of the No Child Left Behind (NCLB) legislation endorsed by both Republican and Democratic legislators ratcheted up the skill requirements for mass education of the workforce and the abstract knowledge needed by those expected to manage and lead competitive corporations. Although the NCLB can claim faithfulness to the government's concern for equity because it demands that *all* students show progress, a more cynical view is that NCLB legislation increases the power of the federal and state governments to privatize public schooling in the interest of efficiency and to give entrepreneurs a greater share of the nearly 1 trillion dollars available annually for educational expenditures.[1]

Underlying curriculum political issues is the question about the role that schools should serve. There are those who want schools to prepare workers needed for the U.S. economy to expand in the face of globalization. They want a curriculum that leads to the preparation of top professionals and scientists (about 20% of expected employment opportunities), as well as those who will take technical and white collar jobs. Schools are to give less emphasis to preparing students for low-paying service positions or for the declining number of factory jobs.

Many parents and students also navigate the curriculum for economic reasons rather than for broader educational values.[2] Even curriculum in the arts is increasingly justified for its contribution to the economic well-being of communities great and small and to the employment opportunities afforded artists in entertainment and other industries. The arts are now justified as leading to more employment opportunities than physics and other prestigious disciplines.

Contrary to those who give priority to economic purposes there are those who still see schools and curriculum as necessary for civic and personal goals. They abhor the idea of students being valued on the basis of their contributions to the economy and regarded chiefly as means, tools, or products. These humanists view learners as ends to be valued for their humanity. Instead of chasing externally imposed standards their political agency centers on having students reach their own standards.[3]

Similarly, those of the democratic persuasion face concerns about civic solidarity and the democratic process. They want to know that free market schools will deal with the emerging problems of multiculture, multifaith, and the inequalities that are transforming the U.S. society.

In an effort to show the possibility of creating a political movement on behalf of local democratic power and opposing the dominant economics-driven curriculum, Michael Apple and his international collaborators have given accounts of "decentralized unities" showing that local social movements can resist state-mandated curriculum.[4]

[1]G. W. Bracey and Michael Apple, *The State and the Policies of Knowledge* (New York: Routledge Falmer, 2003).
[2]Anthony P. Carnevale and Donna M. Desrochers, *Standards for What? The Economic Role of K–16 Reform* (Princeton, NJ: Educational Testing Service, 2003).
[3]Brooks Grennon and Jacqueline Grennon, *Schooling for Life: Reclaiming the Essence of Learning* (Alexandria, VA: Association for Supervision and Curriculum Development, 2002).
[4]Michael Apple, *The State and the Politics of Knowledge* (New York: Routledge Falmer, 2003).

Among these accounts there is a case where students overcame an attempt by a school to impose a curriculum that they saw as a government policy designed to channel them into factory jobs. In another instance, a Brazilian workers' party mobilized and created a publicly funded school where students rebel against commodification of life by addressing their own problems and interests.

Elsewhere, Apple has explained how reactionary and conservative voices have become the loudest in educational discussions and most influential in shaping federal policies.[5] He attributes the "right" turn in education to a broad alliance among neoliberals, neoconservatives, authoritarian populists, together with middle-class managers and professionals:

- *Neoliberals* are advocates of school choice, believing schools will become innovative and efficient by competing in the marketplace of education. Neolibs also regard students as "human capital" important for economic gain and they embrace "scientific" testing as an effective tool in awarding merit.

- *Neoconservatives* see the need for strong state guidance to control and return curriculum to its traditional Western cultural values and to promote character education by fostering exemplars of disciplined behavior.

- *Authoritarian populists* include religious fundamentalists, conservative evangelicals, and the "Christian Right." Although within this group there are wide differences on particular issues, many of its members are opposed to secular religion in the curriculum and instead want God returned to public institutions. A recent faith petitioner urged Christian parents to remove their children from public schools and advised parents to assume responsibility for the moral education of their children. However, the denominational authority rejected the petition on the grounds that such a decision should rest with parents. Within the growing evangelical movement there are those who value the public school as an institution that promotes religious, political, and economic freedom for all peoples and those that advocate neither a particular morality nor traditional gender roles in the family. There are authoritarians in largely white middle social classes who support fixed content standards as representing legitimate knowledge and who view regular testing as desirable in order to ensure the importance and attainment of the standards.

- Members of the *managerial and professional new middle class* have the technical expertise for introducing and monitoring schools and curriculum reforms based on business models. As experts in efficiency, management, testing, and accountability, they are key players in showing business and governmental interests how to centralize control of curriculum goals while decentralizing the means for their attainment.

---

[5]Michael Apple, *Educating the "Right" Way: Markets, Standards and Inequality* (New York: Routledge Falmer, 2001).

CURRICULUM POLICY

Curriculum policy is seldom rational or based on research. Decisions are not often based on careful analysis of content in the disciplines and on societal needs, or on studies of the learning process and concerns of learners. The official curriculum—the content found in standards, frameworks, curriculum guides, tests, texts, and the like—is not neutral knowledge. It is knowledge that has been selected by some individual or group and implies a particular vision of what society should be like.

The Politics Involved

Curriculum decision making is a political process. Different pressure groups are proposing competing values about what to teach. For example, a state board is confronted with deciding whether to give in to efforts to have the biblical version of human origin, the creation theory, become part of the content in the school or to follow the pressure of those who want only the Darwinian evolutionary theory to be taught. Members of state and local public agencies legally responsible for these decisions regularly are accepting and rejecting different values in some way. They may bargain and permit new values to enter the program on a piecemeal basis. They may give lip service to the new values, indicating their importance in general terms but not providing concrete ways for their fulfillment. They may reject a proposed curriculum because it does not meet their view of a school's functions. The decision to accept or reject a proposal often depends on the decision maker's own view as to whether the school should emphasize individual growth and enrichment, transmission of subject matter, or preparation for life in the community.

> *Some idea of the complexity of curriculum policy making can be gained from this paragraph by Kirst and Walker:*
>
> *A mapping of the leverage points for curriculum policy making in local schools would be exceedingly complex. It would involve three levels of government, and numerous private organization foundations, accrediting associations, national testing agencies, textbook-software companies, and interest groups (such as the NAACP, the PTA, and the Heritage Foundation). Moreover, there would be a configuration of leverage points within a particular local school system including teachers, department heads, the assistant superintendent for instruction, the superintendent, and the school board. Cutting across all levels of government would be the pervasive influence of various celebrities, commentators, interest groups, and the journalists who use the mass media to disseminate their views on curriculum. It would be very useful if we were able to quantify the amount of influence of each of these groups of individuals and show input–output interactions for just one school system. Unfortunately this is considerably beyond the state of the art.[6]*

Political Decisions about What Will Be Taught

Several definitions of curriculum would alter most analyses of curriculum making. To say that the curriculum is what the learner actually experiences from schools—the outlooks, predispositions, skills, and attitudes—implies that the learner personally has a major role in determining the curriculum. Individual learners can decide at least to some extent what

---

[6]Michael W. Kirst and Decker F. Walker, "An Analysis of Curriculum Policy Making," *Review of Educational Research* 41, no. 5 (1971): 488. Copyright 1971, American Educational Research Association, Washington, DC.

they will learn. To say that curriculum encompasses everything that influences learning in the schools increases the range of curriculum makers by including peers, custodians, visitors, and cafeteria workers. Furthermore, the definition means that anyone whose actions affect the school experience, either fortuitously or deliberately, is engaging in curriculum making.

For this analysis, I will treat curriculum decisions as conscious policy choices that affect what is learned. These decisions pertain to the nature of programs, preinstructional plans, materials, or activities that delineate organized educational programs of the school or classroom instruction. Curriculum policy making is indeed anticipatory. However, plans and materials are not always used as intended. Also, learner differences make it difficult to ensure that all will derive the same meaning from a common experience or opportunity.

Not everyone who influences the curriculum does so in the same way. A school superintendent who persuades his or her board to install a prekindergarten program is influencing the curriculum. Testing agencies that determine what will be measured on standardized tests, thereby guiding the instructional program, are also making curriculum decisions. When deciding to substitute projects that improve life in the community instead of textbook assignments, the teacher is engaging in curriculum policy making because each of these learning opportunities probably will lead to different outcomes. The authoritative decision to advance one goal over another is policy making.

CONCEPTS FOR INTERPRETING THE PROCESS OF POLITICAL DECISION MAKING

Certain ideas and issues provide a framework for understanding the politics of curriculum decision making. Some of these come from studies by sociologists and some from insightful educators observing how curriculum decisions are being made.

The Professionalization of Reform

The professionalization of reform is the notion that efforts to change the American social system (including schools) have been undertaken by persons whose profession is to reform. National curriculum reform is spearheaded by persons like Dennis P. Doyle (technology and data-driven decisions), Linda Darling-Hammond (teacher development), and Theodore Sizer (curriculum improvement). Professional reformers tend to measure their success by the number of changes they originate.

Examples of professional reformers in action are found in specific studies: (1) J. Hottois and N. A. Milner's research citing evidence that the initiative for introducing sex education came from educators, although the educators themselves claimed that sex education was added in response to public demands for it[7]; (2) D. Nelkin's complaint that, in connection with the nationwide introduction of the curriculum *Man: A Course of Study*, "an elite corps of unrelated professional academics and their government friends run things in the school"[8]; (3) Norman Drachler's account of how a U.S. Commissioner of Education established the Right to Read program with overtones of a political manifesto, including demands for accountability, minority teachers, cultural pluralism in the curriculum, bilingual education, voucher plans, and competency-based teacher certification[9]; and (4) descriptions of the Reverend Jesse Jackson's Push for Excellence program with funding from such sources as the Ford Foundation and the federal government.[10]

[7]J. Hottois and N. A. Milner, *The Sex Education Controversy* (Lexington, MA: Heath, 1975).

[8]D. Nelkin, "The Science-Textbook Controversies," *Scientific American* 234, no. 4 (April 1976): 36.

[9]Norman Drachler, "Education and Politics in Large Cities, 1950–70" in *The Politics of Education, National Society for the Study of Education Yearbook* (Chicago: University of Chicago Press, 1977),188–219.

In his analysis of professional reformers, William Boyd sees them as a controversial force in educational policy making, pursuing their visions of equal opportunity and a more just society, convinced of their expertise and its prerogatives, armed with "solutions looking for problems," assisted by an educational research establishment with its built-in incentive to discover failure. All of this justifies even more research, supplied by federal and foundation funding, and stimulated by the civil rights discovery of new classes of disadvantaged students and those discriminated against, such as the non–English-speaking, the handicapped, and victims of sex discrimination.[11]

Sizer's reform has been likened to a revitalization movement including a charismatic leader, Utopian orientation, and allegiance to a common belief system, disciples, and mass followers.[12]

Forces of Stability

In contrast to professional reformers, many communities, school boards, school administrators, and teachers are more interested in maintaining the social values of the current curriculum and the structure of the schools. To them, carrying out the curriculum changes proposed by professional reformers is too costly to coordinate, too difficult to guide, and too controversial to avoid conflict. The power of the forces for stability may be eroding, yet Lawrence Iannaccone and Peter Cistone testified to the strengths of constraint in innovation: "Two decades of effort in the area of race, equality, and curricular revision with more federal input than impact speak loudly enough for those who will listen. Schools today are more like the schools of twenty years ago than like anything else."[13]

Similarly, Larry Cuban has revealed how little instruction changes at the classroom level in spite of changes at the rhetorical level.[14] The pronouncements made in writing and speeches and those given in official statements are not necessarily translated into action. Reform policies that are acted on tend to be policies with which principals and teachers feel comfortable.

The pressures from key figures in the Excellence Movement of the 1980s for more academically oriented high schools, for instance, were well received by teachers prepared and disposed to teaching academic subjects.[15] It is recalled that the Excellence Movement was initiated with the U.S. Department of Education Report *A Nation at Risk: The Imperatives for Educational Reform*. Shortly after this report numerous commission reports and state level actions created a new political agenda.

The more frequently acted on curriculum reforms of the Excellence Movement were the adding of courses in computer literacy, adopting textbooks with no stereotypes, adopting special textbooks for disadvantaged and gifted students, increasing requirements in math, science, and English, offering foreign languages to elementary students, and increasing homework.[16]

[10]Barbara Sizemore, "Push Politics and the Education of America's Youth," *Phi Delta Kappan* 60, no. 1 (1979): 364–370.

[11]William L. Boyd, "The Politics of Curriculum Change and Stability," *Educational Researcher* 8, no. 2 (Feb. 1979): 15.

[12]Donna E. Munsey and Patrick J. McQuillan, "Education Reform as Revitalization Movement," *American Journal of Education* (Aug. 1993): 393–491.

[13]Lawrence Iannaccone and Peter J. Cistone, *The Politics of Education* (Eugene, OR: ERIC Clearinghouse on Educational Management, University of Oregon, 1974).

[14]Larry Cuban, *How Teachers Taught: Consistency and Change in American Classrooms, 1890–1980* (New York: Longmans, 1984).

[15]Susan Fuhrman and William H. Clune, "Research on Education Reform: Lessons on the Implementation of Policy," *Teachers College Record* 90, no. 2 (1988): 237–257.

[16]William W. Wayson, *Up From Excellence: The Impact of the Excellence Movement on Schools* (Bloomington, IN: Phi Delta Kappa Education Foundation, 1988).

Constraints on Policy

Constraints on policy for curriculum innovation occur through non–decision making, conflict avoidance, the threat of controversy, and loose coupling.

Non–Decision Making This term refers to the ability of powerful interests to control the decision-making agenda, preventing the discussion of "undesirable issues." Wilson Riles, while California State Superintendent of Public Instruction, along with leaders from the California educational establishment avoided public exposure of a campaign to place a school voucher initiative on the ballot. A low profile strategy was laid out at a meeting of educational groups at which they also agreed to step up propaganda efforts to improve the public image of public education. Riles turned down numerous invitations to debate the voucher question, saying, "If we were to get into a knock-down drag out fight, it would get attention. If they (voucher advocates) are going to get publicity, they are going to have to do it on their own." Non–decision making is a formidable barrier to change by keeping potential issues from being discussed or recognized.

Conflict Avoidance Conflict avoidance refers to educators' unwillingness to introduce curriculum changes that conflict with community values and are likely to arouse controversy and opposition. William Boyd found that the degree of latitude for local educators in effecting curriculum change depends on the community. In general, rural school districts and those in the "sunbelt" of the United States are more restrictive about the content of courses such as social studies, literature, and biology. Prevailing controversies center on evolution, obscenity, sex education, and religious views. Methods of teaching reading or mathematics are also sometimes a matter of public controversy, especially in conservative communities.

The Politics of Controversy A technique used by those with a minority viewpoint to control the majority is called the politics of controversy. Using a squeaky wheel tactic, those opposed to a curriculum innovation create a controversy in the hope that school authorities will back off from it. Textbook publishers, for example, are known to be sensitive about introducing into their materials content that is likely to be controversial. Thus the threat of controversy results in nonpublication and weak pabulum in the curriculum.

Loose Coupling The goals set by reformers (the ideal curriculum) may not be faithfully followed by local school boards (the formal curriculum) and certainly are not likely to be attained by the procedures of teachers in the classroom (the actual curriculum). Awareness of loose coupling, or the inability of policy makers to implement their curriculum plans, has resulted in what Arthur Wise calls "hyper-rationalization." Because teachers have failed to attain the goals, they must be made accountable for the goals. For example, classroom methods and procedures for treating handicapped children are now specified in detail by federal and state agencies and by the courts. Compliance is sought through program evaluation, site visits, reviews of classroom records, and learner verification—that is, pupils both displaying desired competencies and reporting. to authorities about teachers' practices. Policy makers in federal or state governments now mandate measurable goals (narrow, selective, and minimal) and demand frequent testing of student achievement with respect to these goals. Additional control over curriculum occurs through special development of experienced teachers and standards-based education for novices—both types of training programs consistent with the curriculum goals of the centralized planners.

PARTICIPANTS IN DETERMINING CURRICULUM POLICY

School-Based Political Participants

Teachers The teacher is a crucial maker of curriculum policy. Even in such a seemingly clear-cut subject as elementary arithmetic, the teacher is not simply an implementer of policy. Teachers decide whether to spend time on drill or problem solving. Teachers have considerable freedom to use their own notions of what schooling ought to be even when subjected to the external pressures of state standards and textbooks and district curriculum guides. In deciding which student will get what kind of curriculum content, the teacher takes on a political role.

At the classroom or instructional level, most teachers have the opportunity to define instructional objectives within an overall framework that indicates what is to be taught. Often they design and order learning activities to achieve these ends. They make important curriculum decisions when they decide to group activities around particular organizing centers such as a theme, problem, project, subject title, unit, or an area of inquiry. However, a teacher's freedom in curriculum development varies. Many years ago, Virgil Herrick proposed three positions, or different degrees of teacher responsibility for making curriculum decisions. At position 1, teachers do little more than follow the state standards and school policies. At position 2, teachers take responsibility for decisions regarding learning activities, the time to be spent on particular subjects, and how to evaluate students. Teachers at position 3 go beyond standards and textbooks, selecting concepts to be taught, designing learning activities, and creating smooth transitions between steps.

Table 10.1 illustrates the degrees of responsibility taken by teachers for curriculum decisions.

A radical proposal for curriculum decision making was made by Hilda Taba in 1962. She called for a deliberate inversion of the common procedure. Instead of starting with a general design in which curriculum began at the societal level and rippled down through institutions to the classroom, Taba proposed that curriculum making start at the teaching level with the planning of specific units of instruction. The results of experimenting with these units then would provide a basis for a general design to be created later. Taba's strategy was calculated to infuse theory into the operation of the practitioner from the outset.[17] Heidi Hayes Jacobs's mapping from students to standards, (Chapter 7), is a similar notion. However, school or district-wide coordination of curriculum by teachers is unlikely as long as teachers focus only on their own classrooms instead of collaborating in curriculum development.

Usually, teachers want the authority to choose the appropriate method for teaching a course. In general, teachers desire to have a modest amount of influence over school policies and practices, particularly those affecting their classrooms. They expect to be consulted and to have the opportunity to initiate change as it affects their own classroom. The current consensus in educational literature is that authority should be diffused to individual schools, teachers, and students. Teachers should have more say in how their school is run, particularly in decisions related to curriculum, instruction, staffing, and resources. However, teachers need the time and resources for this additional participation.

Some teachers write op-ed pieces and go online, attempting to change views of the world and perceptions of reality by challenging mythologies about the cultural supremacy and the nature of capitalism. However, more teachers are likely to express their policy views through their unions.

---

[17]Hilda Taba, *Curriculum Development: Theory and Practice* (New York: Harcourt Brace and World, 1962), 529.

Table 10.1 Positions of Teacher Responsibility for Curriculum Decisions

Decisions	I	II	III
Concept to be taught	Content standards from state and district	Content standards adapted to classroom context	Teacher and student social analysis and teacher expertise in subject matter, knowledge of "big ideas"
Materials and activities	Textbooks, workbooks, recitations, direct instruction	Textbooks, supplementary material, teacher-directed learning opportunities— projects, units, student discussion, and small group participation	Multiple primary and secondary sources, data collection and analysis, investigations in real world, peer-assisted learning, student-led inquiry coupled with whole class review
Evaluation	Observations, embedded assessments, end-of-chapter tests, feedback—scores and grades	Benchmark measures, unit and performance tests, portfolios of student work, final exam, feedback—scores matched to rubrics and criteria, suggestions for improvement, grades for course	Exhibitions, poster sessions, documentaries, published reports, self-assessment with peer reviews using agreed-on criteria, suggestions for improvement
Continuities and next steps	Content standards, textbook	Sequenced performance standards, benchmarks	Students select what they want to do and analyze what knowledge would be necessary

Teacher organizations are beginning to look at curriculum issues. Accountability procedures, differentiated staffing, schools of choice, and other innovations affecting teachers force them to take positions on what shall be taught. Until recently, however, demands from such organizations focused primarily on benefits such as pay, class size, and extra assignments. Increasingly, teachers are expected to use this organized power in the interests of curriculum, exercising authority over such matters as textbooks and other resource materials as part of the negotiated contract. Individual teachers usually establish what knowledge students should derive from course assignments and give priority to their own preferred concepts and values.

Increasingly, collective bargaining is influencing curriculum. For example, innovative programs are being traded for smaller classes and guaranteed jobs for experienced teachers. Collective bargaining has raised the issue of whether public interests in curriculum— the interests of students, parents, and others—might be trampled on if disproportionate powers are given at the bargaining table to board and teacher groups. A bilingual program in the Los Angeles City Schools was threatened when local teacher' groups opposed bonus payments planned to attract bilingual teachers to poverty areas, and charter schools with site-based management by teachers has challenged union protection of tenure, seniority, and common work rules. Teachers' organizations also have much influence at the state and federal levels. Teacher political action committees are active in nearly all states, raising funds for politicians friendly to teachers' causes.[18]

[18]Dennis Carlson, *Leaving Safe Harbors: Toward a New Progressivism in American Education and Public Life* (New York: Routledge, 2002).

In general, teachers have played a secondary role to business interests in recent school state reforms. When the reform carries increased education funding and has the support of business elites, teacher associations suppress their antagonism.[19]

Principals Despite the formal job description as curriculum leader, the principal is often a middle person between the central office, parents, and the staff in implementing curriculum. Most principals are burdened with such a multitude of managerial activities that it is extremely difficult for them to devote the time and effort required for innovation on a substantial scale. Principals can be actively engaged in curriculum making only in schools in which their planning responsibilities can be carried out without heavy managerial responsibilities.

The role of the principal in curriculum making is not settled. Some people think that the principal should initiate curriculum change. Others believe that principals can be more effective and influential by implementing curriculum decisions already made. One would expect principals working in centralized school systems to be more likely to accept the latter role. To date, however, they have not. Although the principal now has the power to make some decisions that were formerly made at the central office, accountability is still directed upward, not toward the community. Decentralization made principals more responsible to their communities, yet held them accountable to systemwide goals and standards. Under decentralization, the principal has to tailor local school interests and activities to the system's goals.

The roles of principals have shifted.[20] Unlike in the 1980s, principals now are more likely to see themselves as educational leaders rather than administrators. They prefer management by empowerment to management by control, redirecting their energy to purpose, defining and getting teachers, parents, and students to support academic achievement as well as to decide what the school should be.

Superintendents The superintendent influences curriculum policy by responding to matters before the board of education, initiating programs for professional development, making district personnel aware of changes occurring in other schools, and moderating outside demands for change. The superintendent takes the curriculum demands from state and federal governments and makes them acceptable to the local population. School board members tend to feel that superintendents are poor in curriculum planning. Superintendents also rate themselves weakest in curriculum and instruction, as opposed to performance in finance or physical plant management. Nevertheless, the superintendent is the key figure in curriculum innovation and educational decision making. In large cities, assistant superintendents for curriculum and instruction attempt to influence the curriculum through their work with committees of teachers and their preparation of guidelines, bulletins, and professional development sessions.

The superintendent, like the principal, appears to be losing control over the curriculum to the centralizing forces of state and federal legislators and to the courts. On the other hand, local control of the curriculum is more prevalent in those communities with superintendents whose values are consonant with those predominant in the district. Superintendents are fired when they stray from community values. A case in point is the celebrated Joseph Fernandez who was ousted as New York City School Chief for his speaking out about the need for a strong multicultural emphasis, developing an antibias curriculum, and promoting "Children of the Rainbow" (a resource guide that helped teachers learn to explain homosexual lifestyle to young children). As urban problems worsened in the early 1990s

---

[19]Lorraine M. McDonnell and Anthony Pascal, *Teacher Unions and Educational Reform* (Santa Monica, CA: Rand Corporation, 1988). Prepared for the Center for Policy Research in Education.

[20]Robert Rothman, "Changes in Policy Social Conditions Reshaping High Schools," *Education Week* (April 21, 1993): 8.

and federal aid failed to keep up, superintendent dumping accelerated. The average urban superintendent lasted 2 years, as against 5 for the rest of the country. The state has taken much control out of the hands of local superintendents. In addition, new structural layers—specialists in different areas—dilute the influence of the superintendent and local school board. The salaries of these specialists come from state categorical funds, which help to insulate them from the superintendent's influence.

Students Students seldom have formal influence over course content. There are, of course, schools in which provisions are made for some genuine self-government by students. Student officers can be elected and appointed to policy boards. They may even participate in approving faculty appointments and determine course offerings and academic requirements. The extent of control given students is usually a function of the maturity that they have attained and the nature of the particular community. Student policy making is generally derivative rather than absolute, a privilege granted by higher powers and subject to revocation by them. Often student government is an administrator's or teacher's means of securing student cooperation.

Informally, however, students have much influence over what is taught. Often they can vote with their feet by refusing to enroll in courses that feature the curriculum of academic specialists. The failure of students to respond to a Physical Science Study Committee's "physics" was an argument for curriculum change. Alternative schools and underground newspapers are other examples of student power. The late 1960s saw both college and high school students rebelling against their role as captive audience and asking for both a social curriculum—to confront the facts of war, racism, oppression—and a personal curriculum—to help them discover themselves.

With the advent of the 1990s, one reads of students protesting assignments involving animal rights (biology and the dissection of frogs) and attempts to teach attitudes (sensitivity games in social studies). An example of student sophistication in politics involved the "Cash for Caps" program, which rewarded schools that increased their scores on the state's achievement tests. Seniors in one school threatened poor performance on the test unless school officials agreed to remove speed bumps from the school's parking lot and to permit the senior class to have a field trip to the beach. When administrators failed to meet the demand, students carried out their threat, losing the district $70,000 because students chose not to perform on the tests. Professional political movements of the twenty-first century are engaging students through conditions with union members, environmentalists, and others. An unresolved issue in these alliances is whether they should focus on broad curriculum issues or have specific targets. The curriculum trend to the social construction of knowledge in the classroom, which emphasizes student negotiating, meaning, and placing authority on evidence and logic rather than text and teacher, will greatly enhance student power.

Community Participants

Local School Board Political analysis shows local boards of education playing a diminishing role in actual decision making. Members of these boards often rubber-stamp the professionals' recommendations. Board members often lack the technical competence they need to decide on specific programs. Hence, they vote on intuition or the advice of others. Also, growing state and federal pressure has weakened local jurisdiction, and in large districts at least, the less specific policies are not carried out according to the board's mandates. Usually the smaller the community, the more likely the public is to believe that school board members are primarily concerned with the welfare of children. Residents of large urban centers tend to see board members as persons seeking prestige and power.

The actions of legislators, judges, and lay groups have taken much of the control from local school boards. The courts are the focus in the struggle for control. Special interest groups prefer to go to court if board policies are not to their satisfaction rather than to discuss board policy at public board meetings. Lawsuits are especially popular with those who cannot prevail in ordinary political decision making.[21] Similarly, legislation is viewed as a last resort for the citizen who is in opposition to the local board. The instances of Massachusetts legislation on the local policy for the assignment of pupils to special classes and of Florida legislation in opposition to a district's policy regarding sex education are examples of laws that began with parents seeking a change.

School board members tend to give themselves failing or barely passing grades in such core areas as their influence on other decision makers, ability to provide policy oversights, involvement of parents and community members, and planning and goal setting. In addition they involve themselves too much in the day-to-day management of schools.[22]

Briefly, state and federal professionals seem to be determining the curriculum, and the board is serving as an advisor. The realities of implementing federal and state directives and court orders tend to make board members more dependent on experts, especially those with legal expertise.

Proposed school board reforms have focused on better selection procedures for school board members (election or appointment); altered roles and responsibilities (transform local boards into policy boards without involvement in daily administration); and state and mayoral takeover of the authority for the local school system, that is, eliminating school boards, replacing them, or restricting the board to an advisory role.[23]

The Public   The role of the local lay community in formulating curriculum is minimal. The public knows little about course content and is not involved with general curriculum issues. Guns, vandalism, drugs, and discipline tend to be seen as problems, not as curriculum issues. Until relatively recently, local communities left curriculum planning to professionals. Only occasionally did the public get involved in curriculum. These occasions are viewed as episodic issues that emerge under special conditions and shortly subside. Thus it is not textbooks that cause concern, but a particular textbook under a special set of circumstances.

Community participation in local curriculum making was thought to increase because of the establishment of such innovations as local school advisory bodies charged with representing community needs and interests and local school site management. However, studies of such councils have shown that most participation came from parents of successful learners and that not much improved by virtue of the school councils. This may have been due either to the school boards' lack of specificity in stating what they mean by participation or to the reluctance of educators to share in decision making. The idealized vision of a school community where all constituents have a respected voice in school politics did not happen. Some parents were more equal than others. Alienated parents and community members are likely to be the poor and those least served by the existing social and political arrangements.

Chicago experimented with decentralization, establishing local school councils in each of Chicago's 595 buildings. Each council consisted of six parent representatives, two teachers chosen by their peers, two representatives chosen by the community at large, and

---

[21]Michael A. Robell and Arthur R. Black, *Educational Policy Making and the Courts* (Chicago: University of Chicago Press, 1982).

[22]Michael W. Kirst, *Task Force on School Governance* (Palo Alto, CA: Stanford University Press, 1992).

[23]Deborah Land, "Local School Boards under Review: Their Role and Effectiveness in Relation to Students' Academic Achievement," *Review of Educational Research* 72, no. 2 (summer 2002): 229–279.

the building principal. Each council drew up a school improvement plan and assumed much of the responsibility for budgetary planning and oversight.[24]

Pauline Lipman taught in Chicago inner schools during the period when some decisions from the district bureaucracy were made by local communities and schools. She also worked under a later policy change that gave control of the "citizen schools" to its mayor. The mayor introduced high-stakes testing, standards, accountability, and centralized regulation of schools and teachers. Lipman argues that the accountability policy exacerbated social inequalities, widening the gap between schools serving low-income students of color and schools serving mixed and high-income populations.

Lipman claims the accountability policy undermined efforts to help students develop the social critique and cultural identities needed to survive and challenge new inequalities. She attributes the policy and its adverse effect on students of color to pressure for a labor discipline in a global economy that demands an uninterrupted flow of low-wage jobs.[25]

Citizen participation in curriculum policy making tends to be minimal, perfunctory, reactive, and superficial. Citizens take part very early when general goals are being established or very late when most of the preparation for change has been completed. Citizens can, however, be influential when they become activated. When significant conflicts arise between citizens and the school board, lay groups usually win. Most active parent groups represent special interests in the curriculum, working for such programs as those on behalf of the handicapped or those that will strengthen the fields of athletics, art, and music. Together with the professional educator associated with those particular programs, they engage in campaigns to protect and enhance their interests.

Most citizen groups active in school affairs are not parents, however, but members of noneducational organizations, such as business associations and property owners' groups. They are more interested in school policies bearing on taxes and the prestige of the school in connection with property values than in decisions about course content.

State Agencies

The states have increased their role in educational policy at the expense of local school districts. This growth was a result of an increase in the states' fiscal capacity to regulate education and the activities of interstate policy issue networks that influence federal funding and educational directives.[26]

States exercise leverage on the curriculum in many ways. State legislatures frequently prescribe what shall be taught. Driver training and courses on the dangers of alcohol and narcotics have long been mandated. Law enforcement, insurance, oil, and automobile interests, too, have influence in such matters. Professional organizations, like Business Roundtable and special interest groups, long ago cemented links within state departments of education and state legislatures.

The most noteworthy of state control of curriculum is through mandatory testing of the basic skills and academic content standards. The standards movement is concerned with assessing all students at elementary and secondary school levels. States have adopted legislation on this testing and through their state boards of education set tougher standards— more mathematics, sciences, English, and foreign languages.

Unlike the federal government and its chief reliance on fiscal control, states use many controls in shaping the process and quality of the curriculum. Required tests, mandated testing, and requirements for teacher certification and competency are some of their means

---

[24]Chris Pipho, "Sorting out Local Control," *Phi Delta Kappan* 70, no. 6 (Feb. 1989): 430–431.
[25]Pauline Lipman, *Inequality, Globalization and Urban School Reform* (New York: Routledge Falmer, 2004).
[26]Michael W. Kirst, *The State's Role in Educational Policy: Innovation* (Palo Alto, CA: Stanford University Press, 1981).

of control. The monitoring mechanisms are also more informal than those of the federal government—informal conciliation, district self-review, and management by media.

The NCLB federal legislation gave to the federal government greater control of elementary and secondary education. Although this act had as its stated purpose the academic achievement of *all* students, maintaining the equity goal of the 1960s, the president and Congress expected states to expand efforts at teacher preparation, assessment, and ongoing technical assistance to districts and schools. The goals of the legislation are ambitious, and it is questionable if states and districts can reach them.

The power of the federal government goes beyond setting the requirements for instructional materials that can be used in federally funded programs. States and districts tend to use these "approved" materials throughout their programs.

Some states use accreditation procedures to maintain a particular curriculum. Accreditation may be done by the state department of education itself, by an association of professional educators (such as the National Association of School Principals), or by a private regional accrediting organization (such as the North Central Association of Colleges and Secondary Schools). Usually these agencies require site visits and evidence of a school's adherence to each of their detailed standards. One of their standards might read, "English courses are organized by themes or experiences with a minimum of emphasis on type or chronology." A standard for social studies might read, "Social studies offerings assist pupils in understanding ideologies that differ from democracy."

Testing Agencies

Testing agencies have helped make a "national" curriculum. Standardized tests for college admission have defined what students going to college must know in the way of understanding and reasoning. (See *The College Board Specification of Outcomes*, Chapter 8.) Furthermore, national standardized reading and math tests given in the elementary schools determine much of the specific content of the curriculum. The Educational Testing Service, with an annual budget in the millions, dominates the testing industry and administers a broad range of vocational and college placement tests. Its SAT test has been considered the most important test the company has, although ETS's acquisition of the National Assessment Contract might rival the SAT in importance. About 1.5 million students take the SAT test each year.

In 2003 controversy raged about the SAT as an admission criterion, and it was recommended that it be replaced as an assessment of aptitude (perhaps a measure of intelligence) by tests that measure achievement in specific subject areas. Subsequently, ETS made changes to enhance curriculum alignment with the skills used in college and high school work, such as math questions that require students to produce their own solutions rather than select from multiple choices.[27]

Test publishers say they try to hold a middle ground, try not to freeze the secondary school curriculum, and try not to adopt innovations too quickly. Their practice of involving professionals from secondary schools and colleges in the preparation and review of the tests is intended to keep the achievement tests abreast of important trends.

Publishers

Book publishers are the gatekeepers of ideas and knowledge. Most teaching in our schools is from textbooks or other curriculum material, such as guides, workbooks, and laboratory apparatus. Nearly 75% of students' classroom time and 90% of their homework is spent with

[27]Rebecca Zwick, ed., *Rethinking the SAT: The Future of Standardized Testing in University Admissions* (New York: Routledge Falmer, 2004).

instructional materials.[28] Student achievement—what students acquire from instruction—mirrors to a substantial extent the content in the textbook. Students are more likely to learn what they find in their textbooks than in something else. After an item of content has been included in a text as important for children to use, Walker and Schaffarzick long ago found that:

> *the multiple resources of the curriculum in use and the variety of active student learning processes combine to produce a level of achievement that is usually greater than any additional increment that might be produced by any further refinement of the curriculum or any improvement in teaching style or method or medium of instruction or organizational change in the school or classroom.[29]*

Sometimes the textbook publisher is only a disseminator, and the actual product is developed by professionals in regional laboratories, universities, and nonprofit organizations paid by agencies of the federal government, private foundations, and professional and scientific associations. At other times, the publisher contracts directly with teachers to develop the company's products. There is pressure on publishers from state curriculum commissions and groups demanding emphasis on certain content. The list of topics to be avoided in textbooks is getting longer every day: the supernatural, war, sex, suicide, and sadness have been added to junk food, treatment of animals, and racial, gender, and age stereotyping. Publishers also use their sales organizations for information and guidance in the revision and production of texts. "Strangely enough this network of salespeople is the only reasonably dependable comprehensive mechanism for compiling the preferences and prejudices of schools on curriculum matters."[30] Even so, textbook content is generally one decade behind the scholarly fields with respect to knowledge and interpretation.

The Courts

The involvement of the courts in curriculum matters has become a critical issue. Some curriculum specialists are disturbed by what they see as a trend in the courts to exceed their authority in curriculum matters.[31] Recent court decisions have mandated specific tests, methods, and materials that schools must use. Some courts have even mandated achievement goals in desegregation cases which, in effect, have made them the evaluators of school curriculum and programs. For example, in San Diego, a judge ordered a controversial approach to teaching reading involving mastery learning. In Tucson, a specific teaching method was mandated for use with minority pupils; and in Detroit, a judge ordered school officials to submit an instructional plan for use by all teachers in the system.

The explosion of school lawsuits is over. At the federal level, the number of opinions declined in the 1990s in all categories except special education. In state courts there has been a refocusing of court attention from area to area, such as from dress codes in the 1970s to drug and alcohol abuse in the 1980s, to suspension for security reasons—guns and violence—in the 1990s. Each issue seems to have a life of its own and then fades in importance.

---

[28]Michael Apple and Linda Christian-Smith, eds., *The Politics of the Textbook* (New York: Routledge Falmer, 1993).

[29]Decker Walker and Ion Schaffarzick, "Comparing Curriculum," *Review of Educational Research* 44, no. 1 (1974): 101.

[30]Kirst and Walker, "An Analysis of Curriculum Policy Making," 497.

[31]Nicholas G. Crisculo, "Seven Critical Issues Facing Today's Schools," *Catalyst for Change* 12, no. 2 (winter 1983):28–30.

As a knowledge institution, the school confronts conflicts that rage between other institutions that vie for influence on the school's curriculum. For example, conflicts between religious and scientific institutions regarding creationism and evolution present a dilemma for the school. In such cases, schools turn to the courts to resolve the issue.

Authority to control public school curriculum resides as a matter of state law primarily with state education officials. There are, however, two practical and legal ways for anyone to deal with challenges to curriculum content such as occurs in censorship and the exclusion of ideas:

1. Consider the fundamental First Amendment principle of nonsuppression of ideas. "Our Constitution does not permit the official suppression of ideas."

2. Recognize that materials used in public schools must be educationally suitable. That is, the decision to accept or reject material must not be on the basis of ideas expressed but on whether the material fosters or hinders the intellectual, emotional, and social development of students.

Although he was referring to universities when he made his important statement on the issue of "politically correct speech," the remarks of Chief Justice Rehnquist have implications for all schools. "Ideas with which we disagree—so long as they remain ideas and not conduct which interferes with the rights of others—should be confronted with argument and persuasion, not suppression. Individuals should decide for themselves—stimulated by free discussion—which ideas and viewpoints to adopt and which to reject."[32]

The Federal Government

In the 1960s and 1970s, the federal government had a very powerful influence on the kinds of materials used in schools. Mainly through the National Science Foundation (NSF) and the U.S. Office of Education (USOE), it dwarfed all previous curriculum development efforts by states, districts, and private enterprise. Federally supported regional laboratories, academic scholars, and nonprofit organizations produced curriculum materials that have been used in most of our schools. Generally, this material modified the content of existing subject matter—mathematics, science, English, and reading. Also, by specifying the use of standardized tests for evaluating the projects they finance, federal agencies fostered national objectives.

Initially the government seemed to be interested in increasing the number of curriculum options available to schools. Later, however, there were deliberate efforts to ensure that schools used the new curriculum through evaluation requirements and special monies given to disseminate materials developed with federal funds. The government became more interested in producing change than in merely making change possible.

The 1977 federal policy established equalization of educational opportunity for minorities, women, non–English-speaking persons, the poor, and the geographically isolated as the focus of federal curriculum development (instructional improvement) efforts. Nevertheless, there was little consensus about the proper role of government in curriculum development, particularly in the areas in which values are so prominent: social studies, moral education, and sex education. The educational community feared that federal sponsorship of development, demonstration, dissemination, and teacher training activities was an illegitimate attempt to weaken state and local control over the school curriculum.

In the 1980s under President Reagan, there was a shift in federal curriculum policy. New organizational structure was created to implement President Reagan's call for a return

---

[32]Justice William H. Rehnquist, address delivered at George Mason University, Washington, DC, May 23, 1993.

to traditional values, recognition of the primary rights and responsibilities of parents in the education of their children, and a focus on private and parochial as well as public schools.[33]

Exemplary curriculum programs that had been disseminated to local educational agencies were discontinued because they seemed to allow for changes in attitude and critical outlook toward existing social structures and might have fostered moral relativism.[34]

The network of conservative think tanks and policy institutes have produced a steady flow of activities, reports, and op-ed pieces for the media decrying the inadequacies of the "failing" public schools, joining business leaders and governors in making neoconservative views become widespread and influential.

Congressional initiatives in curriculum were made less likely by the fact that state governors have gained visibility and power in educational policy making and are not influenced as in the past by "education senators and representatives."[35] However, with the NCLB legislation, Congress and the president restored the federal government's role in elementary and secondary education.

Former President Clinton's educational policies centered on national standards and testing, seed money to states to help them develop reforms, funding for school-to-work programs to be developed by a consortium among the states, and seeing that more poor students were the target of federal funding. Noteworthy was President Clinton's policy that only parents who chose to send their children to public school should get government money. This policy was in direct contrast to the policy of President G. W. Bush who favors public funding for schools of choice.

Foundations

Foundations are a major source of funds and influence on the curriculum. The Ford, Rockefeller, Carnegie, and Kettering foundations have been very active in curriculum development. Foundations have made deliberate efforts to change the habits of school systems and to modify the curriculum by underwriting the production of locally made curriculum materials. Their efforts are only partially successful, mostly in suburban school districts.

In recent years, the Heritage Foundation, composed of conservative activists, has gained curriculum power. The foundation claims that almost two-thirds of its 2000 recommendations had been or were transformed into policy by the end of President Reagan's first year in office. This foundation issued an influential document entitled *Mandate for Leadership.*[36] Among the recommendations were those calling for (1) more parental control over their children's education, (2) constitutional amendments to permit school prayer, and (3) an end to federal intervention in state and local school matters related to the educational opportunities of black Americans, handicapped persons, women, and new immigrant populations. The document designated the federal role in schools to that of pressing for improved academic performance and traditional values as defined by conservatives. The foundation's techniques for managing policy changes include staffing federal agencies with "credible" personnel who support conservative ideological views of what education is for and who should be educated. Accordingly, the president is to use appointments over

[33]Marvin Pasch and Bert I. Green, "A Case Study in Curriculum Decision Making and Federal Education Policy," *Educational Leadership* 42, no. 2 (Oct. 1984): 43–47.

[34]Onalee McGraw, "Reclaiming Traditional Values in Education: The Implication for Educational Research," *Educational Leadership* 42, no. 2 (Oct. 1984): 39–42.

[35]David L. Clark and Terry A. Astuto, "The Significance and Permanence of Changes in Federal Education Policy," *Educational Research* 15, no. 8 (Oct. 1986): 4–13.

[36]Stuart M. Butler, Michael Sanera, and Bruce Weinsrad, *Mandate for Leadership II: Continuing the Conservative Revolution* (Washington, DC: Heritage Foundation, 1984).

budgetary control to weaken equity programs that enjoy congressional support. Federal influence over state and local practices is to be exercised by controlling information and focusing public opinion on getting the desired action from state and local officials.

Special Interests

Kirst and Walker have differentiated between two separate policy-making processes: normal policy making and crisis policy making. Groups such as the John Birch Society, Chamber of Commerce, National Association of Manufacturers, and AFL-CIO are regarded as relatively weak in normal policy making but very powerful in crisis policy making.[37]

International academic competitiveness, drug abuse, war, depression, violence, energy, and natural disaster are examples of crises that draw the response of different groups. Then there are organizations like ACHIEVE, which lobbies for the teaching of fundamental, intellectual subjects, and the American Education Association which is against sex education and atheistic ideas. The political workings of the National Association for the Education of Young Children illustrate a single cause approach.[38] Also, some causes invite the combined pressures of many different groups. Virtually every organization working for the advancement of African-Americans, whether militant or moderate, has demanded a more adequate treatment of Blacks in books and courses dealing with the history of the United States. Similarly, in protecting against the secular offerings of public schools, members of conservative religious groups challenge the notion that schools teach the truth and that there is such a thing as objective knowledge.

Special interest groups follow a common strategy in influencing curriculum content: (1) they offer their own evaluation criteria for judging instructional materials, in contrast to the criteria given by the state; (2) they address the school board politically rather than going through the bureaucratic structure of the school; and (3) they rely on moral arguments and their own moral positions.

As indicated previously, Michael Apple has identified a conservative alliance whose policy is based on a close relationship between government and the capitalistic economy. He also notes a decline in the power of political democracy. The alliance combines economic and political elites with white working-class and middle-class groups who are concerned about security, the family, traditional values, and knowledge. This coalition has partially succeeded in shifting the democratic goal of expanding equality of opportunity to economic goals, such as expansion of the free market and reduction of government responsibility for social need, and to attacks on the poor and disenfranchised for their supposed lack of values and character.

Blame for unemployment, loss of economic competition, and declining traditional values has been placed on the schools and other public agencies, not on the economic, cultural, and social policies of dominant groups. Consequently, Apple sees educational policy favoring more marketization, privatization, and standardized testing. "Freedom" and "choice" in the new educational market will be for those who can afford them. There will be a less regulated and privatized sector for the children of the better off but the schools for the urban poor will be more tightly controlled, more policed, and their curriculum will be underfunded and unlinked to decent paid employment. Further, Apple believes that schools for those whose economic status and racial composition make up the urban areas will not encourage student participation in creating new meanings and values for our culture.

---

[37]Kirst and Walker, "An Analysis of Curriculum Policy Making," 498.

[38]Barbara Miller, "Expanding Our Child Advocacy Efforts: NAEYC Forms a Public Network on Children," *Young Children* 38, no. 6 (Sept. 1983): 71–74.

CONFLICTS IN CURRICULUM CONTROL

The control of curriculum in the United States is a shared responsibility. Authority is dispensed throughout three levels of government—local state, and federal—and curriculum mandates are issued from all three branches of government—legislative, executive, and judicial. These mandates include (1) federal court actions such as those pertaining to meeting the language needs of non–English-speaking persons and of children with specific handicaps; (2) federal legislation giving funds to school districts if they agree to meet certain conditions for their use (examples of such funding are those for disadvantaged children, for science, mathematical, and environmental education, ethnic studies, vocational education, career education, gifted education, and consumer education); (3) state court decisions relating to school financing, planning, and implementation of educational programs (these have triggered mandates that increase state control of programs formerly delegated to local school authorities); and (4) court decisions giving participation privileges to parents and students as well as increased use of legal contracts (collective bargaining) which result in mandates directly or indirectly affecting curriculum, preempting the control by local boards and educators.

Shared control has produced conflict. Federal mandates often combine both educational and social or political goals, as in grant programs for special groups. While these mandates draw attention to the poor, the minorities, and the handicapped, they also conflict with traditional views of how best to develop understanding, skills, and attitudes among learners. For example, children sometimes are required to travel to distant schools, losing instructional time in order to satisfy arbitrary racial composition percentages.

Contradictory mandates from different levels of authority sometimes occur. For example, the federal requirement demands quotas in vocational education, quotas which often conflict with state guidelines on whom is to be eligible for such programs. Mandates for the federal and state governments on behalf of certain special interests have resulted in competition with other special interests and with regular programs, resulting in program fragmentation in the local school. Conflict is triggered by the failure of federal and state authorities to consider the ability of local authorities to carry out the mandates. Although financial incentives are given for starting some curriculum programs, these mandates assume that other agencies will provide the necessary funds, or that the local school can implement the mandate without additional resources.

Conflicts over noncompliance are associated with shared control. Intentional and unintentional deviation from the goals and guidelines of a mandate create tensions. Even when there is surface compliance, the intents of the mandate may not be fulfilled. As critics have pointed out, "We have some perfectly legal but perfectly horrible federal programs in our state."

Mandates cannot create commitment. The motivation of local participants to comply with mandated objectives and their willingness to achieve the project's goals are essential if the project is to succeed. More regulations governing implementation is not the answer. The difficulties arising from increased bureaucratic red tape actually hinder attaining the intent of the mandates. It is true, however, that fiscal audits and compliance reviews are influential in shaping administrative behavior.[39]

Recent studies of shared control, though, are not all pessimistic. Michael Knapp and others, for example, have found that over time, local problem solving and accommodation reduce the conflicts of an external mandate.[40] Most of the burden of particular laws, for

---

[39]Mary T. Moore et al., "Interaction of Federal and State Programs," *Education and Urban Society* 15, no. 4 (Aug. 1983): 452–478.

[40]Michael S. Knapp et al., "Cumulative Effects at the Local Level," *Education and Urban Society* 15, no. 4 (Aug. 1983): 479–499.

instance, diminishes after the first year or two. Although intergovernmental conflicts exist, they are neither massive nor common across all programs.

Suggestions for improving shared curriculum control include an idealistic proposal to limit the authority of each agency so that there is no conflict in power.[41] Other more feasible suggestions call for employing implementation strategies emphasizing local technical assistance and capacity building rather than depending on regulatory- or compliance-oriented strategies. At least, implementation rather than compliance strategies should be used after a mandatory program has been established. Flexibility for local decision making in designing, managing, and delivering services is a key factor in the quality of education provided under mandates. Similarly, federal mandates should encourage flexibility in responding to the wide variance among states and local communities.

CONCLUDING COMMENTS

The debate over the proper division of responsibility among federal, state, and local governments shows no sign of being settled. Issues such as a federal mathematics and science program, tax credits, and school prayer keep the focus on the federal role. The tendency of states to require more of everything—legislated excellence—is strong. The need for local commitment on every undertaking gives support for adaptive policies of implementation and local initiative. Intergovernmental relations will remain numerous and complex.

Many groups and individuals are interested in having a say about what should be taught. No single source believes that it has enough influence or power. Each tends to feel that another element is in charge. In reality, it is a standoff. The curriculum decision of a board of education, a federal agency, a state department of education, or a legislature can be changed in spirit and in fact by principals and teachers. Although students are often thought to be without much power in deciding what will be taught in schools, they have a great deal to say about what is learned.

The political link of special interest groups within professional education to those in government is not too different from the more exposed business and government ties. Most curriculum decisions, however, reflect conflicts among persons and groups. Like most political solutions, the curriculum comes about through compromise, bargaining, and other forms of accommodation. School organizations are not equal in their ability to balance conflicting pressures. Those schools that conduct more community meetings about curriculum issues have to satisfy fewer demands of special interest groups. Public meetings offer opportunity for citizen defense of challenged school policies. The formulation of curriculum policy does not follow a tidy rational procedure resting on the evidence from research. Curriculum, it seems, will continue to be developed by those who have little idea of its effect in the classroom.

QUESTIONS

1. Would you choose a moral, principled, and legal model of curriculum making in which curriculum decisions are made by authorities on the basis of logic and with the guidance of experts? Or would you prefer a model that depends on agreement among different political interests and seeks no more than an imperfect justice because there is no other kind?

2. Which forces appear to have the greatest effect on what is taught in a situation familiar to you?

[41]Edmund C. Short, "Authority and Governance in Curriculum Development: A Policy Analysis in the United States Context," *Educational Evaluation and Policy Analysis* 5, no. 2 (summer 1983):195–205.

3. What will be the likely outcome of the collision courses among the forces pushing for more power to teachers, those favoring strong state control, and those seeking to restore the federal government's role in curriculum making?

4. Democratic policies see the curriculum as a means of reducing inequality; capitalists see the curriculum as a commodity giving selective advantages in the competition for market rewards. Under what conditions will the respective views dominate?

5. Who should control our schools?

6. Are we ready as a nation to support state and federal efforts to offer choices and to privatize the curriculum or do we still believe in a publicly funded, publicly operated school system?

SUGGESTED STRATEGIC RESEARCH

ANALYZING POWER IN MAKING CURRICULUM POLICY

Select a politically charged issue, such as sex education—abstinence versus information. Describe how this issue is treated in a school or district. What policy is emerging? Why? What group or which individuals are most powerful in shaping this policy? What arguments are most telling?

DETERMINING THE IMPACT OF A COURT DECISION

Studies are needed to show the impact of the U.S. Supreme Court decision *Zelman v. Simmons-Harris*, which holds that vouchers do not violate the Constitution in its separation of church and state. Obtain from your city the number of applications for vouchers that followed from this decision and try to determine the forms of schooling chosen by those with vouchers.

ADVANCING DEMOCRACY AT A SUPERNATIONAL LEVEL

Education is a public good when students and teachers work together for social justice. Identify the information networks that are assisting public citizens within the United States as they participate with those in Third World countries. What causes are they undertaking? Are they successful in making authorities more accountable? Are participants learning how to become active global citizens?

REVEALING CURRICULUM INTERESTS OF PROMINENT FOUNDATIONS

Consider some of the prominent foundations that fund educational programs. What are their expressed and latent interests? For example, the C. S. Mott Foundation's effort to infuse school-day content into after-school programs could be studied. Or data can be collected about the impact of the Ewing Marion Kauffman Foundation's programs to teach students how to become entrepreneurs. The goals and workings of the Melinda and Bill Gates Foundation as well as other new foundations are candidates for analysis.

SELECTED REFERENCES

APPLE, MICHAEL W. *Official Knowledge: Democratic Education in a Conservative Age*. New York: Routledge, 1993.

FLODEN, ROBERT E., ED. "Policy Tools for Improving Education," *Review of Research in Education* 27. American Educational Research Society, 2004.

FUSARELLI, BONNIE C., AND WILLIAM LOWE BOYD, EDS. Politics of Education Association Special Issue, "Theme-Curriculum Politics in Multicultural America," *Educational Policy* 18, no. 1 (Jan. and March): 2004.

SPRING, JOEL. *Intergovernmental Organizations, NGOs and the Decline of the Nation State*. Mahwah, NJ: Lawrence Erlbaum, 2004.

PART IV

ISSUES AND TRENDS

Do you believe that students can be taught *how* to think or only *what* to think? Is the United States falling behind other countries in academic achievement and not keeping up with other countries' concern for lifelong learning beyond test scores? Can the curriculum serve both vocational and academic interests? And what about moral and character education? Is it feasible for a school's curriculum to ensure that students care about and do the right thing?

It is difficult to imagine a curriculum without subject matter but what subject matter? For whom and in what form? What is the latest in math? What counts as science, history, the arts and the like along with the fields of literacy, health, and physical education? Is curriculum in the subject fields going backward to traditional approaches such as more grammar in the teaching of writing?

Are the trends going in the direction of accommodating to multiculturalism and its press for new content and outlooks and a future orientation for students who will live in an uncertain world?

If you and your peers think and talk about such questions, you might create a mindset for reading the next two chapters, and then, after reading, perhaps you will see how your answers have changed and what new questions have arisen.

CHAPTER 11

CURRENT ISSUES DEMANDING RESPONSES

CRUCIAL CURRICULUM issues—development of thinking, competition in education with other nations, vocational education, moral education, and school safety—are examined in this chapter. No definite set of solutions to the issues is given. Instead, a range of views on each problem is offered so that readers can discover for themselves the grounds for choosing one position over another. The purpose is not to argue for one view but to consider the factors that apply to each situation and each potential resolution.

Although each issue is important in its own right, you may regard those discussed here as just a sample of the many issues demanding curriculum responses. You may wish to examine the issues from the perspective of different curriculum conceptions or note how traditional curriculum questions are being answered by the proponents involved. For example, using a knowledge of curriculum conceptions, you might try to analyze vocational education critically from the academic conception or consider different views of moral education from the humanistic perspective. You may wish to treat the issue of safe schools by comparing the likely responses of those with academic, systemic, and social reconstructionist views of curriculum.

CURRICULUM FOR THINKING

The curriculum has long been associated with the aim of developing mental power. One view is that thinking—the intellectual power of memorization and reasoning—can best be developed through the right kind of subject matter. Another is that no subject is inherently intellectual. As Dewey says, "Any subject, from Greek to cooking, and from drawing to mathematics, is intellectual, if intellectual at all, not in its fixed inner structure, but in its functions—in its power to start and direct significant inquiry and reflection."[1] Exponents of the doctrine of formal discipline have long argued that the study of Latin and other difficult subjects would develop the ingredients to learn and think in any domain.

In 1894, the Committee of Ten held that the chief purpose of education was to "train the mind," and, although the members differed among themselves as to which subjects were best for this purpose—languages and the classics or math and the sciences—they compromised by saying that all the principal subjects might accomplish this purpose if consecutively taught so that they would enhance the process of observation, memory, expression, and reasoning.

[1] *We Think* (Boston: D. C. Heath, 1933), 46–47.

Shortly after the committee's report, there were attacks on the doctrine of formal discipline, including the idea that instruction is abstract and that rule systems can affect reasoning about everyday life. William James presented a withering critique of faculty psychology, the idea that mental abilities consist of faculties such as memory and reasoning and that the mind could be improved by mere exercise as muscles are (an idea that has resurfaced in light of neuropsychological findings of how mental exercise builds neurons and associations). Subsequently, Edward Thorndike's research found little transfer across tasks. For example, from estimating areas of rectangles of one size and shape to estimating areas of rectangles of another size and shape, he concluded that learning is specific rather than a matter of mental discipline. Transfer can occur but not because of the disciplinary value of classical study, but only if the old and new activities share a common element such as content or method.[2] Other psychologists added to doubt about mental discipline, holding that learning how to solve one problem produces no improvement in solving other problems without an identical formal structure.[3]

Since the late 1980s, the goal of teaching thinking, reasoning, and problem solving has been pursued with new vigor. This renewal follows changes in society that make it necessary for people to think for themselves and to solve novel problems. Assessments suggesting that students may be failing to develop effective thinking is another reason.

New theories for the teaching of thinking stress that knowledge is not important as a "mental discipline" but as a way to conceptualize situations, to identify patterns, and to organize the information so that new problems in the subject area can be solved. Also, today's psychology emphasizes teaching students the kinds of problems for which the subject matter is useful and the condition under which the formal knowledge applies. Psychological findings that reasoning can be taught and that different subject matters teach different kinds of reasoning support the view that thinking can be improved through the curriculum.

Darrin Lehman, Richard Lempert, and Richard Nisbett found that some of the inferential rules that people use to solve everyday problems are improved by formal training.[4] Although the rule systems of mathematics and formal logic contribute little to everyday reasoning, pragmatic rule systems do. Examples of pragmatic rule systems include (a) *the law of large numbers* (extreme values for a sample are less likely to be excessive when a new sample is observed); (b) *casual schemas* (identify what is necessary and sufficient, what is necessary but not sufficient, and what is neither necessary nor sufficient); and (c) *contractual schemas* (before taking action A, one must satisfy preconditions, and the occurrence of one event obligates another).

Different kinds of education produce different effects on reasoning about various life events. Lehman and associates investigated the effect of studying psychology and medicine (probabilistic science), chemistry (nonprobabilistic science), and law (a nonscience), finding that the probabilistic training produced large effects on statistical and methodological reasoning, that both probabilistic and law training produced effects on the ability to reason about logic of the conditional, and that chemistry had no effect on the types of reasoning studied. Also, Raymond Nickerson found that teaching the strategies of reasoning to elementary school children can improve their performance on IQ tests. Among the strategies taught were how to use dimensions, how to analyze and organize, how to extrapolate different types of sequences, how to see the structure of simple propositions and analyze complex arguments, and how to evaluate consistency.[5]

---

[2]Edward L. Thorndike, *The Principles of Teaching* (New York: A. G. Seiler, 1906).

[3]S. R. Reed et al., "Usefulness of Analogous Solutions for Solving Algebra Word Problems," *Journal of Experimental Psychology: Learning, Memory, Cognition* 11 (1985): 105–125.

[4]Darrin R. Lehman et al., "The Effects of Graduate Training on Reasoning," *American Psychologist* 43, no. 6 (June 1988): 431–442.

[5]Raymond Nickerson et al., *The Teaching of Thinking* (Hillsdale, NJ: Lawrence Erlbaum, 1985).

The renaissance of the doctrine of formal discipline confronts students of the curriculum with questions about which dimensions of thinking should be targeted, which curriculum programs have beneficial effects, and whether it is better to teach thinking as part of traditional content courses or as stand-alone programs for thinking.

The Focus of a Thinking Curriculum

Social Reconstructionists' Goals of Thinking   Social reconstructionists favor critical thinking and want students to show a healthy skepticism about the world, their community, and their schooling. The liberatory curriculum and critical inquiry described in Chapter 2 illustrated the preferred approach. Another is to teach directly such topics as the need for definition, logic, and the weight of evidence, the nature of evidence, deductive and inductive inferencing, and propaganda analysis.

Robert Ennis has proposed a critical thinking curriculum aimed at helping students analyze arguments, look for valid evidence, and reach sound conclusions.[6] Donald Macedo argues for "literacy for social justice," based on critical inquiry into European and American colonial contexts and oppressive repercussions, asymmetrical resources around the world, silencing language policies, and the need for political action.[7]

Humanistic Goals for Thinking   Humanists value creative thinking—the ability to form new combinations of ideas to fulfill individual needs. A great deal has been said regarding teaching strategies and conditions conducive to creative thinking. The importance of psychological safety, freedom, and stimulation is well known. Vera John-Steiner's account of how creative people engage in thinking is an excellent source of understanding the origins and elaboration of creative thought.[8]

Various curriculum projects offer exercises in exploring the unfamiliar and creating something new. Usually creative programs call for *fluency* (through such techniques as brainstorming), *flexibility* (changing the focus of thought), *exploring* (confronting paradoxes), *elaborating* (adding new material to existing ideas), and *risk taking* (trying out a new idea). William Gordon's *Synectics* has been useful in developing curriculum for creativity in English, science, social studies, and writing.[9]

Unresolved are questions whether any formal curriculum would work for Mozart or any other creative genius and whether divergent thinking exercises and programs for learning to use various analogies are as important as equipping minds with the information, principles, concepts, and theories with which to think about something in a new way.

Academicians' Goals for Thinking   Academicians prize the paradigmatic or logico-scientific mode of thinking. This mode is based on categorization, conceptualization, and the operations for establishing and relating categories. In trying to develop academic minds, three kinds of knowledge are taught: (1) basic operations such as classifying, generalizing, deducing; (2) problem-solving strategies; and (3) domain-specific knowledge.

Curriculum for Teaching Basic Operations   Programs for teaching basic operations are numerous. *Science—a Process Approach* is a successful curriculum focusing on eight basic processes of science.[10] This curriculum represents an integrated approach to

[6]Robert E. Ennis, "A Taxonomy of Critical Thinking Disposition and Abilities," in *Teaching Thinking Skills: Theory and Practice*, J. Baron and R. Sternberg, eds. (New York: Freeman, 1987).

[7]Donaldo Macedo, "The Illiteracy of English-Only Literacy," *Educational Leadership* 57, no. 4 (Dec. 1999/Jan. 2000): 62–67.

[8]Vera John-Steiner, *Notebooks of the Mind: Explorations of Thinking* (Albuquerque: University of New Mexico Press, 1985).

[9]Bruce Joyce and Marsha Weil, *Models of Teaching,* 5th ed. (Boston: Allyn and Bacon, 1996), 233–263.

[10]H. J. Klausmeir, *Learning and Teaching Concepts* (New York: Academic Press, 1980).

teaching intellectual skills in the context of learning science. In contrast, *Instrumental Enrichment* is almost free of specific subject matter.[11] This curriculum offers a 3-year series of experiments involving classification, orientation in space, logical reasoning, and the like through paper and pencil exercises followed by discussions about how the respective thinking processes might be applied in and out of school.

Students of curriculum might weigh the advantages for teaching both processes in the context of content-rich material which provides a link for relating the thinking skills to a given domain and the advantage of separate programs that explicate processes without presuming any specialized background knowledge on the part of students and which removes the conceptual distraction often found in content-rich exercises.

Curriculum for Teaching Problem Solving　Curriculum for the teaching of problem solving is based on studies of how experts elaborate and reconstruct problems and how they look for solutions by reasoning from analogies. Typically, students learn the heuristics of diagramming, breaking a problem into subproblems, finding analogous problems, and working backward. An example of a problem-solving curriculum is *The Productive Thinking Program,* which has been used successfully in middle school. With this curriculum, students show gains in both the quantity and quality of their ideas (fluency) and improvement in intellectual independence and self-confidence.[12]

Edward de Bono has constructed a curriculum, *Cognitive Research Trust* (CORT), that aims at having students take a broader view of formally posed problems without being restrained by conventions in their thinking.[13] Lessons in this program focus on the perceptual aspect of thinking. Inasmuch as de Bono wants to develop the habits of mind and thinking techniques that can be applied in any subject area, his curriculum emphasizes generalizable strategies rather than specific subject matter.

The emphasis on metacognitive knowledge as an aid to problem solving sets the current thinking skills movement apart from earlier similar movements. Metacognition training involves teaching students how to manage their own cognitive resources and to monitor their own intellectual performance. Students are taught to use such strategies to access task-relevant information, to recognize when something requires clarification, and to make hypotheses and predictions, revising them on the basis of new information.[14]

Evaluation of programs for the direct teaching of problem solving gives mixed results. Usually students acquire the strategies taught but fail to use these heuristics in other contexts and courses. As with the teaching of the basic processes, results as measured by performance on standardized tests are proportional to the similarity of standardized tests and program practice items, suggesting that the results are attributed more to familiarity with tasks than to changed cognitive functions. Frank Smith has misgivings about the teaching of generalizable problem-solving skills. He believes that problems are context bound and if we do not solve a problem it is for lack of knowledge, not lack of skill.[15]

Domain-Specific Knowledge　Whereas experts tend to organize their knowledge on the basis of abstractions that reflect deep understanding of a subject, novices are more likely to organize their conceptions of the problem around literal objects and relationships explicitly mentioned. Students acquire knowledge but do not apply it. Hence, the current

[11]Reuven Feuerstein et al., *Instrumental Enrichment* (Baltimore: University Park Press, 1980).

[12]M. V. Corrington, "Strategic Thinking and Fear of Failure," in *Thinking and Learning 1*, J. W. Segal et al., eds. (Hillsdale, NJ: Lawrence Erlbaum, 1985), 389–411.

[13]*CORT Thinking Program* (Elmsford, NY: Pergamon, 1994).

[14]M. Scardamalia and C. Bereiter, "Fostering the Development of Self-Regulation in Children's Knowledge Processing," in *Thinking and Learning Skills: Research and Open Questions 2*, S. E Chapman et al., eds. (Hillsdale, NJ: Lawrence Erlbaum, 1999), 563–577.

[15]Frank Smith, *To Think* (New York: Teachers College Press, 1990).

focus in curriculum for thinking is not on the acquisition and coverage of subject matter but on how the subject can be taught so that students think about the content in fresh ways and acquire intellectual tools that can be useful in other contexts.

In brief, the challenge is to develop curriculum that will deemphasize student reproduction of knowledge, which tends to remain inert, and to treat knowledge as a stimulation to inquiry and reflection. There should be opportunities to expose one's own and others' beliefs and opinions to criticism and to know how and when to use the formal and informal tools of thought.

Contrast in Goals for Thinking   Nel Noddings, for example, calls for a curriculum where students explore issues affecting their lives and the world.[16] Accordingly, in a study of war, students examine its psychological responses and justifications, including an in-depth analysis of factors that lead to atrocities and strategies for compassion.

In contrast with the traditional academic emphasis on reasoning and logic, social reconstructionists and humanists want students to think about the social, cultural, historical, and aesthetic aspects of the issues, using the lenses of those involved—their historical theories or perspectives in order to understand the complexities.

CURRICULUM COMPETITION: AN INTERNATIONAL COMPARISON

At the start of the twenty-first century, some in the United States see a nation losing educational status. Scientists report that the United States ranks twenty-fourth among nations whose 18- to 24-year-olds are earning advanced science or engineering degrees, whereas in 1995 the United States ranked third. Although the United States outpaces the rest of the world in expenditure in research and development, the gap is narrowing.[17] News accounts report that the supply of great scientists is so limited by nature that K–12 schools should put more effort into finding, nurturing, and unleashing the power of the brightest if the United States is to keep its dominant position.

On the other hand, the Rand Corporation reports there is no shortage on the horizon for scientific, technical, engineering, and mathematical personnel in the U.S. workforce. Others also argue that schools are producing more knowledgeable workers than can be employed, creating a labor excess economy that keeps costs down and productivity high.

Is the curriculum in U.S. schools lagging behind those in other countries? If so, why, and what should be done about it? These questions are controversial. Some view Japanese and Chinese increases in educational productivity—particularly in science and mathematics—in contrast to declining test scores in the United States as a grave national concern. Others say that the data on the comparisons are questionable and that illustrations of the weaknesses of the American educational system create the false impression that American education should imitate the practices of competing nations.

Invidious Comparisons

H. W. Stevenson and J. W. Stigler contend that their interviewing and testing of students in China, Japan, Taiwan, and the United States as well as observing in classrooms and interviewing teachers and mothers in these countries lead to the conclusion that American

---

[16]Nel Noddings, "War, Critical Thinking, and Self-Understanding," *Phi Delta Kappan* 85, no. 7 (March 2004): 488–495.
[17]Gerald W. Bracey, *On the Death of Childhood and the Destruction of Public Schools: The Folly of Today's Education Policies and Practices* (Portsmouth, NH: Heinemann, 2004).

students are not competitive with Asian peers.[18] For example, using their own tests in reading and mathematics based on analysis of the textbooks used by children, Stevenson and Stigler repeatedly tested fifth graders in Minneapolis with those in Taiwan, widening the gap between their performance and that of the American students. In reading, the Chinese students continued to receive the highest scores, and the American students had slipped to third place. Stevenson attributes the poor showing of the Americans to the American parents holding lower standards for academic achievement than parents in Asia and to the additional functions required of American teachers. He urges more training of teachers in what is to be taught and how to teach it.

The Trends in International Mathematics and Science Study (TIMSS) in 1999 examined video samples of eighth-grade lessons in eight countries, revealing striking national differences but showing that the teachers in high-achieving countries have one thing in common: they focus on rich math problems that connect math concepts rather than focus, as do lower achieving U.S. teachers, on procedures for solving the problems.

Consequently, many U.S. teachers are studying the videotaped lessons of high-technology teachers in other cultures and trying to implement in their own classrooms the practices of the high-achieving teachers. Usually these practices call for a coherent curriculum in which math topics relate to other subjects. In contrast with the typical U.S. practice of having students learn a particular solution, strategy, or procedure and then practice using it, high-performing Japanese teachers first engage students in devising their own solutions to problems they have never seen before, followed by peers and teacher exchanging solutions.

On the other hand, Gerald Bracey disagrees with Stevenson's generalizations and recommendations. Bracey faults Stevenson for basing his study on noncomparable groups of students—the American students, for instance, consisted of poverty students and many of them were from non–English-speaking homes. Also, Bracey points to inconsistencies between Stevenson's findings and the findings from international studies reporting that the scores of the upper 5% of virtually all countries are nearly identical.[19]

Elsewhere, Bracey admits that the results of the TIMSS, which tested eighth graders and their progress over 4 years, show that U.S. students are not leading in the areas of math and science although they exceed the international average attained by 38 nations. He attributed this to U.S. math and science textbooks that feature coverage rather than in-depth understanding and to U.S. teachers concentrating on procedures and algorithms (skills) instead of focusing on understanding or relating concepts as do teachers in the high achieving countries.

Table 11.1 shows how eighth-grade U.S. students compare with their peers in math and science. Table 11.1 does not show the complexity of the data, such as the performance of ethnic groups. While U.S. students may exceed the international averages in math and science, the performance of U.S. African-Americans and Hispanics below the poverty line is lower than nearly all of the compared nations.

As indicated previously, the top 5 to 10% of all students (the elite) at the end of secondary education perform at nearly the same level whether they attend a selective or common school. Opportunity to learn is the single most important factor in accounting for differences in achievement, not just money. Economically poor Cuba, for instance, has attained world-class educational achievements while, according to an UNESCO comparative study, scoring higher than their peers in 12 other Latin American countries in reading and math. The connection between schooling and a nation's economic prosperity is unclear. Which is cause and which is effect?

Opportunity to learn is the single most important factor accounting for differences in achievement. For example, in looking at the results of achievement in French as a foreign

[18]H. W. Stevenson and J. W. Stigler, *The Learning Gap* (New York: Summit, 1992).

[19]Gerald W. Bracey, *On the Death of Childhood and the Destruction of Public Schools: The Folly of Today's Education Policies and Practice* (Portsmouth, NH: Heinemann, 2004).

Table 11.1   Results of the Trends in International Mathematics and Science Study (TIMSS)

Mathematics			Science	
Nation	**Average**		**Nation**	**Average**
Singapore	604[a]		Chinese Taipei	569[a]
Republic of Korea	587[a]		Singapore	568[a]
Chinese Taipei	585[a]		Hungary	552[a]
Hong Kong SAR	582[a]		Japan	550[a]
Japan	579[a]		Republic of Korea	549[a]
Belgium-Flemish	558[a]		Netherlands	545[a]
Netherlands	540[a]		Australia	540[a]
Slovak Republic	534[a]		Czech Republic	539[a]
Hungary	532[a]		England	538[a]
Canada	531[a]		Finland	535[a]
Slovenia	530[a]		Slovak Republic	535[a]
Russian Federation	526[a]		Belgium-Flemish	535[a]
Australia	525[a]		Slovenia	533[a]
Finland	520[a]		Canada	533[a]
Czech Republic	520[b]		Hong Kong SAR	530[b]
Malaysia	519[b]		Russian Federation	529[b]
Bulgaria	511[b]		Bulgaria	518[b]
Latvia-LSS	505[b]		United States	515
United States	502		New Zealand	510[b]
England	496[b]		Latvia-LSS	503[b]
New Zealand	491[b]		Italy	493[c]
Lithuania	482[c]		Malaysia	492[c]
Italy	479[c]		Lithuania	488[c]
Cyprus	476[c]		Thailand	482[c]
Romania	472[c]		Romania	472[c]
Moldova	469[c]		Israel	468[c]
Thailand	467[c]		Cyprus	460[c]
Israel	466[c]		Moldova	459[c]
Tunisia	448[c]		Republic of Macedonia	458[c]
Republic of Macedonia	447[c]		Jordan	450[c]
Turkey	429[c]		Islamic Republic of Iran	448[c]
Jordan	428[c]		Indonesia	435[c]
Islamic Republic of Iran	422[c]		Turkey	433[c]
Indonesia	403[c]		Tunisia	430[c]
Chile	392[c]		Chile	420[c]
Philippines	345[c]		Philippines	345[c]
Morocco	337[c]		Morocco	323[c]
South Africa	275[c]		South Africa	243[c]

[a]Average is significantly higher than the U.S. average.
[b]Average does not differ significantly from the U.S. average.
[c]Average is significantly lower than the U.S. average.

language, the United States (in which only 2 years of high school French are required) recorded a dismal score, whereas Romania, which requires 6 years of French, was at the top.

Low standards are not the most serious problem in schooling. The most serious problem for all industrialized nations is the rise of a new educational underclass—those who from the very beginning tend to be failures in school. The key question is how to give an advanced education, one formerly available only to a small social and intellectual elite, to the educationally underprivileged—those who do not have the advantage of a background that stressed academics.

Similarly, in his analysis of data collected in the Second International Math Study (SIMS), Ian Westbury found that the investigators had administered an algebra test to eighth graders and a calculus test to twelfth graders, creating a test/curriculum mismatch for many American students who take algebra in the ninth grade and calculus in college.[20]

Obviously, American students in remedial and regular eighth-grade math performed below the Japanese, all of whom take algebra. The international study does, however, give rise to the question of whether all American eighth graders should be taught algebra and, if so, why?

The International Association for the Evaluation of Educational Achievement offers international comparisons of achievement. One study concluded that U.S. 9- and 14-year-olds compared favorably with counterparts in other industrialized nations in reading. In science and math, however, studies indicate that Japanese students excel the grand mean when compared with students in 14 other industrialized countries, whereas American students score near the grand mean. Japanese students score higher than students in other countries both on items that require functional information as well as on items that test understanding, application, and higher scientific thought (e.g., hypothesis formulation). The higher Japanese scores may be attributed to the requirement of the Japanese Ministry of Education that 25% of classroom time in lower secondary schools be devoted to science and mathematics. (Nearly all Japanese students are exposed to this much science and mathematics through the ninth grade.) In their three years of high school, nearly all college-bound Japanese students (about one-third of the total) take three natural sciences courses and four mathematics courses through differential calculus.

However, partly on the basis of an international study which found that their high achievers in math and science hated these subjects, the Japanese Ministry in 2003 embarked on curriculum reform: a reduction in curriculum content by 30%, more electives, at least three hours a week of flexible time, integrated learning based on student projects, and more autonomy for national universities. However, many parents are resisting the reform because they fear their child will be less prepared to compete on university entrance examinations (and thus suffer loss of social mobility). Also, a public perceives a rise in deviancy among the country's youth.

Other countries with high academic achievement are moving away from defining quality education as performance on traditional tests of school knowledge. High achieving nations like Singapore and Korea, for example, are trying to change from a "learn and drill" approach to what used to be an American-style progressive student-centered approach. In the "Asian Tiger" nations, there are now more student-initiated projects with creativity and individual enterprises as the goals. Development of business plans by students is an alternative to memorization of factual knowledge. Leaders in these countries see that their national interest rests on transforming the curriculum from one that centers on academically smart people to developing an enlarged population (human capital) that is inquisitive, creative, and entrepreneurial if the nation is to compete globally.

As indicated in Part 2, CIDREE, a European consortium, is developing curriculum that prepares students to act in the world and contribute to social values. A new system of international assessment matches this effort. The "Program for International Studies

---

[20]Ian Westbury, "Comparing American and Japanese Achievement: Is the United States Really a Low Achiever?" *Educational Researcher* 25, no. 5 (1992): 18–24.

Assessment (PISA) has gone beyond assessing only reproductive knowledge and comparing test scores. PISA is collecting and comparing test data to find out how what happens in schools affects lifelong learning and performance in a range of human behavior.[21]

PISA is a collaboration of nearly 40 countries from the Organization for Economic Cooperation and Development (OECD) together with some nonmember countries that conduct ongoing studies of achievement and learning. PISA 2000 looked at 15-year-olds' capabilities in reading literacy, mathematics literacy, and science literacy as well as collecting information on students' learning strategies and functional skills. They also asked, "Were students able and willing to apply their knowledge to personal concerns, life, health, the environment, and technology?"

The results of PISA 2000 show considerable differences between countries in terms of whether socioeconomic backgrounds of students and schools affect student performance. In contrast with the United States, countries such as Finland, Hong Kong, and Korea ameliorate the influence of social background and are able to maintain exceptionally high achievements and at the same time ensure high performance for most, leaving few behind.

Fifteen-year-olds in the United States performed in reading as well as peers in 27 participating countries but behind Canada, Finland, and New Zealand. In math and science, the U.S. students performed at the OECD average but were outperformed by eight countries. Across countries, girls excel in reading; boys in math.

"Knowledge and Skills for Life, the First Results from PISA 2000" indicates that the following factors are necessary for success both in school learning and in continued study and learning:

- Using strategies for learning—review what has been learned, test oneself, and relate what is learned to other experiences and to goals.

- Enjoying reading—one's ability to read can compensate for poor instruction and schools.

- Taking responsibility for reaching both goals set by teachers and one's own goals.

- Believing in one's ability to learn and achieve.

- Knowing situations where cooperative or competitive learning is more appropriate.

The Educational Testing Service conducted an international assessment of skills in mathematics and sciences achieved among 13-year-olds in five countries and seven Canadian provinces. This study is noteworthy for its use of questions adapted for cultural differences derived from the National Assessment of Education Project (NAEP).[22] With respect to science achievement, the ETS study found diversity among the achievement of 13-year-olds across populations. Table 11.2 depicts the percentage of students from each population who have acquired the science knowledge and skills reflected at defined levels of achievement.

The poor performance of U.S. students on conceptual tasks may reflect U.S. teachers' traditional practice of emphasizing procedures rather than connecting concepts. School curriculum, time devoted to science, and types of classroom activities are all considerations for study. Other variables such as socioeconomic conditions, level of parents' education, and the societal value placed on the study of science also may be considered.

Caution in making too much of the findings of the NAEP study is voiced by Richard Wolfe. Wolfe believes that the findings are exaggerated because the measurements of each

[21]National Center for Educational Statistics, *Program for International Student Assessment (PISA)* (Washington, DC: U.S. Department of Education, 2000).

[22]Archie E. Lapointe et al., *A World of Differences* (Princeton, NJ: Educational Testing Service, 1989).

Table 11.2 Percentages Performing at or above Each Level of the Science Scale, Age 13•

Country or Province	Know Everyday Facts Level 300	Apply Simple Principles Level 400	Analyze Experiments Level 500	Apply Intermediate Principles Level 600	Integrate Experimental Evidence Level 700
British Columbia	100	95	72	31	4
Korea	100	93	73	33	2
United Kingdom	98	89	59	21	2
Quebec (English)	99	92	57	15	1
Ontario (English)	99	91	56	17	2
Quebec (French)	100	91	56	15	2
New Brunswick(English)	99	90	55	15	1
Spain	99	88	53	12	1
United States	96	78	42	12	1
Ireland	96	76	37	9	1
Ontario (French)	98	79	35	6	<1
New Brunswick (French)	98	78	35	7	<1

•Jackknifed standard errors for percentages range from less than 0.1 to 2.6.

Source: From Archie E. Lapointe et al., *A World of Differences* (Princeton, NJ: Educational Testing Service, January 1989).

skill are composites of different items and fail to show the means of the test items across countries. Some parts of the test are more difficult for students in some populations. The international comparisons are very much determined by how the topics were sampled from the small number of items, and researchers asked, "If the problem of achievement varies between countries, how can there be a single comparative scale?"[23] Also, across countries, students are given different topics to learn.

Comparative data are used to strengthen political agendas. Ludger Woessmann, for example, used TIMSS data and other sources to show that spending did not account for differences in performance. Woessmann concluded that achievement in math and science was greater when a system had these features:

- External examinations.
- A private school sector.
- School autonomy in hiring and rewarding teachers.
- Individual teacher autonomy in selecting a teaching method and influencing the enacted curriculum (in contrast with the negative effect of a teacher collective's or a union's influence on the curriculum).

Woessmann predicted positive effects when those involved have an incentive to improve student performance.[24]

Likewise in a climate of public school bashing, the media ignored a U.S. success story in an international comparison. The Progress in International Reading Literacy Study (PIRLS) that measures reading comprehension at the fourth grade placed U.S. students

[23]Richard Wolfe, *Reading to "A World of Differences"* (Toronto: Ontario Institute for Studies in Education, 1990).
[24]Ludger Woessmann, "Why Students in Some Countries Do Better: International Evidence on the Importance of Education Policy," *Education Matters* (summer 2001): 67–74.

ninth among 35 countries with only three countries scoring higher (the United States was only 19 points out of first place on a 600 point scale). U.S. blacks and Hispanics from poverty sectors underperformed while the affluent whites and Asians outscored the winners.[25]

VOCATIONAL EDUCATION

Vocational education is being transformed. Its new name "career and technical education" reflects the change. High school and two-year college students are introduced to "hot" technologies—robotics, microchip manufacture, nuclear medicine, and nanotechnology— while taking related courses in astronomy, mathematics, and chemistry. Conversely, universities are greatly expanding their career oriented classes, such as vocational courses in business, public health, and journalism. New York University's "Professional Edge," for example, offers an interschool program that prepares liberal arts students for the job market. Accordingly, a history major might learn how to appraise art, and a foreign language student might take courses in how to become a translator.

Curriculum developers confront three non-exclusive approaches in relating school and employment:

1. *Education "through" work.* Students acquire academic subjects that are coordinated with work-related experiences so that aspects of learning in out-of-school situations are incorporated into the school's curriculum. Cooperative education is an example. In co-op curriculum, students are trained in the context of a paid job while being helped by teachers in the school to learn from the job and to contribute to the workplace. Some schools offer on-site work, such as running a store, producing goods or services for sale, using work experience as a vehicle for showing the utility of academic knowledge, and ensuring greater understanding, retention, and transfer of subject matter concepts.

2. *Education "about" work.* Students examine the world of work, learning about career ladders, glass ceilings, rights in the workplace, and the social skills of getting and keeping a job. Throughout this approach, students may become aware of career choices and the technical training that is necessary. Brief work site visits, job shadowing, and career planning are common in this approach.

3. *Education "for" work.* Students are prepared for entry into a "family" of occupations for specific careers. Emergent programs are characterized by aligning secondary and postsecondary curriculum that is expected to lead to a career and incorporate academic as well as technical content. "Tech Prep" is an example of a program that links 2 years of secondary curriculum in math, science, and communication to the first 2 years of a postsecondary curriculum or apprenticeship, usually culminating with a degree or certificate in a specified occupational field. Tech Prep is found in about half of the nation's high schools and in a majority of 2-year colleges.[26]

Four issues face curriculum planners in vocational education:

1. *Purpose.* Should vocational education aim at broad intellectual development and guidance, helping individuals make decisions about careers, or should it aim at preparing students with marketable skills?

---

[25]Gearld W. Bracey, "PIRLS Before Press," *Phi Delta Kappan* 84, no. 10 (June 2003): 795.
[26]U.S. Department of Education, *National Center for Vocational Statistics: Vocational Education in the United States through the Year 2000* (Washington, DC: NCES, 2003).

2. *Access.* Should vocational education be open to the slow as well as to the gifted? Should vocational education prepare one for college or for the world of work? Is the notion of courses limited to either male or female obsolete?

3. *Content.* How well does the content of vocational educational programs match the present and future needs of the economy?

4. *Organization.* Should vocational education be restructured in order to close the gap between the vocational programs of the school and the requirements of work?

CONTRASTING PURPOSES FOR VOCATIONAL EDUCATION

Americans have long been divided on the relative value of the liberal arts, which seem to have little practical value, and vocational studies, which promise to be immediately useful. During the first 100 years of American secondary education, for example, an elite group attended the Latin Grammar School which featured the classics, while commoners chose "venture schools," which, for a fee, taught a directly useful skill of a technical or applied variety, such as bookkeeping, navigation, or surveying.

Many who oppose vocational education reflect a traditional European view of education for different classes of students in which the most prestigious subjects are nonutilitarian.

The nonutilitarian view continues to resurface. A. Graham Down of the former Council for Basic Education, for example, expresses this viewpoint with new arguments: "The idea that a school should prepare students for an entry level job is dear to many hearts, particularly if the vocational training is for somebody else's children. But in today's world, the rudimentary skills needed for success in a first job soon become inadequate. Both change and technology demand highly intellectual skills and adaptability. As Cardinal Newman once put it, 'a liberal education is the only practical form of vocational education.'"[27]

Early Rationale The justification for vocational education does not rest on usefulness alone. The leading advocate for the comprehensive high school in the late 1950s, James B. Conant, regarded vocational education as an incentive, ensuring student participation in the general educational program. He believed that for certain kinds of people vocational education provided the only motivation to keep them in school where they would benefit from education for citizenship.[28]

Early advocates of vocational education offered manual training as complementary to academic studies and necessary for the balanced education for all students. Manual training was a more meaningful way of learning by doing. Similarly, proponents of modern career education are less interested in teaching specific skills than in erasing the differences between vocational and academic education, relating English, reading, writing, and mathematics to practical applications in careers.

Current Thinking about Purposes of Vocational Education The current rationale for vocational education rests on three arguments—national interest, equity, and human development. Federal aid to vocational education began with the desire to conserve and develop resources, to promote a more productive agriculture, to prevent waste of human labor, and to meet an increasing demand for trained workers.[29] Presently, the government

[27]A. Graham Down, "Inequality, Testing, Utilitarianism: The Three Killers of Excellence," *Education Week* 3, no. 6 (Oct. 1983): 20, 21.
[28]Robert L. Hampel, *American High Schools Since 1940* (Boston: Houghton Mifflin, 1984).
[29]U.S. Congress, House Committee on National Aid to Vocational Education, 63rd Congress, 2nd session, 1914, 410–493.

is interested in having scientists and engineers as well as workers with upgraded work-force skills that allow the United States to compete in the international marketplace. The latter skills are defined by employer groups as ability (1) to organize resources; (2) to demonstrate interpersonal skills; (3) to communicate information and use the computer in processing information; (4) to select appropriate technologies; and (5) to understand and design new systems. The national concern for both scientific literacy and technical competence is a priority.

Federally funded vocational education encourages "pipeline" programs with foundation technical training and academic courses in high school and advanced courses at the college level, with work-related experiences. In 2004, the Bush administration reduced federal funding for vocational education and proposed the Secondary and Technical Education Excellence program, which requires that school districts share funding with at least one postsecondary institution, trade or technical college, university, or an apprenticeship program.

Equity in vocational education suggests that it should help the young, refugees, and the hard-to-employ to find a place in the economy. This goal includes training students in specific skills, in general occupational skills, and in the ways of the working world. Students enrolling in specialized programs do so to increase their chances of obtaining and keeping a job. In their view of vocational preparation, employers have conflicting ideas. Some feel that the school should prepare students with the vocational skills for entry-level employment. Others think that the school should emphasize reading, writing, computation, and social skills, leaving specific skill preparation to employers.

Proponents of equity for at-risk students and others who are not in an academic track are advocates for a "new vocationalism" where the goal goes beyond job specific training. Career academics illustrate the concept. Such academics have a broad career focus and offer all students both academic and vocational education integrated around a career theme often in partnership with a business or ties to a postsecondary program.

Equity is not always achieved even when there are articulated agreements between institutions for course credit. Faculty in community colleges sometimes impose additional placement tests and require more foundation courses, thereby delaying and preventing students from continuing the program.

Human development in vocational education underscores the intrinsic value of work. Students gain a sense of how things work—televisions, cars, businesses. Thus the social environment is made more understandable and the learner acquires a feeling of control. Aesthetic values—the satisfaction of creative expression through the construction of a product—is another dimension in human development through work. Vocational education as exploration of different occupational areas—the arts, industry, business—is a means for both creating interest and expanding it. Through vocational education, students may learn to ask questions about (1) the processes through which work roles and their benefits are constructed: (2) how jobs are related to society, the environment, and their own development; and (3) what it means to have a job. Vocational exploration helps learners discover a broad range of possible careers and find which one suits them. Experiential vocation education, in which students engage in projects such as constructing a house, raising livestock, conducting community service, and programming a computer, points to the highest of educational ideals—knowledge of the relationship between effort and consequences, teamwork, and sensitivity to community needs.

Access to Vocational Education

Vocational education has been accused of maintaining class divisions; in other words, working-class children are kept in school but do not receive an academic education. While the poor learn the attitudes and skills for work, middle- and upper-class children have access to the more prestigious academic curriculum. Jeannie Oakes, in her study of the relation between race and vocational education, found restrictions in access to such education for certain students, not only to academic programs, but even to higher status vocational programs.[30] Oakes analyzed vocational programs in 25 secondary schools. She found that on the average white schools and those with a substantial nonwhite population give about equal emphasis to vocational education. However, the characteristics of the program vary according to racial and ethnic composition. Students at the white schools had more extensive business and industrial arts programs than those attending nonwhite or mixed schools; whereas students in the latter schools had greater access to military training and home economics.

Within categories of programs, differences also are found in opportunity. In business programs, for example, courses in management and finance were offered predominantly at white schools. Only in the white schools were students offered courses in banking, taxation, the stock market, data processing, and business law. Keyboards, shorthand, bookkeeping, and office procedures were available in both nonwhite and white schools. Students at white schools could attend courses in marine technology, aviation, and power mechanics; students in nonwhite schools were offered cosmetology, building construction, institutional cooking and sewing, printing, and commercial photography. Nonwhite students were more likely to be enrolled in courses teaching basic skills, many of which are lengthy and off campus.

Clearly curriculum planners may play a part in restricting the access of certain students to future opportunity. Less clear is whether the restriction is a conspiracy or whether it results from well-intentioned efforts to offer "realistic" career choices in a stratified culture.

Discrimination appears also in vocational education according to ability. The new focus in vocational education is on the gifted. Whether existing programs will be redirected or new ones created for these students is not known. Some schools are offering courses stressing high technology and carrying academic prerequisites. Former courses in auto mechanics have been converted to engineering principles, computer science, and electronics, which are usually given in a technology center or in partnership at a company's work site. Selectivity is illustrated by a Ventura, California, school district that opened a technology center with an emphasis on media as a way to address "needs" of middle-ability students. High school faculty and counselors were surprised when their honors and advanced placement courses lost enrollment when the brightest were drawn to the new vocational program.

Schools have discouraged members of both sexes from entering programs that traditionally are the realms of the opposite sex. Courses for skills traditionally thought to be male prepare students for jobs that pay more. The vocational preparation of girls in rural areas presents a particular challenge. As a group, rural women tend to focus their attention on the family, yet they have strong career goals. The rural labor market offers very few choices to most women. Those girls who depart from "sex appropriate" programs such as consumer and homemaking education may experience conflicts in the community and uncertain employment. One answer is a curriculum composed of courses that are sexually neutral and attract both males and females, such as programs in food service, graphics, commercial horticulture, and data processing. These fields lessen the conflict between community approval and self-esteem.

Currently, public schools are becoming more vocational, while private schools are continuing their academic emphasis. In her role as co-chair for the Commission on the

---

[30]Jeannie Oakes, "Beneath the Bottom Line: A Critique of Vocational Education Research," *Journal of Vocational Research*, 11, no. 2 (1986): 33–53.

Skills of the American Workforce, Hillary Rodham Clinton held that by age 16, or soon thereafter, all students should meet a national standard of academic excellence and then choose a structure that will enable them to make a transition to work. The commission suggested work-based learning, alternative paths to college, on-the-job training, and programs that will certify mastery of industry-based standards across a range of occupations. Clinton's proposal would offer mobility both horizontally among occupations and vertically into options for further training or study, avoiding dead ends.

The Oregon Educational Act for the 21st Century incorporated many of Clinton's recommendations. The plan calls for the creation of academic standards to support a certificate of initial mastery that students must attain by age 16, and a certificate of advanced mastery on completion of a program for a given occupation.

Content of Vocational Education

A central question in vocational education is determining the best response to the needs of students who go directly into the job market. For a substantial number, preparation in high school is all they get. For those who think the best preparation is training in the basic skills of reading, writing, mathematics, and science, the problem is already solved.

Advocates of higher standards for all, such as business leaders and state governors in ACHIEVE, want high school exit exams to be strengthened beyond pre-algebra and ninth-grade reading and math to more challenging measures for admission to college and the workplace. Nevertheless, there are concerns that the higher standards may not accommodate late bloomers who do not test well and those who are experiencing poverty, unstable family, and other factors that hinder academic achievement. Also the idea that all decent jobs require a college education has been refuted. There are rewarding jobs available for those whose literacy is at the ninth-grade level and who have good social skills and work habits. There is a marked increase in "creating one's own job," especially by minority women starting their own businesses.

Although in general those in the professional fields earn more money, changing markets upset predictions. During California's recession and real estate boom in early 2000, the highest paid occupations required no university degree—financial officers, real estate agents, insurance sales persons, elevator repairmen, and police, fire, and penitentiary guards.[31]

Skeptics believe the press for higher vocational qualifications is not because jobs require higher level skills, but because corporations want greater numbers of the best employees applying for employment.

The advocacy of increased mathematics and science in vocational education rests on the belief that future job opportunities will be in high technology and that the nation will need analytical or synthetic thinkers who can provide creative solutions to problems and bring forth the innovations necessary for keeping the United States competitive.

Daniel Hull and Leno Pedrotti have suggested a means of designing a curriculum for high tech occupations.[32] They recommend (1) a common core consisting of basic units in mathematics, the physical sciences, communications, and human relations; (2) a technical core of units in electricity, electronics, mechanics, thermics, computers, and fluids; and (3) a sequence on specialization in lasers or electro-optics, instrumentation and control, robotics, and microelectronics. Obviously, industry must play a part in assisting schools with the personnel and expensive equipment required for such a program.

---

[31]U.S. Department of Work, 2004.
[32]Daniel M. Hull and Leno S. Pedrotti, "Meeting the High-Tech Challenge," *Vocational Education* 58, no. 4 (May 1983): 28–31.

Curriculum developers in the vocational field of industrial arts are responding to the newer demands by introducing curricula that relate industrial arts to science and technology. Students design models using principles from these disciplines. Here, too, a broad base of knowledge and an understanding of basic processes are required.

Not everyone believes that vocational education must focus on high technology. The major demand for workers will not be for computer scientists and engineers but for janitors, nurse's aides, sales clerks, cashiers, nurses, fast-food preparers, secretaries, truck drivers, and kitchen helpers. The idea that if young people have skills on leaving school, they would also have jobs is refuted when the economy is poor. Vocational education may increase the competitiveness of individuals in the context of job scarcity, not educational reform. An unpredictable economy means that vocational education might adapt to a diversity of skills rather than focus on training students for a career in a single field. Accordingly, students require a broad base of technical knowledge and the ability to communicate. Specific training likely will follow high school and at regular intervals throughout a person's career.

Although employment nationwide is likely to be in service industries, such as health care, trade, and education rather than in manufacturing, farming, mining, and construction, curriculum developers try to balance demands for responses to national needs with the requirements of the local communities that many vocational programs are designed to serve.

Reorganizing Vocational Education

Reorganization represents an effort to close the gap between the vocational programs of schools and the requirements of work, as in the "cluster-of-skills" approach whereby students are trained in several occupational areas. A day care program that converts to human service by offering courses in caring for children, the physically disabled, and the elderly is an example.

A second kind of reorganization is to add programs to meet expanding industries. "Quick start" programs, which offer customized training for a growing industry, are popular in states that desire to strengthen school ties with the private sector and influence local economic development. Curriculum that includes important export courses, international marketing, and distribution is a response to a changing world economy.

Partnerships between industry and the public schools represent a third type of reorganization. Usually partnerships concentrate on a particular problem or population. For example, a group of Texas business executives have launched a program to do something about the disproportionately small number of minority students in engineering. About 70 mathematicians and scientists from business and industry serve as tutors and role models, lecturing and conducting tours for students. About 6000 students have been enrolled in the program, and an 80% increase in minority students going to engineering colleges has been seen.

Internships without pay, which give students on-the-job experience, are a form of partnership popular for talented students. In one executive internship, students spend one semester working a four-day week for a sponsoring organization in their field of interest. Each student functions as a special assistant to the sponsor, attending meetings and conferences and becoming involved in everything from answering telephones and typing to devising computer programs and preparing reports and studies.

The responsibility of business and industry to provide its own training and development is an issue. U.S. business has been slow to respond to changing workforce needs. A 1992 study by Jobs of the Future found that less than 5% of the nation's companies were doing significant training, and what training was actually going on was targeted almost exclusively on management.[33] Of the $30 billion spent annually by business on training, $27 billion comes from 15,000 employers—about 0.5% of U.S. businesses.[34]

Trends in Vocational Education

Vocational education in schools is responding to two contradictory impulses. On the one hand, it is a progressive innovation that introduces broad content—the development of attitudes toward work, basic communication skills, and knowledge of mathematics and science. On the other hand, it is dictated by economic rationalism aimed at sorting and ranking students as productive workers. National and local interests influence decisions about the particular occupations or fields that vocational education should serve. Congress, through its vocational education acts, has influenced curriculum by demanding that recipients of vocational education funds teach job-specific skills and assist students from low-income families to go straight from high school into the job market—a current influence on academic as well as technical preparation and postsecondary education.

Today's programs go beyond teaching simple vocational tasks and include problem solving and team work. Specialization in a specific occupation tends to be seen as the responsibility of employers and the more than 8000 private technical and modern venture schools.

Current players struggle with how best to respond to the young people who enter the workforce directly after high school or who drop out before graduation and do not have the skills for earning a good living in a high tech economy. In 2002, only about 30% of high school graduates went directly to college and nearly half of them did not complete the college program. Internships, apprenticeships, pre-employment training, adult education programs, specialist schools, and distance education are a few of the structural changes redefining the whole role of vocational education.

MORAL EDUCATION

Phenix's Basic Questions in Moral Education

The late Philip Phenix defined the basic question in moral education as one about the values, standards, or norms, and the sources and justification for these norms.[35] He saw four approaches that can be taken: the *nihilistic* position (morality is meaningless), the *autonomic* position (each individual must create his or her own values), the *heteronomic* position (the laws of God should rule human conduct), and the *telenomic* position (morality must continually be discovered).

The Nihilistic Position The nihilistic position is a denial that there are any standards of right or wrong. Nihilists hold that all human endeavor is meaningless and without purpose. This position contradicts the notion of education as a purposeful improving activity.

---

[33]Jonathan Neisman, "Skills in the Schools: Now It's Business's Turn," *Phi Delta Kappan* 74, no. 5 (Jan. 1993): 367–369.

[34]Economic Change and the American Workforce, *Research and Evaluation Report Series 92-b* (Washington, DC: U.S. Department of Labor, Employment and Training Administration, 1992).

[35]Philip H. Phenix, "The Moral Imperative in Contemporary American Education," *Perspectives on Education* 11, no. 2 (winter 1969): 6–14.

The Autonomic Position The view that norms or values are defined by each person is the cornerstone of the autonomic position. The individual invests in existence with meaning. Advocates of this view believe that values are created by individuals and social groups and that all standards are relative to the persons and societies that make them. The implications of this position for curriculum are many. Inasmuch as human beings make their own values, their schools should *not* teach people how they *ought* to behave. All one can teach is how a particular person or group has decided to behave. Students then learn to adjust to a variety of values to maintain a harmonious society. As Phenix says, "It is not a question of learning what is right or wrong, but what is socially expedient." This position transforms ethical issues into political ones without reference to moral ends. It is not a question of what is good or right but of who has the power to prevail. Also, it causes the curriculum to be judged in terms of its effectiveness in promoting autonomous interests and demands.

The Heteronomic Position The heteronomic position asserts that known standards and values can be taught and can provide clear norms of judgment for human conduct. People do not make values, they discover them. These moral laws are sometimes seen as originating from a divine source. Sometimes they are regarded as rationally and intuitively deduced demands, apprehended by moral sensibility. Curriculum persons who hold the heteronomic position urge the adoption of strong religious or ethical programs to restore lost values to the young. They also have a pedagogical commitment to transmit established standards of belief and conduct.

Phenix himself believed that each of the previously mentioned positions fails to provide a basis for moral education. The nihilistic position cuts the nerve of moral inquiry and negates moral conscience. The autonomic position substitutes political strategy for morality and allows no objective basis for judging the worth of human creations. The heteronomic position is characterized by ethnocentrism and is untenable in light of the staggering multiplicity of norms by which people have lived.

The Telenomic Position The telenomic theory holds that morality is grounded on a comprehensive purpose or *telos,* which is objective and normative but forever transcends concrete institutional embodiment or ideology. It rests on the belief that persons should engage in a progressive discovery of what they ought to do—a dedication to an objective order of values. The moral enterprise is seen as a venture of faith but not a blind adherence to a set of precepts that cannot be rationally justified. People preserve what is right through the imperfect institutions of society. They know, however, that these institutions are subject to criticism and held up to an ideal order that can never be attained. A curriculum in accordance with the telenomic outlook would foster moral inquiry as a lifelong practice. This person would want to do right, not merely be satisfied in getting his or her own way. A person who holds the telenomic position would also see that what is right is a complicated matter, that personal judgments are made on the basis of his or her experience, and that these judgments are extremely partial and unreliable. Hence, a person needs to associate with others who can correct his or her misunderstandings and introduce other perspectives. The learner also would perceive that every value determination is subject to further scrutiny and revision in light of new understandings.

In the domain of moral education, the schools develop skills in moral deliberation through focus on personal and social problems, offering relevant perspectives from a variety of specialized dimensions. For example, sex education is considered with the knowledge of biologists, physicians (conception, abortion, pathologies), psychologists (affect, motivation, sublimation), social scientists (family, patterns of sexual behavior in diverse cultures), humanists (literary meaning of sex, historical perspectives), and philosophers and theologians (creation, nature, the destiny of the person, the meaning of human relations, the sanctity of the person, the significance of loyalty). In the end, persons respond in conscience to the issue. What matters from an educational standpoint is that the decision emerges from a well-informed mind, not from haphazard impulses or personal history.

Kohlberg's Theory of Moral Development

Much of the current writing regarding moral education in schools features the work of Edward Wynne, Kevin Ryan, and the late Lawrence Kohlberg, who offer contrasting views of moral development. Their approaches, however, are not as comprehensive as Phenix's, which deals with all dimensions of moral behavior, not merely the intellectual. Kohlberg attempted to define stages of moral development ranging from the learner's response to cultural values of good and bad to the making of decisions on the basis of universal principles of justice.[36] He regards his stages as stages of moral reasoning. Thus his assessment of the learner's status is made by analyzing the learner's responses to hypothetical problems or moral dilemmas. Kohlberg admits that a person can reason in terms of principles and not live up to these principles. He defends his work by claiming that the narrow focus on moral judgment is the most important factor in moral behavior. Other factors, which admittedly influence moral behavior, are not distinctly moral because there can be no moral behavior without informed moral judgment.

In trying to stimulate moral development, Kohlberg and his followers expose the learner to the next higher stage of moral reasoning, present contradictions to the child's current moral structure, and allow a dialogue in which conflicting moral views are openly compared. Furthermore, their curriculum in English and social studies centers on moral discussions and communication and on relating the government and justice in the school to that of the American society and other societies.

The chief criticism of Kohlberg's view of moral education is that he has omitted important dimensions of the subject. He does not allow for utilitarian ideas of morality in which principles of justice can be problematic. As will be discussed in the next section, several prominent women scholars assert that his theory does not take into account girls' and women's moral perceptions. In addition, Kohlberg has been faulted for not emphasizing the need for conventional morality among all citizens in order for a society to function. He fails to appreciate that moral rules often have to be learned in spite of the temptation to ignore them. He has not attended to the affective dimensions of morality such as guilt, remorse, and concern for others, and he offers no suggestions for developing other factors, such as will, which are necessary in moral conduct.

Caring Responses to Kohlberg's Theory Carol Gilligan, in her book *In a Different Voice*, provided the seminal feminist critique of Kohlberg's theory, arguing that this model rests on limited psychological perspectives going back to Sigmund Freud, Jean Piaget, and Erik Erikson that privilege male conceptions of self and justice. Rather than accepting Kohlberg's hierarchy, based on upholding principles of justice as the highest standard for morality, Gilligan, drawing on a number of psychological research studies, argues that girls and women tend to value relationships and make moral decisions by weighing contexts and relationships, rather than following absolute moral principles.[37] Here she distinguishes two types of "moral judgment" or "moral voices," one based on "care" and the

[36]Lawrence Kohlberg, "The Claim to Moral Adequacy of a Highest Stage of Moral Judgment," *Journal of Philosophy* 70, no. 18 (Oct. 25, 1973): 631–646.

[37]Carol Gilligan, *In a Different Voice: Psychological Theory and Women's Development* (Cambridge: Harvard University Press, 1982).

other on "justice." According to Gilligan, "One voice speaks of connection, not hurting, care, and response; and one speaks of equality, reciprocity, justice, and rights."[38] She continues, "The activities of care—being there, listening, the willingness to help, and the ability to understand—take on a moral dimension, reflecting the injunction to pay attention and not turn away from need." While avoiding absolutes, Gilligan concludes that these conceptions are "gender related," with women tending to focus on care and men on justice.[39] Further research is needed to see whether these distinctions between "care" and "justice" also apply in a range of cultures.

CHARACTER EDUCATION

During the 1960s through early 1980s, values clarification dominated moral education and the teaching of ethics. In values clarification the teachers draw out the child's opinion about issues in which values conflict, rather than impose their opinions.[40] Values clarificationists think that the exploration of personal preferences helps people to (1) be more purposeful because they must rank their priorities; (2) be more productive because they analyze where their activities are taking them; (3) be more critical because they learn to see through the foolishness of others; and (4) be better able to handle relations with others. An individual has a value when a choice or belief is chosen freely from alternatives and after careful consideration of the consequences of each alternative; when the value is prized and publicly affirmed; and when it is acted on regularly. This approach has been criticized for not going beyond helping students become more aware of their own values and for assuming that there is no single correct answer. Learners discuss moral dilemmas to reveal different values. Other criticisms center on its reliance on peer pressure (the bias of many of the questions used in the process), its premature demand for public affirmation and action, and its moral relativism.

However, during the late 1980s, as leading values educator Howard Kirschenbaum recounts, a major shift occurred from values clarification to character education. In the early 2000s, character education continues to gain predominance in K–12 schools in the face of youth violence, moral relativism, changing sexual mores, unchecked materialism, and civic apathy.[40]

In the 1980s character education had a more limited focus, which currently some of the more conservative approaches still share. Edward Wynne and Kevin Ryan represent the traditionalists in their character education approach.[41] Their curriculum consists of eight ethical ideals—such as justice, fortitude, faith, and duty—derived from Judeo-Christian values and the Greek-Roman tradition that enriched them. Students are to know the moral heritage or principles and learn to apply them in various situations. Students are to be introduced to literature that reflects the desired moral facts and ideals, including those that would envelop them with heroic individuals and images. The lives and works of contemporary people exemplifying virtue are to be examined, and students are expected to take moral action in the classroom by doing their assignments well, volunteering to help the

---

[38]Carol Gilligan, "Remapping the Moral Domain: New Images of Self in Relationship," in *Mapping the Moral Domain: A Contribution of Women's Thinking to Psychological Theory and Education*, Carol Gilligan et al., eds. (Cambridge: Harvard Center for the Study of Gender, Education and Human Development, 1988): 8.
[39]Ibid., 16.
[40]Howard Kirschenbaum, "From Values Clarification to Character Education: A Personal Journey," *Journal of Humanistic Counseling, Education, and Development* 39, no. 1 (Sept. 2000): 4–20.
[41]Edward A. Wynne and Kevin Ryan, *Reclaiming Our Schools: Teaching Character, Academics, and Discipline*, 2nd ed. (Upper Saddle River, NJ: Merrill, 1997).

teacher or others, and participating respectfully in ceremonies such as reciting the Pledge of Allegiance.

The focus of this type of character education differs from other forms of moral education in that it endorses a specific content of moral virtues (honesty, kindness, courage) to be learned, whereas other approaches emphasize reason and value selection. Proponents of character education do not always agree on the values to be taught or the meaning of given values; "Does 'honesty' only involve no lying or does it also require volunteering the truth when the situation calls for it?"[42] A second area of controversy surrounding more limited forms of character education is the concern that it indoctrinates students. The student is taught to behave in specific ways without a self-conscious understanding of why and without the option of questioning, accepting, or rejecting the beliefs.

During the 1990s, character education became more expansive in its goals and approaches. Newer programs, which have continued into the new millennium, expand the more traditional focus on values, virtues, and justice to also embrace caring social relationships, personal and civic responsibility, democratic ideals, and multicultural understandings.[43] Beginning with respect for each person's cultural identity and unique background, David W. Johnson and Roger T. Johnson's comprehensive human relations program focuses on respect across cultures, cooperation, peacekeeping, civic values, and increased understandings by honoring diversity.[44] There is also an increase in integrated approaches—that is, using literature and history to probe moral ambiguities and provide ethical lessons to inspire learners with the virtuous qualities of the men and women studied. Character education has taken on increased importance in terms of building positive social relationships in schools.

SCHOOL SAFETY*

While school safety has always been a major concern to educators, the shattering events at Columbine High School in 1999 changed forever how Americans view public schools. Numerous administrators, security, and counseling changes have occurred in schools after the Columbine shootings to prevent weapons on campus and provide early interventions. In addition, this tragic event gave rise to new challenges for curriculum planners.

Recent practice, research, and theory on school safety stress the need for comprehensive approaches that address the complexities of youth violence. Administrators Jerome R. Belair and Paul Freeman believe that each school must focus on physical, emotional, and social safety and "create a learning space in which children—their bodies, hearts, and minds—are protected."[45] In addition to security measures, equally important for a safe school, according to Belair and Freeman, are a positive school culture, respectful interactions, caring, responsive adults, and a curriculum that seeks "to empower the students themselves, to make them actors rather than victims within the school."[46] In a 2002

---

[42]Ivor Pritchard, *Character Education: Analysis of Research Projects and Problems* (Washington, DC: Office of Educational Research and Improvement, U.S. Department of Education, April 1988).

[43]Edward F. DeRoche and Mary M. Williams, *Educating Hearts and Minds: A Comprehensive Character Education Framework*, 2nd ed. (Thousand Oaks, CA: Corwin Press, 2001).

[44]David W. Johnson and Roger T. Johnson, *Multicultural Human Relations: Valuing Diversity* (Boston: Allyn and Bacon, 2002).

*School Safety was written by Jaye Darby and is included with her permission.

[45]Pam Schiffbauer, "A Checklist for Safe Schools," *Educational Leadership* 57, no. 6 (March 2000): 72–74.

[46]Jerome R. Belair and Paul Freeman, "Protecting Bodies, Hearts, and Minds in School," *Middle School Journal* 31, no. 5 (May 2000): 3.

research review of successful prevention programs for peer violence and suicide, Richard J. Hazler and Jolynn V. Carney also report the significance of approaches that increase student empathy, initiative, and empowerment.[47]

Reece L. Peterson and Russell Skiba stress the importance of improving "school climates" to create safe schools. They offer a comprehensive schoolwide approach through five integrated components: (a) parent and community involvement, (b) character education, (c) violence-prevention and conflict-resolution curricula, (d) peer mediation, and (e) bullying prevention.[48] Peterson and Skiba also found that school policies and programs that focus on prevention, rather than punishment, provide early interventions, teach conflict resolution, help young people learn alternatives to violence, and create a sense of community are integral to school safety.[49] According to Bonnie Bernard, a growing body of research on nurturing children's and adolescents' development from "at-risk" to resilient supports the crucial importance of supportive school environments and caring relationships.[50]

While a number of school safety programs exist, two focus on empowerment and strive to change hearts and minds by actively engaging young people in alternatives to violence and conflict. These are Students Against Violence Everywhere (SAVE) at West Charlotte High School in memory of Alex Orange, a 17-year-old football player, shot trying to stop a fight at a party. Since then SAVE has grown into a national program that encourages active student involvement in school safety through three core areas: crime prevention, conflict management, and service projects.[51] Within these areas, SAVE offers a range of student-centered, student-initiated approaches to peer mediation, respectful peer relations, conflict resolution, civic responsibility, nonviolence, and community service. At the elementary school level, children study safety issues in integrated content units and coconstruct safety rules with their teacher. At the middle school and high school level, young people with chapter advisors participate in extracurricular chapter activities and community service projects.

The Tariq Khamisa Foundation recently developed a nonviolence program for San Diego schools to encourage peaceful resolutions and help young people choose alternatives to violence. Like SAVE, this program began with a tragedy. In 1995, Tariq Khamisa, a 21-year-old college student, was delivering pizzas in a San Diego neighborhood when he was gunned down by Tony Hicks, a 14-year-old boy in a gang. Guided by a spirit of forgiveness and a desire to break the cycle of youth violence, Tariq's father, Azim Khamisa, a Muslim businessman, believed there were "victims at both ends of the gun." He then worked with Tony's grandfather, Ples Felix, to found the foundation in memory of Tariq to stop youth violence and promote peace.[52] To further the foundation's mission, "Building a New Generation of Peacemakers," Khamisa and Felix developed the Violence Impact Forum (VIF) for San Diego schools, grades 4–7. Through the stories of Tariq and Tony and the example of the two men, this forum first helps students understand the devastating consequence of gun violence to both the victim and the perpetrator and then offers nonviolent, peaceful alternatives to gangs, violence, and vengeance.[53]

---

[47]Richard J. Hazler and Jolynn V. Carney, "Empowering Peers to Prevent Youth Violence," *Journal of Humanistic Counseling, Education, and Development* 41, no. 1 (fall 2002): 129–149.

[48]Reece L. Peterson and Russell Skiba, "Creating School Climates That Prevent School Violence," *The Clearing House* 74, no. 3 (Jan./Feb. 2001): 156.

[49]Russ Skiba and Reece Peterson, "The Dark Side of Zero Tolerance: Can Punishment Lead to Safe Schools?" *Phi Delta Kappan* 80, no. 5 (Jan. 1999): 372–376, 381–382.

[50]Bonnie Bernard, *Resiliency: What We Have Learned* (San Francisco: WestED, 2004).

[51]National Association of Students against Violence Everywhere, URL: http://www.nationalsave.org.

[52]Azim Khamisa with Carl Goldman, *Azim's Bardo: A Father's Journey from Murder to Forgiveness* (Los Altos, CA: Rising Star Press, 1998).

[53]Tariq Khamisa Foundation, URL: http://www.tfk.org.

CONCLUDING COMMENTS

Curriculum issues regarding thinking, vocational education, international comparisons, moral and character education, and safe schools point out the serious problems that schools everywhere face—how to design instruction that will enable underprivileged students to have success with content formerly available only to an elite population. At this point, both the democratic proponents of equality and participatory politics and the capitalistic proponents of individual excellence favor intellectual achievement of everyone—the former because such achievement promises access to power, the latter because they view the intellectual development of workers as a key to international market competition.

Concern about an underachieving curriculum and the restructuring of vocational education reflects the economic and liberatory perspectives. Comparative education studies show the United States lagging behind other competing nations in addressing concerns for student willingness and ability to use school in lifetime learning.

The moral curriculum raises old curriculum questions: What is the meaning of morality? Should morality be taught? Can it be taught? Is it possible to teach in an amoral manner? Alternatives to school violence are important because they fit in with a growing interest in the rights of children and because they give us a chance to redefine the purpose of schools.

Most curriculum issues involve two fundamental concerns. Dedicated persons have sensed that aspects of the curriculum are not consistent with the premise that every human being is important, regardless of racial, national, social, economic, and mental status. Exploitation of learners by the denial of minority values and a stratified and narrowly defined vocational curriculum are a few examples. Also, more persons are aware that the opportunity for wide participation in the cultural resources of the society is a fundamental right. Hence, a broader vocational education, an emphasis on thinking, and multicultural education are offered as new resources for the creation of knowledge as well as access to wider cultural capital.

QUESTIONS

1. Can we teach students to use critical thinking in challenging their self-interests?

2. How can curriculum best help students realize their potential as thinkers?

3. Should trade, proprietary schools, or industry itself rather than the public schools be responsible for specialized training? Why or why not?

4. It is often assumed that vocational education can contribute to the learning of mathematics and science. How could vocational education be planned in order to enhance academic development?

5. What are the likely consequences of using each of the following approaches to moral education?

   a. Cognitive—students are encouraged to use moral reasoning.

   b. Commitment—personal and social action projects help students put their values into practice.

   c. Inculcation—students observe good models and are reinforced for certain desirable social human behavior.

   d. Clarification—through such exercises as thinking about things in their lives that they would like to celebrate, students are led to define their values.

SUGGESTED STRATEGIC RESEARCH

EXPLORING CRITICAL THINKING IN COMPULSORY CLASSROOMS

If our goal is to open minds and motivate students to think critically or to learn to think critically about their lives, students need an opportunity to engage in great issues that concern them, not just memorize and be tested on facts and events nor forbidden to think about controversial topics such as war, parenting, religion, and cultural differences. Choose an issue and form a focus group(s) comprising a teacher and four randomly drawn students. Determine the balance given to facts, events, and ideas versus reflecting on the meaning of this issue as it relates to their concerns and the human condition. To what extent does the classroom free students from the bias of official textbooks and the school curriculum? Are teachers liberating students' minds from cultural narrowness and awakening intelligent thought?

COMPARING LOCAL PERFORMANCE STATISTICS WITH PISA INTERNATIONAL RANKINGS

Obtain PISA performance statistics from the U.S. Office of Statistics and then compare performance in a given domain on the same measures from a school district or school of interest to you. Consider the implications of your findings and appropriate audiences.

VALIDATING A HIGH SCHOOL, COMMUNITY COLLEGE, AND INDUSTRY VOCATIONAL ALIGNMENT PROGRAM

Select a vocational program that aligns secondary school curriculum with postsecondary courses and apprenticeships leading to a certificate or purporting to offer a clear path to a community college education and a technical occupation. Determine the percentage of high school students who participated in the programs and how many continued. How many finished? How many secured a degree or found employment? Do completers differ from the dropouts? Why did students drop out? What are the employment opportunities for completers versus dropouts?

UNDERSTANDING A SCHOOL'S APPROACH TO MORAL DEVELOPMENT

Although historically teachers have been given the responsibility for moral development, state and district policies may have usurped teacher efforts. Form a research team to find out in a school what teachers of science, math, history, physical education, literature, and the like are doing about the political and moral issues provoked by these subjects—the environment, nuclear energy, biological life and experimentation, health, and the like. Is there commonality in their approaches? How do they take into account the views of parents or administrators regarding moral issues?

HELPING MARGINALIZED STUDENTS RECLAIM THEIR VOICE

Schools are unhappy places when some students are marginalized because of race, gender, and social class. After being marginalized, many students try to find a place for themselves in an environment where school subjects and the prevailing stereotypes held by teachers and peers impact negatively. To what extent might marginalization exist in a school or classroom of your interest? How are different aspects of student identity affirmed, rejected, or normalized in this situation? Is there (mis)behaving as a consequence? What do the marginalized say and do? What is said about them? Can you improve the situation by helping all imagine new possibilities?

SELECTED REFERENCES

THINKING

BLAKE, NAGEL, PAUL SMEYERS, RICHARD SMITH, AND PAUL STANDISH, EDS. *The Blackwell Guide to the Philosophy of Education.* Oxford: Blackwell, 1994.

WILSON, DAVID C. *A Guide to Good Reasoning.* Boston: McGraw-Hill, 1999.

VOCATIONAL EDUCATION

BAILEY, THOMAS R., KATHERINE L. HUGHES, AND DAVID THORNTON MOORE. *Working Knowledge: Work-Based Learning and Education Reform.* New York: Routledge Falmer, 2004.

CSIKSZENTMIHALYI, MIHALY, AND BARBARA SCHNEIDER. *Being Adult: How Teenagers Prepare for the World of Work.* New York: Basic Books, 2000.

WASHINGTON, WARREN. *An Emerging and Critical Problem of the Science and Engineering Labor Force.* Washington, DC: National Science Foundation, May 2004.

COMPARATIVE EDUCATION

DE LAKER, GARY. *National Standards and School Reform: Japan and the United States.* New York: Teachers College Press, 2004.

GOODMAN, ROGER, AND DAVID PHILLIPS, EDS. *Can the Japanese Change Their Educational System?* Oxford Studies in Comparative Education. Oxford: Oxford Symposium Books, 2003.

MORAL AND CHARACTER CURRICULUM

DEROCHE, EDWARD F., AND MARY M. WILLIAMS. *Educating Hearts and Minds: A Comprehensive Character Education Framework*, 2nd ed. Thousand Oaks, CA: Corwin, 2001.

JACKSON, PHILLIP W., ROBERT E. BOOSTROM, AND DAVID T. HANSEN. *The Moral Life of Schools.* San Francisco: Jossey-Bass, 1993.

JOHNSON, DAVID W., AND ROGER T. JOHNSON. *Multicultural Education and Human Relations: Valuing Diversity.* Boston: Allyn and Bacon, 2002.

SCHOOL SAFETY

BARNARD, BONNIE. *Resiliency: What We Have Learned.* San Francisco, CA: WestED, 2004.

National Association of Students against Violence Everywhere. URL: http://www.nationalsave.org.

CHAPTER 12

DIRECTIONS IN THE SUBJECT FIELDS

THE MATERIAL in this chapter is arranged chronologically, though more in the sense of trends than as a detailed recital of events. The chapter is intended to reveal the nature of the various subject fields in the past, describe the directions they are now taking, and provoke a consideration of the forces that should and should not shape them in the future.

It is pointed out that swings in emphasis within the subject fields reflect a difference of opinion about the nature of knowledge. Some view knowledge of subject matter as a tool for resolving problems; others think of it as a series of disciplines for developing the intellect; and some think that subject matter knowledge means access to one's own accrued and personally organized resources. Furthermore, it will be seen how political compromises made by policy makers to accommodate those of different curriculum orientations have resulted in conflicting purposes and incoherent programs. It should be clear that a trend at the policy level is not always reflected at the classroom level.

Discrepancies in subject fields can be viewed in a positive manner. The conflicts are evidence that there are no universal principles that fix curriculum in one direction. Instead, the contradictions can be seen as opportunities for creating dialogue, for considering new possibilities, and for clarifying one's own understanding of the subject.

MATHEMATICS

Mathematics in Our Schools

Before the 1950s, schools commonly taught mathematics around one central theme: student mastery of basic computational skills. This practical yet simplistic approach to mathematics instruction did not suit the nation's increasing need for theoretical mathematicians and scientists. By the early 1960s, a new trend in mathematics instruction had emerged—student acquisition of mathematics as a discipline. Two influences helped set this trend in motion.

The first influence reflected the above-mentioned need for competent and creative scientists. The other influence on the mathematics curriculum was the belief that everyone could profit by acquiring knowledge of mathematics as a discipline. Briefly stated, the belief was that math and other subject matter fields should introduce students to the general concepts, principles, and laws that members of a discipline use in problem solving.

The new math consisted of the fundamental assumptions and conceptual theories on which every scientific enterprise is based. Unfortunately, it was deprecated for being abstract, just as the old math was criticized for being boring. For the average student, sophisticated conceptual theories had little practical relevancy. Instruction in topics such as set theory and use of bases other than the generally used base 10 replaced practice in the basic skills needed for everyday problem solving. Developers of the new math paid too little attention to the practical uses of mathematics in the student's present and future life. Hence, many specialists in mathematics argued that the school should stress a knowledge of mathematics as an end in itself, as a satisfying intellectual task. On the other hand, in order for knowledge to be meaningful, it must be applied. The main question regarding the mathematics curriculum is whether it can be useful both for development of the intellect and for the necessities of a technological era and still avoid a meaningless idealism on the one hand and a strict vocationalism on the other.

Both modern and traditional mathematics are found in today's schools. The move toward traditional mathematics results from the emphasis on basics such as computational skills, whereas the move toward modern mathematics results from a concern for bright students. A survey of the status of mathematics in secondary schools indicates that traditional mathematics courses—courses that feature drill and practice, computation, and memorization—are taken by slower students and students not planning on college, not by students who tend to major in mathematics.[1] The latter still take modern mathematics, algebra, geometry, and optional fourth-year courses which place strong emphasis on structure, definitions, properties, sets, proofs, and other abstract concepts.

Trends in Mathematics

To facilitate the application of knowledge, three new directions have been suggested for future trends in mathematics. The first trend is an integration of mathematics with other subject matter. Opponents of the new math from its inception have proposed that mathematics be studied not as a separate theoretical discipline but as an integrated part of liberal education. Integration of subject matter facilitates the application of mathematical skills to a variety of situations. The importance of mathematical skills in all subjects from homemaking to physics should be stressed.

Increased use of educational technology is a second trend through which mathematics can be made more relevant. The U.S. Department of Education has funded programs to develop a television series on mathematics designed to show how it may be applied to all occupations and problem-solving situations. The series supplements the teacher, who continues with regular computational skills. It is staged with characters using basic mathematical skills to solve problems relating to measurement, quantity, estimation, and so forth. Technology in the larger sense is also having an effect on the mathematics curriculum. The mathematics educators recommend that calculators and computers be introduced into the mathematics classroom as early as possible.[2] Young children are expected to understand negative numbers and exponents. The use of calculators in all classes requires emphasis on the language of calculators—on decimals, fractions, and algebraic symbols. Less emphasis is placed on pencil and paper arithmetic and more opportunity given for

[1]Nathalie J. Gehrke, Michael S. Knapp, and Kenneth Sirotnik, "In Search of the School Curriculum," in *Review of Research in Education* (Washington, DC: American Educational Research Association, 1992), 51–111.
[2]Patricia F. Campbell and James T. Fry, "New Goals for School Mathematics," in *Content of the Curriculum*, Ronald Brandt, ed. (Alexandria, VA: Association for Supervision and Curriculum Development, 1989).

mental arithmetic, estimation, and approximation. The availability of calculators allows expansion of the traditional program to include numbers of greater magnitude. Teachers are able to spend more time on concrete representations of concepts because they can check instantly for student understanding. Patterns can be detected more easily.

Community participation in curriculum planning and implementation is a third way of increasing the relevancy of instruction in mathematics. In the elementary school, use of parents as tutors, teacher's aides, and resource persons not only helps to reduce cost but also provides a balance between classroom and community perspectives. When middle school students in a poverty area became disturbed by 13 liquor stores in the neighborhood of the school and decided to do something about getting officials to address the blight, they had to decide how to present their findings—should it be with percentages, decimals, or fractions? What would make the best impression in this presentation? By the way, as a result of their effort, two liquor stores were removed and a city resolution was passed requiring no liquor store within 600 feet of the school.[3] In the secondary school, visiting mathematics lecturers from industry and opportunities for work experience can narrow the gap between classroom theory and practical application.

Concerns about curriculum content and about ways to develop ideas appropriate to the child's level persist. In their attempts to teach computation, some people ignore concepts and processes for developing proficiency, defining the curriculum as a series of isolated skills to be taught by drill. Also, the role of application and problem solving is far from clear. Incidentalists argue that systematic instruction in abstractions should be replaced by general problem-solving experiences from the real world. Mathematics, they believe, should be taught in relation to other areas such as cooking, building, and sewing. Others advocate experience in mathematical areas that closely resemble the physical world, such as measurement and geometry.

The immediate solution for these issues and concerns seems to be in the direction of a balanced curriculum. Content will be broadened beyond the teaching of whole number ideas in the primary grades. Ideas of symmetry and congruence will be explored. Shapes will be discussed and classified, and measurement and graphing will be popular. Metrics, of course, is necessary. Informal experiences with important mathematical ideas may contribute to greater success in future learning and to application in daily life. A balanced point of view also implies the use of different instructional procedures. No single mathematics program is suitable for all children. Briefly, the balanced curriculum means overcoming an undue focus on skills, mathematical content, and application. Evaluations confirmed that the "back to basics" movement produced improvement in precisely those mathematic abilities that are least important in a rapidly changing, technological society. Computational facility improved, but children failed to solve problems in mathematics. Teachers who follow the policies of the National Council of Teachers of Mathematics (NCTM) stress the interdependence of the following three factors. First, techniques are designed to help learners focus on specific elements and solve problems on their own. Second, a variety of strategies or ways to solve problems are encouraged. Third, children are given opportunities to relate events to mathematical models by estimating, applying estimated abilities in other situations, developing criteria for comparing lengths, noting the regularities of the coordinate system in the real world, and modifying or imposing order on a real situation and then summarizing it in mathematical form.[4] Indeed these guidelines were the basis for the National Standards for Mathematics in the 1990s. It is important to note that the NCTM has wanted valid math content for all students, not just the college-bound.

---

[3]Stephen Pape et al., "Realizing Reform in School Mathematics," *Theory into Practice* 40, no. 2 (spring 2001).
[4]National Council of Teachers of Mathematics, *An Agenda for Action: Recommendations for School Mathematics of the 1980s* (Reston, VA: National Council of Teachers of Mathematics, 1983).

Reaction to the math standards of the 1990s was mixed. Traditionalists were uncomfortable that the standards did not lay out topics to be covered at every grade but instead included discrete math, statistics, and math models applied to the real world across all grades. Geometry patterns and statistics at the elementary school were an innovation as was decreased attention to long division. Some were concerned about a loss of computational skills. Many teachers were unprepared to abandon their sharing of procedures for solving decontextualized problems and to use construction methods whereby students in groups tackle real-world math problems by sharing and justifying their ideas, with the teacher introducing his or her ideas for consideration. A backlash led to revising the math standards whereby content was clarified by grade level and teachers were given examples of problems, student work, and illustrative classroom dialogues.[5]

In higher education, the supremacy of calculus in the freshman and sophomore mathematics curriculum is being challenged in part because computer sciences changed the mathematical needs of students. Colleges and universities are initiating experimental courses in discrete mathematics, which deal with individual values and quantities. Whether discrete mathematics courses will be offered as an alternative to the traditional curriculum or integrated with it remains to be seen.

The transformation of the mathematics curriculum by which students learn mathematics as it is practiced in the discipline calls for students to evaluate their own assumptions and those of others about what is mathematically true; to reason and to engage in mathematical argument as the basis for legitimacy is underway.

Reason and argument—not the teacher or the textbook—as the basis for an idea's legitimacy is something new in the elementary mathematics classroom. Replacement units offer teachers curriculum models for teaching in accordance with the new views. These units focus on a key mathematical topic, such as multiplication, and integrate other math ideas—geometry, probability, statistics, functions—in teaching the topic. Throughout the unit, students create their own theories, investigate patterns and procedures needed to solve problems, and listen to others' perspectives in trying to construct their understanding of the topic. The replacement unit is a general plan, not a recipe; it features detailed classroom examples of student thinking and teacher responding, inviting teachers to adapt, mold, and personalize the unit to their own contexts.[6]

Three ideas that are driving changes in the mathematics curriculum are the following:

1. The American math curriculum has a great deal of repetition and review, with the result that topics are covered with little intensity. There is a loss of the notion of "a spiral curriculum," in which key concepts are revisited at deeper and more complex levels. Instead there is repetition of the same information about a difficult concept.

2. The sudden shift in focus from arithmetic to algebra is confusing to students. For example, in arithmetic, students are taught that an equation is an action statement: "Do this to these numbers, and you will get an answer." But in algebra, the notion of equivalence is often the central focus: "You can make the same change to each side of the equal sign, and the equivalence does not change."

3. Similarly, the deep and persistent misconceptions of students about mathematical operations and concepts have insidious consequences. In concluding that mathematics is a collection of procedures that have to be learned, many students do not construct the powerful meanings for the concepts and the ability to use them in real-world situations.

[5]National Council of Teachers of Mathematics, *Principles and Standards of School Mathematics* (Reston, VA: National Council of Teachers of Mathematics, 2000).

[6]*They're Counting on Us! Mathematical Power for Our Children's Future* (Santa Barbara, CA: Coalition for Mathematics, 1993).

Two national efforts to transform the mathematics curriculum are those by the National Council of Teachers of Mathematics (NCTM) and the National Academy of Sciences (NAS). NCTM's Curriculum Standards Committee has set five general goals for students in K–12 math education: (1) becoming a mathematical problem solver, (2) communicating mathematically, (3) valuing mathematics, (4) developing confidence in math, and (5) reasoning mathematically.[7]

The Mathematics Science Education Board of the NAS explored the math curriculum for the year 2000.[8] This board issued a prototype of what it expected students to be able to do.[9] Also, the National Science Foundation (NSF) supported projects aimed at finding ways to revamp the elementary curriculum by integrating calculators and computers, introducing statistical thinking, and introducing algebra early.

As indicated in Chapter 11, international comparisons of math achievement are centering less on the learning of procedures and algorithms independent of context and more on whether students are acquiring the functional skills and willingness to use math in reaching their own goals and pursuing educational and employment opportunities. Priority is given to students' ability to use math knowledge to solve conceptual problems. In light of cultural diversity and inequity, the United States has a major challenge in how to connect math practices with local communities and diverse cultures.[10]

SCIENCE

Evolution of Science Teaching

All branches of the scientific enterprise depend on the principles and laws of mathematics as a foundation for both theory and methodology. Because of this dependency, curriculum trends in the sciences often parallel those applied to mathematics. Science subject matter in the early 1960s was shaped by the same forces that influenced mathematics, namely, the proposal to teach subjects as disciplines and the push toward specialization. These forms particularly affected the sciences because it was felt that advancements in a technological society required the training of highly skilled scientists and technicians.

Science subject matter at this time was conceptually and theoretically sophisticated. Students were introduced to the principles of science through the discovery process of simple experimentation. This instructional approach replaced the more traditional process of memorizing theorems and laws. It was hoped that this approach would endow students with the inquiry mode of thought used by specialists in the scientific disciplines. Science projects in the early 1960s were heavily funded and resulted in a number of new programs. Children were encouraged to participate in scientific research on a very theoretical level. Science fairs enabled more advanced students to gain recognition as practicing members of the science discipline.

During the late 1960s, the discipline approach to science instruction was criticized for dwelling too long on theory and ignoring the need for practical application. Science in schools had been too specialized to be successfully applied to anything other than scientific research. For students uninterested in pursing science as a career, the new subject matter

[7]*Curriculum and Evaluation Standards for School Mathematics* (Reston, VA: National Council of Teachers of Mathematics, 1989).

[8]*Moving Beyond Myths: Revitalizing Undergraduate Mathematics* (Washington, DC: National Academy Press, 1991).

[9]*A Measuring Up: Prototypes for Mathematics Assessment* (Washington, DC: National Academy Press, 1992).

[10]"Diversity, Equity, and Mathematical Thinking," *Mathematical Thinking and Learning* 4, nos. 2 and 3 (2002).

had little practical relevancy. The average student could not identify the role of science in the common affairs and problems of people. Also, Americans were becoming increasingly concerned about societal implications of the scientific enterprise. Prior demands for research relating to space exploration and national defense had distracted scientists' attention from the problems of air pollution, overpopulation, and depletion of natural resources. Scientists had neglected to study the relationship of research to the individual's place in the universe.

As a result of this neglect, a new trend to humanize the sciences emerged in the 1970s. Accordingly, some multidisciplinary approaches to instruction appeared. Basic laws of science were applied to a variety of situations in subjects other than science. Science teachers sometimes worked in teams with teachers from other disciplines and helped students relate principles of science to current social, political, and economic problems. Students majoring in social science studied the relationship of scientific discoveries to industrial and technological revolutions. The role of the scientific enterprise in international policy making was sometimes studied in political science courses. However, by the mid-1970s, significant numbers of citizens felt that support for curriculum in science was misdirected, if not in error. In the elementary school, the press for higher scores on tests and an emphasis on isolated skills of reading and mathematics meant that science was seldom taught at all. Enrollment in high school science courses steadily decreased, with more than 50% of high school students taking no science after the tenth grade. By the late 1970s, science courses had given way to rote learning, with 90% of teachers using only a traditional textbook approach. By 1984, it was clear that there was a crisis in science education. The U.S. Government Printing Office announced the following about the status of the science curriculum:

1. A mismatch exists between the science curriculum and that which 90% of the students want and need.

2. Nearly all science teachers have goals that are directed only toward preparing students for the next academic level. Science is viewed as specific content to be mastered.

3. Nearly all science teachers use a textbook 95% of the time. Science is virtually never being learned by direct experiences, and most students never experience a real experiment throughout their school program.

4. No attention is given to the development of a science curriculum; the textbook is the course outline, the framework, the testing, and the view of science.

5. The science program is ineffective in influencing interest in science or scientific literacy. Teaching by textbook summarizes the status of science education; to compound the problem, the textbooks in the early 1980s were inadequate.[11–13]

Terminology was the central feature in most science textbooks. The new vocabulary in typical science classrooms exceeded the vocabulary necessary for mastering a foreign language. Indeed, more than 10,000 specialized terms were introduced in the typical chemistry course in high school, which is high considering that foreign language specialists suggest that the learning of vocabulary words in a foreign language should be limited to no more than 2000 new words a year. Too many terms were introduced apart from their meaning.

---

[11]Norris C. Harms and R. E. Yager, *What Research Says to the Science Teacher* (Washington, DC: National Science Teachers Association, 1981).
[12]R. E. Stake and J. Easley, *Case Studies in Science Education* (Urbana: University of Illinois, 1978).
[13]I. R. Weiss, *Report to the 1977 National Survey of Science, Mathematics, and Social Studies Education* (Research Triangle Park, NC: Center for Educational Research and Evaluation, 1978).

New Approaches in Science Education

As indicated in Chapter 4, experts in science education in an undertaking called Project Synthesis predicted that the life science curriculum of the future will be organized around the theme of human adaptation in both the scientific and social senses, and that the use of ethics and values as well as biological knowledge in making decisions will be an important goal of programs dealing with social problems. Scientific topics will be presented from the human point of view. Principles of science will be learned, not as ends in themselves, but as means of coping with personal and social concerns.

The multidisciplinary approach is frequently offered as a possible solution to the problem. In addition to drawing from several scientific disciplines, this approach involves inquiry and outreach to the community, thus serving two purposes. First, it brings new depth to all disciplines. Second, it reminds us of science's relation to the political, economic, and social affairs of humankind. A major goal of science teachers in the twenty-first century will be to provide students with the basic problem-solving skills they will need to cope with an often dehumanizing technological society.

One effort in this direction is the Inquiry Training Project of Port Colborne, Ontario, Canada. This project hopes to improve students' abilities to solve problems which a person might encounter now and in the future. To this end, instead of teaching students a single direct path between questions and answers, teachers engage students in dealing with questions that give rise to a number of plausible alternatives whose desirability must be thought out and ranked. The program attempts to have children analyze cause and effect relationships, a technique that has been profitable in the sciences. With respect to method, children are given simple scientific equipment and materials from the world around them and are encouraged to experiment. A typical activity is the raising of green plants under different conditions and observing and recording the results. Another favorite practice involves fermentation. In this project, pupils are given yeast, sugar, tubing, and a few other materials. They are asked to keep track of how the rate of fermentation is affected by changes in the amount of water used and the temperature, in order to learn about control of variables and effects of such controls. Ecological projects are also popular in science courses. As they progress, children using the inquiry method are exposed to the basic concepts of many sciences, from botany and biology to physics, chemistry, and astronomy.

The broad recommendation is toward more inquiry in the science class. Two obstacles are economic and instrumental considerations. Initial investment in equipment for courses emphasizing experimentation can run as high as $500 per classroom. Also, teachers must know enough about the principles and teaching materials involved to be able to use them. One of the biggest problems in teaching science in the early grades is the teacher's insecurity about the subject matter.

Secondary schools are likely to continue to offer a few advanced science courses of high quality for the most talented students. These courses will probably be organized around the traditional topics of biology, chemistry, and physics. Although this fragmented model is under attack, such programs are now designed for a minority of students. Indeed, data from the National Longitudinal Study of the High School Class show that entry into prestigious fields of biological sciences, business, engineering, physical sciences, and mathematics can be predicted by the science and mathematics courses taken in high school.

Only 20% of all high school graduates take physics, primarily because it is usually the last course in the science sequence of biology and chemistry and, in fact, is an elective course for the sophisticated student.[14] The issue of whether science should be for the few

[14]Michael Neuschatz and Maude Covalt, *Physics in the High School* (New York: American Institute of Physics, 1989).

or the many is alive. One study concludes that science at the K–12 level should enlarge the pool of science learners rather than offer opportunities for the most able students to embark on a scientific career.[15] On the other hand, many school districts have concentrated the best science students in magnet or controlled environments, which emphasize science and attenuate the distractions that interfere with learning science.

The assumption that the best course for those with science aptitude is advanced placement is now questioned. J. Myron Atkin, for example, thinks that the high school years should be used for broad intellectual exploration rather than preparation for college-level specialization. An opportunity to study topics of special interest in depth might be a better use of high school time than a course focused on examinations.[16]

Recommendations for the Future Science Curriculum

There are several recommendations for improving the traditional courses. It is suggested that new materials be developed for use by the 70% of students now being inadequately served. These materials would deal with new areas of modern science and also would contain less encyclopedic content and detail that have little relevance to students' present problems of living. Instructional activities would be tied to the ongoing scientific enterprises in the community. Science would be treated less as an end in itself than as a field related to other aspects of life. There would be more emphasis on the power, responsibilities, and limitations of science.

The idea of having the local community serve as a learning laboratory is another recommendation. The Education Development Center in Newton, Massachusetts, has developed science projects related to issues with social implications. In one such project, *The Family and Community Health,* students have health care experiences in schools, families, and agencies in the community. Units treat such topics as adolescent pregnancy, drinking, stress, and environmental and consumer health. These projects combine ideas and skills from the natural sciences, humanities, and social sciences.

Two documentaries are shaping the science curriculum. The first is "Science for All Americans," a reform blueprint issued by the American Association for the Advancement of Science.[17] The second is "Content Core" from the Scope, Sequence, and Coordination Project of the National Science Teachers Association. The latter project is an effort to replace the current U.S. model of teaching each science in a fixed sequence—biology, chemistry, and physics—with an integrated approach.[18] Accordingly, each of the three subjects plus earth and space science is taught each year, usually starting in the seventh grade and employing hands-on approaches to problems whereby students draw on theories from any of the subjects.

Science for All Americans is the first phase of *Project 2061: Education for a Changing Future.* Instead of viewing high school science as a diluted version of college science for college-bound students, the new view is that the science curriculum should represent a common core of knowledge for all students. The blueprint of what scientifically literate persons need to know does not dwell on rote learning of classification lists but recommends that more time be given to understanding concepts such as the interdependency of living things, the flow of matter and energy, how heredity works, and what cells do.

[15]Robert Rothmer, "NSF Urged to Boost K–12 Effort," *The Scientist* 10, no. 5 (1987): 7.

[16]J. Myron Atkin, "The Improvement of Science Teaching," *Daedalus* 112, no. 2 (Spring 1983): 167–187.

[17]*Science for All Americans: Project 2061. Report on Literacy Goals in Science, Mathematics and Technology* (Washington, DC: American Association for the Advancement of Science, 1989).

[18]B. Aldridge, "Project on Scope, Sequence and Coordination: A New Synthesis for Improving Science Education," *Journal of Science Education and Technology* 17 (1992): 13–22.

Other recommendations of this first phase of Project 2061, which draws its name from the year Halley's comet returns, include the following: (1) integrating science and math with history and other disciplines (however, anathematizing science should be avoided when it makes learning science more difficult); (2) preparing students to be inquisitors and critical thinkers rather than emphasizing right answers; (3) focusing on the connections of science to the social issues of the day—population growth, environmental pollution, waste disposal, energy production, and birth control.

Instead of attempting to cover too many topics or to provide detailed knowledge of the scientific disciplines, the curriculum might help students develop a set of cogent views of the world. Such views include the structure and evaluation of the universe, the general features of the planet, basic concepts of matter, energy, force, and motion, the living environment, biological evolution, the human organism, the human life cycle, physical and mental health, medical techniques, cultural dynamics, social change and conflict, and the mathematics of symbols.

Project 2061 has indicated what progress students should make by the end of grades 2, 5, 8, and 12.[19] The project also is issuing curriculum models from which local designers can construct alternative curriculums.[20]

In 2004, the NCLB legislation altered science teaching by requiring testing of students in science by 2007. The emphasis on testing influences teachers to use direct methods of instruction instead of hands-on inquiries. The textbooks and transmission of subject matter become more important than the generating of new knowledge. However, many teachers prefer to continue lab experiments after students are introduced to basic scientific concepts. A series of undertakings by the National Research Council is underway to explore how students can learn science more effectively and how it is best taught.

Worldwide there are differences between females and males in their expected scientific occupations. Twenty percent of females expect to be in life science or health related programs compared to only 7% of males. Male students more often expect careers associated with physics, mathematics, or engineering (18% of males versus 5% of females).

International achievement in scientific literacy is determined by measures of student understanding of scientific concepts, recognizing scientific questions, and identifying what is involved in scientific investigations. Students are judged by their ability to

- use scientific evidence in making claims and drawing conclusions.
- create or use conceptual models in predicting and giving explanations.
- compare data in evaluating alternative viewpoints.
- make scientific arguments or to describe in detail with precision.

PHYSICAL AND HEALTH EDUCATION

Its Place in the Curriculum

In the early 1960s, President John Kennedy proposed a national standard of physical fitness. Shortly thereafter, most elementary and secondary students were required to participate in annual assessments of physical fitness. This period also saw the flourishing of international sports events. Participation of highly trained foreign athletes in these events aroused American interest in the development of physical education programs.

---

[19]*Benchmarks for Science Literacy* (Washington, DC: American Association for the Advancement of Science, 1994).

[20]Andrew Ahlgren and F. James Rutherford, "Where Is Project 2061 Today?" *Educational Leadership* 50, no. 88 (May 1992): 19–22.

Unfortunately, physical competition as part of the 1960s sports ethic produced disappointment and humiliation for many children. Being good was often not good enough; excellence was the goal. Physical education offerings were limited to traditional team sports, and often aggression and competitiveness were the prerequisites of sportsmanship.

Throughout the 1960s, physical education offerings gradually expanded. Communities requested that more emphasis be placed on lifelong sports. As a result, courses in scuba diving, bike riding, and golf were added to the curriculum. The direction was not away from strenuous exercise, but simply away from the harshness of competition. Competition as an American virtue was slowly being replaced by collaboration and individual choice. Physical education established a new flexibility in course offerings. Less rigid views on sexual roles also provided new opportunities for girls. Students, for the first time, chose from a variety of programs best suited to their interests.

The role of physical education in the classroom has become a controversial issue nationwide in the face of budgetary cutbacks and the demand for renewed emphasis on basic educational forms. Nevertheless, there are national concerns about students' lack of fitness.

Early in the twenty-first century many cash-strapped schools have cut physical education or maintain bare bones programs. Some do little differently than schools did 20 years ago. Increasingly, however, physical education in kindergarten through high school is going through an evolution with team sports and lap running giving way to in-line skating and snorkeling classes that emphasize fun, movement, and individual skills. A private school in Hawaii includes everything from fencing to Frisbee golf.

A national average of 15% of U.S. students being overweight or obese prompted Congress in 2000 to award grants supporting innovative physical education (PE) programs for lifelong healthy habits. The American Alliance for Healthy Physical Education, Recreation, and Health and the National Association for Sports and Physical Education continued to assist schools with lesson plans and criteria for quality physical education programs. National guidelines recommend 30 minutes per day for elementary school students and 45 minutes daily for middle and high school students. The guidelines call for a variety of activities to develop a range of skills, and for students to learn how exercise affects the body.

Innovative programs have (a) fitness labs with elliptical trainers, stationary bikes, treadmills, stair climbers, and weight machines and (b) strength and cardiovascular equipment and activities such as yoga, cycling, and urban hiking as well as traditional sports, such as volleyball.

Elementary schools teach about cardiovascular health and how to maintain a target heart rate. The importance of good nutrition as well as how exercise helps both the body and the brain is coupled with the use of stability balls for balance, juggling for hand–eye coordination, and wall climbing for risk taking and strength.

Guidelines for Future Physical Education Programs

The American Alliance for Health, Physical Education, and Recreation (a 50,000-member professional organization) has suggested five guidelines for future physical education programs:

1. Break down current mass education techniques.
2. Increase flexibility of offerings and teaching methods.
3. View sports as more than athletic competition.
4. Increase coeducational classes, sailing, camp counselor training, and self-defense.
5. Promote physical activities that support the desire to maintain physical fitness throughout life.

The association recommends that teachers emphasize activities that can serve as vehicles for education of the whole person. Activities should be designed to introduce students to the subtle and often overlooked potentials of the human body. Here are some suggested activities for a humanistic curriculum in physical education:

Movement education: The objective is to develop an understanding of creative and expressive movement. Five-year-olds can be asked to proceed down a marked line in any fashion they desire. Some balance carefully, some run, some crawl, but all experience their own style.

Centering oneself: The student develops a state of alert calm by becoming aware of physical energy in and outside the body.

Structural patterning: Students become aware of variations in the way people move.

Relaxation techniques: By means of rhythmic breathing, the student learns how to gain control over habitual tensions.

Similar guidelines have been issued by the National Association for Sports and Physical Education, which has defined the "physically educated person" as one who has learned the skills to perform a variety of physical activities, to keep themselves physically fit through programs of training and conditioning, and to know the benefits of physical activity.[21] The Association is issuing the referenced document, including its listing of exemplary performance levels for students in 20 key physical activities, as the basis for proposed national standards.

Illustrative of newer curriculum in health is the Health Activities Project (HAP) developed by the Lawrence Hall of Science, University of California, Berkeley. This program offers an activity-centered health curriculum for pupils in grades 5 through 8. The goal of the project is to create a positive attitude toward health by giving pupils a sense of control over their own bodies and by imparting understanding about the body's potential for improvement. HAP activities, organized into modules treating such topics as fitness, interaction, growth, decision making, and skin care, supplement existing programs in health, physical education, and science.

New textbooks encourage students to evaluate their own food and fitness habits and develop better ones. Texts are beginning to reveal the role of the food industry in shaping the American diet and to feature the future of women in sports and the effects of advertising on self-image.

Those planning the health curriculum confront concerns about AIDS, drug abuse, stress, and human sexuality. Social ambivalence toward drugs as well as difficult home lives are factors in such programs. So, too, are the images students have of themselves. The role of the health curriculum has been chiefly that of helping students learn how to deal with potential problems posed by dangerous practices such as alcohol abuse. Peer counseling projects, in which students work with other students in helpful relations, have replaced the use of stern lectures and frightening stories to discourage youths from abuse.

Discouraging results from earlier efforts at drug and alcohol education have provoked a new social-psychological approach which shows some promise. Social-psychological prevention programs strengthen resistance to peer pressure to use drugs and alcohol and to smoke. They also help students to cope with interpersonal relations and to reduce stress. Elements in these programs include (1) working with families, community groups, and the media to influence policies and cultural norms associated with smoking and other negative health behaviors; (2) recognizing that substance abuse is intertwined with other problem

---

[21]Mary A. Steinhardt, "Physical Education" in *Handbook of Research on Curriculum*, Philip W. Jackson, ed. (New York: Macmillan, 1992), 964–1001.

behaviors, such as dropping out, teen pregnancy, and delinquency; (3) focusing on specific knowledge and attitudes about alcohol and drugs by the fourth grade; (4) giving information about physiology (genetic predispositions), high-risk populations (medications), psychosocial correlates (family influences), and role of the community and media as related to alcohol and drugs so that young people can estimate their personal risk for developing substance abuse problems; (5) focusing on short-term social consequences important to the students; and (6) attitudinal inoculation, including role playing and Socratic discussions for dealing with overt and covert pressures.[22]

Sex education sometimes suffers attacks from conservative political groups, although even a majority of conservative groups supports sex education. Investigators are surprised at the various aspects of sexuality. Although sex education is only one factor, some draw a connection between it and the incidence of teenage marriage, divorce, unwanted pregnancy, abortion, and venereal disease. Sweden, which has compulsory sex education, has the lowest incidence of such problems, and the United States which has no systematic program, has the highest. Although nearly every state has endorsed sex education, the curricula used often omit important information about sexual behavior, fantasy, homosexuality, masturbation, contraception, and abortion.[23]

National Health Education Standards include having students acting as civic activists, advocating for personal, family, and community health.[24] To this end many schools are partners with a public health agency or a university whereby students participate in research and community projects, such as surveys of the effectiveness of a school's health policy and the health assessment of a neighborhood.

By way of illustration, "False Shock" was a partnership which involved four teachers from math, humanities, history, and science in a semester-long course where students developed their own health research projects. The students used their newly acquired content knowledge as they studied health issues in the community, including ethical and legal difficulties. Results of these studies were presented to the school, health agency, and the community.[25]

ENGLISH

English as a Subject

According to Arthur N. Applebee in his seminal history, *Tradition and Reform in the Teaching of English*, English as a school subject has a short tradition, just over a century old.[26] In fact, when Benjamin Franklin proposed his English academy in 1747, his curriculum was considered quite radical because it stressed English, instead of Latin and Greek, the language of learning at the time.[27] In 1865, according to Applebee, a variety of studies of English included "rhetoric, oratory, spelling, literary history, and reading."[28] In the

[22]Bonnie Bernard et al., "Knowing What to Do and Not to Do Reinvigorates Drug Education," *Curriculum Update* (Feb. 1987): 1–2.
[23]*Unfinished Business: A Siecus Assessment of State Sexuality Education Programs* (New York: Siecus Publications, 1994).
[24]*National Health Education Standards* (Washington, DC: Centers for Disease Control and Prevention, 2001).
[25]Jenny Smith, *Education and Public Health: Natural Partners for Life* (Alexandria, VA: Association for Supervision and Curriculum Development, 2003).
[26]Arthur N. Applebee, *Tradition and Reform in the Teaching of English: A History* (Urbana, IL: National Council of Teachers of English, 1974). The authors are indebted to this work for the section on English.
[27]William J. Reese, *The Origins of the American High School* (New Haven, CT: Yale University Press, 1995), 29.
[28]Applebee, *Tradition and Reform*, 13.

following decades, these traditional offerings were united under the teaching of a single subject—English—with literature, language, and composition forming the major components of the subject. While English eventually replaced Latin and Greek, the study of English continued to be heavily influenced by European classical writers and English authors.[29] Beginning with the election of Rewey Belle Inglis in 1928 as the first female president of the National Council of Teachers of English, women educators, such as Ruth Mary Weeks, Stella Stewart Center, Dora V. Smith, Angela M. Broening, Marion C. Sheridan, Lou La Brant, Luella B. Cook, Helen K. Mackintosh, and Ruth G. Strickland, played crucial roles in the development of the field of English education in public schools.[30]

As Applebee further chronicles, early in the twentieth century educators made efforts to emancipate the teaching of English in the high schools from the college program. These efforts took the form of rejecting a traditional body of literature as the sole purveyor of culture, giving up an analytical approach to literary studies in favor of studying types of literature. In the early 1920s, there was a functional emphasis on English; committees attempted to identify the skills learned in English classes that were most useful to people in a range of social positions. An experience curriculum in English, influenced by John Dewey, was also introduced, which emphasized writing rather than grammar.[31]

The 1940s saw teachers of English trying to adapt their content to adolescent needs, the problems of family life, international relations, and other aspects of daily living. English became guidance. In the late 1950s, an academic resurgence occurred with attacks on such a conception of English. English as a discipline in the high schools soon followed the model of academic work in college. Language, literature, and composition remained the tripod of English. Influenced by new criticism, teachers were expected to teach pupils how to engage in close analysis of what was read and how to respond to questions about form, syntax, and meaning. Literary values once again prevailed over personal interpretations and reading for enjoyment.[32]

With the Civil Rights and Women's Rights movements, the mid-1960s ushered in a major push to make the English curriculum more relevant and meaningful to all students, especially those traditionally underserved. Rather than literary classics, young adult literature became valuable resources for engaging students.[33] The emphasis also shifted to contemporary writing, including selections by culturally diverse and female authors. In literature, English educators moved toward topical units in the junior high school and thematic units in the senior high school. Adolescents often studied a theme like justice or love as treated by poets, playwrights, and novelists over the years. Reading literature was considered more important than reading what was said about it.

A conference on the teaching of English at Dartmouth College in 1966 brought American specialists in English in contact with British influences.[34] Applebee recounts the British had "a model for English" with an emphasis on "the personal and linguistic growth of the child." Hence, many teachers of English began to adopt the British practice of offering "improvised drama, imaginative writing, personal response to literature, and informal classroom discussion."[35] There was a turn away from more formal literary approaches and history.

[29]Ibid., 13–43.
[30]Jeanne Marcum Gerlach and Virginia R. Monseau, eds., *Missing Chapters: Ten Pioneering Women in NCTE and English Education* (Urbana, IL: National Council of Teachers of English, 1991).
[31]Applebee, *Tradition and Reform*, 79–137.
[32]Ibid., 138–183.
[33]Daniel N. Fader and Morton H. Shaevitz, *Hooked on Books* (New York: Berkley, 1966).
[34]John Dixon, *Growth through English* (Reading, PA: National Association for the Teaching of English, 1967).
[35]Applebee, *Tradition and Reform*, 229–330.

In the 1980s, after the publication of *A Nation at Risk*, the field once again returned to basic skills. Many freshmen were required to take a basic grammar and composition course before enrolling in an English course in college. The basic skills movement gained support among students, teachers, parents, and administrators. The basic skills movement in English was a demand for more history of classical literature, more traditional grammar, and a greater emphasis on formal rather than personal writing. There was a return to the workbook and the hardcover anthology. Debates over standard English as the criterion for social advancement also became hotly contested in terms of access to language. Elective programs were dismantled, accused of fragmenting and diminishing the goals of a comprehensive approach to English. Opponents of the basic skills movement urged English teachers not to succumb to pressures that would have them teach trivia because trivia can be easily measured, but to teach so that reading and writing would help students find personal meaning in life. The social reconstructionists called for a critical study of the media, particularly television, and of topics closely related to quality of life.[36]

At the beginning of the 1990s, compromise was evident. Basic English skills were taught in conjunction with those themes in literature affecting all humanity. The great-theme approach focused attention on the most profound and universal questions of all time—for example, people's response to nature, to one another, to beauty, and to the relationship between fate and free will. In contrast to teachers focusing on isolated skills and neglecting to show how these skills relate to current social realities, other teachers considered how skills may be applied in situations relevant to students' lives.

Current Trends in the Teaching of English

The range of activities in the English class continues to reflect tradition, multiculturalism, and other intellectual forces. In 1996, the International Reading Association and National Council of Teachers of English issued *Standards for the English Language Arts*. These standards represent a significant shift in the conceptualization of English and language arts with their focus on helping students become literate for the future.[37] Here, the standards define literacy as understanding and using language effectively in a plurality of settings. The standards call for literary and media analysis of various genres from a range of cultures, reading comprehension for different types of texts, multiple forms of writing and speech, inquiry and research skills, multimedia development, and innovative use of technology.[38]

Teachers, in general, want students to become involved with literature at a personal level and to use it to focus on their own lives, peers, and community. Since the 1980s, reader response or transactional theory, first developed by Louise Rosenblatt in the 1930s and popularized in 1978 in *The Reader, the Text, the Poem*, has become one of the dominant approaches to the teaching of literature.[39] This theory holds that readers actively interact with texts and construct meaning as they read, based on their own experiences and backgrounds. Thus, a single authoritative interpretation of a text does not exist but many interpretations are possible.[40] Questions are based on both interpretations and the readers'

---

[36]George Hillocks, Jr., ed., *The English Curriculum under Fire: What Are the Real Basics?* (Urbana, IL: National Council of Teachers of English, 1982).

[37]International Reading Association and National Council of Teachers of English, *Standards for the English Language Arts* (Urbana, IL: National Council of Teachers of English, 1996).

[38]Ibid., 25.

[39]Louise Rosenblatt, *The Reader, the Text, the Poem: The Transactional Theory of the Literary Work* (Carbondale: Southern Illinois University Press, 1978).

[40]Violet J. Harris, "Literature-Based Approaches to Reading Instruction," in *Review of Research in Education* 19, Linda Darling-Hammond, ed. (Washington, DC: American Educational Research Association, 1993), 269–297.

experiences. Approaches also include the integration of the arts—for example, students dramatize a key event in a novel, create a sound track for a play, or make a quilt to represent significant events in a protagonist's life. Recently, multicultural literature is also playing an increasingly important role in the teaching of English.[41]

English teachers and curriculum workers still debate whether courses should feature great works of literature or emphasize contemporary problems and modern psychological interpretations. The popular response is to try to include both the traditional and contemporary. One chooses important themes dealing with the human condition, such as justice, and then selects material from traditional and modern diverse literature, folklore, and mythology that helps illuminate the theme. Selectivity should govern both the scope and the details selected.

Writing   The precedence to literature, "to reading and responding to texts written by others," has been broadened to include writing. In the 1990s, the National Council of Teachers of English stressed the importance of writing in its call for a consistent English curriculum from the early grades through undergraduate years.[42] Accordingly, students at all levels practice writing in different styles for different purposes.

Also, the move toward seeing writing as a process, which gained momentum in the 1970s and continues today, has encouraged students to begin writing as soon as they grasp a pencil. The current writing process approach, according to Joseph Milner and Lucy Milner, has been extended from the earlier one to emphasize a range of activities: "inventing, arranging, drafting, uniting, proofreading, peer reviewing, revising, editing, refinishing, evaluating, and publishing."[43] Students are encouraged to do what real writers do. Real writers develop their own frameworks, take time to think and talk about their work, and constantly revise to clarify their ideas and to reflect on what they have learned from writing. Grammar and usage are integrated into editing and revision. However, with the recent move toward standardized testing, teachers often feel caught between focusing on students' creativity, analytical thinking, and linguistic fluency, encouraged by process writing, and the counterpressure to teach prescribed five-paragraph essays and standardized usage.[44]

READING

The Curriculum of Reading

The curriculum for the teaching of reading in America from 1600 to the present has reflected different goals. The initial goal was religious. Children were expected to learn to read the word of God directly. With the forming of a new nation, reading was taught to help build national strength and unity—to instill patriotism. From 1840 to 1890, the teaching of reading as a means for obtaining information was the primary goal. This emphasis on enlightenment was an extension of nationalism—from patriotic sentiment to the ideal of an intelligent citizenry. To awaken a perennial interest in literary material was the overriding goal in the late 1890s and until about 1918. Thereafter, utility rather than aesthetics had

[41]Jim Burke, *The English Teacher's Companion: A Complete Guide to Classroom, Curriculum and the Profession,* 2nd ed. (Portsmouth, NH: Heinemann, 2003).

[42]Richard Lloyd-Jones, ed., *The English Coalition Conference: Democracy through Language* (Urbana, IL: National Council of Teachers of English, 1989).

[43]Joseph O'Beirne Milner and Lucy Floyd Morcock Milner, *Bridging English*, 3rd ed. (Upper Saddle River, NJ: Merrill Prentice-Hall, 2003), 295–296.

[44]For insightful discussions of these issues, see *English Journal*, "Special Issue: Teaching Writing in the Twenty-First Century," 90, no. 1 (Sept. 2000): 29–126.

priority. Reading selections were oriented more to the events of daily living than to literary appreciation.

Currently, there are several emphases in the teaching of reading. One emphasis focuses on word recognition and reading comprehension. These skills are taught without considering the purpose for which they will ultimately be used. A second traditional emphasis focuses on the specific kinds of situations in which the student is to apply reading skills—reading want ads, Yellow Pages, job applications, and newspapers. The latter emphasis reflects a concern for those who are said to lack the reading competencies necessary to function successfully in contemporary society. A third emphasis is to teach reading as conceptual development in which a person's background of experience is made use of in the process so that the reader creates meaning from text. A fourth emphasis is critical reading—the deconstructing of text—including the hidden political agenda.

Trends and Directions

Trends in the teaching of reading during the early 1990s followed those in the other language arts. Instruction in reading was influenced by scholarship, technology, and humanistic concerns.

Among the directions in the teaching of reading were the whole language movement, the interactive view of reading, critical reading, and literature-based reading. Proponents of whole language view reading as part of general language development, not as a discrete skill isolated from listening, speaking, and writing. Beginning in kindergarten, children compose stories and learn to read from their writing. They also engage in shared reading of literature. Whole language with older students allows for learners' choice of the areas in which to become literate and encourages voices that are authentic to local reality.

The interactive view of reading is that the reader creates meaning by combining text with previously acquired experiences. Learners can be helped in the process by being taught metacognitive skills (how to monitor their understanding of the text), how to use their prior knowledge in reading, and how to integrate text with their background knowledge. Critical reading by which students "unravel" the text by noting the author's inconsistencies is gaining interest at the secondary school level. Accordingly, students attend to what the author has *not* said, to the author's uncertainties as reflected in the footnotes, to identifying the discourse or central questions that the author purports to answer, and to the adequacy of the contribution.

The driving force behind whole language reading and critical reading is teacher and student empowerment. With these approaches, they are not dependent on text written by others. On the other hand, the emphasis on teaching as comprehension or thinking is supported by the belief that higher level reasoning abilities are required in today's technological and communication society. Finally, the trend to place literature at the core of the reading program often reflects a conservative social view—that of the advocates of cultural literacy, such as E. D. Hirsch, who want all readers to amass a shared content that reflects the traditions of the dominant class.

At the beginning of the twenty-first century, the reading curriculum and the reading field were stymied by a conflict between phonics and whole language proponents. The controversy over method diverted discussion about the kinds of readers wanted and what should count as literacy.

Focus on tests of decoding ability and the making of "correct" inferences from contrived passages substituted for conversations about *multiple literacies* (multicultural and computer), *purposes* (functional, critical, informative, recreational, inspirational, therapeutic), and *forms* (graphs, diagrams, schematics). At the same time that the press reported 35% of the fourth graders at the lowest level of reading achievement, a survey by the

National Endowment for the Arts found that, for the first time in modern history, fewer than half of the adult population in the United States read literature for pleasure.[45]

A national reading panel had sparked a battle between the phonics and whole language proponents and (mis)directed attention to alphabetization instead of literacy.[46] The panel examined published studies of the effects of different approaches in learning to read. The findings of the panel gave more support to the teaching of phonemic awareness and phonics than to whole language methods when decoding was the goal, but did not show the connection of alphabetization methods to reading comprehension. Reid Lyon, Chief of the Child Development and Behavior Branch of the National Institute of Child Health and Human Development, used the report as a springboard to promoting federal government policies that funded alphabetization programs and materials based on "scientific research" purporting to advance reading, restricting funding for programs that were not "validated."

The narrowing of attention to decoding in learning to read avoided confronting underlying issues—English language learners, the disconnect between school literacy and multicultural literacies in homes and local neighborhoods.

Responses to both the panel and to Lyon centered on the limitations of the panel's membership and questionable methodologies for assessing the effects reported by studies. Gearld Cole, for example, critiqued the handpicked panel, the report, and its influences on Reading First legislation.[47] Cole revealed research that was ignored by the panel and which showed the importance of children's immersion in a written language environment. Forgotten, too, was the fact that the best predictor of reading comprehension is the student's background of experience.

Narrowing of the reading curriculum is evidenced by how powerful groups are evaluating the standards states are setting for reading. In their analysis of reports from four groups and the orientations of their consultants, Sheila Valencia and Karen Wixson found marked differences as illustrated below.[48]

a. The *American Federation of Teachers* wants a core curriculum with both content and skills allocated by grade level, elementary through secondary school. The reading skills are specific and narrow, namely, "First graders should be able to spell single words that have *r* controlled vowels, initial consonants *f, l,* and *g,* and have *ck* as the final consonant."

b. The *Fordham Foundation* takes points off if standards encourage students to use their own language if different from English. Older students also should not make multiple representations of text or personal responses as such practices "undermine the very capacity of a literary work to help readers transcend their limited experiences," and although literary movements should be studied, contemporary social issues should be avoided. A canon of English and "American" literature should be taught and the quality of independent reading specified.

c. *Achieve* wants parents and teachers to have a specific guide to suitable content and standards and believes that standards must be measurable. "'Read for enjoyment' is virtually impossible to measure so it can't be a standard; but 'define a simile' is fine."

---

[45]*Reading At Risk—A Survey of Literary Reading in America* (Washington, DC: National Endowment for the Arts, 2004).

[46]National Reading Panel, *Teaching Children to Read: An Evidence-Based Assessment of the Scientific Research Literature on Reading and Its Implications for Reading*, Report of the Subgroup (Washington, DC: National Institute of Child Health and Human Development, 2000).

[47]Gearld Cole, *Reading the Naked Truth: Literacy, Legislation and Lies* (Portsmouth, NH: Heinemann, 2003).

[48]Sheila Valencia and Karen K. Wixson, "Inside English/Language Arts Standards. What's in a Grade? *Reading Research Quarterly* 36 (April/May/June 2001): 202–207.

d. Although the *Council for Basic Education* closed its doors in 2004, it advocated for good standards that were clear and specific but need not dictate instructional practice—"read aloud with accuracy, fluency, and comprehension."

The focus and differences among these influential organizations raise questions regarding the future reading curriculum:

Are the standards to be the curriculum or distinct from it?

Should content be in terms of processes and skills or a prescribed canon?

Should only measurable outcomes be standards?

Should teachers be free to use any method or must they follow prescribed approaches?

HISTORY AND SOCIAL STUDIES

History as a Subject

The "new" history of the 1960s, both its subject matter and methodology, evolved from the same forces that had affected other subject matter fields, that is, the teaching of separate disciplines and the push toward specialization. The subject matter of history was chosen in order to provide students with a conceptual foundation on which specialization could be based. Emphasis was placed on historian's methods of research, analysis, and interpretation. Students were no longer required to memorize sheer facts or chronology, but to express an understanding for general sociological theories. This conceptual approach encouraged students to doubt and openly criticize textbook interpretations of history. Students drew their own conclusions and often found previous perspectives biased and unreliable.

Campus demonstrations in the late 1960s reflected a general lack of confidence in politicians and governmental agencies. Students had been taught to examine, analyze, and interpret, and they freely applied these skills to national policy making. The Vietnam War was history in the making, and students were determined to make known their interpretations of the facts.

Public concern about campus protests resulted in a demand that history be taught in a manner that would make it applicable to constructive resolution of community problems. To accommodate this demand, curriculum specialists suggested integrating the study of history with other subjects and to life in the present. Therefore emphasis was placed on building a basic understanding of the historical influences on community life. Suggested learning activities included studying the influence of science and technology on various periods of history, identifying the relationship between historical movements and developments in the arts, and investigating the effects of business and industry on local history.

An Evaluation of History Curriculum

Appraisals of the curriculum in history during the 1980s were negative. Teachers were accused of having an unintegrated interpretation of history, a limited range of teaching strategies, and a narrow conception of the students' responsibilities.[49] Curriculum consisted of a prescribed, fragmented body of material to be absorbed and repeated to the teacher. Whether the focus was the Federal Reserve Act, current events, or World War II, the material was not related to the lives of students or to the larger historical process.

---

[49]Paula M. Evans, "Teaching History in Libertyville," *Daedalus* 112, no. 3 (spring 1983): 199–229.

The appraisal of elementary and secondary history textbooks was also negative.[50] The texts were unrealistic, although they showed the present as a "tangle of problems" and, paradoxically, were sanguine about the future. Economic history was conspicuously absent, an analysis of ideological conflict was missing from discussions of American wars, and the authors did not attend to continuity. "Politics is one theory to them, economics another, culture a third.... There is no link between the end of Reconstruction in the South and the Civil Rights movement of the sixties.... History is just one damn thing after another. It is, in fact, not history at all."[51] Frances Fitzgerald attributes the lack of interest in academic competence in history to the societal demand that the curriculum promote good social behavior and learning for strictly practical purposes.

History and Geography in the 1990s

At the start of the 1990s, there was renewed emphasis on history and geography, a new look at the primary curriculum, the integration of literature with history, and a more in-depth study of both the history of the world and the history of the United States. These directions are illustrated by the California curriculum for history, which was developed to meet the standards of the Bradley Commission, a group of historians.[52]

Most students study American history in grade 5 (pre-Columbian societies to 1850), grade 8 (growth and conflict, 1783–1914), and grade 11 (continuity and change, 1900 to present); world history in grade 6 (ancient civilizations), grade 7 (medieval and early modern times), and grade 10 (culture and geography of the modern world). Those in the elementary grades learn about local, family, and state history by studying the achievements of great men and women of different cultures. Controversial issues usually are reserved for grades 10 and 11, and high school seniors study economics and government.

In addition to emphasizing historical chronology and continuity, the California curriculum features stories (fairy tales, myths, legends, and biography) in the early grades and literature, including sources from the social sciences, in the secondary school units. This curriculum stresses the rights and responsibilities of citizens, contrasts government in different societies, and fosters individual initiative for historical change.

Most reviewers approve of the new framework's efforts to involve students in historical events by telling stimulating stories of colorful persons and dramatic episodes and having students react to what they would have done in the situations. Nevertheless, there is concern that this program will selectively reinforce a cultural memory that is univocal and uncontested. In trying to give students a solid introduction to their national past and to build national pride in American achievements, the history curriculum might ignore the conflicting voices and heterogeneity of the American experience. Furthermore, in focusing on history, less attention was given to the study of current problems and the development of sociological, anthropological, and economic interpretations.

In New York state, a 1989 Task Force on Minorities Report explored a multicultural history curriculum, pointing to Eurocentric history as contributing to low self-esteem among minority children.[53] Historians who wanted to further a dominant cultural literacy—D. Ravitch and A. Schlesinger—opposed viewing history as a form of therapy whose function

---

[50]Frances Fitzgerald, "Prizewinning Author Charges History Textbooks' President Distorted Picture," *ASCD News Exchange* 21, no. 4 (summer 1979): 1, 7.

[51]Ibid., 7.

[52]*Building a History Curriculum: Guidelines for Teaching History in Schools* (Washington, DC: Educational Excellence Network, 1988).

[53]David Sobol, "Revising the New York State Social Studies Curriculum," *Teachers College Record* 95, no. 2 (winter 1993): 258–273.

is that of raising self-esteem.[54] Therapy is, of course, a pejorative expression for the idea that history might have personal meaning for students, contributing positively to the development of their identity.

Paradoxically, the Bradley Commission and those favoring a national cultural literacy support such a use of history—"history to satisfy young peoples longing for a sense of identity and of their time and place in the human story." The debate is, of course, not over the teaching of history to enhance identity and self-concept, but over which of the many possible identities should be emphasized—a predetermined national identity or separate identities for women, workers, African-Americans, Native Americans, and others. The practice of helping students see historical events from a variety of perspectives is one way of dealing with the conflict. The Westward Movement, for example, can be seen from the perspectives of European Americans, Native Americans, Mexicans, Chinese, and the like. Further, when students read different historical texts about the same event, they learn to participate in the conversations of historians, evaluating the interpretations of the new social historians, revisionists, and cultural literacy and multicultural proponents.

In their draft of National History Standards the National Center for History in the Schools, scholars and teachers attempted to make history more balanced and inclusive by introducing historians that have been silent and by including the history of women and ethnic and religious minorities.[55] Reactions to these standards were mixed. The U.S. Senate passed a resolution advising review panels to refuse certification of the new history standards. Critics faulted the lack of references to traditional historical figures and objected to promoting inquiry and critical thinking rather than indoctrination.

History and the Social Studies in the Standards Movement

The current National History Standards call for teaching five core subject areas and have provoked controversy about what students should be taught about their country's past and place in the world. States, such as California, have prepared detailed state history frameworks that go well beyond frameworks that lay down general guides but leave curriculum development and instruction to local educators. Instead, frameworks for the standards curriculum are prescriptive, mandating specific outcomes as well as outlining items to be learned and assessed. Curriculum content has been intensified. Districts and schools have modified their curriculum to align with the standards and the measures. Classroom instruction, teacher preparation programs, university faculty, and publishers all have been exposed to the standards and are adapting to them.

In California, the authors of the history–social studies curriculum tried to keep historical thinking as well as transmission of content in their framework. For example, teachers are encouraged to use primary sources in the telling of historical stories. However, the content is overwhelming as the authors have tried to respond to confrontational audiences and interest groups. The disciplines of history, geography, economics, the arts, civics, and government are drawn on as well as numerous mandated topics such as the Holocaust.

Although the standards call for integrating history and other disciplines, no guidance is given on how to achieve it. That might be a good thing when teachers bring their own passion and knowledge to bear. One teacher introduced an inquiry-based activity concerning the Chinese Examination System to add life to the standards' scant outline for the required teaching of the history of medieval Chinese. Other teachers turn to experts, such

---

[54]D. Ravitch and A. Schlesinger, "Statement of the Committee of Scholars in Defense of History," *Perspectives* 28 (1990): 7–15.
[55]"U.S. History in Grades 5–12," Los Angeles, CA: National Center for History in the Schools, 1995.

as an expert on maps, who make their Web sites available or to cooperative projects with university students who develop and help implement history lessons related to their subject fields. One example is a project where music is connected with the historical theme of cultural change, geography, and the environment. Guest artists engage the students in the study of the evolution of musical instruments and the influence of historical environmental factors as the instruments changed.

The separate disciplines have vied for inclusion. Economics has emerged as a central study with specified performance objectives throughout the K–12 curriculum. Students at all grades are expected to progress on key topics, such as cost–benefit analysis. Kindergarteners, for instance, are introduced to the topic as they acquire related concepts of work, scarcity, choice, and personal responsibility. Throughout the curriculum students pursue economic topics and learn how they as human capital must advance their skills in order to enhance success.[56]

Social Studies

Social studies is a broad term covering several subject matters including history and the social sciences. Originally, the purpose of the social studies curriculum was the "creation of rich and many-sided personalities, equipped with practical knowledge and inspired by ideals so that they can make their way and fulfill their mission in a changing society which is part of a world complex."[57] Today, there is disenchantment with the stated purpose. It is too vague, and there is doubt that those in the social sciences are able to furnish knowledge with which to resolve complex social issues like racial strife, war, and economic depression. Indeed, social scientists have inflated hopes and made promises beyond the means of their knowledge and capacities.

In the 1950s, the curriculum of the social studies was varied. The authors of some programs aimed at social literacy. They wanted learners to understand social change as responses to the problems and needs of human beings throughout the world. Others said their mission was to help learners develop socially desirable behavior; social scientists felt they were demonstrating social processes, promoting understanding and skill in dealing with social problems. A common curriculum premise of that time was that the social studies program should combine both content and process. Students should have the opportunity to make decisions regarding personal and social problems using the generalizations from the social sciences.

In the 1960s, more than 40 major social studies curriculum projects were financed by the federal government, foundations, and institutions of higher learning. Authors of these projects all emphasized an academic structure but did not share a common view as to what the structure was. They tended to define structure loosely as generalizations, concepts, or modes of inquiry. There was little agreement on which concepts or ways of working in the social sciences are most fruitful and representative of structure. Like most other curriculum programs of the 1960s, social studies projects stressed inductive teaching. Students were expected to make generalizations from data. Typical goals for the social studies during this period were to interpret problems of world citizenship using concepts from the behavioral sciences; to interpret social behavior using concepts from a variety of disciplines; to analyze public controversies using the method of discussion and argument; and to recognize objective evidence using concepts from philosophy, psychology, law, and other social sciences.

---

[56]Jim Charkins, "Economics: Not Just for High School Anymore," *Social Studies Review* 46, no. 1 (winter 2003): 57.
[57]Charles Beard, *The Nature of the Social Sciences* (New York: Scribner, 1938), 179.

In the 1960s, the social studies curriculum was in disarray. On the one hand, there were those who advocated drawing substantially from a wide range of social science disciplines in developing new social studies programs. On the other hand, there were those who recommended studying non-Western societies and organizing curriculum content around the study of world cultures and international affairs.

Today, the social studies curriculum in schools is still more social studies than social science, with history, government, and geography as the dominant subjects. Although economics is gaining in importance in elementary schools, the social studies receive little attention, serving primarily as another opportunity to teach reading and writing skills. At all levels the social studies curriculum is a textbook curriculum; the textbook is used to organize courses, and its content is the focus for student concentration. Few teachers have ever heard of approaches oriented toward the social sciences, and fewer still use them. They also seldom connect the course with anything in the students' life, with events familiar to them, or with a study about the contributions of the students' ancestors. The basic skills movement has weakened efforts to promote inquiry and problem analysis. There is little agreement among teachers, advocates, and analysts within the field as to what purposes the social studies should serve or the most appropriate subject matter to teach.[58]

Janet Alleman and Jere Brophy compared elementary school social studies units on the same topic—transportation—written 71 years apart.[59] Whereas in the past, social studies was the center of the instructional day—a way to introduce the fundamentals—today the subject has limited time for in-class instruction and teachers chiefly present disconnected lessons to satisfy requirements and to practice for assessments. In the old social studies curriculum, in contrast, students built their model farms and cities and as they enacted their work encountered problems, such as how to get their crops to market, and teachers observed the learners to identify their readiness for learning key concepts and operations along with "just in time" instruction.

Today's units place the concept first as the target to be learned and expect the teacher to use prior knowledge of students along with discussion and assigned tasks to teach the concepts, making it less clear to students on why they are acquiring the concept in the first place or how it serves their purposes for knowing.

After her analysis of elementary social studies materials, which revealed incoherence (disconnected facts) and too much breadth and not enough depth, Jere Brophy made a recommendation for improvement: shift from content coverage (lists of specific topics and skills to be "covered") to more general goals expressed as student capacities of dispositions to be developed, such as "understanding how the social world works, how it got to be that way, and what this implies for personal and civic action."[60]

The Future of Social Studies

Problems concerning the social studies curriculum of the future center on the following observations. Rational discourse, critical inquiry, opportunity to exercise the skill of autonomous judgment, and other featured values in social studies programs seem to be no guarantee of behavioral change or even increased happiness of the individual or society. Inasmuch as human beings may act irrationally on impulse, emotion, pride, and passion,

[58]Howard D. Mehlinger, "The Reform of Social Studies and the Role of the National Commission for the Social Studies," *The History Teacher* 21, no. 1 (Feb. 1988): 195–207.

[59]Janet Alleman and Jere Brophy, "Comparing Transportation Units Published in 1921 and 2002—What Have We Learned?" *Journal of Curriculum and Instruction* 19, no. 1 (fall 2003): 5–27.

[60]Jere Brophy, "The De Facto National Curriculum in United States Elementary Social Studies: Critique of a Representative Sample," *Journal of Curriculum Studies* 24, no. 5 (1992): 401–477.

social studies programs that feature only facts and interpretations should not be expected to contribute much toward making students more reasonable about human and social behavior. Consequently, the future will see a movement in the direction of the affective realm. As described in Chapter 11, international tests assess willingness to use knowledge as well as knowledge acquired. Values and attitudes will become more important, and efforts will be made to involve students in ecological and political matters of personal interest. There might be a return to the project method, and we are already seeing more problem-based learning, stressing ways to participate in acts of citizenship and to improve and perfect our government system, an emphasis that may overcome students' loss of confidence in the American political system.

By way of example, eighth graders in Walnut, California, participated in an applied social studies program "We Care" and undertook such projects as simplifying voting procedures, revamping fire drill regulations, and promoting water conservation.[61] Each class selected a project to improve life in their community and state. In dealing with water conservation, the students made use of abstract principles of conservation in writing legislation requiring the state to use water-saving plants for landscaping. They launched a campaign for getting statewide support for the legislation by lobbying, disseminating information through newspapers, and engaging in other forms of political behavior.

The need to construct a better world will force those in the social studies to focus on social problems rather than on transmitting knowledge. These kinds of problems require the student to draw the best current thinking from both the natural and the social sciences. Hence we see attempts at developing an integrative curriculum. The task is difficult. Teachers, for example, are not always comfortable with the inquiry methods and concepts of a single social science. Now they are asked to gain competency in several disciplines. Also, we know that scholars in a single social science have difficulty in agreeing on the goals and content for course materials, and those in different fields have to learn each other's languages in order to communicate.

In the short run, pressures continue to make the social studies curriculum respond to the needs of special groups. Business interests are influencing legislators to mandate instruction on the free enterprise system; Jewish groups effect legislation to require detailed study of the Holocaust. Nuclear curricula, economic, education, global education, and law-related studies are examples of topics that have been included in the social studies curriculum in response to special interests. The social studies curriculum across the land might be a hodgepodge of programs, but the topics can be regarded as vehicles for helping students acquire the overarching ideas of citizenship and skills for participating in public affairs and its elements of understanding the premises of American liberty. Social studies could also be an opportunity for students to apply the concepts and generalizations acquired from concurrent study of history, geography, government, or other disciplines.

However, fragmentation in secondary school social studies is more likely. National and state standards are being set by separate groups. There are standards in geography prepared by the National Council for Geographic Education; standards for history issued by the National Center for History in the Schools; standards for civics developed by the Center for Civics Education; and standards for economics from the National Council on Economic Education. The standards for social studies from the National Council for the Social Studies are noteworthy for their comprehensiveness and as exemplars of curriculum development on the basis of principles rather than prescribed outcomes. The NCSS Standards for Social Studies connect with the standards from other areas of education and are adaptable to either the single discipline or other curriculum configurations.[62]

[61]Alan Haskvitz, "A Middle School Program That Can Change Society," *Phi Delta Kappan* 70, no. 2 (Oct. 1988): 175–178.
[62]*Curriculum Standards for Social Studies* (Silver Spring, MD: National Council for the Social Studies, 2004).

FOREIGN LANGUAGE

The Rise and Fall of Foreign Language

In 1951, six years before Sputnik, the Modern Language Association of America expressed the conviction that we were not teaching foreign languages to enough people. National concern for the advancement of scientific and technological research in the late 1950s accentuated the need for international exchange of knowledge. Hence, the study of one or two foreign languages became a requirement of most secondary schools and universities. Over 8000 elementary schools began to offer instruction in foreign languages.

An instructional method sometimes called the American method or the audiolingual approach for teaching foreign languages became popular at this time. This method was derived from the science of structural or descriptive linguistics that had proved useful in courses offered to the military during World War II. The basic principle of the method is that students' language must be learned as a system of communication by sound from mouth to ear. Students and teacher who used this method spoke the foreign language; they did not only talk about it. The first 300 to 400 hours of language learning were devoted to acquiring a skill rather than a body of facts. During this initial period, students began to comprehend the spoken word and to speak after listening; reading and writing were not emphasized. Students then practiced actively and aloud until they gained some control over the language patterns. The opportunity for such practice was generally provided by language laboratories in which the students heard recordings of a native speaker and tried to model their speech after the speaker's.

Interest in foreign languages began to decline in the mid-1960s as the national concern for space exploration subsided, and with it the push for communication with foreign scientists. Studies in language were criticized for being too specialized to be applicable. Foreign language requirements were eliminated in many colleges and secondary schools. By 1980, only 15% of high school students were enrolled in foreign language courses. Indeed, a presidential commission reported that only 4% of pupils graduating from high school had studied a foreign language for as long as two years. One-fifth of United States public high schools offered no courses in foreign language at all. Among those that did, Spanish, French, and German were most often offered, in that order. A national sampling by the University of Michigan found that more than 52% of Americans who were questioned would like to study a foreign language in the future, but nearly 49% opposed making it a requirement in high schools.

Efforts to Revive Language Instruction

To counteract the loss of student enrollment, advocates of foreign language attempted to concentrate on the human aspects of their discipline in hopes of regaining student interest. Language departments expanded their course offerings in order to meet the needs and interests of students. In discussing ways to do this, teachers typically suggested integration of language study with other subject matter areas, early introduction of language arts, and student participation in curriculum development. Subject matter integration is accomplished by introducing students to the contributions of language to all subject areas. English classes study the contribution of foreign languages to the development of American English; music classes study lyrics of foreign folk songs; and art classes share their work with those in foreign countries. The latest innovation for integration is to teach the academic subjects in a foreign language.

The 1990s saw a shift from an emphasis on grammar and culture to communication and practical language skills. Whereas formerly students had few opportunities to speak the new language in situations that involve genuine communication and instead spoke the language in dry grammar exercises as an abstract activity, the communicative approach encouraged the instrumental value of language, including occupationally oriented foreign language, language learning for immigrants, and language for meeting one's own needs.

Features of the communicative approach include language in use; using language to explain the learner's environment at home and abroad; learning to learn independently; and using media in ways and for purposes which the learners' themselves have determined. Two models of language instruction now vie for ascendancy in the United States: the *monitor model* and the *proficiency-oriented model*. The former assumes that acquisition begins with listening comprehension and that speed emerges spontaneously in natural stages. The latter focuses on discrete proficiency levels at which the speaker's ability to handle function, content, and accuracy are consolidated. Proponents of the monitor method sometimes charge that those using the proficiency method are overly concerned about grammatical accuracy and, in turn, proficiency oriented scholars criticized the monitor method for apparently condoning inaccurate language. In practice, most teachers are eclectic in their methods and are more concerned with how to articulate gaps between elementary and secondary programs and between the programs in secondary schools and higher education. Practical secondary school communication skills come up against grammar-based placement exams and courses in college.

The early introduction of foreign languages has gained general support from everyone concerned with the development of language skills. Young children between the ages of 4 and 10 learn foreign languages easily. Children are usually flexible, uninhibited, and eager to explore different languages. Early introduction of languages also enhances cultural awareness among children. Languages may be used to explore the typical experiences in different cultures (cooking styles and names of foods, folk songs, games played in foreign countries). Among the innovations suggested for stimulating language learning are bilingual nursery schools, home visits by bilingual teachers, tutoring of younger children by trained school-age peers during play, and mobile classrooms to teach foreign languages.

Students are now being encouraged to participate in the planning of new language courses. This trend emerged from the need to make the language arts relevant to the needs of students. In addition, it is now realized that optimum learning takes place when the learner is meaningfully involved in determining what is to be learned and how it is to be learned. A teacher who encountered resistance in teaching academic English to Spanish speakers responded by engaging them in a study of how Spanish and English are being used. Students visited, observed, recorded, and analyzed language and language registers (formal and informal use of language) in a variety of situations—media, law and medical, offices, and soccer fields. Achievement and positive attitudes toward language learning accelerated.

Such practices contrast with efforts to entice students toward second language learning through exposure to language and culture by way of games. If students are shielded from the serious mental effort required for learning a language, the subject may be trivialized and fail to gain student respect.

Although language learning probably will include basic speaking as well as reading and writing, the teaching of foreign language may follow Israel's changes in language learning policy. As indicated in Chapter 8, Israel's new national English as a foreign language program builds from authentic language situations where teachers ask, "What do you want to do?" and not "What do you want to learn?" Students choose the goal they have for speaking a foreign language and aim at acquiring knowledge in four domains—social interaction, access to information, presentation, and appreciation of literature, each of which draws from the traditional language skills and grammar as needed for attaining the learner's purpose.[63]

---

[63]"Seeing the 'New' in Light of the 'Old': Evolving Interpretations of a New English Curriculum," *Journal of Curriculum Studies* 36, no. 3 (May 2004): 321–339.

Resource persons can bring life to the languages. Non–English-speaking persons in the community may be invited to participate in classroom learning activities. Community businesses that employ bilingual persons may be encouraged to offer internship experiences. Field trips and opportunities for travel can be used to introduce students to the language in use, making language studies alive and vital.

Among the new methodologies is the *confluent approach* drawn from the humanistic orientation. Accordingly, students participate in group activities designed to elicit open interpersonal communication. Students in such classes explore and discuss various aspects of themselves, as well as less personal information, in the foreign language. The most original of the new methods is *suggestopedia,* which uses hypnotic and subliminal learning techniques, such as sleep learning.

Optimism for increased instruction in foreign language is found in such recent developments as the reinstatement of foreign language as a graduation requirement and as a college entrance requirement, language instruction beginning in the fifth and sixth grades, and the public's general awareness of the commercial and social value of learning another language.

There are, however, marked changes in the language taught in schools as evidenced by increased percentage rates of students studying true foreign languages (Japanese, Chinese, Korean, and the like) relative to changes in percentages of students studying the cognate languages (French, German, and Italian). In part, the fastest growing offerings reflect the changing diversity of the United States and the number of people who speak a foreign language at home. For example, Spanish speakers have increased 50%, Chinese 98%, Tagalog 87%, Korean 127%, Vietnamese 150%, and Japanese 25%, while Italian speakers declined 20%, German 3.7%, and Greek 5.4%.[64]

The year 2003 saw the highest enrollment ever in university foreign language classes. The percentage of elementary schools offering foreign language went up to 30%, secondary schools 90%. Under the NCLB, foreign language in the K–12 program is considered a "core academic program." Concerns for national security and globalization have brought the need for increasing fluent speakers of languages other than English, resulting in Congress's proclaiming the year 2004–2005 as "year of foreign language study" and the expansion of the foreign language programs in K–12 schools.

The goals of the program are to encourage multilingualism, enhance the learning of intercultural understanding, and to advance the concept that every American should develop proficiently in both English and another language.

Bilingual education is an issue. The conflict between English-only instruction versus initial instruction in one's native language is being redefined. Some states have legislated English-only with waivers on parental request. Others have traditional bilingual programs that give instruction in the child's home language while transitioning them to English instruction. Also, there are partial and full immersion programs that teach English as a second language, and there are now more two-way bilingual programs where, for example, English and Spanish speakers together learn each other's language while engaging in common tasks, recognizing that key concepts are attainable in either language.

Underlying the changes in bilingual education are such factors as:

- Immigrant parents who fear that isolating their children from ESL (English as a Second Language) learning will cut them off from U.S. integration and social mobility.

- Findings about the time it takes to transition students to fluency in a second language. Immigrants vary from 3.6 to 7.4 years in becoming fluent even if they are born in the United States but are living in a linguistic enclave.

[64]*Language Spoken at Home and Ability to Speak English for United States, Regions, and States* (Washington, DC: Population Division, Statistical Information Office, Census Bureau, 1990).

- The desire of second generation immigrants to receive and give information in English.
- The finding that bilingualism enhances cognitive functioning.
- The economic advantage of being bilingual.

THE ARTS

The visual and performing arts have always played a role in American education, although often with different, sometimes competing aims. The 1800s and early 1900s provided multiple views of arts education that have dominated the field for over a century, sometimes to the detriment of arts education. In the 1830s and the 1840s, Horace Mann and the Common School Movement promoted the utility of arts in public education, with an emphasis on drawing to enhance handwriting and manual skills.[65] In addition, studies provided professional art instruction in drawing and painting after the Civil War while colleges and universities stressed art history.[66] Also, in the eighteenth century, Amos Bronson Alcott and Elizabeth Peabody, transcendentalists, provided a more aesthetic rationale by emphasizing art's potential for creation and beauty.[67] In the early 1900s, John Dewey supported arts production as intrinsically meaningful to children, and the 1930s saw the arts as integral to "creative self-expression."[68] Certainly, these multiple aims remain today.

However, during the second half of the twentieth century, the arts began to enjoy support for their role in intellectual development or what Elliot Eisner calls "the growth of the mind."[69] Much of this new thinking is based on the work of Ernst Cassirer, Susanne Langer, Nelson Goodman, and later Howard Gardner who advanced the idea that meaning occurs through a variety of symbol systems, including writing, mathematics, and the arts, which are cognitively based.[70] This line of inquiry led to Harvard University's Project Zero, a major research center for arts and learning. Intellectual legitimacy for the arts moved arts education out of the realm of frill to necessity.

The idea that the arts merit attention in all schools underlies the National Standards for Education in the Arts, which views arts instruction as integral to every person's complete education. These standards emphasize long-term, well-developed programs, not merely artistic exposure. Each art form standard focuses on three areas of competence: creating and performing, perceiving and analyzing, and understanding cultural and historical contexts.[71] Critics of the standards, while applauding their commitment to furthering the arts in schools, sometimes question their rigidity.

The issue of whether the arts are academic or creative is clearly seen in two distinctly different approaches that are revitalizing the American art curriculum. On the one hand, the Getty Center in Los Angeles advocates a discipline-based curriculum in which the arts are approached primarily as a cognitive discipline through the teaching of art history, criticism, and aesthetics along with production, that is, with the goal to learn about art, not merely to "do" art. Through these "disciplinary lenses," students become versed in styles and techniques before they produce their own works. For example, sixth graders may study

[65]Frederick M. Logan, *Growth of Art in American Schools* (New York: Harper and Brothers, 1955): 16—24.
[66]Ibid., 43—65.
[67]Arthur D. Efland, *A History of Art Education: Intellectual and Social Currents in Teaching the Visual Arts* (New York: Teachers College Press, 1990), 115–121.
[68]Ibid., 170 and 210.
[69]Elliot W. Eisner, *The Arts and the Creation of the Mind* (New Haven, CT: Yale University Press, 2002), xi.
[70]Howard Gardner, *Art, Mind, and Brain: A Cognitive Approach to Creativity* (New York: Basic Books, 1982), 1–79.
[71]John O'Neil, "Looking at Art Through New Eyes: Visual Arts Program Pushed to Reaching New Goals, New Students," *Curriculum Update* 32, no. 1 (Jan. 1994): 1–8.

Matisse, then paint in his style.[72] In contrast, many arts centers, including the Lincoln Center in New York, take a more experiential approach that focuses on artistic development first and encourages creative expression as students engage in the acts of performing and creating. Taking a middle view, Steven Zemelman, Harvey Daniels, and Arthur Hyde identified a number of quality markers for what they call "best practice in the arts." These include students having rich opportunities to learn to do the various arts across the curriculum as well as engage in them as disciplines, develop their abilities in a preferred art form, think analytically about art, learn a wide range of art forms, including theater, music and dance, have access to artists in residence, and attend professional shows and performances.[73]

Another current direction in arts education focuses on arts and learning. A 1994 study emphasized the importance of the arts in schools, especially "the arts and equitable access to meaning; the arts as ways to promote student achievement, engagement, and persistence in school," and "the arts as ways to provide authentic multicultural voices, validate students' cultural heritage, and promote cross-cultural understanding.[74] More recently, *Champions of Change*, a research report sponsored by the Arts Education Partnership and the President's Committee on the Arts and the Humanities, also supports the value of arts education, especially music and theater, in a variety of settings, including urban schools.[75] Carolyn L. Piazza offers a range of methods for enhancing the teaching of "*multiple literacies*," which she describes as "the complex amalgam of communicative channels, symbols, forms, and meanings inherent in oral and written language (verbal and nonverbal) as well as the arts— visual arts, music, dance, theater, and film (including television, video, and technology)."[76] While additional research is still needed about arts and learning, a recent Harvard study points to the positive role of drama in increasing students' verbal skills."[77]

Given the competing agendas for arts education, educators face risks that teaching art as an intellectual discipline will undermine its emotional and motivational importance or that focusing solely on emotional aspects will weaken its potential cognitive impact. Thus efforts to renew the teaching of the arts must balance all the positive features that multiple experiences of art education provide children and young adults.

CONCLUDING COMMENTS

Most subjects are influenced by the same social, economic, political, and technological forces. Hence it is no great surprise to see most of them moving in the same direction. We have just undergone a period of great renewal in the academic curriculum. Policy makers have demanded that more students complete more work in the academic subjects, particularly mathematics, science, writing, and the humanities. This renewal was accompanied by three problems: (1) a crisis in purpose, (2) a concern about student interest, (3) and a desire for open access to knowledge.

[72]Stephen Mark Dobbs, *Learning in and through Art: A Guide to Discipline-Based Art Education* (Los Angeles: Getty Education Institute for the Arts, 1998).
[73]Stephen Zemelman, Harvey Daniels, and Arthur Hyde, *Best Practice: New Standards for Teaching and Learning in America's Schools*, 2nd ed. (Portsmouth, NH: Heinemann, 1998), 163–168.
[74]Jaye T. Darby and James S. Catterall, "The Fourth R: The Arts and Learning," *Teachers College Record* 96, no. 2 (winter 1994): 299–327.
[75]Edward B. Fiske, ed., *Champions of Change: The Impact of the Arts on Learning* (Washington, DC: Arts Education Partnership and President's Committee on the Arts and the Humanities, 1999).
[76]Carolyn L. Piazza, *Multiple Forms of Literacy: Teaching Literacy and the Arts* (Upper Saddle River, NJ: Merrill, 1999): 2–3.
[77]Ann Podlozny, "Strengthening Verbal Skills through the Use of Classroom Drama: A Clear Link," *The Journal of Aesthetic Education* 34, nos. 3–4 (fall/winter 2002): 239–275.

There is a revival in all the academic subjects to find clear-cut goals and a body of essential content. In part, this activity is a response to the many incoherent programs developed at a period when individualization was prized. Thus far, there is no final agreement on central purposes in any field. Curriculum policy statements in the respective fields reflect pluralistic interests: functional competency, intellectual development, traditional values, social relevancy, and self-actualization. There is a lack of agreement regarding essential content and strong disagreement between those who prefer the traditional curriculum as the standard of excellence and those who want the academic content to reflect new conceptions of the fields. Even those trying to set national standards and the new college board specialists for college preparation reveal inconsistent expectations, which are more in keeping with political compromise (something for everybody) than an educational philosophy. The existence of separate subjects is an obstacle to interdisciplinary studies.

On the world scene, the problem of globalizing the curriculum for basic literacy and the academic disciplines through systemic accountability and efficiency runs the risk of destroying indigenous values and educational practices. Conversely, there is need to transcend both the separate domains of knowledge and narrow national identities in the interest of world humanistic concerns and environmental survival. As indicated by Kenneth Tye, U.S. schools are still seen as a major force in building national loyalties rather than in increasing knowledge and understanding of world problems and cultures.[78]

A new rationale for redefining goals in academic subjects is needed. It would be better to have individual curriculum programs reflecting specific philosophies—as exist in some distinguished magnet, specialized, and private schools—than to create programs with conflicting purposes unless schools are prepared to make the conflicts themselves the centerpiece for discourse.

Student interest and access reflect the fact that most academic subjects are taught in a sterile manner—primarily textbook information with corresponding emphasis on terminology and definitions. Also, only some students are given the opportunity to pursue subjects in an inspired way, asking new questions, thinking critically and imaginatively.

Studies of fields such as science reveal much student alienation from knowledge. Less than 50% of high school graduates express interest in further study of science, and there is little evidence that school science prepares them either for college or for life. Fewer than 10% of secondary students are interested in the field of science. If additional mandates for more work in the "hard" subjects, such as science, result in more of the same inferior curriculum, the alienation from knowledge is likely to be even greater.

A serious challenge is to design a curriculum that will enable large numbers of students (particularly those from less academically privileged classes) to have success with content formerly available only to an elite group. Obviously, to define subjects in terms of the ways in which experts view their subjects is not enough. Nor is it adequate to offer a subject as a means of advancing up the academic ladder. Students expect to apply what they are learning to current issues and to their personal needs. It is encouraging to note in many of the new trends in the academic curriculum give opportunities for the students' active learning in exploring, drawing inferences, problem solving, collaborative learning, and creativity. The introduction of a multicultural perspective rather than the domination of one culture is an important trend.

Curriculum makers in all fields are trying to enable students to create subject matter for themselves and derive meaning. This effort is putting curriculum makers ahead of academic specialists in the redefinition and integration of subject matter. The relationship of vocational education to academic achievement in mathematics and science is one example.

---

[78]Kenneth A. Tye, "Global Education as a World-Wide Movement," *Phi Delta Kappan* 85, no. 2 (Oct. 2003): 165–168.

It is clear that closer attention might be paid to the relationships among the ideal academic curricula as stated by national and state policy makers, the perceptions of teachers about what they are teaching, and the perceptions of students about what they are learning.

QUESTIONS

1. Sometimes academic trends reflect a desired future; others warn of practices that should be stopped. Identify some trends that you feel contribute to a desirable future and some that you see as dangerous.

2. Try your hand at anticipating a likely future trend in a subject field by (a) identifying or analyzing political, economic, or other social factors that have the potential for shaping curriculum and (b) indicating how this force might affect the curriculum in this field.

3. Subject matter was never really viewed as an end in itself. The learning of a subject is always justified as useful for some social purpose. What social purpose or interest has been served by your academic field?

4. It is sometimes suggested that teachers offer various courses like technology science, surgical science, science and pollution, health care science, and the science of music so that students' interests and local needs are better served. What scientific themes might run through these courses?

5. Are you on the side of subject matter as individual expression and a tool for social change or subject matter as a body of knowledge necessary for participation in an academic community? Why?

SUGGESTED STRATEGIC RESEARCH

BALANCING NATIONAL IDENTITY WITH WORLD CITIZENSHIP
Select a standards framework for a subject and analyze how it responds to the dilemma of indoctrinating students into a national culture and its values versus promoting study of collective global identities and tolerance for cosmopolitan values.

RELATING EARLY EXPERIENCES IN READING WITH LITERARY ACCOMPLISHMENTS
Clues to essential components in learning to read may be gleaned by studying the autobiographies and biographies of distant (John Stuart Mills) and present (C. Nussbaum) persons who represent the highest levels of literacy. What were the major influences on their learning to read? What views of literacy shaped their instruction?

COMPARING FOREIGN LANGUAGE AND SECOND LANGUAGE CURRICULUMS
Foreign languages are usually studied outside the foreign culture, while second language learning takes place within the culture of the new language. Compare textbooks or other materials designed for foreign language instruction with instructional materials for second language learning. After you make a comparative analysis, give an account of why the curriculums differ.

DETERMINING THE DIFFERENTIAL EFFECTS OF SOCIAL CONSTRUCTIONIST PRACTICES IN MATH AND SCIENCE
New math and science curriculums emphasize open problems—many of which are situations in out-of-school contexts and call for peer collaboration and intellectual discussion. Might the negative achievement of different groups be exacerbated by the new practice? How do students who represent different social class, gender, or ethnicity groups respond to the new curriculum? What might account for its varied effects?

SELECTED REFERENCES

MATHEMATICS
Principles and Standards for Teaching Mathematics. Reston, VA: National Council of Teachers of Mathematics, 2000.
STEEN, LYNN ARTHUR, ED. *Heeding the Call for Change: Suggestions for Curriculum Action.* Washington, DC: Mathematical Association of America, 1992.

SCIENCE
CROSS, ROGER, ED. *A Vision for Science Education: Responding to the Work of Peter Fensham.* New York: Routledge Falmer, 2002.
CSERMELY, PETER. Communication in the Life Sciences for Students. URL: http://www.kutdiak.hu. 2004.
HURD, PAUL D. "New Minds for a New Age: Prologue to Modernizing the Science Curriculum." *Science Education* 78, no. 1 (1944): 103–116.
Science for All Americans: Project 2061 Report on Literacy Goals in Science, Mathematics and Technology. Washington, DC: American Association for the Advancement of Science, 1989.

PHYSICAL EDUCATION AND HEALTH
O'NEIL, JOHN. "Physical Education: Promoting Lifelong Fitness for All Students." *Curriculum Update* 30, no. 10 (Dec. 1992): 3.
SMITH, JENNY. *Education and Public Health—Natural Partners in Learning for Life.* Alexandria, VA: Association for Supervision and Curriculum Development, 2003.

ENGLISH
APPLEBEE, ARTHUR N. *Tradition and Reform in the Teaching of English: A History.* Urbana, IL: National Council of Teachers of English, 1974.
BURKE, JIM. *The English Teacher's Companion: A Complete Guide to Classroom, Curriculum, and the Profession,* 2nd ed. Portsmouth, NH: Heinemann, 2003.
English Journal. "Special Issue: Teaching Writing in the Twenty-First Century," 90, no. 1 (Sept. 2000): 29–126.
ROSENBLATT, LOUISE. *The Reader, the Text, the Poem: The Transactional Theory of the Literary Work.* Carbondale: Southern Illinois University Press, 1978.

HISTORY AND SOCIAL STUDIES
EVANS, RONALD W. *The Social Studies Wars: What Should We Teach the Children?* New York: Teachers College Press, 2004.
SEIXAS, PETER. "Parallel Crises: History and the Social Studies Curriculum in the USA," *Journal of Curriculum Studies* 25, no. 3 (1993): 235–250.

ARTS AND MUSIC
CORNETT, CLAUDIA E. *The Arts as Meaning Makers: Integrating Literature and the Arts throughout the Curriculum.* Upper Saddle River, NJ: Merrill Prentice Hall, 1998.
GOLDBERG, MERRYL. *Arts and Learning,* 2nd ed. New York: Longmans, 2001.
Music Educators National Conference. *The Vision for Arts Education in the 21st Century.* Reston, VA: Music Educators National Conference, 1994.
REIMER, BENNET, AND RALPH A. SMITH, EDS. *The Arts, Education, and Aesthetic Knowing,* 91st Yearbook, Part II. Chicago: National Society for the Study of Education (NSSE), 1992.

CURRICULUM INQUIRY: RETROSPECT AND PROSPECT

Although it is time for promoting new curriculum thinking and proposing more curriculum possibilities, the work of an earlier generation of curriculum leaders may help us understand the origins and frameworks that are influencing our curriculum practices. Also, study of the field may help one see what was missing in the early work and perhaps even now needs correcting. Or conversely, what from the past is usable to today's curriculum?

What is current in conceptualizing curriculum? Where is curriculum inquiry going? Who are the curriculum researchers—technical experts who give credibility to particular programs desired by politicians, teachers who are finding better ways to motivate their students, or cultural theorists and activists who are trying to get us to look at our world in new ways? What do they say they are doing in the curriculum? What is said about them?

If you preface reading of these two chapters by recalling your familiarity with curriculum development in the past and your knowledge of key figures moving curriculum in new directions today, your reading of these chapters will be more purposeful.

CHAPTER 13

A HISTORICAL PERSPECTIVE OF CURRICULUM MAKING

THERE ARE at least two reasons for attending to the history of curriculum thought and action. First, a review of the past can help us identify problems with which dedicated persons have struggled and are struggling.

Admittedly, we still have to decide whether these problems are unsolvable, and therefore, should be abandoned as unfruitful areas of inquiry, or whether their very persistence makes them worthy of our attention. For example, the issue of curriculum integration or correlation (the relating of ideas from different subject matter), which is so pressing today, was central in 1895. At that time, correlation was viewed by some with suspicion and as a threat to the inviolability of the basic divisions of subject matter. Others saw it as an answer to the problem of an overcrowded program of studies and of value in helping the child's untrained mind relate an enormous number of topics.

At the start of the new century, as in 1895, some ask not so much whether there should be integration of subject matter but how it should be accomplished. Should we group subjects around problems, using the facts from one discipline to illuminate another, or should we include within a comprehensive course the important generalizations from many fields?

A second reason for studying the history of curriculum thought and practice is to gain a clearer understanding of the processes of curriculum making by examining the work of prominent exponents in the field. By examining what curriculum meant to those who developed the field during the twentieth century, we can see more clearly what curriculum now means. For example, few issues are more important to current theorists than the formulation of an adequate concept of curriculum. Theorists believe that its clarification may contribute to the improvement of curriculum and that it will increase our understanding of curricular phenomena. Some concepts of curriculum include the following:

1. A set of guidelines for developing products, books, and materials for the curriculum.

2. A program of activities; a listing of course offerings, units, topics, and content.

3. All learning guided by the school.

4. The process by which one decides what to teach.

5. The study of the processes used in curriculum making.

6. What learners actually learn at school.

7. What one plans for students to learn.

8. A design for learning.

9. Enactment by teachers and students in the construction of meanings.

10. A conversation about how curriculum shapes a student's identity.

In 1890 extensive professional preparation for curriculum making was nonexistent, and there were no curriculum experts in the United States. Yet less than 50 years later, curriculum was a recognized field of specialization. Two ways to illustrate the development of this field and at the same time to illustrate the value of the specialization is to review the work of those who study the history of American curriculum and to look at the curriculum questions and answers of those persons most associated with the origins of the field.

CURRICULUM HISTORIANS

Years ago, Arno Bellack could point to the ahistorical character of the curriculum field as ignoring the past.[1] It was as if curriculum specialists wanted to escape the past and focus only on creating something better. Of course, there have long been historians who have presented their accounts of the history of education, which included descriptions of what was taught and how at different times and places. What is new is the emergence of scholars who are interested in history as a way of understanding fundamental issues of curriculum and who are also members of a subspecialization within the history of education.[2]

Those writing the history of curriculum reflect widely different orientations and areas of concern. On the one hand, there are curriculum scholars such as Daniel and Laurel Tanner whose history of curriculum focuses chiefly on school reformers of the twentieth century, especially John Dewey.[3] Indeed they use Dewey's writings as the lens for judging curriculum movement and trends past and present. Their interpretations reflect a commitment to the ideal of a common curriculum rather than specialization, a formal curriculum with a balance between academic and practical studies, and an opposition to school reformers who favor child-centered (humanistic) curriculum and radical criticism (social reconstructionism).

On the other hand, Joel Spring represents scholars of curriculum history who look at politics in an effort to show why reformers who announced what is good for students and schools have had little effect on either. Spring's account of what subjects have been chosen to be taught and what has been taught in each subject points to the power of special interest groups, particularly business and politically conservative and right-wing religious organizations.[4]

Increasingly popular among curriculum historians is the effort to show the direction that particular school subjects have taken over time in response to the struggles of different interest groups. David Saxe's *Social Studies in the Schools*,[5] Kerry Friedman's "Art Education,"[6] and George Stanek's *Mathematics*[7] are cases in point.

---

[1] Arno Bellack, "History of Curriculum Thought and Practice," *Review of Educational Research* 39, no. 3 (1969): 283–290.
[2] Herbert M. Kliebard, "Constructing a History of the American Curriculum," in *Handbook of Research on Curriculum*, Philip W. Jackson, ed. (New York: Macmillan, 1992), 157–184.
[3] Daniel Tanner and Laurel Tanner, *History of the School Curriculum* (New York: Macmillan, 1990).
[4] Joel Spring, *Conflict of Interest* (White Plains, NY: Longmans, 1993).
[5] David W. Saxe, *Social Studies in the Schools: A History of the Early Years* (Albany: State University of New York Press, 1991).
[6] Kerry Friedman, "Art Education as a Social Production: Culture, Society, Politics in the Formulation of Curriculum," in *The Formation of School Subjects*, Thomas S. Popkewitz, ed. (London: Falmer, 1987), 63–84.
[7] George M. Stanek, "Mathematics Education in the Beginning of the Twentieth Century," op. cit., 145–175.

There is criticism of both the scholars who study the history of particular school subjects and the scholars who derive their sense of curriculum history from curriculum policy reports found in professional journals, reports of national conventions, prestigious national curriculum committees and government leaders, and professional associations. The chief criticism is that the pronouncements of major curriculum commissions and leaders in the curriculum field were unlikely to be translated into curriculum practice at the classroom level. Indeed, Larry Cuban's study of how teachers taught supports the belief that there has been a great gap between curriculum rhetoric and curriculum practice.[8]

There is need for understanding how the ideas of Dewey and other reformers became institutionalized in specific communities. The reliance on rhetoric instead of practice as sufficient historical evidence of curriculum reality is troublesome. Hence, some curriculum historians are turning to primary curriculum documents—courses of study, samples of students' work (notebooks, exams, projects, and textbooks)—from historical periods. Their work is possible in part because of collections of educational materials that reflect changes in textbooks and curriculum guides. Notable among these collections are those at Teachers College, Columbia University; at Gutman Library at the University of Illinois at Urbana–Champaign; the Center for Research Libraries in Chicago; and the Directory of Historical Curriculum Collections in Virginia Beach. The Emmanuel Textbook Project in Paris is an exemplar for such collections. Emmanuel is a databank that aims at recording and showing the locations of French textbooks published from 1789 to the present.[9] Other resources include oral histories of the Systematic Collection and presentation of recollections of curriculum leaders. O. L. Davis, Jr., and George L. Mehaffy, for example, established an oral history program at the University of Texas in Austin, which collects interviews with major figures in the field of curriculum.[10]

Context for Formulation of the Curriculum Field

By the late 1890s, the conventional classifications of knowledge were seen by many as unsatisfactory in preparing students for new social demands. The curriculum was to respond to vast social changes inherent in industrialization, a large and different school population, and new psychologies emphasizing either fitting the curriculum to the nature of the child (developmentalists) or the training of specific capacities rather than trying to develop the elements of the mind through different subject matters (behavioristic connectionism).

Herbert Kliebard interprets this period as a struggle among different interest groups about what should be taught.[11] He identifies four competitors: (1) *classical humanists,* like Charles A. Eliot, who favored the liberal arts and the transmission of traditional values and culture; (2) *child-centered leaders,* like G. Stanley Hall, who argued that the content of the curriculum could be determined from data of child development (Hall's pedocentric curriculum upset the dominant ideal of fitting the child to the school with the new ideal of fitting the school to the child, encouraging different curriculum for the slow and the fast); (3) *social efficiency* advocates, represented by John Franklin Bobbitt, who saw the curriculum as a mechanism for preparing students for adult roles in the new industrial society. (As described later, his work had great influence on the practice of curriculum development by stressing specifications and responses to current social needs rather than transmitting classical subjects.); and (4) *social reconstructionists,* such as Harold Rugg, who wanted the

---

[8]Larry Cuban, *How Teachers Taught: Constancy and Change in American Classrooms 1890–1980* (New York: Longmans, 1993).

[9]Alain Coppin, "The Emmanuel Textbooks Project," *Journal of Curriculum Studies* 24, no. 4 (1992): 345–356.

[10]O. L. Davis, Jr., and George L. Mehaffy, "An Elusive Quarry: On the Trail of Curriculum History," in *Curriculum History,* Craig Kridel, ed. (New York: Lanham, 1989).

[11]Herbert M. Kliebard, *The Struggle for the American Curriculum, 1893–1951* (Boston: Routledge and Kegan Paul, 1986).

curriculum to provide social change by giving students a new vision of justice and equality with which to remake the society.

According to Kliebard, each of these interest groups was the dominant force at a given time. The classics dominated the nineteenth century; social efficiency and scientific curriculum making were predominant in the first two decades of the twentieth century; child development, with the popularity of the project and activity curriculum, held center stage in the 1920s; and social reconstructionism through critical social studies texts was strongest in the 1930s. Kliebard held that John Dewey did not fit comfortably in any of the four camps, nor did his vision take hold as powerfully as those of the competing factions.

David Larabee has provided additional insights regarding the interest groups identified by Kliebard.[12] Larabee sees these groups caught by two opposing elements in American ideology: *capitalism,* with its emphasis on individualism and competition, and *democracy,* with the pursuit of equality. The classical traditionalists concerned themselves with the college preparatory track, sharpening the differentiation between the college-oriented middle-class top stratum and the vocational working-class stratum. Members of the child-centered group were democratically oriented in their insistence on adapting the curriculum to the heterogeneous needs and capacities of students but in so doing denied many access to prestigious subject matter. Those of the social efficiency group tended to stress the market orientation and preparation of students for the world's work; the social reconstructionists, on the other hand, went against the capitalistic position that school should be responsive to the demands of the marketplace and instead argued for reconstructing the curriculum around the standards of political democracy.

In his study of the Central High School of Philadelphia between 1838 and 1939, Larabee found a shift from preparation for business to preparation for higher education and the professions. A uniform course of study was transformed into a menu of choices arranged in a hierarchy with academic courses for the top stratum.[13] Larabee attributed the shift as a response to the demands of the credential market where the high school diploma could be protected and traded for a thing of value—college, professional status, and high salaries.

In his analysis of the history of the twentieth century American curriculum, Barry Franklin concentrates on the social efficiency interest group and indicates how these curriculum reformers were more interested in promoting socialization than in imparting intellectual content. Franklin advances the thesis that the middle-class intellectuals of the time established the field of curriculum as a way of shaping the curriculum so that it would reconcile traditional liberal democratic values with a transformed American society. He sees social efficiency educators, like Franklin Bobbitt and Warrent W. Charters, as dominating the curriculum field during its formative period and as being preoccupied with the question of how the curriculum (course of study) could socially control the twin forces of urbanization and industrialization. He also believed that the programs that were implemented reflect the interests of several social groups and were not faithful to social efficiency doctrine.[14]

FOUNDERS OF THE FIELD OF CURRICULUM

The immediate focus of the emergent curriculum field in the early 1920s was on how to make the curriculum. For a 2-year period beginning in 1924, major figures from the different interest groups tried to achieve a consensus on the questions that the field should

---

[12]David F Larabee, "Politics, Markets and the Compromised Curriculum," *Harvard Educational Review* 57, no. 4 (1987): 483–495.

[13]David Larabee, *The Making of an American High School: The Credential Market and the Central High School of Philadelphia 1838–1939* (New Haven: Yale University Press, 1988).

[14]Barry Franklin, *Building the American Community: The School Curriculum and the Search for Social Control* (London: Falmer, 1986).

address.[15] Among the questions were the following: How can curriculum best preface effective participation in adult life? Should curriculum makers formulate a point of view concerning the merits or deficiencies of American civilization? Should the school fit students into the social order or educate them to change it? What is the place and function of subject matter in the education process—an end, something to be learned, or a tool for problem solving? What portion of the curriculum should be general, specialized, vocational, and optional? Should the curriculum be made in advance? To what extent is the organization of subject matter to be structured by the learner or constructed by curriculum planners? To what degree should the curriculum provide for individual differences and "minimum essentials"? What use should be made of the spontaneous interests of learners?

In assessing these questions, the participants, though recognizing the importance of organized subject matter of the academic disciplines, favored helping learners to solve problems relevant to their own lives. Hence, they held that content should be drawn in interdisciplinary fashion rather than divided and taught as separate subjects.

In their own work in the curriculum field, early specialists gave different answers to basic questions. The accounts that follow illustrate the contrasts between those who would fit students to an existing order and those who would prepare students to change it.

The persons chosen for review span a period from 1890 to the end of the twentieth century and represent a much larger group of specialists. One basis for their selection is that they both studied the theory of curriculum and engaged in making it. In all instances, these curriculum workers contributed to the development of curriculum as an academic study and established its central questions.

HERBARTISM AND THE MCMURRYS

Charles A. McMurry (1857–1929) and his brother Frank W. McMurry (1862–1936) taught for several years in elementary schools before going abroad to study at the University of Jena in Germany, a mecca for educators in the late 1890s. There, they became profoundly influenced by the pedagogical theory of Johann Herbart whose *Outlines of Educational Doctrine* was the basis for many of the ideas and practices at Jena.[16]

Basic Tenets of Herbartism

Essentially, Herbartism was a rationalized set of philosophical and psychological ideas applied to instructional method. It rested on the assumption that only large, connected units of subject matter are able to arouse and keep alive a child's deep interest. Hence, it stressed "the *doctrine of concentration*," which occurs when the mind is wholly immersed in one interest to the exclusion of everything else. This doctrine was supplemented with the *doctrine of correlation*, which makes one subject the focus of attention but sees to it that connections are made with related subjects.

Instructional Procedure   Specifically, Herbartians recognized five steps as essential in the procedure of instruction:

1. *Preparation*—to revive in the student's consciousness the related ideas from past experience that will arouse interest in the new material and prepare the pupil for its rapid understanding.

---

[15]Harold Rugg, ed., *The Foundations of Curriculum Making, 26th Yearbook of the National Society for the Study of Education, Part 1* (Bloomington, IL: Public School Publishing Co., 1927).
[16]Johann F. Herbart, *Outlines of Educational Doctrine*, Alex F. Lange, trans. (New York: Macmillan, 1904).

2. *Presentation*—to present the new material in concrete form, unless there is already ample sensory experience, and to relate it to the students' past experiences, by reading, conversing, experimenting, lecturing, and so forth.

3. *Association*—to analyze and to compare the present and the old, thus evolving a new idea.

4. *Generalization*—to form general rules, laws, or principles from the analyzed experience, developing general concepts as well as sensations and perceptions.

5. *Application*—to put the generalized idea to work in other situations, sometimes to test it, sometimes to use it as a practical tool.

The Goal of Education   Herbart's followers believed that moral action was the highest educational goal and that education should prepare a person for life with the highest ideals of the culture. Furthermore, they believed that some subjects, such as history and literature, were superior for the development of moral ideas. They thought that if learners were guided by correct ideas and motivated by good interests, they would be prepared to discharge life's duties properly. Among the interests or motives to be advanced were sympathetic interest (a kindly disposition toward people), social interest (participation in public affairs), and religious interest (contemplation of human destiny).

The McMurrys' Thinking

The McMurrys recognized in Herbartian pedagogy a systematic method of selecting, arranging, and organizing the curriculum, something that had been missing in American schooling. On their return from Germany, they joined with others to apply the Herbartian methods and ideals in American schools. During his career, Charles McMurry wrote 30 books and prepared a course of study for the eight elementary grades describing how to select and arrange ideas for instruction. Primarily, he addressed himself to teachers. His own teaching in the schools of Illinois and at George Peabody College for Teachers centered on the making of lesson plans according to the Herbartian five formal steps. He also concerned himself with the special instructional methods required for the teaching of specific subject fields.

Frank McMurry taught and wrote at Teachers College at Columbia University. His students were chiefly teachers who would train and supervise other teachers. His course in general methods reflected the Herbartian concern about the ends of education, the means for their attainment, the relative worth of studies, and the doctrines of concentration and correlation. Both brothers participated in national organizations devoted to the study and improvement of school programs. The effect of their efforts was great. Charles's course of study provided an overall framework for teachers, giving details for conducting lessons, the types of studies, and the special methods thought best for organizing the content in each subject. The McMurrys' influence on lesson planning was especially noteworthy. In the period between 1900 and 1910, "every good teacher was supposed to have a lesson plan for each class period, and the five formal steps were much in evidence."[17] Even today military instructors are expected to design their lessons according to the formal steps outlined by the McMurrys and Madeline Hunter's lessons show their connection to Herbart and the McMurrys. Analysis of the McMurrys' work identifies the questions and answers that define the nature of curriculum thought in this early period.

---

[17]William H. Kilpatrick, "Dewey's Influence on Education," in *The Philosophy of John Dewey*, Paul A. Schlipp, ed. (Evanston, IL: Northwestern University, 1939), 465.

Basic Questions   Implicit in the McMurrys' thinking were five basic questions:

1. *What is the aim of education?* The McMurrys broadened Herbartian concerns for the moral development of the child to include the desire to lead children into the ways of good citizenship and into a wise physical, social, and moral adjustment to the world.

2. *What subject matter has the greatest pedagogical value?* Initially the McMurrys regarded literature as most useful in bringing the aesthetic and the intellectual into helpful association: they saw geography as the most universal, concrete correlating study. When the development of good character was the primary aim, they saw literature and history as the most important subjects. Later, the McMurrys differentiated between subjects that primarily helped the learner to express thought and those that primarily helped the learner receive or furnish thought. They noted that about one-half of schoolwork (i.e., beginning reading, writing, spelling, grammar, music, numbers, modeling, drawing, and painting) depends on the other half for its motive and force. In their later years, the McMurrys came to see that new subjects would claim favor. These new studies were nature study, science, industrial arts, health, agriculture, civics, and modern languages. Indeed, the introduction of new branches of knowledge and activity was seen by them as one of the greatest achievements of the age.

3. *How is subject matter related to instructional method?* The McMurrys believed there were formal elements of method and concepts for each subject, whether geology, arithmetic, or literature. They insisted that the child learn to think with these elements just as the specialists did in these fields and that the learner develop a consciousness of the right method of thinking in each subject. They saw that teachers at that time were not equipped with the fundamental concepts of each subject and, therefore, found it difficult to order instruction to clarify concepts in the respective fields. They were disturbed when curriculum workers ignored the fact that each subject matter makes particular demands on the organization of the curriculum.

4. *What is the best sequence of studies?* The McMurrys thought that suitable subject matter varies according to age and stage of development. Initially, they believed in the *theory of the culture epochs.* This theory holds that the child passes through the same general stages of development through which the race or culture has passed. Hence, what interested humanity at a certain historical stage would appeal most to a child at the corresponding stage of development. It was thought, for example, that teachers should present the stories of Ulysses to younger children. *The Odyssey* was seen as a means by which the heroic impulses of childhood could be related to an ideal person who achieved what the child would like to achieve. This work was deemed of pedagogical value, because it portrayed the primitive human struggle and at the same time revealed a higher plane of reason. Similarly, *Robinson Crusoe* was viewed as a good source for showing humankind's struggle with nature and at the same time helping the learner see that myths were attempts to interpret nature. Myths, legends, and heroic tales were followed by biography and formal history. By 1923, Charles McMurry, at least, saw the theory of culture epochs as vague in its implications and admitted he knew of no sound basis for the placement of studies. For him, any particular scheme for placement of subject matter had come to be no better than the broad plan for organization that ordered it. The importance of organizing studies in relation to the child's mode of thought was seen as the more pressing problem.

5. *How can the curriculum best be organized?* Faced with new school studies and activities, the imposition of scholarly works on children, and the isolation of each study, Charles McMurry gave highest priority to organization of the curriculum. His first

answer was to organize the school studies on a life basis. Knowledge from different subject fields was coordinated into a single project or unit of study. Pupils were to become absorbed in pragmatic life problems or centers of interest. There was, for instance, applied science, like "the problem of securing a pure milk supply"; there were geographic projects like "the Salt River Irrigation Project in Arizona"; and there were historic projects like "Hamilton's project for funding the national debt." Most of these projects drew on history, geography, science, mathematics, and language. Also, each project or series of projects was to reveal the scope and meaning of a larger idea, which "like a view from the mountain top, at one glance brings into simple perspective and arrangement a whole vast grouping of minor facts."[18] The idea of evolution, for example, derived from a series of animal studies, becomes a principle of interpretation for use in other studies of animals and plants. A well-devised continuity of thoughts was kept steadily developing from grade to grade. The growth of institutions in history was one element chosen to ensure continuity over the span of several years of study.

Central Problem of Curriculum Charles McMurry saw that the central problem of curriculum was to select the right centers of organization. These centers were to be points where older forms of knowledge and new studies could be combined. The relationship of centers of organization to the aim of education was most important. Furthermore, McMurry was concerned about who would develop the big topics or themes and organize them into effective instructional plans and materials. Experienced teachers seemed too absorbed with their teaching duties; scholarly specialists were too involved in the academic instruction of university students; and the pedagogical specialists were identified as members of an educational cult dealing solely in generalities and verbal distinctions.

DEWEY'S OPPOSITION TO HERBARTISM

Dewey's School

In his own laboratory school at the University of Chicago, John Dewey introduced manual training, shopwork, sewing, and cooking on the grounds that the traditional curriculum no longer met the needs of the new society created by the forces of industrialism. He wanted the school to take on the character of an embryonic community life, active with occupations that reflect the life of the larger society.

Younger children in the school played at actual occupations, simplifying but not distorting adult roles. Older children followed the Herbartian idea of recapitulating primitive life, but in a childhood social setting as they reconstructed the social life of other times and places. These children were expected to relate their own activities to the consequences of those activities. Primitive human life was supposed to reveal to the child the social effects of introducing tools into a culture. Still older children reflected on the meaning of social forces and processes found in occupations. They were to sense questions, doubts, and problems and to find a means of resolving them.

Dewey used his experiences in the laboratory school in formulating philosophical views that were different from those of the Herbartians. He insisted that the Herbartian interpretations of morality were too narrow and too formal. He protested the teaching of

[18]Charles A. McMurry, *How to Organize the Curriculum* (New York: Macmillan, 1923), 76.

particular virtues without regard for the motives of children. Instead, he proposed that moral motives would develop when children learned to observe and note relationships between the means and the ends in social situations. It was not enough for the teacher to be the model of moral behavior for the children to emulate. Children should be asked to judge and respond morally to their present situations, which are real to them. Indeed, Dewey wanted life in the school to offer opportunities for children to act morally and to learn how to judge their own behavior in terms of the social ideas of cooperation, participation, and positive service. Thus, Dewey challenged the view that morality was an individual matter between oneself and God.

Dewey attacked the view that one's social duty should be done within a traditional framework of values, proposing instead that the method of social intelligence be a critical and creative force. The method of social intelligence means deciding what is right through experimental procedures and the judgment of participants. It requires recognition of different points of view and accommodations of one's own perspective. Whereas the Herbartians relied on ideas as the basic guide to conduct and conceived of knowledge as something to be acquired, Dewey thought more in terms of the child's discovery and evaluation of knowledge than of mere acquisition. He recommended that the learner become the link between knowledge and conduct. His was a relative view of knowledge, not a fixed one. In contrast to the Herbartians' assumption that there was a body of known knowledge, which was indispensable and which could be made interesting to pupils, Dewey argued that subject matter was interesting only when it served the purposes of the learners. Hence, he emphasized learners' participation in formulating the purposes that were the basis for the selection of subject matter.

Dewey's Curriculum

By setting purposes, Dewey meant, however, not only expressing desires but also studying means by which those desires can best be realized. Desire was not the end, but only the occasion for the formulation of a plan and method of activity. Thus Dewey would not have the curriculum start with facts and truth that are outside the range of experience of those taught. Rather, he would start with materials for learning that are consistent with the experience learners already have and then introduce new objects and events that would stimulate new ways to observe and to judge. Subject matter was not to be selected on the basis of what adults thought would be useful for the learner at some future time. Instead, the present experience of the learners was to become the primary focus. The achievements of the past (organized knowledge) were to serve as a resource for helping learners both to understand their present condition and to deal with present problems.

In short, Dewey did not believe that the goal of the curriculum should be merely the acquisition of subject matter. He believed in a new goal for curriculum, namely, that organized subject matter become a tool for understanding and intelligently ordering experience. He generated many of the fundamental questions that guide current inquiries: What is the best way to relate the natural view of the child and the scientific view of those with specialized knowledge? How can knowledge become a method for enriching social life? How can we help learners act morally rather than merely have ideas about morality? How can the curriculum best bring order, power, initiative, and intelligence into the child's experience? How can the teacher be helped to follow the individual internal authority of truth about a learner's growth when curriculum decisions are made by external authority above the teacher?

SCIENTIFIC CURRICULUM MAKING: FRANKLIN BOBBITT AND WERRETT W. CHARTERS

Scientific curriculum making is the attempt to use empirical methods (surveys and analysis of human conduct) in deciding *what* to teach. The history of the scientific movement in curriculum making shows very well that curriculum cannot be separated from the general history of American education or divorced from the broader stream of cultural and intellectual history. Both Franklin Bobbitt and Werrett W. Charters were greatly influenced by these developments in their lifetimes.

Societal Influences on the Scientific Movement

Industrialism   The industrial revolution of the late 1800s meant that large numbers of persons began engaging in manufacturing instead of agriculture. Technology wrought many changes, including a concern for efficiency and economy. For the first time, there was a societal interest in the systematic study of jobs, practices, and working conditions as related to both productivity and what it was that a worker should know and be able to do. There was a concern about how to set standards for both products and processes.

Changing Concepts of School   From an institution with fixed subject matter and with the primary concern of improving intellectual ability by disciplining the mind, the school was increasingly conceived as an agency with no less a goal than satisfying individual and social needs.

Scientific Methods and Techniques   The nineteenth century was characterized by great developments in pure sciences such as biology, physics, and chemistry and in the application of science to agriculture, manufacturing, and almost every other phase of practical life. Yet it was not until early in the twentieth century that the spirit of scientific experimentation began to push its way into the thinking of educators. Bobbitt and Charters brought this way of thinking into the emerging field of curriculum making.

Much of what was called scientific at the time is now labeled scientism, mere technology, or nose counting. Modern critics like to say pejoratively that educational scientists of those days equated efficiency with science. It is true that these early educational scientists were attempting to solve educational problems by means of experimental and statistical techniques. They particularly emphasized the measurement of ability and achievement as they created tests. The zeal for measurement brought forth an abundance of facts about school buildings, school finance, pupil achievement, and pupil traits, as well as the physical, emotional, intellectual, and social growth of students. The field of curriculum also caught this zeal for measurement. Data were collected about the content of textbooks, courses of study, school subjects, and appraisal of results. Studies were undertaken to find out how students learn and to design new methods for overcoming student difficulties.

Key Ideas of Scientific Curriculum Making

Two ideas were frequently associated with the scientific movement in education. One was the idea of an open attitude, the expectation that the school staff would be willing to consider new proposals and be alert to new methods and devices. Teachers, for example, were expected to join their pupils in asking questions. The second idea involved the assumption that natural laws govern not only things and their forces but also humans and their ways. Hence, it was the duty of education to shape the will into a desire to move in harmony with these laws. Science was seen as a guarantor of social progress.

Bobbitt's Contribution to Curriculum Making

Franklin Bobbitt articulated for the first time the importance of studying the processes for making a curriculum. He realized that it was not enough to develop new curricula; there was also a need to learn more about how new curricula can best be developed. This insight came through long experience in curriculum matters.

In his book, *The Curriculum,* Bobbitt tells of a personal experience that caused him to look at curriculum from the point of view of social needs rather than mere academic study.[19] He had gone to the Philippines early in the American occupation as a member of a committee sent to draw up an elementary school curriculum for the islands. Free to recommend almost anything to meet the needs of the population, the committee had the opportunity to create an original, constructive curriculum.

And what happened? The members assembled American textbooks for reading, arithmetic, geography, U.S. history, and other subjects with which they had been familiar in American schools. Without being conscious of it they had organized a course of study for the traditional eight elementary school grades, on the basis of their American prejudices and preconceptions about what an elementary course ought to be.

Bobbitt was lucky. A director of education in the Philippines helped him and the committee to look at the social realities, and they then unceremoniously threw out time-hallowed content. Instead, they brought into the course a number of things to help the people gain health, make a living, and enjoy self-realization. The activities they introduced came from the culture of the Philippines and were quite different from those found in the American textbooks.

From this experience, Bobbitt saw his difficulty: his complete adherence to traditional curriculum beliefs had kept him from realizing the possibility of more useful solutions. He had needed something to shatter his complacency. As Bobbitt himself said,

> We needed principles of curriculum making. We did not know that we should first determine objectives from a study of social needs. We supposed education consisted only of teaching the familiar subjects. We had not come to see that it is essentially a process of unfolding the potential abilities of a population and in particularized relation to the social conditions. We had not learned that studies are means, not ends. We did not realize that any instrument or experience which is effective in such unfoldment is the right instrument and right experience; and that anything which is not effective is wrong, however time-honored and widely used it may be.[20]

Bobbitt was little different from most people who are entering the field of curriculum for the first time today. They are unaware that what they have personally experienced in school may not be the final answer. They have difficulty creating something different and more appropriate.

After his experience in the Philippines, Bobbitt stimulated other workers in the field. His book, *How to Make a Curriculum,* was the forerunner of others on the subject and had great influence on school practice.[21] Students of curriculum now see Bobbitt as the first to recognize the need for a new specialization, the study of curriculum making. It was Bobbitt who saw that professional agreement on a *method* of discovery is more important than agreement on the details of curriculum content. He offered the profession his method with the intention that others would try it, improve it, or suggest a better one. His method was guided by a fundamental assumption that would not be accepted by all curriculum makers

[19]Franklin Bobbitt, *The Curriculum* (Boston: Houghton Mifflin, 1918), 35.
[20]Ibid., 283.
[21]Franklin Bobbitt, *How to Make a Curriculum* (Boston: Houghton Mifflin, 1924).

today—namely, that education is to prepare us for the activities that ought to make up a well-rounded adult life. It is primarily for adult life, not childhood.

Steps in Making Curriculum Bobbitt proposed five steps in curriculum making:

Analysis of Human Experience The first step in curriculum making, according to Bobbitt, is to separate the broad range of human experience into major fields. One such classification includes language, health, citizenship, social life, recreation, religious life, home, and vocation. The whole field of human experience should be reviewed in order that the portions belonging to the schools may be seen in relation to the whole.

Job Analysis The second step is to break down the fields into their more specific activities. In this step, Bobbitt had to compromise with his ideal. He recognized the desirability of using a scientific method of analysis, yet knew that thus far there was not adequate technique for the work. Hence, he tended to fall back on practical and personal experiences to prove that a given activity was crucial to one or more of the categories of human experience.

Bobbitt knew that only a few activity analyses had ever been made and that most of them were in the fields of spelling, language, arithmetic, history, geography, and vocation. He did, however, believe that activity analysis was a promising technique and turned to his colleague, W. W. Charters, for examples of how best to determine specific activities from larger units. Charters, in turn, drew from the idea of job analysis already common in industry. Business and industry at that time made an analysis for each job and prepared training programs for the tasks identified. For the position of application clerk the analysis would include these tasks: meets people who want to open accounts, asks them to fill out blanks, looks up rating in Dunn and Bradstreet. A course of study was prepared to teach future clerks each of the identified duties.

It should be clear, however, that job analysis could result in either a list of duties or a list of methods for performing duties. The procedures for the analysis included introspection, interview, and investigation. Upon introspection, an expert related his or her duties and methods. Then, in an interview, a number of experts reviewed a list of duties to verify the tasks. Finally, the investigator actually carried out the operations on the job. A problem in making a complete analysis occurred in trying to describe the mental operations necessary for the task when one cannot see the steps carried out with the material. The analyses indicated only what the activities were if one were to learn the duties of a position.

Deriving Objectives The third step is to derive the objectives of education from statements of the abilities required to perform the activities. In *How to Make a Curriculum,* Bobbitt presented more than 800 major objectives in 10 fields of human experience. Here is a partial list of the general objectives within a language field: (a) to pronounce words properly; (b) to use voice in agreeable ways; (c) to use grammatically correct language; (d) to effectively organize and express thoughts; (e) to express thought to others in conversation, in recounting experiences, in serious or formal discussion, in an oral report, in giving directions, and before an audience; (f) to command an adequate reading, speaking, and writing vocabulary; (g) to write legibly with ease and speed; (h) to spell correctly the words of one's writing vocabulary; and (i) to use good form and order in all written work (margins, spacing, alignment, paragraphing, capitalization, punctuation, syllabification, abbreviation). These objectives illustrate the level of generality needed to help curriculum makers decide what specific educational results were to be produced. Bobbitt also realized that each of the objectives could be broken down further into its component parts; indeed, he illustrated such detailed analysis.

Selecting Objectives The fourth step is to select from the list of objectives those which are to serve as the basis for planning pupil activities. Guidelines for making this final selection of objectives include:

Eliminate objectives that can be accomplished through the normal process of living. Only the abilities that are not sufficiently developed by chance should be included among the objectives of systematic education. Possibly the more important portions of education are not accomplished in schools but through nonscholastic agencies.

Emphasize objectives that will overcome deficiencies in the adult world.

Avoid objectives opposed by the community. Specific objectives in religion, economics, and health are especially likely to be opposed.

Eliminate objectives when there are practical constraints hindering their achievement.

Involve the community in the selection of objectives. Consult community members who are proficient in practical affairs and experts in their fields.

Differentiate between objectives that are for all learners and those that are practical for only part of the population. Sequence the objectives, indicating how far pupils should go each year in attaining the general goals.

Planning in Detail The fifth step is to lay out the kinds of activities, experiences, and opportunities involved in attaining the objectives. Details for the day-to-day activities of children at each age or grade level must be laid out. These detailed activities make up the curriculum. As project activity and part-time work at home and in the community are introduced, there must be cooperative planning. Teachers, nurses, play activity directors, and parents together should plan the detailed procedures of the courses. Their plans should then be approved by the principal, superintendent, and school board.

Charters's Contribution to the Curriculum Field

Although Charters enunciated a method of curriculum formulation that was very similar to Bobbitt's, he differed in the emphasis on ideals and systematized knowledge in determining the content of the curriculum. Charters saw ideals as objectives with observable consequences. He believed that honesty, loyalty, and generosity contributed to satisfaction. Ideals did not necessarily lead to immediate satisfaction but to satisfaction in the long run or to satisfaction as defined by social consensus. However, he knew of no scientific measurement that would determine which ideals should operate in a school. There was no scientific way to determine whether open-mindedness or artistic taste should be the ideal of the school or student. Hence, Charters thought it defensible for a faculty to vote on the ideals it believed to be most valuable. Faculty selection of ideals was not to be arbitrary, however. The opinion of thoughtful men and women in public and private life needed to be carefully weighed and the needs of the student investigated.

After ideals were selected, they had to serve as standards for actions and were not to be abstracted from activities. The teacher who wished to inculcate ideals in the lives of pupils needed to analyze activities to which an ideal applied and to see that the selected ideal was applied in the pupils' activities. For Charters, the curriculum consisted of both ideals and activities. Unlike Bobbitt, Charters gave explicit attention to knowledge in his method for making the curriculum.[22] He wanted subject matter useful for living and of motivational import to the learner. But he also wanted to reassure those who feared that

[22]W. W. Charters, *Curriculum Construction* (New York: Macmillan, 1923), 103–106.

organized information in such fields as chemistry, history, physics, and mathematics would have no place in a curriculum built around objectives derived from studies of life in the social setting. His answer showed how job analyses revealed the importance of both primary subjects (mathematics and English in application) and derived subjects (subjects necessary for understanding the activity or the reason for the activity). Psychology, for example, was needed in order to explain methods of supervision.

On the one hand, Charters would determine subject material from analysis of life projects in order that one would know which elements of the subjects are most important and require the most attention. On the other hand, he would select school projects that would give instruction in the subject items and allow the pupil to use the knowledge in a broader range of activities.

As representatives of the scientific movement in curriculum making, Bobbitt and Charters brought forth the following conceptions and dimensions of curriculum: It is a process which, if followed, will result in an evolving curriculum. The process of curriculum making is itself a field of study. The relation of goals (ideals), objectives, and activities is a curriculum concern. The selection of goals is a normative process. The selection of objectives and activities is empirical and scientific. Objectives and activities are subject to scientific analysis and verification. The relationship of organized systematic fields of knowledge to the practical requirements of daily living is a central question for students of the curriculum.

IMPROVEMENT OF INSTRUCTION

Local Development of Curriculum

Until the end of World War I, major influences on curriculum came from outside the local school system. Academic scholars set the direction for purposes and content through national committees and textbook writing. Usually, local schools participated only to the extent of deciding which subjects to add and which textbooks to use. The high school curriculum was standardized on the basis of what college presidents thought students needed for college. After 1920, the scientific movement directly influenced the curriculum through new types of school textbooks stressing skills related to the everyday needs of adults and children. College scholars found their power to determine the curriculum challenged by the scientific method of curriculum formulation. The first local systematic curriculum making also began around 1920 when several school systems tried to develop courses of study in single subjects and the study of particular problems, such as learning difficulties in spelling and how to overcome them through instruction.

A course of study was a guide to the teaching of a particular subject or subjects. The course of study included a philosophy, suggested content (topics and their ordering for study), a structure (discipline-centered or interdisciplinary), and the relation of the content to the life of the learner and the larger society. Major themes and other abstractions were outlined for relating activities, and suggested activities and resources were given.

The Course of Study Movement

By 1926, practically all schools were revising their curricula. They attacked the problem of curriculum development in a comprehensive way by defining the general objectives on which the entire curriculum was based and by which all subjects were correlated. It is true, however, that members of state education departments often chose the objectives and left the selection of activities to the teachers. Sometimes, the principals or representatives of teachers selected the objectives according to local needs. In these schools teachers worked in committees in order to list activities to be tested. A director was provided to supervise the preparation of the course of study for an individual school district or an entire state, and a curriculum specialist served as general consultant. Not all professional educators viewed the movement with favor:

> *Too much of the present-day curriculum is amateurish, trifling, and a sheer waste of time—worse than that, an injection of pernicious confusion into what should be orderly progress. The let-everybody-pitch-in-and-help method is ludicrous when applied to curriculum building. It is too much like inviting a group of practical electricians to redesign a modern power plant.*[23]

Caswell's Influence on the Curriculum Field

Hollis Leland Caswell extended our view of the curriculum field through his concern about the relationships between the course of study, teaching, and the learner's role. Caswell was one of the first to see the making of a course of study as too limiting in purpose. He shifted the emphasis from production of a course of study to the actual improvement of instruction. He saw curriculum development as a means of helping teachers apply in their daily tasks of instruction the best information on subject matter, the interests of children, and contemporary social needs. He involved 16,000 Virginia teachers and administrators in making a course of study for that state.[24] His involvement of all teachers instead of just a few selected representatives was a new thrust. Caswell considered the course of study as only one of several aids to the teacher and believed that when teachers made the course of study together they would learn the limits of its usefulness. He looked on the course of study as a means of providing source materials for teachers to use in planning their work rather than a prescription to be followed in detail.

Help for the Teacher in Curriculum Making   Caswell attempted to help teachers improve curricula by providing them with a syllabus of carefully chosen readings under seven topics. These topics or questions are important for what they tell us about the nature of curriculum and the tasks involved in making a curriculum.[25]

1. What is curriculum?
2. What developments resulted in a need for curriculum revision?
3. What is the function of subject matter?
4. How do we determine educational objectives?
5. What is the best way to organize instruction?
6. How should we select subject matter?
7. How should we measure the outcomes of instruction?

The readings Caswell suggested to help teachers answer these questions included a range of sources, some of which gave conflicting opinions. Caswell himself believed that the curriculum is more than the experiences made available to the child; it consists of the

---

[23]Guy M. Whipple, "What Price Curriculum Making," *School and Society* (March 15, 1930): 368.

[24]Mary Louise Seguel, *The Curriculum Field: Its Formative Years* (New York: Columbia University, Teachers College Press, 1966), 148.

[25]Sidney B. Hall, D. W. Peters, and Hollis L. Caswell, "Study Course for Virginia State Curriculum," *State Board of Education Bulletin* 14, no. 2 (Jan. 1932): 363.

experiences the child actually undergoes. Hence, the teacher's interaction with the student is a vital aspect of curriculum. Preparing a course of study is only the starting point for curriculum improvement.

Curriculum Revision Caswell also believed in curriculum revision. He said that curriculum revision is necessary in order for the school to meet new social and personal needs. Curriculum should help sensitize people to social problems and give students experience in social action. Caswell wanted the school to be an avenue of opportunity for all people, contributing to interracial understanding and relations, strengthening home life, stressing democratic ideals, and contributing to the conservation of resources.

Evaluating Demands Caswell thought that the demands for curriculum change must be evaluated. He recommended that any proposed change be screened, and that changes be accepted only if they are (1) consistent with democratic values, (2) consistent with the developmental needs of the learner, (3) something that other agencies cannot accomplish, (4) something that has or will gain the support of leaders in the community, and (5) something that does not replace other existing curriculum areas of relatively higher value.

Curriculum Design Caswell agreed that a curriculum design should synthesize the three basic elements of the curriculum: (1) children's interests, (2) social functions, and (3) organized knowledge. In the tentative course of study for Virginia elementary schools, for example, he helped developers provide scope and sequence. Social functions served as the scope. Some of these functions were protection and conservation of life, property, and natural resources; recreation; expression of aesthetic impulses; and distribution of rewards of production. These functions were worked on in some form in every grade. Sequenced experiences were arranged according to centers of interest. For example, home and school life were studied in the first grade; the effects of the machine on learning in the sixth. Specific activities were suggested to match both the social functions and the centers of interest using the most relevant subject matter.

Caswell saw the central task of curriculum development as synthesizing materials from subject matter fields such as philosophy, psychology, and sociology. "Materials must be so selected and arranged as to become vital in the experience of the learner."[26] Thus he saw curriculum as a field of study that represents no structurally limited body of content; rather, it represents a process or procedure.

RATIONAL CURRICULUM MAKING

In 1949 Ralph Tyler sent to the University of Chicago Press a manuscript, *Basic Principles of Curriculum and Instruction,* a rationale for examining problems of curriculum and instruction.[27] The rationale was based on his experiences as a teacher of curriculum and as a curriculum maker and evaluator. He had been especially active in designing ways to measure changes in learners brought about by schools' new efforts to help learners develop interests and perform more appropriately in society. Since then, more than 100,000 copies of Tyler's rationale have been sold, and it is regarded as the culmination of an epoch of curriculum making.

[26]Hollis L. Caswell and Doak S. Campbell, *Curriculum Development* (New York: American Book Company, 1935), 81.
[27]Ralph W. Tyler, *Basic Principles of Curriculum and Instruction* (Chicago: University of Chicago Press, 1949).

Tyler's Curriculum Inquiry

Tyler assumed that anyone engaging in curriculum inquiry must try to answer these questions:

1. What educational purposes should the school seek to attain?
2. What educational experiences can be provided that are likely to attain these purposes?
3. How can these educational experiences be effectively organized?
4. How can we determine whether these purposes are being attained?

By purposes, Tyler meant a small number of objectives framed at high levels of generalizability, just the opposite of Bobbitt's specific and numerous objectives, and he proposed that school goals would have greater validity if they are selected in light of information about learners psychological needs and interests, contemporary life, and aspects of subject matter that would be useful to everyone, not just specialists in disciplines. In order to select from the many objectives that would be inferred from such information, Tyler recommended that a school staff "screen" them according to the school's philosophy of education and beliefs about the psychology of learning.

Tyler realized that having purposes was only the first step. He used the phrase *learning experiences* to include a plan for providing learning situations that take into account both the previous experience and perceptions that the learner brings to the situation, and whether or not the learner is likely to respond to it mentally and emotionally and in action.

Tyler then turned his attention to ordering the learning situations so that they would be focused on the same outcomes. He was preoccupied with how the curriculum could produce a maximum cumulative effect. He wanted a cumulative plan for organization that would help students learn more effectively.

His answer drew heavily from the early Herbartians' ideas of organization. Like Charles McMurry, he thought organizing elements or controlling ideas, concepts, values, and skills should be the threads, the warp and woof of the fabric of curriculum organization. The use of a concept such as place value in the numeration system, for example, could be enlarged on from kindergarten through the twelfth grade. Such concepts were seen as useful elements for relating different learning experiences in science, social studies, and other fields. He described optional ways of structuring learning experiences both within schools and in the classroom. They could, for instance, be structured within special subject courses, like English and mathematics, or as broad fields, like the language arts. Experience could also be structured within the format of lessons. He showed his own organization and curriculum preference by listing the advantages of relating content to real life through projects that allow for broader grouping of learning opportunities. He also saw merit in organizing courses that span several years rather than a single term.

Finally, Tyler regarded evaluation as an important operation in curriculum development. He saw it as a process for finding out whether the learning experiences actually produced the desired results and for discovering the strengths and weaknesses of the plans. He made a real contribution by enlarging our concept of evaluation. Rather than focusing on only a few aspects of growth, tests should, he believed, indicate attainment of all the objectives of an educational program. Furthermore, he did not believe that tests should be only paper and pencil examinations. He thought that observations of students, products made by learners, records of student participation, and other assessment methods should also be included.

As indicated in Table 13.1, curriculum leaders have addressed questions about what should be taught and why. Their questions range from inquiries about purpose, such as whether morality can be taught, to questions about the selection of content, the relation of

Table 13.1 A Summary of Early Curriculum Theorists' Ideas

Theorists	Purpose, Aims, and Objectives	Content	Method of Instruction	Organization
Charles and Frank McMurry	Moral development Good citizenship	Literature for related aesthetics and the intellectual History and literature for citizenship Geography for correlating studies Later, acceptance of new branches of knowledge	Five formal steps in lesson plans Special methods in each subject field	Studies sequenced according to age and stage of learner development Information organized around problems and projects Activities related by topics and themes
John Dewey	Intellectual control over the forces of humankind and nature Social intelligence Trained capacities in the service of social interest Development as an aim	The intellectual method by which social life is enriched and improved Knowledge from organized fields as it functions in the life of the child	Survey of capacities and needs of learners Arrangement of conditions that provides the content to satisfy needs A plan for meeting needs involving the participation of all group members Intelligent activity, not aimless activity	Life experiences that learners use to carry on to more refined and better organized facts and ideas Curriculum organized around two concepts: that knowing is experimental and that knowledge is instrumental in individual and social purposes
Franklin Bobbitt	Meeting social needs Preparation of learner for adult life	Subject matter as a means, not an end	Deriving objectives from analysis of what is required in order to perform in broad categories of life Detailed activities to be planned by teachers, parents, and others	Specification of objectives to be attained each year Layout of activities involved in attaining objectives

Theorists	Purpose, Aims, and Objectives	Content	Method of Instruction	Organization
Werrett W. Charters	Satisfaction through fulfillment of ideals (e.g., honesty) that sway socially efficient persons	Organized knowledge that can be applied in activities needed for a socially efficient life	Projects and activities consistent with ideals	Experimentation to find the best way to order ideals, activities, and ideas
Hollis Caswell	Fulfillment of democratic ideals (improved intergroup relations, home life, and the conservation of resources)	No limiting body of content Key concepts most helpful in the solution of social problems	Teacher interaction with pupil Teacher applying the best of what is known about subject matter, children's interests, and social needs Key ideas to be woven into the child's performance of social functions	Selected social functions (e.g., the conservation of life) to be worked on in some form in every grade Sequence of activities to be arranged according to centers of interest
Ralph Tyler	No stated purposes Each curriculum person to evolve own purposes through a rational process, involving consideration of learning, social conditions, knowledge, and philosophical position Objectives to be clear, but specifically to depend on one's theory of learning	Subject matter from subject specialists that could contribute to the broad functions of daily living	Opportunity to practice what the objectives of instruction call for Each opportunity to contribute to several objectives Activities that are within the learner's capacity and are satisfying	Provisions for the reiteration of concepts, skills, or values Provisions for the progressive development of the concept, skill, or attitude Correlation of concepts from one field to content in other fields

319

content and method, and the importance of organizing so that learning experiences have a cumulative effect.

In general, the focus is on determining what is most essential in forming identities for participation in society and arranging conditions for attaining these identities, usually as a formal and institutionalized curriculum in contrast with a spontaneous enacted curriculum.

FEMININE ENACTMENT OF CURRICULUM

In much of the history of the curriculum field, women are invisible. The prevailing climate of the time denied women equal access to educational, political, and professional institutions. As just described, leaders in the field centered on goals and effective delivery rather than on the lived experiences of teachers and students. Proposals for orchestrating the institutional curriculum had a masculine bias.

Although Dewey wrote of the need to reconcile children's experiences with organized knowledge, and Tyler considered studies of the learner as a key source of information in deciding what to teach, it was women who early put into practice many of the features that guide today's enacted curriculum, such as learning through projects and problem-based inquiries where by induction students draw generalizations from their own data and discuss with peers their interpretations. Women were pioneers in creating curriculum materials based on children's language and interests, and among the first to put students in touch with ongoing local and world events connected to humanistic and democratic values.

Hilda Taba

Consider Hilda Taba (1902–1967), who regarded facts as chiefly important for the underlying ideas and generalizations students drew from them. More than that, she expected that learner experiences throughout all grade levels could have a cumulative effect if these ideas were linked to powerful abstract concepts and acted on in new and varied situations.[28] Her curriculum is consistent with the bottom-up approach described in Chapter 5 where teachers develop the curriculum instead of following top-down procedures.

Taba was influenced by John Dewey and William Kilpatrick, a leading proponent of real-world projects for learning and integrating subject matters. Her work with Ralph Tyler in the Eight Year Study that evaluated 30 secondary schools that had been "freed" of the curriculum requirements imposed on secondary schools by colleges and universities affirmed her beliefs in the importance of schools developing their own curriculum reflecting differentiated content and context.

Although Taba never received public recognition for her substantial role in the Tyler rationale, her contributions to this work are coming to light, particularly for her emphasis on the following:

- The need and methods for assessing meaningful learning beyond tests and content acquisition.
- Curriculum planning that is coordinated with community organizations.
- Teachers collaborating in linking school subjects and activities to agreed-on powerful themes.[29]

---

[28]Arthur L. Costa and Richard A. Loveall, "The Legacy of Hilda Taba," *Journal of Curriculum and Supervision* 18 (fall 2002): 50–62.
[29]Hilda Taba, The Dynamics of Education: A Methodology Progressive Educational Thought (London: K. Paul, Trench, Truban and Co., 1932).

She regarded curriculum as "a living whole, comprised of experiences actually going on in school. As such it is what it becomes in practice."[30]

Mary Sheldon Barnes

Earlier in the nineteenth century, Mary Sheldon Barnes (1850–1896) rebelled against imparting historical information. Instead she encouraged students to examine a wealth of material and draw their own conclusions. Her curriculum relied heavily on primary sources—documents, illustrations, and artifacts from a range of fields—architecture, literature, and speech. The materials she produced for teachers offered guiding questions; analytical questions for extracting information; synthetic questions that helped students use the information in making a coherent image; and evaluative questions that asked students to reflect on the ideals, character, and moral quality of historical figures and societies.[31]

Modern scholars may fault Barnes for not helping students critique their own nation's racism and other injustices as inconsistent with national ideals, a challenge for curriculum writers at any period; however, her textbooks showed she engaged learners in constructing knowledge instead of memorizing, launching a great debate.

At this time many teachers adopted the source material methodology and its goal of critical thinking; others used the materials as supplements to their textbooks but some were hostile to the practice, saying that students should learn what is in their texts and not think for themselves or have opinions of their own. The critics believed that the main thing was for students to learn what is in the book and to be motivated to learn more.

Lucy Maynard Salmon

Through her own teaching and influence on a national committee that issued guidelines for the secondary school history curriculum, Lucy Maynard Salmon (1853–1927) promoted active learning where students examined the ordinary everyday aspects of life—architecture of the street, newspaper accounts, and backyard searches—as data sources for connecting the past and its present. Unlike Barnes, Salmon's curriculum did not overlook underserved groups—immigrants and women, with a focus on discrimination—but critiqued the society that allowed such injustice. She did not accept the United States as a finished Utopia, but through her curriculum appealed to greater humanistic and cosmopolitan ideals that crossed national boundaries.

Lucy Sprague Mitchell

Lucy Sprague Mitchell (1870–1967) contributed to the progressive elementary school curriculum through a novel teacher education program that featured problem-based learning by children. Mitchell is also known for many accomplishments in higher education on behalf of women and students, and as a pioneer in research on children's development and growth. As a teacher of young children, she became aware of age appropriateness and prepared stories about children's lives and the world about them, replacing the violent and moralistic stories extracted from sagas and epics.[32] Using geography as a subject, Mitchell aimed at helping 9-year-olds become geographers rather than her teaching geography.

[30]Jane Bernard-Powers, "Composing Her Life: Hilda Taba and Social Studies," in *Bending the Future to Their Will*, Margaret Smith Crocco and O. L. Davis, Jr., eds. (New York: Rowman and Littlefield, 1999).
[31]S. A. Anniel, "The Educative Theory of Mary Sheldon Barnes: Inquiry Learning in History Education," *Educational Theory* 40 (1990): 45–52.
[32]Sherry L. Field, "Lucy Sprague Mitchell: Teacher, Geographer, and Teacher Educator," in *Bending the Future to Their Will*, Margaret Smith Crocco and O. L. Davis, Jr., eds. (New York: Rowman and Littlefield, 1999).

She regarded problem solving as a desired outcome from children's experiences with maps as they solved complex problems similar to those that the pioneers faced during Westward Expansion. The children were settlers, traveling by covered wagon trying to find the best route to Oregon or California. A wide range of source materials was discovered related to topography, flora, and fauna, as they sought information from geology, history, science, art, and the like. Students' findings and decisions were continually recorded on a giant relief map to depict the effects of earth forces on topography, vegetation, animals, and people.

As founder of Bank Street College, Mitchell developed a preservice curriculum with the mission of helping new teachers question old practices and to be open to experiments based on observations and the noting of relationships. These teachers were expected to implement a child-centered curriculum based on inquiry, interest, and logical and emotional understanding. Unlike those who would separate curriculum from teaching, Mitchell recognized the need for teachers who both were knowledgeable in subject matters and knew how to relate these subjects to the lives of children.

CONCLUDING COMMENTS

Any new effort in curriculum thought and action must still treat the persistent questions of purpose, activity, organization, and evaluation. The emphasis on these matters and the way they are addressed, however, are changing. The 1970s saw special interest groups and governmental agencies taking over the leadership in program development; fragmentation was the result. The 1980s saw a change in leadership to state government in response to industrial and business interests in academic excellence and a growing concern for a general education that would reflect dominant cultural values. In the 1990s, curriculum development at the local level regained importance in part because central authorities did not want to pay for the activity and would trade freedom to experiment for accountability. Today standardized testing for the masses and advanced academic and technical preparation for the few is challenged but prevails.

How best to balance the demand for programs in response to national and state interests with the requirements of local communities is a common dilemma. The popularity of local curriculum development today rests on the drive for privatization and choice as well as on the desire for effective schools that have a strong sense of community, shared goals, and high expectations for students and staff. Collective decision making in the design of the curriculum at all levels requires deliberation—the coalescence of aims, data, and judgments.

A knowledge of curriculum history, including its theoretical and practical knowledge, may help to improve present reform efforts. For example, what better guidelines for the conduct of local curriculum development can be found than those based in Caswell's experiences? Similarly, the McMurrys' approach to correlation and the value of particular subjects in interrelating knowledge has value for current planners who want to strengthen general education. Also, Dewey's view of moral education is timely as planners consider the best response to public opinion that gives a high priority to education as a moral enterprise.

In contrast with the manifest curriculum set by authorities and approved texts, there is concern about how curriculum engages with learners' purposes, relation with others, cultural familiarity with topics, language, and other factors. Knowing the evolution of student experiences across the years and in different contexts may suggest better ways to organize curriculum and its connection to continued learning.

We expect to see women educators continuing to find new ways to bring students and subject matter together as the curriculum changes from the new goals of learning for transfer, high order thinking, and lifelong learning. The willingness of women to cross subject matter domains is timely. Also, the old source materials model of Barnes and others has relevancy for today's concern about students' judgments as they gain access to cultural resources through the Internet.

QUESTIONS

1. What are some current answers to the central concerns of prominent historical figures in the field of curriculum?

2. Can you tell a curriculum story? Perhaps include a story about a recent curriculum procedure or a story about practices in a particular school.

3. In what way is the present curriculum situation different from the past? How does this difference make some past ideas of curriculum irrelevant?

4. It is said that a history of curriculum thought and practice cannot be separated from the broader stream of cultural and intellectual history. What conditions, movements, or ideas do you think had the greatest influence on curriculum making in the nineteenth century? What social and also intellectual forces are shaping the curriculum field today?

5. What the McMurrys, Dewey, Charters, Bobbitt, Caswell, and Tyler thought about curriculum is less important than what they make *you* think about curriculum. What do they have to say to you?

6. What is your position regarding the conflict between (a) curriculum historians who have faith in progress and a common curriculum that will serve all and (b) historians who interpret curriculum history as the domination of elites over racial and ethnic minorities as well as the working class?

7. Curriculum is often separated from instruction as a field of study. Is this separation an effort to keep masculine control through institutionalizing apart from female concerns for personalization in learning?

SUGGESTED STRATEGIC RESEARCH

DISCONFIRMING AND SUPPORTING HYPOTHESES REGARDING WOMEN'S CURRICULUM DEVELOPMENT

Why are women more than men associated with curriculum that crosses disciplinary lines and shows concern for humanitarian and cosmopolitan ideals, inductive methods, and student motivation? Is it that more women have not been socialized into a separate academic discipline or that they have been restricted to teaching rather than to policy making? Is there a basis for gender as a determinant, with women predisposed to caring, nurturing, and relationships? Your study might take a historical approach by analyzing prominent women curriculum developers and their lives and circumstances.

MEETING THE CHALLENGE OF AN INQUIRY CURRICULUM

Curricula with a focus on inquiry historically have challenged both learners and teachers:

- Students ask questions that require little effort to answer, rather than those that lead to "big ideas."
- Students have difficulty finding and synthesizing information related to their investigation.
- Students do not design experiments that will provide evidence supporting or opposing a conclusion.
- Teachers lack subject matter knowledge for guiding students for collaborative inquiry.

Organize a panel of successful teachers to identify their special ways that might help other teachers and students meet these challenges or circumstances.

REPLICATING THE HISTORICAL METHOD OF LUCY MAYNARD SALMON IN UNCOVERING AND JUDGING CURRICULUM ARTIFACTS

Seek out a common artifact from the past related to a curriculum—a course of study, policy document, teacher guide, lesson plan, and the like—for a school or community of interest to you. Use this source to tell what the curriculum meant. Who developed it? What interests were served? What is the connection between this historical curriculum as revealed by this artifact and curriculum issues today?

IDENTIFYING CONCEPTIONS OF CURRICULUM IN CHARTER SCHOOLS

Which concepts of curriculum are found in charter or other alternative schools? Does the concept encompass method and teaching or only subject matter to be taught? What is the curriculum role of the teacher—a decision maker or one who implements programs designed off site? Visit several charter schools and determine if there is a pattern.

SELECTED REFERENCES

BOBBITT, FRANKLIN. *How to Make a Curriculum*. New York: Houghton Mifflin, 1924.

CASWELL, HOLLIS L., AND DOAK S. CAMPBELL, *Readings in Curriculum Development*. New York: American Book, 1937.

CHARTERS, W. W. *Curriculum Construction*. New York: Macmillan, 1923.

CROCCO, MARGARET SMITH, AND O. L. DAVIS, JR., EDS. *Bending the Future to Their Will: Civic Women, Social Education and Democracy*. New York: Rowman and Littlefield, 1999.

CROCCO, MARGARET SMITH, PETRA MUNRO, AND KATHLEEN WEILER, EDS. *Pedagogies of Resistance: Women Educator Activists 1880–1960*. New York: Teachers College Press, 1999.

FRANKLIN, BARRY M. *Building the American Community: The School Curriculum and the Search for Social Control*. London and Philadelphia: Falmer, 1986.

KLIEBARD, HERBERT M. *The Struggle for the American Curriculum 1893–1951*. Boston: Routledge and Kegan Paul, 1986.

MCMURRY, CHARLES A. *How to Organize the Curriculum*. New York: Macmillan, 1923.

SEGUEL, MARY LOUISE. *The Curriculum Field: Its Formative Years*. New York: Teachers College Press, 1966.

TYLER, RALPH. *Basic Principles of Curriculum and Instruction*. Chicago: University of Chicago Press, 1949.

CHAPTER 14

THE PROMISE OF THEORY AND INQUIRY IN CURRICULUM

THOSE DOING curriculum inquiry can be divided into various camps. Some are under the banner of quantitative or empirical inquiry. They engage in surveys, experiments, and descriptive observations using questionnaires and statistical methods. Usually, they are attempting to find relationships between curriculum outcomes and curriculum processes—the intensity with which certain content is emphasized, the organization of the curriculum, and the differentiation of instruction applied to different kinds of students. Others are qualitative or interpretive. They are interested in the meanings of interactions among inquiring students, teachers, textbooks, and other aspects of the curriculum. Often they are participant observers, drawing on the concepts and methods of sociology and anthropology. Some within this camp use journals and autobiographies as well as psychoanalysis and meditation with the idea of understanding both themselves and what the curriculum means to students. Critical theorists are a third category of inquirers. They examine curriculum practices with the purposes of showing the political nature of curriculum and increasing our awareness of historical and ideological influences on our lives.

Curriculum inquiry has multiple purposes: to advance conceptualization and understanding of the field, to conceive new visions of what and how to teach, to influence curriculum policy, to question normative premises about curriculum, and to improve programs for learning.

The massive educational reform bill, known as the No Child Left Behind Act of 2001, requires school districts to offer programs shown to be effective through "scientifically-based research on best practices, programs, and materials to match predetermined outcomes."

Thus far, none have met the requirement standards of being scientifically proven to be effective, nor have there been the types of evaluation studies needed.[1] Programs may be doing a terrific job of helping students, but we are a long way from being able to tell scientifically. Evidence matters, but many factors influence student achievement—students' previous knowledge, teachers' preparation, resources available, and degree of parent and community support—there is no magic bullet. However, we can get clues as to what works most of the time for most students and learn something about adapting programs to students and contexts.

---

[1]Jerry Meurs, "Evaluating Curriculum Effectiveness," *National Research Association Science* 304 (June 2004): 1583.

Arguments for selecting only programs that have been validated through randomized clinical trials rest on the belief that such vigorous evaluation will build public confidence in the curriculum, lower educational costs, eliminate shoddy teaching, and ensure fidelity in implementation. Certainly the movement to evidence-based decision making supports the alignment of standards, instruction, and assessment.

The "what works" approach may not work in the long term. Best practices become obsolete with changing circumstances, and research should look forward to opening doors for new possibilities rather than closing the search for innovation.

"Scientific research" may influence curriculum choices, but a variety of nonscientific adversarial and stakeholder dynamics are more likely to determine what gets implemented. Those using qualitative methods warn that the narrow focus on randomized controlled studies is an effort to discredit discovery of inequities in social life and the real reasons programs do not work for some students.[2] Others argue that research should foster debate rather than set policy and practice. If research is to generalize, it must go beyond science in considering the contexts that make generalization possible.[3]

In this chapter, we begin by looking at progress in six areas of curriculum research. The contributions of the various research orientations to these areas will be apparent. Later, the nature of curriculum inquiry is illustrated by work of selected productive scholars and practitioners, and by the different forms of inquiry used. Finally, several types of curriculum inquiry that are flourishing today are featured, raising the question of whether different approaches expand our vision or if commitment to a particular paradigm leads to intolerance and restricted horizons.

STATE OF THE FIELD

In 1960 and again in 1969, John Goodlad appraised the status of curriculum research in terms of the curriculum needs for (1) theoretical constructs, (2) concepts that identify major questions, (3) determination of what can best be taught simultaneously, (4) arrangement of material for effective learning, (5) analysis of objectives, and (6) studies indicating the relationship between specific instructional variables and the outcomes from instruction. As benchmarks to progress, let us look at each of Goodlad's 1960 concerns and the status of research in each area in 1969 and the present.

The Need for Curriculum Theory

Status of Curriculum Theory in 1969   Between 1960 and 1969, little was added to our knowledge of how to derive educational purposes. Elizabeth and George Macia and others attempted to adopt theories from outside the field of education to conceptualize phenomena related to curriculum.[4] One consequence was the differentiation of four kinds

[2]Yvonna S. Lincoln and Gaile S. Lannella, "Qualitative Research: Power and the Radical Right," *Qualitative Studies* 10, no. 2 (April 2000): 175–251.
[3]Richard J. Shavelson and Lisa Town, eds., *Scientific Research in Education* (Washington, DC: National Academy Press, 2002).
[4]Several papers are of interest, particularly those by Elizabeth Macia, George Macia, Robert Jewett, and others treating educational theorizing through models (Columbus: Bureau of Educational Research and Service, Ohio State University, 1963–1965).

of curriculum theory. *Formal curriculum theory* involves theorizing about the structure of the disciplines that will constitute the curriculum. Elizabeth Macia would leave this theorizing to the philosophers and members of the disciplines. *Valuational curriculum theory* involves speculation about the appropriate means to attain the most valuable goals and to present the best content in a curriculum. *Event theory* is very much like scientific theory in that it tries to predict what will occur under certain conditions. *Praxiological theory* is speculation about the appropriate means to attain what is judged to be valuable. Praxiological theory forms the theoretical base for determining curriculum policy, the decision to adopt certain goals and practices. In a seminal paper, the late Joseph Schwab said that theoretical pursuits were not appropriate in the field of curriculum. He urged instead direct study of the curriculum: what it is, how it gets that way, and how it affects the students and the teachers.[5]

Present Status of Curriculum Theory   Curriculum theory parallels the major curriculum orientations. Among the more important theories for those with an academic orientation is that academic knowledge is socially constructed by scholars in a community of discourse, and that effective learning by students requires their active construction of knowledge. If academic authority comes from agreeing or shared assumptions and reasoning about their consequences, then students should learn to participate in particular academic cultures, learn the discourse of the arguments and the conjecturing that takes place among scholars, and shift the authority of what is knowledge from textbooks and teacher decree to the sense making and reasoning of the individual. The implications of this theory for curriculum in the classroom are now center stage.

Those with a humanistic orientation have many theories to draw on. There is feminist theory, which raises consciousness concerning the role of emotions, compassion, and human relations in knowing. Using this theory, researchers draw on theater, history, autobiography, and the like to connect themselves to what they seek to know and to understand. Phenomenological theory is used by teachers in understanding their relations with children, raising such questions as "What do I do?" (describe); "Why have I decided to do this?" and "What is the meaning of what I do?" (inform); "What forces have shaped this decision?" (confront); and "How might I do it differently?" (action). Humanists are concerned about the theory–practice relationship, condemning the traditional use of theory as a controlling stick by those with greater political power. They prefer to look for the differences between theory and practice as a way to disclose the limitations of each.

Social reconstructionists as represented by critical theorists are trying to free themselves from the deterministic theories that predict the inevitability of injustice in a capitalistic society where the curriculum contributes to cultural reproduction. Signs of more hopeful critical theories are found in the work of Henry Giroux, who emphasizes the potential for creating new possibilities in school, and of teachers like Gerald Graff, who put cultural and academic conflicts at the center of their curriculum as the best way to help students pursue knowledge and to create new cultural perspectives.

It should be noted that the theories of humanists and social reconstructionists are likely to conflict with the systematists' view that curriculum must be shaped in accordance with institutional definitions of what shall count as knowledge.

The Need for Curriculum Conceptions

Status of Curriculum Conception in 1969   General theory and conceptualizations in curriculum had advanced very little in the decade before 1969. John Goodlad tried to bridge theory and practice with a conceptual scheme for rational curriculum planning.

---

[5]Joseph J. Schwab, *The Practical: A Language for Curriculum* (Washington, DC: National Education Association, 1970).

His categories and suggested processes, which build on the Tyler rationale of 1949, were intended to stimulate research and organize thinking in the curriculum field. However, he later saw no evidence that the intent was fulfilled. Also, Dwayne Huebner elaborated on a concept of curriculum as a field of study. He criticized the means–ends concept of curriculum and argued that curriculum should be conceived as a political process for effecting a just environment. One of the major questions he would have the curriculum workers ask was, "Does the present educational activity reflect the best that humans are capable of?"[6]

In 1979 Goodlad called for more attention to personal and experiential knowledge as a basis for making curriculum decisions, and to recognize the role that values and special interests play in all curriculum decision making. At about the same time, a group of curriculum specialists (later to be called reconceptualists) addressed problems with the traditional model for developing curriculum. They saw the need for drawing on other intellectual sources (psychoanalytic theory, existentialism, and literary discourse) in doing curriculum. Their monograph *Reschooling Society* presented an alternative conception of curriculum,[7] and their ideas were extended to reconceptualism through conferences and publications organized by William Pinar.[8]

Among the intellectual concepts and methodologies introduced to the curriculum field by the reconceptualists were political analysis (social consciousness of cultural politics), aesthetic criticism, phenomenological studies, historical studies, and feminist studies.

Present Status of Curriculum Conceptions In 1992 Philip Jackson reviewed conceptions of curriculum and found the variety of intellectual pursuits of curriculum inquiry so vast as to be daunting. The boundaries of the field are so diffuse that one wonders whether it has any boundaries at all.[9] The volume that Jackson edited was vast (1000 pages, small print, double-columned, nearly 3000 topics and 4000 referenced scholars).

As indicated in Chapter 13, the fundamental curriculum questions have been about purpose, content, method of instruction, and organization of the curriculum. The reconceptualists extended these questions by asking: What are our value commitments, and what is our view of the nature of man? What are the socioeconomic forces operating in our society that we would maximize or perpetuate? How is human experience related to learning? Critical theorists added the question, Who benefits and who does not from the curriculum?

In *Understanding Curriculum* (1995), Pinar and others[10] present several perspectives or forms of text for interpreting curriculum—political, racial, gender, phenomenological, poststructural, deconstructivist, postmodern, autobiographical, aesthetic, theological, and institutional. In recent years, many reconceptualists have attended annual conferences at the Berjano Center in Dayton, Ohio, where they present papers and discuss curriculum from these diverse perspectives. These "Berjano theorists" show new possibilities for teacher education and describe groundbreaking practices in K–12 and higher education, countering a prevailing view that reconceptualists have nothing to do with real school practice.[11]

Pinar thinks of curriculum as an edifying conversation where people listen to each other and dialogue using different perspectives to illuminate problems and to propose possible changes in both society and the curriculum. He casts the curriculum leader as a

[6]Dwayne Huebner, "Curriculum as a Field of Study," in *Precedents and Promise in the Curriculum Field*, Helen Robinson, ed. (New York: Columbia University, Teachers College Press, 1966), 107.

[7]James B. MacDonald, Bernice J. Wolfson, and Esther Zaret, *Reschooling Society—A Conceptual Model* (Washington, DC: Association for Supervision and Curriculum Development, 1973).

[8]William Pinar, ed., *Curriculum Theorizing: The Reconceptualists* (Berkeley, CA: McCutchan, 1975).

[9]Philip W. Jackson, "Conceptions of Curriculum and Curriculum Specialists," in *Handbook of Research on Curriculum,* Philip W. Jackson, ed. (New York: Macmillan, 1992), 3–40.

[10]William Pinar, Patrick Slattery, and Peter Taubman, *Understanding Curriculum: An Introduction to Historical and Contemporary Discourses* (New York: Peter Lang, 1995).

[11]Craig Cridel, "The Reconstructivists and Berjano Theorists," *Journal of Curriculum Theorizing* 14, no. 1 (Spring 1998): 49–52.

"public intellectual" who is attempting a curriculum renaissance by critiquing the society and showing how its deficiencies contribute to ineffective curriculum. For example, Pinar uses historical, psychoanalytic, and phenomenological forms to reveal the nation's problems in coming to terms with sexuality and how suppression of the issue has been disastrous for efforts at overcoming violence and racism in the society and in enacting antiracial programs in school settings.[12]

Curriculum visionaries oppose the worldwide dominance of the systemic curriculum and its penchant for measuring human capital in the interests of consumerism and education for economic gain. Others with alternative metaphors to the mechanized instructional curriculum include[13]:

- C. A. Bowers who is concerned with sustainability of life and would have curriculum leaders engage indigenous people in resisting commodification and destruction of common public spaces.
- Deborah Britzman who questions the value of having students acquire knowledge without wisdom.
- Hongyu Wang who envisions a curriculum that openly reaches to the "others" and the world with love and hope.

In his review of curriculum research methodologies, Decker Walker saw confusion and misdirection in the field.[14] Walker would return to the traditional goal of learning how to build a better curriculum rather than trying to build either a science of education or a brave new world.

Walker once said that five questions should guide curriculum inquiry:

1. What are the significant features of a given curriculum?
2. What are the personal and social consequences of a given curriculum feature?
3. What accounts for stability and change in curriculum features?
4. What accounts for personal judgment of the merit and worth of various features?
5. What sorts of curriculum features should be included for a certain purpose or situation.[15]

In his own work, Walker sees curriculum as a practical activity where one studies the deliberative process of making decisions about curriculum; tests propositions, such as whether similar deliberations produce similar designs; and establishes connections among design variables and outcomes.

Noteworthy among evolving concepts of curriculum is the view that curriculum is enactment, the meanings that teacher and students construct as they interact with each other in the classroom situation.

The Need for Studies of Correlation and Integration

Status of Correlation Studies in 1969   Goodlad omitted any mention of studies during the review period that treated the effects of concurrent offerings. By 1980, however, concern for general education, and for a more integrated view of knowledge, and for a focus on larger social questions had created increased efforts to correlation studies.

---

[12]W. Pinar, *The Bending of Racial Policies and Violence in America: Lynching, Prison Rape* (New York: Peter Lang, 2001).

[13]William E. Doll, Jr., and Noel Gough, eds. *Curriculum Vision* (New York: Peter Lang, 2002).

[14]Decker Walker, "Methodological Issues in Curriculum Research," in *Handbook of Research on Curriculum*, Philip W. Jackson, ed. (New York: Macmillan, 1992), 98–119.

[15]Decker Walker, "What Are the Problems Curricularists Ought to Study?" *Curricular Theory Network* 4, no. 2–3 (1974): 217–218.

Academic alliances were formed as sociologists, psychologists, biologists, and chemists sought answers to closely related questions. Development of curriculum that would relate literature, language, composition, and popular culture began without a unifying theory. Although an emphasis on the interrelationships of things through curriculum invited inquiry about the effects of correlation, there were those who viewed the activity as a false hope that curriculum developers could effect an integration of knowledge.[16] Curriculum scholars may encourage interdisciplinary approaches to a problem or area of interest, but they are unlikely to integrate knowledge or synthesize concepts from various disciplines to create a set of new concepts.

Present Status of Integrated Studies Nathalie Gehrke found that teachers' conceptions of integrative curriculum are vague because they have not experienced an integrative curriculum. Gehrke is one of the first investigators to observe the behaviors of those engaged in integrative curriculum development. She learned that the process was not much different from other curriculum development but is tied to assumptions about what constitutes integration.[17]

Integration is seen as more than a device for the organization of content. To some, it is a way to help students sort out the information that is most relevant and useful. To others, it is a way to transcend conceptual blinders by relating intuition and intellect as problems and ideas become the conscious focus.[18]

As described in Chapter 7, J. Beane and W. Ullrich clarified the concepts of thematic, interdisciplinary, and multidisciplinary approaches to curriculum organization and enlarged on the concept of an integrative curriculum as one that begins with learners' own meanings before expanding them.

Although the nation's need for real-world problem-based learning makes interdisciplinary programs essential, the standards movement with its testing of knowledge in separate fields is inconsistent with this need. The cultural bias of those in academic disciplines and their sometimes fraudulent concepts of reality are barriers to collaborative endeavors. A committee of the National Research Council emphasized that even if students are given more curriculum options, these options should be mutually reinforced.[19]

Practical accounts of integrated curriculum are increasing. Andrew Kaplan's "Galileo," an experiment in interdisciplinary curriculum planning by an entire faculty, as described in Chapter 7, is an excellent example.[20] Kaplan emphasizes the need for training teachers in the deliberative process required for developing such a curriculum.

The Need for Studies of Sequence

Status of Studies Treating Sequence in 1969 The quest for the best arrangement of material in a field was very much alive in 1969. There were many experiments with different sequences in programmed and computer-based instruction. Robert Gagné's work stimulated several investigations to assess the effects of scrambled versus hierarchical orderings of learning tasks. The findings were mixed, indicating that increasing complexity is not always the best criterion for ordering material.

---

[16]Richard L. Derr, "A Note on Curriculum Integration," *Curriculum Inquiry* 11, no. 4 (1981): 387–392.

[17]Nathalie Gehrke, "Developing Integrative Curriculum: Some Discoveries on Process" (paper presented at annual meeting of American Educational Research Association, New Orleans, 1988).

[18]Andrew Kaplan, "The New Disciplines of Liberal Education," *Curriculum Inquiry* 22, no. 3 (Spring 1992): 47–65.

[19]*Transforming Undergraduate Education for Future Research,* National Research Council, BIO 2010 (Washington, DC: National Academy Press, 2003).

[20]Andrew Kaplan, "Galileo: An Experiment in Interdisciplinary Education," *Curriculum Inquiry* 18, no. 3 (1988): 255–287.

Present Status of Studies of Sequence In 1976 George Posner and Kenneth Strike completed an extensive categorization scheme for sequence after which the research interests shifted to the problem of coherence of texts and programs. James Kallison, Jr., provided evidence that the most important way to judge sequence is whether it reveals the relationships among parts.[21] Developmentalists, however, continue to take into account the cognitive capacities of learners, emphasizing that sequence should be planned from the learner's point of view rather than a priori. Many ideas about the cognitive capacities of learners at different ages are being challenged.

The structure of the student's thinking is as important as the logic of the discipline. Today, there is less sequencing by assumed stages of development, such as Piagetian operations, and more recognizing that appropriate content depends on the guidance (scaffolding) from teachers and peers as well as on the student's own goals for learning. Although direct teaching, repealed practice, and the maximization of error by arranging tasks hierarchially is effective in teaching sample tasks, the acquisition of powerful concepts, long-term retention, and transfer of learning is best achieved by initially introducing challenging complex tasks and recognizing that student errors and mistakes and essential components of powerful learning. Yet the old idea of curriculum as structured knowledge located in separate subjects and disciplines and ordered in a sequential way dies hard. Even progressive curriculum specialists, like Elliot Eisner, who puts student interest first, see value in the traditional concepts of scope (breadth) and sequence (order of learning) when he says that one cannot paint well without prerequisite knowledge of color and darkness.

THE NEED FOR ANALYZING EDUCATION OBJECTIVES (STANDARDS)

Status of Taxonomical Analysis of Objectives in 1969 The pioneer taxonomy or classification of objectives in the cognitive domain was completed in 1956, and taxonomies in both psychomotor and affective realms were developed after 1969. Furthermore, there was much research treating how best to refine educational objectives into precise behavioral objectives.

Studies of the effects of behavioral objectives on learning were also common. The structural analysis of feelings, attitudes, and values did not keep up with similar research in the areas of mental abilities and personality. J. R. Calder and others found, in the *Taxonomy of Educational Objectives—Cognitive Domains,* that the synthesis and evaluation of the categories did not depend on integration with lower level behaviors.[22] In his critical review of taxonomies of educational objectives, Robert M. W. Travers faulted the Bloom taxonomy for being chiefly an inventory of test items, not a taxonomy of cognitive processes.[23] He viewed Piaget's system, by which knowledge is classified in terms of formal properties, as a better potential basis for developing a taxonomy of cognitive processes. Piaget's framework was used in a number of curriculum projects for analyzing learning activities in terms of the logical operations they involve (Project SOAR at Xavier University of Louisiana, the STAR Program of Metropolitan State College of Denver, Project ADAPT at the University of Nebraska, and an elementary science program developed at the University of California, Berkeley).

[21]James Kallison, Jr., "Effect of Lesson Organization on Achievement," *American Education Research Journal* 23, no. 2 (1986): 337–347.
[22]J. R. Calder, "In the Cells of the 'Bloom Taxonomy,'" *Journal of Curriculum Studies* 15, no. 3 (July–Sept. 1983): 291–302.
[23]Robert M. W. Travers, "Taxonomies of Educational Objectives and Theories of Classification," *Educational Evaluation and Policy Analysis* 2, no. 2 (March–April 1980): 5–23.

Present Status of Analysis of Objectives (Standards) Current research casts doubt on rigid conceptions of skill hierarchies and spiraled curriculum. Although there may be some valid skill hierarchies such as teaching addition before multiplication, little evidence supports hierarchies such as those in Bloom's taxonomy. Although there is little interest today in sequencing, some people believe that increasing the complexity of the content and task, increasing the diversity of applications, and providing adequate support for learning, gradually transferring responsibility from teacher to student (scaffolding), may be helpful.

Indeed, analysis of cognitive processes has been greatly strengthened by studies of (1) metacognitive processes (knowledge of when and why to use various strategies for problem solving),[24] (2) the cognitive processes underlying the act of writing (planning), sentence generations, and revising,[25] and (3) the processes involved in mathematics activities.[26]

As described in Chapter 9, in 2000 Bloom's Taxonomy was revised to reflect the importance of students acquiring metacognitive knowledge and the ability to transfer what is learned to new situations.[27] The new taxonomy goes beyond the surface level of specific objectives, activities, and test items to determine the level of cognition in each. As such it becomes a tool for aligning standards, instruction, and assessment by their common intellectual challenge and may lead to creating and using new ways to assess higher order thinking.

Evidence of the change in curriculum development as a result of cognitive psychology supplanting behaviorism and its focus on task analysis can be found also in military curriculum development.[28] The old methodology for analyzing the task requirements of a job and developing curriculum geared to those requirements is limited by the problems of high cost and a failure to analyze the mental structures that underlie competence. The new methodology is more interested in analyzing what must be learned in specific situations, emphasizing context and content rather than behavior. The new military training programs use simulations to teach principles of operations and reasoning. Students are not presented with physically faithful renditions of what they will be working with but with graphical simulations that exhibit the conceptual components of the phenomenon. Also, simplified versions of the actual equipment are easier to understand and provide better models for reasoning about the task than physically faithful simulators or the real-life equipment. Training now focuses on making relevant knowledge explicit, using problem-solving contexts for instruction in basic principles, and carefully managing information processing during learning.

The Need for Process–Product Research

Status of Process–Product Research in 1969 Process–product research attempts to relate instructional variables to learner achievement and the curriculum planning process to improved instruction and learning. Much process–product research between 1960 and 1969 dealt with instructional objectives. Most curriculum materials investigations dwelt on specific treatment variables associated with the materials (e.g., organizers, relevant practice, knowledge of results, and prompts). Goodlad realized, however, that there

[24]Lauren Resnick, ed., *Cognition and Instruction Issues and Agendas* (Hillsdale, NJ: Lawrence Erlbaum, 1987).

[25]John R. Hayes and Linda S. Flower, "Writing Research and the Writer," *American Psychologist* 41, no. 10 (Oct. 1986): 1106–1114.

[26]H. P. Ginsberg, ed., *The Development of Mathematical Thinking* (New York: Academic Press, 1983).

[27]Lorin W. Anderson, ed., "Revising Bloom's Taxonomy," Special issue, *Theory into Practice* 26, no. 4 (Autumn 2002).

[28]Henry M. Halff, "Cognitive Science and Military Training," *American Psychologist* 41, no. 10 (Oct. 1986): 1131–1139.

were two problems with this research. The first was methodological. It was not always clear what constituted the process or treatment, nor was it always established that the treatment had been carried out as stipulated. The second problem was theoretical. It was often difficult to know the significance of a small manageable process–product equation within some large frame of explanation.

Present Status of Process–Product Research   The methodological and theoretical problems of 1969 have not been resolved. However, they are more widely recognized now. Research into instructional effectiveness by means of the input–output approach has not yielded consistent results. Background factors tend to dominate the findings. No single resource or variable is consistently shown to exert a powerful influence on learning. Perhaps one reason for this state of affairs is the emphasis on generalizations independent of contexts. Instead of making the search for generalizations the major priority, investigators might also look for unique personal characteristics and uncontrolled events in situations. Generalizations might be working hypotheses and then researchers look for clues to specific factors that might cause departures from the predicted effects. These factors might be *learner variables*, such as a learner's perceptions of the curriculum events or a learner's cognitive style; *teacher variables*, such as a teacher's attitude toward the curriculum and the learners, or teacher pressure toward student conformity rather than toward independence; and *school* or *classroom ambient variables*, such as peer group interactions, morale, expectations, and consistency with home and community values.

As indicated in Chapter 6, work has expanded from concentration on isolated variables associated with effectiveness to include analyses of life in classrooms and from unambiguous tasks with certain answers to the study of tasks with several possible answers. This work has led to a recognition of the importance of (1) improving instructional materials that carry the major academic content and (2) attending to learning tasks that have the greatest consequences for quality in academic work.

Among current trends in process–product research are the following:

1. Making clearer distinction between curriculum goals and instructional method used. In most instances, curriculum content is held constant in order to study instructional methods.

2. Refining measurement instruments in order to measure how well and not just how often something is done. Considering the limited range of measures that have been used to assess curriculum, it is inadvisable to equate curriculum effects in achievement with effectiveness.

3. Considering untapped questions such as what makes an effective unit of instruction and how best to accommodate individual differences.

Design-based research is a departure in process–product research. Essentially, it is the designing of an instructional program based on a grounded theory of learning, such as social construction and the view that the learner's prior knowledge must be dealt with in learning new concepts, many of which are counterintuitive. Instead of lecture, worksheets, and direct teaching, students are placed in a situation where they have to achieve some interesting goal that requires them to learn whatever is in the curriculum. Real-world problems, case studies, and anchored events are commonly introduced to provoke goal setting.

Designers anticipate learners' goals as the learners might work on the challenge, the strategies they might pursue, and the choices they might make. Learners are expected to think for themselves and how they will get the information they need. Small groups of designers conduct their own inquiry that will contribute to the big idea or problem. Each group reports on their decisions, findings, and what they must learn next. The enactment and analysis of the design lead to redesigning of the program.

A serious problem in process–product research is that researchers assume that certain instructional variables are directly related to student achievement. In fact, the relationships between classroom processes and achievement are usually nonlinear. Too much or too little of a good process is ineffective. Furthermore, a good practice may mask a better one. For instance, time on task is considered beneficial. However, Anne Haas Dyson found that time off task, when children collaboratively engage in spontaneous talk, is often a more intellectually demanding opportunity than time on teacher-directed lessons.[29]

DIRECTIONS IN CURRICULUM INQUIRY

New questions invite new forms of inquiry. Also, as curriculum inquiry is undertaken in schools and classrooms by teachers, both the purposes and methodologies for research are altered.

Forms of Inquiry

Edmund Short has edited *Forms of Curriculum Inquiry,* a text that illustrates 17 forms of curriculum inquiry.[30] Short and his contributors take the view that curriculum research is related to a cluster of practical activities for conceiving, expressing, justifying, and enacting educational programs. They assume that there should be a matching between the research question and the form of inquiry selected. That assumption may be challenged by showing how some questions can be answered by using a variety of forms. Nevertheless, as seen in Table 14.1, their illustrations of questions and forms are good introductions to the available range of inquiries and methods.

Synoptic Activity as Curriculum Inquiry

An important direction in curriculum inquiry is to bring together widely separated fields into a larger common area. The curriculum person's competence may lie not in unearthing new knowledge but in putting together many of the findings from other disciplines. The curriculum expert can take a number of narrow perspectives and unite them by applying them in the development of school programs that help students learn things that will be helpful to them and to society. The kinds of research borrowing that are useful in curriculum synoptic activity are the following:

1. *Concepts.* There are more concepts, such as concepts of motivation (locus of control) and concepts of learning (learned helplessness), than anything else that can be used. Developers of new courses use such concepts in their developmental efforts.

2. *Generalizations.* Although there is growing concern that few generalizations have broad applicability and that generalizations depend on conditions that may not be present in particular school settings, generalizations can direct attention to factors that may be important locally.

3. *Facts.* General facts are often less useful than generalizations. Particular facts have to be collected for each situation.

---

[29]Anne Haas Dyson, "The Value of Time Off Task: Spontaneous Talk and Deliberate Text," *Harvard Educational Review* 57, no. 4 (Nov. 1987): 396–420.
[30]Edmund C. Short, ed., *Forms of Curriculum Inquiry* (Albany: State University of New York Press, 1991).

Table 14.1   Forms of Inquiry Applicable to Different Curriculum Questions

Questions	Method or Form of Inquiry
How is "curriculum" defined in different situations? Where does this definition take us? Where does it come from and why?	Analytical
What warnings can I offer about a curriculum trend or practice?	Speculative
What are the historical antecedents to classroom grading practices?	Historical
Does reciprocal teaching improve the reading comprehension of limited English speakers?	Scientific (experimental)
Which factors improve or inhibit teacher participation in curriculum development by a team?	Ethnographic
How have my views of curriculum changed over the last 15 years and what have been the factors in these changes?	Narrative
What are the salient qualities of selected text material?	Aesthetic
What does the student perceive and feel when learning mathematics?	Phenomenological
What is the meaning of testing in school X?	Hermeneutics
What is the validity of the concept "curriculum design" in relating all aspects of a curriculum including normative, practical, and structural dimensions?	Theoretical
On what premises should curriculum be created?	Normative
What are the contradictions and inconsistencies between fundamental norms (e.g., equal access to knowledge) and existing curriculum policies and practices?	Critical
Does a curriculum guide or framework enhance or inhibit curriculum enactment?	Evaluative
What works in promoting attitudinal change?	Integrative (summary of findings)
What kinds of grounds should be given greater weight in justifying our curriculum decisions?	Deliberative
What is happening? What should we do about it?	Action

Source: Adapted from Edmund C. Short, ed., *Forms of Curriculum Inquiry* (Albany: State University of New York Press, 1991), 17–19.

4. *Methods.* Problem-solving procedures are borrowed from disciplines and applied to curriculum problems. For example, the anthropologist's use of naturalistic observation is currently applied in studies of classrooms.

5. *Values and attitudes.* A willingness to put one's deepest beliefs to the test of practice, a commitment to the facts, and an active skepticism are needed to solve curriculum dilemmas.

Examples of synoptic activity in curriculum, illustrating the contributions of different subject matter fields to curriculum development, are seen in borrowings from *social psychology* with its concepts about peer group learning in the selection of learning opportunities; borrowings from *personality psychology* with its notion of human needs and the self, particularly in designing curriculum for moral development; borrowings from *sociology* with its concepts of social class and social mobility; and borrowings from the *psychology of learning* with its concepts and findings about the learning process and their implications for curriculum and instruction. Synoptic activity is predicated on our willingness to question what our curriculum is doing and what we know about the changes we propose. It means using research from many sources, including historical research, in guiding our efforts.

INQUIRY IN THE SCHOOL AND CLASSROOM

The fashion in curriculum research is now moving away from the search for broad generalizations and abstract principles of guiding practice. Instead, it is moving closer to the individual school and classroom. Empirical studies that use methods such as content analysis, expert ratings, and meta-analysis, and that seek findings for wide applicabilities, of course, continue. For example, studies such as "Toward a Knowledge for School Learning" identify factors that exert the greatest and least influence on school learning, contributing important information both for policy and for classroom practice.[31] However, local inquiries are increasing because of dissatisfaction with generalized findings independent of particular contexts, the growing desire to have practitioners "own" and therefore act on the ideas from research, and the belief that teachers should create their own knowledge. Narratives, qualitative inquiry in school settings, and action research are prominent approaches at the local level.

Narrative

D. Jean Clandinin and E Michael Connelly have promoted the idea of teachers researching their own practice.[32] Usually a researcher works with a teacher or a group of teachers for the purpose of having the teachers tell their story about what is happening in their classrooms—their observations, interpretations, concerns, beliefs, and feelings about subject matter, children, and other instructional factors. At other times, teachers tell their own stories, indicating the complexity of curriculum decision making as curriculum is enacted. Generalizations from these stories occur as readers of the narratives identify with the account and see its relevance to their own situations.

Qualitative Inquiry in School Settings

In the past few years, curriculum inquirers have placed themselves in direct and continuous contact with the objects of curriculum investigation: instructional materials, classroom interactions, and their meanings for learners. Often these investigators use ethnographic methods. Basic to this kind of inquiry is the nature of the interpretations given to classroom observations. Gail McCutcheon has illustrated how researchers construct meaning by relating their knowledge to the observations made.[33] McCutcheon recognizes that many qualitative researchers use a phenomenological approach. They interpret events in light of the meanings participants make of those events. Others use a critical stance, such as a Marxist orientation, and interpret events in light of wider considerations. McCutcheon offers the example of the influence of a researcher's orientation on inquiry by examining

---

[31]Margaret C. Wang, Geneva D. Haertel, and Herbert J. Walberg, *Review of Educational Research* 63, no. 3 (fall 1993): 249–295.

[32]D. Jean Clandinin and F. Michael Connelly, "Narrative and Story in Practice and Research," in *The Reflective Turn: Case Studies of Reflective Practice*, Donald Schon, ed. (New York: Teachers College Press, 1990).

[33]Gail McCutcheon, "On the Interpretation of Classroom Observations," *Educational Researcher* 10, no. 5 (May 1981): 5–10.

three approaches to the study of the 45-minute period of instruction so common in secondary school. A systematist concerned with achievement and teaching effectiveness might approach the situation by considering the time spent on tasks within the 45 minutes; a phenomenologist might wonder what meaning 45-minute periods have for participants; and a critical scientist might ask about the origin of 45-minute periods and how such time affects what students learn or how the time allocation denies some students access to knowledge, thereby producing social injustice.

McCutcheon refers to three ways in which interpretations are made. The researcher may look for patterns in the observations. There may be an unconscious order in classroom practices (raising hands, asking questions, assigning projects, grading responses). Observations may also be interpreted for their social meanings. For instance, what does movement of the students' heads mean? Boredom? Agreement? Trying to please the teacher? Fatigue? Social meanings may be interpreted by asking the teacher or students to justify an action or to describe what a particular statement *really* meant. In a third type of interpretation, the facts of a classroom are related to a theory. For example, they might be related to psychological theories of learning, to a historical movement or theme, to a particular educational philosophy, or to a theory of social classes.

The validity of interpretations depends on the reasoning used in arriving at the interpretation, the amount of evidence that supports the interpretation, and the extent to which the interpretation seems to fit with other knowledge of the real world. How far can one generalize from a single case study? The answer is similar to the answer for how far can one accept truths in great literature. It rests on the assumption that others can apply the findings to their own situation.

Action Research as Curriculum Inquiry

A popular view is that action research practitioners put the findings of research into effect in order to resolve their own areas of need. Originally, practitioners used action research in attempting to study their problems systematically, and the value of such research was not determined by the discovery of scientific laws or generalizations but by whether the application led to improvement in practice.

In the mid-1950s, teachers began using action research to improve their curricula. Gordon MacKenzie, Stephen Corey, and Hilda Taba were among those curriculum specialists who involved teachers in the research process. Teachers under their direction accumulated evidence to define their problems, drew on experience and knowledge to form action hypotheses to improve the situation of their daily work, tested promising procedures, and accumulated evidence of their effectiveness. The rationale and technical procedures for conducting such research are still available from several sources.[34,35] Three forces aborted the growth of action research. First, the academic curriculum reform of the 1960s put little emphasis on local development of curriculum. Standardization was prized over uniqueness. Second, educational researchers in universities, who in the 1950s might have been willing to work with teachers in curriculum inquiry, found themselves in the 1960s attending instead to the interests of government agencies that were funding politically motivated research. Third, many persons in the 1960s believed that problems of curriculum and instruction would best be resolved by the discovery and application of generalizations and laws of learning, not by individual teachers in unique situations.

---

[34]*Research for Curriculum Development* (Washington, DC: Association for Supervision and Curriculum Development, 1957).

[35]Stephen M. Corey, *Action Research to Improve School Practice* (New York: Columbia University, Teachers College, 1953).

Currently, it is again being recognized that teachers (as well as students and persons not directly involved in the school) are theorists and researchers in their own right. There are signs of a shift of responsibility for curriculum development from colleges and laboratories to classrooms and communities. There are networks representing scholarly efforts aimed at helping teachers rather than at producing research for fellow scholars.

Enthusiasm for action research is cresting. Action research projects, textbooks, and journal articles on actions abound.[36,37] However, Wilfred Carr has illuminated problems with this activity.[38] Carr points out that action research now means different things to different people. While all action researchers have a contempt for academic theorizing and are disenchanted with "mainstream" research, they are divided on what the practical purposes of action research are. Some regard action research primarily as a way to deepen teachers' understanding, whereas others stress the researcher's role in stimulating improvement and change. Still others see action research as an effective way to communicate research findings to teachers. Carr warns against action researchers using the language and evaluative standards of positivist conventional research. The old practices of action researchers engaging in systematic and methodological processes for acquiring knowledge is faulted because it falls into the positivist tradition with its separation from philosophical questioning and its indifferences to major social, political, and moral concerns. A contrary view is that action research is a dialogical or reflective process of democratic discussion and philosophical critique. By way of example, Richard Winter describes how action research need not be confined to revealing teachers' interpretive theories but revealing to them aspects of their practices in a way that makes practice amenable to critical transformation.[39] Instead of being primarily concerned with explicating or testing teachers' implicit theories, action research can be concerned with establishing the conditions that enable teachers to reflect critically on the contradictions between their educational ideas and beliefs and the institutionalized practices through which the ideas and beliefs are expressed. A practical illustration of this perspective is found in the work of Carr and Kemmis.[40]

According to these researchers, action research is a critical inquiry controlled by practitioners who are committed to social as well as curriculum change. Teachers reflect on the justice of their social and educational practices, their understanding of these practices, and the situation in which these practices are carried out. The latter relates to understanding the influence of broader sociocultural and political structures on the educational environment.

In *Sources of a Science of Education*, Dewey made these points[41]:

1. An inquirer can repeat the research of another to confirm or discredit it. Moreover, by using this technique, the inquirer discovers new problems and new investigations that refine old procedures and lead to new and better ones.

2. No conclusion of scientific research can be converted into an immediate rule for educators. Educational practice contains many conditions and factors not included in the scientific finding.

3. Although scientific findings should not be used as a rule of action, they can help teachers to be alert to discover certain factors that would otherwise go unnoticed and to interpret something that would otherwise be misunderstood.

---

[36]Stephen Kemmis, ed., *The Action Research Planner* (Victoria, Australia: Deakin University Press, 1988).

[37]D. Hustler et al., eds., *Action Research in Classrooms and Schools* (London: Allen and Unwin, 1986).

[38]Wilfred Carr, "Action Research: Ten Years On," *Journal of Curriculum Studies* 21, no. 1 (1989): 85–90.

[39]Richard Winter, *Action Research and the Nature of Social Inquiry: Professional Innovation and Education Work* (Aldershot, England: Avebury, Gower, 1987).

[40]Wilfred Carr and Stephen Kemmis, *Becoming Critical: Knowing Through Action Research* (Victoria, Australia: Deakin University Press, 1983).

[41]John Dewey, *The Sources of a Science of Education* (New York: Horace Liveright, 1929).

4. The practitioner who knows a science (a system) can see more possibilities and opportunities and has a wide range of alternatives to select from in dealing with individual situations.

5. In education, practice should form the problems of inquiry. The worth of a scientific finding is shown only when it serves an educational purpose, and whether it really serves or not can be found only in practice.

6. Research persons connected with school systems may be too close to the practical problems and the university professor too far away from them to secure the best results.

7. Curriculum problems arise in relations with students. Consequently, it is impossible to see how there can be an adequate investigation unless teachers actively participate.

Perhaps the most eloquent argument for action research as a form of curriculum inquiry is found in John Dewey's answer to the question of how educational objectives are to be determined. He thought it false to say that social conditions, science, or the subject matter of any field could determine objectives. He conceived education as a process of discovering what values are worthwhile and to be pursued as objectives.

> To see what is going on and to observe the results of what goes on so as to see their future consequences in the process of growth, and so on indefinitely, is the only way in which the value of what takes place can be judged. To look at some outside source to provide aims is to fail to know what education is as an ongoing process.... Knowledge of the objectives which society actually strives for and the consequences actually attained may be had in some measure through a study of the social sciences. This knowledge may render educators more circumspect, more critical, as to what they are doing. It may inspire better insight into what is going on here and now in the home or school; it may enable teachers and parents to look farther ahead and judge on the basis of consequences in a longer course of development. But it must operate through their own ideas, plannings, observations, judgments. Otherwise it is not educational science at all, but merely so much sociological information.[42]

CONCLUDING COMMENTS

In this chapter, the state of the curriculum field was appraised by reviewing the status of curriculum research in six areas. Curriculum theory is divided among traditionalists, scientists, and reconceptualists. A lack of common ground of professional action and responsibility is a source of concern. The status of conceptual systems for identifying major curriculum questions shows more attention to the role of the learner as a decision maker in curriculum, the impact of social political forces in curriculum making, and curriculum criticism as a mode of inquiry in its own right. There is much activity attempting to show how best to arrange material for effective learning. Work regarding educational objectives or standards, which has dominated much of curriculum thought and practice, is being extended to reveal reasons for the learner's inability to use the knowledge acquired and the relationship between content objectives and the cognitive processes that underlie competent performance.

Process–product studies are revealing useful information such as findings showing the minimal influence of policy solutions—restructuring, site-based management, evaluation, and tracking—and the importance of students using metacognitive strategies and building their own knowledge structures.

---

[42]Ibid., 74–76.

Long-range work regarding educational standards will look for the reasons learners are unable or unwilling to use knowledge in the real world and in their lifelong learning. Present research on the relationship between content standards and the cognitive processes underlying competent performance is a major advance.

Future directions in curriculum theory promise to be fruitful. The reconceptualists are drawing attention to both the political and moral aspects of curriculum making. Empiricists are expanding curriculum design experiments to inform us on how best to prepare students for group participation in the social construction of their knowledge. Many will study the incoherent state of curriculum brought by (a) multicultural influences; (b) the state-imposed standardization of skills and separate subject matters; and (c) the variety of new options for learning through the Internet and alternative institutions of choice.

Anyone wishing to do curriculum inquiry in schools and classrooms will be helped by the guidance of those advocating qualitative inquiry, synoptic activity, narratives, and action research. You can decide whether the many research paradigms are broadening or whether they are so self-contained that they neglect important questions outside their field, clouding our visions.

QUESTIONS

1. How might scientific-based research for validating programs be strengthened by (a) empirical studies of curriculum design, (b) critical analysis of the curriculum, and (c) the researcher's personal awareness of self?

2. Given the enormity of curriculum problems and the shortage of resources, it is imperative that topics for inquiry be selected carefully. What criteria should guide the selection of a topic for inquiry?

3. Do you see curriculum inquiry as the search for answers or at best a way to gain ideas, insights, and a different approach to a familiar problem?

4. Which of the six curriculum concerns used to appraise the status of curriculum research shows the least progress? What might account for the difference in progress?

5. In curriculum, are you a serialist who proceeds from certainty to certainty with information acquired in small well-defined steps at a sequentially ordered pace? Or are you a holistic starter who experimentally tries to understand an overall framework or big problem and then starts to fill in the details?

6. Donald Chipley at Pennsylvania State University once gave three reasons for undertaking curriculum research. One reason is to make an inventory of the content that is offered and the resources that are invested in particular educational developments. Another reason is personal curiosity. An investigator has an interest in exploring new ideas and extending generalizable knowledge about curriculum relationships. The third reason is decision making. A person assesses various curriculum alternatives in order to make more rational decisions in specific situations. Which of these motives is closest to your own?

SUGGESTED STRATEGIC RESEARCH

GOING BEYOND CONFLICTING CONCEPTIONS OF CURRICULUM
Much of curriculum discourse is about opposing views—either–or—yet efforts to form a more inclusive view are part of the history of the curriculum field. Consider a conflict, such as a social reconstructivist versus a humanistic curriculum; curriculum as an instrumental commodity versus curriculum as a moral or life-sustaining venture; or curriculum delivered by direct teaching versus an inquiry approach. Propose an overriding concept or situation and show how it would benefit from both positions.

DETERMINING THE BALANCE AMONG FOUR CURRICULUM FORMS

Andrew Seaton has proposed four curriculum forms—each of which has a particular significance and complements the others[43]:

> *Focused learning*—subject matter concepts unlikely to be learned in out-of-school contexts.
>
> *Transdisciplinary investigations*—complex active learning units based on important questions or problems and requiring knowledge from several subject areas.
>
> *Curriculum development*—real-life projects with public consequences for a community.
>
> *Personal learning projects*—students (individuals or group) initiate and direct problem-based or purpose-based projects.

In what kind of school or classroom do you find the four curriculum forms? What makes it possible to enact the four forms? What are the consequences of using four rather than fewer?

CHILDREN'S STORIES OF THEIR CURRICULUM

We have learned much about both the institutional and the enacted curriculum from narratives by teachers. Where are the stories by children telling of their present life in the classroom (not reminiscing as adults)? What might children's narratives reveal about curriculum as experienced by diverse learners? What frameworks do they use in interpreting the curriculum as enacted? Consider different ways of eliciting stories—oral and written stories, "talk alouds," visuals, and dramatics. Who do they want to hear their stories?

RECOGNIZING A CURRICULUM PERSON

Curriculum is sometimes thought to be a discourse or conversation in which curriculum workers critique their situation as a basis for transforming the institutional curriculum and having an impact on learning experiences and outcomes. As a participant observer of conversations with peers, colleagues, or others, identify potential and active curriculum leaders. Some clues to use are

- Passionate about his or her beliefs and values.
- Communicates ideas with confidence, but also considers the views of others.
- Willing to collaborate with everyone in all areas of curriculum activity.
- Problematise matters related to curriculum.
- Raises difficult questions rather than providing easy answers about curriculum issues.
- Seeks relationships—past–present–future, society–school–learners.

SELECTED REFERENCES

JACKSON, PHILIP W., ED. *Handbook of Research on Curriculum*. American Educational Research Association. New York: Macmillan, 1992.

JONASSEN, DAVID H., AND SUSAN M. LANDS. *Theoretical Foundations of Learning Environments*. Mahwah, NJ: Lawrence Erlbaum, 2000.

LINDBLOOM, CHARLES E. *Inquiry and Change: The Troubled Attempt to Understand and Shape Society*. New Haven: Yale University Press, 1990.

SHAVELSON, RICHARD J., AND LISA TOWN, EDS. *Scientific Research in Education*. Washington, DC: National Academy Press, 2002.

SHORT, EDMUND C., ED. *Forms of Curriculum Inquiry*. Albany: State University of New York Press, 1991.

---

[43] Andrew Seaton, *The Key Abilities Model: Curriculum Organization for a Society of Autonomous Learners*, retrieved November 2001 from http://www.tpg.com.au/users/aseaton/kam.

NAME INDEX

A

Adler, M., 73
Agassi, J., 122
Aiken, W. M., 163
Airasian, P., 210
Alcott, A. B., 294
Alexander of Macedon, 80
Alleman, J., 135, 289
Amis, K., 18
Amsein, A., 55
Anyon, J., 31–32
Apple, M., 30, 221–222,
    237
Applebee, A. N., 279, 280
Aquinas, T., 81
Archimedes, 80
Aristotle, 18, 72, 79–80
Arnold, M., 82
Atkin, J. M., 275
Augustine of Hippo, 37
Aurelius, M., 17
Ausebel, D., 78
Ayres, E., 69

B

Barnes, M. S., 321
Beane, J., 165, 330
Belair, J. R., 263
Bell, L., 12
Bellack, A., 302
Bennett, W. J., 177
Ben-Zui, A., 164
Berend, M., 184
Berliner, D., 55
Bernard, B., 264
Bernard, C., 73
Bjork, R., 164
Black, P., 211
Bloom, A., 71
Bloom, B., 131

Bobbitt, J. F., 99, 303–304,
    310–314, 318
Bode, B. H., 99
Bonser, S., 108
Bowers, C. A., 32, 41, 329
Boyd, W., 225, 226
Boyle, R., 81
Boyost, I., 140
Bracey, G., 248
Bradford, J., 78–79
Brameld, T., 38
Brecht, B., 157
Brewer, W., 124
Britzman, D., 329
Broening, A. M., 280
Brophy, J., 135, 289
Bruner, J., 64–65, 67
Bryk, A., 196
Buber, M., 13
Burns, M., 129–130
Bush, G. W., 236
Butler, G., 141

C

Calder, J. R., 331
Carmon, A., 11
Carney, J. V., 264
Carnoy, M., 56
Carr, W., 338
Carroll, J., 164
Cassirer, E., 294
Caswell, H. L., 315–316, 319
Center, S. S., 280
Charters, W. W., 304, 310,
    312–314, 319
Cheney, L., 71
Chinn, C., 124
Cicero, 80
Cistone, P., 225
Clandinin, D. J., 336

Clinton, B., 17, 236
Clinton, H. R., 257
Cohen, S. A., 49
Cole, G., 284
Cole, M., 35–36
Comenius, J. A., 118, 150
Comer, J., 177, 178
Comer, R., 176
Conant, J. B., 254
Conlan, J. B., 68
Connelly, E. M., 336
Conrad, M., 134
Cook, L. B., 280
Corey, S., 337
Counts, G., 38
Cronbach, L. J., 201
Csermely, P., 145
Csikszentmihalyi, M, 14, 15
Cuban, L., 195, 225, 303

D

Daniels, H., 295
Davis, O. L., Jr., 303
de Bono, E., 123, 246
Dewey, J., 9, 19, 37, 243, 280,
    294, 302–304, 308–309,
    318, 339
Down, A. G., 254
Doyle, D. P., 224
Doyle, W., 121
Drachler, N., 224
Dyson, A. H., 334

E

Eidelson, J., 35
Eidelson, R., 35
Einstein, A., 5, 16, 57, 123
Eisner, E. W., 95, 204–205,
    294, 331
Eliot, C. A., 303

Eliot, T. S., 147
Elliot, C. W., 83
Emerson, R. W., 19
English, F., 137
Ennis, R., 245
Erasmus, 18
Erikson, E., 11–12, 160, 261
Euclid, 80

F
Faraday, M., 82
Felix, P., 264
Fernandez, J., 229
Festinger, L., 77
Fetterman, D., 208
Finn, C., Jr., 73–74
Fitzgerald, F., 286
Frankenstein, M., 30, 31
Franklin, B., 279, 304
Freeman, P., 263
Freire, P., 27, 28, 41
Freud, S., 37, 261
Freyberg, P., 167
Friedman, K., 302

G
Gagné, R. M., 162, 330
Galen, 72
Galileo, 157
Gamoran, A., 184
Ganiel, V., 164
Gardner, H., 64, 177, 294
Gee, J., 140
Gehrke, N., 158, 330
Gibbon, P., 17
Gilligan, C., 261–262
Giroux, H., 30, 141, 327
Goethe, J., 63
Good, T., 120
Goodlad, J., 91, 120, 173, 326–328, 332–333
Goodman, N., 294
Goodman, T., 69
Gordon, C. W., 193
Gordon, W., 245
Gowin, D. B., 65
Graff, G., 327
Grallert, M., 10

Graman, T., 110
Grundy, S., 108

H
Habermas, J., 106–107
Hall, G. S., 303
Hamilton, D., 199
Hart, T., 140
Harvey, W., 73
Hazler, R. J., 264
Heidegger, M., 13
Herbart, J., 305–306
Herrick, V., 227
Hicks, T., 264
Hirsch, E. D., Jr., 74–75, 178, 283
Hirst, P., 63–64
Horace, 80
Horst, D., 214
Horton, M., 26
Hottois, J., 224
Hubbard, R., 193
Huebner, D., 6–7, 328
Hull, D., 257
Hunter, M., 306
Hutchins, R. M., 75
Hyde, A., 295

I
Iannaccone, L., 225
Illich, I., 39
Ingersoll, R., 191
Inglis, R. B., 280

J
Jackson, J., 224
Jackson, P., 328
Jacobs, H. H., 163, 227
James, W., 244
Johnson, D. W., 263
Johnson, R. T., 263
John-Steiner, V., 123, 245
Joyce, B., 160

K
Kallison, J., Jr., 331
Kant, I., 18
Kaplan, A., 330

Keislar, E., 9
Kemmis, S., 338
Kennedy, J. F., 80, 276
Kerr, S., 141
Khamisa, A., 264
Khamisa, T., 264
Kierkegaard, S., 13
Kirschenbaum, H., 262
Kirst, M. W., 104, 223, 237
Kliebard, H., 303–304
Knapp, M., 238
Kohlberg, L., 160, 261

L
La Brant, L., 280
Langer, S., 294
Larabee, D., 304
Lawton, D., 96
Lehman, D., 244
Lempert, R., 244
Levin, H., 176, 178
Lipman, P., 232
Liston, D., 41
Lock, E. A., 56
Locke, J., 18, 81
Loeb, S., 56
Lyon, R., 284

M
Macedo, D., 245
Macia, E., 326–327
Macia, G., 326
MacKenzie, G., 337
Mackintosh, H. K., 280
Mann, H., 37, 294
Marx, K., 37
Marzano, R., 49
Maslow, A., 14–16, 20, 140
May, R., 16
McCarty, F. H., 20
McClintock, B., 61
McCutcheon, G., 336–337
McLaren, P., 40
McMurry, C. A., 305–308, 317, 318
McMurry, F. W., 305–307, 318
McNeil, L., 120, 193
Mehaffy, G. L., 303

Mendel, G. J., 73
Metfessel, N., 212
Michael, W. B., 212
Milner, J., 282
Milner, L., 282
Milner, N. A., 224
Milton, J., 82
Mitchell, L. S., 321–322
Montaigne, M., 18
Moss, D., 13
Muller, C., 134

N
Nelkin, D., 224
Nevo, D., 203
Newton, I., 81
Newman, R., 197
Nickerson, R., 244
Nisbett, R., 244
Noddings, N., 11, 247
Nussbaum, M., 94

O
Oakes, J., 183, 256
Olson, D., 174, 175
Orange, A., 264
Orff, C., 150
Orr, D., 11
Osborne, R., 167
Ouhi, W., 175
Owen, R., 38–39

P
Parker, F., 19, 37
Patton, M., 213
Peabody, E., 294
Pedrotti, L., 257
Peltier, G., 180
Perls, F., 16
Pestalozzi, J., 18–19
Peterson, R. L., 264
Petrarch, 18
Phenix, P., 10, 63, 259, 260
Piaget, J., 77, 160, 261, 331
Piazza, C. L., 295
Pinar, W., 32, 328–329
Plato, 18, 37, 79–80
Pope, A., 82

Popham, W. J., 202, 214
Porter, A., 164
Posner, G., 331
Postman, N., 33
Powell, R., 35
Prigo, R., 119
Purves, A., 111

R
Ravitch, D., 73, 286–287
Reagan, R., 235, 236
Rehnquist, W. H., 235
Reich, W., 16
Reid, W., 175
Reigeluth, M., 162
Resch, K., 10
Riles, W., 226
Riordan, R., 175
Rochester, J. M., 40
Rogers, C., 15–16
Rosenblatt, L., 281
Rousseau, J., 18–19
Rugg, H., 38, 303–304
Ryan, K., 46, 261–262

S
Salmon, L. M., 321
Santayana, G., 208
Sartre, J., 13
Sax, D., 302
Schaffarzick, I., 234
Schlesinger, A., 286–287
Schneider, B., 196
Schniedewind, N., 12
Schultz, A., 37
Schwab, J., 327
Schwebel, M., 174
Schweder, R., 37
Scott, J., 110
Scriven, M., 208
Seligman, M. E. F., 16
Shakespeare, W., 82
Shane, H. G., 33
Shapiro, S. B., 5, 6, 17
Sheridan, M. C., 280
Shor, I., 28, 29, 159
Short, E., 334
Simanton, D. K., 122–123

Sirotnik, K., 205
Sizer, T., 173, 176–178, 224, 225
Skiba, R., 264
Slavin, R., 176–177, 184
Smith, D. V., 280
Smith, F., 246
Socrates, 18
Spring, J., 302
St. Vincent Millay, E., 147
Stake, R. E., 204
Stanek, G., 302
Stark, R., 81
Stern, S. S., 162
Sternberg, R., 123
Stevenson, H. W., 247–248
Stigler, J. W., 247–248
Stipek, D., 120
Strickland, R. G., 280
Strike, K., 331
Stufflebeam, D., 203

T
Taba, H., 227, 320–321, 337
Tanner, D., 302
Tanner, L., 302
Thorndike, E., 244
Tobias, S., 119–120
Torrance, E. P., 123
Travers, R. M., 331
Tye, K., 296
Tyler, R., 101–104, 118, 208, 316–320

U
Ullrich, W., 165, 330

V
Valencia, S., 284
Virgil, 80
Von Baer, K. E., 73
Vygotsky, L. S., 36–37, 119

W
Walker, D., 104, 223, 234, 237, 329
Walker, J., 41
Wang, H., 329

Webb, N. M., 184
Weeks, R. M., 280
Westbury, I., 250
White, A., 11
Wiggins, G., 210
Wiliam, D., 211

Willinsky, J., 109
Winter, R., 338
Wise, A., 226
Wixson, K., 284
Woessmann, L., 252
Wolfe, R., 251, 252

Wordsworth, W., 10
Wright, W., 140
Wynne, E., 261–262

Z
Zemelman, S., 295

SUBJECT INDEX

A

Ability groupings, 183–184
Academic curriculum, 60–84
  approaches to, 62–3
  and closing of academic
    gaps, 1
  criticisms of, 75
  cultural literacy approach to,
    73–75
  developing instructional
    materials for, 129–130
  fallacy of content in, 75
  fallacy of universalism in, 75
  forms of knowledge
    approach to, 63–64
  historical antecedents to,
    79–83
  humanistic factors in, 6
  instrumentalism in, 60–61
  liberal arts approach to,
    71–73
  and multiculturalism, 61–62
  obstacles to implementing,
    61
  organizational patterns in,
    156–158
  and postmodern thinking, 61
  psychological foundations of,
    77–79
  responses to criticisms of,
    75–77
  structure in disciplines
    approach to, 64–71
  teaching of thinking in,
    245–247
  technology in, 144–145
Academic gaps, 1
Accelerated School Programs,
  57
Accelerated School Project, 176,
  178

Accommodation, 77
Accountability Movement, 220
Accountability systems:
  in systemic curriculum,
    45–46
  for urban schools, 55
ACHIEVE, 48, 237, 257, 284
Achievement, motivation for, 9
Achievement tests, 57
  high stakes related to, 55–56
  public support for, 56
  quality of, 55
  in systemic curricula, 53–54
ACLU (American Civil Liberties
  Union), 209
Action research, 337–339
Activism, technology and,
  140–141
Activity, new psychological
  criteria for, 132
Adaptability of activities, 134
Adaptation of instruction,
  115–116, 119
Administrative structure, 111.
  see also Managing curriculum
Adult literacy, 27, 28
Advanced Placement (AP)
  tests, 55
Advisory councils (vocational
  training), 105
AET, 55
Affect, measuring, 213–214
Affective dimension (of learning
  styles), 119
Affective domain:
  in curriculum, see
    Humanistic curriculum
  in self-directed curriculum, 9
Affiliation, 94
Age appropriateness (reading),
  160–161

Albert Einstein College of
  Medicine, 4
Alexandria (Egypt), 80
Algebra Cognitive Tutor, 142
Alignment:
  of psychological assumptions
    and learning theories, 52
  in systemic curriculum, 45,
    49–50
  of teaching standards and
    goals, 116
Alternative schools, 187–188,
  230
Amelioration function, 93
American Alliance for Healthy
  Physical Education,
  Recreation, and Health, 277
American Association for the
  Advancement of Science, 275
American Civil Liberties Union
  (ACLU), 209
American Education
  Association, 237
American Federation of
  Teachers, 284
American ideals for education, 3
American Institute for Research,
  177
Amherst College, 151
Ancient Greeks, 17, 18, 78–80
Ancient Romans, 17, 78–80
Anticipatory set (lesson plans),
  153
Application(s):
  as category of objective,
    206–207
  organizing by, 158
Apprenticeship-based projects,
  132
Appropriate practice principle,
  118

The arts:
    as academic disciplines, 81
    in humanistic curriculum,
        7–8
    in self-directed learning, 10
    in social reconstruction
        curriculum, 25
    trends in, 294–295
Arts Education Partnership, 295
ASCD, *see* Association for
    Supervision and Curriculum
    Development
Asian Tiger nations, 250
Assessment:
    authentic, 210–211
    evaluation vs., 200
    as learning, 211–212
Assimilation, 77
Association for Supervision and
    Curriculum Development
    (ASCD), 29–30, 100, 175
Association of Literary Scholars
    and Critics, 72
Association of Rhetorical
    Societies, 80
Attainability of standards/
    objectives, 103
Attraction function, 93
Attributive theory, 9
Authentic assessment,
    210–211
Authoritarian populists, 222
Autonomic moral education,
    260
Awareness, 16

B
Balanced curriculum, 270
*Basic Principles of Curriculum
    and Instruction* (Ralph Tyler),
    104, 316
Basic skills movement, 281
Behaviorism:
    and systemic curriculum, 51
    and third force psychology,
        13–14
    and value of learning activi-
        ties, 131

Beliefs:
    and knowledge, 123–125
    as predictor of academic
        success, 78
    student-generated, 110
Benchmarks, 153, 206–208
Berjano Center (Ohio), 328
Bias, 103
Bilingual education, 293–294
Biofeedback, 88
Biological Science Curriculum
    Study, 76
Bloom's Taxonomy, 332
Boston school and neighborhood
    project, 25
Bottom-up approach, 154
Bradley Commission, 286, 287
Broad fields structure, 151, 157

C
C. Everett Koop Institute, 4
CAI (computer-assisted instruc-
    tion), 129
California:
    administrator training centers
        in, 179
    cultural literacy approach
        in, 74
    history curriculum in,
        286, 287
    management of schools
        in, 175
    state control in, 53
    systemic curriculum in, 47
    vocational technology center
        in, 256
    "We Care" program in, 290
Capitalism, curriculum and, 304
Career and technical education,
    253. *see also* Vocational
    education
Carnegie Foundation, 236
Carnegie schools, 175
Carnegie units, 181, 183
Cash for Caps program, 230
Catholic schools, 190
Centers, organizing, 146–148,
    150

Center for Civics Education, 290
Center for Educational Policy
    and Research (University of
    Oregon), 47
Center for Research Libraries
    (Chicago), 303
Center for the Study of
    Evaluation (UCLA), 45
Central High School
    (Philadelphia), 304
Centralized educational
    systems, 91
Champions of Change, 295
Character education, 262–263
Charter schools, 187, 189
Check for understanding (lesson
    plans), 154
Chicago, decentralization in,
    231–232
Chicken Book, 157
Child-centered leaders, 303
Children's interests, 9
China, literacy campaign in, 28
Chinese Examination System,
    287
Choice (as motivational princi-
    ple), 116
Chronological ordering, 150, 157
CIDREE, 250
CIPP model, 203
Classical humanists, 303
Classicists, 63
Classroom learning opportuni-
    ties, *see* Learning opportunities
Classroom level, structure at,
    151
Classroom practices, effective-
    ness of, 193
Closed view of learning activi-
    ties, 131
*The Closing of the American
    Mind* (Allan Bloom), 71
Coalition for Evidence-Based
    Policy, 135
Coalition of Essential Schools,
    55, 57, 173, 176, 178, 183
Cognition and Technology
    Group (Vanderbilt), 143

Cognitive dimension (of learning styles), 119
Cognitive dissonance, 77
Cognitive domain, 9
Cognitive learning, 161
Cognitive mapping, 78
Cognitive psychology:
  and systemic curriculum, 51–52
  and technological curriculum, 162
Cognitive Research Trust (CORT), 246
Cognitive tutors, 142
Cognitivism, value of learning activities and, 131
Cohesion, 88
Colleges and universities:
  admission requirements of, 47
  career-oriented classes in, 253
  curriculum functions and conceptions for, 95
  instrumentalism in, 60
  liberal arts curriculum in, 71–73
Columbia University, 303
Columbine High School shootings, 263
Committee of Ten, 83, 243
Common education, 94
Common School Movement, 294
Communicative approach to language, 292
Community college curricula, 93
Community involvement:
  in math curriculum, 270
  in policy making, 231–232
  in social reconstruction curriculum, 25–27
Community of persuasion, 38
Comparisons, international, 247–253
Competency-based education, 47
Competition:
  constructive, 78
  curriculum on, 12–13
  international, 247–253

Complexity, 14–15
Comprehensiveness:
  of disciplines, 63
  of standards, 103
Comprehensive School Reform Program (CSRP), 177, 178
Computer-assisted instruction (CAI), 129
Computer-Supported Intentions Learning Environment (CSILE), 144
Concentration(s):
  doctrine of, 305
  organization by, 157–158
Concepts. *see also specific curricula*
  of curriculum, 327–329
  as organizing element, 147–149
  spontaneous vs. nonspontaneous, 77
Conceptual maps, 78
Conceptual understanding, 142, 143
Concern, curriculum of, 6
Concerns conferences, 98
Concrete to abstract sequencing, 150
Conditions of use (learning activities), 134
Conflict:
  avoidance techniques for, 226
  beliefs leading to, 35
Confluence, 119, 161, 292
Confluent curriculum, 5–6
Connoisseurship model, 204–205
Conscientization, 27
Consciousness curriculum, 6–8
Consensus models, 200–204
Consistency of standards/objectives, 103
Constructivists, 129–130
Consummation functions, 95–96
Contemplative knowledge, 80
Content:
  fallacy of, 75
  new psychological criteria for, 132
"Content Core," 275

Contexturalization, 208
Contradictory ideas, responses to, 124–125
Control:
  of curriculum, 238–239
  as systemic curriculum theme, 44
Cooperative communities, 38–39
Cooperative experiences, 78
Coordination of curriculum, 192–194
Core curriculum:
  for higher education, 71–72
  structure of, 151
Core Knowledge Foundation, 74
Corporate training, 4, 89
Correlation:
  doctrine of, 305
  studies of, 329–330
CORT (*Cognitive Research Trust*), 246
Council for Basic Education, 73, 285
Council of Great City Schools, 55
Course, defined, 92
Course of study, 314–315
Court involvement in curriculum, 234–235, 238
Creativity, 3
  learning opportunities for, 120–125
  teachers' avoidance of, 120
  in thinking curriculum, 245
Crisis policy making, 237
Criterion-referenced tests, 209
Critical awareness, 6
Critical-democratic pedagogy, 159
Critical inquiry:
  in the classroom, 109
  in curriculum making, 106–107, 109
  evaluation as, 205
Critical reading, 283
Critical thinking curriculum, 243–247
Cross-disciplines, 158
CSILE (Computer-Supported Intentions Learning Environment), 144

CSRP, *see* Comprehensive School Reform Program
Cuba, 28, 248
"Cult of efficiency," 53
Cultural analyses, 96
Cultural change, accommodation of, 62
Cultural epochs, theory of, 150, 307
Cultural literacy, 73–75
Cultural Literacy Foundation, 74
Cultural pluralists, 97
Cultural psychology, 35–37, 78
Cultural reproduction, 30–32, 40
"Culture, Ideal, and Values" program, 71
Curriculum. *see also specific topics, e.g.:* History of curriculum making
  balanced, 270
  functions of, 94–96
  hidden, 193
  levels of, 91–92
  organization of, *see* Organization of learning opportunities
  revision of, 316
  of rhetoric vs. practice, 91
  structure of knowledge in, 65
  teachers' modifications of, 115–116
  textbook as, 142
Curriculum Alignment, 162
Curriculum conceptions, 327–329
Curriculum design outline, 151
Curriculum essentialists, 118
Curriculum evaluation, 199–218
  and assessment as learning, 211–212
  authenticity in, 210–211
  consensus models for, 200–204
  controversial technical issues in, 206
  criterion-referenced tests, 209
  data collection for, 212–217
  goal-free, 208

  and invasion of privacy, 209–210
  norm-references tests, 208–209
  outcomes measurement, 208
  pluralistic models for, 204–205
  and statements of objectives, 206–208
The Curriculum (Franklin Bobbitt), 311
Curriculum historians, 302–304
Curriculum inquiry, 325–340
  action research as, 337–339
  context of, 66, 67
  correlation/integration studies, 329–330
  curriculum conceptions, 327–329
  curriculum theory, 326–327
  directions in, 334–336
  narrative in, 336
  process-product research, 332–334
  purposes of, 325
  qualitative inquiry in school settings, 336–337
  sequence studies, 330–331
  standards analysis, 331–332
  state of field, 326–334
"Curriculum of concern," 6
Curriculum planning and development, 89–113
  determining what to teach, 96
  disjointed incrementalism in, 107–108
  emergent approaches in decision making, 108–110
  and functions of curriculum, 94–96
  futuristic model for, 100–101
  institutional, 93–94
  levels of decision making in, 89–91
  local, 93
  materials development, 92–93
  models of decision making, 97–107

  needs assessment model for, 97–100
  range of activities in, 92
  rational model for, 101–105
  regional, 93
  rules for, 111
  state, 93
  vocational training model for, 104–107
Curriculum policy, 92
Curriculum theory, 326–327
Custodial function, 95

D
DAN (Direct Action Network), 141
Data collection techniques, 212–217
Decentralization, 229, 231
Decision making. *see also* Curriculum planning and development
  on achieving stated purposes, 111
  disjointed incrementalism in, 107–108
  futuristic model for, 100–101
  levels of, 89–91
  needs assessment model for, 97–100
  non-decision making, 226
  optional bases for, 174
  as political process, 223–224. *see also* Politics of curriculum making
  rational model for, 101–105
  vocational (training) model for, 104–107
Deductive reasoning, 80
Dehumanization, beliefs leading to, 35
Deliberative model (mathematics), 111
Delphi method, 101
Democracy, curriculum and, 304
Department heads, curriculum management and, 181
Dependent factors, sequencing of, 150
Depersonalization, 8–13

Deschooling theory, 39–40
Design-based research, 333
Development. *see also*
  Curriculum planning and
  development
    of learning opportunities,
    125–130
    of materials, 92–93
Developmentalism, value of
  learning activities and, 131
Developmental stages, 160–161
Diagnosis (in lesson plan), 153
Direct Action Network (DAN),
  141
Directory of Historical
  Curriculum Collections
  (Virginia Beach), 303
Disciplines. *see also* Structure in
  disciplines approach
    the arts as, 81
    comprehensiveness of, 63
    as form of curriculum organi-
    zation, 156
    social utility of, 63
    substantive structure of, 65
    syntactical structure of, 65
    unified, 158
Disjointed incrementalism,
  107–108
Dissonance, 77
District-level curriculum plan-
  ning, 90–91
Doctrines of concentration/
  correlation, 305
Domain-specific knowledge,
  246–247
Drug and alcohol education,
  278–279
Durability of learning activities,
  134

E
"Earth centered" curriculum, 11
Economics, 288
Education. *see also specific*
  topics
    American ideals for, 3
    bilingual, 293–294
    character, 262–263

common, 94
competency-based, 47
equity in, 235, 255
moral, 259–262, 308–309
training vs., 104
vocational, 253–259
Educational acceptance for cre-
  ating the future, 100
Educational objectives, 206
Educational Products
  Information Exchange Institute
  (EPIE), 134
Educational purposes:
    formulating, 101
    framing, 96
    in social reconstructionist
    learning activities, 127
Educational Science Reform
  (ESRA) Act of 2002, 134, 135
Educational Testing Service,
  233, 251
Education Commission of the
  States, 176
Education Development Center
  (Massachusetts), 165–166,
  275
Effectiveness, administration for,
  191–196
Efficiency, testing, 53
Ego development, 9
Eight Year Study, 320
Electronic readers, 140
Elements, organizing, 147–150
Elementary schools:
    common curriculum in, 53
    foreign language instruction
    in, 292
    instrumentalism in, 60–61
    liberal arts in, 73
    open structure at, 152–153
    reform movements for, 176
    social reconstruction curricu-
    lum in, 25
    social studies in, 289
    "teaching to the test" in, 56
Elements of Geometry (Euclid),
  80
Elitism, 79
E-mail, 140

Emmanuel Textbook Project
  (Paris), 303
Emotional competence/control,
  17
Enacted curriculum, 174, 175
Ends-means planning, 101
English. *see also* Literature
    confluent teaching of, 6
    transpersonal techniques in, 8
    trends in, 279–282
Enlightenment, education dur-
  ing, 81–82
Environmental reconstruction,
  32
EPIE (Educational Products
  Information Exchange
  Institute), 134
E-portfolios, 139–140
Equalitarian programs, 39
Equalization of education, 235
ESALEN, 20
ESRA, *see* Educational Science
  Reform Act of 2002
Essential Schools Projects, 180
Evaluation:
    assessment vs., 200
    of curriculum, *see*
    Curriculum evaluation
    of demands for curriculum
    change, 316
    of progress toward goals, 111
    of teachers' curriculum
    plans, 117
    of technology by students,
    141
Event theory, 327
Excellence Movement, 220, 225
Executive training, 4–5
Experienced curriculum, 92
Exploration (as curriculum func-
  tion), 95
External variables, 193

F
Facilities management, 186
Faculty psychology, 243
Fallacy of content, 75
Fallacy of universalism, 75
"False Shock," 279

Familiar to unfamiliar sequencing, 150
The Family and Community Health, 275
Federal government:
  control of educational policy by, 233
  mandates from, 238
  and No Child Left Behind, 47
  and systemic curriculum of 1960s, 54
Feminist teaching, 72
Film production, 141
First Amendment, 235
Flow experiences, 14, 15, 119, 161
Fluid blocks, 184–185
Focused leadership, 179
Ford Foundation, 236
Fordham Foundation, 284
Foreign languages, trends in teaching, 291–294
Formal curriculum, 91
Formal curriculum theory, 327
Formal discipline, 244–245
Formative evaluation, 201–202
Forms of Curriculum Inquiry, 334
Fostering Communities of Learning program, 61
Foundations, 236, 284
Fourth force psychology, 16
Foxfire Network, 176
Frames of reference, shared, 35
France, centralized educational planning in, 91
Freedom schools, 188
Free-form structure, 151. *see also* Open structure
Freudian psychology:
  and social reconstruction, 37
  and third force psychology, 13–14
Functions of curriculum, 94–96
Functional creativity, 122
Futuristic curriculum development model, 100–101
Futurologists, 32–34, 40

G
Gain scores, 215
Galileo (interdisciplinary course), 157–158, 330
Gender:
  and expected scientific occupations, 276
  and feminine enactment of curriculum, 320–322
  in planning for success, 120
  and vocational education, 256
General education, 94
Generalizations:
  knowledge as, 79, 80
  as organizing element, 147
Geography:
  curriculum continuity in, 164
  trends in teaching, 286–287
Getty Center (Los Angeles), 294
Global School Bus, 144
Goals, 96, 206–208. *see also* Objectives
  clarity of, 99
  in confluent curriculum, 6
  in needs assessment, 97–99
  new psychological criteria for, 132
  obtaining consensus on, 101
  selecting among, 102–103
  in student-generated curriculum, 110
  in systemic curriculum, 44–45
  for teaching of thinking, 247
  teaching standards aligned with, 116
  unrealistic (in *Goals 2000*), 107
Goals 2000, 107
Goal-free evaluation, 208
Grade-equivalent scores, 215
Grade inflation, 55
Great Books of Western civilization, 72
Great City Schools, 55
Grouping of students, 183–184
Guided practice, 154

Gullett Elementary School (Texas), 32

H
The Handbook of Humanistic Psychology, 16
HAP (Health Activities Project), 278
Harvard University:
  curriculum at, 71–72, 82
  Project Zero, 294
Hawthorne effects, 215
Health Activities Project (HAP), 278
Health education, 276–279
Herbartism, 305–309
Heritage Foundation, 236
Heroes, study of, 17
Heteronomic moral education, 260
Hidden curriculum, 193
Hidden functions, 95–96
Hierarchical sequence studies, 164
Higher education, *see* Colleges and universities
Higher-order skills/thinking:
  learning opportunities for, 120–125
  and structure in disciplines approach, 68
Highlander Folk School (Tennessee), 26–27
High schools:
  general systemic curriculum for, 47
  houses in, 191
High/Scope Educational Research Foundation (Michigan), 160
High Success Network, 55
Historical antecedents:
  to academic curriculum, 79–83
  to humanistic curriculum, 17–19
  to social reconstruction curriculum, 37–40
  to systemic curriculum, 52–54

History of curriculum making, 301–323
  curriculum historians, 302–304
  Dewey's school, 308–309
  founders of field of curriculum, 304–305
  Herbartism, 305–308
  improvement of instruction, 314–316
  rational curriculum making, 316–320
  scientific curriculum making, 310–314
  women in, 320–322
History (subject area):
  in cultural literacy approach, 73–74
  in self-directed learning, 11–12
  structure of discipline approach to, 70
  trends in teaching, 285–288
Holism, 208
Holocaust curriculum, 11–12
Holtsville, Alabama, 39
How to Make a Curriculum (Franklin Bobbitt), 311, 312
Humanists, teaching standards and, 117–118
Humanistic curriculum, 3–21
  academic knowledge and personal development in, 10–12, 20
  and American ideals, 3
  benefits of, 3–4
  and closing of academic gaps, 1
  confluent curriculum, 5–6
  connecting individual and social learning in, 12–13
  consciousness curriculum, 6–8
  criticisms of, 19–21
  developing learning activities for, 126–127
  historical antecedents to, 17–19
  open structure for, 152–153

  organizational patterns in, 160–161
  prevalent forms of, 5–6
  psychological foundations of, 13–17
  purpose of, 5
  recent applications of, 4–5
  responses to depersonalization in, 8–13
  role of teacher in, 5
  self-directed learning in, 8–10
  student-generated, 110
  teaching of thinking in, 245
  technology in, 139–140
  and third force psychology, 13–17
Humanistic Mathematics Network Journal, 11
Hypermedia, 142
Hyper-rationalization, 226

I
Ideal curriculum, 91
IES (Institute of Educational Science), 135
ILEARN telecommunication, 145
Illiteracy, 28
In a Different Voice (Carol Gilligan), 261–262
Incongruity, 119
Independent practice, 154
Indicators, 206–208
Individualism, 19–20
Inductive reasoning, 80
Information processing theories, 51
Innovation, 3
Inquiry. *see also* Curriculum inquiry
  in science, 274
  types of, 325
Inquiry Training Project (Canada), 274
Institute of Educational Science (IES), 135
Institutionalized curriculum, 173–174

Institutional level:
  of curriculum planning, 90, 93–94
  structure at, 151
Instructional alignment, 49–50
Instructional effectiveness, administration for, 191–196
Instructional level of curriculum planning, 90
Instructional materials:
  for academic curriculum, 129–130
  costs of, 133–134
  criticisms of, 135–136
  development of, 92–93
  "kid rating" of, 134
  political standards for, 133
  scientifically based criteria for, 134–135
  systemic criteria for assessing, 131–132
  for systemic curriculum, 128
Instructional objectives, 207
Instructional Systems Design, 162
Instructional units, 92
Instrumental Enrichment, 246
Instrumentalism, 60–61
INTASC (Interstate New Teaching Assessment and Support Consortium), 116
Integrated studies movement, 83
Integration:
  achieving, 166–167
  in confluent curriculum, 6
  in middle school curriculum, 165, 166
  in social reconstruction curriculum, 25
  studies of, 329–330
Intelligence, multiple forms of, 64
Intelligent Tutoring Systems (ITS), 142
Intentional world, 36
Interactive view of reading, 283
Interdisciplinary organization, 165, 166
Interdisciplinary studies, 60

Interests, as motivational principle, 116
Internal supports, 195
International Association for the Evaluation of Educational Achievement, 250
International competition/comparison, 247–253
International Mathematics Study of 2002, 55
International Math Trail, 145
International Reading Association, 281
Internet:
    in humanistic classrooms, 140
    in social reconstructivist classrooms, 141
Internships, 258
Interrupted time series design, 202
Interstate New Teaching Assessment and Support Consortium (INTASC), 116
Intuitive receptive training, 7–8
Israel, English teaching in, 180–181, 292
Issued-based spaces projects, 132
ITS (Intelligent Tutoring Systems), 142

J
Japan:
    academic achievement in, 250
    centralized educational planning in, 91
Jasper Woodbury Series videos, 143
Jesuit schools, 52
Job analysis, 312
Job descriptions, 105–106
Jobs of the Futures, 258
Joint fact finding, 109
Judgment of projected trends, 100

K
Kettering Foundation, 236
Key School (Indianapolis), 152

"Kid rating" (of textbooks), 134
Kids Network Curriculum, 144
KIE (Knowledge Integration Environment), 61
Knowledge:
    Aquinas' view of, 81
    Aristotle's views of, 80
    conflicting views of, 69–71
    creation of, 123–125
    defined, 62
    domain-specific, 246–247
    fallacies concerning, 75
    fundamental rational structure of, 63–64
    means of connecting, 165, 166
    multiple forms of, 64
    Plato's views of, 79–80
    as predictor of academic success, 78
    structure of, 65–68
    teaching forms of, 83
Knowledge acquisition, 142, 143
Knowledge core, 178
Knowledge Integration Environment (KIE), 61
Korea, academic achievement in, 250

L
Lake Washington School District (Washington state), 101
Language arts, *see specific areas, e.g.:* Reading
Latent functions, 95–96
Latin Grammar Schools, 82
LBD (Learning by Design), 132
Leadership:
    focused, 179
    shared, 179–181
Learners:
    deriving standards/objectives from, 102
    and structuring of learning opportunities, 167–168
Learner centered leadership, 180
Learning:
    academic, 77–79
    acceptable vs. observed states of, 97

assessment as, 211–212
    as making of connections, 149
    mastery learning, 50
    teaching vs., 3–4
    theories of, 132
Learning by Design (LBD), 132
Learning environment, 126
Learning Laboratory initiative, 183
Learning opportunities, 115–137
    appeal of, 75–77
    and criticisms of textbooks, 135–136
    and differences in achievement, 248, 250
    for higher order thinking, 120–125
    in lesson plan, 154
    organizing, *see* Organization of learning opportunities
    principles for developing, 118–120
    procedures for developing, 125–130
    selection criteria for, 130–136
    and standards for teaching, 116–118
    and teachers' curriculum modifications, 115–116
    teaching standards and student perceptions of, 117
Learning styles, 119
Learning through service, 34
Legal constraints, 111
Lesson plans, 92, 153–155
Liberal arts curriculum, 62, 71–73
Lighthouse Schools, 177
Lincoln Center (New York), 295
Link to values (as motivational principle), 116
Literacy:
    campaigns, 27–28
    cultural, 73–75
    defined in standards, 281
    enlightenment forms of, 82
    multiple, 295

Literature:
changes in emphasis on, 280
in cultural literacy approach,
73–74
in liberal arts curriculum, 62
pleasure reading of, 284
in self-directed learning, 10
trends in teaching, 281–282
Literature-based reading, 283
Local curriculum planning, 93
Logical dependency, 157
Loose coupling, 226
Los Angeles City School
District, 175, 228
Los Angeles Leadership
Academy, 25–26
Los Angeles Unified School
District, 47
Louisiana School for Math,
Science, and the Arts, 189

M
MACOS, *see Man: A Course of
Study*
Macroclasses, 185
Magnet schools, 187–189
Maharishi International
University (MIU), 7
Man: A Course of Study
(MACOS), 67–68, 224
Managerial and professional
new middle class, 222
Managing curriculum, 173–196
administrative arrangements
for, 181, 183
alternative schools, 187–188
charter schools, 187, 189
in context of restructuring,
175–179
directions in reform, 190–191
and enacted curriculum, 174,
175
and facilities management,
186
and institutionalized curriculum, 173–174
for instructional effectiveness, 191–196
magnet schools, 187–189
middle school development,
186–187

nongrading, 186
roles in, 179–182
specialist schools, 187,
189–190
staffing patterns and schedul-
ing, 184–185
stratifying students, 183–184
supplementary personnel in,
185–186
Mandates, 238
Manipulative variables, 193
*Manpower Report of the
President,* 105
Mapping, 137, 162
Masconomet Massachusetts
Regional School district, 185
Massachusetts, mandated exit
test in, 140
Massachusetts Institute of
Technology (MIT), 144
Mastery learning, 50, 162, 164
Materials, *see* Instructional
materials
Math by All Means (Marilyn
Burns), 129–130
Mathematics:
industry—school partner-
ships for, 258
and international competi-
tion, 247–253
models and teaching of,
111–112
in self-directed learning,
10–11
sources of difficulty with,
119–120
traditional vs. structure of
discipline approaches to, 70
trends in, 268–282
U.S. performance in, 251
in vocational education, 257
Math Trail Web site, 145
Meaning, social negotiation of,
79
Means-end view of planing, 118
Media, student learning about,
141
Medical education, humanistic
curricula in, 4
Mentors, 145
Metacognition, 79

Metacognitive strategies, 148
Michigan, elementary school
math study in, 164
Middle class, new, 222
Middle schools:
curriculum organization in,
165, 166
development of, 186–187
houses in, 191
interdisciplinary teaming in,
184
Minnesota, Internet projects
partnership in, 189
Mismatched comparison groups,
215
MIT (Massachusetts Institute of
Technology), 144
MIU (Maharishi International
University), 7
Modeling:
in lesson plans, 154
as motivational principle,
116
Modern Language Association,
72, 291
Modern Red Schoolhouse, 177
Modifications of curriculum,
115–116
Modules, 156
Monitor model (language
instruction), 292
Moral development:
in self-directed curriculum, 9
theory of, 261–262
Moral education, 259–262,
308–309
Motivation:
for achievement, 9
principles of, 116
Multiculturalism:
and academic curriculum,
61–62
and cultural literacy
approach, 73–74
Multidisciplinary organization,
165, 166
Multidisciplinary science education, 274
Multidisciplinary seminars, 100
Multiple approaches principle,
120

Multiple literacies, 295
Multiple outcomes principle, 120
Muses, 79
Mysticism, 7–8

N
Nabisco Foundation, 176
NAEP, *see* National Assessment
    of Educational Progress
NAS (National Academy of
    Sciences), 272
NAS (New American Schools),
    48
National Academy of Sciences
    (NAS), 272
National Assessment of
    Educational Progress (NAEP),
    55, 56, 203, 251
National Association for Sports
    and Physical Education, 277,
    278
National Association for the
    Education of Young Children,
    237
National Association of State
    Boards of Education, 183
National Board for Professional
    Standards (NBPT), 116
National Center for Educational
    Statistics, 55
National Center for History in
    the Schools, 287, 290
National Center on Education
    and the Economy, 48–49
National Commission for
    Excellence in Education, 54
National Content Standards, 49
National Council for Geographic
    Education, 290
National Council for Social
    Studies (NCSS), 90, 290
National Council for the
    Accreditation of Teacher
    Education (NCATE), 116
National Council of Teachers of
    English, 281
National Council of Teachers of
    Mathematics (NCTM), 270,
    272
National Council on Economic
    Education, 290

National Education Association,
    183
National Endowment for the
    Arts, 284
National Government
    Association, 177
National Health Education
    Standards, 279
National-level curriculum plan-
    ning, 90
National Longitudinal Study of
    the High School Class, 274
National Math Trail, 145
National Research Council
    (NRC), 8, 55, 69, 135, 330
National Science Foundation
    (NSF), 56, 67, 68, 83, 235
National Science Teachers
    Association, 275
National standards:
    for the arts, 294
    for health education, 279
    for history, 287
    for math, 55, 270–271
    for science, 55
    for social studies, 290
    for teachers, 116
Nation at Risk report, 54
Native Americans, suicide
    reduction curriculum for, 11
Naturalistic model (mathemat-
    ics), 111
NBPT (National Board for
    Professional Standards), 116
NCATE (National Council for
    the Accreditation of Teacher
    Education), 116
NCLB, *see* No Child Left
    Behind Act of 2001
NCSS, *see* National Council for
    Social Studies
NCTM, *see* National Council of
    Teachers of Mathematics
Needs assessment model,
    97–100
Neoconservatives, 222
Neoliberals, 222
Neo-Marxism, 29–32, 40
Neptune Project, 145
Network of ideas, 181, 182

New American Schools
    Development Corporation, 176
New American Schools (NAS),
    48
"New basics," 55
New Harmony (Indiana) cooper-
    ative community, 38
"New Standards" program,
    48–49
New York:
    history curriculum in,
        286–287
    Regents Examinations in, 54
    systemic curriculum in, 47
New York University, 253
Nicaragua, literacy campaign in,
    28
Nihilistic moral education, 259
No Child Left Behind (NCLB)
    Act of 2001, 44, 46–47, 134,
    216, 221, 233, 276, 292, 325
Noncomparable groups, 215
Non-decision making, 226
Nongrading, 186
Nonjudgmentalism, 208
Nonspontaneous concepts, 77
Norm-group comparisons, 215
Norm-referenced tests,
    208–209
NSF, *see* National Science
    Foundation

O
OBE, *see* Outcome-based educa-
    tion approach
Objectives. *see also* Goals
    analysis of, 331–332
    deriving, 312
    discriminating among, 99
    form of, 206–208
    in lesson plan, 153
    obtaining consensus on, 101
    rational model for deriving,
        101–102
    selecting among, 102–103,
        313
    terminal, 162
    for training courses/pro-
        grams, 105–106
    Tyler vs. revisionist genera-
        tion of, 105

Occupational targets, determining, 105
Open classrooms, 161
Open Courseware (MIT), 144
Open structure, 151, 152
Open view of learning activities, 131
Operational curriculum, 92
Opportunities for learning, *see* Learning opportunities
Options systems, 188–191
Oracle Education Foundation, 145
Ordering, 149, 150
Oregon Educational Act for the 21st Century, 257
Organizational structure (of disciplines), 65
Organization of learning opportunities, 146–148
  in academic curriculum, 156–158
  at classroom level, 152–156
  and curriculum concepts, 156
  by developmental stages, 160–161
  in humanistic curriculum, 160–161
  at institutional level, 151
  issues in, 165–168
  key concepts in, 146–149
  in open classrooms, 161
  organizing centers, 146–148, 150
  organizing elements, 147–150
  principles for, 150
  in social reconstruction curriculum, 158–160
  structures for, 150–151
  studies of patterns for, 163–166
  in systemic curriculum, 161–163
Organizing centers, 146–148, 150
Organizing elements, 147–150
Organizing structures, 150–151
  at classroom level, 152–156
  at institutional level, 151

Original creativity, 122–123
Outcomes, measurement of, 208
Outcome-based education approach (OBE), 47–48, 164
Outlines of Educational Doctrine (Johann Herbart), 305
Outward Bound, 4–5

P
Pacing guides, 137
Paideia Proposal, 73, 75
Partage, 110
Participation (in confluent curriculum), 6
Partnerships, industry—school, 258
PBS programs, 143
Peace Corps, social reconstructionism in, 26
Pedagogy. *see also* Organization of learning opportunities
  critical-democratic, 159
  in enacted curriculum, 175
  Herbartian, 305–306
  nature as guide to, 118
People's Global Action, 140
Perceived curriculum, 91
Perceived purpose (in lesson plan), 154
Performance:
  acceptable level of, 98
  and long-term retention and transfer, 149
  student orientation toward, 119
  teacher proficiency standards, 116
Personal growth and development:
  Freire's approach to, 28–29
  in humanistic curriculum, 10–12, 20
Personalized systematic instruction (PSI), 50–51
Personal level of curriculum planning, 90
Persuasion, community of, 38
PEW Charitable Trust, 176

Phenomology, 208
Philosophical criteria for activity selection, 130
Physical education:
  transpersonal techniques in, 8
  trends in, 276–279
Physical manipulation, 119
Physical Science Study Committee (PSSC), 68
PIRLS, *see* Progress in International Reading Literacy Study
PISA, *see* Program for International Studies Assessment
Planning, *see* Curriculum planning and development
Plato's Academy, 79
Pluralistic models, 204–205
Pluralistic view of evaluation, 200
Policy(-ies):
  constraints on, 226
  critical inquiry in setting, 109
  curriculum, 92
  for curriculum reform, 96
  effectiveness of, 194
  methods and materials included in, 90
  normal vs. crisis making of, 237
  in systemic curriculum, 45–49
Politics of controversy, 226
Politics of curriculum making, 220–239
  book publishers, 233–234
  community policy making participants, 230–232
  and concept of public school, 220–221
  and constraints on policy, 226
  in control of curriculum, 238–239
  court involvement, 234–235
  in decision making, 223–224

federal government involvement, 235–236
and foundation funding, 236–237
in learning activity selection, 133
local social movements, 221–222
power of forces for stability, 225
professionalization of reform, 224–225
and role of schools, 221
school-based policy making participants, 227–230
special interests, 237
state agencies, 232–233
testing agencies, 233
Positive psychology, 16
Positivism, 82
Postmodern thinking, 61
Posttests, 202, 215, 216
Practicality, as opportunity selection criterion, 133–134
Practical knowledge, 80
Practical reasoning, 94
Pragmatic rule systems, 244
Praxiological curriculum theory, 327
Prescriptive lesson structure, 154
Presentism, 106
President's Committee on the Arts and the Humanities, 295
Pretests, 202, 215, 216
Pretest/posttest control group design, 202
Primary schools, *see* Elementary schools
Principals:
in curriculum management, 179–181
and curriculum policy, 229
effectiveness of, 193
Privacy issues with testing, 209–210
Private schools:
academic emphasis in, 256
options in, 190
origin of, 82

Problem solving:
curriculum for teaching, 246
emphasis on teaching, 244
learning opportunities for, 78, 120–125
Process:
evaluation of, 203
process-product research, 332–334
The Process of Education (Jerome Bruner), 64–65
Product:
evaluation of, 203
process-product research, 332–334
The Productive Thinking Program, 246
Professionalization of reform, 224–225
Proficiency-oriented model (language instruction), 292
Programs of study, 92
Program for International Studies Assessment (PISA), 250–251
Progress in International Reading Literacy Study (PIRLS), 252–253
Progressive formulation, 154
Project 2001, 101
Project Ixtliyollotl (Mexico), 26
Project Synthesis, 274
Project Talent, 202
Project 2061, 276
Project Wild, 32
Project Zero, 294
Properties of Matter curriculum, 70
Pseudoacademic essentialists, 118
PSI, *see* Personalized systematic instruction
PSSC (Physical Science Study Committee), 68
Psychoanalytical psychology, 37
Psychological criteria for activity selection, 130–132
Psychological dimension of learning styles, 119

Psychological foundations:
of academic curriculum, 77–79
of humanistic curriculum, 13–17
of social reconstruction curriculum, 35–37
of systemic curriculum, 51–52
Public Broadcasting System (PBS) programs, 143
Public schools:
concept of, 220–221
options in, 189
vocational emphasis in, 256
Publishers:
decision making by, 90
influence on educational policy, 233–234
Push for Excellence program, 224

Q
Quaker schools, 180
Qualitative inquiry, 336–337

R
Race, in planning for success, 120
Rand Corporation, 247
Range of knowledge, 3
Rational curriculum development model, 101–105
Rationale (Ralph Tyler), 101, 103–104
Reader response, 281–282
Reading. *see also* Literature
age appropriateness for, 160–161
Freire's vs. conventional approach to, 27, 28
literacy campaigns, 27–28
trends in, 282–285
U.S. performance in, 251–253
Realms of Meaning (Philip Phenix), 63
Reasoning, 244
Reflective deliberation, 108–109

Reform:
  abolition of Carnegie unit,
    181, 183
  directions in, 190–191
  for elementary schools, 176
  in managing curriculum,
    190–191
  policies for, 96
  professionalization of,
    224–225
  state-mandated, 181
Regional curriculum planning,
  93
Relevance, 6
Religious issues:
  in cultural literacy approach,
    74
  with transcendence, 7
REM Research Corporation, 214
Renaissance (Italy):
  classical schools in, 81
  humanism in, 18
"Reproductive" theory of cur-
  riculum, 30–32, 40
Republic (Plato), 79
Research on curriculum, *see*
  Curriculum inquiry
Resource unit, 155
Responsibility, avoiding, 89
Responsive evaluations, 204
Restricted curriculum develop-
  ment, 92
Restructuring of schools,
  175–179
Retention, long-term, 149
Reverse citations, 141
Revisionists, objectives genera-
  tion by, 105
Rhetoric, 80
Right to Read program, 224
Rochester City school district,
  178–179
Rockefeller Foundation,
  175–176, 236

S
Safety:
  of learning activities, 134
  in schools, 263–264

St. John's College (Maryland), 72
Sampling, 214
San Andres (Mexico), 26
San Diego nonviolence pro-
  grams, 264
Satisfaction principle, 119
SAT (Scholastic Assessment
  Test), 55
SAVE (Students Against
  Violence Everywhere), 264
Scenario writing, 100
Scheduling, 184–185
Scholastics (as term), 81
Scholastic Assessment Test
  (SAT), 55
Schools. *see also specific types,*
  e.g.: Elementary schools
  authority in, 174
  changing concepts of, 310
  concept of, 173
  private, 82, 190, 256
  public, 189, 220–221, 256
  restructuring of, 175–179
  roles of, 221
School boards, policy making
  and, 230–231
School cultural approach,
  192–194
School Development Program,
  176, 178
School-level curriculum planning, 91
School safety, 263–264
SchoolWorld, 145
Science:
  Biological Science
    Curriculum Study, 76
  industry—school partner-
    ships for, 258
  and international competi-
    tion, 247–253
  in self-directed learning, 11
  sources of difficulty with,
    119–120
  structured approach to,
    66, 67
  structure in disciplines
    approach to, 68
  trends in, 272–276

  U.S. performance in, 251,
    252
  in vocational education, 257
Science—a Process Approach,
  245–246
Science for All Americans,
  275–276
Science of Creative Intelligence,
  7
Scientific curriculum making,
  310–314
Scope, Sequence, and
  Coordination Project, 275
Secondary and Technical
  Education Excellence program,
  255
Secondary schools. *see also*
  High schools; Middle schools
  curriculum functions and
    conceptions for, 95
  influences on curriculum in,
    54
  instrumentalism in, 60–61
  liberal arts in, 73
  social studies in, 290
Second International Math Study
  (SIMS), 250
Self, in confluent curriculum, 6
Self-actualization, 3
  in humanistic curriculum, 5
  Maslow's view of, 13
Self-development:
  and academic knowledge, 10
  Keislar curriculum model
    for, 9
Self-directed learning, 8–10
Self-regulation, 17
Sense Maker, 145
Sequence:
  instructional research on,
    163–166
  and intellectual conflicts
    among experts, 167
  studies of, 330–331
Sequencing centers and activi-
  ties, 150
Sex education, 260–261, 279
Shared control, 238–239
Shared leadership, 179–181

Shared values, 192–193
Significant others, interacting with, 119
Simple to complex sequencing, 150, 157
SIMS (Second International Math Study), 250
Simulation modules, 143–144
Singapore, academic achievement in, 250
Situational approach (mathematics), 111–112
Skills, as organizing element, 147–148
Social activities, 9
Social adaptation:
    in early 20th century, 39
    needs assessment use in, 99
    social reconstruction vs., 34
Social class, reproducing maintenance of, 31–32, 40
Social conditions, deriving standards/objectives from, 102
Social efficiency advocates, 303
Socializing function, 95
Social learning, 12–13, 78
Social reconstruction curriculum, 24–42
    and closing of academic gaps, 1
    criticisms of, 40–41
    developing learning activities for, 127–128
    examples of, 25–27
    Freire's approach to, 27–29
    futurologist approach to, 32–33
    historical antecedents to, 37–40
    humanistic factors in, 6
    and institutional purposes, 94
    neo-Marxist, 29–32
    objectives in, 24–25
    organizational patterns in, 158–160
    and psychoanalytical psychology, 37
    psychological foundations of, 35–37

purpose of, 24–25
role of teacher in, 25
social adaptation vs., 34
student-generated, 110
teaching of thinking in, 245
technology in, 140–141
Social reconstructionists:
    and history of curriculum, 303–304
    and teaching standards, 117
Social science (in self-directed learning), 11
Social studies, trends in teaching, 287–290
Social utility (of disciplines), 63
Societal level of curriculum planning, 90
Socioeconomic success factors, 120
Sources of a Science of Education (John Dewey), 338–339
Special interest groups, 232, 237, 290
Specialist schools, 187, 189–190
Specialization, as curriculum function, 95
Specific subjects structure, 151
Spirituality:
    students' rating of importance of, 8
    in transcendental movement, 19
Sponsor speakups, 98
Spontaneous concepts, 77
Staffing patterns, 184–185
Standards, 206–208
    analysis of, 331–332
    for the arts, 294
    for English teaching, 281
    for health education, 279
    for history, 287
    for math, 270–271
    for physical fitness, 276
    rational model for deriving, 101–102
    selecting among, 102–103

for social studies, 290
teaching, 116–118
Standards-based curriculum, *see* Systemic curriculum
Standards for the English Language Arts, 281
Stanford Achievement Test, 55
Stanford University, 71
States:
    competency-based and outcome-based education approach, 47–48
    content standards of, 46–47, 55, 57–58
    control of curriculum in, 53
    curriculum mandates from, 238
    curriculum planning by, 90, 91, 93
    role in educational policy, 232–233
States of consciousness, 7
Statistics curriculum (Frankenstein), 30–31
Status variables, 120
Stereotyping, beliefs leading to, 35
Stoicism, 17
Strategic teaching, 122
Strategy Planning Network, 100–101
Stratification of students, 183–184
Structures, *see* Organizing structures
Structure in disciplines
    approach, 60–61, 64–71
    reaction against, 66–68
    revival of, 68–71
Students. *see also* Learners
    and curriculum policy, 230
    stratification of, 183–184
Students Against Violence Everywhere (SAVE), 264
Student-centered learning, 132
Student-generated curriculum, 110
Student-teacher relationships, 5
Student Web sites, 141

Subject matter areas. *see also*
  Subject matter trends
    adult vs. student views of, 83
    comprehensiveness of, 63
    curriculum standards for, 46
    lack of appeal of, 75–77
    national-level planning for, 90
    political decisions about,
      223–224
    prerequisite, 63
    social utility of, 63
    structure of, 64–65. *see also*
      Structure in disciplines
      approach
Subject matter experts/specialists:
  deriving standards/objectives
    from, 102
  students working with, 145
Subject matter trends, 268–297
  the arts, 294–295
  English, 279–282
  foreign languages, 291–294
  history and social studies,
    285–290
  mathematics, 268–282
  physical and health educa-
    tion, 276–279
  reading, 282–285
  science, 272–276
Substantive structure (of disci-
  plines), 65
Success (as motivational princi-
  ple), 116
Success for All, 176, 178
Success principle, 119–120
Sudbury Valley School, 190
Suggestopedia, 292
Summative evaluation, 201, 202
Superintendents, curriculum pol-
  icy and, 229–230
Supplementation (as curriculum
  function), 94–95
Synoptics, 167
Synoptic activity, 334–336
Syntactical structure (of disci-
  plines), 65
Synthesis, instructional research
  on, 163–166

Synthesizers, 162–163
Systems approach (curriculum
  coordination), 192
Systematic Collection (oral histories), 303
Systemic curriculum, 44–58
  accountability in, 45–46
  alignment in, 45
  for avoiding responsibility,
    89
  and closing of academic
    gaps, 1
  consequences of, 54–57
  control in, 44–45
  "data driven" decisions for,
    99–100
  developing learning activities
    for, 128–129
  development of, 49
  historical antecedents to,
    52–54
  instructional alignment in,
    49–50
  learning opportunities selec-
    tion for, 131
  lesson plans in, 153–154
  mastery learning, 50
  organizational patterns in,
    161–163
  personalized systematic
    instruction, 50–51
  policies for, 46–49
  psychological foundations of,
    51–52
  technology in, 142–144
Systemic Initiative Program
  (NSF), 56

T
Tariq Khamisa Foundation, 264
Task analysis, 106, 128
*Taxonomy of Educational
  Objectives,* 206, 331
Teachers' roles:
  in curriculum decisions,
    227–229
  in curriculum development,
    115–116

  in curriculum management,
    180–181
  in enacted curriculum, 175
  in humanistic curriculum, 5
  in social reconstructionist
    curriculum, 25, 30
  in students' creation of new
    knowledge, 125
  in systemic curriculum, 49,
    56–57
Teaching:
  humanistic view of, 126
  paradigms for, 137
  strategic, 122
  team, 184
Teaching standards,
  116–118
Teaching the Holocaust curriculum, 11–12
"Teaching to the test," 49–50,
  56
Team teaching, 184
Technology, 139–145
  in academic curriculum,
    144–145
  computer-assisted instruc-
    tion, 129
  high-tech vocational training,
    257–258
  in humanistic classrooms,
    139–140
  and learning/transmission of
    culture, 175
  in social reconstruction cur-
    riculum, 140–141
  and structure of disciplines
    approach, 61, 69
  student evaluation of, 141
  in systemic curriculum,
    142–144
Telecommunications projects,
  145
Telenomic moral education,
  260–261
Television (as curriculum), 33
Terminal objectives, 162
Testing agencies, 233
Test levels, 215

Textbooks:
criticisms of, 135–136
grade-level, 142
for health and physical education, 278
history of changes in, 303
Themes:
as organizing element, 147
in social reconstructionist curriculum, 159–160
Theoretical knowledge, 80
Theory, curriculum, 326–327
Theory of cultural epochs, 150, 307
thinkcycle.org, 144
Thinking, curriculum for teaching, 243–247
ThinkQuest, 145
Third force psychology, 13–17
Third space, 153
TIMSS, *see* Trends in International Mathematics and Science Study
TM (transcendental meditation), 7
Top-down approach:
in curriculum making, 103
in lesson plans, 154
"Toward a Knowledge for School Learning," 336
Tracking, 183–184
Tradition and Reform in the Teaching of English (Arthur N. Applebee), 279–280
Training, education vs., 104
Training curriculum development model, 104–107
Transactional theory, 281–282
Transcendency, 16
Transcendental meditation (TM), 7
Transcendental movement, 7–8, 19
Transfer, 121–122
long-term, 149
research on, 244
Transformist conception, student-generated, 110

Transpersonal techniques, 8
Trends:
in academic curriculum, 60
futurologists' study of, 33
judgment of projected, 100
in subject matter, 268–297
Trends in International Mathematics and Science Study (TIMSS), 248, 249, 252
Trust, 5
Truth, knowledge as, 75
Tutoring, 185, 186

U
Understanding Curriculum (W. Pinar, P. Slattery, and P. Taubman), 327–329
UNESCO study, 248
Unified disciplines, 158
United Federation of Teachers (New York), 47
U.S. Department of Education, 177, 269
U.S. Department of Labor, 105
U.S. Office of Education (USOE), 67, 235
Unit structure, 155–156
Universalism, fallacy of, 75
Universities, *see* Colleges and universities
University of California, Berkeley, 278
University of Illinois at Urbana-Champaign, 303
University of Iowa, 84
University of Texas in Austin, 303
Unobtrusive measures, 213
Unrestricted curriculum development, 92–93
Urban schools, accountability systems in, 55
Usefulness, ordering by, 150
USOE, *see* U.S. Office of Education
Utility (as motivational principle), 116
Utopianism, 32, 38, 141

V
Valuational curriculum theory, 327
Values:
in character education, 262–263
in moral education, 259–262
as organizing element, 148
in rational curriculum planning method, 103, 104
shared, 192–193
Values clarification, 262
Value added assessment, 216–217
Vanderbilt Cognition and Technology Group, 143
Victorian age, 82
Video disks, 143
Video games, 140
Video presentations, 139
Violence Impact Forum (VIF), 264
Vision logic, 16
Visualization, 143–144
Vocational curriculum development model, 104–107
Vocational education, 253–259
access to, 255–257
content of, 257–258
contrasting purposes for, 254–255
issues in planning, 253–254
reorganization of, 258–259
trends in, 259
Volunteering, 27, 34
Voucher plans, 190

W
Waldorf schools, 190
Web sites, 145
for academic curriculum, 145
student, 141
"We Care" program, 290
West Charlotte High School, 264
Westward Movement, 287
Whole language movement, 283
Whole to part structure, 157

Women in curriculum field,
320–322
Workshop in Learning Design
(Wild), 32

World Future Society, 32
Writing, teaching of, 282
The Writing Partner, 145

Z
Zones of proximal development
(ZPD), 36, 37